Christianity and the Christian Church of the First Three Centuries

Christianity and the Christian Church of the First Three Centuries

FERDINAND CHRISTIAN BAUR

Edited by Peter C. Hodgson
Translated by Robert F. Brown and Peter C. Hodgson

CASCADE Books · Eugene, Oregon

CHRISTIANITY AND THE CHRISTIAN CHURCH OF THE FIRST THREE CENTURIES

Copyright © 2019 Peter C. Hodgson and Robert F. Brown. All rights reserved. Except for brief quotations in critical publications or reviews, no part of this book may be reproduced in any manner without prior written permission from the publisher. Write: Permissions, Wipf and Stock Publishers, 199 W. 8th Ave., Suite 3, Eugene, OR 97401.

Cascade Books
An Imprint of Wipf and Stock Publishers
199 W. 8th Ave., Suite 3
Eugene, OR 97401

www.wipfandstock.com

PAPERBACK ISBN: 978-1-5326-3234-1
HARDCOVER ISBN: 978-1-5326-3236-5
EBOOK ISBN: 978-1-5326-3235-8

Cataloging-in-Publication data:

Names: Baur, Ferdinand Christian, 1792–1860. | Hodgson, Peter Crafts, 1934–, editor and translator. | Brown, Robert F., 1941–, translator.

Title: Christianity and the Christian church of the first three centuries / Ferdinand Christian Baur ; edited by Peter C. Hodgson ; translated by Robert F. Brown and Peter C. Hodgson.

Description: Eugene, OR: Cascade Books, 2019. | Includes bibliographical references and index.

Identifiers: ISBN: 978-1-5326-3234-1 (paperback). | ISBN: 978-1-5326-3236-5 (hardcover). | ISBN: 978-1-5326-3235-8 (ebook).

Subjects: LCSH: Church history—Primitive and early church, ca. 30–600.

Classification: BR165 B3 2019 (print). | BR165 (epub).

Manufactured in the U.S.A.   06/04/19

A translation of Ferdinand Christian Baur, *Das Christenthum und die christliche Kirche der drei ersten Jahrhunderte*, 2nd ed. (Tübingen: L. F. Fues, 1860).

Unless otherwise noted, biblical quotations are taken from the New Revised Standard Version Bible, copyright © 1989 National Council of the Churches of Christ in the United States of America. Used by permission. All rights reserved worldwide.

Contents

Editor's Foreword | xi
Preface to the First Edition | xxiii
Preface to the Second Edition | xxvii

Part 1: The Entrance of Christianity into World History; Primitive Christianity

The Universalism of the Roman Empire as a Preparation for Christianity | 3
Christianity and the Pre-Christian Religions | 7
Greek Philosophy | 11
Judaism | 17
Primitive Christianity and the Gospels | 21
The Consciousness of Primitive Christianity and Its Principle | 24
The Teaching about the Kingdom of God | 30
The Person of Jesus and the Messianic Idea | 32
The Death and Resurrection of Jesus | 36

Part 2: Christianity as a Universal Principle of Salvation: The Antithesis of Paulinism and Judaism, and Its Equilibrium in the Idea of the Catholic Church

I. The Antitheses | 41
    The Jerusalem Congregation and Stephen | 41
    Paul the Apostle to the Gentiles, and the Earlier Apostles | 42
    The Opponents of the Apostle Paul | 49
        In Galatia | 49
        In Corinth | 52
    The Epistle to the Romans | 55
    The Final Journey to Jerusalem | 60
    The Height of the Antithesis; The Gospel of Luke | 62
        Marcionite Paulinism | 66
        The Jewish Tenor of the Book of Revelation | 67

Papias and Hegesippus | 69
The Ebionites of the Clementines, and Simon Magus | 72

II. The Mediation | 78
    The Difference between the Viewpoints | 78
    The Elements of the Mediation | 82
    Baptism Replaces Circumcision; Peter the Apostle to the Gentiles | 83
    The Influence of Jewish Christianity on the Configuration of the Church | 87
    The Mediating Tendency of the Post-Apostolic Canonical Scriptures | 89
        The Epistle to the Hebrews | 89
        The Epistles to the Ephesians, the Colossians, and the Philippians | 94
        The Pastoral Epistles | 98
        The Epistle of James, and First Peter | 98
        The Book of Acts | 101
    The Writings of the Apostolic Fathers | 104
    Justin Martyr | 108
    Peter and Paul in Brotherly Unity | 112

III. Johannine Christianity | 116
    The Apostle John; the Apocalyptic Writer and the Gospel Writer | 116
    The Gospel of John | 118
        The Complete Break with Judaism; Its Antithesis | 118
        Christ the True Passover Lamb | 120
        The Passover Controversy | 123
        The Form of Christian Consciousness Surpassing Judaism and Paulinism | 133
    Review of the Course Taken by the Development; the Ebionites | 135

Part 3: Christianity As Ideal World-Principle and as Real, Historically Conditioned Phenomenon, or Gnosis and Montanism, and the Catholic Church as the Antithesis to Each of Them

I. Gnosis and Montanism | 141
    1. Gnosis | 141
        The Concept and Nature of Gnosis | 141
        The Origin of Gnosis | 145
        The Main Elements: Spirit and Matter; the Demiurge and Christ | 148
        Early Gnostic Sects | 153
            Cerinthus | 153
            Simon Magus and the Simonians | 153
            The Ophites | 155
            The Peratai | 156
            Summary | 158
        The Major Christian Gnostics | 158

    Valentinus | 159
    Basilides | 165
    Marcion | 172
    The Pseudo-Clementine Homilies | 176
   The Three Basic Forms of Gnosis | 181
   Docetism | 183
  2. Montanism | 189
   Gnosis and Montanism | 189
   Belief in the Parousia | 189
   Chiliasm and Prophecy | 190
   The Reactionary Tendency of Montanism | 193
   Montanism Compared with Gnosis | 195
   The Origins of Montanism | 197
 II. The Catholic Church as the Antithesis to Gnosis and Montanism | 198
  1. The Dogmatic Antitheses | 198
   The Idea of the Catholic Church | 198
   The Stance of the Church Fathers toward Gnosis | 200
    Clement of Alexandria, Origen, and Their Relation to Gnosis | 200
    The Opposition of Irenaeus and Tertullian to Gnosis and to Philosophy | 203
    Scripture and Tradition; Catholicism and Heresy | 206
  2. The Hierarchy as Antithesis | 209
   The Local Authority and Autonomy of the Churches | 209
   The Clergy, the Presbyters, and the Bishops | 214
   The Episcopate | 216
    The Concept of the Episcopate | 216
    The Origin of the Episcopate, from Concern for Unity and in the Opposition to Heresy | 218
    The Pastoral Epistles | 220
    Pseudo-Ignatius and Pseudo-Clement | 221
    The Most Exalted Idea of the Episcopate and the Principle of Its Unity | 226
   The Throne of Peter | 228
   Montanism and the Episcopate | 230
   The Bishops as Instruments of the Spirit | 235
   The Church Councils (*die Synoden*) | 238
  3. The System of the Hierarchy | 240

Part 4: Christianity as the Highest Principle of Revelation, and as Dogma

The Transition to Dogma | 245

The Christology of the Synoptic Gospels, and Paul's Christology | 248

The Christology of the Book of Revelation | 254
Christology in the Epistle to the Hebrews, and in the Deutero-Pauline Epistles | 256
The Johannine Concept of the Logos | 260
The Apostolic Fathers and the Early Church Fathers | 265
The Monarchians | 271
    First Group | 271
        Praxeas and Callistus | 271
        Noetus | 272
        Sabellius | 273
    Second Group | 276
        Theodotus of Byzantium, and Artemon | 276
        Beryllus of Bostra | 280
        Paul of Samosata | 281
The Further Development of the Doctrine of Christ's Divinity | 284
    Origen | 284
    Arianism | 287
    The Teaching of Arius' Opponents | 289
    The Nicene Dogma | 291
The Big Picture: the Doctrines of God, Moral Freedom, and the Church | 294

Part 5: Christianity as a Power Dominant in the World, in Its Relation to the Pagan World and to the Roman State

The Transition to a Position of Power | 301
I. The Internal Aspects of Christianity's Relation to the Pagan World and to the Roman State | 303
    The World-Consciousness of Christians | 303
    The Hostility of the Pagans, and the Power of Christianity Quietly at Work | 305
    The Apologists | 308
    The Philosophically Educated Opponents of Christianity | 311
        Celsus | 312
            The Significance and the Structure of Celsus' Book | 313
            The Initial Attack from the Jewish Standpoint | 313
            Celsus' Disdainful Verdict | 316
            Celsus' Opposition to Revelation | 318
            Various Arguments of Celsus in Line with Polytheism, or else with Platonism | 321
            Demonology as a Major Element of Affinity and of Difference | 326
            Christianity: Deceit and Delusion, Albeit a Force to Be Reckoned With | 330

Lucian of Samosata | 332
    How Lucian Compares with Celsus | 332
    Lucian's *Peregrinus Proteus* | 333
    The Fanaticism of Christianity | 336
  Philostratus | 337
    Philostratus' *Life of Apollonius of Tyana* | 337
    Religious Syncretism | 340
  Porphyry | 341
    Porphyry's Polemical Work | 341
    The Critical Stance of Neoplatonism | 343
  Hierocles | 346
  The Authority of Tradition and the Principle of Religious Freedom | 347
II. The External Aspects of Christianity's Relation to the Pagan World to the Roman State | 350
  Tiberius, Claudius, and Nero | 350
  Trajan, Hadrian, and the Antonine Emperors | 355
  Septimus Severus, Heliogabalus, and Alexander Severus | 362
  Decius and Gallienus | 363
  Diocletian | 365
  The Religious Edicts of the Roman Emperors | 369
    The First Edict, from Galerius, Constantine, and Licinius | 369
    The Second and Third Edicts of Constantine and Licinius | 371
  Constantine | 373
    Constantine's Concern for Unity | 374
    Constantine's Politics and His Religious Sentiments | 376
  Christianity Victorious | 378

Part 6: Christianity as a Moral and Religious Principle, in Its Universality and Its Limitations at This Time

Introduction | 385

The Universality and the Energy of Christianity's Moral and Religious Principle | 386

The Good Features of the Christian's Approach to Morality | 387
  Aversion to Shows or Spectacles | 388
  Withdrawal from Political Affairs; the Closeness of Their Own Community | 389
  Marriage and Domestic Life | 391

The One-Sided and Restrictive Character of Christian Morality | 395
  The Fear of Demons | 395

      Moral Rigorism Clashes with the Pagan World | 396
      The Dualistic, Ascetic View of Life | 398
      Marriage | 400
           The Gnostic View of Marriage | 401
           Tertullian | 405
      Clerical Celibacy | 409
      Mortal Sins and Venial Sins | 412
      Good Works | 415
      The Idea of the Church as the Principle of Moral Action | 417
The Purer Moral Principles of Clement of Alexandria | 419
More Lenient Moral Practices | 422
The Christian Cultus | 424
      The Original Elements | 424
      The Eucharist and the Love-Feast | 425
      The Passover Feast, Sunday, and the Sabbath | 427
      Further Forms of the Cultus | 428
      The Cultus of the Saints | 430

Index of Persons | 433
Index of Subjects | 439

Editor's Foreword

Peter C. Hodgson

Baur published *Das Christenthum und die christliche Kirche der drei ersten Jahrhunderte* in 1853. It was followed by a second, revised edition in 1860 (the year of his death), which was reprinted as a third edition in 1863 with a revised title, *Kirchengeschichte der drei ersten Jahrhunderte*.[1] The title was revised to accord with the issuing of the remaining volumes of his church history by his son Ferdinand Friedrich Baur and his son-in-law Eduard Zeller. The last two volumes (from the Reformation to the middle of the nineteenth century) were based on Baur's lecture notes; the third volume (on the middle ages) on a manuscript Baur prepared for the press before his death; and the first two volumes on his own published editions.

Allan Menzies (1845–1916), a Scottish pastor and later a professor of divinity and biblical criticism at the University of St. Andrews, translated the third edition of the first volume as *The Church History of the First Three Centuries*.[2] Menzies, who a few years earlier had translated Baur's *Paul the Apostle of Jesus Christ*, revised and completed an earlier version of the church history started by the Oxford philosopher T. H. Green.[3] The Menzies translation is written in a rather stilted Victorian English, and it often uses circumlocutions or introduces terms into the translation that are not found

---

1. *Das Christenthum und die christliche Kirche der drei ersten Jahrhunderte*, 1st ed. (Tübingen: Fues, 1853); 2nd ed. (Tübingen: Fues, 1860); 3rd ed., identical with the 2nd, published under the title *Kirchengeschichte der drei ersten Jahrhunderte* (Tübingen: Fues, 1863). Reprint of the 2nd ed. in *Ausgewählte Werke in Einzelausgaben*, ed. Klaus Scholder, vol. 3 (Stuttgart–Bad Cannstatt: Frommann, 1966). For a bibliography of works by and about Baur, see *Ferdinand Christian Baur and the History of Early Christianity*, ed. Martin Bauspiess, Christof Landmesser, and David Lincicum; trans. Robert F. Brown and Peter C. Hodgson (Oxford: Oxford University Press, 2017), 391–401. The German edition, without a bibliography, is *Ferdinand Christian Baur und die Geschichte des frühen Christentums* (Tübingen: Mohr/Siebeck, 2014).

2. 2 vols., London and Edinburgh: Williams & Norgate, 1878–79.

3. On Green's involvement, see the "Note by the Translator" at the beginning of vol. 2, and the remark by James Carleton Paget in *Ferdinand Christian Baur and the History of Early Christianity* (n. 1), 319.

in the German text, most notoriously in a few instances the category of "race."[4] Its translation of the title of the third edition obscures the fact that Baur himself intended to distinguish between "Christianity" as the original phenomenon and the "church" as the institution that arose from it.[5] For these reasons, we have decided it would be worthwhile to prepare a new translation of the first volume, called *Christianity and the Christian Church of the First Three Centuries*, based on the second edition of 1860, to accompany our translation of the final volume, called *Church and Theology in the Nineteenth Century*.[6] Another consideration is that a group of German, British, and American scholars has recently produced a volume of essays that we have brought out in English as *Ferdinand Christian Baur and the History of Early Christianity* (see n. 1). It has reawakened interest in the way Baur interprets the period covered by the present book.

In his Preface to the First Edition, Baur says he holds to the convictions set forth the previous year in *Die Epochen der kirchlichen Geschichtsschreibung*,[7] which is intended as an introduction to the present work and explains the general principles that guide his treatment of church history. In his other historical studies, whether of the history of Christian dogma, or of specific doctrines, or of the New Testament, Baur provided an introduction that surveys the history of the discipline in question. In the case of the church history, he published a separate book that identifies six "epochs" in the writing of church history: the supernaturalist or old Catholic view of history (from Hegesippus to the Middle Ages, with a focus on Eusebius), the Reformation and the old Protestant view of history (the *Magdeburg Centuries*, written by Matthias Flacius and others), Catholic and Protestant opposition to the *Centuries* (Caesar Baronius and Gottfried Arnold), the gradual transition from a dualistic worldview to a conception of historical development (J. L. Mosheim, J. S. Semler, C. W. F. Walch), the pragmatic method of historiography (L. T. Spittler, G. J. Planck, H. P. K. Henke), and the quest for an objective view of history (Philipp Marheineke, August Neander, J. K. L. Gieseler, Karl Hase). While the focus is Germanic, the work does provide information not generally accessible to English readers. The final chapter of "conclusions and suggestions" sets forth Baur's own methodological principles.

---

4. Compare Menzies' translation of a passage on pp. 17–18 of vol. 1 with the German text on pp. 16–17 and our version below, p. 17.

5. In the Preface to the First Edition, Baur writes that the church "takes shape" from Christianity (p. xxiv); and in Part Three that the idea of a catholic church "emerges" from Christianity (p. 142).

6. *Kirchengeschichte des neunzehnten Jahrhunderts*, ed. Eduard Zeller, 1st ed. (Tübingen: Fues, 1862); 2nd ed. (Leipzig: Fues's Verlag [R. Reisland], 1877). Reprint of the 1st ed. in *Ausgewählte Werke* (n.1), vol. 4 (1970). ET of the 1st ed.: *Church and Theology in the Nineteenth Century*, ed. Peter C. Hodgson; trans. Robert F. Brown and Peter C. Hodgson (Eugene, OR: Cascade Books, 2018).

7. Tübingen: Fues, 1852. Reprint in *Ausgewählte Werke* (n. 1), vol. 2 (1963). Translated by Peter C. Hodgson as *The Epochs of Church Historiography* in *Ferdinand Christian Baur: On the Writing of Church History* (New York: Oxford University Press, 1968). The translation has deficiencies but is still usable.

In his Preface to the present volume, Baur says that he simply deals "with what is purely historical, what is historically given, insofar as it is possible to understand it in its pure objectivity." As a summary of his interpretation of history, this statement is very limited and misleading. The question is what constitutes the "pure objectivity" of the historically given. From the *Epochs* it becomes clear that this objectivity does not simply consist of empirical facts as opposed to the subjective biases and interests of "pragmatic" historiography. The objectivity of history is constituted by the interweaving of what is called "the idea" with the various historical materials in which it manifests itself. "The history of the Christian church is the movement of the idea of the church, and therefore consists of something more than a succession of changes following one another at random." This idea "must possess within itself the living impulse to go out from itself and to become actualized in a series of manifestations."[8] The difference between pre-Reformation and post-Reformation historiography is that, in the pre-Reformation period the idea of the church simply merges into identity with the historical Catholic Church, while after the Reformation there is an endeavor "just as much to retract the idea from the reality of the visible church" and to hold idea and reality both together and apart in a dialectical tension.[9] This tensive relationship of idea and reality (or manifestation) is the key to Baur's historiography.

What is the idea of the church? The following passage from the *Epochs* provides a crucial explanation:

> The church is the real form (*reale Form*) in which Christianity is made manifest (*zu seiner Erscheinung kommt*). If we inquire about the idea of the church, we inquire, therefore, about Christianity itself. . . . Christianity can be essentially nothing other than that which the Christian consciousness of all times, in whatever form it may have occurred, has perceived (*angeschaut*) in the person of Christ: the unity and union (*Einheit*) of God and the human being. However else we may conceive the essence of Christianity—as everything it is intended to be for human beings in its various aspects, such as the revelation of absolute truth, the establishment of redemption, reconciliation, blessing—it has its absolute conception and expression in the unity and union of God and

---

8. *Epochs*, 241–42. In a footnote Baur says that this view represents a progression from the "empirical" standpoint to what Schelling called the "universal" or "absolute" standpoint. He quotes a lengthy passage from Friedrich Schelling's *Vorlesungen über die Methode des akademischen Studium* (Stuttgart and Tübingen: Gotta'schen, 1803), 216 ff., which ends as follows: "History does not satisfy reason until the empirical causes that satisfy the understanding have served to disclose the works of a higher necessity. Treated in this way, history cannot fail to strike us as the greatest and most marvelous drama, which only an infinite spirit could have composed" (translation from *On University Studies*, trans. E. S. Morgan [Athens: Ohio University Press, 1966], 107). This quotation demonstrates the extent to which Baur was influenced by Schelling's interpretation of history (see esp. chaps. 8 and 10 of the *Vorlesungen*) before he found confirmation and elaboration of it in Hegel. On Schelling, Hegel, and Baur, see Martin Wendte, "Ferdinand Christian Baur: A Historically Informed Idealist of a Distinctive Kind," in *Ferdinand Christian Baur and the History of Early Christianity* (n. 1), ch. 3.

9. *Epochs*, 243.

> the human being, as that unity is perceived in the person of Christ, and in this perception becomes a fact of Christian consciousness.[10]

The church is the "real form" in which Christianity is made manifest or comes into historical appearance. Actually, the person of Christ is the paradigmatic form, to which all the others are subordinate. Baur goes on to say that the major components in the historical development of the church are also "forms" in which the idea realizes itself. These major forms are *dogma* (doctrine, theology, thought), *institutional governance* (*Verfassung*, meaning the episcopal hierarchy for the Catholic Church and congregational-synodal governance for the Protestant churches), *external relations*, and *moral-religious and cultic practices*. All of these forms are present in every period of the church, but one predominates in each period. As we shall see, this becomes a structuring device for the church history as a whole.[11]

So the idea of the church is the idea of Christianity itself, the idea of God in reconciling communion with human beings as perceived in Christ. This idea does not float above history or intervene in the historical nexus as a supernatural or miraculous causality. Rather it is *constitutive* of Christian history itself, indeed of history as such because the idea is perceived in other forms and figures as well. Baur's conception is remarkably similar to what Hegel says in his philosophy of world history, that the divine idea and human passions "form the weft and the warp in the fabric that world history spreads before us." The divine idea is like a shuttle that drives back and forth across the warp of human passions, weaving the fabric of world history, which gradually assumes the pattern of ethical freedom. History is a divine-human production in which the idea provides the guiding propulsive power and the passions the material substrate.[12] The "perception" (*Anschauung*) human beings have of this idea is not a sensible perception but rather an intellectual vision or intuition, a spiritual knowing that entails faith.

Baur rarely if ever makes reference to Hegel's philosophy of world history, and in *Christianity and the Christian Church of the First Three Centuries* he downplays his philosophical views because here he wants to stress his historical-critical, scientific method. He is sensitive to the charge of "Hegelianism," and he defends the Tübingen School against the accusation that it constructs history a priori. The rigor of his historical approach is evident in all his writings. He is able to follow the historical evidence wherever it leads him because he is confident that history is the medium of divine revelation and the manifestation of divine purpose, no matter how tragically

---

10. *Epochs*, 244, slightly revised.

11. *Epochs*, 244–45. In the *Epochs*, only the first two forms are mentioned, but it became evident as Baur wrote the first volume of the church history, and as he acknowledged in the Preface to the First Edition, that an analysis focusing on dogma and governance alone is insufficient.

12. G. W. F. Hegel, *Lectures on the Philosophy of World History*, vol. 1, *Manuscripts of the Introduction and the Lectures of 1822–3*, ed. and trans. Robert F. Brown and Peter C. Hodgson (Oxford: Clarendon, 2011), 147.

entangled it becomes as a result of human frailty. In this sense his Schellingian and Hegelian "panentheism" is a liberation that allows him to engage freely in New Testament criticism and church-historical research.

Baur famously wrote in an early publication that "without philosophy, history remains for me forever dead and mute."[13] An eloquent elaboration of this conviction is found much later in his lectures on church and theology in the nineteenth century.

> What would the metaphysical truth be without its historical mediation, if it did not actualize itself in the consciousness of humanity by appearing in history, and doing so not merely in scattered individuals but in the organic nexus of historical development, thus emerging out of the abstract region of philosophy into the concrete life of religion, and becoming part of the collective consciousness of a religious and ecclesial community? And what, on the other hand, would the historical aspect be—everything that has objectified itself in such a broad scope in the history of humanity and has been incorporated into human consciousness—how subjective and contingent would it be in all its external objectivity if it could not also be grasped in its true objectivity, and thus in the final analysis as a metaphysical truth grounded in the essence of God himself? Thus it is always a matter here of the vital conjunction of the two opposed aspects, the metaphysical and the historical.[14]

Metaphysical truth is historically mediated, and historical events are metaphysically grounded. Expressed in theological terms, God is in history, and history is in God. God is in history as the ideality that moves history (non-coercively) toward freedom, redemption, and reconciliation. History is in God as an aspect of the divine milieu in which the ideality of God assumes real form. Contingency and chance play a role in history, but they do not define its meaning and purpose. Human passions and interests often disrupt the trajectory of history, but they cannot permanently reverse it. History is animated by conflicts, struggles, and resolutions between competing positions. God is not an abstract supreme being externally related to the world but its inner ideal power, its beating heart. This metaphysical interpretation remains for the most part behind the scenes in Baur's historical-critical writings. It makes an appearance in prefaces, polemical writings, and rare passages such as the one quoted above. It is more evident as a structuring device than in the detailed examination of evidence.

Baur published a revised second edition of *Christianity and the Christian Church* in 1860. It adds about thirty pages of text, mostly through revisions to Part 2 and 3 and additional footnotes. The Preface to the Second Edition evidences a certain weariness of conflict on Baur's part. His health was failing and he died later the same year. He notes that critics do not object in principle to understanding Christianity as a historically given phenomenon, but when it comes to its origins they are reluctant

---

13. *Symbolik und Mythologie oder die Naturreligion des Althertums*, pt. 1 (Stuttgart: Metzler, 1824), xi.

14. *Church and Theology in the Nineteenth Century* (n. 6), 64.

to surrender a supernatural causality. Baur insists on the consistent application of scientific principles; for him *Wissenschaft* (science) includes both empirical research and a philosophical worldview. He does not describe the latter here but says merely that "genuine historical actuality exists only where there is life and movement, coherent and progressive development, and a more profound disclosure of the antitheses that first have to be undergone through struggle and conflict if they are to be overcome and reconciled." In the latter part of the Preface he becomes entangled in a not-very-edifying dispute with Heinrich Ewald over the origins of Christianity and its relation to the history of Israel. Ewald, a former colleague in Tübingen and now at Göttingen, attacked him quite viciously and personally, and Baur shows that he is a masterful polemicist himself.

Christianity and the Christian Church of the First Three Centuries comprises six major parts. Part One treats the historical emergence of Christianity as a new world religion out of its historical context and background: the pre-Christian religions, Greek philosophy, and Judaism. The teaching and person of a Jew, Jesus of Nazareth, appeared as something new in this context and served as the essential foundation of Christianity. This new thing was not supernatural or miraculous but rather a radical appeal to moral-religious consciousness and a proclamation of God's righteousness and the coming of God's kingdom—assertions for which Jesus was crucified. These factors led early Christian believers to perceive in Christ the reconciling unity of God and humanity. This perception constitutes the origin of Christianity along with the figure of Jesus himself.

Parts Two and Three describe the transition from Christianity to the Catholic Church in terms of two epic conflicts. As we have noted, history is not based on harmonies and happiness but comes about through conflicts, struggles, and resolutions. These resolutions eventually break down and new issues arise. Baur discovered this truth about history through historical research and did not first learn it from Hegel's philosophy.[15] The principal conflict in the earliest church was between Jewish-Christian and Gentile-Christian interpretations of salvation. The concrete issue concerned whether Christians must be circumcised. Paul, the Apostle to the Gentiles, argued that Christianity offers universal salvation and is open to believers from all nations without the specific ritual requirements of Judaism. He was opposed by the Apostle Peter, who not only insisted on circumcision but also questioned Paul's credentials as an apostle since he had not known Jesus in the flesh. Baur describes this conflict and then shows how it was "mediated" in the second century, when baptism replaced circumcision as the initiating ritual, and when the roles of Peter and Paul were eventually reversed,

---

15. See his discussion of factions in the Corinthian Church, "Die Christuspartei in der korinthischen Gemeinde, der Gegensatz des petrinischen und paulinischen Christenthums in der ältesten Kirche, der Apostel Petrus in Rom," *Tübinger Zeitschrift für Theologie* 4 (1831) 61–206 (reprinted in *Ausgewählte Werke* [n. 1], vol. 1 [1963]). Hegel wrote that "in history the periods of happiness are blank pages, for the object of history is, at the least, change" (*Lectures on the Philosophy of World History* [n. 12], 172).

especially in the Book of Acts and later writings. The conflict could be resolved only when it was believed that the principal antagonists themselves resolved it. The Gospel of John is treated as a synthesis, achieved toward the end of the second century, that surpassed both Jewish and Pauline Christianity in a universal, idealized vision of God as love and Christ as the incarnate Logos. But in the process the concrete historical figure of Jesus was obscured.

The other major conflict was over the ideality and historicality of the church and is based partly on the influence of pagan ideas. The Gnostics and Montanists argued, in different ways, that Christianity is a world-principle and that its true existence is not found in an empirical institution. Baur explains the difference between Parts Two and Three as follows:

> The issue is no longer whether Christianity is one particular principle of salvation, or is instead a universal principle of salvation. The concern is no longer the condition for a person to gain the blessedness that Christianity imparts. The issue is no longer merely one of breaking through, and setting aside, the barriers preventing Christianity from evolving in a freer and more universal way. The horizon is quite different here. People now see themselves in a setting where the concepts and antitheses are those of God and world, spirit and matter, absolute and finite; of the world's origin, its development, and how it will end. In short, Christianity is to be understood as a world-principle rather than as a principle of salvation.

The Catholic Church, through the development of its hierarchical institution, had to resist this tendency toward historical evaporation:

> The church has the important task of holding fast to what are positive elements in Christianity. It is a "catholic" church as such, only inasmuch as it is a central, focal point reconciling all the different perspectives, a center staying just as far from one extreme as it does from the other. On the one hand, if the idea of a catholic church, an idea emerging from Christianity, had not overcome the particularism of Judaism, Christianity itself would have become just a Jewish sect. On the other hand, the threat posed to Christianity by paganism was the equally great danger of generalizing and watering-down its contents by ideas so boundlessly expanding Christian consciousness that it would have had to completely lose its specific, historical character.

These two statements, found at the beginning of Part Three, are as clear a summary as any of Baur's perspective on the formation of the early Catholic Church. Catholicism played an indispensable role in the history of the church until its internal tensions and immoral excesses led to a breakdown in the late Middle Ages. This is quite a different view from that which postulates a "fall" of the church with the emergence of early Catholicism and its recovery only in the Reformation. The view also obviously differs from the Catholic Church's own self-understanding.

Parts 4, 5, and 6 of our text treat the major forms by which the idea of Christianity takes shape: thought, governance, external relations, and practices. (Governance or institutional hierarchy is actually already addressed at the end of Part Three.) In the ancient period thought or dogma was the principal form, and it is elaborated in Part Four under the theme of "Christianity as the highest principle of revelation and as dogma." At the beginning of Part Four Baur provides another helpful summary of his argument:

> In reviewing the presentation thus far, we see that in this sphere there are two outlooks or ways of thinking in which the idea immanent in Christianity realized itself in Christian consciousness. The limitation that the particularism of Judaism wanted to impose on the Christian principle of salvation had above all to be overcome, and Christian universalism established. This could only happen by doing away with the wall of separation between Judaism and paganism or the Gentile world, and by regarding the entirety of humankind as both needing Christian salvation and being receptive to it—as the wide domain in which the idea of Christianity should actualize itself. In this regard, however, just as Christianity had from the outset the tendency to expand into a universal movement, it on the other hand had, from this universal standpoint, an equal concern to hold firmly to its specific content and character. In wanting to be just as specific—that is, personal, individual, and historically concrete—as it was universal, Christianity had to relate these two aspects adequately to each other.

In Part Four the presentation is no longer chronological but thematic. It argues that christology was the major focus of dogmatic development during the first three centuries, and it traces this development from its beginning in the Synoptic Gospels and Paul (a still substantially "Jewish form of christology") through the formation of the Catholic dogma of Christ (the incarnation of the divine Logos) to the controversies that led to the Council of Nicaea in 325.

Part 5 treats Christianity as a "power dominant in the world." In order to realize the "absolute idea" that is its "essential content," and to become a universal religion accessible to all peoples, Christianity had to become a dominant world power. This power put it into conflict with paganism, and into both competition and cooperation with the Roman Empire. Baur discusses these two relationships in terms of their internal and external aspects. Internally he highlights Christianity's critique by and defense against philosophical opponents, and externally, its engagement with Roman politics and emperors up until the conversion of Constantine.

Regarding the conversion of Constantine, Baur offers a helpful glimpse into his way of understanding the relationship between individual figures and the objective course of events. He cites the historian August Neander, who explains the conversion through a psychological interpretation of the legend that Constantine perceived the sign of the cross in the shape of the clouds. Baur comments: "Those who set more emphasis on minor personal matters than they do on the larger course of history, and give more weight to what is fantastically miraculous than they do to the simple truth of historical facts, may find this account satisfactory." But the historian cannot. The simple truth is that Christianity had become an objective force by this time and could no longer be constrained or persecuted. What made Constantine a world-historical figure is simply that he recognized this fact and understood the age in which he lived. He knew how to reconcile his own personal convictions with the spirit of Christianity, even though his principal motive was political—reestablishing the threatened unity of the Roman Empire. For the achievement of unity the episcopal system of the Catholic Church was the ideal instrument.

Part 6 takes up Christianity as a moral and religious principle and its cultic practices. By "moral and religious" Baur means a religious principle with a moral focus or emphasis. Religion proves its truthfulness by the moral transformation it is capable of producing in the world, and Christianity did so to an eminent degree. It brought about an inward renewal of consciousness in relation to God and produced a genuine community of the faithful. It had an aversion to shows and spectacles, withdrew from pagan politics, and emphasized marriage and domestic life. Baur writes: "The aristocratic and despotic spirit of the ancient world, which considered the individual to be simply an instrument serving the general purposes of the whole, . . . had to give way to a more humane and less harsh way of thinking, one recognizing that all had equal rights and respecting the human dignity of even the humblest and lowliest ones." In this respect the new religion contributed to the abolition of ancient slavery.

But in the early centuries especially, Christian morality also exhibited a one-sided and limited character, as evidenced by superstition, a widespread fear of demons, the moral rigorism exhibited by Tertullian in particular, and a dualistic, ascetic view of life. Marriage was often interpreted in terms of the antithesis of matter and spirit, with the sensuous dimension pitted against the spiritual, and chastity defended as the higher ideal. These "catholic" tendencies are contrasted with "the purer moral principles of evangelical Christianity" on the part of Clement of Alexandria, who set forth a moral vision without Montanist fanaticism. But as time went on, more lenient moral practices settled into place; martyrdom was no longer considered a virtue, and people turned their attention "to what was feasible in practice and suited to their circumstances."

Finally, the origins of the Christian cultus are explored, including the Eucharist understood not as a sacrament but as an agape or love-feast in remembrance of the Lord's death, the complex issues related to the Passover (a summary of the earlier discussion), the relative values of Sunday and the Sabbath, more developed cultic forms (incorporating pagan and Jewish practices), and the creation of a cult of saints (also influenced by paganism).

The organizing structure of thought, governance, external relations, and religio-ethical practices is carried over into subsequent volumes of the history of the Christian

Church, with modifications. Volume 2, which covers the period from the fourth through the sixth centuries, is divided into four main parts: Christianity's relationship to paganism; dogma; hierarchy; the Christian cultus and ethical life.[16] Volume 3, on the Middle Ages, has the same four parts, presented in two main periods divided by the papacy of Gregory VII. In the second main period, hierarchy attains ascendency over dogma as the principal form.[17] In Volumes 4 and 5, from the Reformation to the middle of the nineteenth century, the forms are still present, but are accommodated to the division between Catholicism and Protestantism.[18] With Protestantism the emphasis shifts from dogma and hierarchy to faith and spiritual communion with God. It is true that Baur's church history is written from a Protestant perspective, but he attempts to do justice to the Catholic Church in its historically essential role. In this respect his approach is quite different from subsequent Protestant historians such as Adolf Harnack,[19] who regarded Catholicism to be an expression of an alien Greek spirit in opposition to the faith of "the Gospel." Baur in fact is seeking a mediation between the objectivity of Catholicism and the subjectivity of Protestantism. He seems to be looking toward a time when the truth of Protestantism becomes an integral part of the church universal.[20]

∽

Robert F. Brown is mostly responsible for the translation of this volume. The hundred pages I contributed have been revised and improved by him. My efforts have been directed rather to editorial and publication matters. *Church and Theology in the Nineteenth Century* (n. 6), the final volume in the church history series, was based on Baur's manuscripts and published posthumously by Eduard Zeller. Consequently, most of the footnotes are editorial, and others are designated as coming from [*Baur*] or [*Zeller*]. By contrast, the present volume was published by Baur himself with a good many footnotes, and editorial notes are designated as such, either by [*Ed.*] for our own notes or additions to Baur notes, or simply by square brackets for insertions into Baur notes. (We supplement Baur's bibliographic information silently.) With this exception, the two volumes are edited similarly. We have introduced subheadings into the text from the table of contents, and have broken up Baur's long paragraphs into shorter ones. We have included some Greek and Latin in the text, but with longer

---

16. *Die christliche Kirche vom Anfang des vierten bis zum Ende des sechsten Jahrhunderts in den Hauptmomenten ihrer Entwicklung* (Tübingen: Fues, 1859).

17. *Die christliche Kirche des Mittelalters in den Hauptmomenten ihrer Entwicklung*, ed. Ferdinand Friedrich Baur (Tübingen: Fues, 1862).

18. *Kirchengeschichte der neueren Zeit, von der Reformation bis zum Ende des achtzehnten Jahrhunderts*, ed. Ferdinand Friedrich Baur (Tübingen: Fues, 1863). For vol. 5, see n. 6.

19. See Daniel Geese in *Baur and the History of Early Christianity* (n. 1), ch. 14.

20. See *Lehrbuch der christlichen Dogmengeschichte*, 2nd ed. (Tübingen: Fues, 1858), 56–58. ET: *History of Christian Dogma*, ed. Peter C. Hodgson, trans. Robert F. Brown and Peter C. Hodgson (Oxford: Oxford University Press, 2014), 87–89.

quotations of passages in Greek or Latin only an English translation is provided. For citations of patristic writers, see the bibliography in our translation of Baur's *History of Christian Dogma*.[21] References to *The Ante-Nicene Fathers*[22] are abbreviated *ANF*, although these translations are often modified by us into more contemporary English, so the references are given partly just for informational purposes. Loeb Classical Library editions, which we occasionally cite, are abbreviated LCL.[23] We hope this new version of one of Baur's most important books will make it more accessible to the public.[24]

I end on a personal note. The book we have translated was published in 1860, just before the beginning of the American Civil War, and the remaining volumes of Baur's church history appeared during the War. Whether Baur would have attended to this tragic and bloody conflict on another continent is unknown since he also died in

---

21. *History of Christian Dogma* (n. 20), 372–79.

22. *The Ante-Nicene Fathers: Translations of the Writings of the Fathers down to A.D. 325*, ed. Alexander Roberts and James Donaldson, 10 vols. (Edinburgh: T. & T. Clark, 1867–73). American edition by the Christian Literature Company, reprinted by Eerdmans and other publishers. A few references to the First and Second Series of *Nicene and Post-Nicene Fathers*, ed. Philip Schaff and Henry Wace, 14 vols. (Edinburgh: T. & T. Clark, 1886–1900), are abbreviated $NPNF^1$ and $NPNF^2$.

23. They were published in Cambridge, Mass., and London, and are referenced by volume name rather than series number. The volumes containing Eusebius' *Ecclesiastical History* appeared in 1926; and those containing Tacitus' *Histories* appeared in 1951–52.

24. Brown contributes the following remark: The term *Religionsphilosophie* (literally, "philosophy of religion") in Baur's works can pose a problem for someone translating them into English. He uses this same term for two somewhat different things that, in some contexts at least, are best kept distinct. — (1) Philosophy of religion as a topic to which someone who is primarily a philosopher might chose to give attention, by analyzing and/or criticizing religion or particular features of it. The philosopher assuming this role can incidentally be (but may not be and often is not) a religious believer or someone sympathetic to religion. In this sense of the term, and in this role, the philosopher is not operating as a believer any more than a philosopher of art is, or operates as, an artist. Examples of such philosophers of religion from the ancient world discussed by Baur here include Plato, Epicurus, and Plotinus.—(2) The same term, *Religionsphilosophie*, Baur (and others) often apply to the work of a religious believer or sympathizer who uses philosophical concepts and methods to describe and/or construct the beliefs or belief system of that specific religion, as well as defending it against criticism. This practice might just as well be called "religious philosophy" or "philosophical religion" or "philosophical theology." In fact, we frequently use the term "religious philosophy" for it in translating Baur into English here, and in our previous Baur translation, *Church and Theology in the Nineteenth Century* as well. — Most Anglo-American philosophers of religion practice the first type of philosophy of religion, and regard it as significantly different from this second type. Hence the value of having a separate term for the latter when making an English translation. Of course, the boundary between the two types is not always clear-cut, and individual judgment is called for regarding the use of terminology. For instance, consider Schelling and Hegel. With his right-leaning Hegelianism, and his almost exclusively religious focus on the works of these two philosophers, Baur might regard them in the second sense as philosophers of religion who are "religious philosophers" or "philosophical theologians." On the other hand, someone of a different mindset, and with a more wide-ranging interest in the other works of these two philosophers, might say they are simply doing philosophy of religion in the first sense.—In the big picture, it is all indeed "philosophy of religion" in the broadest sense. However, in translating Baur into English, we think it important to be clear about this difference between two uses made of the term *Religionsphilosophie*, and to reflect that difference in the translation.

1860, but his focus, in addition to religion, was always on antiquity and Europe.[25] This war and its aftermath certainly tested Baur's Hegelian-inflected views about the role of the idea in history, but Lincoln seems to have come to a similar conclusion when he proclaimed at Gettysburg "a new birth of freedom." The struggles following the Civil War and up to the present day illustrate how difficult a birth this has been. The same is true of the birth of Christianity and the Christian Church many centuries ago.

---

25. See his remarks on ancient slavery in Part Six, n. 15.

Preface to the First Edition

For a long time various groups have desired to have a survey of the results brought to light by the most recent critical investigations in the field of early church history. The material itself can also call for such a presentation, since a domain of historical research that constantly requires more intensive reworking has many features that seem unimportant or superficial when looked at in isolation, but are only seen in their true light when placed in their broader context and comprised within the unity of the whole.

Providing such a survey is the main purpose of the present work. But it is not its sole purpose, for this book is not, as one might have anticipated, just a reiteration of what was already known. While I recapitulate my previous investigations by drawing together their main elements, I not only reexamine them in the light of several new perspectives, but also enhance them with additional material providing both new investigations of the sources and new source documents. The new sources include, in particular, the *Philosophumena*,[1] allegedly written by Origen. It is very important for the history of Gnosis and of early dogmas, and I have now made very extensive use of it for the first time. In addition to it I have utilized the quite remarkable *Pistis Sophia*,[2] a Gnostic text heretofore largely ignored. The main thing, however, is that I have not just made needed rearrangements of, and additions to the whole. Parts Five and Six of the present text go beyond the range of my previous authorship on the apostolic and post-apostolic times, since I have now included aspects of the church's initial emergence that must also be considered if the overall picture of the Christian Church in the first three centuries is to be as complete and comprehensive, as clear and concrete, as it possibly can be.

My consistent standpoint over these many years is well-known, and need not be explained again in detail here. I hold firmly and candidly to the convictions set forth last year in *Die Epochen der kirchlichen Geschichtsschreibung* (Tübingen, 1852),[3] which

---

1. [*Ed.*] See Part 3, n. 11. The Oxford edition (1851) ascribed it to Origen. The Göttingen edition (1859) attributed it to Hippolytus, as did the English translation published in vol. 5 of the *Ante-Nicene Fathers* (1886).

2. [*Ed.*] See Part 3, n. 40.

3. [*Ed.*] *The Epochs of Church Historiography*, in *Ferdinand Christian Baur: On the Writing of*

states my overall view as to how to treat church history and the general principles that guide it. That work may be regarded as an introduction to this one, which can therefore omit all these general considerations. Briefly put, from my standpoint I deal solely with what is purely historical, what is historically given, insofar as it is possible to understand it in its pure objectivity.[4] However successful I have been at this, I am in any event not consciously trying to do anything else. This awareness sufficiently shields me from any suspicions, from all those wrongheaded and malicious pronouncements that are the predominant tenor of an age caught up in its limited, partisan concerns. If we disregard all that which still inherently bears the obvious marks of one-sidedness, and which has the effrontery to treat history superficially, then certainly no one can fail to recognize what demands the most important period in the history of the Christian Church always still places on those who research and present it in historical terms. There is no mistaking the task at hand if one is just to approach more satisfactory explanations than those provided so far.

If we take the best and most current portrayals of the early history of Christianity, and look more closely at how they bring the historical materials, with their heterogeneous and far-flung components, into a unified whole, what do we see? We see how insular and fragmentary, how limp and lifeless, how vague and unclear they appear to us in so many respects. This lack of unity quite naturally becomes more apparent the farther we go back toward the points on which one first of all had to make up one's mind, and arrive at a definite view, if any historical vision of Christianity taking shape as the church is said to be possible. Any attempted investigation, in more detail and depth, of the foundation that must first of all be laid—and which no one can lay otherwise than history itself in its unchangeable truth has laid it—can only be justified by carrying it out. Such an investigation will bring coherence, steadiness, and unity to the whole; will separate out, with their differences, the various concurrent factors, and the forces and principles at work, that produced the outcomes of the first three centuries; and will track, in their reciprocal relations, all the individual features belonging to the character of a time embracing such momentous developments, thus unifying them as much as possible in an internally harmonious picture. Accordingly, insofar as it is not too deficient in all the requisites for the possibility of completing its task, such an investigation will, as I said, only be justified by carrying it out. It is from this perspective that I wish to see the present work judged, by those who are sufficiently impartial and knowledgeable to be able to appreciate such an enterprise.

Church History, ed. and trans. Peter C. Hodgson (New York, 1968). See the Editor's Foreword.

4. [*Ed.*] In the *Epochs* Baur writes: "The historian can be equal to his task only in so far as he transposes himself into the objective reality of the subject matter itself, free from the bias of subjective views and interests, . . . so that instead of making history a reflection of his own subjectivity, he may be simply a mirror for the perception of historical phenomena in their true and real form" (241). These phenomena can only be determined by historical science, but they also constitute the dialectical movement of spirit in history, which enables the historian to grasp the overall coherence of events.

Preface to the First Edition

Whether I shall in the future go farther along the path I have here begun—even if not to provide a detailed history, yet to indicate the points that my studies and investigation lead me to think most important, in order to follow the general course of development of the Christian Church—remains to be seen. In any event, the present work forms a presentation that stands on its own.

Tübingen, September 1853

Preface to the Second Edition

I am pleased to bring my book, *Christianity and the Christian Church of the First Three Centuries*, back to the public once again after the first edition has run its course. The first edition set forth the results of many years of study that I value and cherish because of my long engagement with, and personal interest in, the subject matter. This new edition gives me a suitable opportunity to reexamine and improve it, and to fill out the presentation there with all that seems noteworthy, in part from my own further research and in part from other literature. As should be expected, my own view of this history overall remains the same. Even where I found it advantageous to rework larger parts, as was the case most of all for Part Two, I did so only to expand upon one point or another, to emphasize the main features more sharply and define them more precisely. Overall, I endeavored to make the presentation more lucid, more precise, and to lay it out more clearly.

Since the appearance of the first edition, it has become increasingly customary to designate the standpoint I champion, in interpreting early Christianity, as that of the "Tübingen School." Some who call it by this name regard this standpoint not as wholly unjustified, yet as something one could just resist rather than assenting to it. That has in large measure also been my previous experience. Nothing deemed a product of the Tübingen School has ever lacked opponents and challengers. Although it seems that people often gladly avoid engaging in a more exacting scientific discussion of the disputed issues, they have very few reservations about behaving in a distrustful and suspicious, disparaging and reprehensible fashion. With people frequently delivering verdicts of this sort, they have envisaged the difference between the two standpoints as extraordinarily great and profound. Yet as soon as it comes to understanding this as a difference in principle, they at least want to see it basically in a different light. I can only describe my own standpoint as purely historical. Accordingly, the task is to understand Christianity as, already in its origins, a historically given phenomenon and, as such, to comprehend it in historical terms. People have no general objection to this, and are often happy and willing to agree in principle. So it surprises me when one of my most recent critics, indeed in his review of my book on the Tübingen School,[1] declares in opposition to me:

1. *Die Tübinger Schule und ihre Stellung zur Gegenwart* (Tübingen, 1859 [2nd rev. ed., 1860]).

The issue is whether or not we have the right to view early Christianity from the same standpoint of historical development as that otherwise generally applicable to secular history. At least Protestant research agrees that this standpoint holds good for all other areas of church history. . . . We do not want to believe that someone is seriously inclined to push the antithesis to this extreme. In any event it is so very obvious that, if research should no longer retain the right to comprehend the supernatural too as in turn at the same time something natural, therefore entering [as supernatural] into, and developing within, the historical setting, then the most advisable course would be to dispense with all further scientific investigation of it. This would of course be a very fundamental reversal for science, and many gentlemen would certainly find nothing more desirable than seeing the mouths of the malevolent critics shut forever.

If people are not arguing with me about the principle, then the only question concerns how consistently they adhere to the principle and put it into practice. In fact there is no other issue. Everything just depends solely on whether people also remain faithful to the principle they recognize, when it is a matter of applying it in practice to a specific area of historical research. Yet this very thing is so often their stumbling-block. For what is a scientific view worth if it is not also supported by a scientific frame of mind in the one who holds it? Suppose that one directly seeks to circumvent the principle one has only just established, and to substitute for it something entirely different that is its direct opposite. Or that one is alarmed by the difficulty following from its application, a difficulty one can take as a candid acknowledgment of how things stand. Or if one concocts hypotheses in order to avoid the difficulty, ones too untenable to be seriously intended. Or if one emphasizes minor details in order to camouflage agreement with the principle, under the pretext of differing with it. Or, finally, even not shying away from obvious contradictions. How can such strategies involve anything other than holding two very widely divergent views, despite all the pretense of their unity in principle? In the end, whatever involves such a contradiction with its own principle can only collapse internally.

Genuine historical actuality exists only where there is life and movement, coherent and progressive development, and a more profound disclosure of the antitheses that first have to be undergone through struggle and conflict if they are to be overcome and reconciled. Thus one cannot contest the way I present things here. It relies on a view of history that, by consistently applying its principle, is sufficiently fertile and vigorous that it does not shy away from comparisons with opposing views.

It contains a detailed discussion of the aforementioned issues. [*Ed.*] Reprint of the 2nd ed. in *Ausgewählte Werke in Einzelausgaben*, ed. Klaus Scholder, vol. 5 (Stuttgart–Bad Cannstatt, 1975). The term "Tübingen School" was first coined by Baur's opponents. He wrote this book in response to an 1858 essay by Gerhard Uhlhorn (also reprinted in *Ausgewählte Werke*, vol. 5), who claimed that the School was in the process of breaking up. Baur does not identify the author of the review.

Without hesitation, I leave it to the future to judge which of the two approaches will be acknowledged as having had the truth overwhelmingly on its side.

Recently, in the final volume of his *Geschichte des Volkes Israel*, Ewald dealt with a part of the same period I discuss in this work.[2] So I am tempted to compare his understanding of history with my own. I will remark here on just this one point. We can already see, from the organization of his work, what an unclear conception this historian of the people of Israel has of Christianity's relation to the people of Israel. According to their titles, the first four volumes were said to just go up to Christ, whereas the fifth volume also adopted *Die Geschichte Christus' und seine Zeit* into the overall plan. A new body of material was added in volume 6, with the account of the apostolic age up to the destruction of Jerusalem, and the sequence concluded with volume 7 [1859], *Geschichte der Ausgänge des Volkes Israel*. This account of the ending of an era also appeared again with a twofold title. The full title, as it was put in place only after the final printing of the work, does not just include "the endings of the people of Israel," but instead is *Geschichte der Ausgänge des Volkes Israel und des nachapostolischen Zeitalters*. Ewald states in the preface (p. ix) that he "decided to call attention to the twofold content of this volume, at least on the book cover, simply for the sake of many who want to close their eyes to it, for it is self-evident that this is the end of an era in a twofold way, an ending in perdition and another one leading to a new, eternal salvation."

What is the need for a twofold title when the matter is self-evident? It seems that Ewald has been unable to wholly conceal the internal deficiency of his not-very-organically generated work in the indicated way. What is the point of referring twice here to the ending? Must we not think that, with a work said to have its natural conclusion, an author who must instruct the reader so emphatically about the endings does not rightly know himself how matters in fact stand with them; that in order to extricate himself from the different paths on which he wanders, he must first search for the ending himself. It is as though, based on different endings, we were to hear the call, "Can I just find the ending!" That is in fact the case. Whoever, like Ewald, has hardly made it clear how Christianity relates to the history of the people of Israel, where Christianity is anchored in this history, and how Christianity separates and detaches itself from it—whoever, with the vague, indeterminate concept of the truly consummate religion, as this vague concept is said to have been in the possession of

---

2. [*Ed.*] In what follows, Baur responds to Heinrich Ewald (1803–1875), Orientalist and biblical scholar, who taught for ten years in Tübingen (1837–47) before returning to his native Göttingen, where he had studied with J. G. Eichhorn. He engaged in a bitter personal controversy with Baur over the origins of Christianity, leading to an attack in the last volume of his *Geschichte des Volkes Israel*, 7 vols. (Göttingen, 1843–59). Ewald was also the editor/author of the *Jahrbücher der biblischen Wissenschaft*, in which he attacked Baur for many years. Ewald believed that divine providence assigned a special task to each of the nations of antiquity. The history of Israel was the history of how humanity acquired the one true religion, beginning with the exodus and culminating with Christ and Christianity. Ewald had a reputation for aggressive and often personal polemics.

the people of Israel from the outset, believes he has captured the guiding thread right up into the first Christian century; and who just knows how to repeat the stock phrase about the truly consummate religion and its eternally same essence, where it is not merely a matter of recounting events and calls for thoughtful consideration at critical points—does not of course know where the one ceases and the other one begins. How externally do the two endings stand vis-à-vis each other here? At what point, and on what basis, have these religions then separated into these two side-by-side paths? In the same manner as the ending of the people of Israel is also said to be the ending of the post-apostolic age, could one not also have made the entire histories of the world and of the church into an appendix to Ewald's history of the people of Israel?

Ewald's entire presentation of Christianity in this period accords with this vague concept of the ending. Here Christianity still appears in some fashion interlaced and entwined with Judaism, as though it would have been incapable of any independent action of its own, and that it could only have enjoyed the fresh air of a free existence, not merely after the destruction of Jerusalem but also when the last Jewish uprising under Bar Cochba had been entirely suppressed. Hence Ewald, in the best fashion of a pragmatic historiography according to a well-known but now superannuated Göttingen specimen,[3] holds forth most especially about the immeasurable consequences for Christianity that the destruction of Jerusalem supposedly had for "the everywhere tenuous groundwork of the apostolic church"—and doing so in a flurry of words whose pathos, with its persistent, and ever more forcefully intensified excitement, is of course not in itself the mindset of a calm and objective historian.

Ewald has, in the customary way, combined with the preface to this seventh volume, a survey of the entire literary and political world, an overview he had to be especially inclined to provide then, right at the pinnacle where he stood in concluding a work that, in the "more than thirty years in which he directed his mental labors to the topic, and the nearly twenty years he set his hand to the task of writing about it," embraces such an extensive and eventful period of time—and fully conscious of "the recognition the now concluded work has gained." Naturally, I am fittingly included among the harmful influences of our time that oppose his views, and he cannot sufficiently bewail their fundamentally destructive impact as compared with his own influence, which alone is salutary. This time he gives me such extensive attention, since I did indeed just recently venture to say something judgmental about him.[4] Yet

---

3. [*Ed.*] Baur's reference here is perhaps to Gottlieb Jakob Planck (1751–1833), one of Ewald's predecessors at Göttingen, a "rational supernaturalist" whose method is described in Baur's *Epochs of Church Historiography* (p. xxiii n. 3) as "subjective pragmatism at its peak" (184 ff., esp. 185 n. 29).

4. *Die Tübinger Schule* (n. 1), 119–68. Among other things, he states his views about this in his preface ([to vol. 7], p. xviii), that what I have to say in detail against others, and express in a "feebler" and briefer way against him, is so completely vacuous, but also so completely foolish and undoubtedly off the mark, that in saying this I have just provided a reminder of my own unscientific methods. In a subsequent article in the *Jahrbücher der biblischen Wissenschaft* Ewald adds that one need not waste one's time evaluating such "Tübingen scribbling." The way he seeks to find solace here, in the impression this little text has made on him, is too ingenuous, as is his wish to rise above this treachery. He

everything he has to say in reply just confirms what I said. Now he can only scold and belittle, and just give new proof of his utter inability to even stand apart from himself and his own subjectivity, as rational reflection calls for in opposing its enemies. It is truly ridiculous how, in painting the darkest picture of my entire life and influence, in attributing to me superficiality, fundamental perversity, rashness, laziness, and appalling consequences of my own making, he reproaches me for extremely pernicious errors and false aspirations. He supposes he can, at a single stroke, cancel out my entire life's activity.

Does he then believe it all comes down to railing haphazardly, in the crudest and most vulgar way, against the opponent so that the whole world would believe it too? I am a public figure just like he is. Anyone who knows me can judge my writings, my scholarly activity; and I do not even in the least fear comparison of what someone says about me with what I am in reality and what influence I have. I can only be amazed at his failure to see how, in saying nothing about others, he leaves himself open by such a lack of critical judgment. Just how has it impressed any one of my opponents when, among so many disparaging and defamatory things he has long said about me, he also, in his *Jahrbücher der biblischen Wissenschaft*, has for years, in the most absurd way, also denied that I have any ethical consciousness? How does it vouch for the objectivity of his historical judgment when, where everything is laid out and all can judge for themselves, he hardly knows himself how to distinguish his own subjective notions, his set ideas, the products of his own malicious passions, from the true state of affairs? There can be nothing vaguer, more trivial, more pointless, than such an exhibition of Ewald's calumny, the kind he reiterates in his most recent preface. From it one can simply see how little he even knows what he is talking about. It is a forewarning of the contradictions in which he gets himself embroiled.

On p. xvi [of vol. 7] Ewald brags about never having in the least done anything contrary to freedom and science. Yet there can be nothing more high-handed than the peremptory way he treats all his opponents (and of course all who find themselves opposing him in any sort of difference of opinion, and do not unconditionally embrace his own views and perceptions, are opponents), and how he wants to dominate, in the manner of a despot, by claiming absolute authority. In his love for the freedom of science, he also calls upon the Swabians to make even greater efforts than previously to liberate their Tübingen from such a reputation (as I have given it and Tübingen has acquired because of me)! It is surely obvious what kind liberation he has in mind,

---

supposes I could just publish "feebler" thoughts, although all those besides himself are feebler than he, the unparalleled one. While he supposes he would be exempted from what I say against him more briefly than I say it about others, one can nevertheless state briefly what hits the nail on the head. However, if he should once try to rebut just one sentence of this "scribbling" of mine—naturally not in everyday expressions that are of course always at hand, but in a scientific way, with reasons and proofs—that will show whether or not he is in a position to do so. [*Ed.*] In *Die Tübinger Schule*, Baur describes and criticizes Ewald's attempt (in the fifth volume of his history of Israel) to harmonize the Gospel of John's portrayal of Christ with that found in the Synoptic Gospels.

from how he has depicted my influence, mine alone, and from what he can hope for from the Swabians he has called upon to support him.

If anything Ewald says about me, and considers to be the basically destructive feature of my influence, has any sort of rational sense behind it, that could only be related to my disputing the apostolic origin of several of the canonical scriptures. But does he not do the same thing himself? Indeed, he too declares that a number of canonical epistles are pseudo-apostolic writings: Ephesians, the three Pastoral Epistles, and Second Peter. And if one cannot speak of "pseudo-apostolic" scriptures without employing the correct concept of pseudonymity, in the ancient sense, then he certainly has the same view of it (see 7:139, 231, 248, 315, and 321) as the one I have long held. So what is the point of this overly fanatical opposition to me, as though the issue involves the most absolute antithesis!

Let him express himself and blow off steam howsoever he will, about important and unimportant matters in the political and literary world as well as about me, under the cover of a freedom that no rational person can be envious of. All this is not in the slightest way a verdict calling for my attention. In his most recent preface he recalls our previous collegial relations, in order to inform me that, as he is now proud to say, back then he thought our collegial friendship was bogus. That statement gives me greater insight into the cause of the hatred he now bears, not merely against me but also against Tübingen in general. The cause lies in what he calls my philosophical presuppositions[5] ([vol. 7], p. xvi). For him, to be sure, the direct opposite is the case—the absence of what, very understandably, seems to him a very extraneous presupposition, whereas here in Tübingen it is still always counted among the requisites of a scientifically educated theologian. He was supposedly less bitterly enraged in 1848, the year he broke free from his captivity in Tübingen.

The fate of the view of history I have championed is that it has to fight its way past opponents of all kinds. So the reader may excuse me for using this space to present the foregoing account, which had to be stated in the interest of truth, and to publicly express the moral contempt that such conduct deserves from all educated people.

The struggles I have previously endured have hardly disheartened me. Instead I felt the desire and fortitude to continue the history of the early church up to the end of the sixth century, with the continuation appearing in 1859 as a companion to this book.[6] I also plan to venture on to the medieval church and to follow out the history

---

5. [Ed.] Ewald regarded Baur's philosophical presuppositions, based on Schelling and Hegel, to be atheistic because they did not allow for a supernatural causality. Rather for Baur the divine idea operates *within* the historical nexus and does not interrupt natural causality. He believed that every historian makes at least implicit philosophical assumptions.

6. [Ed.] *Die christliche Kirche vom Anfang des vierten bis zum Ende des sechsten Jahrhunderts* (Tübingen, 1859). Baur prepared the third volume, on the medieval church, for the press, but it was not published until after his death. He suffered a severe stroke in July 1860, followed by a second fatal stroke in late autumn. The last two volumes, from the Reformation to the middle of the nineteenth century, were based on lecture notes, edited by F. F. Baur and E. Zeller.

of its development in similar fashion, to the extent that my already aging powers still permit it.

Tübingen, February 1860

Part 1

The Entrance of Christianity
into World History;
Primitive Christianity

The Universalism of the Roman Empire as a Preparation for Christianity

In no area of historical examination does everything that belongs to a specific series of historical phenomena depend so much on the starting point from which it proceeds as it does in the history of the Christian Church. Thus nowhere else does so much depend on the representation we form of that point from which the entire historical course takes its beginning.

The historian who enters upon the object of his presentation with the faith of the church is confronted at the very outset with the miracle of all miracles, the primal fact of Christianity—that the only-begotten Son of God descended to earth from the eternal throne of the Godhead and became human in the womb of the Virgin. Whoever regards this as simply and absolutely a miracle immediately steps completely outside the nexus of history. Miracle is an absolute beginning, and to the extent that such a beginning conditions everything that follows, the whole series of phenomena that belong to the field of Christianity must then bear the same miraculous character. That is because severing the historical connection at the outset makes it possible to do so again. Therefore a truly historical examination or reflection (*die geschichtliche Betrachtung*)[1] very naturally is concerned to draw the miracle of the absolute beginning into the historical nexus and to resolve it, insofar as possible, into its natural elements.

People have often attempted to do this, and various objections have been brought against their attempts, but the task itself remains always the same. By just asking why

---

1. [Ed.] *Betrachtung* is the term Baur typically uses for critical, scientific (*wissenschaftlich*) historical method. It has both an empirical and a speculative (reflective) component, as our double translation suggests. Empirically, it investigates the wealth of historical materials and follows where they lead regardless of the historian's subjective interests. Speculatively, it knows "how to grasp historical phenomena as appearances of the idea objectifying itself within them, and how to comprehend them as moments of the idea's immanent working within history" (*Kirchengeschichte des neunzehnten Jahrhunderts*, ed. Eduard Zeller, 1st ed. [Tübingen, 1862], 416. *Church and Theology in the Nineteenth Century*, ed. P. C. Hodgson, trans. R. F. Brown and P. C. Hodgson [Eugene, OR, 2018], 385.). This immanent working does not sever, but rather constitutes, the historical nexus (*Zusammenhang*). When the systematic meaning is not so evident, *Betrachtung* is translated as "consideration," "view," "perspective," etc.

the miracle with which the history of Christianity begins has entered into the nexus of historical events precisely at this point in world history, we have already raised a series of questions that can only be answered by means of historical examination and reflection. Therefore the first task in a history of Christianity, or of the Christian Church, can only be to orient ourselves to Christianity at the point in time when it enters into world history. So we ask whether we can recognize, on the one hand, something here that belongs to the essence of Christianity itself, and on the other hand, something here that expresses the general character of the age in which Christianity appears. Where such common points of contact emerge, they shed light on the historical origin of Christianity itself.

In doing so, early Christian apologists already found it especially significant that Christianity appeared precisely at the point in time when the Roman Empire reached the zenith of its worldly dominion. They inferred from this that, even in the eyes of the pagans, a religion could not but appear auspicious whose epoch coincided with the fullest flourishing of the Roman Empire. This coincidence of Christianity with the Roman world monarchy[2] appeared to them so remarkable that they could not attribute it to chance.[3]

The true point of contact between Christianity and the Empire, however, is the universal tendency of both. It is a reflection of genuine significance for world history that, at the same point in time when the Roman Empire united all the peoples of the then-known world in a universal monarchy, the religion that subsumed (*aufhob*)[4] all religious particularism into universality began its course in the world. Thus the universalism of Christianity was comparable to the stage already attained by the power and genius of Rome with its world monarchy. This was in fact the time when universal world-consciousness first made this momentous advance. As the barriers and divisions between peoples and nationalities vanished before the encroaching power of the Romans, and people became aware, through their subjection to a common head, of the unity subsuming their differences, spiritual consciousness as such was proportionately enlarged and led more and more to disregard the particular traits that separated one group from another, and to elevate itself to a universal perspective.

The general striving of the age toward an all-encompassing unity, into which everything particular and individual might be resolved, found its most imposing expression in the universalism of the Roman Empire. This universalism was the very goal toward which the course of world history had aimed for many centuries. Alexander the Great had opened to the West the portals of the East; and, by means of so

---

2. [*Ed.*] Baur uses the term "monarchy" here and several times below, although the Romans were very clear that the emperor was not a "king." The Roman Republic had replaced the earlier kings, and the Romans wanted no more of that kind of monarchy.

3. See the fragment of the *Apology* of Melito of Sardis in Eusebius, *Ecclesiastical History* 4.26; and Origen, *Against Celsus* 2.30.

4. [*Ed.*] The verb *aufheben* means both to annul and to preserve or take up. Thus particularism does not simply disappear but is "taken up into" universality.

many newly-opened routes for the lively and diverse intercourse of peoples, the Greek language and culture had spread throughout the known world. It was but the next step on the same road of world-historical development when the Roman dominion gave all these peoples a new bond of political unity in forms never seen before. This all-encompassing unity found its basis in Roman civilization and law, and operated through the vast and highly organized Roman state. Under the empire, not only was there a reduction in the former hostility among its constituent peoples; but also everything national and individual increasingly resolved itself into a universality that smoothed over their differences.

A group that from its beginnings had kept itself apart from other peoples by the distinctiveness of its national character, and that had clung to this distinctiveness in the most obstinate and persistent way, nevertheless could not remain outside this general unity, which bound peoples together not merely politically but also in a new spiritual bond. After the Jewish state had twice been destroyed,[5] the Jews were forced to associate with other peoples in the wider world. When the successors of Alexander founded their own kingdoms, in those cities that became the chief centers of political and intellectual intercourse among peoples, Jews were an important part of the population. These Jews became Hellenists and assimilated the most diverse elements of Greek culture. Ultimately they were also drawn into the ever-widening net of Roman dominion. So it came about that the birthplace of Christianity on Jewish soil was already in contact with the power that was said to be its forerunner on the road to world conquest.

Thus the universalism of Christianity has its essential presupposition in the universalism of Roman world dominion. But in considering how these two world powers came into contact with each other, we must not think in customary teleological terms. We must not think that, in these external circumstances and connections, Christianity entered into the world by the special favor of divine providence—a providence that, so the supposition goes, could have selected no more appropriate a time than this for the accomplishment of its purposes. On that view the major consideration is merely the fact that so many new routes of communication facilitated the diffusion of Christianity throughout the provinces of the Roman Empire, and that the protection of the Roman legions and civil order removed many obstacles the messengers of the gospel otherwise could have faced.[6]

5. [*Ed.*] Through the Assyrian and Babylonian conquests.

6. See Origen, *Against Celsus* 2.30. To the objection of Celsus that the sun first displays itself by illuminating all other things, and that the Son of God ought to have presented himself in the same way, Origen answers that he in fact did so. "For righteousness has arisen in his days, and there is abundance of peace, which took its commencement at his birth, God preparing the nations for his teaching, that they might be under one Roman emperor, and that it might not, owing to the want of union among the nations, caused by the existence of many kingdoms, be more difficult for the apostles of Jesus to accomplish the task enjoined upon them by their Master, when he said, 'Go and teach all nations.' Moreover it is certain that Jesus was born in the reign of Augustus, who, so to speak, fused together into one monarchy the many populations of the earth. Now the existence of many kingdoms would

The bond that connects the two powers is based, far more deeply and inwardly, on the general spiritual and intellectual movement of the time. The main point is that Christianity could not have been the universal form of religious consciousness that it is had the entire development of world history, up to the time when it appeared, not prepared the way for it. First came the general intellectual culture that the Greeks made the common property of the nations, then Roman rule uniting the nations, with its political institutions serving as the basis for universal civilization. Roman rule removed the limitations of national consciousness and set aside the many differences that had kept peoples separate, not merely in their outward relationships but even more so inwardly. The universalism of Christianity could never have passed over into peoples' general consciousness had not political universalism prepared the way for that to happen. Christianity is itself essentially the same form of general consciousness to which the development of humankind had already advanced at the time of Christianity's appearance.

have been a hindrance to the spread of the doctrine of Jesus throughout the entire world; not only for the reasons mentioned, but also on account of the necessity of men everywhere engaging in war, and fighting on behalf of their native country, which was the case before the times of Augustus, and in periods still more remote, when necessity arose, as when the Peloponnesians and Athenians warred against each other, and other nations in like manner. How, then, was it possible for the gospel doctrine of peace, which does not permit men to take vengeance even upon enemies, to prevail throughout the world, unless at the advent of Jesus a milder spirit had been everywhere introduced into the conduct of things?" [*Ed.*] Rather than translating Baur's German version, we have for the most part used the text translated from Greek in *ANF* 4:443–44.

Christianity and the Pre-Christian Religions

By viewing Christianity as a universal form of religious consciousness that corresponds to the spirit of the age, and for which the entire previous historical development of peoples has been preparing, we have grasped it at the point where it enters into world history. But what gives Christianity this universal form? It appears as the universal form of religious consciousness because it increasingly overcame the other religions, absorbed them, and transcended them by its universal dominion over the world. As opposed to those particular forms of religion, it is the absolute religion. But what is it in Christianity that gives it its absolute character? The first answer to this question is that Christianity rises above all the defects and limitations, the one-sidedness and finitude, that constitute the particularism of those other religious forms. It is not polytheistic like paganism; it does not, like Judaism, attach itself to outward rites and ordinances, or to the positive[7] aspects of a purely traditional religion. Speaking generally, it stands above them as a more spiritual form of religious consciousness.

This, however, is saying very little and is self-evident as soon as we compare Christianity with the other two religions it encountered [paganism and Judaism]. When Christianity attained its world-historical significance, these two religions had long fallen into decay. They had become empty, inwardly dying, purely external forms that had lost their hold on the religious consciousness of their peoples. Paganism had sunk to the level of a spiritless folk religion. With all educated people, belief in the old gods had become more or less disconnected from religious consciousness. The myths in which the simpler faith of earlier times had expressed its finest religious intuitions seemed now mere fables in which there was no longer a spiritual bond joining form and content into a harmonious unity; they were merely pictorial forms for ideas that had grown up from a totally different soil. The only thing that maintained general interest in the national religion was that, as the religion of the state, it was closely intertwined with all the institutions of political life, and not easily separable from them.

Judaism, to be sure, rested on a wholly different religious foundation. For the Jews "the religion of their fathers" was never a meaningless expression, and religious

---

7. [*Ed.*] The tension between "the positive" (historical and authoritative) and "the spiritual" (ideal and inward) is a constant theme of this volume. Both are present in every religion, but the balance between them shifts as we move from Judaism to Christianity, and within Christianity itself.

worship continued undiminished, with all of its elaborate ceremonies. But the fragmentation into so many sects and parties that hardly agreed on the most important issues, clearly shows that here too the national religion was tending toward dissolution.

These two religions had been making way in this fashion for a new religion; and if we look at the situation from the teleological point of view, we can only regard it as a special dispensation of divine providence that Christianity came into existence at precisely the point in time when there was so great a void to be filled in the religious life of the ancient world. But this point of view also fails to provide deeper insight into the inner connection of Christianity, as a new form of religious consciousness, with the preceding development of religion.

In addition to everything that constituted a more or less harsh antithesis between the pre-Christian religions and Christianity, their main point of contact has generally been taken to be how these earlier religions were negatively related to Christianity and the religious feelings and needs awakened thereby. People said that disbelief and superstition (*Unglaube und Aberglaube*) were of course two forces in the paganism and Judaism resistant to Christianity. Yet these forces also involved factors that facilitated the transition to Christianity and made souls receptive to it. There was also a disbelief sustained simply because the need to believe could not be satisfied by anything the ancient world could offer in terms of religion and philosophy. For human nature has an undeniable desire to know the supernatural and be in communion with it. So when disbelief is all-encompassing, that only intensifies the desire to believe. The same was the case to a large extent with superstition, at the root of which lay a need that looked for satisfaction and could find it only in Christianity—the need for deliverance from a deeply felt disconnect, for reconciliation with an unknown God whom people were looking for, whether consciously or not.[8]

Here some interpreters resort to immediate religious feeling as the source of people's receptivity for Christianity. Christianity too undoubtedly has its roots, like every other religion, in this primary ground of all religious life. But to just trace Christianity back to this feeling still leaves us very much in the broad and ill-defined realm of subjective contexts. The question is not what distinctive frame of mind might dispose this or that individual to adopt Christianity, or what individual circumstances might make a person more or less receptive to its content. The question rather is how Christianity, objectively considered, relates to everything constituting the religious development of the world, not merely in its negative but also in its positive aspects. The universal tendency of Christianity presupposed the universalism to which the

---

8. See August Neander, *Allgemeine Geschichte der christlichen Religion und Kirche*, 2nd ed., 4 vols (Hamburg, 1842–47), 1:7 ff and 56ff. [*Ed.*] ET: *General History of the Christian Religion and Church*, trans. Joseph Torrey (London and Boston, 1849–51), 1:5ff. and 46ff. August Neander (1789–1850), born David Mendel, converted to Christianity under the influence of Schleiermacher, and was a popular and prolific professor of church history at the University of Berlin. Baur became increasingly critical of Neander's partisanship in later years. See his discussion of Neander in *Kirchengeschichte des neunzehnten Jahrhunderts* (n. 1), 223ff., 369, 380, 382, 384 [ET 209ff., 339, 350, 352, 354].

collective consciousness of the age had already expanded under the influence of the Roman world empire. If this is the case, then the overall religious and spiritual development of the world must be inwardly and objectively related to everything that constitutes not merely the universal, but also the absolute, character of Christianity.

Here, however, it is of first importance to not understand this absolute character of Christianity too narrowly and one-sidedly. Some have thought to find the absoluteness merely in the fact that Christianity welcomes, and most fully satisfies, the human longing for belief; or in its being a supernatural revelation, a universal arrangement for the reconciliation of human beings with God; or because it sets before us, in the person of its founder, one who is the Son of God and the God-man, in the sense the church uses these words. But these answers just lead us to ask what it is about these features of Christianity that makes it superior to the other religions, for the pre-Christian world believed it had more or less analogous features. Every religion claimed to be a supernatural revelation, and there were numerous procedures for reconciling human beings with God. People thought that fellowship with God was provided by beings whose functions were nearly the same as those of the Christian Son of God. What is it then that gives Christianity its peculiar and specific superiority over everything that more or less resembled it in the pre-Christian world? Christianity may be regarded under various points of view, each of which always exhibits only one of the various aspects we can distinguish in it as such. But what forms Christianity's common and all-encompassing unity?

In brief, it is the spiritual character of Christianity as such. We take into account the fact that it is far freer than any other religion from everything merely external, sensible, and material. It has a deeper basis than any other in the innermost substance of human nature and in the principles of moral consciousness. It says that it knows no worship of God other than "worship in spirit and truth."[9] When we fix our attention on its spiritual character as such, the absoluteness of its essence in this broadest and most general sense, how then is Christianity linked to the pre-Christian world and the world contemporaneous with it? What features do we find in the general development of the world that are closest and most related to it, ones that are preconditions for it in regard to its inner essence?

The two religions preceding Christianity, as we have already noted, were in such a condition of decay and dissolution that, at the time they came into contact with Christianity, no one who had become aware of their imperfection and finitude, or who had seen them as they really were, could come away without the feeling of an infinite void, a craving for satisfaction that could not be filled by anything in the entire sphere of these religions, the longing for a positive point of contact to which religious consciousness might attach itself. But what had caused such decay and dissolution in these religions and brought them to ruin? How could this have happened even before the arrival of Christianity? Some other power, a greater power than they, must have

---

9. [*Ed.*] John 4:24: "God is spirit, and those who worship him must worship in spirit and truth."

come over them. It is a common and very serious mistake to suppose that periods of transition, such as occurred during the time of the appearance of Christianity, are simply times of decay and dissolution, times of a completely moribund spiritual and religious life. The forms of previously active religious life do indeed become increasingly decadent until they are completely emptied of the content that once filled them. But the reason for this is that they have become too narrow and limited for the spirit whose religious consciousness they had served to mediate. When something old collapses, something new is always already there to replace it; the old could not decay if the new had not arrived, even if only as a seed, and had not been long laboring to undermine and render meaningless the previously existing structure. It may take a long time for a new form of religious and spiritual life to take shape in an outwardly evident way, but the spirit doing the shaping is nevertheless silently long at work; there is already fermentation in the depths, and the vital process moving ahead in its unbroken continuity cannot rest until it has brought forth a new creation.[10]

---

10. [*Ed.*] This is a very Hegelian perception, as expressed for example in Hegel's lectures on the philosophy of world history. See G. W. F. Hegel, *Lectures on the Philosophy of World History*, vol. 1, ed. Peter C. Hodgson, trans. Robert F. Brown and Peter C. Hodgson (Oxford, 2011), 107–10, 155–66 (passages on historical development, transitions, and progression). At the very end of his discussion of the Greek World, Hegel refers to the circumstances described by Polybius in which "good and practical persons must either despair or withdraw. And such circumstances, together with such personalities, call for a power to which they themselves finally succumb—a power that judges and discloses the impotence of the old way. Over against these parochial concerns, and the fixation in these finite circumstances in which all that is particular in states and personalities rigidifies itself, a destiny appears that can only negate what has gone before; it is blind, harsh, and abstract. And the Roman Empire plays the role of this fate" (425). It is under this fate that Christianity arrives in the world, introducing a new principle antithetical to the Roman principle, the principle of freedom as opposed to that of dominion and servitude (447ff.).

Greek Philosophy

The decay of paganism is not to be dated from the time when Christianity appeared, and it is certainly not brought about by Christianity. It had been under way from the beginning, from the time when there was not simply a Greek religion but also a Greek philosophy. This philosophy not only offered critical reflection on the popular religious myths but also constituted for itself a world independent of the myths, in the realm of free thought. In this world, the spirit that could no longer find an adequate form for its consciousness in the myths of the popular religion was elevated to a new sphere of its own thinking and intuition.

Thus, in addition to the religious teaching of the Old Testament, Greek philosophy provides the only other spiritual point of contact between Christianity and the pre-Christian historical development of humankind. Its relation to Christianity has always been taken into account, first and foremost, when people have tried to get their bearings on Christianity's place in world history. But the negative rather than the positive aspect of this relationship has customarily been emphasized far more. Despite its apparent defects and biases, people simply give the edge to Platonism. It spiritualized religious thought; it turned away from polytheism to a secure unity of God-consciousness; it stimulated many ideas akin to Christianity, such as the idea of redemption as a deliverance from the blind force of nature that opposes the divine; in Christianity it elevated people to the standpoint of a divine life, beyond the influence of natural powers.

Both Epicureanism and Stoicism[11] are regarded as much less likely candidates. It is said to be self-evident that a system of atheism and eudaemonism such as the Epicurean philosophy can have nothing whatsoever to do with Christianity. And there is the strongest possible contrast between the proud self-sufficiency of the Stoic sage and

---

11. [*Ed.*] Epicureanism is a system of philosophy based on the teachings of Epicurus (c. 307 BC), which advocated "pleasure" as the greatest good, but a pleasure that can be achieved only by living modestly, gaining knowledge of how the world works, and limiting one's desires. It originally challenged Platonism but later became the main opponent of Stoicism. Stoicism is a system of Hellenistic philosophy that flourished throughout the Greek and Roman worlds for about 600 years, so-called because its founder, Zeno (c. 308 BC), taught under a colonnade (*stoa*) in Athens. It offered a system of personal ethics based on accepting what is given by life and not indulging one's desire for pleasure or fear of pain.

the humility of the believing Christian. We cannot judge otherwise as long as we focus only on the points where the contrasts are most extreme. Our task, however, is not to focus on individual instances, but to place all the phenomena under the universal perspective of historical development. The question, therefore, is how Greek philosophy, from its principal epoch onward, has been related to Christianity.

The question appears in quite a different light when we recall the well-known parallel so often drawn between Christ and Socrates.[12] There is some truth in it, for Christianity culminates an orientation in the field of pagan religion and philosophy that began with Socrates. All the principal ensuing forms of Greek philosophy serve a mediating function for Christianity. The more closely we follow the course taken by the thinking spirit in this most important period of Greek philosophy, the more clearly we also see why Christianity entered into world history at just this point in time. If the essence of Christianity is located solely in its character as a supernatural revelation, then there is no point in considering its appearance in a broader context, and looking back to the period beginning with Socrates. But in any event Christianity has a genuinely human side; and the more sharply we bring into view its origin, the manner and means by which it introduced itself into the world and sought to gain entrance into human hearts, the more directly it appears to us in its genuinely human character. The first words it proclaims are the demand that human beings must look within themselves (*Insichgehen*) and repent (μετάνοια). These words already articulate how Christianity addresses human beings and the entire standpoint from which it understands their relationship to God. Above all it earnestly calls human beings to direct their gaze within, to turn within themselves, to plumb the depths of their own self-consciousness. In this way they are to learn what their relationship to God is, and what it ought to be, and to become aware of everything in their moral nature that awakens, in all its depth and intensity, the need for redemption. In short, it rests on everything that makes Christianity to be religion in the absolute sense—that human beings know themselves as moral subjects. If human moral consciousness had not already been fully developed in all those aspects that concern its deeper significance [as it had with Socrates], Christianity could not have appeared in human history with its own distinctive character as a genuinely moral religion.

Human beings first became moral subjects, however, when they became aware of the concept of the subject, the principle of subjectivity. This is the truly epochal significance of Socrates.[13] [He was the first to demand] that the subject look within, that

---

12. [*Ed.*] Socrates (c. 470–399 BC) was the teacher of Plato and Xenophon and the chief protagonist in Plato's dialogues, through which he is known to the world, since he is not known to have written anything himself.

13. See my book, *Das Christliche des Platonismus, oder Socrates und Christus* (Tübingen, 1837), 20ff.; and Zeller, *Die Philosophie der Griechen in ihrer geschichtlichen Entwicklung*, 2nd ed., vol. 2 (Tübingen, 1859), 78ff. [*Ed.*] Eduard Zeller (1814–1908) was Baur's student and son-in-law. He taught theology in Bern and Marburg before shifting to philosophy because of church opposition. Subsequently he taught philosophy in Heidelberg and Berlin, and became best known for his history of

human beings go within themselves, that the mind or spirit withdraw from the outer world to the interior world of subjectivity, so as to apprehend what is intrinsically true and actual in the contents of conceptual thought. Likewise, in the practical arena, by referring virtue back to knowledge, we have the demand for moral self-knowledge, the intensifying of moral consciousness within itself, so as to find the norm of action in the inner self-certainty of the subject. From this point forward we find a series of developments—the epistemological theories of Plato and Aristotle concerned with the general nature of things, the ethical systems of the Stoics and Epicureans, and the later orientations of Skepticism and Eclecticism[14]—in which practical interests increasingly predominated over theoretical ones, and the moral nature of human beings became the chief object of reflective thought in the same way that Christianity must understand it. The Stoics and Epicureans applied themselves most directly and earnestly to the moral task of human beings and the conditions under which it is accomplished. All those frequently discussed questions about the idea of the good, or the highest good, the relation of virtue to happiness, the value of moral action, and so on, are simply the ethical expression of the same major issue that Christianity poses to humanity from its religious point of view. Divergent as these two orientations [Stoicism and Epicureanism] were, the very opposition between the two systems served to arouse moral consciousness and to expand and shape it from all sides such that the ground was already prepared on which Christianity could accomplish its higher moral-religious task.

Given the rigor and purity of its moral principles, Stoicism may certainly seem superior to Epicureanism; but it has been rightly acknowledged[15] that the latter, which leads human beings back from the outer world into themselves, and teaches them to seek the highest happiness in the splendid humaneness of an inwardly satisfied and cultivated mind, has contributed just as much, in its more sensitive fashion, as Stoicism has in its more rigorous way, to a free and universal ethical life (*Sittlichkeit*). Both systems start from the same guiding idea of post-Aristotelian philosophy—the requirement that the subject withdraw into its pure self-consciousness in order to find its unconditioned satisfaction there. According to the one, humanity's vocation and happiness are found only in the subordination of the individual to the reason and law of the whole, which is virtue; according to the other, they are found in the independence of the individual from all that is external, in the awareness of this independence, in the undisturbed enjoyment of individual life, and in freedom from pain. Thus both strive for the same goal in opposite ways, namely the freedom of

---

Greek philosophy, which was translated into English.

14. [*Ed.*] Pyrrho of Elis (365–275 BC) is generally credited with founding the school of Skepticism. Eclecticism comprises a group of Greek and Roman philosophers who selected from existing beliefs those that seemed most reasonable to them. Cicero was one of the best-known Eclectics.

15. Zeller, *Die Philosophie der Griechen* (n. 13), 1st ed., vol. 3.1 (1852), 263ff.

self-consciousness; and this led them to a position that contrasts very sharply with the fundamental religious consciousness of Christianity.

The Stoic and Epicurean sages are ideals equally foreign to Christianity. The common endeavor of both systems is to put human beings on their own (*frei auf sich selbst*) and, through the infinitude of their own self-conscious thinking, to make them utterly independent of external factors; and that is opposed to Christianity's feeling of dependence (*Abhängigkeitsgefühl*).[16] But even the Stoics found it necessary to descend from the heights of their moral idealism and to acknowledge its limits by returning to practical needs. Skepticism was the next stage Greek philosophy took in its development. We see from this process that the unbounded character of consciousness ultimately led, through the contradiction of opposed and mutually annulling tendencies, to an awareness of the limitations of knowledge and to consciousness withdrawing into itself by completely abandoning knowing. The subject withdraws into itself, but it cannot remain so utterly inactive in its abstract and self-imposed subjectivity as not to resort to one form or another of what was called "the probable."[17] Thus Skepticism in its turn gave birth to Eclecticism. This mode of thought moderated the harshness and one-sidedness of the earlier schools by choosing the best ideas available and lifting individual ones out of their systematic settings. It was also well-suited for conjoining religious and practical concerns. At the time of the appearance of Christianity, Eclecticism was the most widely-held way of thinking, and it had taken the form of a popular philosophy and natural theology. The writings of its chief representatives—Cicero, Seneca, Epictetus, and Marcus Aurelius[18]—contain many elements related to Christianity. Their views and doctrines not only present us with the most well-established and practical concerns, mainly drawn from all their predecessors. They also already seem to place us on the soil of Christian religious and moral teaching, and we often come upon sentences whose Christian tone we find surprising.

The firm basis for Eclecticism, which required a standard for testing different opinions, is articulated by Cicero, the best known and most popular writer of the school. This basis is found in immediate consciousness, inner self-certainty, the natural instinct for truth, or innate knowledge. The seeds of morality are innate in us; nature has not merely given the human mind a moral faculty but has bestowed on it the fundamental moral conceptions as an original endowment prior to any instruction;

---

16. [*Ed.*] Baur here employs the term famously associated with Friedrich Schleiermacher's *Glaubenslehre*. See *Christian Faith*, trans. T. N. Tice, C. L. Kelsey, and E. Lawler, 2 vols (Louisville, 2016), 1:18 (§4). Even as he transitioned to Hegel, Baur continued to incorporate important elements from Schleiermacher (and from Kant and Schelling).

17. [*Ed.*] This is an allusion to the teaching of Carneades (c. 214–293 BC), a dialectician and head of the New Academy.

18. [*Ed.*] Marcus Tullius Cicero (106–46 BC) was one of Rome's greatest orators and prose stylists. Lucius Annaeus Seneca (4 BC–AD 65) was a Roman philosopher, statesman, and dramatist. Epictetus (c. AD 50–135) was a Greek-speaking Stoic philosopher. Marcus Aurelius (AD 120–181) was a Roman emperor whose *Mediations* is a source for understanding Neo-Stoic philosophy.

our task is simply to develop these innate conceptions. The closer an individual stands to nature, the more clearly these conceptions will be reflected in him; we learn from children what is in conformity with nature. Belief in divinity rests on a similar foundation. By virtue of the human mind's affinity with God, God-consciousness is given directly with self-consciousness. Humans need only to recollect the mind's origins in order to be led to their creator. Nature itself, therefore, teaches us of the existence of God, and the strongest proof of this truth is its universal recognition.[19] In these few sentences we see clearly traced the outlines of a natural theology, which subsequently was elaborated on within Christianity itself on genuinely Christian grounds. The view that self-consciousness is at the same time God-consciousness is ultimately on the way to regarding its original knowledge as something merely given to it and, in the immediate consciousness of a higher source of knowledge transcending the finite subject, to receiving the revelation of divinity. In its longing for a higher communication of truth and an immediate revelation, Greek philosophy finally concluded its course of development in Neoplatonism.[20]

In summary, when Christianity is viewed from this angle, all these elements indicate to us how it entered into the general history of humanity at a point when preparations had been made for it in many important ways. This is the very point when the profound significance of moral consciousness had dawned on the pagan world—a time when the most spiritual and the most practically important results that Greek philosophy produced in the entire sweep of its ethical endeavors had become the essential content of the general consciousness of the age. It was a generally acknowledged truth that the human being is a moral subject with a specific moral role to play in life. Christianity is itself the key point at which the various orientations pursuing the same goal coalesced, in order to find their specific conceptuality and richest expression in Christianity. When approached from the side of paganism, this is Christianity's position in the nexus of world history. As the absolute religion, however, it likewise unites

---

19. See Zeller, *Die Philosophie der Griechen*, 1st ed. (n. 15), vol. 3:1, 371ff. [He says:] the natural theology that arose on the foundation of Stoicism appears in its purest form, and the one most analogous to the teachings and principles of Christianity, in the writings of Seneca. Compare my essay, "Seneca und Paulus, das Verhältniss des Stoicismus zum Christenthum nach den Schriften Seneca's," *Zeitschrift für wissenschaftliche Theologie* 1 (1858) 161–246, 441–70. A peculiar characteristic of Seneca's Stoicism is his tendency to approach the Christian religious mode of perception to the same extent that he departs from the old system of the Stoa. I have pointed this out under the following aspects: 1. God and the feeling of dependence. 2. Human beings and their need for salvation. 3. The relationship of human beings to each other. 4. Belief in a future life. 5. The difference in principle between the Stoic and Christian worldviews. At the same time I have tried to show how unjustified the rash but popular conclusion is that this tendency must be ascribed to Seneca's acquaintance with Christianity as he heard it proclaimed.

20. [*Ed.*] Neoplatonism was a philosophical tradition arising in the third century AD and lasting about 300 years. Plotinus and Proclus were among its most important thinkers. Despite a great diversity of views, most Neoplatonists saw the whole of reality as subordinate to, and dependent on, a single principle, "the One." Many Christian theologians through the ages have been influenced by Neoplatonism.

the other two religions, paganism and Judaism. Let us therefore consider its relationship to Judaism in order to observe how, in this respect too, Christianity comprises everything that has attained a higher spiritual significance.

Judaism

Christianity arose on Jewish soil, and it is far more closely and directly connected with Judaism. It professes to be nothing other than spiritualized Judaism; its deepest roots originate in the soil of Old Testament religion. In paganism, Greek philosophy developed the content of moral consciousness to the stage at which Christianity could consolidate with it, whereas Judaism shares the same religious concerns with Christianity. The specific superiority of Judaism vis-à-vis all the religious forms of paganism is its pure and refined monotheistic concept of God, which from the earliest times was the essential foundation of Old Testament religion. In its consciousness of God, therefore, Christianity knows itself above all to be at one with Judaism. The God of the Old Testament is also the God of the New, and all the teaching of the Old Testament concerning the essential distinctness of God from the world, and the absolute transcendence and holiness of God's being, is also an essential part of Christian doctrine. But on the other hand the Old Testament concept of God bears such a truly national stamp that the particularism wholly connected with, and springing from, this feature placed Judaism in the most decisive contrast with Christianity. If the Old Testament God-concept was ever to be an adequate form of religious consciousness for Christianity, with its universal and absolute standpoint, this concept first had to be liberated from, and purged of, everything one-sided and deficient, that is, freed from everything just belonging to the limited perspective of Jewish theocracy, and from the anthropomorphic and anthropopathic views inherent in antiquity.

The course taken by the history of the Jewish people involved, of its own accord, various modifications in their religious views generally, and this led to a gradual broadening and spiritualizing of their religious consciousness. Yet on the other hand the fortunes of the people only led them to cling more tightly to their narrow particularism, and to their nationalistic preconceptions and legalistic tradition. A comprehensive change in their outlook first occurred when the Jews found themselves living in kingdoms founded after the death of Alexander the Great, specifically in Egypt and in a city such as Alexandria. In Alexandria, Judaism was reshaped, first of all, by becoming open to the influence of new ideas, ones originally foreign and contrary to it, ideas leading it to abandon its narrow national and political isolation.[21] The Jew-

---

21. See Georgii, "Die neuesten Gegensätze in Auffassung der alexandrinischen Religionsphilosophie,

ish diaspora among foreign peoples had already produced a new hybrid group that blended Judaism with Greek practices and culture. This naturally had to become very important for their general spiritual and religious development. The Hellenism that arose in this way acquired its great world-historical significance when it generated an entirely new form of consciousness, based on the Greco-Jewish philosophy that took shape in Alexandria. In such a setting the Jews were powerfully influenced by Greek thinking, and they could hardly resist the temptation to become more closely acquainted with the ideas and teachings of Greek philosophy. Such an interest could not have arisen without transcending the standpoint of pure Judaism; and the more deeply they occupied themselves with Greek philosophy, the more they had to feel the conflict with their national religious consciousness. On the one hand they could not rid themselves of their interest in the new ideas; on the other hand, their ancestral faith asserted its ancient inalienable authority. This contradiction had to be resolved one way or another.

As is well-known, they reconciled the two by the allegorical interpretation of scripture. According to the way the Jews viewed their sacred books, nothing could be true that was not already contained in them, so scripture had to be the source of the new ideas people had adopted. All that was necessary was to find the right key for the interpretation of the Old Testament writings, and then the interpreter could draw forth from the scriptures the same ideas he himself had unconsciously put into them. In this way an entirely new form of Judaism arose. People believed they were simply holding on to the old faith, whereas they had in fact substituted something entirely new for it. So the writings of the Old Testament that were said to also contain the new content became the mere form for something that far surpassed them. The distinctive character of this Alexandrian Judaism consisted in its breaking through the limits of the old Jewish particularism, in setting them aside as far as this could be done without completely abandoning the standpoint of Old Testament religion. Its teachings took on a greatly modified and generally freer and more spiritual shape. New ideas were introduced that came from a worldview completely different than that of Judaism; and in particular the Old Testament concept of God was raised far above all those elements that belonged merely to the limited sphere of Jewish theocracy. The profound influence that the Alexandrian philosophy of religion—in its highest and most elaborate form as it appears in the writings of Philo[22]—later exercised on Christian theology is the clearest proof that the mode of thought on which it was based had great affinity with the spirit of Christianity. Here, however, we need merely trace the influence of Philo's writings in the sphere where they came into the closest contact

---

insbesondere des jüdischen Alexandrinismus," *Zeitschrift für die historische Theologie* 9 (1839) nos. 3 and 4. [*Ed.*] Ludwig Georgii (1810–96), a theology student in Tübingen, later a pastor in Württemberg.

22. [*Ed.*] Philo of Alexandria (c. 50 BC—c. AD 25) was a Hellenistic Jewish philosopher whose allegorical exegesis was important for Christian theologians but had little influence on Rabbinic Judaism.

with Christianity on its original soil. When looked at in this way, the sects of the *Therapeutae* and the *Essenes*,[23] especially the latter, are a very noteworthy phenomenon.[24]

The Therapeutae are the link between Greco-Alexandrian Judaism and the Essenes of Palestine. However, although closely related to the Egyptian Therapeutae, the Essenes are associated with the sects into which Palestinian Judaism divided. They represent the form in which the Greco-Alexandrian way of seeing things became for Palestinian Jews as well a profoundly religious view of life. This is what puts the Essenes in such a close relationship with Christianity. Of course we should hardly suppose that Christianity itself sprang from Essenism; yet it cannot be denied that the religious view of life of the Essenes is far more closely allied with the original spirit of Christianity than are all the features that marked the sectarian character of the Pharisees and Sadducees. The Essenes certainly attached great value to outward practices, but they were not caught up in the rules and traditions of Pharisaic Judaism or in the external forms of Levitical temple worship. Their religious piety had a more spiritual and inward character, and a thoroughly practical orientation. Their highest goal in life was to rise above material and sensuous things, and to make all their activity the constant practice of all that could lead them to this one end.

The name "Essenes" indicates that they are "physicians of the soul." They sought to use all the means that seem suited to promote the soul's healthy and therapeutic life, and to keep one always open to the influences and revelations of the higher world. Their many features that remind us of the spirit of primitive Christianity include the prohibition of oaths, zealous practice of the duties of benevolence, and collective ownership of goods. One of their distinctive characteristics is their principle of voluntary

---

23. [*Ed.*] The Therapeutae were a Jewish sect that flourished in Alexandria and other parts of the diaspora of Hellenistic Judaism. The primary source concerning them is the account *De vita contemplativa* purportedly by Philo, where they are an example of contemplative life as opposed to the active (but ascetic) life of the Essenes. The Essenes were a Jewish sect that flourished from the 2nd century BC through the 1st century AD. The Dead Sea Scrolls were discovered in what is believed to be an Essene library.

24. On the Essenes, see Zeller, *Die Philosophie der Griechen* (n. 13), 3.2:583. Ritschl, in the *Theologische Jahrbücher* 14 (1855) 315–56, and *Die Entstehung der altkatholischen Kirche*, 2nd ed. (Bonn, 1857), 279ff., traces Essenism to an endeavor to realize the ideal of the priestly kingdom held up before the people of Israel (Exod 19:6), and to form a society of priests answering to it. Zeller opposes this view and argues (*Theologische Jahrbücher* 15 [1856] 401–33) for the commonly accepted view of a connection between Essenism and the Orphic-Pythagorean ascetic discipline and way of life that were so widely diffused in the ancient world and also had an influence on Judaism. The reasons he adduces are enough to refute Hilgenfeld's view that Essenism arose from apocalyptic prophecy (*Die jüdischen Apokalyptik in ihrer geschichtlichen Entwicklung* [Jena, 1857], 245ff.); and these reasons are likely to prevail against any similarly eccentric theories in the future. [*Ed.*] Baur is referring here to a dispute within his own school. On Zeller, see n. 13. Albrecht Ritschl (1822–89) studied at Bonn, Halle, Heidelberg, and Tübingen, where he came under the influence of Baur. But he diverged from the Tübingen School with the 2nd ed. of *Entstehung*, and developed his own theological views, influenced by Kant, Schleiermacher, and Hermann Lotze, when he taught at Bonn and later Heidelberg. For Baur's critique of this work, see Part 2, n. 74. Adolf Hilgenfeld (1823–1907) studied at Berlin and Halle and later taught New Testament at Jena. He was a member of the Tübingen School but did not study under Baur.

poverty—a view of poverty that says it is better to be poor and possess as little as possible in this world, so as to be all the richer in the goods of the world to come.[25] This is the same sense of poverty that we find in Christianity when its first followers are called "blessed" because they are poor in spirit (Matt 5:3). We may reasonably assume that Essenism also had friends and followers who did not share every one of its features. It was a widespread way of thinking and view of life practiced with various modifications and different degrees of rigor. All those who embraced the general turn of religious piety from the external world to inwardness were touched to some degree by the Essene spirit. Thus it is certain that Essenism is one of the most truly spiritual points of contact between Judaism and Christianity. In addition to these affinities in the religious life as such, there is the external factor that the Essenes had their settlements in the same Jewish outlying areas inhabited by a population also including Gentiles, places where Christianity preached the blessedness of the poor. Where else could this gospel of the poor have found such receptive hearts than among those meek of the land whose piety was in so many ways the basis from which Christianity itself arose?

Thus all these various movements, starting from such different quarters, repeatedly meet at the same point; and Christianity, when it is placed in its world-historical context, appears as the natural unity of all these elements. Various and manifold as they are, they belong to one and the same process of development. This process, which moves gradually forward and increasingly eliminates everything that simply bears the marks of what is particular and subjective, can only start out from where the origins of Christianity lie. On what ground, therefore, can we regard Christianity itself as a purely supernatural phenomenon, as an absolute miracle introduced into world history without any natural agency, and thus incapable of being grasped in any historical connection, when wherever we turn we find so many points of connection and affinity linking Christianity most intimately with the entire history of the development of humanity? It contains nothing that was not conditioned by a preceding series of causes and effects; nothing that had not been long prepared in different ways and brought forward to that stage of development at which it appears in Christianity; nothing that had not previously demanded recognition, in one form or another, as a result of rational thinking, as a need of the human heart, or as a requisite of moral consciousness. How then can it be surprising that what had so long been in different ways the goal of all rational striving, and had been forcing itself increasingly and with inner necessity on the developing consciousness of humanity as its most essential content, should have at last found its simplest, purest, and most natural expression in the form in which it appeared in Christianity?

25. See my commentary *De Ebionitarum origine et doctrina ab Essenis rependa* (Tübingen, 1831). Note the passages I have quoted there (p. 30) from Philo, *Quod omnis probus liber*, ed. Mangey, 2:457, and *De vita contemplativa*, Mangey, 2:473; and from Josephus, *de Bello Judaico*, 2.8.3. See also A. F. Dähne, *Geschichtliche Darstellung der jüdisch-alexandrinische Religionsphilosophie* (Halle, 1834), 1:476ff. [*Ed.*] Titus Flavius Josephus (37–c. 100 AD) was a Romano-Jewish historian, best known for his *Jewish Wars* and *Jewish Antiquities*.

Primitive Christianity and the Gospels

However, the essential nature of Christianity itself involves many different aspects, ones that cannot all be placed under the same heading. The question arises, therefore, as to whether what has been said holds good for Christianity in its whole scope and extent, or only for a specific aspect of it, and whether it applies to what we must regard as its authentic kernel and substantial center. When Christianity is considered from the viewpoint set forth above, it is of course self-evident that this means sticking to all those points of connection and affinity that tie Christianity so closely and internally with the whole preceding history of human development.

But does this aspect then constitute the original and substantial essence of Christianity? Perhaps this historical setting is just a secondary factor. Is it possible to speak of the essence and contents of Christianity as such without making the person of its founder the main object to be considered? Must we not recognize its distinctiveness in that everything that Christianity is, it is solely through the person of its founder? If so, is not understanding the essence and contents of Christianity in terms of its world-historical connection of little consequence? Is not its entire meaning and significance so conditioned by the person of its founder that historical examination and reflection can only start out from him?

These questions lead us to the sources of the gospel story (*Geschichte*), and to the distinction that the most recent critical investigations must draw among these scriptures.[26] The sources of the gospel story are the four gospels. The major question concerns the relationship of the Fourth Gospel to the first three. It is obvious that our way of understanding Christianity will be essentially different depending on whether we assume that the four gospels agree with each other throughout, or instead recognize that the differences between the Gospel of John and the three Synoptic Gospels amount to a contradiction that cannot be resolved in historical fashion.[27] If we assume

---

26. Compare my work, *Kritische Untersuchungen über die kanonischen Evangelien, ihr Verhältniss zu einander, ihren Charakter und Ursprung* (Tübingen, 1847); Köstlin, *Der Ursprung und die Composition der synoptischen Evangelien* (Stuttgart, 1853); Hilgenfeld, *Die Evangelien nach ihrer Entstehung und geschichtlichen Bedeutung* (Leipzig, 1854). [*Ed.*] On Hilgenfeld, see n. 24. On Karl Reinhard Köstlin see Part 2, n. 30.

27. The main question of concern here is not the authenticity of the Johannine Gospel. Regardless of who wrote the Gospel, whether the Apostle John or someone else, the obvious fact cannot be denied

that the four gospels can be harmonized, then the absolute significance that the Johannine Gospel assigns to the person of Jesus must be utterly determinative of how we understand the gospel story. From the fact of the incarnation of the eternal Logos, we must regard Christianity as a miracle in the strictest and most absolute sense. The human dimension vanishes into the divine, the natural into the supernatural; and, despite all the differences between the first three gospels and the Fourth Gospel, the authority of the latter must be decisive. This amounts, however, to an abandonment of the historical treatment of the gospel story, and miracle becomes so overwhelming and overriding that we completely lose any firm historical footing. As a consequence, allowing the Fourth Gospel its claim to absolute miracle means downgrading the historical credibility of the other three gospels to the point where they basically no longer serve as historical sources.

The only way to escape these difficulties is to be convinced that the Johannine Gospel is related to the other three gospels in a wholly different way than has been customarily assumed. Whether we look to its differences from the Synoptics, or to its general spirit and character, how can a gospel such as John possibly be regarded also as a purely historical portrayal, simply in the sense in which the Synoptics can be called historical? So even with all their differences as to the gospel story, we take our stand [as historians] only on the side of the Synoptics. In doing so, we gain a firmer historical foundation; whereas placing John on the same level as the Synoptics can only serve to call the whole gospel story into question, owing to the arguments justifiably favoring John over the Synoptics, or vice versa.

However, here we must further circumscribe what can count as critical historical analysis. The most recent investigations into the mutual relations of the gospels show that the Synoptics cannot all be approached in just the same way. The Gospel of Mark is so largely dependent on the other two that we cannot regard it as an independent source at all.[28] The Gospel of Luke is stamped by the Paulinism of its author, the key to

---

that the gospel story in the Fourth Gospel is essentially different from that in the first three gospels. Since this historical difference must either be acknowledged or denied, we have here the parting of two roads that lead in essentially different directions, and whose divergence extends to the whole conception of church history. Whoever overlooks this divergence from a dogmatic point of view will also view the entire history of the church quite differently from one who is not invested so heavily in this principle, and who regards what is historically given from a purely historical point of view. As for the question of authorship, the more the well-known critical dilemma of the Johannine authorship of the Gospel and of the Apocalypse [the Book of Revelation] is faced (as Lücke rightly does in the second edition of his *Einleitung in die Offenbarung des Johannes* [Bonn, 1852], 659–744), the less will any sophistry be able to prevent assigning most of this evidence to the Apocalypse, when the external testimonies for the Johannine origin of the two works are impartially weighed. [*Ed.*] Baur's view is that the Book of Revelation could well have been written by the Apostle John, but not the Gospel of John, which arises from a different *Sitz im Leben* in the second century and has a distinctive worldview. Friedrich Lücke (1791–1855) was a professor of exegesis, dogmatics, and ethics in Göttingen, and a friend of Schleiermacher, to whom the latter wrote his "open letters" concerning the *Glaubenslehre*.

28. See my book, *Das Markusevangelium nach seinem Ursprung und Charakter* (Tübingen, 1851). Also my "Rückblick auf die neuesten Untersuchungen über das Markusevangelium," *Theologische*

its own distinctive portrayal. So we are thrown back on the Gospel of Matthew as the relatively most genuine and trustworthy source for the gospel story.

But if we examine more closely the contents of the Gospel of Matthew, we must distinguish two different elements in it, the content of the teaching and the purely historical narrative. The early tradition about the Apostle Matthew states that he wrote down the λόγια, the sayings and discourses of Jesus, for the Hebrews and in the Hebrew language.[29] Now the main content of our Greek Gospel of Matthew, its actual substance, consists of the discourses and sayings of Jesus, as can be seen above all from the Sermon on the Mount, which is such a meaningful beginning for his public ministry. We may justly conclude from this that the author placed his emphasis from the beginning on treating Jesus' life, and what he manifested, from this point of view. This Gospel differs greatly from the Gospel of John, where the teaching serves to reveal Jesus' personal identity itself and its supernatural standing. What the discourses in Matthew present is the human and familiar face of Jesus, his direct appeal to the moral and religious consciousness, his simple answer to the first and most pressing question as to what one's intentions must be, and what one has to do, in order to enter the kingdom of God. This is not to say that the Gospel of Matthew fails to also ascribe full significance to the person of Jesus, or that this significance is not also perceptible in the Sermon on the Mount. But in the whole of the Sermon on the Mount the personal element remains as it were in the background; it is not the person who gives the discourse its meaning, but rather the content-laden discourse that first reveals the person in his true light. The inner power of truth, directly impressed on the human heart, is Jesus' subject matter here—truth proclaimed here in its world-historical significance.

Jahrbücher 12 (1853) 54–94; and Köstlin, *Ursprung und Composition* (n. 26), 310ff. [*Ed.*] Baur endorsed the so-called Griesbach hypothesis, which accorded priority to the Gospel of Matthew, followed by Luke, and regarded Mark as dependent on both. He had many reasons for doing so, which are elaborated in his *Kritische Untersuchungen über die kanonischen Evangelien* (n. 26) as well as in *Das Markusevangelium*. For a summary, see the chapter by Martin Bauspiess on Baur's view of the Synoptic Gospels in *Ferdinand Christian Baur and the History of Early Christianity*, ed. Martin Bauspiess, Christof Landmesser, and David Lincicum; trans. R. F. Brown and P. C. Hodgson (Oxford, 2017). Today the two-source hypothesis (Mark and Q) is favored over the Griesbach hypothesis, but the issue is still debated. On purely literary-critical grounds, Mark can be placed either first or last.

29. [*Ed.*] Papias, Hegesippus, and other church fathers bear witness to this. See Eusebius, *Ecclesiastical History* 3.39.16.

The Consciousness of Primitive Christianity and Its Principle

Now what does this direct and original element, this principle of Christianity, consist in, as it is expressed in the Sermon on the Mount as well as in the parables and the whole of the teaching contained in the Gospel of Matthew? It may be summed up briefly in its main elements.

The beatitudes of the Sermon on the Mount (Matt 5:3–12) offer the deepest and most comprehensive insight into the central way of looking at things and frame of mind from which Christianity emerged. What is behind all those pronouncements—"Blessed are the poor in spirit, those who mourn, the meek, those who hunger and thirst after righteousness, the pure in heart, the peacemakers, those who are persecuted for righteousness' sake"—but a consciousness feeling most profoundly the pressure of finitude and all the contradictions of the present day, yet a religious consciousness that, in this feeling, is infinitely exalted above, and extends far beyond, all that is finite and limited. The most pregnant expression of this primitive Christian consciousness is the poverty of those poor in spirit, which rightly comes first in this recitation of all the blessings.[30]

As opposed to the customary interpretation, the poor spoken of here are not to be understood as merely those who feel inwardly poor and empty in the awareness of their spiritual needs. Outward, bodily poverty is an essential part of the conception of this poverty. We ought not overlook this aspect of it because the parallel passage in Luke (6:20) speaks not of the πτωχοὶ τῷ πνεύματι (poor in spirit) of Matthew but simply of the πτωχοί (poor); and because historically the gospel found its first adherents almost exclusively among the poor. That being so, we see that, when looked at in spiritual terms, this poverty in spirit is exactly the opposite of what it appears to be outwardly. Since these poor accept their poverty readily and voluntarily, and of their own free will choose to be none other than what they are, their poverty becomes to them a sign and proof that, though outwardly poor, in themselves they are not poor. Here [on earth] they are the poor who have nothing, in order that there [in heaven]

---

30. See my *Kritische Untersuchungen* (n. 26), 447ff. [*Ed.*] See Matt 5:3. See also Baur's *Lectures on New Testament Theology* (n. 41), 106–8.

they are all the more certain to be the opposite of what they are here. They are the poor who have nothing and yet possess everything. They have nothing because, being poor in physical terms, they have no worldly possessions; and what they may count as their possessions in the world to come are for them simply something in the future. In having nothing, their existence and their lives are simply the longing and desire for what they do not have; but in this longing and desire they already have in themselves everything that is the object of such longing and desire. As having nothing, they have everything; their poverty is their riches; the kingdom of heaven is already now their most intimate possession because, as surely as they have nothing here, so surely they have everything there.

In this contrast of having and not having, of poverty and riches, of earth and heaven, of present and future, Christian consciousness attains its purest ideality; it is the ideal unity of all the antitheses that press upon temporal consciousness. It comprises all that the most elaborated dogmatic consciousness can include; and yet its entire meaning consists in its being the immediate unity of all antitheses. However diverse they sound, all the beatitudes are simply different expressions of the same original and fundamental outlook and sentiment of Christian consciousness. What they express is the pure feeling of the need for redemption, though as yet undeveloped, a feeling that contains in itself implicitly the antithesis of sin and grace, a feeling that already has in itself the whole reality of redemption. Because all antitheses are held together here in their unity, this original consciousness is so vigorous and rich in content. It is not only the most intensive self-consciousness but also the most wide-ranging world-consciousness. We see this from the words Jesus himself uses immediately after the beatitudes (Matt 5:13–16), when he calls his disciples "the salt of the earth," which must not lose its savor if the world is not to be deprived of the sustaining power that holds it together and preserves it from decay. Jesus says: "You are the light of the world," which must not be set "under a bushel," but must "shine before others so that they may see your good works," the works of those who let their light shine, and "give glory to your Father in heaven."

The beatitudes of the Sermon on the Mount describe, in an absolute manner, the innermost self-consciousness of the Christian as something that subsists in itself (*das an sich Seiende*). Likewise, the original element of Christianity, its principle, appears in the form of the absolute moral command, both in the parts antithetical to the Pharisees and elsewhere in the Sermon on the Mount. Here Jesus insists emphatically on one having a pure heart and the right disposition (*Gesinnung*), on a morality that consists not merely of the outer deed but the inner disposition; and on an earnest and moral observance of the law that can admit of no arbitrary exception or limitation, no toleration of false hypocritical pretenses, no half-heartedness and partiality. But to what extent is Christianity setting up a new principle? Jesus declared at the outset that he had come not to destroy the law and the prophets but to fulfill them (Matt 5:17). So he seems to have taken up a purely affirmative relationship to the Old Testament. One could say that the only difference between the teaching of Jesus and the law or the Old Testament is quantitative, not qualitative.[31] On this view no new principle is advanced; rather the moral precepts already contained in the law are extended to include the whole of the moral sphere to which they are applicable. Jesus simply includes under the law what should never have been excluded from it. He makes explicit the extension and generalization of which it is inherently capable. This interpretation of the Sermon on the Mount is supported by the fact that Jesus always just speaks about individual commandments, so as to give them a significance corresponding to their original sense in the law, or to the moral consciousness.

The sermon never enunciates a general principle applicable in all cases. Nevertheless, the individual stipulations for fulfilling the law, for what alone gives moral worth to human acts, always revert to the difference between the outer and inner aspects, between the mere deed and one's inner disposition. So we cannot but recognize in this a new principle, and one that differs essentially from the Mosaic law. What the law indeed contains, but only implicitly, now explicitly becomes the main thing and is enunciated as the principle of morality. The quantitative extension of the law becomes of itself a qualitative difference. The inner is opposed to the outer, the disposition to the deed, the spirit to the letter. This is the essential, basic principle of Christianity, and by insisting that the absolute moral value of human beings depends simply and solely on their disposition, it is an essentially new principle.

In this way the affirmative relationship Jesus adopted toward the law also includes a contrasting aspect, an antithesis to the law; and it is difficult, therefore, to understand how Jesus could say that not a letter of the law, not the least of its commandments, should be taken away (Matt 5:18). How could he say this, when the very opposite came about so soon afterwards, and the whole law was declared to be abolished?[32] How can he have affirmed the continuing validity of all the injunctions of the law, when we think, for example, of the one injunction of circumcision?[33] It is unthinkable that Jesus himself was so little aware of the principle and spirit of his teaching; and the only choice seems either to understand his words as exclusively about the law's moral content, leaving aside the ritual law, or else as being cast in this strict Jewish form only later. Jesus' stance toward the Old Testament was as affirmative as it could be, and he did not oppose the traditions of the Pharisees, and their additions to the law, to the point of demanding an open break with them. Even when he set aside their

---

31. See Ritschl, *Die Entstehung der altkatholischen Kirche* (Bonn, 1850), 27ff. Ritschl changed his views in the 2nd ed. (Bonn, 1857), although the position characterized above retains its value as a precise formulation, as an inherently possible way of understanding this passage. [*Ed.*] On Ritschl and this work, see n. 24.

32. [*Ed.*] See various passages in Galatians and Romans. In Rom 8:2–3 Paul says that the law of the Spirit has "set you free" from the law of sin and death, and that God has done what the law "could not do."

33. [*Ed.*] Compare what Paul says about circumcision in Rom 2:25–9, namely, that "real circumcision is a matter of the heart." Also, Gal 5:2–6.

excessive scrupulosity and countered it with inherently reasonable practices as being one's inalienable and incontrovertible right, he nevertheless recognized the Pharisees as the legitimate successors of Moses. Examples of this include Jesus' action seeming to violate the Sabbath law (Matt 12:1–14), and his defense against the Pharisees' unwarranted expectations (e.g., Matt 9:14; 15:1).[34] He said the Pharisees and the scribes sit in the chair of Moses, the seat of the teacher and legislator, and the people are required to follow their precepts, if not their example. Jesus does not reject out of hand even the most petty regulations Pharisaic scrupulosity devised for obedience to the law (Matt 23:1ff., 23).[35]

It is also true, however, that he declares the Pharisaic requirements to be heavy and intolerable burdens, and it could not have been his intention to allow this oppressive weight on the people to continue (Matt 23:3).[36] He also said, when speaking out against the Pharisees, "Every plant that my heavenly Father has not planted will be uprooted" (Matt 15:13). His actions were in great measure directed to this end, for he made it one of his most important tasks to challenge the Pharisaic attitude at every opportunity he had. When we think of how antithetical the two sides really were in principle, we can understand how Jesus regarded it as unnecessary to speak in generalities or to derive specific consequences from this antithesis. Instead he could leave to the further development of the spirit of his teaching everything that it involved and that must follow from the teaching itself. That he himself was quite aware of the difference in principle, and of its necessary consequences, is evident in the saying in Matt 9:16,[37] where he not only declares that the spirit of the new teaching is incompatible with that of the old, but also intimates that, although he himself had held as far as possible to the old traditional forms, thus putting new wine into old wineskins, he had done this with the specific awareness that the new contents would soon break through the old forms.

But what all-encompassing content in the new principle breaks through the old forms? It could be nothing other than going back to the inward disposition, to everything that expresses itself as inherently existent in a person's entire consciousness, as its absolute content. Since one's disposition ought to be pure and simple, free from

---

34. [*Ed.*] In Matt 12:1–14 the Pharisees criticize the disciples for picking grain on the sabbath, and Jesus himself for healing on the sabbath, to which Jesus responds that "it is lawful to do good on the sabbath." Matt 9:14ff. is concerned with fasting, and 15:1ff. with purification rituals; in the latter case Jesus accuses the Pharisees of hypocrisy.

35. [*Ed.*] Jesus says, "The scribes and Pharisees sit on Moses' seat; therefore do whatever they teach you and follow it; but do not do as they do, for they do not practice what they teach." (Matt 23:2–3).

36. [*Ed.*] Jesus continues (Matt 23:4, 23). "They tie up heavy burdens, hard to bear, and lay them on the shoulders of others; but they themselves are unwilling to lift a finger to move them. . . . Woe to you, scribes and Pharisees, hypocrites! . . . You have neglected the weightiest matters of the law: justice and mercy and faith."

37. [*Ed.*] Matt 9:16–17. "No one sews a piece of unshrunk cloth on an old cloak, for the patch pulls away from the cloak, and a worse tear is made. Neither is new wine put into old wineskins; otherwise, the skins burst, and the wine is spilled, and the skins are destroyed; but new wine is put into fresh wineskins, and so both are preserved."

all self-seeking, and since it alone is the root from which the good can proceed as its fruit, human consciousness as such ought to be directed to the one thing that it recognizes as its absolute content. This is the fundamental idea that runs throughout the whole of the Sermon on the Mount. The sayings in it that strike us as most significant are those that forever present most directly this absolute character of Christian consciousness. As the sayings in Matt 6:19–24[38] demand, this consciousness excludes all half-heartedness and ambivalence, all detachment and diffidence. This is just the requirement in Matt 7:12,[39] to which so many have looked for a principle of Christian morality, for its foundational significance. If Christians are conscious of their absolute standpoint, they must be able to stand apart from their own ego, and to know themselves as so much one with all others that they regard everyone else as subjects equal to themselves. This is exactly what Jesus means when he says of this requirement that it is the sum and substance of the law and the prophets; that it has the same meaning as the Old Testament commandment to love your neighbor as yourself.[40] Those who love their neighbors as themselves must renounce everything egotistical, subjective, particular. Above the multiplicity of individual subjects, each of whom is the same as we are, there stands on its own the objectivity of the universal, which subsumes everything particular and subjective. This universal [principle] is the form of the action in accord with which we do unto others what we wish others would do to us. The moral good is thus what is equally right and good for all; in other words, what can be the same object of everyone's action.[41]

Here we see the distinctiveness of the Christian principle expressed once again. It looks beyond the outward, contingent, and particular, and rises to the universal, the unconditioned, to what is existent in itself (*an sich Seiende*); it locates human moral value solely in what intrinsically has absolute value and content. This same energy of consciousness, which finds the substantial essence of the moral life solely in the innermost core of the disposition, makes itself felt in the demand to lift the individual ego up to the universal ego, to the ego or self of the whole of humanity that is identical

---

38. [Ed.] "Do not store up for yourselves treasures on earth, where moth and rust consume, and where thieves break in and steal; but store up for yourselves treasures in heaven. . . . For where your treasure is, there your heart will be also. The eye is the lamp of the body. So, if your eye is healthy, your whole body will be full of light; but if your eye is unhealthy, your whole body will be full of darkness. . . . No one can serve two masters; for a slave will either hate the one and love the other, or be devoted to the one and despise the other. You cannot serve God and wealth."

39. [Ed.] "In everything do to others as you would have them do to you; for this is the law and the prophets."

40. [Ed.] Matt 22:37–9: "'You shall love the Lord your God with all your heart, and all your soul, and all your mind.' This is the greatest and first commandment. And a second is like it: 'You shall love your neighbor as yourself.' On these two commandments hang all the law and the prophets."

41. [Ed.] Baur here uses a very Kantian formulation. As he says in his *Lectures on New Testament Theology*, ed. Peter C. Hodgson, trans. Robert F. Brown (Oxford, 2016), 106: "This is a formal principle of action that essentially coincides with the Kantian imperative so to act that the maxim of your action can be the universal law of action." The will of God is the universal law of action, but also more than that, as Baur explains below in the discussion of righteousness and the kingdom of God.

with itself in all single individuals. This requirement differs from the commandment [in Matt 7:12] only in that the commandment is its simplest practical expression.

Thus the absolute content of the Christian principle finds its expression in the moral consciousness. What gives human beings their highest moral value is simply the purity of a genuinely moral disposition that rises above everything finite, particular, and purely subjective. This morality of disposition is also the definitive standard for the human being's relationship to God. What gives human beings their highest moral value also places them in an adequate relationship to God that corresponds to the idea of God. When they are viewed in terms of their relationship to God, the supreme task of the moral consciousness appears in the requirement to be perfect as God is perfect (Matt 5:48). The absolute character of the Christian principle comes to its most direct expression in this requirement. Christianity has no other standard for human perfection than the absolute standard of God's perfection. If people are perfect as God is perfect, then in this absolute perfection they stand in an adequate relationship to God, which is described by the concept of righteousness (*Gerechtigkeit*). Righteousness in this sense is the absolute condition for entering into the kingdom of God. In the context in which Jesus speaks of righteousness in the Sermon on the Mount, we can only understand righteousness as the complete fulfillment of the law—but of course only in the sense in which Jesus speaks in general terms of the continuing validity of the law. If we ask how human beings can attain this righteousness, we find it a distinctive feature of Jesus' teaching that it simply assumes the law can be fulfilled; it assumes that the will of God will be done on earth as it is in heaven, and doing so will attain the righteousness that puts human beings in an adequate relationship to God.

It appears, however, that a forgiveness of sins on God's part is an essential element by which the shortcomings in human conduct are offset and made good, as becomes clear from the Lord's Prayer, in which the forgiveness of sins is something one asks for oneself [Matt 6:12]. Therefore, one cannot be related to God as God wills unless one is also forgiven for one's omissions and sins. Since the teaching of Jesus in principle defines the moral value of human beings as based not on external deeds but only on one's disposition, his teaching can only locate the righteousness consisting in conduct adequate to the will of God in the disposition—the disposition by which people completely cease to will on their own and surrender unconditionally to the will of God. This is worked out in the teaching about the kingdom of God,[42] which is found principally in the parables.

---

42. [*Ed.*] Baur understands this "kingdom" (*basileia*) not in political terms as the territory ruled by a king but in moral terms as a spiritual fellowship of those who are righteous in the eyes of God. He interprets the teaching of Jesus generally in moral and religious rather than political or eschatological categories.

The Teaching about the Kingdom of God

In the kingdom of God, where every individual is absolutely required to fulfill the will of God, what God wills becomes the common task of a specific community in which all together are to actualize within themselves the purpose established by the will of God. The more closely they are bound together, the more fully they do so. The shared or communal element that comprises the essence of religion is also the essential aspect of the kingdom of God. The Old Testament concept of theocracy is spiritualized in the teaching of Jesus, so that everything concerning the relationship of human beings to the kingdom of God is based purely on moral conditions. The moral dimension is so exclusively the condition here that there is not yet any mention of those objective means that later were thought to enable the acceptance of people into the kingdom of God or for fellowship with God. It is simply assumed that partaking of all that God's kingdom has to offer depends solely on human beings themselves, on their own volition.

How clearly and vividly this simple truth is portrayed in the parable of the sower![43] What makes a person fit for the kingdom of God is the Word, the embodiment of all teachings and precepts a person heeds to actualize the will of God. The Word is given to human beings; they can hear and understand it, but everything depends on how they receive it. What does ordinary experience show us? That, as the scattered seed cannot grow and bear fruit unless it falls on fertile soil, so the subjective capacities of human beings to receive the Word are very diverse. A few may receive the Word in a right spirit, but it is always their own fault when the Word does not produce in people what it is intrinsically capable of producing. The reason lies simply in their lack of receptivity, and they need only will to be receptive for their part. Such is the simplicity of the human relationship to God. Their entry into the kingdom of God depends only on themselves, on their own will, their own natural capability and receptivity.

For this reason, the whole relationship of human beings to the kingdom of God can only be thought of as a moral one. Hence what matters, first and foremost, is that people recognize this, and not suppose that their participation in the kingdom of God depends on anything other than what is of a purely moral nature. The first requirement made of them, therefore, is that they renounce everything on which they might

43. [*Ed.*] Matt 13:1–9; Mark 4:1–9; Luke 8:4–8.

rely as giving them merely an outward claim to the kingdom of God—that they should simply go back into themselves and, only in themselves, in their inner nature and moral consciousness, become aware of whether they are fit for the kingdom of God. If they rid themselves of everything that would put them in a merely external relationship to the kingdom of God, and face the kingdom of God with this mindset that makes no claims and looks purely within itself, then their receptivity can all the more surely consist in their being entirely receptive to what the kingdom wants to provide for them. This is the meaning of the words in which Jesus deals with all the claims the Jews, with their prevailing notions, make about the kingdom of God. In Matthew 18:3, Jesus says: "Unless you change and become like children, you will never enter the kingdom of heaven." To become like children is to cease wanting to be something on our own, and to remain rather in that purely natural condition that just makes us aware of our dependence and need. The less we have within ourselves what we ought to have, the more clearly we long for what only the kingdom of God can give, and the more surely we come to recognize the kingdom of God as possessing the highest, the absolute, value. This truth is evident in the parable of the pearl of great value, for which the merchant sold all that he had and bought it (Matt 13:45–6). There can be no doubt that the parables dealing with the subjective stance of human beings toward the kingdom of God, and portraying the moral conditions for one's participation in it, are, together with the Sermon on the Mount, the most genuine and original materials that have come down to us from the content of Jesus' teaching.

The Person of Jesus and the Messianic Idea

If we view everything discussed thus far as the most original and direct content of the teaching of Jesus, we see that it contains only what is clearly focused on morality, and its aim is simply to restore our focus on our own moral and religious consciousness. People only need to become aware of what their own consciousness expresses as its highest moral goal, and thus that they can actualize this goal by their own efforts. Regarded in this fashion, Christianity in its earliest elements is a purely moral religion; its highest and most distinctive aspect is that it bears a thoroughly moral character that is rooted in the moral consciousness of human beings.

Faith in the person of Jesus does not yet emerge here as the essential condition of the new relationship to God into which people should enter through Jesus—at least not in the sense that the Gospel of John makes this faith the precondition for everything else. Other elements belong to the character and content of Christianity, and the relation they have to its most original and immediate aspect may be variously described. But there can be no question that the purely moral element from which Christianity springs constantly remains its substantial foundation. Christianity has never been dislodged from this foundation without denying its true and proper character. People have always been compelled to return to this foundation whenever they went astray in excessive dogmatism from which they drew conclusions undermining the innermost basis of moral-religious life. This original moral element, its significance in principle, has remained the same despite all changes, and, as the very foundation of Christianity's truth, can also simply be regarded as Christianity's proper substance.

And yet had Christianity been nothing more than a teaching of religion and morality such as we have described, what would it have amounted to, and what would have come of it? Although it may, as such, be the sum and substance of the purest and most immediate truths given expression in moral-religious consciousness, and may have made them accessible to the general consciousness of humankind in the simplest and most popular way, this moral Christianity still lacked the form appropriate for concretely shaping religious life. A firm center was needed around which the circle of its followers could rally as a community able to gain supremacy in the world. When we consider the way in which Christianity developed, we see that its entire historical significance depends solely on the person of its founder. How soon would all the true and meaningful teachings of Christianity have taken their place among the now mostly-forgotten sayings of the noble humanitarians and philosophic sages of antiquity, had not its teachings become words of eternal life as spoken by its founder?

But we cannot help asking what we should see as the actual foundation of Christianity's world-historical significance with regard to the person of Jesus himself. However much we emphasize the total impact of Jesus' person, we see that he must have affected the consciousness of the age from an already existing perspective, if a world-historical development could emerge from the appearing of an individual. Here then is the place where Christianity and Judaism are so closely intertwined that Christianity can only be understood in terms of its connection with Judaism. Succinctly put, if the national idea of Judaism, the messianic idea, had not been so identified with the person of Jesus that people could find in him the fulfillment of the ancient promise of the Messiah, a Messiah coming for the salvation of his people, then faith in Jesus would never have attained such a great world-historical significance. The messianic idea first gave the spiritual content of Christianity the concrete form in which it could embark on the path of its historical development. People's consciousness of Jesus was thus able to expand into a general world-consciousness, via the route of Judaism's national consciousness.

The gospel story itself supplies us with an abundance of evidence for the great national importance the messianic expectations had at the time of Jesus, not only for individual pious souls but also for the faith of the Jewish people as a whole. The greater the discrepancy between the present condition of the Jewish people and the theocratic idea basic to their entire history, the more they looked back to a past in which, at one point at least, albeit for just a short time, the theocratic ideal appeared to have been actualized.[44] But after that one time things were in fact quite different from how they ideally should have been. People expected, even more confidently, that the near or distant future would bring what the past had failed to realize. They handed down, from generation to generation, the promise given to their forefathers, and longed for its fulfillment. It is a characteristic of Judaism that, because of the continuing, ever more apparent, contradiction between idea and actuality, Judaism became principally a religion of the future with its belief in a Messiah who was still to come. Thus nothing of greater import could take place on the soil of the history of the Jewish people and the Jewish religion without being connected with the messianic idea or introduced by it. It also prescribed the course that Christianity must take. The Synoptic account of the gospel story introduces Jesus with all the miracles that were said to proclaim him to be the long-expected and now-appearing Messiah, and to be the Son of God in terms of the Jewish outlook.

From the standpoint of critical reflection we can only ask how it came to be an established fact in Jesus' consciousness that he was called to be the Messiah. Three elements in the gospel story merit special attention in this regard: the title υἱὸς τοῦ

---

44. [*Ed.*] The time of the monarchy from Saul to Solomon.

ανθρώπου, "Son of Man," which Jesus applies to himself; the group of narratives comprising the confession of Peter, the scene of the transfiguration, and the first announcement of his approaching death; and Jesus' entry into Jerusalem. The manner in which Jesus applies the title υἱὸς τοῦ ἀνθρώπου to himself is so unusual that, however we define its meaning more precisely, we must assume he intended some reference to the messianic idea when he used it.[45] Such a reference is even clearer in the aforementioned group of narratives. If we follow the gospel story up to the point where we find these narratives, which are so interrelated both externally and internally, we clearly see that Jesus' cause has reached a decisive turning point. Both he and his disciples are now expressly aware that he is the Messiah.[46] It certainly remains quite inconceivable how at that point in time this belief could still require confirmation, when the gospel story has already provided a number of such evident proofs of Jesus' messiahship. But it is of all the greater historical significance that, in a presentation such as that of the Synoptic Gospels, such information could have been convincing only in the wake of the prior established facts.

The most unambiguous demonstration of Jesus' messianic consciousness, however, is furnished by his presence in Jerusalem, even apart from the specific scene of his entry. After his extended activity in Galilee,[47] and after all his experiences of people accepting his teaching and of the opposition to it by the adversaries he met up with there, he resolved to leave Galilee and go to Judea, to appear in the capital itself at the seat of those rulers against whose prevailing system his entire activity up to now had been most decisively opposed. He can only have taken such a momentous step based on the conviction that his cause had now necessarily come to a head. People must either accept or reject his teaching and his person; the whole nation must in fact declare whether it will persist in its traditional messianic belief, inherently bearing the sensuous marks of Jewish particularism, or will acknowledge the kind of Messiah he was and had shown himself to be, in his whole life and influence. The only answer

---

45. It is very doubtful that this expression was applied to the messiah at the time of Jesus. The most apparent explanation is that, in contrast to the Jewish υἱὸς θεοῦ, "Son of God," and its associated images, Jesus intended to allude all the more emphatically to the genuinely human character of his appearance and vocation. [*Ed.*] Cf. Baur, "Die Bedeutung des Ausdrucks: ὁ υἱὸς τοῦ ἀνθρώπου," *Zeitschrift für wissenschaftliche Theologie* 3 (1860), 274–92.

46. *Theologische Jahrbücher* 12 (1853), 77ff. [*Ed.*] Article by Baur, "Rückblick auf die neuesten Untersuchungen über das Markusevangelium," 54–94.

47. The duration of this activity is one of the unsettled points in the life of Jesus about which in its external outlines we know so little. The usual assumption of a teaching activity lasting three years is based only on the number of festival journeys mentioned by John, and this depends on the way the Johannine question is settled. The great weight of the tradition of the early church is that Jesus taught only one year. This one year, however, is the ἐνιαυτὸς κυρίου δεκτός of Isaiah 61:2 ["the year of the Lord's favor"], cf. Luke 4:19; and it is doubtless only a dogmatic assumption. It is not in itself probable that the public activity of Jesus extended over so short a period. Cf. Hilgenfeld (n. 24), *Die clementinische Recognitionen und Homilien* (Jena, 1848), 160ff.; and *Kritische Untersuchungen über die Evangelien Justins* (Halle, 1850), 337; and my *Kritische Untersuchungen über die kanonischen Evangelien* (Tübingen, 1847), 363ff.

to this question could be the one he himself had long accepted, consciously and with complete self-assurance.

The Death and Resurrection of Jesus

What seemed to be on its surface just ruin and annihilation was never turned into such a decisive victory, and breakthrough to life, as this happened in the death of Jesus. Before now there had still been the possibility that belief in the Messiah might be the bond linking Jesus with the people, that is, with the people acknowledging him to be the one supposed to come to fulfill the nation's expectation, and the contradiction between his messianic idea and the Jewish messianic faith still being amicably resolved. But his death caused a complete breach between Jesus and Judaism. A death like his made it impossible for Jews, as long as they remained Jews, to believe in him as their Messiah. To believe in him as the Messiah after such a death would have of course required eliminating from the Jews' notion of the Messiah everything inherently of a Jewish and fleshly nature. A Messiah whose death denied everything Jews expected of their messiah—a messiah who died to life in the flesh—was no longer a Χριστὸς κατὰ σάρκα, an "Anointed One according to the flesh" (2 Cor 5:16), as the Messiah of the Jewish national faith had been. Even to the most faithful adherent of Jesus' cause, what could a Messiah be who had himself fallen prey to death? Only two alternatives were possible: either with his death faith in him must be extinguished; or this faith, if it were firm and strong enough, must necessarily break through even the bonds of death and press on from death to life.

Only the miracle of the resurrection could dispel these doubts that seemingly had to cast faith itself out into the eternal night of death. What the resurrection is in itself lies outside the sphere of historical investigation. Historical reflection has to stick just to the fact that, for the faith of the disciples, the resurrection of Jesus had become the most secure and most incontestable certainty. Christianity first attained the firm ground of its historical development in this faith. For history the necessary presupposition of all that follows is not so much the fact of the resurrection of Jesus itself as it is the belief in the resurrection. We may regard the resurrection as a miracle occurring objectively, or as a subjective psychological miracle. But if we assume the possibility of such a subjective miracle, no psychological analysis can penetrate the inner, mental process by which, in the consciousness of the disciples, their disbelief upon the death of Jesus became belief in his resurrection. In any case it is forever only through the consciousness of the disciples that we have any knowledge of what was, for them, the object of their faith. We can say no more than that, whatever the means that produced this faith, the resurrection became a fact of their consciousness, and had for them all the reality of a historical fact.

However great the significance of this fact, and however much it had to make the disciples who believed in Jesus break decisively with Judaism, we still must ask: What would this belief in the risen one have amounted to if he had just passed from death to life and risen from earth to heaven, so as to return, after a short interval, the same as he had been before, now just as one seated on the clouds of heaven and clothed with all the power and majesty that belonged to the Son of Man, so as to realize at last what his early and violent death had left unaccomplished? The initial followers thought that the Lord's second coming, which was to be the consummation of the whole world, would occur soon after his departure from the earth.[48] So their faith in the risen one was simply a new and stronger form of the old messianic hope. The only difference between the believing disciples and their unbelieving compatriots was that, to Jesus' followers, the Messiah was one who had already come, and to the latter he was one who was still to come. Had this latter view prevailed, the Christian faith would have become the faith of a Jewish sect in which the entire future of Christianity would have been placed in question. What was it then that first invested the belief in the risen one with a significance enabling the principle that had entered the world in Christianity to develop into the great and imposing network of phenomena that shaped its historical existence? What enabled it to overcome all the restrictive limits on its all-inclusive universalism?

---

48. Cf. Matt 24:29; Acts 3:19–21.

Part 2

Christianity as a Universal Principle
of Salvation:
The Antithesis of Paulinism and Judaism,
and Its Equilibrium in the Idea
of the Catholic Church

I. The Antitheses[1]

THE JERUSALEM CONGREGATION AND STEPHEN

Proof of the strong faith of the disciples, and of their great confidence in the cause of Jesus, is found in the fact that immediately after his death they neither dispersed outside Jerusalem nor gathered at a distant place, but made Jerusalem itself their permanent center. They formed the first Christian community here, and the Jerusalem congregation continued to be regarded by all Jewish believers in Jesus as the headquarters.

Recent critical investigations show that the reports in the Book of Acts about the earliest community of disciples provide only a very meager and unclear picture, with little that is reliable and historically coherent to offer for historical examination. We stand on firmer historical ground for the first time with the appearance of Stephen and the persecution directed at him (Acts, chs. 6 and 7). Here two things are especially noteworthy. The charge brought against Stephen,[2] which is strikingly similar to that brought against Jesus at his own trial, and that cannot in either case have been an entirely baseless statement on the part of false witnesses, already shows the seeds of an opposition that could only find its further development in Paulinism. The more spiritual worship of God, which Stephen opposed to the externality of the existing temple cult, had to lead beyond Judaism. Stephen's entire demeanor, with his confrontational style, makes him look like a forerunner of the Apostle Paul.

It is important to notice, however, that this opposition to Judaism, which first came to light in Stephen, seems to have already divided the Jerusalem congregation itself into two different factions. Stephen was a Hellenist, and it cannot be accidental that his Hellenism gave him a more liberal tendency. From him we see that Hellenists also belonged to the earliest congregation in Jerusalem, and that is confirmed

---

1. [*Ed.*] *Die Gegensätze.* The term *Gegensatz* means "antithesis" or "opposition." Occasionally Baur uses its Latinate equivalent, *Antithese.*

2. [*Ed.*] Stephen was charged with speaking "blasphemous words against Moses and God" (Acts 6:11).

by express statements in Acts (8:4; 11:19–20).³ When all the members of the congregation fled from the persecution following Stephen's martyrdom, and were scattered throughout the regions of Judea and Samaria, not only did these fugitives bring Christianity to Samaria, to the towns of the seacoast and even farther to Cyprus and Antioch, but some of them, Cypriots and Cyreneans, thus being Hellenists, also took the important step in Antioch of preaching the gospel to the Gentiles. Antioch thus became the seat of the first community of Gentile Christians, just as Jerusalem was the mother community of the Jewish Christians.

Acts 8:1 states that only the apostles remained in Jerusalem during the persecution, but this is unlikely. Subsequent events show that this persecution was not aimed at the community as a whole but rather at the Hellenists who sympathized with Stephen in his more liberal orientation and his consequent hostility toward Judaism. Thus Stephen's story affords clear evidence that the Jerusalem congregation had all along consisted of two different components, the Hebraists and the Hellenists, which now outwardly parted ways.⁴ From then on the congregation in Jerusalem consisted only of Hebraists. The Hellenists, however, were already widespread before this time. It can only have been the Hellenism of the more liberal tendency, first expressed by Stephen, that also gave birth to Gentile Christianity. Nevertheless, within the set of events centering around Stephen, the first martyr, the Apostle Paul was in fact the first herald of Gentile Christianity. He established its basic principles.⁵

PAUL THE APOSTLE TO THE GENTILES, AND THE EARLIER APOSTLES

The history of the development of Christianity, after the departure of Jesus, found in Paul a new beginning point, from which we are able to trace not only this history's external features but also its inner connections.

We can only regard what the Book of Acts reports about the conversion of the Apostle as the outward reflection of an inner spiritual process, which is best explained by the Apostle's own individuality as we have it set before us in his own [authentic] epistles. In speaking of the period immediately preceding the great turning point of

---

3. [*Ed.*] These are references to "those who were scattered" because of persecution. In 11:20 they are called "Hellenists."

4. [*Ed.*] For an analysis and critique of this claim, see Anders Gerdmar, "Baur and the Creation of the Judaism–Hellenism Dichotomy," in *Ferdinand Christian Baur and the History of Early Christianity*, ed. Martin Bauspiess, Christof Landmesser, and David Lincicum; trans. R. F. Brown and P. C. Hodgson (Oxford, 2017), ch. 5.

5. See my book, *Paulus, der Apostel Jesu Christi: Sein Leben und Wirken, seine Briefe und seine Lehre* (Stuttgart, 1845). [*Ed.*] Eduard Zeller issued a 2nd ed. incorporating revisions Baur was making at the time of his death (2 vols., Leipzig, 1866–67). ET of 2nd ed., *Paul the Apostle of Jesus Christ*, trans. Allan Menzies (2 vols., London and Edinburgh, 1875–76). For an analysis of Baur on Paul see Christof Landmesser, "Ferdinand Christian Baur as Interpreter of Paul: History, the Absolute, and Freedom," *Baur and the History of Early Christianity* (n. 4), ch. 7.

his life, he says (Gal 1:14) he was a great zealot for the traditions of the fathers, and that he surpassed many of his contemporaries in his knowledge of the Jewish religion. Based on this, he saw more clearly than many others how the direction the new teaching took would undermine Judaism. The characteristic feature of Christianity no doubt appeared to him in what Stephen, and Jesus himself, were mainly charged with doing—disengaging true religious piety (*Religiosität*) from specific ordinances and localities. This conviction motivated religious consciousness to detach itself from the soil of traditional Judaism. Thus it was the natural consequence of his temperament that he employed the same severity in opposing Judaism on principled grounds as a Christian, that he previously had shown as a Jew in persecuting Christians. In this regard, nothing is more remarkable about his conversion, as he himself describes it in Galatians 1:15–16, than that the revelation in which God disclosed his Son to him, and the call he received in this disclosure to proclaim the gospel among the Gentiles, were for him one and the same spiritual act. He did not merely become a disciple of Jesus, like other converts to the Christian faith: he was also aware of being an *apostle* of Christ, such as the earlier apostles were, yet quite differently from them since he believed his apostolic calling to be one that could be fulfilled only in the Gentile world. Thus not only was he called to state, explicitly and definitively, that Christian universalism is fundamentally distinct from Jewish particularism; for also, from the outset, he made it the task and main criterion of his apostolic activity, to be aware, as a Christian, that the two things are inseparable, his call to the apostolic office, and Christianity's destiny to be the universal principle of salvation for all peoples of the world.

If we cannot call Paul's conversion, his sudden transformation from being the most vehement opponent of Christianity into being its boldest herald, anything other than a miracle, then this appears an even greater miracle because, in this sudden new awareness, he broke through the limits of Judaism and annulled Jewish particularism in the universal idea of Christianity. And yet this miracle, great as it is, can only be conceived as a spiritual process, and for this reason there must be a mediating element between the one extreme and the other. No analysis, either psychological or dialectical, can plumb the inner mystery of the act by which God disclosed his Son to Paul; yet we can rightly ask whether the mediating aspect of this transition could be anything other than the powerful impact with which the great event of the death of Jesus confronted him in a flash. From the moment of the revelation in which the Son of God was disclosed in him, Paul lives only with his eyes on the Crucified One; he knows no other, he is crucified with him, his whole system of thought turns on this one event. The death that was to the Jews a stumbling block and to the Greeks foolishness [1 Cor 1:23] is for him the sum and substance of salvation, and it is so in its most immediate and material form as the death on the cross, for which reason Christianity is called the word of the cross. In what other way can Paul have overcome his Jewish hatred and repugnance toward Christianity than by an involuntary, inner spiritual pressure to carefully consider this death? The very thing that was most intolerable to the Jewish imagination, a crucified Messiah, became, in his more deeply reflective mind, the idea that what was most repugnant to the sensible consciousness of human beings could turn out to be what is most profoundly and essentially true. What was intolerable became tolerable, and death could be taken up (*aufgehoben*) into life. A Messiah who has died in the flesh cannot indeed be a Χριστὸς κατὰ σάρκα (one anointed according to the flesh) in the sense of Jewish national ideas. Yet all the more surely, in his stature as one who has died to the flesh and been transfigured to a higher life, he is a redeemer far exceeding all the limitations of Judaism.

There could be no place in the thinking of the Jewish nation for a death that ran so directly counter to all that it assumed to be true. Such a death would have a significance far transcending Jewish particularism. There can be no doubt that this was the basic idea in terms of which the Apostle first elucidated the truth of Christianity. It was the idea that shaped his perception of the person of Christ and from which the entire dialectical development of Pauline Christianity proceeded. The Christian universalism that in this way became a certainty for the Apostle, sooner than for the others, entailed from the start a much greater break with Judaism than might have first seemed to be the case. This is the only explanation for Paul going his own independent way from the first moment of his conversion, by intentionally and on principle avoiding contact with the earlier apostles. He made a short visit to Jerusalem, during which he did meet with Peter, but he leaves us completely in the dark about his relationship with Peter, other than the brief but significant indication that he just went there to make Peter's acquaintance. After that he seemed to turn his back on Judaism forever (Gal 1:17–24).[6]

But the Apostle positions himself freely and independently over against not merely the earlier apostles but also the person of Jesus himself. How are we to understand this circumstance? The Apostle Paul seems to have been the first one to state what Christianity essentially is as distinct from Judaism. How far apart are the founder of Christianity and Paul, who first appeared outside the circle of the earlier apostles? Did Paul first introduce Christianity to the world as a universal religion, without any help from the twelve disciples? Was he the first to articulate the full meaning of Christianity as the universal religion?

What we see in Jesus' person are two constitutive elements that are properly related to each other. One is the morally universal and divinely exalted aspect that embraces all humanity, and that gave his person its absolute significance. The other one is the limiting and restrictive aspect of the national Jewish messianic idea, which was the form in which the first element necessarily had to appear in the person of

---

6. Cf. Dr. Holsten, *Inhalt und Gedankengang des Briefs an die Galater* (Rostock, 1859), 4ff., 17ff. This work is markedly superior to ordinary commentaries in its logical precision and evidence of development [in Paul's thought]. [*Ed.*] Karl Christian Johann Holsten (1825–97), professor in Bern and Heidelberg, influenced by, but not a student of, Baur.

Jesus himself, in order to have a point of contact where it could develop in history and find the way to become a consciousness embracing all humanity. What then could be more natural than for one group of his followers to hold to the national aspect manifested in Jesus and, because of their dependence on it, not know how to rise above Jewish particularism; while another group of his followers expressed, more specifically and energetically and in a different venue, the other one of the two elements directly united in the person of Jesus.[7] In this way each group found its natural point of departure in the life and work of the founder.

The only remaining question is why, in his epistles, the Apostle Paul seems to be so indifferent to the historical details of the life of Jesus. He seldom appeals to the traditions [about Jesus] that, even for him, had to be the presupposition of his apostolic activity. Especially when it comes to his teaching, he hardly appears to be a disciple who can only have received the doctrines and principles he espouses from the master whose name he invokes.

But this just shows us how grand and spiritual Paul's conception of Christianity is. For him the individual and particular aspect disappears in his way of looking at the whole. Christianity stands before him as a historical phenomenon that can be understood and conceptualized only in its unity and in the immediacy of a divine revelation. The great events of the death and resurrection of Jesus make it what it is. His entire Christian consciousness depends on what they mean. For him, Christianity's entire content takes the shape of a conception of Jesus' person that stands in no need of historical commentary. Why should he turn to first-hand accounts of what Jesus did and said, to what Christ was in the flesh, when he has seen Christ himself in the spirit? Why should he first ask whether what he is teaching agrees with the authentic teaching of Jesus, and with the sayings and discourses handed down about him, when in the Christ who lives and works in him he hears the voice of the Lord himself? Why should he draw from the past what the Christ who is present in him has made to be the direct testimony of his own consciousness?[8]

---

7. See my work, *Die Tübinger Schule und ihre Stellung zur Gegenwart* (Tübingen, 1859), 30ff.

8. Nothing could be more trifling than the way people fill the supposed gap in the Apostle's credentials, by establishing from his epistles as many citations of the words of Jesus as possible, and by asserting that the Apostle's confidence that he has not worked in vain means that he also must have been fully informed about the historical teaching of the historical Christ. Otherwise, it is said, he must have been proclaiming himself a second, better Christ, a sort of Montanist Paraclete. See especially Heinrich Paret, "Jesus und Paulus. Einige Bermerkungen über das Verhältniss des Apostels Paulus und seiner Lehre zu der Person, dem Leben und der Lehre des geschichtlichen Christus," in the *Jahrbücher für deutsche Theologie* 3 (1858) 1–85. These attempted proofs are so deficient and unsatisfying that it must be said, if the Apostle himself had felt the need for such a confirmation of his teaching, he would have expressed himself quite differently in his epistles; and it would be utterly inexplicable why, just at the time when he should have made it his task above all to be as fully informed as possible about the teaching of Jesus, he could be so unconcerned about the sources that first reported it, if he wanted to learn about Jesus' teaching from the most authentic and reliable sources. It can be seen clearly enough from Gal 1:11–12 that he owed nothing to the earlier apostles for the substance of his gospel. He would have regarded what they had to offer as merely a human mediation, which could not

Fourteen years had passed since the Apostle's conversion. He had begun his apostolic activity, had founded Gentile Christian communities, and made Antioch the mother city for these communities. Then an issue apparently left in abeyance thus far, and one Jesus never had the occasion to address, suddenly became of very serious practical importance. Heretofore Paul and his apostolic associates had unhesitatingly drawn Gentiles to the gospel without requiring them to be circumcised, and thus comply with the law, in order to share in the messianic blessings. But as the number of Gentile converts increased, and as the efforts of those who carried the gospel to the Gentiles disseminated it more widely in the Gentile world, the Christians of Jerusalem became alarmed. They could not stand by silently when they saw a Gentile Christian community of equal standing arising alongside the Jewish Christian community, but disregarding the ordinances and privileges of Judaism.

Members of the Jerusalem congregation came to Antioch, as the Apostle himself reports (Galatians, ch. 2). He calls them "false brothers,"[9] intruders who jealously spied on the freedom enjoyed and claimed as a Christian right in Antioch, and who aimed to enslave them under the law. The matter appeared so important to the Apostle that he went to Jerusalem himself[10] and discussed the issue on the spot where it had been raised, and where alone it could be decided. Circumcision was the major issue of direct, practical significance. Therefore the Apostle took with him not only Barnabas but also Titus, who was uncircumcised, in order to plainly demonstrate the strength of resistance to the Jerusalem demand. But who were the opponents that so strenuously resisted Paul and Barnabas? Who else other than the earlier apostles themselves? We would have a strange picture of the Jerusalem congregation and the position of the earlier apostles in it if we thought that they took virtually no part in a controversial question of this importance, and that the originators of the dispute were merely certain extreme Judaists with whose assertions and demands the apostles themselves

---

be connected in any way with his awareness of the immediacy of the ἀποκάλυψις Ἰησοῦ Χριστοῦ, the revelation of Jesus Christ, to him. From this we can only conclude that we would have a false notion of what his apostolic consciousness was if we assume he must have relied solely on what are the limited sources for our own historical knowledge. We have only to consider what is involved in his wanting to be not merely a disciple of Jesus but also an apostle with the full autonomy of apostolic authority. Compare the discussion (which the author of the above-named article has left quite unnoticed) I provide on the Apostle's principle of authority in my "Beiträge zur Erklärung der Korinthierbriefe" in the *Theologische Jahrbücher* 11 (1852) 32ff., and on his ecstatic experiences in 9 (1850) 182ff. [*Ed.*] This article on Corinthians extends over two volumes of the *Theologische Jahrbücher* 9 (1850) 139–85; vol. 11 (1852) 1–40, 535–74. Galatians 1:11–12 reads: "For I want you to know, brothers and sisters, that the gospel that was proclaimed by me is not of human origin; for I did not receive it from a human source, nor was I taught it, but I received it through a revelation of Jesus Christ."

9. [*Ed.*] See Gal 2:4–5: "But because of false brothers secretly brought in, who slipped in to spy on the freedom we have in Christ Jesus, so that they might enslave us—we did not submit to them even for a moment, so that the truth of the gospel might always remain with you."

10. Ἀνέβην κατὰ ἀποκάλυψιν ("in response to a revelation") says the Apostle in Gal 2:2. Here we see very clearly into the psychological background of such ἀποκαλύψεις (revelations), in which Christ himself appeared to him.

did not agree. Had this been the case, how easy it would have been to arrive at an understanding. This view is clearly contrary not only to the way things were but to the clear meaning of the Apostle's own words. It has often been repeated,[11] but it can never amount to anything more than an unjustified claim, replacing the original account—obviously true on its face—with a narrative inconsistent with it and obviously tending to cast things in a false light.[12] We need only consider how Paul intentionally describes the subjective standpoint of his opponents with the words οἱ δοκοῦντες, δοκοῦντες εἶναί τι, οἱ δοκοῦντες στύλοι εἶναι,[13] thus showing that the earlier apostles themselves were the authorities for the view [about circumcision] he was contesting. We can see his awareness of independence vis-à-vis the Apostle Peter and the outcome of the entire procedure (Gal 2:7–10). The three principal representatives of the Jerusalem congregation did indeed extend to Paul and Barnabas the right hand of fellowship, but their reconciliation simply consisted in the recognition that each party had the right to go its own way, separate from and independent of the other.

Thus there were now two gospels, one for the circumcised and one for the uncircumcised, a mission to the Jews and a mission to the Gentiles. The two groups were to work alongside each other, separately and independently, without crossing each other's paths. Their only link was a shared concern to support the poor of the

---

11. A principal authority for this view, which is totally opposed to sound historical insight, is a book by Lechler that was awarded a prize by the Teyler Theological Society, *Das apostolische und nachapostolische Zeitalter mit Rücksicht auf Unterschied und Einheit zwischen Paulus und den übrigen Aposteln, zwischen Heidenchristen und Judenchristen* (Haarlem, 1851). In the second and revised edition (Stuttgart, 1857), Lechler has simply repeated his former assertion, as was to be expected, without bringing forward better evidence to support it. See Hilgenfeld, *Der Galaterbrief übersetzt, in seinen geschichtlichen Beziehungen untersucht und erklärt* (Leipzig, 1852), 128; and *Zeitschrift für wissenschaftliche Theologie* 1 (1858) 54ff., 377ff. No recent writer has pointed out the un-Pauline conception of this passage with greater acumen and evidence than Holsten in the work mentioned above (n. 6), p. 46. [*Ed.*] Gotthard Victor Lechler (1811–88) was a disciple of August Neander and belonged to the extreme right of the school of mediating theologians. On Adolf Hilgenfeld, see Part 1, n. 24. The article to which Baur refers is "Das Urchristenthum und seine neuesten Bearbeitungen von Lechler und Ritschl."

12. This is one of the points where the question of the relation between the narrative in the Book of Acts and the Apostle's own statements is of greatest importance. Everything that needs to be said on this topic is found in my work on *Paulus, der Apostel Jesu Christi* (Stuttgart, 1845) (n. 5), and especially in Zeller, *Die Apostelgeschichte nach ihrem Inhalt und Ursprung kritisch untersucht* (Stuttgart, 1854). Here if anywhere there is a conflict of principles [with Lechler] that cannot be resolved. The two views simply confront each other as the critical and the uncritical. The critical view is based on differences that actually lie before our eyes. The uncritical view seeks, in the interest of the apostles, to smooth over these differences in a manner that can be satisfying only to those who accept the apostolic viewpoint as the standard of truth. See my *Paulus*, 164ff.; and Zeller, *Die Apostelgeschichte*, 215ff. [*Ed.*] On Eduard Zeller, see Part 1, n. 13. His work is translated by Joseph Dare as *The Contents and Origins of the Acts of the Apostles, Critically Investigated*, 2 vols. (London and Edinburgh, 1875–76); the reference is to 2:8ff.

13. [*Ed.*] "The leaders, the supposed leaders, the leaders who were pillars." These phrases are found in Gal 2:6 and 9: "And from those who were supposed to be acknowledged leaders (what they actually were makes no difference to me; God shows no partiality)—those leaders contributed nothing to me. . . . And when James and Cephas and John, who were acknowledged pillars . . . ."

original Jerusalem community. The two standpoints were firmly opposed: on the one side was the Apostle Paul, steadfastly refusing to waver, even for a moment on any point undermining his principles, in order to accommodate the demands made of him; on the other side were the earlier apostles clinging tenaciously to their Judaism. During the long period of fourteen years these apostles had not taken a single step beyond their Jewish particularism. They still maintained the principle of circumcision as a fundamental condition for the messianic community. In view of the success of the conversion of Gentiles, which indicated God's blessing on the endeavor, and in face of the cogent arguments of the Pauline dialectic, they could find no objection to the unhindered continuation of the mission to the Gentiles. But this was essentially only a concession, out of step with their own religious thinking. In fact the two parties were soon on the verge of having to reassert their differences.

We see this when Peter and Paul met in Antioch. Shortly before this [in Jerusalem] they had extended the right hand of fellowship. But now, in Antioch, a very different scene unfolded. Peter was of two minds. When he arrived in Antioch he ate first with the Gentile Christians. But then, when some persons came from James, and by their presence reminded Peter of the principles so rigorously upheld at Jerusalem, he gave up sitting at table with the Gentile Christians. In drawing this distinction between Jewish and Gentile Christians he practically declared that he no longer recognized the latter to be on the same level as the former. The Apostle to the Gentiles felt his own principles to be so deeply compromised that he confronted the head of the earlier apostles very energetically before the assembled community. From the standpoint of the Jerusalem agreement, people could see that the only option left open to the Apostle Peter was either to completely do away with the distinction between Jewish and Gentile Christians, or to remain in this respect a Jew and deny to the Gentile Christians the rights that would place them on the same level with Jewish Christians.

For his own part Paul took a step that had to have further consequences. With incisive energy he pointed out to Peter how his inconsistent and half-hearted Jewish-Christian position, which tied the [Jewish] law to the [Christian] faith, was a logical as well as a moral error, a contradiction in which he stood self-condemned. He then went on to show the inherent, strict consistency of the Christian principle, where, in abolishing the law, Christ is no promoter of sin. Paul says that, instead of rebuilding what was destroyed, "through the law I died to the law, so that I might live to God."[14] The words and the whole tone of the Apostle make us feel how forcefully the two apostles must have collided in person. So it cannot be a surprise that the scene in Antioch made a deep impression on the age that followed and had lasting effects. None of the epistles of Paul give any indication that the two apostles were reconciled in the years that followed. The Book of Acts passes over the scene in Antioch with a resolute silence, which shows clearly enough how recalling it did not fit with its own tendency to harmonize differences. From a work written in the second half of the

---

14. For an interpretation of the passage in Gal 2:15–21, see Holsten, *Galater* (n. 6), 22ff.

second century, the *Pseudo-Clementine Homilies*, we learn that even then the Jewish Christians could not forget the harsh words the Apostle Paul had spoken about the person they regarded as the chief of the apostles.[15]

THE OPPONENTS OF THE APOSTLE PAUL

In Galatia

We have seen that at the very outset of the controversy, as soon as the question of circumcision had arisen, people once again appeared on the scene who had come from the Jerusalem congregation and openly sought to foment a reaction (Gal 2:4, 12). We meet with the same phenomenon in the Gentile Christian communities founded by Paul. Judaists of the same stamp appeared in these communities, and made it their business to discredit Pauline Christianity, and to undermine what the Apostle had founded and built up as his own work, apart from the law and in opposition to the law. They did this in order to rebuild Christianity on the basis of the law.

The first actual proof of this systematic opposition to the Apostle Paul appears in the Epistle to the Galatians, which he wrote because of this very opposition. This was a few years after the scene at Antioch, and after the Apostle had made his second missionary journey. The whole arrangement and tendency of the Epistle show that the Apostle deemed the matter to be of great importance and saw that this was a very significant contest of principles. For this reason he even went back to the time of his conversion to Christianity, in order to separate his whole relationship to Christ from his relation to the earlier apostles. By a purely objective presentation he provides an incontrovertible proof that from the very outset he has in various ways asserted decisively and successfully the independent legitimacy of his gospel. The opponents who came forward against him in the Galatian congregation were a new branch of the opposition he had fought with before. They had confused the conscience of the Galatian Christians by asserting that, without observing the law, their achievement of salvation rests on a totally false foundation; and the Galatians were at the point of falling away from the teaching of the Apostle, and of allowing the whole yoke of the law, including

---

15. *Homilies*, 17.19: "But if you say that I am condemned, you bring an accusation against God, who revealed the Christ to me" [*ANF* 8:324], Peter says to Simon Magus, with an obvious allusion to the words of Paul in Gal 2:11: "[when Cephas came to Antioch,] I opposed him face to face, because he stood self-condemned." The tradition of the church that brought the apostles together again places the final reconciliation of the two at the end of a long period of separation. "When a long time had passed," the *Predicatio Pauli* says in the passage that has been preserved in the treatise *De Rebaptismate*, ch. 17, appended to the works of Cyprian (*Cypr. Opp.*, ed. Baluz, 365ff.), "Peter and Paul—after the gospel was collated in Jerusalem, and after a mutual understanding and settling of their altercation, and agreeing on what was to be done—met in the city, becoming acquainted as though for the first time" [cf. *ANF* 5:677]. [*Ed.*] The anonymous *Treatise on Rebaptism* was probably aimed at Cyprian, who favored the rebaptism of heretics. It cites the obviously apocryphal *Preaching of Paul* just prior to this passage. On the *Pseudo-Clementine Homilies*, see n. 54.

circumcision (Gal 5:2), to be imposed on them. Such was the impression made by these Judaists even in a community consisting mostly of Gentile Christians—a community that, so Paul declares, had received his gospel of freedom from the law with such lively interest and with such warm affection for him personally (Gal 4:12–19).

No other epistle affords such deep insight into the significance of the ever-widening struggle and the religious motives that operated on both sides. The Judaists maintained the absolute validity of Judaism, namely that without the law and circumcision no one can be saved, while Paul set forth the antithesis, that "if you let yourself be circumcised, Christ will be of no benefit to you" (Gal 5:2). According to the Judaists, it is pointless being a Christian if one is not also a Jew; whereas according to the Apostle, it is pointless being a Christian if as a Christian one chooses to be a Jew as well. And since one cannot be a Jew without circumcision, and along with it the obligation to keep the whole law in all its details, the contradiction and division into which one falls by taking this path are evident. But the Apostle is not content with exposing this contradiction to the Galatians, and showing them how untenable and irrational this course of action would be. He goes to the root of the matter and attacks Judaism itself, showing that its being a religion of law reduces it to a minor and secondary position in the history of humankind's religious development.

Even in Jewish religious history the law is not what is primary and original. Above it stands the promise given to Abraham, which points forward to a time when the same faith that was "reckoned to Abraham as righteousness" will become the blessing of all peoples. This promise can only be fulfilled when the law, whose curse extends to "everyone who does not observe and obey all the things written in the law," gives way to faith. Through faith in him who has "redeemed us from the curse of the law," we receive the very object of the promise given to Abraham, the Spirit. Thus the Apostle has placed the law and the promise in such direct opposition to each other that he can only ask what the law as such is, what purpose it serves, if because of its inability to give life, righteousness also could not in fact come by it. The answer he gives is that, because of transgressions—not to prevent them but that in them sin might attain to its full manifestation and existence—the law was interposed between the promise and the time when faith should arrive. This was the interval for the discipline of the law, in which sinful human beings were to be imprisoned until they became mature enough to be adopted into the children of God through faith in Christ and be free from sin.[16]

Thus Judaism is only the religion of the law in contrast to Christianity as the religion of the spirit. Judaism's position in the world and its inner constitution are indicative of its mediating and interim character. It is there just to exercise the stern severity of one who watches over transgressions, and to keep promise and fulfillment apart until the promise can be fulfilled in the world order, at God's appointed time for it (the πλήρωμα τοῦ χρόνου, "the fullness of time," Gal 4:4). Indeed, the Apostle denigrates Judaism even more. Not only does it put human beings under the yoke of

---

16. [*Ed.*] See the whole of Galatians, chs. 3–4.

the law, but also, like paganism, it has its religious institutions and forms of worship that are bound to specific times, days, months, years. Thus it binds human beings to the same elementary and material powers of nature, the veneration of which is characteristic of the pagan nature religions, and in this respect at least it stands at the same level of religious development as paganism.[17] The divine world order assures that there is a progression from the immaturity and dependence of childhood to the maturity of adulthood, from slavery to freedom, from the flesh to the spirit. So Christianity certainly stands high above Judaism. Falling back from Christianity to Judaism can only be regarded as an irrational inversion of the relationship ordained by God.

Such is the lofty standpoint from which the Apostle here appears to us when we see him for the first time developing, in more specific dialectical terms, the reasons for refuting his Judaizing opponents. Not only does he repudiate as completely unjustified their demand regarding circumcision; he also denies that the law possesses the absolute right the Jews ascribe to it. He considers Judaism and Christianity from a religio-historical perspective, and with a worldview subsuming Jewish particularism into its universal idea. The demand made of Gentile Christians amounts to none other than the contention that, by submitting to circumcision, they also acknowledge the absolute superiority of the Jewish nation, as God's chosen people, over all other peoples. The cardinal point of Paul's dialectical polemic, however, is to be found in the passage [Gal 3:25–29] where, from the previous discussion of the law and the promise, he draws the conclusion that all who are baptized into Christ by that very fact enter into a new community, in which everything that separates one person from another in outer life-circumstances is removed; there is no longer any difference between Jews and Greeks, between circumcision and uncircumcision, and all may regard themselves as children of Abraham. All are one in Christ, in the faith that manifests itself by love.

The inner power of truth and the acuteness of his dialectical development give the Apostle a decisive superiority over his Judaistic opponents. But what could all this avail if the Christian principle of truth depended only on apostolic authority; and if, when Paul was compared with the earlier apostles, they were seen to be the immediate witnesses to the truth proclaimed by Christ, whereas the autonomy of his apostolic authority could only be based on the self-certainty of his own apostolic consciousness? We of course see clearly enough in the Epistle to the Galatians how Paul is very

---

17. The Apostle's object is simply to define the place of the law in the divine governance of the world. See the very acute and appropriate analysis of the course of the Apostle's thought in Holsten, *Galater* (n. 6), 30ff., where the result is summed up as follows on p. 48. The law is no longer the absolute purpose of God but only a relative one; it is subsumed under the absolute purpose as a means. Thus while it is distinguished from the promise, its unity with the promise is maintained. In God's salvific will the νόμος is distinguished from the ἐπαγγελία, but in the economy of salvation they are united. [*Ed.*] Baur continues by quoting phrases from Gal 3:19–21, which reads in translation: "Why then the law? It was added because of transgressions, until the offspring would come to whom the promise had been made, and it was ordained through angels by a mediator. Now a mediator involves more than one party; but God is one. Is the law then opposed to the promises of God? Certainly not! For if a law had been given that could make alive, then righteousness would indeed come through the law."

much aware that the truth of his gospel and the assertion of his apostolic authority are very closely connected, are inseparable. He could only maintain the truth of his gospel by legitimizing his own position as an apostle over against the earlier apostles. What then are his apostolic credentials; and when he affirmed that he alone was the true apostle of Jesus Christ, how did things stand with the earlier apostles, who made the same claim for themselves? Thus the dispute that had arisen about the necessity of circumcision and the continuing validity of the law must naturally have had further consequences.

In Corinth

Whatever success the Apostle may have had with his Epistle to the Galatians and in his controversy with opponents in the Galatian congregation, it is only a further development of the same controversy when we encounter not long thereafter, at another juncture of his apostolic activity, adversaries who pursued the same interests in opposing him.

If there is not any doubt that the Apostle wrote the Epistle to the Galatians during the earlier part of his residence in Ephesus from 54 to 57, then our First Epistle to the Corinthians was composed during the latter part of the same period. It was occasioned by reports indicating that Paul should expect similar experiences in Corinth as those he had encountered in Galatia. Judaizing teachers had made their way here too and had made people hesitate about accepting Paul's version of the gospel. There were divisions and factions, but the main opposition originated with a party that bore the name of Peter—although Peter himself was doubtless never in Corinth—and it took a position opposed to those members of the Corinthian congregation who remained faithful to the principles of Pauline Christianity.[18] The factional interests that moved the community in various directions undoubtedly had their basis and origin in the same antithesis with which the Epistle to the Galatians was concerned.

It is remarkable, however, that in the two Epistles to the Corinthians there is no longer any discussion of the law and circumcision. A very personal issue has now come to the fore of the controversy, one that was inevitable. How could someone who had not become an apostle as the earlier apostles did claim authority as an apostle? It could be dubious as to whether he should rightly be called a true and genuine apostle. The Apostle Paul does not directly address this most important question until the end

---

18. I am still of the opinion that the only view of the Corinthian factions that will explain both the epistles of the Apostle and the factions in Corinth generally is that the party of Cephas [Peter] and the so-called party of Christ were essentially one and the same. See *Paulus, der Apostel Jesu Christi* (n. 5), 26off. [ET 1:261 ff]. [*Ed.*] In this text Baur refers in a footnote to his path-breaking article, "Die Christuspartei in der korinthischen Gemeinde, der Gegensatz des petrinischen und paulinischen Christenthums in der ältesten Kirche, der Apostel Paulus in Rom," *Tübinger Zeitschrift für Theologie* (1831) no. 4, 61–206. See 1 Cor 1:12: "What I mean is that each of you says, 'I belong to Paul,' or 'I belong to Apollos,' or 'I belong to Cephas,' or 'I belong to Christ.'"

I. The Antitheses

of the second Epistle; but it is readily apparent that, through the whole course of the two Epistles, he never loses sight of it, and that he takes every opportunity to prepare the groundwork and speak on his own behalf, so that he could decisively refute his opponents' charges. He asserts in the most emphatic way that he is as much an apostle as any other, and is not in the least inferior to those "super-apostles" supposedly more authoritative than him. Although he can only speak ironically about the formal prerogatives of the Jewish nation, in pitting himself against his opponents[19] he offers real arguments on which he rests his case. They are the actual results to which he can point: the ever-widening sphere of his gospel's influence, all those painful experiences in which he proved himself a servant of Christ, and finally the visions and revelations of the Lord of which he can boast. The Apostle could not leave the last point unmentioned once the question of his apostolic calling had been so pointedly raised. He might appeal with the greatest justice to the success of his missionary activity,[20] but it was self-evident that only a person who had been called by Jesus Christ himself could be an apostle of Christ.

In First Corinthians (9:1) he had insisted emphatically that, as an apostle, he too had seen the Lord, and so the visions and revelations of the Lord of which he speaks, toward the end of Second Corinthians (12:1–10), are evidence of his apostolic calling. They have the same significance for him as the direct call by Jesus himself during his earthly life has for the earlier apostles. To the Apostle himself, this was the most immediate and convincing proof of his apostolic calling, but it was also the most subjective proof he could offer on his behalf. It consisted of ecstatic experiences, vivid inner perceptions, and facts of consciousness that could have no objective reality for anyone other than the immediate subject himself. And nothing is more natural than that opponents who could never bring themselves to accept the truth of the Apostle's teaching should also have refused to grant those premises on which the teaching was based. They directed their attacks chiefly at this point—where the Apostle had to feel himself most vulnerable. He could not conceal the peculiar situation in which he found himself vis-à-vis the opponents because of this factor. In opposing them, we see him especially agitated and irritated, and that is mainly the expression of his uneasiness in having to do what was inherently impossible, namely, to prove objectively what was purely subjective in nature. This impossibility confronted him most acutely at the point where his own personal interests were concerned.

From this perspective the opponents' concern also appears in a different light from how we generally view it, when we judge it entirely by the very unfavorable way

---

19. 2 Cor 11:21–22. [*Ed.*] "But whatever anyone dares to boast of—I am speaking as a fool—I also dare to boast of that. Are they Hebrews? So am I. Are they Israelites? So am I. Are they descendents of Abraham? So am I." On the "super-apostles," see 2 Cor 11:5.

20. See especially such passages as 1 Cor 9:1–2; 15:10; 2 Cor 2:14–17; 3:2–3; 10:13–18; 11:23. In the same way he cites as proof of the reality of his apostolic calling that "he who worked through Peter making him an apostle to the circumcised also worked through me in sending me to the Gentiles" (Gal 2:8).

the Apostle describes his opponents. Maybe human passion and partisanship led to such indecency in their opposition to the Apostle. But why should we assume that all the wrong was on their side, when they resisted not only Paul's contention that he was called to apostleship, but also his consistent assertion that he has an apostolic authority superior to all the early apostles taken together? Whereas he appealed to his inner certainty of being called by Christ and of his apostolic consciousness, they in turn were actually linked to Christ on the soil of history. Thus one principle stood opposed to another, and only further developments could determine which of these two principles would attain dominance over the other. In the meantime, the attacks made on the person of the Apostle and on his apostolic authority form a new and noteworthy epoch in the controversy between Judaism and Paulinism. The very serious manner in which the Apostle confronted these opponents is indicative of their importance. We would have a very erroneous picture if we regarded this as merely an isolated phenomenon, the arbitrary action of a few individuals who were driven by merely fortuitous and personal motives to disrupt and hinder the Apostle's effectiveness. Everything combines to show that they had a powerful faction behind them and that they believed they were justified in stepping up as the agents and emissaries of that faction.

The name of the Apostle Peter at the forefront of their efforts served to identify their orientation and made their cause appear as a cause common to all Jewish Christians. However, as we learn from the Apostle Paul himself (2 Cor 3:1), these opponents also brought letters of recommendation with them that left no doubt as to their party affiliation. Who else could send such letters of recommendation other than those who were of sufficient importance within the mother community to be also recognized elsewhere? These letters are an additional proof of growing factional interests, of the opposing position of the two parties, and of their efforts in carrying on local battles. The letters were also a new manifestation of the difference in principle between the two contending parties. In the final analysis, the Apostle could offer nothing other than the autonomy of his own self-consciousness over against the external principle of authority that legitimated his opponents. This is what he does in the passage where he speaks of these letters recommending his opponents (2 Cor 3:1–18).[21]

In dealing with the opponents in Corinth, he assumes a higher religio-historical perspective, as he did in the Epistle to the Galatians. Judaism and Christianity are related to each other as the old and the new διαθήκη (covenant); the old one is antiquated and has expired, but the new one is bright and luminous. The justification for his apostolic authority lies in this distinction between these covenants and in the Spirit as the principle of Christian consciousness. Judaism is veiling and subjection, a limited and finite religious consciousness. Christianity is opposed to this; it opens up the religious consciousness to perfect clarity and self-certainty, and does not rely on any external mediation. This is the very principle of Paul's apostolic authority. Against

---

21. See my "Beiträge zur Erklärung der Korintherbriefe," *Theologische Jahrbücher* 9 (1850) 165ff.

those who refuse to recognize him as an apostle, he can only argue that their religious consciousness is imperfect. The veil[22] is the symbol of Mosaism. The opponents' Jewish consciousness is still veiled, and they cannot see that the end of the old religion is already at hand. The principle of Paulinism could not be expressed more purely than the Apostle himself does in this setting when he summarizes his argument stating the antithesis between the old covenant and those who, with their Christian consciousness, still stand within it. He says: "The Lord is the Spirit, and the Spirit is freedom" (2 Cor 3:17).[23] That is to say, the principle and essence of Paulinism is the emancipation of consciousness from every external authority that is only exercised by human beings. It is the removal of all confining barriers and the elevation of the spirit to a standpoint where everything is unveiled and opened up in luminous clarity to the eyes of spirit. It is the autonomy and immediacy of self-consciousness.

THE EPISTLE TO THE ROMANS

The Apostle rebuts the opponents of his teaching and his apostolic authority by demonstrating the imperfection, the narrowness, and the finitude of the religion of the law. But to completely undercut the particularism that was so closely interwoven with Judaism—the Jewish national pride that led Jews to regard themselves as better and more privileged than all other human beings—it was necessary to attack it more directly, to lay the ax more sharply to its root. What this especially required was a more in-depth and focused engagement with moral consciousness, via a discussion basically sticking to an abstract and theoretical level. In the Epistle to the Romans we see the Apostle proceed to do this, as the third and most important stage of the long and hard struggle by which his principle first had to work its way through so many antitheses. Regarded from this perspective, the Epistle to the Romans is to be seen not merely as a compendium of Pauline theology but also as a historical source of great importance.[24]

What led the Apostle to write to the Roman congregation and to address it in such an epistle as this? As a rule he only wrote to congregations that he himself had founded. The Roman congregation was not one of his, but neither is it known whether any of the other apostles was directly involved in its founding. We can only suppose that it formed on its own as a result of the frequent contacts that the large Jewish

---

22. [*Ed.*] See 2 Cor 3:14–16. When the people of Israel "hear the reading of the old covenant, that same veil is still there [that Moses put over his face], since only Christ can set it aside. Indeed, to this very day whenever Moses is read, a veil lies over their minds; but when one turns to the Lord the veil is removed."

23. [*Ed.*] This is an abbreviated version of the passage, which in the NRSV reads: "Now the Lord is the Spirit, and where the Spirit of the Lord is, there is freedom."

24. See my article, "Ueber Zweck und Gedankengang des Römerbriefs," *Theologische Jahrbücher* 16 (1857) 60–108, 184–209.

population, long in Rome, maintained with Judea and Jerusalem.[25] It was not even a Gentile Christian community but was mainly composed of Jewish Christians, and its prevailing character was Jewish Christian. It has indeed been generally assumed that the Roman Christians to whom the Apostle to the Gentiles wrote must have been Gentile Christians; but the entire tendency of the Epistle, the main purpose to which it is directed, and the greater part of its contents, make it no longer possible to doubt that the Apostle is dealing mainly with Jewish Christians. This is exactly why he wrote the Epistle to the Romans. The Apostle addressed himself to them as Jewish Christians, but also because he saw them as the community that, located in the capital and having numerous and influential members, could be the leader of the non-Palestinian communities, and thus be representative of all the Jewish Christians living among Gentile peoples. But what may have especially motivated the Apostle to keep his eyes on this community for a long time, and even made him want to visit it, as he says in Rom 1:13, was undoubtedly that he had more latitude here. That was because he had not yet come into any personal contact with opponents here, as he had in battles in the Galatian and Corinthian communities. Much in the earlier epistles involved subjective, personal, and nettlesome factors. But with the Roman community he could treat the same questions far more unselfconsciously and objectively. He could pose the controversial issues in more multifaceted and detailed ways, and that facilitated a much more favorable response from the opponents. Precisely at the main points of his argument the Apostle adopted a milder, more conciliatory, more sympathetic tone than he had done before. This, certainly, is only part of the picture. The rest, the other side, apparently very different and yet closely connected with the first, is a keenness in dialectical polemics, penetrating more deeply than in any of the previous epistles, so as to cut off the justification of Jewish particularism at its roots. These two features—the mild spirit with which he confronts his opponents in order to engage with their standpoint and not judge it too harshly, and the keenness with which he confutes them—give the Epistle to the Romans its peculiar interest and make its contents the deepest and most comprehensive foundation of Pauline universalism, in contrast to Jewish particularism. This and nothing else is the actual theme of the Epistle.

People could no longer cling with their former tenacity to their prerogative as circumcised Jews over uncircumcised Gentiles, nor close their eyes to the law being insufficient for salvation. They were not offended at the admission of Gentiles to the messianic blessings, and could even dismiss the scruples and objections people formerly had regarding the apostolic calling and authority of the Apostle. But one issue still made them uneasy. Since the conversion of Gentiles had occurred on a large scale and was continuing at an increasing pace, there was now an evident incongruity

---

25. [It was] a clear proof of Christianity's inherent impulse to communicate and propagate itself. In this regard we should not ascribe too much to the direct personal activity of the apostles. There is no evidence that the apostles ever visited some regions, such as North Africa and Spain, where there seem to have been numerous Christian communities from very early times.

affecting the Gentile and Jewish worlds. How explain the fact that, although the Jewish people was from ancient times the chosen people of God and the object of God's promises, a great part of that people had no part in the salvation that had appeared in Christ, and that Gentiles were instead occupying the place vacated by God's own people? This question grasps, in the most purely religious terms, everything that Jewish particularism could claim as its absolute right, and even the Apostle would have had to deny his own national feeling had this issue not moved him to the depths of his heart. The question appeared to him so important that he attempted not merely to remove the obstacle it presented to a frank recognition of Christian universalism, but also to come to an understanding with his Jewish compatriots. He delves into the issue with deep sympathy for the salvation of his own people; but the more deeply he goes into it the more he becomes aware that it is simply another form of the old claim of a national prerogative, which as such lies at the basis of Jewish particularism. Is it really the case, when the question is considered from the moral-religious point of view, that Jews are better and more favored than other peoples? Do not all the advantages the history of their people has given them over others instead make them more responsible for their guilt before God?

This is the point from which the Apostle sets out in his Epistle. At the forefront of his argument, as his leading idea, is the righteousness of God contrasted with the unrighteousness of human beings, which is obviously a notorious fact of history applicable to Gentiles and Jews alike. In this respect Gentiles and Jews are on the same level. If what makes the immoral actions of the Gentiles inexcusable and worthy of punishment is that they did these things despite their own better knowledge and conscience (Rom 1:19–23), the same is true of the Jews. If there is any difference, it can only be found in the degree of awareness with which people do what they ought not to do. But it is all the worse for the Jews. The Gentiles are not without a law; they have the law of their conscience; and if the Jews have the advantage of an additional law, all that they boast about in relying on it only counts against them. They are not better than the Gentiles, but rather are worse and more culpable to the same degree that they know better than the Gentiles, knowing clearly and completely from their own law what they should do, while in fact doing the opposite. Since the true moral worth of human beings consists in their doing what their consciousness tells them they should do, this one consideration puts an end to setting Jews apart from Gentiles It is all the same whether one is or is not circumcised. It matters not what Jews are outwardly, just what they are inwardly, in their hearts, before God (Rom 2:25–29). If Jews still seek a privileged position, they are to be referred to scripture, which itself testifies that Jews and Gentiles are under sin; and what scripture or the law says, it says to them who are under the law. All the passages of scripture lamenting the depravity of human beings apply to the Jews first of all, and these passages altogether only show that no one can be justified before God by works of the law. The law just brings one to recognize one's own sin.

If there is then any righteousness, it is only the righteousness of God through faith in Jesus Christ, which excludes all boasting. Faith alone corresponds to the universal idea of God. If one could be justified and saved through works of the law, as the Jews suppose, then only the Jews would have this righteousness, and God would be God of Jews alone. But God is God of the Gentiles as well as the Jews (Rom 3:21–31). In faith, then, the distinction between circumcision and uncircumcision disappears. Given the universal sinfulness of humankind, there is no route to salvation other than the righteousness of God through faith. Thus the universalism of Christianity is certainly established in its full significance, as the Apostle expresses it by saying that God is not the God of the Jews only, but also of Gentiles [3:29]. This universalism has its deepest foundation in the irrefutable fact of the moral consciousness, that Jews as well as Gentiles simply know themselves to be sinners and under the judgment of God.

The whole force of the Apostle's argument depends on assuming the objective truth of the new way of salvation he proclaims. So his epistle has the further task of aligning this way of salvation with the religious consciousness of Jews and Jewish Christians, and of removing the scruples and objections that still stood in the way of their receiving it (Rom 4:1—8:39). There are three steps in this argument.

1. The religious worldview of Judaism already contains all the aspects of the Apostle's teaching. The history of humanity from Adam to Christ divides into two opposing periods, each of which has its own distinctive principle determining every part of it. Thus we see that world history and the history of revelation call for not only a condemnation to death but also a justification to life (Rom 4:1—5:21).

2. The moral requirement of the law loses none of its force because of the teaching about faith, as the opponents claim (cf. Rom 3:8). The believing Christian and sin have nothing whatever to do with each other: the death of Christ has absolutely dissolved the bond connecting human beings with sin, and also dissolved their bond with the law by which sin first comes to life (Rom 6:1—7:6).

3. At the same time sin and law are not identical. The law in itself is good and holy; in its inner essence it is spiritual, and only in its relation to nature and to human consciousness does it give rise to a conflict between flesh and spirit. In this conflict the religious ego of Judaism remains in the condition of an unhappy consciousness, and it cannot break through the barrier that separates Judaism from Christianity.

Only in Christianity is the flesh encountered by the spirit, the principle that overcomes the flesh. Thus only when human beings receive the spirit are they adopted by God, and in this adoption, in their unity with Christ, everything is removed that separates them from God and from God's love in Christ. Delivered from the dominion of the powers that ruled in the pre-Christian world—the powers of the flesh, sin, and the law—and set free to live the life of the spirit, human beings can, by reason of the indwelling spirit, now know themselves to be spiritually one with God (Rom 7:7—8:39).

It is at this point (Rom 9:1ff.) that the Apostle, looking back on all the blessed and saving effects of faith that he has been describing, expresses the most tender sympathy for his Jewish compatriots, and labors with all his heart to show them that the participation of Gentiles in the kingdom of God does not take place at the expense of Israel. But he cannot do this without denying the primacy of the Jews over the Gentiles, something he has had to contend with all along. He denies it even in its mildest, purely theocratic form where it applies simply to the faithfulness and truthfulness of God. For what advantage has the Jew over the Gentile if there is no such thing as righteousness based on works of the law? It is true that the promises of God cannot remain unfulfilled, but they are fulfilled without any human cooperation. What justifiable claim can humans assert against God, if God can do what God wills according to his pleasure and can make of humans either a vessel of mercy or a vessel of wrath? If human beings disregard faith, they can only be reminded of their utter dependence on God; but if faith is taken into account, then it is the "stumbling stone" for Israel.[26] All guilt consists simply in unbelief. The Apostle expresses a hope that finally, after the fullness of the Gentiles has been gathered in, the promises will also be fulfilled by the conversion of Israel. Born as an Israelite, as a descendant of Abraham and of the tribe of Benjamin (Rom 11:1), Paul finds it hard to abandon this hope. However, he bases it not upon Jewish nationality and everything connected with it, but on the general truth that sooner or later all things must return to that God from whom and through whom all things are, and in whom all things have the final purpose of their being and subsistence (Rom 9–11).[27]

So Jewish particularism lacks any justification on external or internal grounds. The absolute nullity of all its claims is the basic idea running through the whole of the epistle in its two main parts (chapters 1–8, 9–11), connecting them not merely externally but internally. From a closer analysis of its contents it is clear that its great significance lies not so much in what it says dogmatically about the doctrine of sin and grace, but rather in its practical bearing on the most important question of the time, the relationship of Jews and Gentiles. How could the two peoples have ever come together in the unity of one Christian church, had not the particularism of Judaism, with all its prejudices and pretensions, its presumed privileges and superiority, and which

---

26. [*Ed.*] See Rom 8:31–33. The Jews did not succeed in fulfilling the law because "they did not strive for it on the basis of faith, but as if it were based on works. They have stumbled over the stumbling stone, as it is written [in Isa 8:14–15, 28:16], 'See, I am laying in Zion a stone that will make people stumble, a rock that will make them fall.'"

27. This belongs to the Apostle's universal worldview. The ἥττημα (defeat) of the Jews and the πλήρωμα (riches) of the Gentiles (Rom 11:12) arrive at the same end, because each has its own time period; and as God has imprisoned all in disobedience, so God will be merciful to all (11:32). The Apostle can think only of a final salvation for all. The dogma of eternal punishment belongs only to Judaism.

opposed the Gentile world so brusquely and offensively, been thus uprooted and exposed to the world? This is what the Apostle's magnificent dialectic accomplished.

We do not know what impression and effects this epistle had on the Roman congregation. But we can scarcely be wrong in assuming that, in a community in which (as we may infer from the epistle itself) the antagonism between the two factions had already been mitigated to some degree, an epistle of so significant and comprehensive a character did not fail to have the desired effect (Rom 1:13).[28] It must also have contributed to the Roman community's more open, more conciliatory, and mediating posture that subsequently made it so important. Despite the challenges it poses, the epistle unmistakably has a conciliatory character. It shows the Apostle not only as very sympathetic toward the salvation of his Jewish compatriots, but also having a heartfelt need to approach them rationally and affectionately in every respect, and to clear away completely all remaining barriers. It is as though the Apostle had turned to the Roman community with the confidence that it was especially fitted to undertake the role of mediator, as it were, on the great issue of his apostolic calling, where so many bitter opponents and persecutors still confronted him. When we consider the circumstances in which the epistle was written to the Roman congregation during his last residence in Corinth, it appears very likely that the Apostle was occupied with thoughts like these, and was seeking to do everything in his power to get the cause for which he was working dealt with in a conciliatory and loving spirit, and so brought to a final decision.

THE FINAL JOURNEY TO JERUSALEM

Paul was on the point of setting off for Jerusalem once more, indeed in connection with a matter in which he had for some time taken a deep interest because it seemed to provide an appropriate means for drawing Gentile Christians and Jewish Christians closer together, and for making his peace with the Jerusalem congregation.

In the Epistle to the Galatians (2:10) he states that ever since the assembly in Jerusalem he had never lost sight of a work by which the communities now divided might be reunited, namely, the support of the poor in Jerusalem. In the period during which the two Epistles to the Corinthians were written, he had given special attention to this undertaking (1 Cor 16:1–4; 2 Cor 8–9). Since the monetary contribution was such an important purpose for his journey, he desired that it should be as large as possible. It must have been his uncertainty on this point that made him think at first of sending the contribution by delegates to be chosen by the Corinthians, who would carry an epistle from him to the Christians at Jerusalem. He adds, however (1 Cor 16:4), that if the matter is worthwhile, that is, if the gift is generous enough

---

28. The last two chapters of the epistle are not genuine but an addition by a later hand. Thus the long list of those who are greeted at the end provides proof that the Apostle's epistle did not fail to attain its goal.

to help him with the purpose he had in mind, he would go with them himself. That his purpose was not merely the material sustenance of the poor, that he had another aim more closely connected with his apostolic calling, he himself states very clearly in Second Corinthians 9:12–13. He says (v. 12): "For the rendering of this ministry not only supplies the needs of the saints but also overflows with many thanksgivings to God." He adds that the Christians of Jerusalem praise God that the confession of the Gentile Christians is so entirely obedient to the gospel of Christ, that they seek to be nothing but true confessors of the gospel of Christ. And as they recognize in this gift the heartfelt fellowship that the Gentile Christians offer, their heart turns to them, their prayers for them express the yearning they feel toward them, because the grace of God has been demonstrated in them in such a superabundant way. So this was supposed to be an attempt to remove the wall still dividing the Jewish and the Gentile Christians, and to win for Pauline Christianity the recognition that was still denied it. The Apostle believed he could break through the mistrust and prejudice still existing on the part of Jewish Christians, due to the former circumstances; that the love-offering the Gentile Christian communities were sending to the Jerusalem congregation in token of fraternal unity, would produce such an impression. It was no doubt in furtherance of this plan, and with the contribution that had been collected, that he soon afterwards set out on his journey to Jerusalem. But how painfully he was disappointed in these hopes!

It is not necessary to detail the circumstances under which the Apostle met his well-known fate in Jerusalem. There is just one question of special interest: who stirred up those tumultuous episodes in which the Roman military authorities had to intervene in order to rescue the Apostle from the rage of his opponents? Were they Jews, or were they Jewish Christians? They were zealots for the law who saw in the Apostle a transgressor of the law, an apostate, a declared enemy of the national religion. But such zealots were not merely Jews; they were rather Jewish Christians, even more so than Jews, because for them the mission to the Gentiles had made the question of the law a matter of the keenest factional interest. Even in the narrative of the Book of Acts,[29] which conceals the true state of affairs as much as possible, we see that the Jewish Christians were not as uninvolved in the outbreaks of hatred to which the Apostle fell a victim as is generally supposed. Under the protection of his Roman citizenship the Apostle was removed to Rome after two years' imprisonment in Caesarea. According to Acts [28:30] his house arrest in Rome lasted for an additional two years, but we are not told when or how it ended. Even if we assume the genuineness of the epistles that are alleged to have been written by the Apostle during his captivity in Rome, we have no certain or noteworthy information about this period. The most important fact is that the terminus of these two years coincides with the great fire of Nero and the persecution of Christians to which it led. It is very unlikely that the Apostle survived this fateful period.

29. [*Ed.*] See chs. 21–28. The Book of Acts places the blame squarely on the Jews.

THE HEIGHT OF THE ANTITHESIS; THE GOSPEL OF LUKE

Up to the time when the Apostle disappears from the stage of history, we just see disagreements and antitheses, with no sure path to compromise and reconciliation. The [Gentile-Christian] side, whose existence led to the rift in the religious consciousness still shared by Jews and Jewish Christians, certainly felt the need for rapprochement and reconciliation, but there was no corresponding response from the other side.

There were as yet only Jewish Christians and Gentile Christians, with divergent tendencies and interests. There was still no unifying ecclesial community. Nor has history yet been able to point to anything of greater significance that might have been able to effect the bridging of the great gulf, which since the events in Antioch had continued to exist between the Apostles Peter and Paul, the heads of the two parties. As we saw earlier, there must have been reconciling elements in the Roman community, which Paul influenced by both his epistle and his personal presence there. And how could the martyrdom of the great Apostle to the Gentiles, in one way or another ending his work in Rome, leave behind it anything other than a healing influence for the future? A suggestive legend, which however arose at a much later time, connects the brotherly unity of Peter and Paul with this death. What primarily contravenes treating this as established fact in the further developing history of this relationship, in the interim after the death of the Apostle Paul, is that so many elements proceeded in different directions, and historical development is able to arrive at this goal only by a longer road.

As we may infer from the result, the main tendency must have been to bring the two opposing parties closer to each other by balancing out their differences and mediating their opposing principles as much as possible. This tendency must, from the nature of the case, have become increasingly prevalent and predominant. But if we are to follow it in its whole range, we must first of all obtain a clear view of those points where the existing opposition is most extreme. This is mainly the case where the antagonism is conscious and intentional; where each of the two parties aims to maintain what separates it from the opponent, and to adopt an antithetical stance, thus removing the goal of a possible union to a distant future. Are there then, we must ask, phenomena of such a kind even after the death of the Apostle Paul—instances in which Paulinism takes an antithetical stance toward Jewish Christianity, or in which Jewish Christianity keeps up the same opposition against Paulinism that it had originally directed against the Apostle Paul?

Next to the epistles of the Apostle Paul, the Gospel of Luke[30] is the most consistent and most important source for knowledge of Paulinism. It contains special

---

30. See my *Kritische Untersuchungen über die kanonischen Evangelien* (Tübingen, 1847), 427; and my *Das Markusevangelium nach seinem Ursprung und Charakter* (Tübingen, 1851), 191ff. See also K. R. Köstlin, *Ursprung und Composition der synoptischen Evangelien* (Stuttgart, 1853), 132ff.; and A. Hilgenfeld, *Die Evangelien* (Leipzig, 1854), 220ff. Köstlin does not see in Luke the sharp and outspoken opposition to the Judaism of the Gospel of Matthew that I do, and this appears to me to be a

references to the destruction of Jerusalem, so it must at any rate have been written later than the year 70. From earliest times it counted as a Pauline gospel, but only very recently have people appreciated the specific way in which its Pauline character sets it apart from the other two Synoptic Gospels. This point is so closely connected with the question as to the overall makeup of the gospel that we can only touch on its most general features, but here too its Pauline tendency is unmistakable. Just as we can only grasp the structure and tendency of the Gospel of Luke in terms of its relation to the Gospel of Matthew, so too the Jewishness of Matthew provides our best measure for determining Luke's Pauline character. In Luke Jesus is not merely the Jewish Messiah of Matthew, for he is the redeemer of humanity as such, and in this sense he is the Son of God. In accord with his universal vocation, the entire representation of his person is more exalted and more comprehensive. In all that he does—his teaching, his miracles (especially his power over demons), and the whole of his self-revelation—he operates as a superhuman person. This is the reason why the Gospel of Luke, in its comprehension and portrayal of the gospel story, has already taken the decisive step, one that enables it to transcend the perspective of Matthew and move toward the Gospel of John. It abbreviates the Galilean ministry of Jesus as much as possible, while correspondingly extending that in Judea and Jerusalem. The announcement of the death and resurrection of Jesus as the final outcome and decisive goal of his whole earthly activity appears much earlier in Luke (9:22, 51) than in Matthew. In his struggle with his adversaries Jesus takes the offensive, and the struggle is more pronounced and uncompromising. The demonic power that uses these adversaries as its instruments intervenes at definite moments in the course of the story (Luke 4:13; 10:18; 22:3, 53). By this device, and by his repeated declarations, Luke clearly sets forth the truth: that Judaism as such is not the proper and actual arena for the accomplishment of Jesus' work.

However, if we restrict ourselves here to the main point, its Pauline universalism—the fundamental perspective of this Gospel—has the following major features. Unlike Matthew, Luke does not have Jesus saying anything with a particularistic ring,[31] and it makes Christian universalism a special topic of several of its narratives and parables. The Jews reject the gospel, whereas the Gentiles openly and willingly accept it. Although Jesus himself does not yet proclaim the gospel message in Gentile lands, he virtually inaugurates the mission to the Gentiles by his travels to Samaria, which, according to Luke's Gospel (9:52; 17:11), he [twice] entered from Galilee. The choice of the seventy [Luke 10:1], moreover, shows that the gospel was intended not exclusively for the twelve tribes of Israel but for all Gentile peoples. It is equally indicative of

defect in his understanding. On the other hand, the anonymous author of the work, *Die Evangelien, ihre Verfasser und ihr Verhältniss zu einander* (Leipzig, 1845), has stated this antithesis too broadly, but he has the merit of having been the first to pose the question in all its sharpness. [*Ed.*] Karl Reinhard Köstlin (1819–84) was one of Baur's former students, a member of the Tübingen School, and later a professor of aesthetics.

31. See Köstlin (n. 30), 178ff.

the Pauline character of Luke that it is oblivious to the identity of the teaching of Jesus with the law and the Old Testament, as the Gospel of Matthew asserts. The Gospel of Luke does not contain the statement so characteristic of the Gospel of Matthew, about the fulfillment of the law and its continuing validity. While the Gospel of Matthew [5:16] says that "not one stroke . . . will pass from the law," the Gospel of Luke, according to the original reading,[32] applies this statement instead to the words of Jesus (Luke 16:17). It even makes Jesus declare that, with the appearance of John the Baptist, the Mosaic law has come to an end, and that since that time the law has been replaced by the proclamation of the kingdom of God (16:16).[33] Again, this Gospel speaks of the earlier apostles in a way that can only be explained by supposing that it sought to place them in an unfavorable light so as to promote, at their expense, the authority and apostolic stature of the Apostle Paul.

A very significant instance of this is that the Gospel of Luke entirely ignores Jesus' declaration in the Gospel of Matthew [16:16–19] that is so important for Peter, in which Peter is called blessed because of his confession [that Jesus is the Messiah]; a passage declaring that he is the rock on which Jesus' church is to be built, so the gates of hell shall not prevail against it, and that the keys of heaven are to be given to him with power to bind and loose. The Gospel of Luke could not of course acknowledge such a primacy of Peter. In the same way Luke omits the authority given to the twelve (Matt 18:18) to forgive or not forgive sin, along with other related powers. Moreover, in many passages it presents the earlier apostles in a very unfavorable light, so as almost to suggest that, if the original twelve disciples were no better than this, then Jesus still had no true and proper disciples until the Apostle Paul came along.[34]

---

32. Investigations of the Marcionite Gospel have been taken up again by Albert Schwegler in the *Theologische Jahrbücher* 2 (1843) 575ff. and in *Das nachapostolische Zeitalter* (Tübingen, 1846), 1:26off.; and by Albrecht Ritschl, *Das Evangelium Marcions und das kanonische Evangelium des Lukas* (Tübingen, 1846). Thorough discussions of the question have also been undertaken by Gustav Volkmar in the *Theologische Jahrbücher* 9 (1850) 110ff., and in the book *Das Evangelium Marcions* (Leipzig, 1842); and by Adolf Hilgenfeld in the *Theologische Jahrbücher* 12 (1853) 194ff. These studies have led to the conclusion that the Marcionite Gospel contained not only alterations Marcion introduced intentionally but certainly also readings that in all probability are more original than those in our canonical text. I think there is good reason for adding to the latter passages the one I have cited above from Luke 16:17, which, in accord with Hilgenfeld (231ff.), Ritschl (201), and Volkmar (258), I read as τῶν λόγων μου. On the Gospel of Marcion, see my *Markusevangelium* (n. 30), 191ff. [*Ed.*] Thus according to Baur the original version of Luke 16:17 reads, "It is easier for heaven and earth to pass away, than for one stroke of a letter of my word to be dropped," as compared with the canonical version, ". . . than for one stroke of a letter in the law to be dropped." Marcion published the earliest extant collection of New Testament books, including an abridged version of Luke. See also Baur, *Lectures on New Testament Theology*, ed. Peter C. Hodgson, trans. Robert F. Brown (Oxford, 2016), 311–12.

33. [*Ed.*] Luke 16:16: "The law and the prophets were in effect until John came; since then the good news of the kingdom of God is proclaimed."

34. Cf. my *Kritische Untersuchungen* (n. 30), 435ff. According to Köstlin, *Ursprung und Composition* (n. 30), 200ff., the author of the Gospel of Luke did not intend to downgrade the twelve; he only wished to bring out as strongly as possible the exalted nature of the Christian revelation, and for this purpose he dwelt so frequently on their failure to understand Jesus. He opposes the claim put forward

I. The Antitheses

We cannot assume that the Gospel of Luke rests on a purer historical tradition than that of Matthew, or that, where significant differences occur between it and the other two gospels, Luke gives the truer and more faithful presentation of the gospel story. Thus these differences result from Luke's efforts to establish the justification in principle for Pauline universalism, by understanding the gospel story, indeed as to Jesus' person itself, from this perspective. The Gospel of Luke thus testifies to the vigorous self-consciousness with which the Pauline spirit lived on in his faithful adherents after the death of the Apostle himself. It makes no secret about what people later sought to conceal regarding Paulinism's view of [Paul's] personal relation to the earlier apostles; its necessary assumption is that, as Paulinism was superior to Jewishness [i.e., to Jewish Christianity], so Paul stood higher than the earlier apostles. The markedly Paulinizing tendency of this Gospel is such a distinctive phenomenon that, whenever the Pauline spirit subsequently manifested itself ever more forcefully, it turned to this Gospel to find itself purely expressed there. It counted so heavily as the Apostle Paul's gospel that church fathers such as Eusebius[35] thought that, when Paul spoke in his epistles of his gospel, as in 2 Tim 2:7,[36] he must have been referring directly to the Gospel of Luke.

---

by the twelve of being the only persons commissioned to proclaim Jesus. But what purpose do the new proclaimers of the gospel serve if their predecessors were quite capable, and the new ones were merely so many more of the same kind? Köstlin even thinks (267) that the introduction of the seventy points to a Gospel of Peter as the source of our Gospel of Luke. The writing in which the seventy originally appeared, he believes, must have been one that sought to assign the Jewish and the non-Jewish missions to different followers, with the twelve assigned exclusively to the people of Israel, and at the same time showing that care had been taken for the instruction of the Gentile world. But when we consider that, after the idea of the mission to the Gentiles had occurred to the Jewish Christians (even Peter had not entertained the idea at first, Gal 2:7), they set to work to make Peter an apostle to the Gentiles, we cannot consider it likely that a Petrine gospel first introduced the seventy into the evangelical tradition. But from whatever source the Gospel of Luke derived its seventy disciples, the antithesis to the twelve that the 10th chapter presents is perfectly clear, and it is impossible to ignore the Pauline interest on which it is based. So what use is it for Köstlin to say that so obviously singling out the seventy makes it all the more striking that very little is reported about them, and that when they return (Luke 10:20) Jesus somewhat severely exhorts them to be humble? Notwithstanding this admonition, how could they be exalted more highly than when they are told that their names are written in heaven (cf. Rev 21:12)? The very fact that nothing more is said about them—when we regard it in the light of what is the only possible meaning of the words of Jesus in 10:20, that the important thing is not what they have now accomplished, the evident success of their activity, but rather what their names gain in heaven—clearly shows that they embody an idea that ought to be brought to light. This idea could be realized only in Paulinism, as opposed to Judaism. In dealing with passages likes these, where the antitheses are pointedly expressed, it is not in the interests of gospel criticism to iron out the antitheses and neutralize them, especially if this is done by so obviously supporting a new hypothesis about the possible sources of a gospel. On the contrary, these passages serve to explain those where the tendency is less evident. With regard to Luke 8:54, I cannot but think it an arbitrary proceeding to remove the apostles from the πάντες (all) whom Jesus addresses upon leaving. Who is left to be the πάντες if, as we are told in v. 51, there was no one there but the three apostles and the parents of the child? (cf. Köstlin, 196).

35. *Ecclesiastical History* 3.4.

36. [*Ed.*] Baur's reference must be to 2 Tim 2:8: "Remember Jesus Christ, raised from the dead, a

Marcionite Paulinism

No one placed Luke higher than Marcion[37] did. In the early history of Paulinism, next to the author of the Gospel of Luke, Marcion is the most characteristic representative and champion of the purely Pauline principle.[38] Whatever the status of the Marcionite gospel, Marcion is by no means a mutilator and falsifier of the Gospel of Luke in the sense in which the church fathers said he was. In many passages there can be no doubt that his text is the authentic and original one. Even in cases where he has undeniably taken liberties by abridging or altering it in the interests of his Paulinism and of his Gnostic system, we should look at this differently than people usually do. We should deem this practice comparable to how the authors of our canonical gospels stand to one another. Each successive evangelist takes the substantial content of the gospel story, which he supposes to remain always unchanged, looks at it from a different point of view, and presents it in a different form. Thus in each instance the negative, antithetical, critical tendency of Marcion's Gospel bears witness to a decidedly rigorous Paulinism. His aim was to excise from the gospel, as far as possible, everything that merely bore the stamp of Judaism, and to exhibit the full extent of the gospel's antithesis to the law and the Old Testament. The work that accompanied his Gospel under the title *Antitheses* had a similar purpose, which indeed is plainly indicated by its name. It consisted of a juxtaposition of passages from the Old Testament with passages from the Gospel of Luke, in such a way as to place at once before our eyes the antithesis between the law and the gospel. It was intended as an introduction to his Gospel, to establish the correct approach to it.[39]

Marcion deliberately placed the Epistle to the Galatians first in his collection of the Pauline epistles as the *principalis adversus Judaismum Epistola* ("the epistle most decidedly against Judaism").[40] (It could also have been the first one chronologically.) He held Paul to be distinctively and even exclusively the true apostle. Thus Marcion

---

descendant of David—that is my gospel."

37. [*Ed.*] On Marcion, see Part 3, n. 62.

38. This is very clearly not to be understood in the sense that Ritschl (*Die Entstehung der altkatholischen Kirche*, 2nd ed. [Bonn, 1857], 311) imputes to me, as if Paulinism had developed into Marcionism, and this heresy had preserved the pure root principle of Paul. Ritschl might have spared himself the further remark that monotheism and the recognition of the unity of the Old and New Testaments, which is connected with the idea of the promise, are such inseparable elements of the purely Pauline view that, although Marcion intended to agree with Paul, he in fact did so just superficially and apparently. It is a well-known fact that Marcion was not only a Paulinist but a Gnostic, although this does not hinder his antinomianism from being genuinely Pauline, and he is entitled to a place in the history of Paulinism.

39. See Tertullian, *Adversus Marcion*, 4.1: "To encourage a belief *of this Gospel* he has actually devised for it a sort of dower, in a work composed of contrary statements set in opposition, thence entitled *Antitheses*, and compiled with a view to severing the law from the gospel" [*ANF* 3:345]. See also my work, *Die christliche Gnosis, oder die christliche Religions-Philosophie in ihrer geschichtlichen Entwicklung* (Tübingen, 1835), 249ff.

40. Tertullian, *Adversus Marcion*, 5.2 [*ANF* 3:431].

had fewer reservations than any other Gnostic about bringing up the controversy at Antioch as the most trenchant argument against the Judaism of the earlier apostles. The Marcionites accentuated this point as showing that, in separating the law from the gospel, Marcion had not so much set up a new principle as he had simply gone back to the pure and original gospel.[41] His Gnostic dualism necessarily led him to a much more pronounced antithesis to the Old Testament than that of the Apostle Paul. His position on the Old Testament did not allow resorting to allegorical interpretation, since allegory only served to connect the two testaments and iron out their differences. Even the Apostle Paul made use of allegory for this purpose, which makes it all the more remarkable that Marcion rejected allegory on principle.[42] But while his Paulinism led him to fully insist on the distinctions between the law and the gospel, it was inconsistent with his way of thinking to admit distinctions within the soil of the gospel itself. We can only see this as Marcion's consistent Pauline universalism, resulting from what he took to be people's basic consciousness of the gospel. He refused in any way to countenance that separation of catechumens from believers, that outward distinction of ranks and classes, in which the foundation of an ecclesiastical institution molded after the spirit of the Jewish hierarchy was already beginning to appear.[43]

The Marcionite movement with all these features is the phenomenon in the early church where Paulinism developed its anti-Judaic tendency with the greatest energy. Marcion seems from all accounts to have exercised a remarkable influence on the Christian Church of the second century. His adherents were widespread, and some of them formed communities of their own not just in Rome and Italy but also in the East, even into the fourth and fifth centuries.[44] All this is to be attributed to the Pauline element that Marcionism contained. In the same way that Jewishness asserted itself, it was also necessary for Paulinism to coalesce and become more profoundly self-aware. However, the expression that it found in Marcionism was extreme, and linked it to the Gnostic heresy. The inevitable result was that, together with Marcionism, this brand of Paulinism was suppressed and increasingly relegated to a minor role.

The Jewish Tenor of the Book of Revelation

One of the earliest writings of the New Testament canon tells us something about the opponents Paulinism had to contend with after the death of the Apostle Paul. Who are the opponents the Book of Revelation attacks so vigorously in its letters to the seven

---

41. Ibid., 1.20: "For they allege that Marcion did not so much innovate on the rule of faith by his separation of the law and the gospel, as restore it after it had been previously adulterated" [*ANF* 3:285].

42. Origen, *Commentariorum in Matthaeum*, 15.3: Μαρκίων . . . φάσκων, μὴ δεῖν ἀλληγορεῖν τὴν γραφήν ("Marcion . . . claims we should not allegorize the writings").

43. Jerome, in his *Commentary on Galatians*, 6.6; cf. Tertullian, *De praescriptione haereticorum*, ch. 41.

44. *Die christliche Gnosis* (n. 39), 297ff.

churches of Asia Minor, and especially in those to the communities of Pergamum and Thyatira, the ones it calls Balaamites or Nicolaitans, and the followers of "that woman Jezebel"?[45] Besides fornication, they are charged with eating meat offered to idols (Rev 2:14, 20).

The question whether Christians are allowed to eat such meat had first arisen when members of the Corinthian congregation posed it to the Apostle Paul [1 Cor 8]. He had discussed its various aspects, and had applied the standards of Christian freedom and the enlightened views of a Pauline Christian. He ruled against eating such meat, but he allowed exceptions in individual cases where doing so was inconsistent with Christianity yet might not be regarded as a sin. It is very likely that many Pauline Christians were led by their more liberal views, as we see with the Christians of Corinth in 1 Cor 8:1ff., to go further than Paul contemplated, and to observe no very strict rule on this point in their relations with Gentiles. Thus, in the eyes of Jewish Christians, who regarded the Apostle Paul with hostility, the eating of meat offered to idols could become a distinctive mark of the more lenient Pauline Christianity that was on such good terms with paganism.

Hence one could see these passages cited in the Book of Revelation as directed against Pauline Christians, without their blameworthy abuse of Christian freedom being laid at the door of the Apostle himself. But there can be little doubt that the writer had his eye on the Apostle Paul himself as the originator of a teaching from which this spurious Christianity had sprung, and that he regarded Paul as a teacher whose apostolic authority was by no means a settled issue. The Judaistic character of Revelation not only makes this very likely. Direct evidence for it is found in 21:12–14, where the author speaks of the twelve apostles, and of their twelve names corresponding to the twelve tribes of Israel, names written on the twelve foundation stones of the heavenly Jerusalem. Here the Apostle Paul is obviously excluded from the number of the apostles. And to whom can the author be referring in 2:2 but the Apostle to the Gentiles and his apostolic assistants, when he commends the community in Ephesus because it "tested those who claim to be apostles but are not, and have found them to be false"?

The locale to which this passage applies makes it even more important evidence as to the Judaistic reaction against Pauline Christianity. In addition to Corinth, the city of Ephesus had long been the Apostle Paul's headquarters. Here a "wide door" had been opened to him for his apostolic labors (1 Cor 16:9), and one should have thought that nowhere was Pauline Christianity established more firmly than in the communities of Asia Minor, where the Apostle had lived so long. But at the close of his residence there he had already begun to complain of the many adversaries who opposed him (16:9). There were no doubt Judaistic partisans of the same sort as those at Corinth, and here they had found an even more favorable field for their operations. Not long after the Apostle Paul left Ephesus and the theater of his operations, we meet

---

45. [*Ed.*] See Rev, chs. 1 and 2, esp. 2:14–15, and 20.

the Apostle John at the same place. The Book of Revelation was written, according to its own statement, at or near Ephesus. The tradition of the church was that he lived here many years, and that, as highly respected, he was the leader of congregations for miles around until he died at an advanced age. Tradition traced back to his teaching those ecclesiastical practices that were distinctive of the church of Asia Minor. Given all that we know about the Apostle John—his antagonism, as one of the pillar apostles at Jerusalem, toward Paul, and all the features marking him as an apocalyptic thinker—is it so unlikely that he also mainly came to reside in Ephesus, where Paul had been previously, so as intentionally to make it the center of widespread operations for Jerusalem Christianity in opposition to the encroachments of Paul's Christianity? In despising everything that savored of paganism, he had to judge the Paulinizing communities of that region mainly by how far they were tainted with paganism. This is the context for understanding the specific meaning of John's words praising or reproaching people, according to whether their zeal for pure and authentic Christianity is more ardent and active, or more lukewarm and lackluster.

Nothing can show more distinctly the wide difference there is between Pauline and apocalyptic-Johannine views than the conception that the apocalyptic writer has of the whole Gentile world. Paganism and Judaism are poles apart in his eyes; paganism is simply the kingdom of the Antichrist, and the Gentiles exist only to share the fate of the Antichrist. Side by side with the positive element of the Mosaic law, the Apostle Paul sets, as equally important and valid, the law of nature derived from the natural God-consciousness and from the moral consciousness expressed in one's conscience. In the one God he sees the God of the Gentiles as well as the God of the Jews. The apocalyptic writer, on the contrary, recognizes no religious tendency or receptivity that might lead the Gentiles to Christianity. For him each successive plague God sends upon them only makes them more hostile to God, and more blasphemous.[46] For Paul the body of Gentiles first enters into the kingdom of God, after which Israel is converted and the promises to it are fulfilled. But the apocalyptic writer cuts off all possibility of a historical development since, with the world's denouement imminent, Judaism is to celebrate its triumph upon the ruins of the pagan world. With such a testimonial to Jewish particularism, can it be surprising that John, the apocalyptic writer, would, as leader of the communities of Asia Minor, have opposed Pauline Christianity?

Papias and Hegesippus

In any case the Christianity in that part of Asia Minor now was no longer Pauline, but just Johannine. The church writers subsequently belonging mainly to this region either do not mention the name of the Apostle Paul at all, or do so just in a hostile sense.

---

46. Rev 9:20; 16:9; 11:21.

Papias, who took so much interest in the immediate successors of the apostolic era, in the well-known passage[47] nevertheless does not mention either the Apostle Paul or anyone of his circle. Even in Justin's writings, in many passages where we should expect to hear of the Apostle Paul, his name never occurs. There can be no doubt that the Apostle's writings were widely known then, and Justin was well aware of the Revelation of John. His strange silence about the Apostle Paul and his epistles certainly suggests that Justin meant to ignore them.

The first reference to the Apostle Paul after this is in Hegesippus,[48] a Jewish-Christian writer, who lived about the middle of the second century, and who does not have a favorable opinion of Paul. While not mentioning the Apostle's name, Hegesippus refers to the words Paul uses in 1 Cor 2:9, saying they are untrue and in conflict with divine scripture. To them Hegesippus opposes the words of Jesus in Matt 13:16.[49] Given this view regarding the apostolic qualifications of the Apostle Paul, we must include Hegesippus among the Apostle's most pronounced opponents. According to these words of the Lord, those only are to be called blessed who have seen with their eyes and heard with their ears. Paul therefore cannot belong to these blessed ones, and accordingly he cannot have been called to be an apostle.[50] What we know in other ways of the character of this defender of the Jewish Christian party fully bears out this view. As its representative, he traveled to communities abroad during the years 150–160 and talked to a number of bishops, in particular those at Corinth and Rome. The satisfying outcome of his travels was that "in each city things are as the law, the prophets, and the Lord preach."[51] From this we may conclude that even in such a community as that of Corinth the Jewish-Christian or Petrine party had gained a decided ascendency over the Pauline faction. In another passage of the same work, all our knowledge of which comes from the fragments preserved in Eusebius, Hegesippus seems to have depicted the apostolic age as the time when "the church remained a pure and uncorrupted virgin," and to have dated the entrance of godless error from the time when, after the sacred band of the apostles had all died, the generation of those who had been privileged to hear the divine wisdom with their own ears had passed away.[52]

---

47. Eusebius, *Ecclesiastical History* 3.39. [*Ed.*] Papias, bishop of Hierapolis (c. 60–130 AD), wrote an *Exposition of the Sayings of the Lord*, now lost except for fragments in Irenaeus and Eusebius.

48. [*Ed.*] Hegesippus (c. 110—c. 180), possibly a convert from Judaism. His *Memoirs* have been entirely lost except for fragments in Eusebius.

49. [*Ed.*] In 1 Cor 2:9–10, Paul quotes Isa 64:4: "'What no eye has seen, nor ear heard, nor the human heart conceived, what God has prepared for those who love him'—these things God has revealed to us through the Spirit." In Matt 13:16, Jesus says, "But blessed are your eyes, for they see, and your ears, for they hear."

50. See my book, *Paulus, der Apostel Jesu Christi* (n. 5), 221ff. [ET 1:225].

51. Eusebius, *Ecclesiastical History* 4.22.

52. Ibid., 3.32.

But when we look more closely at this passage we see that it by no means excludes the possibility of there having been, even during the time of the apostles, such a false teacher as the Apostle Paul was in the eyes of these Jewish Christians. It says that only upon the death of the apostles did false teachers appear openly and undisguised, with their false, so-called Gnosis, which opposed the preaching of the truth. But Hegesippus also says that, even during the lifetime of the apostles, there were persons who indeed sought to remain concealed in the shadows, but still were aiming at undermining the sound canon of saving doctrine. This remark seems to be about Paul more than anyone else. He was not one of those who had heard the divine wisdom with his own ears. While Paul's mode of operation hardly was to teach error covertly, Hegesippus may have said this about it both because Paul's teaching vanished as darkness vanishes before the brightly shining sun of the holy band of the apostles, and because it did not appear in its true light until the Gnostic errors emerged from it.

It is clear enough that what Hegesippus says here makes personal reference to the Apostle Paul. The same thing just gets fully expressed in reports that the Ebionites considered Paul an apostate and false teacher, rejected all his epistles, and said a great many slanderous things about him.[53] The Jewish-Christian opposition to the Apostle Paul, evident from his epistles, we see in its extreme form in the Ebionites' outspoken hatred of him. The Ebionites are usually regarded simply as heretics; but their connection with the original Jewish Christianity is unmistakable. Thus their view of the Apostle Paul is no mere isolated phenomenon.

The Ebionites of the Clementines, and Simon Magus

An important source for our further knowledge of these relations is the Pseudo-Clementine writings, the *Homilies* and the *Recognitions*.[54] In these works we become ac-

53. Irenaeus, *Against Heresies* 1.26; Eusebius, *Ecclesiastical History* 3.27; Epiphanius, *Against Heresies* 30.25.

54. The relation of these writings to each other and to an older work, a monument of the Petrine party, the Κήρυγμα Πέτρου or "Preaching of Peter," has lately been the subject of a very thorough and elaborate discussion, in which, however, divergent views have emerged. See A. Hilgenfeld, *Die clementinischen Recognitionen und Homilien nach ihrem Ursprung und Inhalt* (Jena, 1848). After him A. Ritschl took up the subject in his *Die Entstehung der altkatholischen Kirche*, 1st ed. (Bonn, 1850), 153ff. Lastly, G. Uhlhorn, *Die Homilien und Recognitionen des Clemens Romanus nach ihrem Ursprung und Inhalt* (Göttingen, 1854); and Hilgenfeld, *Theologische Jahrbücher* 13 (1854) 483ff; cf. his *Die apostolische Väter* (Halle, 1853), 287ff. It is especially noteworthy how, as Hilgenfeld has pointed out, Clement of Rome is introduced at a later stage, on the basis of the original Pseudo-Clementine text. We have here the important factor that, in the person of this Clement, we have the progression from the narrowness of the earlier text, still Jewish and excluding all Gentile Christianity (*Epistle of Peter to James*, ch. 1; *Contest. Jac.*, ch. 1), to a more advanced stage. [*Ed.*] On the *Pseudo-Clementine Homilies*, see Part 3, n. 66. The Clementine literature consists of both the *Homilies* and the *Recognitions*, the former preserved in its original Greek, the latter only in Latin translation. They partially overlap in content. Gerhard Uhlhorn argued that they were both recensions of an earlier book, the *Kerygma Petrou*. The source of the two quoted passages below is the apocryphal *Epistle of Peter to James*, which prefixes the *Homilies*. The first, brief one is from ch. 1 of the *Epistle*, and follows the translation of *ANF*

quainted with the teaching and viewpoint of a party that flourished about the middle of the second century, and subsequently formed the most outspoken opposition to Pauline Christianity. The Apostle Paul is not mentioned by name, but the reference to him is so unmistakable that the deliberate omission of his name makes the polemical tendency of this work all the more telling. In the epistle prefixed to the *Homilies*, Peter, in the course of sending his sermons to James the bishop of Jerusalem, recommends that he not pass them on to the Gentiles, but only share them with his fellow countrymen who adhere firmly to the teaching about the unity of God, "after the manner in which Moses delivered his books to the Seventy who succeeded to his chair." He continues:

> If this is not done, our doctrine of truth will be divided into a multitude of opinions. I know this not only as a prophet, but because I already see the beginning of the evil. For some of the Gentiles have rejected the lawful preaching that was delivered by me, and have received the lawless and worthless teaching of the enemy. And even in my lifetime some have attempted to pervert my words by cunning interpretations into abolishing the law, as if I myself held such opinions, and did not teach sincerely or honestly, which is far from me. To do this is nothing else than to act against the law of God, which was given by Moses, and attested by our Lord when he said of its permanent duration: "Until heaven and earth pass away, not one letter, not one stroke of a letter, will pass from the law" [Matt 5:18]. But those who profess to set forth, I know not how, my thoughts, and think they can interpret the meaning of the discourses they have heard from me better than I can myself, say to those who have been instructed by me, that my doctrine and opinion is so and so, a thing that never entered into my mind. If they venture to tell such lies against me while I am still living, how much more will they when I am gone?

Who can this enemy have been, whose lawless doctrine is being accepted among the Gentiles, but the Apostle Paul?

It is a curious phenomenon, moreover, that in the *Homilies* and *Recognitions*, Paul appears in the character of Simon Magus, and as a Samaritan. Peter obviously refers to the same Paul when he says that Simon went to the Gentiles before him, and that he followed and came after Simon as light comes after darkness, knowledge after ignorance, healing after sickness. "As the true prophet said, it was necessary that the false gospel should come first, by a false teacher, and that afterwards, after the destruction of the holy place, the true gospel should be sent forth secretly, for the refutation of future heresies."[55] The reference to the Apostle Paul is still clearer when we find the Apostle Peter arguing with Simon Magus as follows:

8:215. The second, long one is from ch. 2 of the *Epistle*, and we translate Baur's German version rather than using the text in *ANF* 8:215.

55. *Homilies*, 2.17.

> Even though our Jesus appeared to you in a vision, made himself known to you, and spoke to you, he was angry with you as an adversary, and therefore spoke to you through visions and dreams, or it may be outward revelations. But can anyone be commissioned to the office of a teacher by a vision? And if you say it is possible, why did the teacher go about constantly for a whole year with people who were not wide awake? And how should we believe that he revealed himself to you? How can he have appeared to you, who have views contrary to his teaching? If you really did become an apostle by his appearing to you and instructing you for one hour, then expound his sayings, preach his doctrine, love his apostles, and do not dispute with me who was with him! For you have striven against me as an adversary, against me, the firm rock, the foundation of the church. If you were not an adversary, you would not vilify and abuse me and my preaching, so that people will not believe me when I say what I heard from the Lord himself when I was with him, while it is clear that I who am condemned am worthy of praise. If you call me worthy of condemnation, you accuse God who revealed Christ to me, and attack him who called me blessed on account of this revelation.[56]

Here we meet the same accusations that the Jewish Christians had brought against Paul from the very first. The great cause of offense here is Paul's teaching about the law, that his is a lawless teaching. It does not obligate the Gentiles to observe the law, and it asserts that it is possible to be saved apart from the law. But whoever contradicts the true apostles by teaching something so false cannot be a genuine apostle. Thus the main attack is directed against the person of the Apostle himself. Not only is his apostolic authority expressly denied; the very thing on which he believes he can alone base his contention is in principle challenged. Pointed reference to the Apostle Paul is obvious in this sweeping denial of the value of revelations such as he asserted that he had received in visions, ecstasies, and dreams. In contrast, is not direct personal contact with Jesus during the whole period of his public ministry the only way to gain the apostolic office, the sole criterion of apostolic authority? We even see here clear evidence of how hard the Jewish Christians found it to forgive the Apostle Paul his conflict with the Apostle Peter. They remembered the scene at Antioch, and what Paul said there about Peter [cf. Gal 2:11–21].

But how are we to explain this identification of Simon Magus with the Apostle Paul? The simplest explanation seems to be that the narrative recounted in Acts 8:9ff.,[57] of the encounter of the two apostles Peter and John with Simon Magus, had

---

56. Ibid., 17.19. [*Ed.*] Quoted by Baur in German; cf. *ANF* 8:323–24.

57. [*Ed.*] Acts 8:9–24 describes the encounter of the apostles with Simon Magus, a magician who had amazed people in Samaria with a reputation for great feats. After his conversion to Christianity, and witnessing how the Spirit was received with the laying on of the apostles' hands, Simon offered money to Peter and John for the power to perform the same "trick." Traditions about Simon survived in later orthodox texts by Irenaeus, Justin Martyr, and others, where he was commonly described as the source of all heresies. In apocryphal texts such as the Clementines he appears as a great sorcerer

been reapplied to the Apostle Paul. Such a transference would be a very striking proof of the bitter hatred of the Apostle that animated the Jewish-Christian party, and that gave rise to the *Homilies*. That still will not tell us when this hatred arose, nor how widespread it was among the Jewish Christians. But when we take into consideration the notorious character of the Book of Acts as a [reputedly] historical work, and the likelihood that it was written at a comparatively late period, we are led to ask if the identification may not be accounted for in another way. Instead of the story of Simon having been transferred to Paul, maybe the occasion for the entire legend, its original source, is to be sought in the Apostle Paul. The historical existence of the Magus is, on a closer look, very doubtful. He may be nothing but a caricature of the Apostle Paul. This theory would explain both the great hatred of Jewish Christians for the Apostle Paul, and their motive for it, in pursuing him from the outset. All the distinctive features of the Simon of Acts, and of the legend as afterwards elaborated, thus fully correspond to definite facts of the Apostle's life story. So they not only afford a glimpse of the process by which the legend first arose, but also furnish evidence as to the early times to which this hatred is traceable, and how deliberately everything was done that could intensify it.

What the opponents of the Apostle considered to be his first and more grievous offense was, as we might have expected, his assertion that the Lord himself had appeared to him, and had called him, in such a unique and direct way, to be an apostle. Paul's opponents took this statement to be so baseless and subjective that, at best, they could only regard it as a delusion, failing any objective criterion of truth. It is obviously this charge against the Apostle that is represented in the ecstatic, visionary, and fantastic character attributed to the Magus. Spoken words are subject to the same misconception. They are not fully convincing because, for all one knows, the person seen to be speaking may be lying. But a vision, as soon as it is seen, convinces someone who has it that it is something divine. In answer to this, the Apostle Peter declares that personal contact, and continuous instruction by teaching and example, are the true criteria that what is communicated is divine. Peter asserts the direct opposite of Simon's view, that whoever puts faith in a vision, or an appearance, or a dream, has no certainty, and knows not in whom that faith is placed.

> For it may be that a wicked demon or a deceiving spirit creates false appearances, and if a person asks who is appearing to him, that spirit can answer whatever he pleases. He remains as long as he pleases, and vanishes like a flash of lightning without giving the questioner the information he desires. In a dream one cannot even ask for what one wishes to know, since the sleeper has no power over his own mind. It cannot therefore be concluded from someone seeing visions, having dreams and apparitions, that he is a good person. Receiving communications from without by visions and dreams is not revelation

---

capable of levitating and flying at will. Baur regards the entire legend as a fiction, intended as a caricature of Paul.

at all, but is a proof of the divine anger, as it is written in the law (Numbers 12:6[58]). Alternatively, when someone sees a vision, he must consider that it proceeds from an evil demon.[59]

What has the Apostle Paul to urge against all this but the assurance of his own self-consciousness?

The Apostle contended, however, that the supernatural appearance vouchsafed to him did not just convert him to faith in Christ, but also called him to be an apostle. This is a further point of contact between the Magus and the Apostle, and indeed the chief one. What the Apostle affirmed that he was, the Magus at least wished to become. His proposal to the two apostles [Peter and John] was simply that they should bestow on him the apostolic office, so that he would be endowed with the Holy Spirit in the same magical way that the Book of Acts links the imparting of the Spirit with the laying on of hands by the apostles. We should have thought that no one could be less suspect than the Apostle Paul of having taken this road to gain apostolic office. But were there no limits to what such malicious adversaries as the apostles might do? They said that, aware of his baseless pretensions, he was nevertheless determined to be an apostle at any price, and to become one via the earlier apostles. The facts out of which this charge arose must have been the two conferences that, according to the Apostle's own narrative, he held with the older apostles at Jerusalem (Gal 1:18 and 2:1), as if his object had been to worm his way into the apostolic group.

But this was not enough. The great crime of the Magus, for which the church called him "the father of simony," was that, by paying money to the apostles, he sought to procure for himself the gift of the Holy Spirit and the spiritual function connected with it, of imparting the Holy Spirit by the laying on of hands. They said the Apostle Paul did this. Here we see most clearly revealed the whole cunning web of hateful charges that the Apostle's Judaistic opponents had from the first been concocting and disseminating. From the narrative in Acts it is impossible to form any clear idea of how the effects of the apostolic imposition of hands so impressed the Magus that it led him to seek to undergo the same rite. Yet this story about the Apostle Paul does give us the key that explains the whole fiction. The only way money was a factor in his relations with the earlier apostles was when he departed from them and promised that, in the Gentile Christian communities where he labored, he would do what he could to support the poor of Jerusalem. When he wrote his Epistle to the Galatians he could already say that he had not neglected this; and his Epistle to the Corinthians

---

58. [*Ed.*] Num 12:6–9: "And he [the Lord] said: 'Hear my words: When there are prophets among you, I the Lord make myself known to them in visions; I speak to them in dreams. Not so with my servant Moses; he is entrusted with all my house. With him I speak face to face—clearly, and not in riddles; and he beholds the form of the Lord. Why then were you not afraid to speak against my servant Moses?' And the anger of the Lord was kindled against them, and he departed."

59. *Homilies* 17.13ff. [esp. 17.14 and 17.17].

contains most convincing evidence of his efforts for this cause.⁶⁰ Now is it not clear that when, at the expense of much labor and with the kindest intentions, the Apostle had collected this subsidy for the congregation at Jerusalem from the congregations of Galatia, Macedonia, and Achaia, his opponents alleged that his objective was simply to buy the favor of the earlier apostles, and thus to attain at last what he had hitherto sought in vain, recognition as an apostle equal to the others? Thus we find the entire figure of Simon Magus, all its characteristic features, to be none other than a picture of the Apostle Paul, a picture distorted by the hatred of his opponents who, as truly Jews, used their imagination to create it. So this is doubtless how the name of Simon Magus came to be a stand-in for the person of the Apostle Paul.

Simon was said to be from Samaria, and to be devoted to demonic magic. This is to be understood in the same sense as a passage in John's Gospel (8:48), where, when the hostility of the Jews against Jesus has reached its climax, the worst they can say against Jesus is that he is a Samaritan, and has a demon. There is no stronger way of saying that Pauline Christianity was pagan and hostile to the law, than to say that it came from Samaria. The Ebionites regarded the Apostle as a Gentile.⁶¹ The Samaritans of course were not actual pagans, they were only half-pagans;⁶² but this made the strictly orthodox Jews hate them all the more, seeing directly in them not only what was false and perverted in paganism, but also the falsification and distortion of divine truth by pagan errors. The *Homilies* state (2.22), in this sense, that Simon Magus disavowed Jerusalem and replaced it with Mount Gerizim. And Hegesippus speaks of the Marcionites, Carpocratians, Valentinians, Basilidians, and Saturnilians, as having come forth from the seven Jewish heresies, to which the Samaritans also belonged, with Simon Magus at the head of them all. He says these are the source of false Christs, false prophets, false apostles, breaking up the unity of the church into sects by their poisonous doctrines.⁶³ Paganism was held to be inherently demonic; and where ecstasies and visions played so great a part, as in the case of the Apostle Paul, it was natural for demonic magic to come into play. As what is ungodly confronts the divine in the form of magic, so the magician, wanting to become an apostle in such a vile way, was just the false Simon in contrast with the true one—the Simon Peter who stood at the head of the apostles. But Peter at once saw through the guile of the false

60. [*Ed.*] See Gal 2:10; 1 Cor 16:1–4.

61. According to Epiphanius, *Against Heresies* 30.16, they maintained that he was not a Jew by birth but a Greek or a pagan; that he was born of pagan parents and only later became a proselyte for Judaism.

62. [*Ed.*] Samaritans claimed descent from different tribes than those of mainstream Judaism, and believed they represented the true Israelites as they were prior to the Babylonian Captivity. They regarded Mount Gerizim as the holy mountain of Israel rather than Mount Zion. They were more disliked cousins than half-pagans.

63. Eusebius, *Ecclesiastical History* 4.22 [LCL, *Eusebius*, 1:376–77]. [*Ed.*] According to this passage in Eusebius, reporting on Hegesippus, Simon was one of several original heretics, and the groups named in our text derived from them. The Samaritans are then mentioned as one of seven sects that existed among the Jews.

Simon and exposed his hypocrisy publicly and incontestably; just as Peter was said to have exposed Paul at Antioch.

Once the fundamental conception of the Magus emerged, many features got added to it. Simon became the great father of heretics. In the imagination and fantasies of the early church fathers, the person of Simon embodied their most extreme conceptions and views of pagan Gnosticism. In a short time no one had any idea who this Simon Magus had originally been. Yet there was a deeper connection grounded in how things stood at that time, for the legend of the Magus was used to represent Paulinism and Gnosis as closely related. The wanderings of the Magus came to an end in Rome, and the fantastic denouement he supposedly met with there to end his career is, in any event, unmistakably just a dim reflection of the story of the Apostle to the Gentiles.[64]

64. The evidence for the assertion that the Simon Magus of the *Clementine Homilies* is not only Marcion but the Apostle Paul I have already set forth in my essay, "Die Christuspartei in der korinthischen Gemeinde," *Tübinger Zeitschrift für Theologie* (1831) no. 4, 136ff. For further criticism of the Simon-legend, see Hilgenfeld, *Die clementinischen Recognitionen und Homilien* (n. 54), 319, and Zeller, *Apostelgeschichte* (n. 12), 158ff. [ET 1:245ff.]. Zeller not only gives a critical analysis of the unhistorical narrative in Acts, but has also strikingly summed up the meaning of the legend in the following words: "If in Acts 8:18ff. we substitute the name of Paul for that of Simon, we have a narrative that says in a historical form what, according to 2 Cor 11:4ff., 12:11ff., 1 Cor 9:1ff., the anti-Pauline Judaists affirmed as a general truth." But it was G. Volkmar who first completed the identification by recognizing in the magician's offer of money the Apostle's subsidy [for the poor]. See "Ueber den Simon Magus der Apostelgeschichte und den Ursprung der Simonie," *Theologische Jahrbücher* 15 (1856) 279ff. Zeller remarks very correctly, p. 173 [ET 266], that "the author of Acts, still aware of the meaning of the legend, nevertheless wished to forestall any application of it to his Apostle even by the position in which he placed it" (prior to the conversion of Paul). Here we have a more recent and very striking proof of the way in which the author of the Book of Acts made his materials serve his own apologetic designs. He adheres to what is historical, but he places it in a new light, and it receives another form in his hands. He could not ignore the Simon-legend: if he had passed over it in silence, that would have been to let its original meaning stand, without saying anything against it. He therefore prefers to mention it; but he gives it such a turn as to make it impossible to think of any reference to the Apostle Paul. Originally he was Simon; but Simon is now quite a different person, and has nothing to do with Paul. —The author of Acts treated the infamous dispute between the two apostles at Antioch in a similar way. This was a tender spot it was desirable to avoid. But he did not merely wish to preserve silence on the subject; he wished to draw off attention from it altogether, and so he substituted for it another incident to suggest that something of the sort had happened at that place, but it did not have the same significance, as Peter was not a participant in it—namely, the dispute between Paul and Barnabas in Acts 15:38–39 (cf. Gal 2:13). This, he suggests, was what happened, not the other account; he knows of a παροξυσμός (disagreement) of apostles at Antioch, and his historical sense does not permit him to omit it altogether; and yet he is silent about the actual disagreement, and covers it up. —In this connection it is impossible to avoid thinking of the Apostle's journey to Jerusalem, Acts 11:29ff. On chronological and other grounds it is impossible to assume that the Apostle was at Jerusalem during the period in which Acts places this journey, between Gal 1:18 and 2:1. At that time he is said to have brought aid from the Christians at Antioch to their brothers and sisters in Judea. But why does the author of Acts speak only of this aid and so studiously ignore the much more important aid that the Apostle prepared for his last journey to Jerusalem, since there can be no doubt that he delivered it? For what other reason than that the Jerusalem aid was the origin of the hateful calumny directed against the Apostle, which Acts wished to ignore? So there was such aid because such a thing was a feature in the Apostle's history; and yet it had no painful memories associated with it. One could

II. The Mediation

THE DIFFERENCE BETWEEN THE VIEWPOINTS

In light of the series of phenomena presented so far, the next set of topics must involve the way in which these two, so extremely divergent, orientations came to unite in conciliatory fashion. A Catholic Church that cut itself off from all extreme positions, and united the antitheses within itself, is the only conceivable vehicle for reaching an equilibrium, one unattainable unless each of the two sides more or less relaxed its strict opposition to the other one.

The issues include the following. How did this change take place? Is one side the main source of the principle leading to this reconciliation? What is the other side's stance on it? How are the various phenomena pertinent to this issue to be grouped and classified? In recent times these have been the topics of the most many-faceted and most strenuous efforts devoted to in-depth research into early Christianity. Not only are there those who generally object to this research, by pitting the utter rigidity and lifelessness of their outdated standpoint against the latest criticism. There are also significantly different views among those who acknowledge that only a more penetrating, critical understanding can shed new light on what is obscure about these matters.

Schwegler first attempted to employ the new critical approach consistently in a presentation covering the post-apostolic period, and he did so with skill and acumen.[65] Ritschl was then the main one to emerge as a most decided opponent of Schwegler.[66]

---

dismiss the one account in favor of the other one.

65. *Das nachapostolische Zeitalter in den Hauptmomenten seiner Entwicklung* (Tübingen, 1846). [*Ed.*] Albert Schwegler (1819–1857) was a student of Baur and a Tübingen historian of early Christianity. When his views came into conflict with the church authorities, he switched from theology to philosophy.

66. Ritschl, *Die Entstehung der altkatholischen Kirche* (Bonn, 1850). Simultaneously with Ritschl, Köstlin published the essay "Zur Geschichte des Urchristentums," *Theologische Jahrbücher* 9 (1850) 1–62, which followed closely Planck's essay, "Über Judenthum und Urchristenthum," which had appeared in the same journal, 6 (1847) 258–93. Köstlin made the course and character of the first two centuries the topic of a new investigation, and did so with reference to Schwegler's presentation. In it he declared that he could hardly agree with the findings on which Ritschl placed the most importance in his opposition to Schwegler, namely Ritschl's contention that there was no element of

Ritschl found fault with how Schwegler defined the task as the plotting of the stages in which the development of Ebionitism led to Catholicism, in that Schwegler had not established a clear concept of either Ebionitism or Paulinism. [He said that Schwegler] debased Jewish Christianity too much, and exalted Paulinism so much, that it was inconceivable how a shared creed could hold the two orientations together, even just outwardly. The spiritual process by which, in Paul, the religion of law is converted dialectically into the religion of freedom, and the bound and unhappy consciousness converted into reconciled self-certainty, appears to find merely external support in the story of Jesus of Nazareth. Thus it is also clearly a contingent fact that the history of Paulinism and the history of Jewish Christianity have something in common. Schwegler's way of understanding how the two orientations in early Christianity are fundamentally related is consistent with applying a quite external pragmatism to the history of reconciliation itself. If no inner drive to form a commonality was acknowledged within these orientations, then blunting the antithesis step by step could only be motivated by their unity being outwardly desirable. To achieve it, the writers who spoke for both parties gradually eliminated the rough edges of their respective positions.

In making this critique of Schwegler's presentation, Ritschl can simply claim that his own view has the merit of grasping correctly, and in greater depth, the inner coherence of this development. Apart from some individual differences, closer examination shows that, on the whole, the two views are not as far apart as they seem to be. Ritschl too proceeds from the fact that post-apostolic Christianity is, in its essentials, traceable back to the Pauline principle. However, Ritschl does not agree with Schwegler that the reconciliation comes about from each party softening its position and entering into an external relation with the other one. Instead Ritschl thinks a change in Paulinism leads the way and that change produces the same result. Ritschl maintains that the Apostle Paul's theological framework inherently presents features that make a one-sided elaboration of its principle inevitable. Although we cannot overlook the fact that the second century saw a decline, among Christians, of the original religious energy, nevertheless the one-sided elaboration of the Pauline principle can only be the effect of its creator, owing to the one-sided stamp he originally placed on it. The confusing views as to how the Christian perspective developed in the post-apostolic period are largely to blame for people not taking into account that, and how, the Pauline orientation had to go beyond the original form in which its creator left his mark on it dogmatically; and that it had been shaped in a way quite discrepant from its original dogmatic character. The clearer dogmatic motive for this change is to be found in the need to shape the Pauline principle into a general and directly applicable norm for living. Two external motives also came into play. On the negative side there was the troublesome and unpopular nature of the Pauline dialectic. On the positive side there

---

Christian development within Jewish Christianity. He says that view is simply the abstract antithesis to Schwegler's position. [*Ed.*] On Ritschl, see Part 1, n. 24; on Köstlin, see n. 30. Karl Christian Planck (1819–1880) was a student in Tübingen and later a philosopher who advanced a theory of naturalism.

was the influence of the evangelical tradition of the teaching of Jesus, for the Pauline theological framework had taken shape quite independently of it.[67]

The change by which Paulinism lost its original contours occurred because faith was no longer subjective belief in Christ's atoning death, apart from the law. Now it was faith in a wider sense in its relation to God, a faith that made room for obedience to God's will, or to Christ's commandments, as the means of justification, redemption, and blessedness in a sense befitting the law. Despite the initial Pauline formulation, this other factor became preponderant over faith [as subjective belief]. People no longer spoke of redemption through Christ's death understood in the Pauline sense. Now they instead spoke of love, of the power of good works, as the route to divine forgiveness for sins. This is essentially the same formulation as πίστις καὶ ἀγάπη (faith and love), which Schwegler takes to be the goal for a developing Paulinism and the basis for reconciling the two opposed parties. Since Paulinism is inherently so one-sided that the general and directly applicable norm for living, which came to replace original Paulinism, could emerge from it only by a leap rather than by its inner development, we therefore have here [with Ritschl] the same externally related elements from the two orientations as we do with Schwegler.

Ritschl explicitly maintains, additionally, that the Pauline theological framework took shape quite unrelated to the teaching of Jesus. So it is not apparent by what right he accuses Schwegler of having understood Paulinism as unrelated not merely to the innermost core of Jesus' life but also to any sort of idea deriving from Jesus' activities.[68] In any event there is no justification for the contention that the gospel tradition or the teaching of Jesus influenced the later configuration of Paulinism, via the Gospel of Luke. For indeed Ritschl himself assumes that the presentation of the gospel story in Luke itself is just a reflection of original Paulinism.[69]

A closer look at Ritschl's presentation makes it even more evident how it dissolves into antitheses in which we fail to see any coherent development. On the one hand we have Jewish Christianity with the thesis: Christianity is the old law. On the other hand we have Paulinism with its antithetical position: Christianity is subjective faith in Christ, apart from the law. Whereas Jewish Christianity is deprived of any capacity for developing internally, and the motive principle is located in Paulinism, this Paulinism also cannot develop in a natural way, since it is too harsh and one-sided to be able to accommodate a general and directly applicable norm for living emerging from itself. Paulinism is of course the more respectable position, although one ought not fail to recognize the case to be made for Jewish Christianity. "For out of respect for the Christianity of those apostles still with a Jewish orientation, one must not assume that the Pauline doctrine is absolutely perfect and complete in the orthodox sense."[70]

---

67. Ritschl, *Entstehung*, 28 and 280ff.
68. *Entstehung*, 20.
69. *Entstehung*, 300.
70. *Entstehung*, 23.

Neither of these two orientations is therefore absolutely true, for each one, with equal justification, stands opposed to the other. "On essential points Jesus was willing neither to oppose Mosaism nor to speak against it. Furthermore, precisely because his teaching has this character, it became the immediate foundation of Jewish Christianity as something steadfastly different from Paulinism."[71] Thus according to Ritschl it is not comprehensible that the dogma and the abundantly articulated, organic structure of the Catholic Church supposedly developed from the entirely Jewish conception that Jesus is the Messiah. When all is said and done, we cannot get past our doubts as to whether Jesus or Paul is in fact the originator of Christianity.[72]

The universally acknowledged representatives of the early Catholic Church—Irenaeus, Tertullian, Clement of Alexandria, and Origen—agree with Justin Martyr in understanding Christianity as law, in the concept of the "new law." This concept supposedly presents to us how the Catholic Church relates to the types of apostolic doctrine, the Jewish Christian and the Pauline models. From this we see that, notwithstanding its opposition to Pauline principles, this side of Catholicism rests not on the Jewish Christian perspective, but instead on the Pauline orientation.[73] However, if the altered form of Paulinism indeed has just the aforementioned external motive, and so did not arise from the essence of Paulinism itself, then one cannot say that the development leading to Catholicism essentially rests on the Pauline orientation. It can just as well be the result of a Jewish-Christian foundation, since the very thing said to be characteristic of Catholic Christianity is the juxtaposition of faith and the practical stance active in works. This feature is very naturally connected with the character of Old Testament religion.

In the end, Ritschl's presentation does not even take into account how the personal antagonism between the two apostles, Peter and Paul, ultimately got smoothed over, an antagonism in which the different orientations were most sharply and directly expressed at the outset. For that very process makes it possible to pinpoint, in the most specific way, the entire transition of the divergent orientations into the unity of a Catholicism reconciling all their mutual antitheses and extreme stances.[74]

---

71. *Entstehung*, 300.

72. *Entstehung*, 19.

73. *Entstehung*, 327.

74. The second, and thoroughly revised, edition of Ritschl's book (Bonn, 1857) is supposedly a recantation of the first edition, since Ritschl now contends that he has come to oppose the Tübingen School, so that he in principle, and sweepingly, disagrees with it (Preface, p. v). Yet the disagreement is neither as much in principle nor as sweeping as Ritschl maintains that it is, nor is his thorough reworking an actual improvement. That is because Ritschl's new approach for his understanding and portrayal of early Christianity has just resulted in an even greater number of contradictions and inconsistencies. He does now think of Jesus' stance toward the law in a directly opposite way than he did before. But as for the rest, this book has utterly the same deficiency his work initially suffered from, namely, how externally he juxtaposes the antitheses, so that no inner, vital development can arise from this. There is supposedly no fundamental antithesis between the original apostles and Paul; and yet there is still the fundamental antithesis between Jewish particularism and Pauline universalism. Any

THE ELEMENTS OF THE MEDIATION

Thus far we have indicated briefly the main points we ought not lose sight of in the following explanation, if it is supposedly equal to the task of tracing out the historical development of all these internally connected antitheses.

Our point of departure is the antitheses as already indicated. The outcome is their being smoothed over and cancelled out. Therefore, mediating elements must lie along the way. Nothing is more likely than that the mediation comes not merely from one of the two sides, but rather from both of them in different ways. Both factions, in being aware to some extent that they belong together, engage each other in the vital process of a reciprocally conditioned historical development.

But how would such a process have been possible, one without which there could never have come about what actually did, the founding of a Christian Catholic Church? How could it occur if both sides, Jewish Christian and Gentile Christian, faced off in such a harsh and mutually repellent way that doing so made all forms of Jewish Christianity incapable of further development? And that, from the Pauline side, what linked Catholic Christianity with apostolic Christianity was just the inability of the Gentile Christians to give a correct and vital account of the Apostle Paul's basic conception of the divine grounding of the religious relationship, something only comprehensible on the basis of the Old Testament? The entire perspective from which these relationships are understood is misguided if we suppose that, between these two opposed parties, it was principally a matter of dogmatic antitheses; of attempting to formulate, in one way or another, how Jewish teaching about the law and the Pauline doctrine of faith are related. We ought not simply seek the motive principle in the realm of abstract conceptions, so unrelated to each other that this cannot beget something new. Instead, look for it in the antitheses in the concrete center, ones that are mutually and vitally engaged—right where Christianity, situated in the midst of the currently dominant powers, had to first struggle for its basic existence, and then had first to create for itself the forms shaping its own historical development.

---

vital principle of historical movement is so very lacking here that Jewish Christianity and Paulinism are declared outright to be equally incapable of any further development (pp. 271ff. and 282). On this and other publications dealing with this same issue, see my book, *Die Tübinger Schule und ihre Stellung zur Gegenwart* (Tübingen, 1859), which was occasioned by Uhlhorn's essay in the *Jahrbücher für deutsche Theologie* 3 (1858) 280–349. In the *Zeitschrift für wissenschaftliche Theologie* 1 (1858), "Das Christenthum und seine neuesten Bearbeitungen von Lechler und Ritschl," Hilgenfeld states very correctly (p. 381) that for Ritschl, as for Lechler, the development of Gentile Christianity and Jewish Christianity into Catholicism seems to occur by blind chance. [*Ed.*] Gerhard Uhlhorn, "Die älteste Kirchengeschichte in der Darstellung der Tübinger Schule."

BAPTISM REPLACES CIRCUMCISION; PETER THE APOSTLE TO THE GENTILES

After Paulinism and Jewish Christianity initially came to oppose each other openly, the operative principle resided with those Judaists who had most decidedly confronted the Apostle Paul at every point of his sphere of influence. There is no greater proof of how capable of development this Jewish attitude was, than the undeniable fact that it had no difficulty surrendering positions it had zealously defended, as soon as it saw that doing so was the way to more successfully maintain its superiority to Paulinism.

This is the only explanation for why baptism suddenly took the place of circumcision. The Jewish Christians of Jerusalem at first absolutely required circumcision, and said the Gentiles too should be circumcised. There is no reason to assume that the older apostles did not originally hold this same view. In the Epistle to the Galatians, Paul's Jewish-Christian opponents are still making circumcision a necessary condition for becoming blessed. But where, after this, is there still talk, in the same principled way, about circumcision as a requirement imposed by the entire Jewish-Christian party? Even in the Pseudo-Clementine writings, circumcision is no longer thought of as a fundamental article of Judaism. Here we only get a glimpse of its former significance, for instance in the *Contestatio* (Adjuration), in the specification that the writings sent by Peter to James should be communicated only "to one who is good and religious, and who wishes to teach, and who is circumcised and faithful."[75] From this we can correctly infer that the Jewish Christians themselves no longer regarded circumcision as necessary. This can only be explained if, after so much progress in converting Gentiles without their being circumcised, the Jewish Christians themselves had to see it was impossible to insist on a requirement now in fact obsolete because of all that had transpired in Gentile Christianity. Howsoever they may have squared this change with their view of the necessity of observing the law, we can only look upon it as a concession made to Pauline universalism.

Apparently closely connected with this concession is the way in which baptism gains religious significance comparable to circumcision, just as circumcision is ceasing to be mentioned. There had to be some sort of formal induction of Gentiles into the messianic community. What other means was able to serve this purpose as well as baptism? No doubt the more widespread practice of baptism, and its heightened religious significance, are very closely tied to the conversion of the Gentiles. The Apostle Paul also seems to indicate as much, when he declares (Gal 3:27) that baptism is requisite for fellowship with Christ, at a time when circumcision was still made the absolute requirement for blessedness. He says that those who "were baptized into Christ have clothed" themselves "with Christ," and there is no longer a distinction between Jew and Gentile (v. 28). Thus, just as circumcision makes one a Jew, so baptism makes one a Christian. Also, in Matt 28:19, in a passage doubtless belonging only to the last

---

75. [Ed.] This is from the *Epistle of Peter to James* (n. 54), ch. 4 (*ANF* 8:216).

recension of this gospel, the instruction to baptize is most closely linked to the command to "make disciples of all nations."

From the *Pseudo-Clementine Homilies* we see how Jewish Christians also recognized this import of baptism, although at first, of course, only the Gentile Christians could have done so. The *Homilies* indeed simply calls baptism the means ordained by God for "casting off" (ἀφελληνισθῆναι) paganism; but it regards baptism as the necessary and sole condition by which human beings can receive the forgiveness of sins and future blessedness.[76] Accordingly the Jewish Christians themselves had discontinued circumcision as soon as there was another form for becoming certain of salvation, a ceremony they themselves recognized as comparable to it. For the Gentile Christians, of its own accord baptism therefore became the replacement for circumcision. Jewish Christians born as Jews had no need for such a replacement. However, as those born as Jews and adopting Christianity subsequently became fewer in number, baptism increasingly had to become the general rite for avowing one's Christianity, in the same way that, for Jews, circumcision was the characteristic mark of their religion.[77]

The absolute dominance of Judaism accordingly gave way first on the issue of circumcision. There still remained Jewish Christians who insisted on the absolute validity of the law for themselves, but also wanted no fellowship with Gentile Christians who did not observe the law in this way as they did. They were only the more unbending group, but another group, in contrast, held more conciliatory views, made no such demands on Gentile Christians, and acknowledged these Gentiles as Christian brethren.[78] Yet this group of Jewish Christians could not excuse Gentile Christians from heeding the law. In opposing complete disregard of the law, they said that the stipulations still in force are those the author of Acts introduces as decisions of the apostolic council he alleges took place. However, it has long been shown[79] that the apostles

---

76. *Homilies* (n. 54), 13.9 and 11.24ff.

77. According to the *Recognitions* (n. 54), baptism was said to be a replacement for the sacrificial offerings. In 1.39 we read: "But when the time began to draw near that what was wanting in the Mosaic institutions should be supplied, as we have said, and that the Prophet should appear, of whom he [Moses] had foretold that he should warn them by the mercy of God to cease from sacrificing; lest haply they might suppose that on the cessation of sacrifice there was no remission of sins for them, he instituted baptism by water amongst them" [*ANF* 8:88]. Looked at in this way, even for Jewish Christians who, as those born as Jews, needed no replacement for circumcision, baptism could gain its religious significance. Without a doubt this has its Essene-Ebionite origins. Their religious ablutions, with their purifying and sin-absolving power, rested on their rejection of the Mosaic sacrificial cultus. This is then also the very natural explanation for how, among the Elkesaites, baptism as forgiveness for sins was even received repeatedly. See Ritschl, *Zeitschrift für historische Theologie* (1853) 582ff.; *Entstehung*, 2nd ed. (n. 74), 188. See also Hilgenfeld, *Zeitschrift für wissenschaftliche Theologie* 1 (1858) (n. 11) 422ff. In no case was baptism's relation to sacrificial offerings a barrier to accepting baptism as the actual replacement for circumcision. (On this passage in the *Recognitions*, see Uhlhorn [n. 74], 251; Ritschl, 239.)

78. See Justin Martyr, *Dialogue with Trypho*, ch. 47.

79. See my book *Paulus, der Apostel Jesu Christi* (n. 5), 104 ff [ET 1:131]. Also see Zeller, *Die Apostelgeschichte* (n. 12), 288ff. [ET 2:27ff.].

could not have issued these decrees in this way, for they just contain the minimum demands of the law that the Jewish Christians imposed on the Gentile Christians in practice. These are the same conditions the Israelites required of foreigners residing among them (Lev 17:8–16; 18:26).[80] From them we see how the Jewish Christians could indeed maintain their legalistic standpoint, and could determine their relation to Gentile Christians only on the basis of such norms as the law established for governing the association of Jews with Gentiles.

But this was as far as the Jewish Christians could go in making concessions to the Gentile Christians. Provided that the Gentile Christians just adhered to these conditions, there were no further impediments to the mutual association of Jewish Christians and Gentile Christians, of the kind the circumcision issue had apparently made so divisive. Thus the Jewish Christians' antipathy to Gentile Christians ended as soon as they could see Gentile Christians as "foreigners residing among them"; and then Jewish Christianity's relation to Paulinism therefore became a matter of taking Paulinism to be just a way of looking at things that is acceptable to the Jewish Christian religious consciousness.

As soon as a new Christian world came into being outside of Judaism and quite independent of it, a world whose existence was a given and no longer in fact something to be undone, the Jewish Christians would even have made Pauline universalism wholly their own, if only its originator had been Peter instead of Paul. For how is it anything other than a transfer of Pauline universalism from Paul to Peter, when the Pseudo-Clementine writings in fact make Peter into the apostle to the Gentiles? They state that Peter is called to journey "to the nations which say there are many gods, to teach and to preach that God is one, who made heaven and earth, and all things that are in them, in order that they may love him and be saved."[81] The Pseudo-Clementine writings describe the Apostle Peter as having the same sphere of activity as that in which the Apostle Paul traveled around among various peoples in order to preach his gospel, so that Peter too, as apostle to the Gentiles, can take his gospel from town to town, from land to land, on a course ultimately just leading on to its end in Rome.[82]

To be sure, since Peter follows on the trail of his adversary Simon Magus, in order to refute his false teaching and to steer these peoples away from it and to the teaching of the true prophets, this gives his mission to the Gentiles the character of a counteroffensive. He wants, first of all, to simply make whole again what the false apostle, who preceded him, had destroyed. But this very approach is simply the form under which

---

80. See Ritschl, *Entstehung* (n. 54), 117ff.; 2nd ed. (n. 38), 129ff. [*Ed.*] The reference is to "4 Mos." (Numbers), but it should be to "3 Mos." (Leviticus).

81. *Homilies* (n. 54), 3.59 [*ANF* 8:249]. See also *Recognitions* (n. 54), 3.56, 7.7, and 10.16.

82. See the *Epistle of Clement to James*, ch. 1, where it states, about Peter, that he, "being fittest of all, was commanded to enlighten the darker part of the world . . . and was able to accomplish it . . . having come as far as Rome, clearly and publicly testifying . . . while saving men by his God-inspired doctrine . . . and by violence left this present existence for life [eternal]" [*ANF* 8:218; quoted by Baur in Greek].

the Apostle of Jewish Christianity was said to make his own what was done by, and to the credit of, the Apostle to the Gentiles. The Jewish Christians are content to accept the current state of affairs. They well know that the time is past for imposing a requirement on the Gentiles that would have made their entry into the messianic kingdom impossible, or far too onerous. Conversion of the Gentiles is an accomplished fact and there is no disputing its reality. It must therefore be acknowledged as such, except that it ought not be said to have taken place owing to an apostle not authorized by the Apostle of Jewish Christianity.

This was not merely an effort to fall in line with what, according to the views and practices of the Apostle's opponents, as known from his epistles, could have been requisite for a justifiable conversion of the Gentiles. Instead it sidelined the true Apostle to the Gentiles himself, in order to erase the memory of him and his name for posterity. They had another figure supplant him, one who can only be the object of universal hatred and loathing—using the name of a false teacher [Simon Magus]. What the legitimate Apostle [Paul] had accomplished in his struggles was said to have been done by this illegitimate, false figure. Simply from a concern to expunge the name of the Apostle Paul from human memory, wherever they could and permanently, the Pseudo-Clementine writings expressed this bitterly hostile hatred, by renewing and intensifying the old and odious charges against the Apostle Paul, at a time when people in the greater part of the Christian world had already gotten past this antagonism.

This is even more remarkable, since the Clement playing such an important role in these writings is not only a Gentile by birth, and the first-fruits of all the Gentiles converted by the Apostle Peter,[83] and thus the natural mediator between Gentile Christians and Jewish Christians; for he is also well-versed in all Hellenic culture.[84] The religious interest awakened in this way led to Christianity. He came to be most closely connected with the Apostle Peter, and personally represented the spiritualization of Christianity via all the better elements it was able to adopt from paganism. In the historical narrative on which the construction of Christianity relies, this religion certainly already appears here as the one bringing together all that is noble in human nature. Those who are cut off and lost on life's most divergent paths come together again, so as to become aware of their kinship in their essential humanity, as members of one and the same family; and in this consciousness to gain peace of soul and the greatest assurance about all directions their lives take.[85] How does all this fit in with such an implacable antipathy toward the Apostle Paul?[86]

83. *Epistle of Clement to James*, ch. 3.

84. *Homilies* 1.3 and 4.7: "Clement—a student well-versed in everything Hellenic" [quoted in Greek].

85. See *Die christliche Gnosis* (n. 39), 372ff.; and Hilgenfeld, *Die apostolische Väter* (n. 102), 297ff.

86. From the demonstration provided about the origin of the legend of Simon [above, pp. 72–77], we see clearly that such fierce hostility toward the Apostle Paul cannot be attributed merely to the specific features distinctive to these writings. Forming a great contrast with the exclusively one-sided opposition to the Apostle Paul, is how very freely the *Homilies* insist on the practical dimension, in

THE INFLUENCE OF JEWISH CHRISTIANITY ON THE CONFIGURATION OF THE CHURCH

In any event one could see in this factor simply evidence of the energy with which Jewish Christianity left no stone unturned in also maintaining, at any price, its claim of superiority to Paulinism, and in not losing its grip on dominance in the Gentile world. But when we judge the situation just in terms of its historical success, such a perspective does not in fact adequately capture the impact of Jewish Christianity on the configuration of the Christian Church.

Judaism first presents itself to us, with the full splendor of its world-historical significance, in its rejuvenation and further development into Jewish Christianity. Where else than from Judaism do there stem all those theocratic institutions and aristocratic forms giving the Catholic Church the elements of an organization incorporating all the prerequisites for a power overcoming the world? With the episcopate being in fact the center and pillar of Catholicism, the organizing and life-giving principle of its whole social body, we therefore already see, in the beginnings of an episcopal system of governance—where, in the most concrete way the bishop was, for each individual congregation, to become verily and conceptually what, based on the Jewish concept of the Messiah, Christ was at the highest level for the church universal—the whole medieval, papal hierarchy right before our eyes. Here we have the endless capacity for development found in Jewish Christianity, the innate drive of Judaism toward a theocratic world-domination that, with the same energy by which it holds fast to the distinctiveness of its own principle, expands outwardly and constitutes itself as a very real world power.

Because of its mission to the Gentiles, Paulinism secured the foundation for Catholic Christianity in the great multitude of those who, from all peoples and races, all nations and languages, joined the early community of those who bore the seal.[87] Whereas Jewish Christianity, with its organizational forms, was what provided the hierarchical edifice of the church. Yet despite the predominant influence of Jewish Christianity on this front, Paulinism also asserted its own hard-won legitimacy, as well as the superiority of its own principle.

From the first, Paulinism made Christian universalism the foundation, in principle, for Christian consciousness in general, by rebutting the aristocratic claims of Jewish particularism and eradicating it at its very roots. Thus, for the entire future

---

superficially treating Christianity's universality as a doctrine in which there ought to be no difference between Jewish Christians and Gentile Christians, or even between Jews and Gentiles, if only they just do as they are directed, and do not hate those they do not know. *Homilies*, 8.4 and 11.16. See *Die christliche Gnosis*, 363ff.

87. Rev 6:9 ["When he opened the fifth seal, I saw under the altar the souls of those who had been slaughtered for the word of God and for the testimony they had given"]. Here the Gentiles are only the great, endless multitude; and the twelve tribes of Israel, each of which has its own specific, numerical position, are set apart from them in truly aristocratic and hierarchical fashion.

of the church, Paulinism stands ready to forever act, with the same harshness and decisiveness, whenever hierarchical Catholicism runs roughshod over evangelical Christianity and encroaches upon the original Christian consciousness in its innermost foundation. In all instances of this kind one could only revert to the same simple and basic truths by which the Apostle Paul has shown, from the standpoint of moral consciousness, that, before God, there is no distinction of Jew from Gentile.

It is rightly said[88] that, in the transition to the Catholic Church, Paulinism developed into a general norm of life, one in which the doctrine of justification became less dominant and faith went hand in hand with works. But doing so is no surrender of its principle, no defection or backward step, for it is only a matter of understanding correctly how the Apostle himself sees the relation of faith to works.[89] Paulinism only emphasizes the rigor of its doctrine of justification when it has to do battle with Jewish Christianity as to the ground of its existence and its validity in principle. Paulinism was able to maintain itself, over against the still so dominant Jewish Christianity, only thanks to the energy with which the Apostle carried on this battle. However, as soon as it was successful in this endeavor, Paulinism too could concede the validity of works in addition to faith, for the Apostle himself had indeed already acknowledged the moral worth of works and not merely that of faith alone. He had also spoken of a faith active through love. The only shortcoming was that Paulinism did not step forward with the same rigorous doctrine of justification as soon as Jewish Christianity had once more become conceptually pervasive in one form or another, as this of course happened in post-apostolic times, in the church's adoption of a hierarchical structure.[90]

Thus we have established the perspective from which we must grasp the self-development of historical Christianity, on the basis of these two elements, as ones of course internally related in their being essentially different but also essentially belonging together. So now our next task is to look at the canonical scriptures most closely linked to the [post-] apostolic age, by doing so from this perspective. Accordingly, we will examine how they relate to one side or the other in this process of mediation or reconciliation. That is, whether an interest in mediation has inherently a more Pauline or a more Judaistic character. Also, to what extent it contains ideas and outlooks that either just pertain more to individual, subordinate factors, or else, by taking a higher standpoint, seek their basis in the need for a unifying and conciliatory mediation.

---

88. See above, p. 79.

89. See my article, "Ueber Zweck und Gedankengang des Römerbriefs" (n. 24), 184: "Die Werke und die Glaube."

90. See *Die Tübinger Schule* (n. 7), 33ff. and 65ff.

II. The Mediation

THE MEDIATING TENDENCY OF THE POST-APOSTOLIC CANONICAL SCRIPTURES

The Epistle to the Hebrews

The Epistle to the Hebrews is doubtless one of the first of these scriptures we are to consider, based on its date and its subject matter.

A large part of the early church regarded this scripture as an epistle by the Apostle Paul. This testimonial seems to support the view that, even if not written by the Apostle himself, it at least is a product of Paulinism. Also, the writer himself seems to foster this belief since, by expressly mentioning "our brother Timothy" (13:23), his intent can only be to identify his epistle as coming from the Apostle Paul's immediate circle. Despite this, when we more carefully weigh how the author looks at things consistently and completely from the standpoint of the ancient people of the covenant, as well as the overall stance and tendency of his epistle, we can certainly have no further doubts about it being a product of Jewish Christianity and not of Paulinism. Nevertheless we should be more specific: the epistle's origin is by no means a harsh and exclusionary Jewish Christianity, but instead a freer and more spiritual version, one broad enough to already presuppose Paulinism itself.

Nowhere in this Epistle do we encounter specifically Pauline concepts and doctrinal formulations, but it also contains nothing contrary to them. It does not explicitly entertain Pauline universalism, nor does it make provision for Jewish particularism. The Epistle is much more completely in agreement with the Apostle Paul in its view that Judaism just belongs to a very subordinate stage of religious development, an imperfect and transitory stage, one that must be followed by a higher and more perfect religious system, an everlasting one. On the whole we therefore have the same antitheses as those the Apostle Paul dealt with. The distinctive feature here is that the author of Hebrews directly mediates the antitheses, and that takes him beyond the Apostle Paul. Of course he only knows how to do so by employing a fundamental outlook that just mediates the antitheses from the vantage point of Judaism. This outlook is, in short, that of the priesthood.

Christ is essentially a priest. Judaism also has its priesthood, so everything distinguishing Christianity from Judaism, and everything uniting them, can be traced back to the essential nature of the priesthood. This deprives the antithesis to be mediated of its sharpest features. It is not such a direct and divisive antithesis as that between faith and works of the law. Instead it is the kind of antithesis that, with all the deeper significance it involves, nevertheless can be taken primarily as a relative opposition, merely a difference of degree. The two components of the antithesis are simply the imperfect priesthood and the perfect priesthood. So Judaism is also inherently the same as Christianity, except that what in Judaism is still just imperfect and deficient, first arrives at its perfection in Christianity.

But the writer of Hebrews does not just stop here. He has something else spanning the imperfect and perfect priesthoods and, as what is higher, uniting the two components of the antithesis. This is the priesthood of Melchizedek. The priesthood of Melchizedek stands above the Levitical priesthood, and the distinction drawn between the priesthood of Christ and the Levitical priesthood is precisely that Christ is a priest "according to the order of Melchizedek."[91] In going back in this way to an Old Testament standpoint lying beyond Levitical and Mosaic Judaism, the writer of Hebrews seems to just follow in the steps of the Apostle Paul, who also did indeed place the faith of Abraham above the law and the righteousness of the law, and saw the promise given to Abraham now being fulfilled in the faith of Christians.

However, this position is essentially different from Paul's. The writer of Hebrews puts the priesthood of Melchizedek, the Levitical priesthood, and Christ's priesthood, together in a single series, where the continuity of the main idea throughout the whole series is quite evident. In contrast, when the Apostle Paul situates the law in between the promise to Abraham on one side, and the fulfillment of the promise in Christ on the other side, we do not see how, with this procedure, the law fits in here. The law certainly just seems to be here in order to keep promise and fulfillment apart. The Apostle himself indicates that the law is merely a stopgap. Even when, to account for this interim role, he says that the law "was added because of transgressions," to let sin run its full course (Gal 3:19–21), this seems to mark a complete break with legalistic Judaism.

This view cannot follow from the standpoint of the Epistle to the Hebrews. The Epistle counters it with the idea of the priesthood, something far removed from the Apostle Paul's range of ideas. For the Apostle, Judaism is essentially law, and he sees the law as just negatively related to Christianity. Even though the author of Hebrews calls the law worldly, "weak and ineffectual (for the law made nothing perfect)" (7:16–19), he gives all this an entirely different meaning by just including it under his assumed idea of the priesthood. He even indicates in striking fashion how his standpoint differs from that of the Apostle, by stating (7:12): "For when there is a change in the priesthood, there is necessarily a change in the law as well." For him the priesthood is therefore primary, and his entire outlook begins with it; whereas the law is secondary, and must take its bearings from the priesthood. For him the idea of the priesthood has such an exalted and absolute significance that it shapes his entire worldview and conception of Christianity.

However, what gives this idea its very real significance is that, for the writer, the "priest according to the order of Melchizedek," and his identity with Christ, show us that what determines the author's standpoint is the typological relation of (proto)type and antitype. Everything belonging in the sphere of Old Testament religion has an ideal, typological, figurative meaning relating to Christianity, except that in the figurative meaning we have to distinguish in turn the archetype from the image. Judaism

---

91. Heb 4:14; 5:6; 6:20; and 7:1ff.

proper is just the image, the shadow or reflection, of an archetypal religion standing over it, and such archetypes as the priest Melchizedek crop up within Judaism. In its true essence, and as distinct from Judaism proper, Christianity is, ideally and in itself, what is contained in that original type. Inasmuch as actual Judaism, the legalistic and Levitical religion, stands in between the Old Testament religion as ideal Christianity, and historical Christianity, Judaism itself just appears to be the falling away from the idea, just the shadow of it, the still untrue shape of the as yet veiled, true religion—something through which the idea must make its way in order to attain its true historical realization, its consummation in Christianity. Thus the whole of world history and religious history is the process of the idea of religion making its way through Judaism and Christianity as its successive moments and, in Christianity, filling itself with its concrete content.

In the Apostle's worldview, Adam and Christ, in other words the First Adam and the Second Adam, have an archetypal unity only in the Second Adam, the "man from heaven" (1 Cor 15:47), a unity in an analogue to Melchizedek and standing above the antithesis—most especially above the antitheses of sin and grace, death and life. From the contrasting standpoint of the Epistle to the Hebrews, the archetype is self-realizing through the mediation of its image. Hence we can describe the difference concisely as contrasting ethical and metaphysical concerns. Paul and the author of Hebrews very much share common ground in seeking to conceive the relation of Judaism and Christianity from the standpoint of a higher worldview, one overarching both religions. However, they part ways on all the individual major points. What for the Apostle Paul has the innermost and most subjective meaning, rooted in ethical consciousness, is for the writer of Hebrews a purely theoretical issue. For this writer everything just boils down in the end to the reflection that it contradicts an objective view of the world if one prefers the imperfect to the perfect, the mere shadow image to the essential being of the thing itself. The author of Hebrews knows nothing of all the moral concepts belonging to Pauline anthropology—nothing of sin's power to make fulfilling the law impossible, or of the flesh's power over the spirit with the universal sinfulness it brings about.

In addition, although Christ's death is an atoning sacrifice, Hebrews does not view Christ as the one who died for all, so that all have died in him. Whereas for the Apostle there is no other sacrifice atoning for sins, so he reckons Old Testament sacrificial offerings as being just "works of the law," Hebrews is all about comparing the Old Testament sacrificial institutions with Christ's sacrificial death. Hebrews does this to show that, while Judaism also already includes, in its own fashion, everything belonging to the essence of religion, Christianity nevertheless has all of it in a far better and more perfect way. An account of religious elements (*Symbolik*) presented in this manner, emphasizing the affinity of the two religious systems, always highlights the quantitative differences and puts the qualitative differences, which in this case can hardly be ignored, in the background.[92] When what is in one is repeatedly said to be in the other, this analogizing overly generalizes and trivializes the specifically Pauline concepts, as we see most clearly with the concept of faith, when there is already the same salvific faith in the old covenant as there is in the new covenant (see all of ch. 11), and when faith's content is only that God exists and those who seek him will be rewarded (11:6 and 26).

This is how, on the basis of the authentically Jewish idea of the priesthood, the relation of type and antitype is the principle determining the worldview of the Epistle to the Hebrews. A further important element belonging to its own distinctive understanding of Christianity is that, for it, the relation of type and antitype also parallels the relation of the present world to the world to come. According to the Epistle's basic outlook, so little is true and enduring in the present, temporal world that everything first becomes perfect in the world to come. But since only that which inherently has the principle of perfection within it can perfect itself, in the final analysis it all goes back to the antitheses of the heavenly and the earthly. The heavenly is what is perfect, what is existent in itself, what is real and archetypal being (9:11 and 24; 10:1). Since the image now stands over against the archetype, and the present world is just the reflection of the archetypal world, everything can attain its reality only in the world to come. Hence even Christianity first has all its reality there; it is identical with the world to come (2:5, 6:5). Thus the writer of the Epistle is so reluctant to assign to Christianity any firm footing in the shaky ground of this transitory, temporal world (12:27), that he even transfers the atoning act from the present world to the world to come. He only allows that Jesus dies here so as to have the blood with which he must enter heaven, as the great high priest.

This is an Alexandrian perspective, not a Pauline position. Alexandrian idealism manifestly governs the Epistle's entire way of looking at things. All the antitheses making up this worldview are just so many ways of determining how Christianity relates to Judaism. They relate as archetype and image, heavenly and earthly, as what is absolute to what is finite. In other words, since the absolute must itself enter into what is finite, and only via mediation of the finite can what is absolute be what it ought to be, Judaism and Christianity relate as the present world and the world to come. From the standpoint of Alexandrian idealism, the temporal earthly world is only a vanishing moment of the ideal world, which is existent in itself. Hence the relation between Christianity and Judaism cannot be otherwise. As the religious system of this real, finite world, Judaism is heading steadily toward its downfall; in itself it is already "obsolete," "growing old," and "will soon disappear" (8:13). Christianity can exist in the present world only insofar as it reaches over from the ideal world, the world to

---

92. Hence the comparisons with Judaism: Christianity is "the introduction of a better hope" (7:19) and "a better covenant" (7:22); Christ has "a more excellent ministry" (8:6), and he entered in "through the greater and perfect tent" (9:11); his "sacrifices" are "better" (9:23). [*Ed.*] Baur gives the Greek of these passages.

come, and makes itself known here subjectively, in "the powers of the age to come" (6:15). The death of Christ does of course mark the division between the two worlds, although Judaism still continues on, for Christianity is not yet present here in its true being. Thus in the present world Judaism and Christianity are interconnected. We see the latter in the former, but only as an image, in a more or less obscure reflection, for this relation is characteristic of the symbolic, allegorical way of looking at things the writer of Hebrews shares with Alexandrian Judaism.[93]

Now we are in a position to state in more specific terms the Epistle to the Hebrews' stance on Pauline universalism. It does not rule it out. Instead it presupposes universalism, but nowhere specifically acknowledges it. Had Hebrews wanted to assign paganism a specific place within its worldview, it could only have put it in the same, both negative and interim, position as Judaism occupies in relation to Christianity. Yet if, despite Judaism's close ties to Christianity, Judaism is just a shadow image of the true essence of things, how little would there have been to say of real substance about paganism? Accordingly, it is part of the Jewish-Christian character of Hebrews that it says nothing about paganism and silently lumps it in with Judaism. On the other hand, however, all that made Judaism as such to be deficient and insubstantial certainly posed no obstacle to its serving, in this transitory order of things, as intermediary for what is ideal and existent in itself. So why should the same not also hold good for paganism itself? Thus if Judaism and paganism be lumped together in the transcendent worldview of Hebrews, then that expresses the universal principle of Christianity as breaking free from the particularism of Judaism. We see this universal principle in Christ, the priest according to the order of Melchizedek, also being the Son of God, who is exalted above everything and embraces all things with his power.[94]

---

93. [Ed.] Jews began settling in Alexandria shortly after its founding (323 BC) and became a large community there, deeply influenced by Greek-Hellenistic culture and learning. Baur gives no names associated with "Alexandrian idealism," but the most prominent Helleno-Judaic thinker was Philo of Alexandria (c. 20 BC—c. AD 50).

94. See Köstlin's essay on Hebrews in the *Theologische Jahrbücher* 12 (1853), 410–28; and 13 (1854) 366–446 and 463–82 [on Köstlin, see n. 30]. Köstlin has very thoroughly demonstrated the Alexandrine origin and character of the Epistle. My only disagreement is with his view that Hebrews is plainly a polemic against a Jewish Christianity clinging to the ritual law; that Hebrews plays a mediating role only insofar as it deigns to give detailed proof of the law's transitory function as well as of how New Testament sources themselves do away with the old covenant; and that there is nothing in Hebrews seeking to bring Jewish Christianity and Paulinism closer together. Hebrews makes no direct attempt at mediation, although, since its Alexandrine character is neither Judaism nor Paulinism because, in standing between them and setting limits to both, it sets itself above them, its conceptualization obviously assumes the nature of a mediation. It is mediating in the same sense as the Alexandrine method has, on the whole, a mediating tendency in the interest of Judaism. Ritschl continues to hold that the premises behind the Epistle's main idea are to be found among the early apostles (*Entstehung*, 2nd ed. [n. 38], 169ff.). But here too this seems to be a very one-sided and limited perspective. See the contrary view of Hilgenfeld, in the *Zeitschrift für wissenschaftliche Theologie* (1858) (n. 11) 104ff.

The Epistles to the Ephesians, the Colossians, and the Philippians

The Epistles to the Ephesians and the Colossians belong to the series of writings [traditionally] assigned to the Apostle Paul. They belong under the same heading as the Epistle to the Hebrews, except that they position themselves on the Pauline side, whereas Hebrews represents the standpoint of Jewish Christianity. They too struggle for an understanding of Christianity in which the difference between Jewish Christians and Gentile Christians, a feature their religious consciousness shares, becomes of its own accord something that vanishes in the concrete vision of a unity standing above the antitheses. Universal reconciliation or reunion of what is separated and discordant is the highest idea of both epistles, and is all-pervasive in their contents. Everything relates to this idea, and the christology of these epistles is its supreme expression.

All things in heaven and on earth are said to be one in Christ. This is God's eternal decree, and it will be fulfilled and realized in Christ at the duly appointed time (Eph 1:10). This is most especially the purpose of his death on the cross. God has willed to reconcile all things through Christ and in relation to him, such that everything has its final purpose in him. Thus "through him God was pleased to reconcile to himself all things, whether on earth or in heaven, by making peace through the blood of the cross" (Col 1:20). This takes place in various ways. These two epistles consider Christ's death to be a battle with a power hostile to God. Placing Christ's person and work under an even higher and more general perspective results in a much more intensified idea of the antithesis. Christ's death is the triumphant defeat of hostile powers and authorities he has disarmed (Eph 2:2; 3:10; 6:12; Col 2:15). So the "rulers of this age" that the Apostle Paul speaks of in 1 Cor 2:8, in an as yet nonspecific way, have become here a supersensible force; and the battle with these powers and authorities, their conquest, is an action affecting the visible world and the unseen world.

What especially has greater affinity with the Pauline theological framework is the assigning of the law's annulment to Christ's atoning work. God nailed the law, the ledger of human guilt, to the cross in order to erase it from the world (Col 2:14). His doing so reconciles human beings with him. The means of the reconciliation was Christ's slain body of flesh. Christ's death removed and took away from us the body of flesh as the locus of sin. The consequence of this reconciliation is that, conscious of our freedom from the law, and of our forgiveness for the guilt of sin, we stand before God, "holy and blameless and irreproachable" (Col 1:20ff. and 2:11ff.).

One particular element in the universal process of reconciliation, consummated in Christ, is the uniting of Jews and Gentiles in one and the same religious fellowship. We should view this very feature as in fact the practical aim of these epistles. Christ's death is God's provision for the appointed purpose of removing the wall dividing Gentiles and Jews, and of reconciling the two groups jointly with God, via the peace established between them. Setting aside the Mosaic law deprives Judaism of its absolute prerogative. Inasmuch as Christ's death therefore does away with all national distinctions and antipathies, with everything in life's various circumstances that otherwise separates people from one another, Christianity thus presents a new self, one that also in practice has to increasingly set aside the old self (Col 3:9; Eph 2:10 and 15; 4:22). The two groups, Gentiles and Jews both, have therefore been united in One Body, have been reconciled with God. In the same spirit, both have access to the Father (Eph 2:16–18).

Because the distinction between Gentiles and Jews ceases in the unity of the new self, Christianity, as the absolute religion, stands above paganism and Judaism. In the terms Ephesians 3:5–10 uses to describe Christianity's absolute sublimity, it is the mystery foreordained before the beginning of the world and infinitely transcending all others, "hidden for ages in God" and formerly "not made known to humankind," first proclaimed by Christ and "revealed to his apostles and prophets by the Spirit."

If Christianity is the absolute religion, then paganism and Judaism have an equally negative relation to it. Yet scripture also speaks in turn of a certain relationship of identity between Judaism and Christianity. Like the Epistle to the Hebrews, Colossians also regards the Old Testament as a shadow image. If the ordinances of Old Testament religion are just a shadow image of what is to come, whereas the true reality is, in contrast, only in Christianity (the body of Christ), then from this we of course recognize that Old Testament religion is just a lesser degree of truth and reality. But since this also involves the relation of image and the thing itself, this weakness and imperfection, as the prototype, is already more directly related to Christianity [than paganism is].

It is in this sense that the Epistle to the Colossians especially seeks to demonstrate analogies between Judaism and Christianity. Judaism is of course deprived of the absolute claim it made with its commandment to be circumscribed. But Christianity also has a circumcision in place of it, although not a circumcision of the flesh, performed by human hands. It is "a spiritual circumcision, by putting off the body of the flesh in the circumcision of Christ," and it takes place in virtue of baptism. In it Christ makes alive again those who are dead in "the uncircumcision of the flesh," so that they rid themselves of all sinful lusts and desires, and become dedicated to a moral and holy life (Col 2:11–14). In this way Judaism and Christianity are indeed drawn closer together and considered to be inherently one.

Ephesians 2:11–22 has this taking place in even more specific terms. In all the time the Gentiles existed without Christ, those of the so-called "circumcision of the flesh" spoke of the Gentiles as "the uncircumcised," as far removed from the citizenry of Israel and ignorant of the promises of the covenant, as existing in the world without hope and without God. "But now . . . you who once were far off have been brought here by the blood of Christ" (v. 13). So this passage just speaks of the Gentiles coming to share in what the Jews already had beforehand. Christianity is not the absolute religion taking up into itself both the Gentile world and Judaism on equal terms. Instead the substantial content of Christianity is Judaism itself; for, in virtue of Christ's death, the universality of Christianity is simply the extension of Judaism to the Gentiles as well. However, although the Gentiles, regarded in this way as apparently being latecomers, are merely conceded a place in Christianity, Ephesians strongly emphasizes the fact that now they have become entitled to fully enjoy equal membership rights; that they are "no longer strangers and aliens, but . . . citizens with the saints and also members of the household of God" (2:19). The writer of Ephesians cannot stress this complete equality of the Gentiles with the Jews any more strongly, than when he says about these ἔθνη that they "have become fellow heirs, members of the same body, and sharers in the promise in Christ Jesus through the gospel" (3:6).

Although the Jewish Christians cannot therefore be deprived of their pride of place, nevertheless they now no longer take precedence over the Gentile Christians. The circumstances of the two groups are quite different from how the author of the Book of Revelation spells them out. While of course he did not wish to regard the Gentiles as excluded from the messianic community, he could think to number among the legitimate members of God's community only those with a legal entitlement, derived from the original twelve tribes of Israel (Rev 7:4).

The fundamental conception proper to the two epistles is that of the body of Christ in which both groups are said to become one body (Eph 2:16); the σῶμα Χριστοῦ as the Christian Church (1:22–23) in which Jews and Gentiles are united into one and the same communion. Aware of the powerful antitheses separating the Jewish and Gentile groups from each other, and of the necessity of neutralizing these antitheses if there is to be a Christian Church as such, the writers of these epistles insist, most earnestly and emphatically, on the unity of the church. Unity is in fact the essential nature of the church. Christianity provides this unity with all of the elements belonging to it: "There is one body and one Spirit, . . . one Lord, one faith, one baptism" (Eph 4:4–6). But this unity is grounded in the death of Christ. The hostility, the wall of separation, all the positive factors that divide the two groups, have ended with Christ's death (Eph 2:14–16).

Starting from this point, the conception becomes increasingly exalted until it arrives at the ground of all unity. The unifying power of Christ's death, in founding a universal communion, is only conceivable based on Christ being, as such, the center of the whole universe, by sustaining everything and holding it all together. As Christian consciousness is increasingly imbued with the absolute content of Christianity, in the conception of the self-constituting church, the more it is inwardly impelled to look upon this absoluteness as something supraworldly and supratemporal. Hence the christology of these two epistles is most intimately connected with the pressing need at that time for uniting under the idea of the one church in which all mutual differences and antitheses are set aside.

We see that these two epistles are looking at things from a genuinely Catholic standpoint. And when we set them alongside the Epistle to the Hebrews on the one hand, and the Pseudo-Clementine writings on the other hand, then altogether we have three fundamentally different views of Christianity. In all three views there is the same striving toward unity, one that seeks to find the supreme expression of unity and how to connect that expressed unity with dogmatics. In Hebrews, Christ is the high priest; in the Pseudo-Clementine writings he is the prophet of truth; in Ephesians and Colossians he is the central being of the universe. Christian consciousness is envisaging the same unity in each of these formulations. The idea of this unity was said to realize itself in the antitheses of the different contending factions.

The catholicizing tendency of Ephesians and Colossians is also clearly recognizable in that they give works, or morality in action, quite independent significance in distinction from faith or belief. The Epistle to the Philippians, which belongs in the same category, does of course obviously emphasize, in 3:9, the Pauline doctrine of justification by faith as opposed to "righteousness from the law." But it does so only in external fashion. Philippians is no longer concerned to establish that faith, as opposed to works in general, is the principle of justification. Ephesians and Colossians simply speak about forgiveness of sins, about redemption, and reconciliation. The fact that we are saved by grace is something Ephesians 2:8 attributes to faith. Yet verse 10 then places the main emphasis on works in addition to faith, even saying that God foreordained them for us.

In the transcendent christology of these epistles, all that bears upon human blessedness lies far above one's temporal existence, and depends on God's eternal decree that is carried out in time. Thus one can only look upon all of it as a free gift of God's grace. Grace is the principle creating human beings anew, through faith in Christ. That is to say, through Christianity a human being must become something new. The old self must be "stripped off" and one must be "clothed . . . with the new self" (Col 3:9–10; also Eph 4:21–24), which is something different from the former self. Yet this is just the renewal, in human beings, of the image according to which God originally created them. While the Apostle Paul held fast to faith as the principle bringing about oneness with Christ, these epistles mainly fix their attention on the moral perfection of human beings that proceeds from faith, a process running its course within the same antitheses of death and life that present themselves in Christ (Col 3:1–4; also, the rest of ch. 3).[95]

The Pastoral Epistles

The repeated reminders of Gnosis and its distinctive teachings to be found in Ephesians, Colossians, and Philippians, obviously show that these epistles belong to the post-apostolic age. The Pastoral Epistles even more directly and definitively take us to

---

95. See my book *Paulus, der Apostel Jesu Christi* (n. 5), 417ff. [ET 2:1–44]. Also see Schwegler, *Das nachapostolische Zeitalter* (n. 32), 2:325ff.

the time of heretical Gnosis. These epistles have a place of their own in the series of efforts striving for unity that come from the Pauline side as well.

The Pastoral Epistles belong to a period in the history of the nascent church's development when the danger already threatening from heretics, and the resistance to them that had become necessary, made it requisite to secure the unity of the church. The imminent challenge was to consolidate the various components of the ecclesial community and to create a church organization embracing all the elements of ecclesial life. The Pastoral Epistles have the same orientation as that of the Pseudo-Ignatian Epistles and the Pseudo-Clementine writings. Since the efforts to give the church an enduring system of governance, one resting on specific principles, initially seemed to come from the Jewish-Christian faction, the Pastoral Epistles therefore attest to a readiness to cooperate on the goal coming also from the Pauline side. They do so by placing in the mouth of the Apostle Paul a series of pastoral instructions that he could not have entertained himself, but that were now enjoined as also being in Pauline interests.[96]

The Epistle of James, and First Peter

The Epistle of James and the First Epistle of Peter fall in a somewhat earlier time period than the Pastoral Epistles. All of these epistles were written by persons other than those whose names they bear. We can only consider these two epistles here with respect to how they relate the two elements of the antithesis conceived as in equilibrium, and to the way a more definite configuration of Catholic Christianity is already recognizable in them.

There is no mistaking the fact that the First Epistle of Peter presupposes [awareness of] the Pauline doctrine of justification. So it can also simply have an anti-Pauline tendency, albeit not one directly aimed at the Apostle Paul himself. It contests a one-sided understanding of Pauline teaching that is detrimental to Christianity in practice. What the epistle expresses, in such a principled way, is that it sets over against the Pauline formula of justification a different formulation in which, because of how faith is related to works, works are equally as real and substantial factors [in justification] as faith is for Paul.[97]

On the other hand, however, the writer of James is also no stranger to the Pauline spiritualizing of the law, i.e. making it inward, since he does not just cite the commandment to love one's neighbor (2:8) as sovereign law; he also speaks of a "law of

---

96. See my book, *Die sogennanten Pastoralbriefe des Apostels Paulus* (Tübingen, 1835).

97. The main point on which they differ is the concept of faith ($\pi i\sigma\tau\iota\varsigma$). As opposed to faith's ideal character for Paul, the writer of the Epistle of James, from the standpoint of his authentically Jewish realism, thinks a faith without works amounts to nothing, is something "dead," is inactive (2:17 and 26). Basically, such faith has no existence at all because, given its purely ideal character, there can be no empirical proof of its reality (2:18). Even though faith in itself is present, faith first becomes truly real in works. In any event it is just "active along with" becoming righteous by works (2:22).

liberty" (2:12), which for him can only have been the law because he knew he was just as inwardly free from the externality of the law as the Apostle Paul knew that from his own standpoint. The same striving to spiritualize the law is evident from the writer locating the principle of blessedness—of course not like Paul, in faith—instead in the word of truth as a principle of rebirth immanent in human beings. The word of truth (λόγος ἀληθείας) is an "implanted word" (λόγος ἔμφυτος), a vital impulse toward fruitful activity implanted in a human being, only when it also yields an inner consciousness of truth corresponding to an outward revelation.

The Epistle of James arose from the endeavor to counteract a tendency toward conceptual formalism and downplaying matters of practice. It sought to influence the Christian consciousness now taking shape in ways consistent with the interests of Jewish Christianity. Hence the writer of the epistle, as defender of Jewish Christianity, presents himself as the highest authority on the Jewish-Christian side, as the James known in other contexts. In writing "to the twelve tribes in the Dispersion" (1:1), that is, the Jewish Christians living among the Gentile Christians, he also presents himself here as the leader of the mother church in Jerusalem.

The writer of James is by no means just engaging in a polemic against the Pauline doctrine of justification. Instead he has taken up the general task of addressing the entire scope of the Christian life from the standpoint of his more liberal and spiritualized Jewish Christianity as it plays out, essentially and practically, in what one undergoes and what one does. He seeks to depict Christians as they ought to be, as complete persons in the fullness of the Christian life, a fullness that can only be thought of as completed in works. This makes it very clear how much the writer was aware of his role at that time, and of the importance of his Jewish-Christian standpoint. He could make a not insignificant contribution to the Catholic Christianity that was taking shape, by his employing in this way the antithesis in his doctrine of works and of practical Christian conduct, an antithesis certainly legitimized from his side and yet keeping its distance from any personal polemic. Since everything here that inherently opposes one-sided positions, and seeks to harmonize each of the two sides by setting them in a suitable equilibrium, is also in the spirit of Catholic Christianity, it would be an injustice to the epistle, in this context, to want to attribute a harshly anti-Pauline tendency to it.

The First Epistle of Peter is closely related to the Epistle of James, whose writer is addressing the Christian churches of the Diaspora. Both epistles have the same characteristics: an explicit avowal of the Jewish-Christian standpoint; an undeniable concern to come to terms with Paulinism and its influence, as well as having their own setting in a later era. Comparison of the ostensibly Petrine theological framework with that of Paul reveals striking similarities. Thus even those who accept both the authenticity of the Epistle and the distinctiveness and independence of a Petrine doctrinal perspective, cannot fail to recognize these similarities. Their explanation for them can only be that the Apostle Paul read and utilized First Peter. But those who date the Epistle in the period of Trajan's measures against the Christians [early second century], when the legend of the Apostle Peter residing in Rome was already established, are even more justified in taking an opposite view. In the Epistle's parallels with Romans and Ephesians they see it accommodating itself to Pauline ideas. In any event the presence of Pauline ideas shows how people on the Jewish-Christian side were inclined to be receptive to such an idea as the Pauline doctrine regarding Christ's death (1 Pet 4:1–2), and to be open to utilizing this theological framework for Christian practical life.

The writer discloses the intent of the Epistle, the direction it takes, at the end (5:12) when he makes Silvanus, the well-known companion of the Apostle Paul, the one to deliver his Epistle. He calls Silvanus "a faithful brother" and states that its purpose is to give those who read it a convincing testimony to the truth of their Christian faith. He says that, whether Jewish Christians or Gentile Christians, they are to be deemed orthodox Christians provided that they simply agree with, and hold firmly to, what he has set forth for them in his Epistle as the true contents of the Christian faith. The predominantly practical concerns of First Peter, and the general conviction gaining force in the current circumstances, namely the conviction that the essence of Christianity consists above all in the moral integrity of good conduct, allow the differences of earlier times to be increasingly disregarded.[98]

The Book of Acts

As the conclusion of First Peter also reminds us, despite all these steps toward convergence and equilibrium, taken by both sides, there was still something remaining that necessarily had to be put aside as well, if the work of unification was not to collapse internally for want of an adequately secured foundation.

How could Jewish Christians and Gentile Christians draw closer to each other and join together in one and the same religious and ecclesial community in these circumstances? How could a Christian Church arising from such a unification even consider itself to be built on the foundation of the apostles, when it had to accommodate an awareness that the two apostles, standing respectively as leaders of the two main parties, had held such opposing views and principles? How could they join together

---

98. As to dating the Epistle of James, and its contents and character, see my *Paulus* (n. 5), 677ff. [ET 2:297]. On First Peter, see my essay ["Der erste petrinische Brief, mit besonderer Beziehung auf das Werk . . . von Dr. Bernh. Weiss"] in the *Theologische Jahrbücher* 15 (1856) 193–240, where I have fully evaluated the work on it by Weiss (Berlin, 1855). It is hard to comprehend how, even today, someone can still make a case for the alleged apostolic origin of writings so transparently pseudonymous, by such baseless and superficial contentions as those found all too often in the pages of Ritschl and Weiss. It is as though such an apologetic was quite intentionally seeking to obstruct the way to gain a historical perspective on the earliest period of the Christian Church that is sound and true to life. It is not worth the effort for me to remark further about vague hypotheses lacking any historical support and coherence. See Hilgenfeld (n. 74), 405ff. [*Ed.*] Bernhard Weiss (1827–1918), New Testament scholar and father of Johannes Weiss, was an opponent of the Tübingen School.

when living with the memory of a gulf that existed between these apostles still not having been bridged? It is clearly self-evident that whatever might bring Jewish Christians and Gentile Christians together has a solid basis only on the assumption that the actual nature of this mutual relation rests on an understanding the Apostles Peter and Paul themselves intentionally entered into.

This is where the Book of Acts has its place, not merely as a literary product but also as an independent historical factor shaping how this relationship unfolded. The most recent investigations[99] have shown incontrovertibly that Acts cannot be regarded as a purely historical document; that instead it is a presentation with a specific tendency or theme. Its actual purpose can thus only have been to resolve the issue that was then of the most widespread concern, by going back to deal with the Apostle Paul's stance toward the earlier apostles. From this perspective our verdict can only be that Acts seems to present just a very modified form of original Paulinism. Yet Acts does most definitely maintain a Pauline character on two points. First and foremost, it does hold firmly to what Paulinism is essentially and in principle: that Christianity is destined to be universal; that Gentile Christianity, freed from the law, is as legitimate as Jewish Christianity. The Paulinism of Acts proceeds from the Lord's answer to the disciples prior to the ascension, when they asked about the restoration of the kingdom to Israel (Acts 1:6–8). Christ says, "You will be my witnesses in Jerusalem, in all Judea and Samaria, and to the ends of the earth" (v. 8). This universalism extends throughout all the elements of Acts' historical account, right up to its conclusion with the Apostle Paul's declaration to the Jews: "Let it be known to you then that this salvation of God has been sent to the Gentiles; they will listen" (28:28). Just as decisively Acts sets the condition to be acknowledged if Christianity is to be capable of fulfilling its universal destiny. Acts indeed allows the Jewish Christians to remain subject to the law as they have been, whereas it relieves the Gentile Christians from that obligation by only requiring them to abstain from practices that are most offensive to the Jewish Christians, and that stand mainly in the way of a mutual coming-together (15:28–30).

To understand correctly the purpose and character of the Book of Acts, one must see things from this central, Paulinist focus. Howsoever much it bends the truth when it comes to depicting the personality of the Apostle Paul himself, Acts does not shortchange anything when it comes to the two aforementioned Paulinist principles. Yet the contrast between the two Pauls is very striking: the depiction of Paul's character and conduct in the Book of Acts, versus the picture we get of his personality from his own writings. Also, according to Acts, Paul supposedly made concessions to the Jewish Christians that he cannot possibly have made, given the principles he himself enunciated most decisively. We find the same phenomenon with respect to the opposing side, for Acts also presents Peter in a light leaving him no longer recognizable to us

---

99. See Matthias Schneckenburger, *Über den Zweck der Apostelgeschichte* (Bern, 1841); my own book *Paulus* (n. 5), 5ff. [ET 1:4ff.]; and Zeller, *Apostelgeschichte* (n. 12), 316ff. and 343ff. [ET 2:139ff., 173ff.].

as the main representative of the Jewish Christianity of Jerusalem. Hence we see that the Book of Acts directly aims at just paralleling the two apostles, so that Peter shall appear to be just as Pauline, on the one hand, as Paul appears Petrine on the other.

In looking at their deeds and their fates, we find the two apostles so much alike that there is no kind of miracle-working performed by Peter, in the first part of Acts, that does not have its counterpart in the second part [where Paul is the main actor]. Even more striking is the fact that, in both parts, the two apostles not only agree on how they present their teaching, and in their apostolic demeanor; they even seem to have switched roles. In the speech of the Apostle Paul in Acts, ch. 13, alongside the proclamation of monotheism in opposition to pagan polytheism, and the preaching about Jesus' resurrection and messianic status, about turning from sin and to good works, there is barely any mention (vv. 38–39) of the distinctive Pauline teaching about the law and about justification. In contrast to this, Peter and even James speak in far more Pauline terms. Peter states that God makes no distinction between Jews and Gentiles (15:9), for the Gentiles too, the unclean ones, are cleansed by faith. He calls the law "a yoke that neither our ancestors nor we have been able to bear" (v. 10). He declares that the Jews as well as the Gentiles can be saved simply through the grace of Christ (v. 11), and that "God shows no partiality, for in every nation anyone who fears him and does what is right is acceptable to him" (10:34). Even James professes Pauline universalism (15:17).

It is no different with other things these two apostles do. Even before [the newly converted] Paul became a factor, Peter performs the first baptism of a Gentile, Cornelius, with the approval of the Jerusalem community [10:48, 11:18]. In contrast to this, Paul himself circumcises Timothy, the Gentile Christian, in deference to his Jewish compatriots, and conducts himself overall as a pious Israelite under the law who, despite the pressing demands of his apostolic function, does not fail to make the traditional journey to Jerusalem. He takes the vow and becomes a nazirite,[100] for the express purpose of refuting the wrongful accusation that he teaches people to forsake the law. He has such great respect for the theocratic privileges of his people that, from first to last, he always initially preaches to the Jews, and only then turns to the Gentiles when forced to on account of the Jews' unbelief and when instructed to do so by God. The two apostles also appear in parallel when Peter, just like Paul, is charged in a vision to be an apostle to the Gentiles (ch. 10).

The only explanation for all this is that the historical facts were altered intentionally, in keeping with the tendency of Acts. Yet this cannot have been done merely for apologetic reasons relating simply to the person of the Apostle Paul. So it is indubitable that the Book of Acts has a conciliatory or irenic tendency. It is not supposed to be merely a personal vindication of the Apostle Paul against the accusations and prejudices of the Judaists, for instead it is supposed to pave the way for receptivity

---

100. [*Ed.*] Acts 18:18 says that Paul "had his hair cut, for he was under a [nazarite] vow." See Acts 21:24 and Num 6:1–21. A "nazarite" is one who is set apart or consecrated.

to Pauline Christianity. To this end Acts not only commended Paul and his cause to the Jewish Christians; it also disseminated on the Pauline side an understanding of Christianity, and a representation of Paul's character and teaching, that, by setting aside or concealing its most objectionable aspects, is more suited to linking it with Jewish Christianity, as the writer endeavored to do.

Hence the Book of Acts is the attempt at conciliation, and the peace overture, of a Paulinist who, by concessions his faction made to Judaism, sought to gain recognition for Gentile Christianity on the part of the Jewish Christians, and in this way to influence both factions. Accordingly, Acts gives us very clear insight into the efforts then aiming at a Catholic Christianity. Yet despite how intentionally and methodically the author worked toward that end, he could hardly avoid the one point on which attaining that goal ultimately depended—that a union of the two factions could actually come to pass only insofar as they had come to think of the two apostles in a way that made a union possible. This is actually the key point of the Book of Acts' very tendentious presentation. What merits particular attention in this regard is how fastidiously Acts avoids even touching upon the provocative elements in the account of its Apostle [Paul]. How striking it is that Acts passes over, in total silence, the conflict in Antioch, which the Clementine writings still recalled so vividly; that it not once mentions the Titus who, as the Apostle's companion and according to Galatians 2:1ff., proved to be so very objectionable to the Jerusalem Christians; and that, instead of these two scenes it recounts the dispute with Barnabas. It is as though this latter and far less important issue was the only thing to be dealt with at that time. It looks like Acts even had to replace the refusal to circumcise Titus when it has its Apostle so willingly accommodate the Jews by circumcising Timothy.

Do we not see clearly here the effort to throw a veil over the past, so that from now on it is buried in the darkness of oblivion? On the other hand, Acts is concerned that its Apostle Paul be in contact with the older apostles at every opportunity. His doing so can only foster the supposition that he had a truly brotherly relation with them. Consequently, people also believed what they wished to believe, and they no longer wavered from believing it. This shows how well the writer of Acts understood the times in which he lived, and how strictly he kept focused on what had to be held to steadfastly, in the general interest.[101]

---

101. Just as the writer of the Book of Acts believed he could tie the efforts at unity in his day simply with the persons of the two apostles, we find the same concern underlying the appearing of so many epistles that can only be regarded as pseudonymous apostolic writings. Since the prevailing outlook could not accept anything not resting on apostolic authority, one had to trace everything of particular concern at that time back to an apostolic reputation, or even to the very mouth of the apostle himself to whose faction one belonged, in an epistle ostensibly written by him. Hence because so many documents from that time period are certainly tendentious in nature, the fact that they are pseudonymous is a matter of course. The pseudonymous character, that is, the authority of a name long known to the public and representing a specific orientation, is the form in which one captures current interest in one's own work, so as to influence other people. At a time harboring such stark antitheses, it is quite natural for there to be so many tendency writings. This is an important factor in understanding

THE WRITINGS OF THE APOSTOLIC FATHERS

The writings of the Apostolic Fathers constitute a group of its own that comes after the canonical scriptures. It is only because of the wide gulf between two different periods of church history that these writings can be viewed as separate from the set of scriptures in the canon, whose reputedly divine inspiration is exaggerated. But since several of the canonical scriptures belong to the post-apostolic age, the transition from one class of writings to the other is initially recognizable only from an external benchmark: the latter group no longer takes their pseudonymous names from the circle of the apostles, but instead takes them from their followers. The most recent research,[102] which is increasingly indisputable, shows that pseudonymity is still prevalent here, and that names such as Barnabas, Clement, and Ignatius do not indicate the true origins of these writings, but just disclose their character and tendency.

Hence the main issue here too is how Paulinism and Jewish Christianity, the two factors in Christianity's historical development, are mutually related; and how their further development toward Catholic Christianity can be followed up in terms of this relationship. Although in this context as well there is, on the whole, just a fleeting distinction between these writings and the canonical scriptures, the writings of the Apostolic Fathers nevertheless do move more decidedly to one side or the other of the antithesis, in a way not open to the canonical scriptures given their character. Even so, that does not answer ahead of time the question about the respective positions of these writings in a way that removes any controversy about the matter. Schwegler[103] has spotted most keenly all of their Ebionite contents, and allows that there are Pauline elements present only to an extent that facilitates the achievement of an agreement between the two parties. Ritschl,[104] who is much opposed to Schwegler's understanding of the post-apostolic age, even goes so far as to assign a Pauline orientation to *The Shepherd* of Hermas and to the writings of Justin Martyr.

The Epistle of Barnabas and the Pseudo-Ignatian Epistles stand most decidedly on the side opposed to Jewish Christianity. The Epistle of Barnabas shares with the Epistle to the Hebrews the standard allegorical view of how Judaism is related to

---

correctly why such an extensive pseudonymous literature appeared at that very time. It is also why—to avoid sharing what is therefore a very narrow and biased view, arising from limited knowledge of the ancient world—pseudonymity is conceptually the same thing as literary deception. On this issue, see Schwegler, *Das nachapostolische Zeitalter* (n. 32), 1:79 ff; my *Paulus* (n. 5), 503 [ET 2:110], and my article ["Die Clementinen nebst den verwandten Schriften und der Ebionitismus"] in the *Theologische Jahrbücher* 3 (1844) 548; Ritschl, *Entstehung*, 1st ed. (n. 54), 195ff. Köstlin (n. 30) has treated it in the most comprehensive and most fundamental way in his treatise, "Die pseudonyme Litteratur der ältesten Kirche, ein Beitrag zur Geschichte der Bildung des Kanons," *Theologische Jahrbücher* 10 (1851) 149–221. There is no other New Testament scripture so susceptible to a demonstration of its specific tendency character as is the Book of Acts.

102. See Adolf Hilgenfeld, *Die apostolische Väter, Untersuchungen über Inhalt und Ursprung der unter ihrem Namen erhaltenen Schriften* (Halle, 1853).

103. [*Ed.*] See n. 65.

104. [*Ed.*] See n. 66.

Christianity; except that Barnabas understands this relationship not as something objective, but rather just from the subjective side. The two are related as image and substance, although the main thing is the consciousness of this relationship. Christianity is not Judaism completed, Judaism arrived at its full reality, for instead Christianity is Judaism unveiled, Judaism become manifest. What in Judaism lay hidden under the veil of types and allegories, but was from the beginning not referring to anything but Christianity, is now disclosed to consciousness and recognized in its true meaning as what it is in itself. Hence Christianity itself is essentially this knowing, a Gnosis in the sense in which this term most especially designates a knowing conveyed via allegorical interpretation.

When viewed from the objective standpoint of Hebrews, the idea realizing itself in Christianity at least shines through within Judaism as in a shadow image. Viewed according to the subjective mode of understanding in the Epistle of Barnabas, Judaism is just related to Christianity as not-knowing is to knowing. Moses simply spoke very much "in the spirit," and his ritual laws thus simply had a strongly allegorical sense. Because the Jews were completely unaware of this allegorical sense, they did not in principle have the law at all. Of course Moses did convey the covenant to their forefathers. But because of their sins they were not worthy to receive it, and that is why Moses smashed the tablets of the law. Now we, as heirs of the Jews, have received the covenant of Jesus, who was appointed to deliver us from darkness and, by his word, to enter into a covenant with us (ch. 14).[105]

From the fact that other peoples too—Syrians, Arabs, Egyptians, all the priests of idol worship—undergo circumcision, we see how little significance circumcision supposedly has in the physical sense Jews attribute to it; for Abraham just practiced circumcision in "looking forward in spirit to Jesus" (ch. 9). All this about physical circumcision falls by the wayside of its own accord as soon as one recognizes its true meaning; and Christianity is a new law that, without the yoke of compulsory circumcision, requires one to present oneself as offered or dedicated to God (ch. 2). The writer of Barnabas indeed skirts so closely to the Gnostic way of degrading Judaism that, in recounting how the warnings of the prophets were completely in vain when it came to conveying a spiritual understanding to Jews caught up in fleshly meanings, he speaks of an evil angel "who deluded them" (ch. 9). Here we see expressed the consciousness of something new, first manifested in Christianity and put in terms that are, in any event, quite kindred with Paulinism.[106]

---

105. [*Ed.*] For The Epistle of Barnabas, see *ANF* 1:137–49.

106. While having this Paulinist foundation, the Epistle is actually said to have an Alexandrine character, like that of Hebrews. See Hilgenfeld, *Die apostolische Väter* (n. 102), 37ff., and his article in the *Zeitschrift für wissenschaftliche Theologie* 1 (1858) 569ff. However Ritschl, who in the first edition of his *Entstehung der altkatholischen Kirche* (n. 54), 276, describes the standpoint of the Epistle as an evolution of the Paulinist principle, no longer acknowledges the writer's Paulinist standpoint in his second edition (n. 38), 570, where he instead takes the view that it already embodies all the marks of Gentile Christianity on the way to being Catholic Christianity. Contrary to Ritschl, Hilgenfeld

This antithetical stance toward Judaism in the Epistle of Barnabas places it closest to the Pseudo-Ignatian Epistles.[107] Their author also expressly recognizes the Apostle Paul as his model and refers to him by name in setting Christianity, in its newness and autonomy, over against Judaism. The writer of these Pseudo-Ignatian Epistles admonishes the followers of Christ that they must also live in keeping with Christianity (κατὰ Χριστιανισμόν); that whoever goes by another name than "Christian" does not belong to God. It is contradictory to call Jesus "Christ" and yet cling to Judaism, for Christianity has not involved belief in Judaism, whereas Judaism has involved belief in Christianity. The truth of Judaism did not already belong in advance to Judaism, for it belonged to Christianity, just as the Old Testament prophets, and those Jews already hoping for Christ before he came, were indeed in those days no longer Jews but Christians. The tendency of the writer of these Epistles is so decidedly anti-Jewish that, in order to distance everything Jewish from the Christian community, and to nail down the difference between the two in external terms, he will give no credence to any other labels than "Christians" (Χριστιανοί) and "Christianity" (Χριστιανισμός).[108] The way in which, without regard for this complete break with everything Jewish, the writer could go on about the foundation of a Catholic Church in forms where Gentile Christians could only join forces with Jewish Christians, is another aspect of these Epistles, and is to be taken up elsewhere in this history.[109]

There are clear indications of Paulinism in the Epistle of Clement of Rome to the Corinthians, as well as in the Epistle of Polycarp.[110] It is noteworthy how Clement not only names the Apostles Peter and Paul together, but also has the fame of Paul overshadowing the fame of Peter (ch. 5). The Epistle of Polycarp praises the blessed and illustrious Paul so much that there can certainly be no doubt about the Pauline character of this text, if one can simply judge it by that feature. The writer states that Paul has no equal in wisdom; that Paul personally instructed the Philippians, with precision and firmness, in the word of truth; that he also wrote letters to them when he was away, ones that, when read, could fortify them in the faith that is the "mother

---

correctly remarks (p. 570 of his article) that the Epistle's statements about the original apostles certainly make the writer's purely Pauline standpoint unmistakable. Who but a Paulinist could have not only linked the twelve apostles so closely with the twelve tribes of the Jews (ch. 8), but also have portrayed them so unfavorably, as having been [chosen from those who were] unimaginably sinful (ch. 5)? Despite what Hilgenfeld and others say about the date of the Epistle, nothing convinces me to change what I stated about that dating on p. 80 of the 2nd ed. (Tübingen, 1858) of my *Lehrbuch der christlichen Dogmengeschichte*. [*Ed.*] See Baur, *History of Christian Dogma*, ed. Peter C. Hodgson, trans. R. F. Brown and P. C. Hodgson (Oxford, 2014), 107, where he says "the letter cannot have been written prior to the year 119."

107. [*Ed.*] For the Pseudo-Ignatian Epistles, see *ANF* 1:49–96.

108. See my treatise, "Ueber der Ursprung des Episcopats in der christlichen Kirche," *Tübinger Zeitschrift für Theologie* (1838) no. 3, 179ff.; and Schwegler, *Das nachapostolisches Zeitalter* (n. 32), 2:163ff.

109. [*Ed.*] See below, pp. 221–23.

110. [*Ed.*] See *ANF* 1:5–21. See also 1:33–36, for an epistle about the martyrdom of Polycarp.

of all." The only qualification here is that the emphatic admonition to do good works and to love carries equal weight with the Pauline sense of justifying faith, so that both orientations fuse into a neutral form in which faith and works are juxtaposed in unmediated fashion.[111]

While the Ignatian Epistles place love even higher than faith, the earlier Epistle of Clement affirms both of them. On the one hand, it states that we are not justified through ourselves—not by our wisdom, insight, or piety, nor by works we have carried out in the holiness of our hearts. On the other hand, however, it just as strongly admonishes us not to become weary in doing good, nor to be wanting in love, but instead to carry out each good work eagerly and willingly, and to obey the divine will with works of righteousness. The Epistle of Polycarp locates edification in the faith that, as "mother of all," is followed by hope and preceded by love.[112]

The Shepherd of Hermas[113] without question belongs to this same category of writings. It is a product of Jewish Christianity and a testimonial to it. Its strictly monotheistic Judaism is expressed in the statement it places at the head [of the second book], as the fundamental article of the commandments imparted to Hermas by the Shepherd and as the entire content of the faith: there is one God who created all things; hence the summons is simply to obey God's will. Some contend that a writing like *The Shepherd* of Hermas could only belong to a circle of Christianity opposed to Judaism, hence the Pauline circle,[114] because it neither declares the law of Christ to be identical with the Mosaic law, nor does it contain the specific Jewish Christian duties—not either circumcision for those who were Jews or the laws governing proselytes for those

---

111. See Köstlin (n. 30), 247ff., especially where concern for the laws and for the Old Testament revelation are also emphasized as characteristic features.

112. See Schwegler (n. 32), 129, 157, and 168. In opposition to Ritschl and to R. A. Lipsius, *De Clementis Romani Epistola ad Corinthios priore disquisitio* (Leipzig, 1855), Hilgenfeld [*Die clementinischen Recognitionen und Homilien nach ihrem Ursprung und Inhalt* (n. 54)], 572ff., regards Clement of Rome as a pure Paulinist, although this Paulinism already and unmistakably takes a direction more moderate and conciliatory with respect to Jewish Christianity than the Epistle of Barnabas does. The inner development of Paulinism here first shows us a conciliatory frame of mind, one with which the still quite heterogeneous, basic outlook of the Rule of Faith from the apostolic age is comfortable. The fact that Jewish Christianity in Rome had a similar conciliatory frame of mind is best demonstrated from the Gospel of Mark, which is Roman in character and belongs to the same time period. All factors were favorable for the two originally antithetical Christian factions to first attain a certain equilibrium in Christian Rome, which at that time was able to maintain a certain independence from the original Jewish-Christian community in Jerusalem, and was predetermined to be the new central point of the Catholic Church. I concur with this view of Hilgenfeld. We see (from p. 132) with regard to the Epistle of Barnabas, that the Epistle of Clement of Rome is not to be assigned a very early date. Determining its date more exactly depends on the further results of investigations initiated by Hitzig and Volkmar concerning the Book of Judith, which is cited for the first time in Clement's epistle. [*Ed.*] Ferdinand Hitzig (1807–1885), biblical scholar; Gustav Volkmar (1809–93), philologist and historian of early Christianity. Both taught in Zürich.

113. [*Ed.*] See *ANF* 2:1–58.

114. Ritschl, *Entstehung*, 1st ed. (n.54), 297ff.; 2nd ed. (n. 38), 288ff.

born as Gentiles. But this just proves that by this time Jewish Christianity has already assumed a more liberal outlook.

As in the Book of Revelation, the underlying vision of *The Shepherd* is that of the twelve tribes of Israel. The believers among the Gentiles are added to the twelve peoples of God's community as replacements filling the gaps left by the unfaithful Jews. Prior to Christ's earthly appearance, the Jewish people were the ones especially overseen and guided by God. So too now, when Christ expiates the people's sins and gives it a new law that leads to life, we are simply to think of this people as the ancient people of God, not as a new people derived from the Gentiles. There are twelve apostles, corresponding to there being twelve tribes, a number emphasized as it is in the Book of Revelation. The result of doing so is the relegation of the Apostle Paul to the series of lesser teachers and proclaimers of the Son of God. The writer's perspective is so completely imbued with the character of legalism that everything just turns on obeying the divine commandments and on the meritoriousness of works. Faith itself stands at the top of the list of commandments. For *The Shepherd*, the universality of Christianity is undeniable only because the law imparted by Christ involves preaching about the Son of God to the ends of the earth, and because *The Shepherd* has the righteous ones of the Old Testament entering into the kingdom of God only after they have been baptized in the underworld, by the apostles and the evangelists.[115]

JUSTIN MARTYR

All of these writings contain, to one degree or another, the elements from which Catholic Christianity emerged. There is no truer representative of this transitional period than Justin Martyr. He stands just as close, on the one side, to the Apostolic Fathers as he does to the fathers of the Catholic Church on the other.

Like the writer of the Epistle of Barnabas, Justin too sees in Christianity a new law, based on Christianity being the first to gain the true understanding of the law, because the Jews misunderstood the ritual laws and religious institutions, which constitute the actual essence of Judaism, by applying them so much to the flesh.[116] Circumcision is not meant for the flesh as the Jews took it, but is instead to be understood only as the spiritual circumcision of removing the foreskin of the heart. The patriarchs had indeed undergone this spiritual circumcision, and Christians now do so by baptism, in which, as sinners, they receive forgiveness of sins by God's mercy.[117]

Everything of this kind—the sabbath and festivals, the dietary laws, the sacrifices and temple rituals—has only a spiritual meaning, one referring to Christianity. Stipulation of all these directives was therefore a merely transitory arrangement; they were

---

115. We see the evidence for this latter point in Hilgenfeld's article in the *Zeitschrift für wissenschaftliche Theologie* (n. 11), 423ff., and in his *Die apostolische Väter* (n. 102), 161ff.

116. See ch. 14 of Justin's *Dialogue with Trypho*. [*Ed.*] ANF 1:194–270.

117. Ibid., ch. 43.

just given because of the people's hardness of heart, and were only supposed to serve, at least in this external way, to prompt the people to think of God. We see most clearly that these practices have no religious value on their own, from the fact that they did not yet exist in the days of the patriarchs. So the patriarchs gained God's favor without them; God certainly counted Abraham as righteous because of his faith, not because of his being circumcised. Since God is forever the same God, is no different in Moses' day than in Enoch's day, all these directives of the Jewish religion can have only been specified for a particular time period.[118] Justin even downgrades circumcision to such an extent that he declares it to be the sign said to have made the Jews stand out from all other peoples, as those who deservedly suffer what others inflict on them.

This sheds light on a general characteristic of Justin's thinking regarding everything of religious significance in Judaism. In Justin's view it all reduces to prophecies, types, and allegories that could only be recognized for what they are, in themselves, from the standpoint of Christianity. He says this of course so that his religious consciousness, finding Judaism repellent, turns all the more to the Old Testament instead. The richer and more profound contents of his Christian consciousness could only connect up with the Old Testament by recognizing its prophetic and allegorical meaning. With all its ties to Paulinism, this stance toward the Old Testament is essentially different from the Pauline one. As in the case of the Epistle to the Hebrews, Justin's stance is not so much Pauline as it is Alexandrian. As is characteristic of Alexandrian Judaism, Justin places greater emphasis on the typological, symbolic, allegorical way of understanding the Old Testament, so that the Old Testament too remains the absolute source of truth. Thus howsoever much Judaism is downgraded in relation to Christianity, and emphasis falls on the full extent of the difference between them, the predominant factor from this standpoint is always a firm grip on Christianity's concern, and identity, with Old Testament religion.

For Paulinism, the absolute content of Christianity is directly in Christianity itself, in the spiritual consciousness awakened by faith and for which everything of an Old Testament character can only have very secondary significance. In contrast, that other view is so imbued with an Old Testament way of looking at things that, for it, even the truth of Christianity is mediated only via the Old Testament; and everything Christian is already to be found in the Old Testament, with the newness of

---

118. Justin distinguishes three elements in the Old Testament, a moral element, a typological element, and a purely spiritual element. In *Dialogue with Trypho*, ch. 44, he says that no one can receive something of the good things bestowed by Christ except those who are, in their minds, like the faith of Abraham and who know all the mysteries. He writes there: "I say that some injunctions were laid on you, in reference to the worship of God and practice of righteousness; but some injunctions and acts were likewise mentioned in reference to the mystery of Christ, on account of the hardness of your people's hearts" [ET from *ANF* 1:217 here and below]. In ch. 45, with reference to the moral contents of the Old Testament, Justin speaks of what "is naturally good, and pious, and righteous," in other words of what is "universally, naturally, and eternally good." This is precisely the main content of the religion of the patriarchs, which is distinct from the purely positive element, which "was appointed to be performed by reason of the hardness of the people's hearts."

Christianity being just the novelty of the consciousness that has arisen by surpassing the [literal] Old Testament. The absolute antithesis Paulinism established between law and gospel thus increasingly became a merely relative and subjective opposition.

Yet as long as people did not know how to say anything different than Justin did, about historical Judaism being meaningful only for a limited time, this view still remained very unstable. Although Justin did also mention the idea that pinpointed in a more specific way the relation of Christianity to the Old Testament revelation, mainly through the idea of the Logos now coming into the picture, this idea is nevertheless just a point of intersection between them. This failure to pinpoint Christian consciousness in stricter terms, a failure that makes Justin's position still so unstable and uncertain, also finds expression in his judgment concerning the Jewish Christians in his day. Given his low estimation of Judaism, one should have expected from him a harsher verdict also regarding the sort of people who, as Christians, were not so much Christians as they were Jews. However, he does not want to deny the hope of blessedness even for those who, while indeed believing in Christ, at the same time observe the Mosaic law, just so long as they do not also wish to make that compulsory for Gentile Christians. He merely disapproves of there also being Jewish Christians who do not want to associate in any way with Gentile Christians. So Justin has no reservations about acknowledging, as true brethren of the Christian community, those with weaker views who believe it necessary to link with hope in Christ, and observing those commandments involving eternal and natural righteousness, all the things Moses ordained on account of the people's hardness of heart—in such a way that these brethren live together with Christians without demanding of them that they be circumcised, and observe the sabbath and other laws of that kind.[119]

Praise for this liberal view taken toward Judaism is undercut, on the other hand, by how strictly Justin rules out everything not in agreement with his view. The more liberal Pauline view regarding eating the flesh of animals sacrificed to idols so little suits him, that he declares this act just as abominable as paganism, and he will have no manner of Christian fellowship with all those who permit it.[120] Although this verdict is not initially directed at Pauline Christians, but only at Gnostics, we see from the general terms in which it is expressed, and from how it contrasts with Justin's verdict about Jewish Christians, that for him what is ultimately decisive always favors Jewish Christianity rather than Pauline Christianity.

On other issues Justin presents us with entirely the same type of doctrine then looked upon as the most generally accepted expression of Christian consciousness. Christ has indeed taken upon himself, in accord with God's will, the curse all human beings bear for transgressing the law, and those believing in him are purified by his blood. However, the condition for forgiveness of sin is not faith in the Pauline sense. It is instead repentance, change of heart, obeying God's commandments, with Justin

---

119. *Dialogue with Trypho*, ch. 47.
120. Ibid., ch. 35.

especially stressing this obedience as the working of a person's own moral power.[121] Hence Christ is not so much redeemer as he is rather the teacher and lawgiver, as Justin expressly calls him.[122]

From all this we see that there is no simple answer as to whether Justin belongs to the Jewish Christian orientation or the Pauline one; whether his dogmatic standpoint is to be called Ebionitism or Paulinism. He cannot be placed definitely on either side, since his overall position is still too indeterminate and uncertain to pinpoint it more precisely. He sets himself apart from the Jewish Christians and declares that he agrees with them more superficially than wholeheartedly. Even more so, however, do we look in vain in Justin for an explicit acknowledgment of Pauline Christianity. Some contend that without a doubt Justin derived his view on Abraham's faith from the Epistle to the Romans and, by emphasizing justification by faith, he wished to present himself in general as a Paulinist.[123] If so, then it must just be all the more striking that not once has he even mentioned the name of the Apostle Paul. It will not suffice to explain this as merely due to Justin showing consideration for the Jews. Therefore if he is in fact a Paulinist, he nevertheless does not want to be called one. What we actually have in his case, though not expressed and openly declared as such, is Catholic Christianity, with the balancing out of the differences and partisan orientations that have been mutually opposed up to now.

We encounter in principle the same phenomenon here as we do in asking about Justin's use of the gospels. While there is no doubt that Justin indeed knew one or another of our canonical gospels, he has mentioned none by name. This is in fact how things stand, but there is not yet any term or name for this circumstance. Since there is no term for it, everything is not yet as established and delimited as the concept of Catholic Christianity calls for. Accordingly, Justin is forever just the transition to Catholic Christianity.[124]

---

121. See Ritschl, *Entstehung*, 1st ed. (n. 54), 310ff.; 2nd ed. (n. 38), 304.

122. *Dialogue*, ch. 18: Ὁ καινὸς νομοθέτης (the new lawgiver).

123. See Ritschl, *Entstehung*, 1st ed., 309; 2nd ed., 303.

124. In the second edition of his *Entstehung*, 310, Ritschl has disputed the position I assign to Justin. Ritschl contends that Pauline ideas are the predominant influence to be seen in Justin, albeit only in fragmentary form because this teacher is the first one to bring to its completion the idea of a new law. With regard to Justin's Paulinism, the following point is to be especially considered. Justin distinguishes just two classes of Christians (*Dialogue with Trypho*, chs. 35 and 80; cf. my article in the *Theologische Jahrbücher* 16 [1857] 219ff.). They are the true believers—who, as followers of the true, pure teachings of Jesus, believe in a resurrection of the flesh and in a thousand-year reign—and those who indeed profess faith in Jesus and call themselves Christians, but eat the flesh from sacrificial offerings to idols and maintain that this does no harm to them, that is, "Gnostics," as Justin afterwards calls them. Thus the question is: to which of these two classes does Justin assign the Pauline Christians? In this connection a further contention is that Justin's verdict about eating flesh from sacrificial offerings to idols could not have been directed against either Paul or a faction of Paul's, because Paul himself refused to approve of it, and because First Corinthians 10:20–21 directly forbids participation in pagan sacrificial meals. The question is whether this is not a very one-sided way of understanding the part of First Corinthians (i.e., chs. 8–10) bearing on this issue. The Apostle Paul did not simply forbid eating

PETER AND PAUL IN BROTHERLY UNITY

We now have to see how this transition took place. If we look back to our starting point, we see that the course of development was specifically influenced not only by the antithesis between two essentially different orientations, but also by the discord between the two apostles serving as their leaders. The two orientations did gradually come closer together, the original acrimony of the antithesis diminished, and people on both sides strove toward a midpoint uniting the antitheses as much as possible. However, it is nevertheless problematic as to how the two apostles, at odds in the controversy, reconciled in turn and came to an understanding. If people cannot be certain that the founders of the church themselves joined hands peacefully and acknowledged each other as brothers, then there is no firm foundation for uniting the two parties and guaranteeing an ongoing unity of the church. People could not remain in doubt about this. The fact that every possible remaining doubt on this point disappeared just when, in [the writings of] its main representatives, the Catholic Church assumed its full form, is the clearest proof that this is where the issue got settled.

We find Irenaeus first stating, as a truth that had already become established fact, that "the very great, the very ancient, and universally known church [was] founded and organized at Rome by the two most glorious apostles, Peter and Paul."[125] Tertullian says about the Roman church: "How happy is its church, on which apostles poured forth all their doctrine along with their blood! Where Peter endures a passion like his Lord's! Where Paul wins his crown in a death like John's!"[126] From this time onward—with Irenaeus and Tertullian, Clement of Alexandria and Origen, all the church fathers of that time, fully agreeing on the doctrine and tradition, and all the principles, of the ecclesiastical functions attesting to the Catholic Church as an ongoing institution—all memory of a split between the two apostles, and of them having disparate views, has completely disappeared. The authority of one apostle is now established as equal to that of the other. The canon of the New Testament scriptures, as the essential foundation of the Catholic Church now taking shape, is gradually established, including in particular the writings of Paul, which were least in doubt as to their canonical standing. Giving the two apostles equal standing is no longer merely something aspired to, as it was for the writer of the Book of Acts. What he envisaged is

---

the flesh from sacrificial offerings to idols, for at the same time he also was open to it and declared it a matter of indifference, both intrinsically and as looked at subjectively. In any event he spoke of it in such a way that one could on good grounds appeal to his authority for the latter view. On this issue, Paulinism and Gnosticism are not far apart. That is why a Christian like Justin, who was so obsessed with the thought of demonic paganism, could harbor doubts about how he had to look upon Paulinism in general. This quite naturally explains his silence about Paulinism by name. But one should not infer from this anything other than that his view about Paulinism was still unstable and indecisive.

125. *Against Heresies* 3.3 [ANF 1:415].
126. *The Prescription against Heretics*, ch. 63 [ANF 3:260].

now actually achieved. What then seemed to be a necessary presupposition, if the idea of the church was to be realized, has now become the widely-held belief in the church.

In the Roman church itself it passes for a historical tradition that each of the two apostles suffered a martyr's death in Rome. In the time of Caius, a Roman presbyter, at the beginning of the third century, people pointed out the place where they were slain as martyrs, and lay buried.[127] If this were clearly historical fact, we would have to just stick with it as simply historical truth. But since, in form and content, this legend is contrary to all historical likelihood, and since one can, for good reasons, also doubt that Peter had ever come to Rome, the historical significance of the legend is precisely in its not being historically true—for a tradition so lacking in a historical basis can only be the product of a special interest.[128] After our preceding discussion, no more need be said as to what that interest was. People wanted to bring the two apostles as close together as they could. Each one was said to share in the other one's merit and renown. As they had collaborated harmoniously in life, so too their deaths were said to attest to, and authenticate, the brotherly communion of their apostolic careers. We need only trace how the legend took shape in order to see how pains were taken to set aside the obstacles to gaining the desired outcome.

The two Epistles of Peter in particular contain noteworthy data that are pertinent. Second Peter is not only definitely pseudonymous, but is also one of the latest writings in the canon. One need only ponder how the writer has the Apostle Peter speaking, near the end, about the Apostle Paul as "our beloved brother" (3:15). He says that Paul, "according to the wisdom given him," has written about the topic discussed in this epistle, the imminent denouement, "speaking of this as he does in all his letters. There are some things in them hard to understand, which the ignorant and the unstable twist to their own destruction" (3:15–16).[129] The Apostle Paul is indeed acknowledged here, in brotherly fashion, as an apostle. What pains his brother and fellow apostle takes to counter the prejudice people might still have harbored toward the Apostle Paul's epistles, and the misconceptions they were exposed to! Indeed, Paul's epistles are even placed here in a single grouping with the canonical scriptures.

Even setting aside other indications of a mediating tendency that can be found in 2 Peter, certainly its testimony to Paul's apostolic authority, set forth so directly in speaking of the Apostle himself, can only mean it has a specific intention in doing this. The Epistle just expresses what the overwhelming majority must have long felt:

---

127. Eusebius, *Ecclesiastical History* 2.25.

128. See my *Paulus* (n. 5), 232–33 [ET 1:233].

129. It is doubtful whether, in 3:16, the text should read ἐν αἷς [referring to the things "hard to understand"] or ἐν οἷς [referring to the letters themselves as "hard to understand"]. But even if we choose the latter of these readings, we see from the following clause, "as they do the other scriptures," that the things to which the relative clause refers can only be things spoken about in Paul's epistles. Thus δυσνόητα ("hard to understand") can only refer to Paul's epistles. What did the writer of 2 Peter have in mind in using this term? Surely Gal 2:11–14 [the conflict between Peter and Paul over circumcision], as well as other passages.

that there was no reason to refuse giving the Apostle Paul the recognition to which he had most legitimately laid claim, because of his writings and all the reminders of his apostolic activity.[130]

This same tendency is also recognizable in 1 Peter and, given the same setting, it probably has this tendency all the more because its apostolic origin is so improbable. If the Apostle Peter cannot possibly have written an epistle widely judged to be so Paulinizing and so strikingly dependent on the epistles of the Apostle Paul, then 1 Peter too can only be looked upon as further documentation of the endeavor to show that there actually was harmony between the two apostles. This is precisely the aim of the explicit statement at the conclusion, that "through Silvanus, whom I consider a faithful brother, I have written this short letter" (5:12).[131] It wholly fits the style of such purportedly apostolic epistles to betray the tendency of their writing also by casually mentioning such incidental factors, by inserting the names of well-known apostolic assistants. So here we have Peter writing his epistle "through Silvanus," the well-known companion of the Apostle Paul, similar to how the Petrine Clement is Paul's co-worker (Phil 4:3), and the same Mark that Peter calls his son (1 Pet 5:13) also appears at Paul's side (Col 4:10). It is as though these companions and co-workers were supposedly the go-betweens for the two apostles. How then could one doubt that the two apostles were on friendly terms, if their friends and associates are so much at home with either of them?

The "Babylon" in which the author writes 1 Peter can only be Rome. So we should assume that the concern for unity giving rise to these Epistles of Peter is also mainly present in the Roman church. The Apostle Paul had indeed counted on a better mutual understanding in the Roman congregation. Thus many writings aimed at the same goal, for instance the Book of Acts, which was probably written in Rome. No other community was so highly motivated to seek such a reconciliation. Here in Rome each of the apostles had equal standing: Paul, owing to the powerful historical memory of his influence; Peter, who early on was considered to be the leader of the Roman congregation. This leadership on Peter's part also fit with the character of the Roman congregation, in which the Jewish-Christian element was predominant from the outset, so that, with all the efforts to give the two apostles parity, the Apostle Peter was nevertheless always given a certain precedence over the Apostle Paul.

---

130. The highest official predicate the Petrine side assigns to the Apostle Paul is "fellow-apostle of Peter." For instance, in the *Apostolic Constitutions* 6.8, Peter speaks of "Clement the bishop and citizen of Rome, who was the disciple of Paul, our fellow-apostle and co-worker in the gospel" [*ANF* 7:453]. Right at the beginning of 2 Peter the writer speaks to the Gentile Christians in the name of the Jewish Christians, as those whose faith has the same value and the same justification as the faith of others. In doing so, however, this Jewish-Christian author, writing under the name of Peter and wanting this work to be recognized as his parting legacy (1:13–15), continually hints at the precedence Peter has as the eyewitness to Christ's glory, and praises Paul only for his wisdom (3:15).

131. See my treatise in the 1856 *Theologische Jahrbücher* (n. 98) 237.

II. The Mediation

We find a territorial division intentionally drawn up in chapter 15 of the Epistle to the Romans, a chapter doubtless added by a later hand. It assigns Paul to the east, only as far west as Illyria, and in the west he just sets his sights on Spain, with the result that he seems to have only passed through Rome (15:24). This division is explainable only as intended to draw geographical lines, so to speak, demarcating two apostolic domains, by reserving to another apostle [Peter] all the land areas in between these lines, that is, Rome, Italy, and neighboring Gaul.[132] Thus the actual apostle of the Roman congregation must forever remain the Apostle Peter. However, if the other side concedes as much, then the bond of brotherly unity becomes all the firmer.[133] The way Catholic consciousness developed so early and so consistently in no other church than the one in Rome fittingly gives it the merit of having first established this essential foundation of Catholicism.

---

132. See my article ["Zur neutestamentliche Kritik..."] in the *Theologische Jahrbücher* 8 (1849) 493ff.

133. According to the *Apostolic Constitutions* 7.46, the first two bishops in Antioch were ordained by Peter and Paul respectively, and the same is true of the first two bishops in Rome. It is clear that the Paulinist bishop Linus was inserted in the list between Peter and Clement only in the interest of parity. In fact, Clement was the Apostle Peter's successor in Rome. See the *Epistle of Clement to James*, chs. 2, 19; Tertullian, *The Prescription against Heretics*, ch. 32; Jerome, *Against Jovinanius*, 1.7, and *De viris illustribus* (On Illustrious Men), ch. 15. In the *Theologische Jahrbücher* 15 (1856) 309ff., and 16 (1857) 147ff., G. Volkmar perceptively conjectures that the key to interpreting the puzzling passage, Phil 4:2, is to be found in the relationship of the two apostles and of their factions.

III. Johannine Christianity

THE APOSTLE JOHN;
THE APOCALYPTIC WRITER AND THE GOSPEL WRITER

Our historical examination now turns from the sphere where the great antitheses, bearing the names of the Apostle Peter and the Apostle Paul, got resolved by developing into the unity of the Roman church. We now look at another dimension of the development, one in which the self-realizing idea of the Catholic Church took a distinctive course.

We still have to ask how things stand with the other pillar of the apostles, the Apostle John. We have to consider him as an added factor alongside Peter, who is now in brotherly unity with the Apostle Paul, and in addition to James, who is just associated with the Jerusalem community. What are we to make of the whole set of phenomena that comes to a head in the Gospel of John? As we have already shown, the Apostle John, as one of the pillar apostles, as Paul's successor in his sphere of influence in Ephesus, and as the author of the Book of Revelation, stands in a different setting from that of the Apostle Paul.

However, the Gospel of John is our main focus here, and it forms a new nexus in the development.[134] At this point the well-known, critical issues concerning this Gospel, questions about its apostolic origin and its relation to the Apocalypse, or Book of Revelation, appear here in their great historical significance, since a gospel such as this one could only take shape, and be conceivable, upon the transition to the Catholic

---

134. On this topic, see the following works: my *Kritische Untersuchungen über die kanonischen Evangelien* (n. 30), 77ff.; K. R. Köstlin's articles ["Zur Geschichte des Urchristentums" and "Die pseudonyme Litteratur der ältesten Kirche"] in the *Theologische Jahrbücher* 9 (1850) 277f., and 10 (1851) 183ff.; Adolf Hilgenfeld, *Die Evangelien nach ihrer Entstehung und geschichtlichen Bedeutung* (Leipzig, 1854), 229ff.; my article "Die johanneische Frage, und ihre neuesten Beantwortungen (durch Luthardt, Delitzsch, Brückner, Hase)," *Theologische Jahrbücher* 13 (1854) 196–287; Karl Hase, *Die Tübinger Schule: Sendschreiben an Dr. Baur* (Leipzig, 1855), 1ff.; my *An Herrn Dr. Karl Hase: Beantwortung des Sendschreibens "Die Tübinger Schule"* (Tübingen, 1855), 8ff.; Hilgenfeld, *Das Urchristentum in den Hauptwendenpunkten seines Entwicklungsganges* (Jena, 1855), 6ff.; my article "Zur johanneischen Frage über Justin den Märtyrer," *Theologische Jahrbücher* 16 (1857) 209–57; and my *Die Tübinger Schule und ihre Stellung zur Gegenwart* (Tübingen, 1859), 83ff.

III. Johannine Christianity

Church, the transition signified for us in the Roman church by the legend regarding the Apostle Peter and the Apostle Paul. The more carefully we trace the course of the historical development, the more we must be convinced that there is such a great difference and antithesis between the Book of Revelation and the Gospel of John, that even the Apostle John's allegedly long life would be insufficient to span the gap between them. Hence the fact that it does not engage with the earlier course of the historical development can only be based on the contents and character of the Gospel of John itself. But if we go by that reasoning, what basis is there for accepting such an early date for the Gospel, when for such a long time period there is not the slightest historical evidence for its existence?

On the other hand, however, it would be just as misguided if, given their differences and opposed perspectives, one were to overlook the close connection between the Gospel and the Book of Revelation, quite apart from the issue of their authors. While it can hardly be accepted that the author of the Gospel is one and the same person as the writer of Revelation, it is almost unmistakable that the Gospel writer thought of himself as writing in the stead of the apocalyptic author, and wanted to utilize, for purposes of his Gospel, the prestige of John, who, as the Apostle, the author of Revelation, and for so many years the leader at the head of the community, had been the highest authority in the church in Asia Minor. Certainly the writer of the Gospel is not merely relying on his use of a much-celebrated name, because there are also internal connections between the Gospel and Revelation. One can only admire the great ingenuity and artistry with which the Gospel writer has adopted elements that lead from the standpoint of the Apocalypse to the freer and higher standpoint of the Gospel, in order to "spiritualize" the Apocalypse into the Gospel. The way the writer positions himself in relation to the Apocalypse is only correctly understood from the Gospel's standpoint.

The Gospel writer had to be aware that his standpoint was new and distinctive, one essentially different from both Pauline and Jewish Christian perspectives. Thus he must have felt the necessity to express this new form of Christian consciousness in an authentically apostolic way. Since the names of the two apostles, Peter and Paul, already represented specific orientations in the Christian world at that time, what better name could serve his purpose but that of the Apostle John? Especially so in the place where the name of the Apostle John held the greatest significance, where the Gospel of John is customarily regarded as having originated; but also because this name provided so many starting points for gaining a higher understanding of Christianity, since the Book of Revelation was in fact deemed, in Asia Minor, to have been written by the Apostle John. Hence, in the context of our treatment of the Gospel of John, we will use the name of the Apostle John simply as a way of designating a new and distinctive form of consciousness, and we have to keep our attention focused above all on how it differs from the two other orientations, the Jewish Christian and the Pauline perspectives.

THE GOSPEL OF JOHN

The Complete Break with Judaism; Its Antithesis

The feature of the Gospel of John that most sets it apart from the other orientations is its idea of the Logos. The writer has expressed the absolute content of his Christian consciousness in the most definite and direct way with this idea. Yet this idea itself is just the [idea of the] unity of the different contexts and antitheses within which the gospel writer situates himself. His way of looking at things completely transcends the other two orientations, in order to embrace them, together with Judaism and paganism, in a higher unity comprising all humanity.

In his view of Judaism, the gospel writer is farthest removed from the author of Revelation. The latter links everything to the prominence of Jerusalem, where, in a nutshell, the absolute significance of Christianity is to be found; whereas for the gospel writer, "the hour is coming when you will worship the Father neither on this mountain [Gerizim] nor in Jerusalem," for the true worshipers of God are only those who "will worship the Father in spirit and truth" (John 4:21, 23). Therefore paganism and Judaism stand in the same negative relation to Christianity as the one true and absolute religion. Of course Judaism does take precedence over paganism because it knows it is worshiping God, for its worship is directed to the true object of religious consciousness (4:22); because, in knowing the one true God there is also eternal life (17:3); because messianic salvation therefore can come only from the Jews (4:22); also because there is ongoing prophecy of, and allusion to, a redeemer of the world in the scriptures of the Old Testament. (John 5:46; 6:45; 8:56; 12:41, and other passages refer to these Old Testament elements.) However, paganism also plays a certain part with reference to this light of the Logos, which from the beginning "shines in the darkness" (1:4, 9). As the gospel writer especially emphasizes in 11:52, if Jesus was not said to die solely for the Jewish people, but instead, by his death, "to gather into one the dispersed children of God," then that must have meant the children of God dispersed in the pagan world as well.

Inasmuch as the Jews have not believed in Jesus, the gospel writer, in authentically Pauline fashion, sees coming to fulfillment in the Gentile world what remained unfulfilled as far as the Jews were concerned. He assumes far greater receptivity for the word of God, and for belief in Jesus, in the Gentile world, and in several passages (see, for instance, chap. 4, as well as 12:20[135]) he explicitly shows preference for Gentiles over Jews. The phrase "one flock, one shepherd" (10:16) indicates as much. If the Jews do not make up the flock all by themselves, for "I have other sheep . . . [and] must bring them also," then these others had to make up more of the flock in proportion as the Jewish people, in its unbelief, responded negatively to the gospel. The unbelief of the Jews at all the stages where it is manifest is certainly one aspect of the Gospel's

---

135. [*Ed.*] Baur writes 12:30. Chap. 4 narrates the story of the Samaritan woman; in 12:20 John says that Greeks were among those who came to the Passover.

main theme. The gospel writer concludes his presentation of Jesus' public activity by emphasizing that, notwithstanding all the disclosures of Jesus' glory, the Jews have not believed in him (12:36–43).

The ultimate consequence of such unbelief, every form of which increasingly grew more intense, could only be the kind of denouement we see in the death of Jesus. Hence his death is simply something orchestrated by the Jews, and the heavy burden of guilt for it falls on them alone. But because the whole power of darkness reveals itself in an unbelief so typified by an entire people, that makes the crisis ensuing in Jesus' death all the more significant. In the Johannine portrayal of the gospel story, the two principles of light and darkness are the moving forces in their antithesis, and are set over against each other in the death of Jesus. Thus the entire period of Old Testament religious history has its terminal point in the moment of this death.

In order that the death of Jesus shall appear in the full meaning of this crisis, the gospel writer quite intentionally brings in whatever in Old Testament passages may make a reference to it. Everything that, in the Old Testament prototypes and prophecies, still looks forward to being finally realized must now be completely realized, so that the scriptures will be fulfilled (John 19:24, 28, 36–37). The writer's leading idea on this matter is expressed in the last words of the dying Jesus himself, in the statement "It is finished" (τετέλεσται, 19:30). What is completed is in fact everything that had to happen to Jesus, as the Messiah, "in order to fulfill the scripture" (19:28) of the Old Testament. We must adopt this grand historical perspective ourselves if we wish to understand correctly the writer's portrayal of the death of Jesus. What ensues in the moment of Jesus' death is the turning point between the two religious forms of life, the sudden change from the Old Testament, Judaic consciousness to the New Testament, Christian consciousness. The old way has run its course and come to an end, and the new one has come into being. With his final words on the cross, he who was sent by the Father has completely met all the demands that Judaism and the Old Testament had justifiably placed on him as the promised Messiah, and now he stands in a completely free relation to all that went before.

Judaism and the Old Testament now belong to a period that has already run its course. We can also take this as simply a sign that this Gospel originated at a later time, from the fact that the writer sees Judaism as something long gone for him. He takes the antithesis of Judaism to Christianity as very much a lifeless, settled historical fact. Everything of a positive nature in Judaism—the sabbath, and circumcision (7:22–23)—is a matter of complete indifference from the writer's standpoint. Most tellingly, he even speaks of the Mosaic law as something that concerns only the Jews, something only they can call their law (8:17 and 10:34: "in your law"). "The law indeed was given through Moses; grace and truth came through Jesus Christ" (1:17). Accordingly, the gospel sets aside the law. Since the Jews have rejected the grace and truth of the gospel so decidedly and openly, Judaism has pronounced judgment on itself.

The gospel writer's consciousness has become so divorced from any connection with Judaism that concern for the Jewish nation—something the Apostle Paul showed in still keeping open encouraging and conciliatory prospects for Judaism, at least in the future—is entirely foreign to him. As a result of the antithetical relation in which he sets Judaism and paganism, when he anticipates in the Gentile world the glorification of the Son of Man that was not accorded him in the Jewish world, the writer can only have the punishment for unbelief fall upon Judaism with the same force that the author of the Book of Revelation has it falling on paganism. Christianity's break with Judaism—something for the Apostle Paul just taking the form of a dialectical process, as only an ongoing interaction—has become, in the Johannine framework, an accomplished fact.

A further element also deserving special attention here is that the author of John is the first one to determine more precisely how the Old Testament is related to Christianity, prophetically and typologically. However much one disparages historical Judaism and looks upon it disdainfully, if one nevertheless sees in the Old Testament the archetypal idea of Christianity—by laying great stress on the Old Testament prophecies, types, and symbols so that, through them, we first know what Christianity is, so that a truly Christian consciousness first emerges in light of them—then Judaism and Christianity have grown so internally connected in content and form that neither can be without the other, that someone can only be conscious of Christianity's contents in the form contained in the Old Testament. The Gospel of John then takes the further important step where, instead of holding fast to the image or type because of the thing it signifies, and viewing the two as essentially one, now the image is declared to be completely obsolete and set aside, a form become entirely meaningless, as soon as the thing it signifies has come on the scene, the full reality that previously had just been there as a type or image.

Christ the True Passover Lamb

For John, the most important and most significant of all the Old Testament symbols in this sense is the Passover lamb. The writer's religious concern is expressed more directly and emphatically in John 19:33–37 than it is anywhere else. The event of Jesus' death has its supreme significance in the fact that blood and water flowed out from Jesus' pierced side. Blood and water could have flowed from Jesus' side only because it had been pierced, and it was pierced because the piercing was done instead of breaking his bones. His bones were not allowed to be broken, because the words of scripture about the Passover lamb[136] had to be fulfilled in his case (v. 36).

Thus Jesus himself is the Passover lamb. But if so, then he can only be the true and actual Passover lamb, as distinct from the mere type in Judaism that has reached

---

136. [*Ed.*] See Exod 12:5: "Your lamb shall be without blemish."

its appointed end; for, as a rule, the image or type ceases to be what it is as soon as the thing to which it refers is present. The moment in which the typified Passover lamb has become the true and actual Passover lamb in the crucified Christ, is the very turning point at which Judaism ceases to be what it formerly was; when its absolute significance has come to an end, and Christianity comes forward in its place, as the true religion. The blood and water flowing from the side of Jesus, as the true Passover lamb, are symbolic of the spiritual life imparting itself in all its fullness to humankind, via the medium of Jesus' death. We see how significant envisaging the true and actual Passover lamb in Christ is for the gospel writer, mainly from the influence this idea has had on his presentation of the gospel story.

This influence is the simple explanation for the well-known difference between John and the Synoptic Gospels as to the day of Jesus' death. If Christ is truly and actually the Passover lamb, then he can only have died on the same day and at the same time when Passover lambs were slain by the Jews following their legal tradition—thus not as the Synoptic Gospels report, according to what is doubtless their historical tradition, on the fifteenth of Nisan, but on the fourteenth. However, if he died as the Passover lamb on the fourteenth, then the consequence is that he cannot have shared in the Passover meal on this day. Therefore if he nevertheless had a meal with his disciples prior to his death, it can only have been held on the previous day, the thirteenth, and for that reason too it cannot have been a Passover meal. This timing is also a feature of the Gospel of John's discrepant account.

Thus for the Christian everything pertaining to the [Jewish] Passover feast utterly has no further significance. It is forever obsolete and set aside, in that Christ himself, as the Passover lamb, died on the eve of that Passover festival. Because of this, Christianity has now for the first time completely divorced itself from its link to Judaism. Here too Judaism and Christianity are related as type or image, and reality. But how can there be any interest in going back to the type and immersing oneself in looking at Old Testament types and symbols, when one has the thing itself? How, when the thing itself so involves what is absolutely real, that in principle nothing except it has any real significance?

There is a new antithesis connected with the idea of Christ as the true and fitting Passover lamb. It is noteworthy that the more objectionable Christian consciousness finds Judaism to be, the more it holds firmly to this idea of the Passover lamb. Whereas, the more it still has a home in Judaism, and regards Judaism and Christianity as essentially one, the more its interest in this idea moves to the background; for even though Christ counts as the Passover lamb, this predicate is just on a par with other types and symbols applicable to him. The first one who called Christ "our" Passover lamb is the Apostle Paul, when he admonished the Corinthians to "clean out the old yeast so that you may be a new batch, as you really are unleavened. For our paschal lamb, Christ, has been sacrificed" for us (1 Cor 5:7). Perhaps it was just by chance that he hit upon this idea, directly connecting different thoughts in writing this Epistle shortly before Easter, and thus simply calling Christ the Passover lamb, just like his applying the image of leaven to Christians. So Paul was the first one to express this idea. Given his view of Judaism, he could not have taken this idea to mean a Christianity holding fast to Judaism; instead, only one separating from it.

Paul draws no further conclusions from this idea. The only thing that could have seemed to relate in any specific way to his idea of the Passover lamb is his description of Jesus' final meal and the instituting of the Lord's Supper; but there he says nothing about it being a Passover meal. Instead, he just speaks of "the night in which he [the Lord Jesus] was betrayed" (1 Cor 11:23). Therefore although Paul certainly knew, from the tradition to which he appeals, that this meal was a Passover meal, this fact still has no further significance for him. In his mind the main thing was not the connection of Jesus' actions with ancient Jewish festival customs; instead it was only the new thing Jesus intended, the instituting of a new covenant. Paul did not agree in general with the practice of "observing special days, and months, and seasons, and years" (Gal 4:10) that was so closely connected to compliance with Jewish festival customs, and he rejected their being bound up with the forces of nature, as an element still clinging to Judaism but unworthy of true religion. Thus he also could not countenance the remembrance of the Lord, which was said to be the aim of celebrating the Lord's Supper, being linked to the annual reenactment of the Jewish Passover festival.

The Pauline author of the Gospel of Luke of course also agrees with the other Synoptic Gospels in describing Jesus' final meal as a Passover meal. He even has Jesus saying, "I have eagerly desired to eat this Passover with you before I suffer" (Luke 22:15). In Luke's recounting this it is as though he has done full justice to Judaism and to the older apostles; however, he then in contrast emphasizes even more the other aspect of Jesus' actions by having the instituting of the Lord's Supper (vv. 19–20) follow after the holding of the Jewish Passover meal (vv. 15–18). This shows that the Lord's Supper replaces the Passover meal and appears as a new and essentially different action on Jesus' part. So this is already the first step in the transition from the Synoptics' portrayal to the Johannine one, which completely cuts itself off from the Jewish seasonal Passover meal.[137]

Accordingly, the Johannine idea of Christ as the true and fitting Passover lamb already has such a point of contact with the Paulinism [in Luke] that there can hardly be any doubt about an inner connection between the two. On the other hand, however, this idea is equally foreign to the two other Synoptic Gospels—which are otherwise so careful to point out the fulfilling of Old Testament prophecies and types in Jesus, yet introduce none of the Old Testament passages referring to the Passover lamb—and to the writer of the Book of Revelation. We can only account for this by pointing to deeper underlying differences between two major orientations. Of course

---

137. See: Hilgenfeld, *Kritische Untersuchungen über die Evangelien Justins* (Halle, 1850), 472ff.; Köstlin, *Die Synoptischen Evangelien* (n. 30), 177; Hilgenfeld, *Die Evangelien* (n. 134), 213ff.

there can still always be a debate about the sense in which Revelation calls Jesus the ἀρνίον ἐσφαγμένον ("slaughtered lamb"; 6:8). Recently there has been very decided support for the view that the writer sought to designate him as the Passover lamb by using this expression.[138]

However, more careful consideration of the pertinent data must lead to a different conclusion. In the Book of Revelation there is no other passage even alluding to the Passover lamb. The expression "slaughtered lamb" is the only one there that can involve such a reference; however, it can equally well be referring to Isaiah 53:7 ["He was oppressed . . . like a lamb that is led to the slaughter"]. The application of this Isaiah passage to Jesus, which has already occurred in Acts 8:32–33, was so commonplace and routine that, where Christ is called "the Passover," it indicates not the slain Passover lamb but instead the prophet Isaiah's "lamb that is led to the slaughter." Thus it is indisputably far more fitting to have this sense in mind in the Book of Revelation too.[139] In Revelation, "led to the slaughter" is certainly predicated of "the lamb" in such an emphatic sense that much more is obviously being said here than just what is involved in the idea of the Passover lamb, which, in the first place, was not even looked upon as a propitiatory offering; furthermore its slaughtering had no special meaning other than what is obviously understood by the act itself. Here the meaning of such a slaughter can only be tied to the entire concept of calmly offering oneself for the sins of humankind, just as this is the main concept in the passage from the prophet.

If we are to ascribe to the Gospel writer the idea that Christ is the true and fitting Passover lamb, and do not attribute it to the author of Revelation, then we gain a perspective from which the two differ. We then see them as mutually antithetical, and very explicitly so.

The Passover Controversy

In Asia Minor, in the second half of the second century, there was a very lively controversy about the Christian celebration of Passover. There were two distinct factions in the Asia Minor church on this issue, and the majority faction in Asia Minor also came out in opposition to Rome. Bishop Polycrates of Ephesus and Bishop Victor of Rome stood on opposite sides at the height of the controversy. From these circumstances we first learn more precisely about the background factors that led to the controversy.

---

138. See Ritschl, *Entstehung*, 1st ed. (n. 54), 146ff., 2nd ed. (n. 38), 121ff.

139. See the passages cited by Ritschl from *The Testaments of the Twelve Patriarchs* (The Testament of Benjamin, ch. 3); Justin Martyr, *Dialogue with Trypho*, chs. 72 and 111; fragment from Clement of Alexandria quoted in the Paschal Chronicle [*ANF* 2:581]. Least probative is the reasoning that "the wrath of the Lamb" (Rev 6:16) would hardly fit with the image in Isaiah of a gentle lamb since, if gentleness and wrath are mutually exclusive, there cannot be any talk of a "wrath of the Lamb." Nor does Jeremiah 11:19, where the prophet speaks of himself as "like a gentle lamb led to the slaughter," a passage the author of Revelation doubtless had in mind, lead us to the Passover lamb.

The issue was initially raised when Bishop Polycarp of Smyrna came to Rome about the year 160, in order to confer with Bishop Anicetus of Rome about various church matters, including the question of the Passover feast. They could not agree. Anicetus could not persuade Polycarp to change his practice [as to the day for observing the feast], a practice he had kept in concert with the Apostle John and the other apostles he had associated with. Nor could Polycarp induce Anicetus to adopt that practice, for Anicetus appealed to the customary practice of his predecessors as what must be upheld. They nevertheless parted amicably and the peace of the church as a whole was not disturbed, even though the church was divided into two factions (those who observed it [the Quartodeciman practice] and those who did not observe it).[140]

But things changed a few years afterward, when an intense controversy arose in Laodicea about the year 170, just at the time when the feast was to be observed. Opinion was now divided even in the church in Asia Minor, and the controversy was pursued in writings about it. Melito, the bishop of Sardis, supported one side and Apollinaris, the bishop of Hierapolis, supported the other. Two fragments have survived from *On the Passover*, written by Apollinaris. Clement of Alexandria was prompted by Melito's text to oppose it and support the view that Apollinaris advocated.[141]

This was all just the prelude to the real dispute, which broke out about 190 and was no longer confined to the church in Asia Minor. The controversy extended to communities in other lands, and the main opposition to the church in Asia Minor was now the Roman church. As Eusebius tells us,[142] many synods met and issued letters about it. The communities of Asia, following their tradition, believed that they must observe the feast of the savior's Passover on the fourteenth day of the month of Nisan, the day on which the Jews were commanded to sacrifice the lamb, for this is the day on which the fast must be ended no matter on what day of the week it falls. On the contrary, the other communities, following the tradition of the apostles, observed what later had become the prevailing custom, that the fast should only be suspended on the day of the redeemer's resurrection.

Palestine, Pontus, Gaul, Osroëne [in Mesopotamia], and Greece took the side of the Roman church, whose bishop then was Victor. On the other side, the church in Asia Minor held most faithfully to the ancient custom. How very important this custom was for those from Asia Minor is apparent from the document Bishop Polycrates of Ephesus addressed to Bishop Victor on behalf of the bishops in Asia. He refers to all the luminaries of his [i.e., Asia's] church, the great princes of the church "sleeping in Asia" who "will rise on the day of the coming of the Lord." They include: the Apostle Philip and his two daughters, sleeping in Hierapolis, and a daughter resting in

---

140. See the letter that Irenaeus sent to Victor, the bishop of Rome, in the name of the brethren of Gaul, cited in Eusebius, *Ecclesiastical History* 5.24–25.

141. Eusebius, *Ecclesiastical History* 4.26. [*Ed.*] For Melito, see *ANF* 8:758; for Apollinaris, *ANF* 8:772–73; for Clement, *ANF* 2:581.

142. *Ecclesiastical History* 5.23.

Ephesus; "John, who lay on the Lord's breast, who was a priest wearing the breastplate, and a martyr and teacher"; "Polycarp at Smyrna, both bishop and martyr"; and many others who have all "kept the fourteenth day of the Passover according to the gospel." Polycrates writes that he too, who has grown grey in the service of the Lord, did not want to deviate from this day. He says: "I . . . have studied all holy scripture, am not afraid of threats," for those "greater than I" have said, "It is better to obey God rather than men."[143]

Because of this, Victor, the bishop of Rome, right away tried to deprive the congregations in all of Asia, and neighboring areas, of unity and fellowship with the church, regarding them as heterodox. He stigmatized them via letters in which he ended ecclesial fellowship with all the brethren there. For doing this, Victor was rebuked by those such as Irenaeus in Gaul, whose view on the substantive issue itself agreed with that of the Roman church, and who likewise maintained that "the mystery of the Lord's resurrection be observed only on the Lord's day."[144]

Since the actual issue in dispute had always been a very thorny one, there could only be a very unsatisfactory resolution. Even today the only correct view is still not so secure that it need not contend with opposition to it. One could have thought that the Asia Minor faction, as a strict Judaizing party, would have observed Passover in just a wholly Jewish fashion. But such was not the case. There is no indication of that in the polemic of its opponents, who could not have kept silent if it were true. In Asia Minor Passover was also the "Passover of the savior" or the "saving Passover," that is, a Christian feast. In it the Jewish Passover had taken on the character of a Christian feast in the form it received from the way Jesus himself had observed it with the disciples prior to his passion.

For those referred to as "Quartodecimans,"[145] the distinguishing feature was specifically their sticking to the fourteenth day of the Jewish month of Nisan, just like the Jews for whom this was the actual day of Passover and from which the following days were customarily distinguished as the feast of unleavened bread. In the history of the controversy this practice is what the constantly recurring expression τηρεῖν (observing) refers to. The complete formulation in the document by Polycrates is: τηρεῖν τῆν ἡμέραν τῆς τεσσαρεσκαιδεκάτης τοῦ πάσχα (observing the fourteenth day of the Passover). It is still not clear from this what significance this day would have had for them. The closest indication is that they declared it was utterly necessary to end the fast on this date, whereas their opponents did not want to cease the traditional pre-Easter fast until the Sunday on which Christ's resurrection was celebrated. So the day

---

143. [Ed.] See Eusebius, *Ecclesiastical History* 5.24.2-7. Polycrates' letter, paraphrased here, is in ANF 8:773-74.

144. [Ed.] *Ecclesiastical History* 5.24.9-11.

145. [Ed.] The term "Quartodeciman" means "fourteenth." Baur goes into this lengthy discussion in order to establish that the Gospel of John, reflecting the influence of the Quartodeciman or Passover Controversy, must have been written in the second half of the second century.

of the resurrection, of course always a Sunday, had an importance for one group that the fourteenth of the month, on whatever day it fell, had for the other group. But what special feature makes the fourteenth of Nisan important for those Christians?

It is too hasty a conclusion to suppose that it is only a matter of the time of Jesus' resurrection versus the time of his death, and that the difference between the two factions simply hinges on where to draw the line where festive joy begins and sorrowful fasting ends: whether already on 14 Nisan or only on Easter Sunday. For the West, the resurrection was the memorable and infinitely important day on which the small band of believers had been freed from all their fears; the day when, after the most horrible doubts and dark days following Jesus' death, they joyfully saw the light of redemption's reality. This day removed a huge burden from the disciples. For them it was truly the day of deliverance. For those in the East, on the other hand, the day of Jesus' death was of primary importance, for it too was extremely significant to them. Up until the onset of death the Lord's suffering was a painfully sorrowful event. But at the moment of his death the Lord's suffering ended, the great work of reconciliation was completed, eternal redemption was established, and Christ's glorification had begun. All this was so even though the disciples were not already clearly aware of it by that very day.

Hence the entire standpoint of the Western observance must be characterized as typically more subjective, personal, and individual, as historically situated and traditional, in sticking as closely as possible to the outer structure of the week's original events. The Eastern standpoint, on the other hand, represents a more objective, dogmatic, universal, and freely-constructed approach, inasmuch as its observance derives from the effort to express the essence or inner meaning of the salvific fact itself, rather than being a form of historical consciousness about this fact in the way it is celebrated. Thus in place of the outer physical structure of the week's events in determining the end point for observers of Christ's death, it adopts as its principle an ideal, religious-philosophical element situated within that week's events.[146]

There is no historical foundation supporting either side. Because of that the whole issue spills over far too much into the domain of a priori assumptions and abstract thinking. One cannot even say that the fasting is generally meaningful only where the leading idea is remembering Jesus' death, and that ending the fast on 14 Nisan could be based on the assumption that Christ died as the Passover lamb, and brought about reconciliation, on the 14th and not on the 15th.[147] There is a difference as to the customary fasting prior to Easter, as Irenaeus says in his letter: "For some think that they ought to fast one day, others two, others even more, [and] some count their day as forty hours, day and night."[148] This customary pre-Easter fast could in any

---

146. K. L. Weitzel, *Die christliche Passahfeier der drei ersten Jahrhunderte* (Pforzheim, 1848), 101, 110, 131.

147. Ritschl, *Entstehung*, 1st ed. (n. 54), 250; 2nd ed. (n. 38), 269.

148. For this statement, see Eusebius, *Ecclesiastical History* 5.24.12, where the Greek ends with: τὴν ἡμέραν αὐτῶν (their day). The meaning can only be that they made a span of forty hours, day and

event only have been with reference to Jesus' suffering and death. But it is also an erroneous conclusion to suppose that, because the fasting is a sign of sorrow, the cessation of fasting, the meal that takes its place, can only be expressing the opposite frame of mind, and that Christians in the East accordingly celebrated the day of Jesus' death as likewise a joyful feast like the day of the resurrection was for those in the West.[149] Even if Jesus' death could only have called to mind the reconciliation it accomplished, the feeling of sorrow had to be so overwhelming that it would be incomprehensible how Christians in the East could have stopped fasting right on the day of Jesus' death, simply in order to already express their joy.

Undoubtedly there must have been a particular motive for ceasing to fast, and the question is: What led them to celebrate this particular day, the 14th, not by fasting but by eating? Also, if they ate rather than fasting on this day, does that not first of all question the assumption that they observed this date as the day of Jesus' death? The answer is not to be found by clever conjectures; it is obvious in the fragments preserved from the *Chronicon Paschale*.[150] The basis for the different view is expressed in the most specific terms in a fragment from Hippolytus who, as a defender of the West's customary observance, has his "opponent" say: "What Christ carried out on that day was the Passover feast, after which he suffered, for which reason I too must in the same way do what the Lord has done." To this Hippolytus replies: "It is wrong to be unaware that, at the time Christ suffered, he had not eaten the law's Passover,

---

night, the measure of their "day"; that they believed they had to fast for forty hours, and they counted these forty hours as just one day. J. C. L. Gieseler (*Lehrbuch der Kirchengeschichte*, 10 vols. [Darmstadt, 1824–57], 1.1:240), wants the text to read: τῇ ἡμέρᾳ αὐτῶν (along with their day). Then his interpretation is that they apportion forty hours along with their day; that is, the fast for the day they celebrate as the Passover, or the day of Christ's death, and then they begin a new forty-hour fast, extending from the hour of his death up to the resurrection. This interpretation is definitely incorrect, since those in Asia Minor ceased fasting on the evening of the 14th.

149. The comments about this fasting that G. Steitz makes in *Theologische Studien und Kritiken* 32 (1859) 728ff., are simply further proof of how generally misguided is his entire view of the celebration of Passover in Asia Minor. He supposes that their fasting on this day would become completely incomprehensible if one assumes that the church in Asia Minor intended its celebration to be the commemoration of the Lord's last gathering with his disciples. For why should these Christians receive on an empty stomach what the Lord had given to the disciples during or after the meal on that evening? Of course that assumption would be exceedingly odd. But who says this? The main element of the view Steitz is contesting is certainly the very fact that the celebration of Passover in Asia Minor does not refer to Holy Communion or the Eucharist as such. Instead it refers to Jesus' final gathering with the disciples. How out of place it therefore is to have in mind the church's rule about not eating prior to communion, and how natural it is instead to regard this fasting as the expression of the sorrowful mood of the disciples on that day, beginning a time when "the bridegroom is taken away" (*sponsus ablatus est*) [an allusion to Matt 9:15, which in the Vulgate reads *auferetur ab eis sponsus*]. This is the same thing Herr Steitz himself says about this fasting (on p. 733), except that the focus is not on Jesus' death but is instead on the Lord who still lingers in the circle of the disciples albeit already undergoing his suffering. Herr Steitz could have spared himself much unnecessary verbiage had he first of all correctly understood his opponents' views.

150. In the Bonn edition of the *Corpus scriptorum historiae Byzantinae*, 2 vols. (1832), 1.13ff. [cf. ANF 8:772–73].

for he was the foretold Passover that was fulfilled on that specific day." In the same sense Hippolytus states, in another fragment: "As the Lord had already said that he no longer would eat the Passover, he ate this meal prior to Passover and did not eat on Passover but instead suffered then, for that was certainly not the time for him to eat it."

From this it is as clear as anything can be that Eastern Christians celebrated 14 Nisan not as the day of Jesus' death, but instead as the day on which he still held the Passover meal with his disciples. The point of controversy with their opponents involved the contrast between doing and suffering, or more specifically, between φαγεῖν (eating) and παθεῖν (suffering, the Passion). If Jesus ate the Passover lamb on the 14th, then he did not die on that day and therefore his death cannot be commemorated on the 14th. Instead one is only obligated to do the same thing he did, thus not to fast but instead to hold a meal too, in commemoration of the Passover meal held by Jesus, one that on its own concluded in this way the customary pre-Easter time of fasting. On the other hand, those in the West drew the opposite conclusion. They held that, because Jesus suffered and died on the 14th, he cannot have eaten the Passover meal on this date. Thus there is no reason to break the fast on the day when the Jewish Passover meal is held, or for 14 Nisan to have any bearing for the Christian celebration of Easter.

The same consequence follows from the fragments of Apollinaris of Hierapolis. His version of the contention of his opponents from the East is quite the same as we find in Hippolytus. He states that they "say that on the fourteenth day the Lord ate the lamb with the disciples, and that on the great day of the feast of unleavened bread he himself suffered; and they quote Matthew as speaking in accordance with their view. Wherefore their opinion is contrary to the law, and the gospels seem to be at variance with them."[151] For Apollinaris this "being contrary to the law" can only mean the contradiction in which, according to the opponents' contention, the gospels stand in contrast to the law. That is so if, following the gospels, Jesus did not die on the day when, as the Passover lamb, he had to have died according to the law's stipulations about the slaying of the Passover lamb. Thus according to the Western side the entire controversy turned on the idea of Christ as the Passover lamb. This very idea is expressed so distinctly in the second fragment from Apollinaris that there can be no doubt as to how very coherent this view is.[152]

---

151. [Ed.] ANF 8:772.

152. *Chronicon Paschale* (n. 150), p. 14: "The fourteenth day, the true Passover of the Lord; the great sacrifice, the Son of God instead of the lamb, who was bound, who bound the strong, . . . who was buried on the day of the Passover" [ANF 8:722–23]. Evidence of this kind comes from Hippolytus, Apollinaris, and Clement of Alexandria. According to a fragment in the *Chronicon Paschale* (p. 14), Clement states that "in the years gone by, Jesus went to eat the Passover sacrificed by the Jews," but on this occasion, on the 13th, "when he had preached, he who was the Passover . . . . On the following day our Savior suffered" [ANF 2:581]. These passages make very clear the point at issue in the controversy. But they also show the significance the information about the Passover controversy has regarding the supposed apostolic origin of the Gospel of John. To dispose of this unavoidable consequence, Weitzel contends ([n. 146,] pp. 16ff.) that we have to distinguish between Catholic and

III. Johannine Christianity

Firmly established above all for the opponents from Asia Minor is the fact that heretical Quartodecimans, and that the evidence from Hippolytus and the others merely refers to the heretical ones. He says that the Passover controversy in the year 170 differs greatly from what it was in 190. In 170 it was not one church against another; instead it was the main representatives of the church against one isolated faction, a few Judaizing Laodiceans who came forward initially in 170 with their Judaizing Passover ritual. But these so-called heretical Quartodecimans (in Weitzel's account) are purely fictional, so lacking in any substantiation that the entire character and course of the controversy instead directly rules out any such assumption. From the [fragmentary, lost] writings of Irenaeus we see clearly that the disputed issue is the same from start to finish [ANF 1:568–69]. The text speaks of the difference between Polycarp and Anicetus as that between τηρεῖν (observing) and μὴ τηρεῖν (not observing), just like it is between Polycrates and Victor in the document by Polycrates. Had it been a matter of heretics, that is, Judaistic Quartodecimans, then their Judaistic concerns would also have had to stand out more clearly. But the issue is not about Passover as such, insofar as it was to be celebrated as a Jewish festival in step with Jews. Instead it just concerned the action Jesus undertook here, that on a Passover he held a final meal with his disciples. Therefore the 14th was said to be observed not on account of Passover, but only as a remembrance of Jesus and what he did, for that is the clear meaning of the evidence cited. So what here was specifically Judaistic and not also applicable to the Catholic Quartodeciman position? We see from a passage in the recently discovered *Philosophumena* 8.18 (in the Miller ed., pp. 274ff.) (Part 3, n. 11), attributed to Origen, how the ancient church hardly knew of any heretical Quartodecimans in the sense proposed here. It speaks of those who observe Passover "on the fourteenth of the first month . . . according to the ordinance of the law" by appealing to the Mosaic law's curse [on those who do not do so], but disregard the meaning of the true Passover sacrifice in Christ and what the Apostle Paul says in Galatians 5:3. Just as Apollinaris and Hippolytus accused their opponents of being argumentative and ignorant, so too these ones are labeled as "contentious by nature but simpletons in knowledge," but not as Judaistic heretics. Rather they are explicitly attested to be completely orthodox on other points: "In other matters, however, these people agree entirely with the apostolic traditions given to the church." [Quotations from the Litwa translation (Part 3, n. 11), 610–13.] —On the Passover controversy, see: my *Kritische Untersuchungen über die kanonischen Evangelien* (n. 30), 269, 334ff., 353ff., and essays in the *Theologische Jahrbücher* 6 (1847) 89ff., and 7 (1848) 264ff.; Hilgenfeld, "Der Paschastreit und das Evangelium des Johannes mit Rücksicht auf Weitzels Darstellung," *Theologische Jahrbücher* 8 (1849) 209ff., and *Der Galaterbrief* (Leipzig, 1852), 84ff. Weitzel's view is repeated by Lechler on pp. 327ff. of his book cited above (n. 11), without his even understanding correctly the point at issue. For many, Weitzel's view is a very convenient authority to invoke in opposing the results of more recent criticism, despite its evidently erroneous assumption. Even in his second and thoroughly revised edition of 1857, Lechler has just set forth again what is known to have been long since refuted. Further literature on this topic includes Steitz, "Die Differenz der Occidentalen und Kleinasiasten in der Passahfeier, auf's Neue kritisch untersucht und im Zusammenhang mit der gesammten Festordnung der alten Kirche entwickelt," *Theologische Studien und Kritiken* (1856) 721ff. On the other side, see my essay, "Zur johanneischen Frage," *Theologische Jahrbücher* 16 (1857) 242ff., and Hilgenfeld, *Galaterbrief*, 523ff. Steitz published further remarks in defense of his view, or of Weitzel's hypothesis, in *Theologische Studien und Kritiken* (1857) 741ff., which I did not let go unanswered, in the *Zeitschrift für wissenschaftliche Theologie* 1 (1858) 298ff. This topic has been investigated so long, and discussed by both sides so exhaustively, that two points are to be regarded as firmly established results, and there is hardly anything essentially new to be said about them. The first one is that the Passover meal on the 14th was not dedicated to the dying or already dead redeemer; instead it was dedicated to the Lord still sitting among his disciples and only then commencing his πάθος, his suffering or passion. (As I have after all emphasized, this is what caused these final moments to be remembered as infinitely precious. Hence those in Asia Minor tied everything to that one day, and they did not want to hear of anything that would have detracted from an outlook so inwardly connected with it. Everything is concentrated so intensely on these few hours of the Passover meal held, following the fast, in memory of Jesus' final meal, that, far from it being a joyful celebration—as people suppose they have to think of this Passover observance as aesthetically antithetical to the concluded period of fasting—it can instead only be observed in the solemn mood

Christ is the true and proper Passover lamb, from which it follows that the type and what it points to, prophecy and fulfillment, must coincide as closely as possible. The necessary consequence is that Christ died on the same date as the Jewish Passover lamb was slain. However, if the 14th was just the day on which Jesus died, and if Jesus died as the Passover lamb only in order that the new [meaning] that was now in place would forever take the place of the old one that had served its purpose, then there would also have been no interest in holding fast to the 14th as the permanent anniversary of Jesus' death. In the calendar of Christian feast days the constant date going forward could only be the Sunday of the resurrection. Whereas for the Easterners, all the other dates had to be fixed in relation to the 14th, which had its set celebration, for those in the West the calendar of feast days was specified by starting from a different point than 14 Nisan. The day of Jesus' death could only be determined based on the day of his resurrection, and thus fell always on Friday just as the resurrection was on Sunday.

Although the custom of the Roman church became ever more predominant, the difference between the two practices still continued for an extended period. It was even one of the issues that led to the Council of Nicaea, for in the East there continued to be several ecclesiastical provinces that observed the feast of Passover according to the Jewish calendar.[153] From the beginning people took offense at the "Jewishness" of the Quartodecimans. Anti-Jewish concerns ultimately got expressed in the Nicene Council's declaration that it would be improper to be guided by the practice of unbelieving and hostile-minded Jews. All the Eastern Christians who up to now had observed Passover in concert with the Jewish custom were supposed to have their future observances conform to those of the Roman church. Indeed, people were so averse to this feast having anything in common with the Jews that, if the Easter full

---

of a certainly sorrow-filled farewell meal, albeit one uplifted by the most inward, pious feeling.) The second, firmly established point is that there is no historical basis of any sort for the existence of an allegedly heretical Quartodeciman element. This notion is truly nothing but an apologetic expedient. In his "final words" on this issue, Steitz completes his examination of the Passover controversy by also taking in the aesthetic aspect; see "Der aesthetische Character der Eucharistie und des Fastens in der alten Kirche," *Theologische Studien und Kritiken* (1859) 716ff. On p. 737 he summarizes his results as follows: "There is every reason not to overrate what Polycarp and Polycrates have to say about John. The church in Asia Minor will have received from the beloved disciple, via the Fourth Gospel, the authenticated fact that Christ died on 14 Nisan, and perhaps it also inherited from it the practice of observing this day as the date set for his death. However, the manner of the observance doubtless belongs to a later time, and has taken its form only in the course of historical development, although probably on the basis of the Fourth Gospel (see John 16:6–7 and 19:30)." From this statement we see how, by confining one's historical outlook to the beloved disciple, the whole business just ends up by simply denying the significance of historical testimonies that cannot serve one's own purposes, such as the evidence from Polycarp and Polycrates. In the end, the issue to be dealt with remains just as unresolved as it was at the outset.

153. See Athanasius, *De synodis* (On the Councils) 1.5: "The Syrians, Cilicians, and Mesopotamians, were out of order in celebrating the Feast, and kept Passover with the Jews" [*NPNF*² 4:452]. See also Eusebius, *Life of Constantine* 3.5.18, and Socrates, *Ecclesiastical History* 1.9.

moon fell on a Sunday, then Easter ought not be celebrated on that day, but instead only on the following Sunday.

As this controversy became more lively and widespread not merely in Asia Minor but in Christian communities generally at that time, it is most noteworthy what role the Gospel of John played in it. John most decidedly favors the Western tradition's side. John's portrayal of Jesus' death quite intentionally seeks to preclude any idea that Jesus' final meal was the Passover meal. In John 13:1–2, it expressly states that Jesus held *a* meal or "supper" (δεῖπνον), not *the* meal (τὸ δεῖπνον), "before the festival of the Passover." Despite how this differs from the account in the Synoptic Gospels, it is likewise his final meal. Other verses referring to the still-approaching festival (13:29 and 18:28) seem designed to leave no doubt that this was the very same meal Jesus shared with his disciples on the evening when he was arrested, just like in the Synoptics but with the difference that it was not the Passover meal. The respective portrayals by the Synoptics and John are so completely different here that, exegetically, it is utterly futile to try to integrate or harmonize them on this one point.

Yet this same Apostle John is also said to be one of the main witnesses supporting the authentically apostolic origins of the tradition of Asia Minor. The venerable Polycrates, the bishop of Ephesus, appealed to the authority of John. With his grey hair and with all that was holy and revered, he made this appeal in a way that assured the historical credibility of his attestation and precluded any objection that could cast doubt on that exegetical result. What other way is there to deal with this obvious contradiction than by assuming that the writer of the Gospel is a different person from the Apostle John who wrote the Book of Revelation?[154]

These reports about the Passover controversy certainly provide us with historical data that just confirm the answer based on so many other incontrovertible sources. Accordingly the Gospel of John can only be dated at a later time; it can only have originated in a setting where the Passover controversy was alive; and it can only have arisen

---

154. According to Gieseler, *Lehrbuch der Kirchengeschichte* (n. 148), 4th ed., 1:241ff., this contradiction would have been very easily resolved. He says that: "In the beginning the Christian communities would have retained the Jewish Passover festival, but celebrated with reference to Christ as the true Passover (1 Cor 5:7). John found this to be the case in Ephesus, and he left the practice unchanged. In his Gospel he just altered it to no longer mean that Christ observed Passover in the Jewish tradition on the day before his death, since John clearly emphasized that Christ was crucified on 14 Nisan. That is why there was no need to change that observance in Ephesus. Instead 14 Nisan was now also the true Passover date for Christians. The fulfillment of the type (the Jewish Passover) fell on the same date as it did." It is as though the very contradiction itself was not in the fact that the greatest importance got placed on the 14th as the date of Christ's death, and yet so little concern was given to how the day itself was to be celebrated! How could John just let the contradiction between φαγεῖν (eating) and παθεῖν (suffering) on the same day stand? How could he allow it by his own participation in the Passover observation in Asia Minor, whereas in his Gospel he does everything to oppose it? How did he come to revise that notion and to contradict the widespread tradition confirmed by the Synoptic Gospels, according to which Christ was said to have died on the 15th? To suppose that one can so easily set aside the self-contradiction on the Apostle John's part is to completely overlook how far-reaching is the difference as to the day of Jesus' death.

from the same concerns that led the Roman church to increasingly take a position antithetical to that of the communities still clinging to the original Jewish Christian tradition. The Quartodecimans of Asia Minor without question had the authority of the historical tradition on their side. We have no reason to doubt the trustworthiness of the testimonies to which they appeal in support of their tradition's apostolic origin. Thus the portrayal of Jesus' death in the Synoptic Gospels, which harmonizes with this tradition, inherently has the character of the earliest historical account coming down to us. All the testimonies in the Synoptics agree that Jesus died on 15 Nisan, and held the Passover meal with his disciples on 14 Nisan.

The other tradition, according to which Jesus died on the 14th, the day of the Passover meal, and that his final meal was not a Passover meal, is manifestly a tradition originating at a later time. In the Roman church Anicetus, in opposing Polycarp, did of course also appeal to the tradition of his predecessors. However, we see from the letter of Irenaeus to Bishop Victor of Rome that the line of Roman bishops—those Irenaeus designated as μὴ τηροῦντες (not observant) although they maintained friendly relations with those who were τηροῦντες (observant)—could not be traced further back from Anicetus, Pius, Hyginus, and Telephorus to Sixtus. Eusebius (*Historia ecclesiastica*, 4.4) dates Sixtus in the time of Hadrian, and says (4.6) that he was the Roman bishop from the third to the twelfth year of Hadrian's reign (c. 120–129). Whatever the causes combining to give the Roman church an increasingly anti-Judaistic orientation in the course of the second century may have been, the core reason was in any event that Christian consciousness developed in a more unhampered fashion—although it mainly came to be expressed with reference to Old Testament typology, by more precisely defining the relation between type and antitype or reality. For instance, despite the fact that Justin Martyr related the Old Testament, as type, to Christ, he nevertheless agreed with the way the Synoptics related the death of Jesus to the day of the Passover feast.[155]

In countering the opponents by placing greater emphasis on the point that Jesus no longer would have held the Jewish Passover meal, one had to cast about for reasons supporting this contention. The only way one could justify it was giving a more precise account of the relation of the type to its antitype or realization. The more completely the two coincide the less the type still has any sort of significance, as soon as the full reality of the antitype has taken its place. This was the underlying idea guiding thinking on this issue as we find it in the Gnostic writers at this time too, when they sought to specify with more precision the significance of Old Testament types

---

155. *Dialogue with Trypho*, ch. 111 [*ANF* 1:254]. In ch. 40 [*ANF* 1:214–15] it is nevertheless especially noteworthy how Justin describes the Passover lamb as the type of Christ. He finds the type-element only in the blood that was smeared on the [Jews'] houses, and in the form of the cross presented by the Passover lamb when it is [placed on the spit and] roasted. Justin leaves entirely unmentioned the very thing to which the Gospel writer attaches the greatest importance, in 19:36. ["These things occurred so that the scripture might be fulfilled, 'None of his bones shall be broken.'"] How is this possible if the Gospel of John was already known to Justin?

and symbols.[156] They took the allegorical interpretation of scripture to be the key to the holy scripture and as being the highest knowledge. Thus those who supposed that they see more deeply into the relation of type and antitype from this perspective also regarded themselves as occupying a higher level of Christian knowledge. This relates to the charge of ignorance and contentiousness made in the fragments of Apollinaris and Hippolytus against their opponents, insofar as the opponents lacked the proper insight—which they alone possessed—into the matter of knowing how to correctly distinguish, and relate, type and antitype. Obstinately clinging to their purported tradition, they contested, on the opponents' part, what these opponents themselves believed they understood far better.

The Form of Christian Consciousness Surpassing Judaism and Paulinism

The Passover controversy, understood in this way, is one of the most important in the series of efforts by which the church of the second century sought to cleanse and free itself from the Jewish features still adhering to it, at the point when the Christian principle had been comprehended in its freer development. Belonging entirely to this setting, the Gospel of John is the purest expression of the higher form of Christian consciousness emerging from this process of development.[157]

The Gospel of John regards the break with Judaism as an accomplished fact, and therefore it also takes an analogous stance toward Jewish Christianity. Since Christ has been sacrificed as the Passover lamb, the Passover meal is no longer of concern to Christians. Passover is now just a purely Jewish festival, one Christians have done away with ("the Passover of the Jews," John 2:13; cf. 6:4 and 11:55), just as this Gospel likewise also speaks of the law as just the law of the Jews. As the character of this Gospel shows, its author can have identified himself with the Apostle John only by being conscious of the higher stage of development that leaves all particularism so far behind it. For him, the highest expression of Christian consciousness is found in none other than the Apostle John, albeit also only in the John who is spiritualized in the tenor of this Gospel. That is why the Gospel of John sets John apart as the beloved

---

156. See in particular the Letter to Flora by Ptolemaeus the Gnostic, according to Epiphanius, *Against Heresies* 33.5.9: "All these things, being images and symbols, were transposed once the truth was revealed. As far as outward appearance goes and the physical carrying out of rites, they have been abolished, but in their spiritual aspect they have been taken up; the names remain the same, while the things have changed." [ET from *The Panarion of St. Epiphanius, Bishop of Salamis*, trans. and ed. Philip R. Amidon (Oxford, 1990), 121.]

157. [*Ed.*] The language about Christianity "cleansing" itself of Jewish features, and of moving beyond Jewish "particularism" (next paragraph), is unfortunate. Baur may regard these terms as simply reflecting the attitude of Catholic Christianity toward Judaism at the end of the second century, but to our ears they sound prejudicial. In other contexts Baur speaks very appreciatively of Judaism's contribution to Christianity, and he by no means simply embraces the Johannine theological framework. The latter is a higher form of consciousness only in terms of the prevailing historical trajectory. On the latter point, see the Editorial Introduction to Baur's *Lectures on New Testament Theology* (n.32), 54.

disciple, the one most trusted by and closest to Jesus. It does so in a way distinctive to this Gospel, so that even Peter needs John as his intermediary and appears quite intentionally to be subordinated to John. This stance on the Gospel's part obviously becomes a protest against the primacy the Jewish Christians accorded to the Apostle Peter.[158]

The John who sets himself even higher than the Apostle Peter is in any event just a sheerly ideal person, not someone historical. Thus for the Gospel writer, the Spirit that came in its fullness only after Jesus' earthly life, as the universal Christian principle, also stands so far above the personal authority of the apostles that, with regard to the antithesis between Judaism and Paulinism in this context, this Spirit itself goes above and beyond Paulinism.[159]

The same is the case with John's doctrinal framework. This too is the higher unity of the Jewish Christian framework and the Pauline framework. Here too faith has the same intense import as it has for the Apostle Paul, except that here faith's object is not the death of Jesus with its sin-forgiving efficacy. Instead faith's object is the person of Jesus as such, as the Logos become flesh, or is God himself since, as the one sent down, Jesus can only be thought of as being in the most direct unity with the one sending him. The relation Jesus, as the Son, has to the Father is the absolute type for the entire relation of the human being to God. Through the Son's mediation, those believing in him should become what he is in an absolute way. Those believing in him are not just related to the Son in the same way as the Son stands to the Father, for, through the Son's mediation, they also stand related to the Father. But the principle determining the entire relationship is the love acting through the unconditional devotion and behest of the divine will. The supreme and absolute principle of this love is the Father's love for the Son, and God's love for the world.

Accordingly, love is everywhere the supreme concept from which the Johannine way of looking at things sets out. Love is the point in which the Johannine theological framework diverges from the Pauline framework. However high Paul places God's love, because of his view of the law Paul still always sets love in contrast to righteousness. One cannot escape the demands of the law unless satisfaction is made for the law's rightful claim against oneself, unless the demand for its payment is eliminated, unless the ransom is paid. From the standpoint of the Gospel of John, on the one hand the law is already so removed from the center of attention that its claims are looked upon as "antiquated," as it were, and there is no need for any special engagement with

---

158. See my *Kritische Untersuchungen* (n. 30), 320ff. and 377ff.

159. The Spirit released to operate most freely following Jesus' glorification, and taking the place of Jesus' personal presence, is foretold by the Johannine Christ himself, who says (7:38): "Out of the believer's heart shall flow rivers of living water." The Gospel transports us into the sphere of pure spirituality. Just as Paul broke through the bounds of the old apostolic circle in virtue of his calling, so those who bear and possess the apostolic spirit are now the believing disciples as such (17:20ff.). Hence in the Johannine view, even the origin of a Gospel such as John's is in no way conditional upon the author being an apostle.

it. On the other hand, from this standpoint the overall view of Jesus' person does not allow for highlighting one individual moment so overwhelmingly that Jesus' death is in fact the crucial point in the entire work of redemption. His death is redemptive only to the same degree as is Jesus' entire appearance in the world. The purely personal element, the person of Jesus in its absolute significance, is for John what the event of his death is for Paul. The way to characterize the relation of the Johannine standpoint to the Pauline standpoint is simply that one must see the Gospel of John as far removed from the antitheses that Paulinism first had to fight its way through. In John, faith and works are taken up into love, as their higher unity. The particularism of Judaism, with all the antithetical baggage it involves, disappears in the universal antithesis of two principles, light and darkness. These two principles stand in the background of the Johannine worldview, and decisively influence the moral world as well.

REVIEW OF THE COURSE TAKEN BY THE DEVELOPMENT; THE EBIONITES

At this point the Christian principle's process of development, which is the topic we have been examining, has reached its specific goal. Christianity is established as the universal principle of salvation, and all the antitheses within Judaism's particularism to which Christianity wished to cling are now abolished in Christianity's universality.

The abolition of Jewish particularism occurs at two points with two series of phenomena, each of which takes its own independent course. One of them lies in the Roman church; the Gospel of John forms the other one. At each point the free development of Christian consciousness has its eye on the same goal: realizing the idea of the Catholic Church. In the Gospel of John this process of development presents itself to us in its ideal aspect, and in the Roman church it presents us with its practical aspect. Whereas the development of Christian consciousness already inherently has the character of a Christian theology in the Gospel, the practical idea of the church and efforts to realize it characterize the Roman church. In the Roman church everything emanates from one specific point, its footing is on the solid soil of historical actuality, and there are definite antitheses that are to be mediated. In the Gospel of John, in contrast, the entire way of looking at things hovers in the realm of a transcendent ideality.

We do not even know where the Gospel of John originated. It has many links to the church in Asia Minor and to the controversial issues that made this church the center of ecclesiastical activity in the course of the second century. Yet on the whole, and in so many of its individual features, John bears such an Alexandrian stamp, and has such close kinship with the later Alexandrian theology, that we can just see it as representing the Alexandrian orientation. Wherever it may have come about, we must look mainly in this Alexandrian direction for the root from which it sprang. However, notwithstanding its ideal and theological character, John does not lose sight of the practical task of the idea of the church, in the one flock and the one shepherd [10:16].

In sharing with the Roman church an anti-Judaistic tendency, it thus has the most direct point of contact with Rome in their mutual opposition to the Jewishness of the Quartodecimans of Asia Minor.

The same striving for unity that had already joined the Apostles Peter and Paul in brotherly fashion in the Roman church did not let this church rest from also pursuing its catholicizing concern for unity against this vestige of tenacious clinging to Judaism. Thus in the future there ought no longer be declared Judaists such as the Quartodecimans. So this was a new element, the exclusion from the Christian Church of what originally connected Christianity with Judaism but with which the church now no longer wanted to have anything in common. Accordingly, whoever in the future held fast, with the old tenacity, to any one of the Jewish elements that Christian consciousness had gradually gotten rid of could, at the very least, no longer be held to be in communion with the Catholic Church. From the end of the second century and going forward, this is the concept linked to the term "Ebionites."

Ebionites in this sense are all those Jewish Christians who, after there was already an existing Catholic Church, retained elements that were originally regarded within the Christian community as essential elements of Christianity but subsequently were no longer recognized as such by the Catholic Church.[160] As a sect later spurned by the Catholic Church, the Ebionites are the same sort as the Jewish Christians who were originally distinct from Pauline Christians. Irenaeus, who was the first to speak of the Ebionites as a sect not belonging to the Catholic Church,[161] and Epiphanius, who describes the vestiges of the Ebionites still carrying on in his day,[162] ascribe to them the same features that were characteristic of Jewish Christians generally. When Irenaeus says that "they even adore Jerusalem as if it were the house of God," he is very emphatically describing their view of the absolute significance of Judaism. Epiphanius says the Ebionites still clung so firmly to circumcision that they considered it to be the seal and characteristic sign not merely of the patriarchs and the righteous ones who live according to the law, but even the seal of Christ's follower who has certainly been circumcised himself.[163]

The Ebionites' hatred for the Apostle Paul and their explicit rejection of his epistles set them apart later on from the more moderate thinking of the Nazarenes, who at least were not so hostile. Also, what is reported about the Passover festival of the Ebionites assumes that they observed the Jewish feast day in the same way

---

160. See my *Lehrbuch der christlichen Dogmengeschichte*, 2nd ed. (n. 106), 64; *History of Christian Dogma* (n. 106), 94.

161. Irenaeus, *Against Heresies* 1.26 [cf. *ANF* 1:352].

162. Epiphanius, *Against Heresies* 30.1ff.

163. See Hilgenfeld's article in the *Zeitschrift für wissenschaftliche Theologie* 1 (1858) 287ff. Contrary to Ritschl, who in *Entstehung*, 2nd ed. (n. 38), 172, understands the Testament of the Twelve Patriarchs as a product of the Nazarenes, Hilgenfeld asserts that the Nazarenes and the Ebionites were not so much two particular sects of Jewish Christians as they were different degrees of the ancient hostility to Paulinism, with the Nazarenes taking a more tolerant stance toward Gentile Christianity.

as the Quartodecimans did. Epiphanius declares that the Ebionite movement began only after the destruction of Jerusalem, but there is no historical basis at all for this statement. It follows only if one assumes that nothing later on counts as heretical if it could originally have been part of orthodox Christianity. Since even Justin Martyr certainly did not yet regard them as a sect, the Ebionites only became one later. For an examination of their principles, teaching, and practices shows us that, in company with so many other groups expressing a markedly sectarian character, they were, to be sure, so identical with the original Jewish Christianity, and so ingrown with it, that it is hardly an unjustifiable use of the term if we designate Jewish Christianity overall as "Ebionite" in a certain sense. In the customary and narrower sense, however, the term signifies the form of early Christianity that withdraws on its own from the fellowship of the Catholic Church because its own members could not fall in line with the developing Christian consciousness that went above and beyond Jewish Christianity.

Part 3

Christianity as Ideal World-Principle and as Real, Historically Conditioned Phenomenon
or
Gnosis and Montanism, and the Catholic Church as the Antithesis to Each of Them

I. Gnosis and Montanism

1. GNOSIS

The Concept and Nature of Gnosis

The term "Gnosis"[1] and the concept of Gnosis take us into a completely different domain of the earliest church from the one we have described thus far. (The reason for juxtaposing Gnosis and Montanism will first become clear from the following discussion.)

The issue is no longer whether Christianity is one particular principle of salvation, or is instead a universal principle of salvation. The concern is no longer the condition for a person to gain the blessedness that Christianity imparts. The issue is no longer merely one of breaking through, and setting aside, the barriers preventing Christianity from evolving in a freer and more universal way. The horizon is quite different here. People now see themselves in a setting where the concepts and antitheses are those of God and world, spirit and matter, absolute and finite; of the world's origin, its development, and how it will end. In short, the concern is to understand Christianity as a world-principle instead of as a principle of salvation.

The phenomena we are speaking about here originate on their own and form such a distinctive array that, what they share with what else belongs to the history of the earliest church, is basically just the name "Christianity." And yet, they are no less significant than the rest for how the history of the Catholic Church unfolded. Of course first and foremost, in keeping with the idea of being "catholic" (or universal), the church must strive to transcend everything particularistic and to elevate it to the universality of the Christian principle. On the other hand, however, the church has the important task of holding fast to what are positive elements in Christianity. It is a "catholic" church as such only inasmuch as it is a central, focal point reconciling all the different perspectives, a center staying just as far from one extreme as it does

---

1. [Ed.] This term (*Gnosis* in German) is capitalized in this translation because Baur uses it to refer not only to the concept of γνῶσις (knowledge) but also to the variety of movements known as "Gnosticism." Gnosis often means not just gnosis but Gnosticism.

from the other. On the one hand, if the idea of a catholic church, an idea emerging from Christianity,[2] had not overcome the particularism of Judaism, Christianity itself would have become just a Jewish sect. On the other hand, the threat posed to Christianity by paganism was the equally great danger of generalizing and watering-down its contents by ideas so boundlessly expanding Christian consciousness that it would have had to completely lose its specific, historical character. Gnosis had this latter tendency. And given this tendency, the most general heading under which we must place Gnosis is that which regards Christianity as the principle governing the world's entire development, rather than see Christianity as, above all, [just] a principle of salvation. So the foundation of Gnosis is not so much a religious interest as it is a speculative, philosophical interest, one that leads back to philosophy as the human mind's supreme creation in the pagan world.

This gives us a general indication as to the nature of Gnosis. However, even with all the discussion of Gnosis, especially in most recent times, it is nevertheless not a very easy or simple matter to define and elaborate on the concept of Gnosis in more specific terms. With so much that is always still ill-defined, vague, merely applicable to one instance, or just partially true about Gnosis, the task is to fix our attention on those points that give us a clear concept of the thing itself.

The most common approach is to understand Gnosis as being mainly theological speculation. Gieseler[3] too describes it in this way. He interprets its philosophical foundation as resting in part on the age-old question about the origin of evil, and in part on the fact that, the more philosophy worked out the idea of the highest divinity, the less philosophy believed it permissible to regard this divinity as creator of the world. Philosophy was inclined to attribute the imperfect goodness in the world to lesser beings, while attributing the evil in the world to an evil principle. These ideas gained a foothold in Christianity, which then in those terms viewed Christianity itself as what is perfect, Judaism as imperfect, and paganism as evil. Neander[4] starts with the aristocratic outlook of the ancient world, with the antithesis between knowledge

---

2. [Ed.] This formulation makes it clear that Baur intended to distinguish original Christianity from the church that arose from it, hence the title, *Christianity and the Christian Church of the First Three Centuries*.

3. J. C. L. Gieseler, *Lehrbuch der Kirchengeschichte*, 4th ed., 6 vols. (Bonn, 1844), 1.1:179. [Ed.] ET: *A Text-Book of Church History*, trans. H. B. Smith, 5 vols. (New York, 1847).

4. August Neander, *Allgemeine Geschichte der christlichen Religion und Kirche*, 2nd ed., 4 vols. (Hamburg, 1842–47), 2:632–36. [Ed.] *General History of the Christian Religion and Church*, trans. Joseph Torrey (London and Boston, 1849ff.), 1:366–68. The translations are our own. August Neander (1789–1850), a convert from Judaism, was a widely influential church historian who emphasized the role of individuality, feeling, and belief in history. See Part 1, n. 8. In *Die christliche Gnosis* (n. 5 below) Baur distinguishes his own approach from that of his predecessors: Neander, Gieseler, and J. Matter. See Volker Henning Drecoll, "Ferdinand Christian Baur's View of Christian Gnosis, and of the Philosophy of Religion in His Own Day," ch. 6 in *Ferdinand Christian Baur and the History of Early Christianity*, ed. Martin Bauspiess, Christof Landmesser, and David Lincicum, trans. R. F. Brown and P. C. Hodgson (Oxford, 2017), esp. 117–26.

and belief, and with the eclectic character of Gnosticism. His particular emphasis is then as follows:

> When Christianity came to terms with the life of the mind, it had to feel the need to become aware of how the truths conveyed by revelation are connected to humanity's already-existing intellectual heritage, as well as of how Christian truth itself is an interconnected, organic whole. However, where such a felt need was forcibly suppressed rather than satisfied, doing so opened the door to Gnosis.

But this statement is rather unclear, and Neander's favorite category of "reaction" can hardly substitute for it. So we look for the solution to the puzzle in the following passage.

> The speculative element in Gnostic systems is not the product of a reason cutting itself off from history and wanting to extract all its contents from reason's own depths. A merely negative philosophy sinking into the void would have to let the mind, which insists on what is real, seek out a more positive philosophy once more. In the Gnostic systems we can discover elements of Platonic philosophy, Jewish theology, and ancient eastern theosophy, all blended together. Yet these systems are never explainable solely as a mixture and combination of such elements. Most of the Gnostic combinations were animated by life-giving principles of their own. They bore the wholly distinctive stamp of their era, and it gave them certain orientations and ideas, ones that exerted great influence on everything at that time. The dualistic principle was influential then, for a dualistic outlook fit well with the prevailing mood and was in turn mirrored in it. The basic tenor of many of the more serious minds at this time was their consciousness of the power of evil, a consciousness on which Christianity too had quite a special impact.

According to this, the origin and essential nature of Gnosis were explainable from the influence of the dualistic principle; and dualism indisputably belongs to the essential character of the Gnostic systems. However, since this influence of the dualistic principle first appears in the Gnostic systems themselves, it cannot serve to explain the essence of Gnosis.

Neander's most accurate statement about Gnosticism amounts only to this:

> Gnosticism has made religious teachings depend on speculative answers to all those questions that speculation has struggled with in vain; and in doing so it wanted to provide, for the first time, a firm foundation for, and a correct understanding of, those teachings. In doing this, Gnosticism was said to teach people for the first time how to comprehend Christianity, and how first to gain firm convictions, ones independent of external considerations.

Put succinctly, Gnosis was therefore a philosophy of religion. But in what sense was it one?[5]

The term "Gnosis" does not just refer to the phenomena we are explaining in historical terms here. There is a general concept of Gnosis, whereas here we have to adopt a more specific definition of it for the special sense Gnosis takes on as Christian Gnosis. Gnosis [in the general sense] is a higher knowing, a knowing aware of its own foundation, of its own transmission; in other words, the kind of knowing or knowledge that is everything it ought to be as knowledge. In this sense Gnosis, as knowledge, is the natural antithesis to Pistis, or belief.[6] If we are to designate knowledge as being specifically different from belief, Gnosis serves this descriptive purpose better than any other term.

However, the knowledge designated as Gnosis in this general sense is already principally a religious knowledge, not a speculative knowledge as such. It is instead the kind of knowledge that has its object in religion. Thus the Apostle Paul indeed employs the term γνῶσις in 1 Cor 8:1–13, which concerns the view about eating food offered to idols that claims validity as more liberal and enlightened, as befitting the essential issue. Also in 12:8, when he speaks of a λόγος γνώσεως (an utterance of knowledge), which can be understood as contrasting with the λόγος σοφίας (utterance of wisdom) only inasmuch as knowledge here has a religious import setting it apart by the depth of its content.

Especially noteworthy for our purposes is the fact that γνῶσις in the special sense is used specifically for a kind of religious knowledge that relies on the allegorical interpretation of scripture.[7] Gnosis and allegory are of course inherently related concepts. For, in most Gnostic systems, and especially in those that present us with the original form of Gnosis, allegory plays a very significant role. So, in them we have a quite specific benchmark that essentially enables us to get closer to the origin of Gnosis in this way.

---

5. On the concept of Gnosis, in addition to my inaugural dissertation, *De Gnosticorum Christianismo ideali* (Tübingen, 1827), and my book, *Die christliche Gnosis, oder die christliche Religions-Philosophie in ihrer geschichtlichen Entwicklung* (Tübingen, 1835), see my essays, "Kritische Studien über den Begriff der Gnosis," *Theologische Studien und Kritiken* 10 (1837) 511–79, and "Ueber den Begriff der christlichen Religionsphilosophie, ihren Ursprung und ihre ersten Formen," *Zeitschrift für speculative Theologie*, ed. Bruno Bauer, 2.2 (1837) 354ff. See also my *Lehrbuch der christlichen Dogmengeschichte*, 2nd ed. (Tübingen, 1858), 69ff. [*History of Christian Dogma*, ed. P. C. Hodgson, trans. R. F. Brown and P. C. Hodgson (Oxford, 2014), 97–102]; and *Die Tübinger Schule und ihre Stellung zur Gegenwart* (Tübingen, 1859), 50ff.

6. [*Ed.*] See Plato, *Republic*, 5.21 (also 6.20–21), where the contrast is between knowledge and opinion (δόξα), with belief (πίστις) a subcategory of δόξα.

7. See *Die christliche Gnosis* (n. 5), 85ff.

I. Gnosis and Montanism

The Origin of Gnosis

As we all know, allegory is the soul of the Alexandrian philosophy of religion. Allegory is so deeply rooted in its very being that we cannot conceive of it as originally other than essentially allegorical. Allegory is, in general, the mediatrix[8] between philosophy and the religion resting on positive, traditional contents. Everywhere wholesale allegorical interpretation emerged, it played this mediating role. At this time, on the one hand, a philosophical way of looking at things had taken shape alongside, and independently of, the existing religion, and on the other hand, there was a concurrent need to harmonize these philosophical ideas and teachings with the contents of religious belief. The simple way to do this was to interpret religious belief in a philosophical sense, so that religious concepts and narratives are given a figurative meaning completely different from their literal contents. The Greeks had already made use of allegory in this fashion.

Plato was the first to be interested in utilizing the myths from popular religion for his philosophical ideas and thus making connections between philosophical consciousness and the popular mind; and the Stoics subsequently did even more along these lines. The Stoic philosophers took the road of allegory, or the allegorical interpretation of myths. In fact the Stoics are well-known for their extensive use of allegory as a way of demonstrating their own ideas in the philosophy of nature, by referring to the gods of the popular religion and the narratives about them.[9]

Allegorical interpretation gained far greater significance in Alexandria, where it had to play the important role of unifying the new ideas of compelling interest to intellectually-aware Jews, with their faith in the authority of their religion's sacred scriptures. Allegory alone made it possible for someone to admire Greek philosophy so much on the one hand, specifically Plato's philosophy, and to adopt this philosophy as one's own; while, on the other hand, being able to revere the Old Testament scriptures as the only source of divinely revealed truth. One need only interpret the sacred scriptures allegorically, and then one could find in these very scriptures anything one wanted to, even the speculative ideas of Greek philosophy.

The writings of Philo are evidence for the extensive use of allegory in Alexandria. In them we see the contents of the Old Testament most closely integrated with all that the Greek philosophical systems had to offer. Yet it would be quite erroneous to suppose that what the allegorical interpretation of scripture gave rise to, and what made it so very influential, was just arbitrariness and the free play of the imagination. For Alexandrian Jews at their current level of intellectual development, a divided consciousness reflecting both ancestral Hebrew thinking and modern Hellenistic philosophy,

---

8. [*Ed.*] By using the feminine form, Baur follows an ancient tradition of representing a purveyor of superhuman wisdom or inspiration as a female figure: e.g., the Muses in Greek and Roman legend, and the Alexandrian Jewish depiction of God's word or wisdom (Sophia).

9. See Eduard Zeller, *Die Philosophie der Griechen*, 3 vols. (Tübingen, 1844–52), 3:113ff.

allegory was a necessary form of consciousness. They scarcely had any intimation that the artificial link between such heterogeneous elements was their own creation. Thus to them, all that they recognized as being truth in the Greek philosophical systems just seemed to be an offshoot of Old Testament revelation.[10]

Since the Gnostic systems also to a large extent make very frequent use of allegorical explanations, this indeed shows us that we have to put them under the same heading as the Alexandrian religious philosophy. So far as we can tell [since most are no longer extant], the writings of the Gnostics were full of allegorical interpretations, but of course not just like those we find in Philo relating to the Old Testament scriptures (since they took a different stance toward them). The Gnostics dealt much more with the New Testament, which functions for them as the Old Testament did for Philo. In order to give a Christian stamp to their own ideas, they interpreted the persons and events of the gospel story as allegorically as possible, especially also the numerical elements present in it. For instance, the Valentinians were said to interpret the number twenty in the New Testament, particularly in Jesus' life (Luke 3:23), as being the number of their Aeons; to hold that the last, wandering sheep (Luke 15:3–7) was the Acamoth; and that even sayings of Jesus containing quite simple religious truths have meanings for them corresponding to the doctrines of their system.

From the recently-discovered *Philosophumena* of the Pseudo-Origen, which undertook the task of refuting all the heresies,[11] we see in more specific terms what extensive use the Gnostics made of their allegorical interpretation. The Gnostics applied this method not only to the scriptures of the Old and New Testaments, but also to Greek literature, for instance to the Homeric poems. Their overall perspective was so completely allegorical that they drew freely from the entire domain of ancient mythology, astronomy, and physical science in order to find re-expressed everywhere the same ideas that were the leading themes of their thought and knowledge.[12]

---

10. [*Ed.*] Some church fathers thought that Jeremiah spent time in Egypt, and that via Egypt the Greeks acquired their "truths" from Old Testament revelation. See, for example, the *Stromata* of Clement of Alexandria (*ANF* 2). In 5.1 Clement writes: "We showed in the first Miscellany [1.16] that the philosophers of the Greeks are thieves, inasmuch as they have taken without acknowledgment their principal dogma from Moses and the prophets." In 5.14 he goes on at great length about how the Greeks plagiarized the Hebrews.

11. Ὠριγένους φιλοσοφούμενα, ἡ κατὰ πασῶν αἱρέσεων ἔλεγχος. E codice Parisino nunc primum edidit Emmanuel Miller (Oxford, 1851). [*Ed.*] ET: *The Refutation of All Heresies*, trans. with an introduction and notes by M. David Litwa (Society of Biblical Literature; Atlanta, 2016). Hereafter this work is referred to in the text and notes as *Philosophumena*, the title Baur uses. It was actually written by Hippolytus of Rome (170–235 or 236), but it was long known and published among the works of Origen (hence the term "Pseudo-Origen"). Because of its then-recent discovery, Baur refers to it frequently in the following pages. He quotes lengthy passages in Greek, for which we use, with permission, the Litwa translation.

12. See *Philosophumena* 5.8.1 (p. 106): "These most wondrous Gnostics follow these and like teachings. As inventors of a new form of literary analysis, they glorify their own prophet Homer, who secretly declared these things. When they amalgamate the holy scriptures into these sorts of meanings, they lord it over the uninitiated" [ET 228–31]. Also 4.46.2 (p. 81): "But in order to make my points clearer to the readers, it seems fitting also to declare the speculations of Aratos about the

However, the allegorical method as such is just the means for giving, to a content made up of various elements, a consistently clear form corresponding to that content, even for a content with the most heterogeneous elements. Thus also in the case of Gnosis, this method looks for the inner nature of the content for which the allegory is in fact just the outward form of its presentation. In this respect too, Gnosis is so closely related to the Alexandrian religious philosophy that, in its essentials, Gnosis is to be regarded as simply a further development of it. Both took their main contents from Greek philosophy. Philo's system can be called a speculative religious system, and the Gnostic systems have a quite similar character. The early church fathers already viewed Gnosis in this light. As one example, Tertullian declared Gnosis to be antithetical to Christianity, to be a worldly wisdom, and he reproached philosophy for being the originator of the heresies.[13]

---

celestial configurations of the stars, since some people allegorize them by conforming them to verses of scripture. They try to seduce the minds of those interested, enticing them to their views with convincing rhetoric, exhibiting a strange wonder—as if those babbled about by them had truly been raised to the stars!" [ET 168–69]. Also 5.20.1 (p. 148), where it says about the Sethians: "Their discourse is concocted from the natural philosophers and from discourses directed toward other subjects. These discourses they convert into their own idiom and narrate as I have described" [ET 320–21]. This passage later continues, 5.20.4 (p. 144): "Their entire teaching about the Word is from the ancient theologians Musaios, Linos, and—the consummate revealer of initiations and mysteries—Orpheus" [ET 322–23]. Also 5.13.12 (p. 127), where it says about the Gnostic sect of the Peratai that they "tell lies about the Name of truth, by proclaiming it as the message of Christ. They discourse about the war of aeons, and rebellion of good powers who turn to evil acts," and so forth [ET 284–85]. The entire fantastic world of the astrologers concerning the stars they interpret in their own sense, from which one can see that "their teachings are undeniably those of the astrologers, not Christ" [ET 284–85]. [*Ed.*] Aratos of Cilicia (c. 315—239 BC) was influenced by Stoicism, produced an edition of *The Odyssey* ("their own prophet Homer" of the previous quotation?), and composed an astronomical poem, *Phaenomena*, to which there are many references in the *Philosophumena*. Musaeus was a mythical singer associated with Orpheus; see Plato, *Republic*, 365e. Linos was the subject of a well-known song named for him. Orpheus was the founder of Orphism, a religious movement; he figures prominently in several major Greek myths.

13. *The Prescription against Heretics*, ch. 7 [ANF 3:246]. "These are 'the doctrines' of men and 'of demons,' produced for itching ears of the spirit of this world's wisdom. The Lord called this 'foolishness,' and 'chose the foolish things of the world' to confound even philosophy itself. For philosophy is the material of the world's wisdom, the rash interpreter of the nature and the dispensation of God. Indeed heresies are themselves instigated by philosophy. From this source came the Aeons, and I know not what infinite forms, and the trinity of man in the system of Valentinus, who was of Plato's school. From the same source came Marcion's better god, with all his tranquility; he came from the Stoics. Then, again, the opinion that the soul dies is held by the Epicureans. The denial of the restoration of the body is taken from the aggregate school of all the philosophers. When matter is made equal to God, then you have the teaching of Zeno. When any doctrine is alleged concerning a god of fire, then Heraclitus comes in. The same subject matter is discussed over and over again by the heretics and the philosophers; the same arguments are involved. Whence comes evil? Why is it permitted? What is the origin of man and how does he arise? There is also the question Valentinus has very lately posed—Whence comes God? His answer is: From *enthymesis* and *ectroma*. Unhappy Aristotle who invented for these men dialectics, the art of building up and pulling down; an art so evasive in its propositions, so far-fetched in its conjectures, so harsh in its arguments, so productive of contentions—embarrassing even to itself, retracting everything, and really treating of nothing!"

The church fathers did not merely derive Gnosis from philosophy in general terms. They also sought to show, on individual points too, from what philosophical systems the Gnostics borrowed the main ideas and principles of their own systems. Following the path laid out by Irenaeus and Tertullian, the author of the *Philosophumena* in particular pursued this line of thinking most extensively. His entire text is organized for this purpose. In aiming at the refutation of the Gnostic heresies, it consists simply in demonstrating that each Gnostic system followed a particular Greek philosopher. For instance, Simon Magus followed Heraclitus "the obscure," Valentinus followed Pythagoras and Plato, Basilides followed Aristotle, and Marcion followed Empedocles. In order to make these pairings as plausible as possible, the writer of the *Philosophumena* sets out the teachings of the Greek philosophers in a sequence from Thales onward. His demonstration is of course not very convincing, since he largely just sticks to isolated points and external analogies. However, on the whole his presentation of this general perspective confirms that the philosophical outlook of antiquity is the foundation of Gnosis, and that this foundation passed over from Gnosis to Christianity. This philosophical outlook blended with Christianity to become a system consisting of various elements but resting on one and the same fundamental way of seeing things. In form and content, Gnosis in the Christian sense is the expansion and continuation of the Alexandrian religious philosophy, which had proceeded on the basis of Greek philosophy.

The Main Elements: Spirit and Matter; the Demiurge and Christ

However, to become better acquainted with its essential nature, we have to analyze the main components of Gnosis in such a way that we can see, for each of its characteristic concepts, whether that concept is more expressive of a pagan outlook or a Christian outlook.

In all of its forms, Gnosis is fundamentally dualistic. Nothing else is so directly indicative of its being a product of the pagan outlook as its sharply-defined, all-pervasive dualism. Pagan antiquity never got beyond the antithesis of spirit and matter, and could never conceive of a world produced by the free, creative activity of a purely personal will. In the Gnostic systems the two principles of spirit and matter likewise form the most general antithesis, the sphere of operations for everything in the world. Since the two principles cannot just be antithetical in an abstract sense, the main content of the Gnostic systems can only be based on the reciprocal engagement of the two principles as initiating the process of world development.

The world is the sum and substance of the relative antitheses that are conditioned and constrained by bounds set to the absolute antithesis. Everything in the world takes its own course as prescribed by how the balance between the two poles of the general antithesis shifts one way or the other. The initiative comes from one pole or the other. If it comes from matter, then matter as active on its own is also the principle of evil, and the process of world development takes the form of the two powers reacting hostilely to each other, an ongoing antagonism. As the realm of darkness, matter's natural impulse is hostility toward the principle of light. If the initial impulse of world development comes from the spiritual principle, then this impulse can only be spiritual in nature. The moving principle is then spirit's involvement with itself, wherein spirit naturally strives to distinguish itself from itself and, in the distinction of the different moments established by its thinking activity, it strives to become self-conscious spirit—spirit reflected within itself. The process of world development goes forward from these great heights of a purely spiritual process and into the sphere of physical and material life, with matter itself just setting bounds to spiritual being, to spirit become objective and external to itself.

However negative this concept of matter is, we still have here at least the dualistic outlook, involving the absolute antithesis of the principles. The principle of matter is already posited in spirit's urge to go out from itself and objectify itself. Here we have self-materializing spirit's path from above to below, a path for which there is no further explanation than this [urge itself]. There is then likewise a strong foundation, in the essence of the spiritual principle, for spirit to free itself in turn from the dominance matter has gained over it; to win absolute ascendancy over any limiting and eclipsing effect on matter's part; and ultimately to end the entire course of world development so that spirit will, as pure spirit, simply return into itself. But when all is said and done, the absolute antithesis of the principles still forever remains, because the same process of world development can always begin anew and follow the same course. The principle of matter can never be so annulled, and the antithesis of the two principles can never just be conceived so abstractly, that there is never again the possibility, or the necessity, for spirit to be drawn, again and again, into the same process of world development, in an endless series of worlds. Matter cannot ascend to a spiritual form (*zum Geist*), but spirit can certainly relinquish (*entäussern*) itself and descend into material form (*zur Materie*). So there are the emanations and projections (προβολαί) of spirit that occupy the infinite gap between spirit and matter, and constitute, to the fullest extent possible, the transitional stages from spirit to matter.

Hence in most Gnostic systems the Aeons, as the forms of the self-objectifying spirit, occupy a very important position, and mainly because of that these systems also bear the marks of the ancient outlook. For the Aeons are none other than the ideas personified, the archetypes of the finite world. They also involve the antithesis of the ideal world and the real world, in other words, the world above and the world below. The latter form of the antithesis has an even more profound significance for the Gnostic systems.

Another major concept of the Gnostic systems is that of the Demiurge. Since the two highest principles are spirit and matter, and that very fact rules out any proper concept of a creation of the world, the Gnostic systems typically tend to set the world's creator apart from the supreme God, and to assign a lesser position to that being, who is not so much a "creator" as he is a "shaper" of the world. But how then do the Gnostics arrive at their notion of a Demiurge? From their identifying him with the Jewish God, one could infer that their systems simply took the Demiurge over from Judaism, and that this concept therefore just belongs to the standpoint of Jewish religion. However, Platonism of course already had its own Demiurge, one playing the same role as the Gnostics' Demiurge.[14] On the one hand the Platonic Demiurge of course stands higher than the θεοὶ θεῶν, the gods of nature religion in the myths. He is the one God and father of the workmanship he has produced[15] and that will not be destroyed unless he wills it. On the other hand, however, he also has a higher principle above him. For this Platonic God is dependent on the Platonic ideas, and can only accomplish his creative workmanship by constantly looking to the never-changing ideas as the archetypes for it. Now since the Demiurge plays the same subordinate role for Plato as he does for the Gnostics, the underlying notion can only be the same in both cases.

For Plato, the mythical domain as a rule also has its own immanent truth. For Plato, inasmuch as myth is a necessary form for presenting abstract philosophical ideas, his Demiurge is also a figure of myth.[16] The creative power of the ideas is personified in the Demiurge. However, this personification is only the form mediating between the mythical notion and philosophical consciousness. The Platonic Demiurge is where mythical polytheism gets resolved into a monotheism, the higher truth of which is the very fact that something utterly one in its nature replaces an indeterminate multiplicity. It is a truth in which of course the oneness expresses the absolute idea, but which does justice to the mythical element as well, because the one world-creator is a freely-acting personal being of the same kind as the gods of the mythical popular beliefs.

The Gnostic Demiurge also is understood from the same perspective. To say that Gnosis took its essential contents from Greek philosophy is just part of the picture. The rest is that Gnosis presented these contents in a form reflecting the mythical outlook of Greek popular religion. Gnosis is not merely Greek philosophy, for Greek mythology is also an essential component of Gnosis. All those beings of the world of the Aeons, beings presenting the idea of the absolute in its various facets, are mythic figures, and the Demiurge stands apart from them in virtue of his lower level, which makes his mythical form even more concrete. He reflects and represents the popular God-consciousness of the myth.

The best reason the Gnostics had for identifying the Demiurge with the God of Judaism is that the Old Testament God is preeminently depicted as the world's Lord and Creator. But this identification also expresses the Gnostics' view of Old Testament religion. They could only assign it to a stage of religious development at

---

14. See my essay in *Theologische Studien und Kritiken* cited above (n. 5), 547ff.

15. [*Ed.*] See Plato, *Timaeus*, 28c, "the Maker and Father of this Universe."

16. [*Ed.*] For Plato, this myth of creation by the Demiurge is not knowledge per se, but is "the likely account of these matters (περὶ τούτων τον εἰκότα μῦδον)," that is, opinion or belief (*Timaeus* 29d).

which religious consciousness had not yet gotten beyond a representation that, like the notion of the Demiurge, still inherently had so many sensuous elements. What we mainly see with the Gnostic Demiurge is that the content of Gnosis is not so much philosophy as it is religion. For what sets religion apart from philosophy is the more concrete and more sensuous form in which the inherently abstract philosophical idea appears when presented by religion. Now since Gnosis assigns a more or less subordinate stage to all representations of this kind, with the more sensuous forms at the lower levels, and with Gnosis itself, as thinking consciousness, positioned above the sphere of mythical-religious modes of representation, Gnosis in itself is for that very reason neither philosophy nor religion, but instead both at the same time. For Gnosis relates its own two elements, philosophical and religious, in such a way that we can only describe the general character of Gnosis as religious philosophy.

The Gnostic Demiurge is a case in point for how the relation between philosophy and religion can be variously defined, depending on whether they are thought of as more or less identical in content and form. As we see with the Platonic Demiurge, the more closely the absolute idea of God is tied to the Demiurge, the more the mythical personal element appears to be an inherently necessary form of its presentation, one inseparably connected with the content. By the same token, the further the Gnostic systems place the Demiurge below the absolute God, and the more sharply this separates them, the more it expresses how decidedly philosophical reflection is dismissive of the sensuous concreteness of the religious mode of representation.

Gnosis settled the issue as to how all these concepts, standpoints, and antitheses are interrelated, by establishing not merely two principles but three principles. It located the domain proper to the Demiurge under the psychical principle, which stands between the pneumatic principle and the material principle. These three principles are the elements of all natural and spiritual being. For instance, they serve to divide human beings into three essentially different classes. A meeting of the spiritual and material principles as such would be possible only via a form, such as the psychical principle, mediating between them. So the psychical is of course a third principle. But since only two of them are principles in themselves, and since the pneumatic principle is in fact the substantial element in the psychical principle, it is the nature of the psychical to ultimately resolve itself, or be taken up, into the pneumatic. The psychical is finite, is transitory, so that indeed the Demiurge's entire world must ultimately come to an end. The distinction between the pneumatic and the psychical, the distinction underlying the difference between philosophy and religion, in the final analysis, therefore rests as such on there being different standpoints from which to consider what is an inherently identical content, but one presenting itself in different forms.

The role played by the Demiurge in the Gnostic systems, when they focus on the downward direction things take, has its counterpart in Christ when their focus is upward. Just as there is descent, there must also be ascent. The Gnostic systems make their Christian character known not merely by giving Christ this specific place in their systematic structure, but also by greatly emphasizing this aspect of it. As this system moves through its various moments, Christ is the turning point. Much of this system is connected with the names Christ and Jesus and the concepts related to these names: everything referring in some way to mediating between one part and another, to maintaining the coherence of the whole, to reconnecting what has come apart, to retrieving the apostate, to moving from the lower world to the world above—in general, to leading everything to where the consummation and conclusion of the entire course of the world is to be found. These names embody the goal toward which the entire development or unfolding of the world is striving.

In the Gnostic systems, what was originally just redemption in the moral and religious sense became the reinstatement and consummation of the entire world order. Just as Christ restored the harmony that was disrupted in the Aeon world, by operating there as a cohesive, stabilizing, and unifying principle, the Jesus born of Mary, and the Soter or Savior in the specific sense, carried out in the lower world this same task of διόρθωσις (correction) or ἐπανόρθωσις (rectification), as the Gnostics designate their concept of redemption.[17] Christ is not so much the principle of salvation as he is instead the universal cosmic principle. In the Gnostic systems, their worldview is said to contemplate and conceptualize the exodus or procession of the finite from the absolute, taking its direction from above to below and descending ever deeper, until finally reaching the point at which the universal reversal must follow. Thus Christianity comprises all that the other and opposite aspect to this involves, in the direction from below to above.

The Pauline theological framework also of course contains reference points and elements for such an understanding of Christianity. In it Adam and Christ each stand at the head of one of the two major world periods. They are juxtaposed as the two principles of the psychic and the pneumatic respectively, of death and life. In Paulinism, Christ is the one to whom everything is subject, in his role as victor over sin, death, and hell, so that God is ultimately all in all. Even more pertinent here are the Epistles to the Ephesians and the Colossians, which give such lofty and universal standing to christology, doubtless under the influence of Gnosis itself. But only in the Gnostic systems is Christ set within a context where his appearing and his effectiveness, in other words Christianity as such, can only be understood from the perspective of a process in which the world's unfolding, from beginning to end, takes its appointed course as conditioned by the antithesis of the principles.

---

17. *Philosophumena* (n. 11) 6.19 (p. 175) [ET 386–91]; 6.32.4 (p. 190) [ET 420–21]; 6.36.4 (pp. 195–96) [ET 436–37].

Early Gnostic Sects

Before we can expound further on the essential nature of Gnosis, we need a brief overview of the different sects, forms, and systems of Gnosticism.[18]

Cerinthus

Cerinthus was a Jewish Christian, and the first prominent Christian Gnostic. As the most recently discovered source for our knowledge of Gnostic teachings confirms,[19] he had already introduced the characteristic feature of Gnosis, by setting the concept of God apart from the concept of the world's creator. He is said to have taught that the world did not come to exist because of the first and highest being. Instead the world was created by a power separate from that universal principle, a power that did not know the God who transcends all things. Cerinthus contended that Jesus, the natural-born son of Joseph and Mary, differed from other human beings only by his greater righteousness and wisdom. This contention expressed the Christian element of his Gnosis. Cerinthus said that, at Jesus' baptism, Christ, who is the Son of the most high God, descended on Jesus in the form of a dove; that he proclaimed the unknown Father[20]; but that Christ ultimately withdrew from Jesus and remained free from suffering while Jesus suffered and was resurrected.

Simon Magus and the Simonians

According to the church fathers, Simon Magus was the first Gnostic and the forefather of all the Gnostic sects, a contention clearly without any basis in fact. If Simon had actually been the originator of all the teachings the church fathers ascribe to him, that would have to push the origin of Gnosis back to a time when there are no historical data to support their supposition. The church fathers' Simon Magus, as forefather of the Gnostics, is an entirely apocryphal and mythical figure that can only be seen as one personification of Gnosis. In alleging that he himself is the most high God, he is just presenting himself as someone conveying the Gnostic idea of the primal being, as personified in himself.

However, the fundamental conception of the Gnosis supposedly symbolized mythically in Simon, and in his consort Helena, is the Gnostic idea of syzygy, or conjunction. Since the Gnostics sought to understand the absolute concept of the primal being as abstractly as possible, and yet also had to presuppose a principle of

---

18. [*Ed.*] Our headings and subheadings from here to the end of the discussion of Gnosticism differ slightly from those found in Baur's table of contents.

19. *Philosophumena* 7.33.1 (pp. 256–57) [ET 566–69]. Cf. Irenaeus, *Against Heresies* 1.25 [*ANF* 1:351–52].

20. *Philosophumena* has τὸν γνωστὸν πατέρα (p. 257) [known Father], but it must be ἄγνωστον [unknown], as in Irenaeus, *Against Heresies*. [*Ed.*] The ET also corrects to "unknown."

differentiation being already present within it, by using their mythical way of thinking they represented the supreme being as androgynous so they could conceive of how it is possible for the finite to arise from the absolute. According to the author of the *Philosophumena*, Simon is said to have declared the following[21] about his highest principle.[22]

> There are two offshoots of all the aeons, having neither beginning nor end. They are from a single root or power, namely, invisible and incomprehensible Silence. One of these appears above: a Great Power, Mind of the universe, pervading all things and male. The other is below: Thought, who is magnificent, female, and generates all things. Hence they correspond to each other and form a pair. In the intervening space, they exhibit an immeasurable expanse of air, which has neither beginning nor end. In this air, the Father upholds all things and nourishes those beings that have beginning and end. He is the One Who Stood, Who Stands, Who Will Stand. He is an androgynous power as is right for the infinite preexisting power having neither beginning nor end and existing in unity. From this power the Thought in the unity came forth and became two.

However, the duality is not said to annul the unity since, as duality, it is also just the one, self-identical principle.[23]

---

21. [*Ed.*] In the quotation that follows, Baur closely paraphrases the *Philosophumena* 6.18.2–4, but without indicating as much or providing a citation. We have replaced Baur's wording with the English of the translation by Litwa (n. 11), 385–87.

22. In the ἀπόφασις μεγάλη (great declaration) ascribed to Simon, this phrase should be taken in the same sense as when Simon himself was said to be the δύναμις μεγάλη (great power). Ἀπόφασις means "negation" [the ET reads "declaration"]. The great negation is doubtless none other than the Gnostic process as it is designated in the two notes following this one—through affirmation and negation, between above and below, proceeding through unity and the duality arising via emanation and projection and, in the world of representation, annulling once more the shapes established in that world and taking them back into itself. In this case too Simon Magus, as the author of such a writing, is just the ideal expression of what people envisaged as the distinctiveness of Gnosis. And if there was in fact no Simon Magus, then there were also no Simonians. The ones people called Simonians were just those who utilized the writings reputedly written by Simon Magus. See Adolf Hilgenfeld, *Die apostolischen Väter* (Halle, 1853), 242ff.

23. *Philosophumena* 6.18.6–7 (p. 173): "... thus there is an androgynous power and Thought. Thus they correspond to each other. This is because power does not at all differ from Thought; they are one. Power is discovered from things above, while Thought is discovered from things below. It works the same way with what is manifested from them. Though one, they are discovered to be two. The androgynous one contains the female in himself. So also there is Mind in Thought. They are inseparable. Although one, they are discovered to be two" [ET 386–87]. Cf. *Philosophumena*, p. 171: "This, he says, is the single power, divided above and below, giving birth to itself, increasing itself, seeking itself, finding itself, being mother of itself, father of itself, sister of itself, partner of itself, daughter of itself, son of itself, mother and father, yet one—the rest of the universe" [ET 382–83 from 6.17.3]. What stands as threefold is said to present the three moments of the primal being existent in itself, proceeding out from itself and taking itself back into itself. As described elsewhere, he is the one "standing on high in unborn power," the one "standing down below in the flowing stream, begotten in images," and the one "having come to stand above, at the pinnacle of blessedness, renouncing images." In other words,

Since the primal being is envisaged as a spiritual principle, the principle of differentiation that the primal being contains is therefore also of a spiritual kind. It is self-moving spiritual activity, presenting itself in the perceptions and images of the finite world of the senses. This ἐπίνοια (thought) is mythically personified, as the representing consciousness and the world of representation, by Helena who stands at Simon's side. This is the Gnostic method of borrowing its pictorial forms from Greek mythology in order to present Gnosticism's speculative ideas.[24]

The Ophites

The oldest Gnostic sects are doubtless those that do not take their names from a specific founder, but instead just express the general conception of Gnosis by their names. They include the Ophites, or Naassenes. The church fathers likened the Ophites, or "Brethren of the Snake," to the serpent [in Genesis 3], in order to point to the dangerous poison of their teaching, and they portrayed the Ophites as the many-headed Hydra that always raised up a new head. But for the Ophites themselves, the serpent was itself the symbol of their higher knowledge. In the story of the Fall, the serpent appears as the intelligent being who knows how to dialectically interweave good and evil, in such a way that this marked the beginning of the process of world history, in the antagonism of the two principles.

According to the author of the *Philosophumena*, the first priests and overseers of this dogma were the so-called Naassenes, a name derived from the Hebrew term for snake [*naas*]. "Later they called themselves 'gnostics,' claiming that they alone know the deep mysteries. From these people, many splintered off and split the heresy into many factions" since they "narrated the same teaching with different terminology."[25]

---

when the one has objectified itself in a real likeness, it goes back from this self-divestment and into the oneness of the principle. [*Ed.*] Baur quotes these passages in Greek. He gives no specific reference for the final set of quotations, and we are unable to locate them.

24. In *Philosophumena* 6.19.1, it says that Simon "invented [things], distorting by his arbitrary interpretation not only the writings of Moses but also those of the poets" [ET 386–87]. In doing so he is also entirely representative of the essence of Gnosis, which appropriates everything via allegorical interpretation. See my *Die christliche Gnosis* (n. 5), 305ff. The essence of Gnosis, as destructive of all that is positive by dissolving it into general ideas and perceptions, is certainly typified in the two figures of Simon and Helena. (Since all the worldly powers wanted to share in her ἐπίνοια, her beauty was said to be the cause of the Trojan War.) See the account in *Philosophumena* 6.18.5–6 (p. 175), of Simon's ἐπίγνωσις, his own knowledge: "Having redeemed Helen, Simon provided salvation to human beings in the same manner: through his own knowledge. Since the angels mismanaged the world on account of their lust to rule, he said that he arrived for its rectification. He transformed and assimilated himself to the rulers, authorities, and angels. He appeared to be human but was not human. He seemed to suffer in Judea, although he suffered nothing. But after appearing in Judea as Son, and in Samaria as Father, and among the rest of the nations as the Holy Spirit, he allowed himself to be called by whatever name people wish to call him" [ET 388–89]. So Gnostic knowledge involves knowing and recognizing the same one religion in all forms of religion, and the same one being in all the spiritual powers of the world.

25. [*Ed.*] Baur's German here is actually paraphrase, turning into direct translation, of

According to Irenaeus and Epiphanius, they had a system, worked out with various elements, that is very similar to the Valentinian one.[26] In the *Philosophumena* their teaching appears to be simpler [than the Valentinians']. Just as Simon purportedly did, the Ophites too characterized the primal being as androgynous, although they call it "Human" and "Human Son," or "Adamas" (Adam). In this Adamas they distinguish three principles: spiritual, psychical, and material. Gnostic perfection was said to begin with knowledge of the Human and to end with knowledge of God.[27] They make Jesus the counterpart of the primal Human. They maintain that everything united in the primal human being—the spiritual, psychical, and material aspects—descended together upon one human person, Jesus born of Mary.[28]

The Peratai

The Peratai have until now not been well-known. The author of the *Philosophumena* first filled out the history of these heretics' teaching,[29] which is similar to that of the Ophites. They affirm three principles: the unborn Good, the self-born Good, and what is born. Everything is divided in a threefold way, and Christ is the sum and substance of all the threefold divisions. The seeds of all possible powers are descended into this world of ours from the two higher worlds, those of unborn and self-born goodness. Christ too came down from the unborn Good, in order by his descent to save everything divided in a threefold way. Through him all that has come down from above returns. The third world [that of the born] must perish, but the two higher worlds are everlasting.

Euphrates the Peratic and Kelbes [actually Akembes] the Karystian, are named as founders of the Peratic heresy. However, the name "Peratai" (Traversers) seems rather to refer to the fact that the Peratai—who alone know the necessary law of what has

---

Philosophumena 5.6.3–4 (ET 194–97), although he does not indicate that or give a citation.

26. See *Die christliche Gnosis* (n. 5), 171ff. [*Ed.*] Cf. Irenaeus, *Against Heresies* 1.30.15.

27. *Philosophumena* 5.6.6 (p. 95). [*Ed.*] Our translation of Baur is guided by, but not quite the same as, the ET (196–99). In his footnote, Baur gives the Greek for the last sentence of this citation. The ET reads that "the Human" is what is androgynous and what is called "Adamas," although its footnotes indicate that scholarly opinion differs as to which element "androgynous" and "Adamas" apply.

28. [*Ed.*] Baur does not mention the very interesting statements that follow this in *Philosophumena* 5.6.7: "These three humans [i.e., aspects of the primal human being] were speaking together at the same time, individually from their own substances to their own people. There are, according to them, three kinds of people in the universe, angelic, animate [i.e., psychical], and earthly. They are called 'the elect,' 'the called,' and 'the captive'" (ET 198–99). Perhaps he omits a reference here because Irenaeus (*Against Heresies* 1.8.3) attributes this view directly to the Valentinians.

29. *Philosophumena* 5.12.1–18 (pp. 123ff.) [ET 276–311]. [*Ed.* The corrections at the end of *Das Christenthum* add the following to this note:] The Peratai were of course already known from Theodoret, *Heretical Tales*, 1.17. However, as G. Volkmar has shown, in *Hippolytus und die römischen Zeitgenossen* (Zurich, 1855), 22ff., in his heresiology Theodoret simply utilized the summation in Book 10 of the *Philosophumena*. Hence we know the special features of the Peratai teaching only from the cited passages of the *Philosophumena* [10.10.1–4].

come to be and by which route human beings came into the world—are also those who claim to be alone the ones able to overcome its transitoriness.[30] The Peratai locate the principle of transitoriness, or destruction, in water, and say that water is the death that overtook the Egyptians in the Red Sea. Someone who is ignorant is "an Egyptian"; so people should "abandon Egypt," that is, leave the body. They regard the body as a "little Egypt," and demand that people pass through the Red Sea, the water of destruction, which is Kronos [or Saturn] and proceed into the desert. By this they mean one should pass beyond the temporal world where all the gods, those of destruction and the God of salvation, are together in one place. The gods of destruction are the heavenly bodies of the changeable world, and they subject to necessity everything that comes into being. Moses called these gods the "biting serpents of the desert" that killed those who supposed they had left the Red Sea behind them. He showed the true serpent to those bitten in the desert, the perfect serpent, and whoever believed in it would not be bitten in the desert.[31] No one but the perfect serpent can save those who leave the land of Egypt, that is, go out from the body and from this world. Whoever sets his hope on this serpent will not be destroyed by the snakes of the desert, that is, by the gods of the temporal world.[32]

These Gnostics have such high regard for the significance of the serpent in several Old Testament passages—as salvific symbol in the desert, as the wonder-working staff of Moses in Egypt (Exod 4:17), and above all in the story of the Fall[33]—that they see in the serpent one of their highest principles. The serpent was the same being as the Son. Between the Father on the one side and matter on the other side, is the Son, the Logos, the serpent, ever moving both toward the motionless Father and toward self-moving matter; now turning to the Father and now turning with these powers to matter. Formless matter receives into itself the ideas from the Son, ideas the Son has had imprinted in himself from the Father. Just as the serpent is the intermediary between the Father and matter, in order to bring the powers of the higher world down into the lower world, so the serpent, or Son, is also the sole saving principle, bringing

---

30. *Philosophumena* 5.16.1 (p. 131). [*Ed.*] Baur's footnote gives the Greek—διελθεῖν καὶ περᾶσει τὴν φθοράν—for "cross over and traverse the destruction" (ET 296–97).

31. [*Ed.*] See Num 21:5–9: "The people spoke against God and against Moses, 'Why have you brought us up out of Egypt to die in the wilderness? For there is no food and no water, and we detest this miserable food.' Then the LORD sent poisonous serpents among the people, and they bit the people, so that many Israelites died. The people came to Moses and said, 'We have sinned by speaking against the LORD and against you; pray to the LORD to take away the serpents from us.' So Moses prayed for the people. And the LORD said to Moses, 'Make a poisonous serpent, and set it on a pole; and everyone who is bitten shall look at it and live.' So Moses made a serpent of bronze, and put it upon a pole; and whenever a serpent bit someone, that person would look at the serpent of bronze and live."

32. [*Ed.*] This passage about the snakes of the desert draws heavily on *Philosophumena* 5.16.6–8 (ET 298–301).

33. *Philosophumena*, 133: "The universal snake, he says, is the wise word of Eve" [ET 300–1 from 5.16.8]. As universal world-symbol, the snake is said to be "catholic" in about the same sense as, in §47 of Theodoret's *Excerpta ex scripturis*, the Demiurge in the higher, universal sense is called καθολικός in distinguishing it from the Demiurge proper.

about the return.[34] Thus, in short, the serpent is the very process of the world's development, winding its way dialectically via the antitheses.

Summary

These teachings, which constantly make reference to the same problems—the oneness, duality, or triplicity of principles; the antitheses and mediation of principles; the descent from the world above into the world below, and the return from it to the world above—have an essential content so universal in nature that these teachings could have been present long before a specifically Christian Gnosis arose. Thus they took on their Christian tenor and modifications only subsequently, as these doctrines increasingly became amplified by the allegorical and syncretistic outlook. That is the form in which we encounter the essence of Gnosis in what are reputed to be the doctrines and teachings of the Simonians, the Ophites, the Gnostics, the Peratai, and the Sethians (who belong in this group too), especially as the *Philosophumena* portrays them—a fluid and muddled Gnosis, attaching itself to any possibility, constantly seeking out new ways of expressing its general, fundamental vision by turning to the whole colorful array of ancient symbols and myths.

The Major Christian Gnostics

A more developed kind of Gnosis, more rigorous and more self-consistent and in a form treating the Christian element as an essential, organic component of the whole system rather than as a separable element, first presents itself to us in those systems known by the names of their individual founders. The most important of these individuals are the three famous leaders of Gnostic sects: Valentinus, Basilides, and Marcion.

This major period of Gnosis begins in the first decades of the second century. The most reliable accounts about the origins of Gnosis agree that the founders of the Gnostic heresies appeared during the reigns of Trajan and Hadrian.[35] Basilides is said to have lived in Alexandria around 125, and Valentinus reportedly went from Alexandria to Rome about 140. About the same time Marcion came to Rome from Sinope in Pontus, and his activities in Rome are dated as occurring during 140–50.[36] Also very

---

34. *Philosophumena*, 135ff. [ET 304–11 from 5.17.2–10].

35. Hegesippus, in Eusebius, *Ecclesiastical History* 3.32; Clement of Alexandria, *Stromata* 7.17. [*Ed.*] Trajan ruled 98–117, Hadrian, 117–38.

36. Regarding the chronological information about Marcion and his appearing in Rome, see Gustav Volkmar, "Die Zeit Justin's des Märtyrers," *Theologische Jahrbücher* 14 (1855) 270–71: "All the earlier fathers of the church, when speaking specifically about the time of Marcion, clearly state that he first appeared in the reign of Antoninus Pius [ruled 138–61], or at the earliest in 135." In the *Libellus adversus omnes haereses*, undoubtedly not written by Tertullian, there is a statement about the occasion leading to Marcion's leaving Pontus and going to Rome: "After him (Cerdo) there emerged

noteworthy for the history of Gnosis is the information that several of these Gnostics were natives of Alexandria, and that Valentinus and Marcion, two very important leaders of Gnostic sects, both headed for Rome.

Valentinus

The profoundest of these Gnostic systems, and the one we have the most detailed knowledge of, is the system associated with Valentinus,[37] although it cannot be determined which elements in the Valentinian system come from Valentinus himself and which ones come from his followers.

The Valentinian system is fully occupied with taking the dimensions of the world of the Aeons, and with the number and categories of the Aeons. There are thirty Aeons in all, and they fall into several basic numerical groups, an ogdoad (of eight Aeons), a decad (ten), and a dodecad (twelve). However, the Aeons always go together in pairs, since the idea of syzygy (conjunction) is a basic concept here too, one on which the system rests. But the question as to whether the highest being itself should also be thought of as together with a female Aeon seemed to elicit various answers from the followers of Valentinus. Some of them wanted to have the Father be utterly alone, whereas others regarded it as impossible that something could have proceeded from a male figure alone. Thus for the Father to be able to become the Father of the whole, they paired him with silence (Σιγή) as his wife (σύζυγος). However, even this silence is but an expression for the abstract concept of his absolute oneness or his being-alone.

Nevertheless, since he did not like solitude and was wholly love, and since love is not love if there is not also love's object, the Father therefore had within him the urge to engender and bring forth the very finest and most perfect of what he had within himself. So, alone as he was, he engendered or produced Nous (mind) and Aletheia (truth), the dyad that is the mother of the Aeons within the pleroma. Nous and Aletheia themselves then produced Logos (reason) and Zoë (life) respectively, and these two then produced Anthropos (humankind) and Ecclesia (the church). To glorify the perfect Father by a perfect number, Nous and Aletheia engendered ten

---

a disciple of his, one Marcion by name, a native of Pontus, son of a bishop, excommunicated because of a rape committed on a certain virgin" [*Against All Heresies*, ch. 6 (*ANF* 3:653)]. It now seems to me (cf. *Die christliche Gnosis* [n. 5], 296) best to interpret the phrase *stuprum virginis* (rape of a virgin) most simply by assuming it was originally just a figurative expression for Marcion's heresy, by which he did violence to the church (ἐκκλησία) as the "pure and incorruptible virgin" (παρθένος καθαρὰ ἀδιάφθορος), as Hegesippus describes it according to Eusebius, *Ecclesiastical History* 3.32.

37. [*Ed.*] Valentinus (c. 100–c. 160) was born in Egypt and received a Greek education in Alexandria, where he became conversant with Hellenistic Middle Platonism and Hellenized Judaism. Later he became a prominent Roman Christian and a candidate for bishop of Rome. He is known mostly through fragments of writings quoted by his opponents (Irenaeus, Tertullian, et al.). Baur does not indicate specific sources. Valentinus had many disciples and his ideas were the most widely diffused of any of the Gnostic systems. The *Gospel of Truth*, attributed to him by Irenaeus, was not discovered until 1945 in the Nag Hammadi Library.

Aeons, whereas Logos and Zoë could only give rise from themselves to the imperfect number of twelve Aeons. Howsoever the Valentinians may have conceptualized the relationships of this dodecad and this decad, in any event the main series of the Aeons is formed by the six primal Aeons, Nous and Aletheia, Logos and Zoë, Anthropos and Ecclesia. But the major factor as the system unfolds further is the well-known myth relating to the Sophia (wisdom).

This Sophia is the twelfth member of the dodecad, the youngest one of the twenty-eight Aeons and, as the weakest and most outlying member of the whole series of Aeons, she is a female Aeon. She was then the one most distant from the primal principle, and as her awareness of this distance grew, she increasingly felt the urge to unite directly with the primal being by leaping over all the other members of the world of Aeons. She leapt back into the depths of the Father and sought, as the Father does, to engender or produce, by herself alone, nothing less than what the Father engenders. She did not know that only what is itself not engendered—being the principle of the whole, the root, the depth, what is ungrounded (*Abgrund*) or the abyss—is able to produce solely on its own. Only in what is not engendered is everything as one, for in what is engendered the female element produces the substance of the product and the male element gives form to the substance the female element produces. So what the Sophia produced was only an ἔκτρωμα (abortion), as the Valentinians call it. Within the pleroma, there was not-knowing (*Unwissenheit*) on the Sophia's part, and formlessness in what she produced. Confusion arose within the pleroma, and the entire world of the Aeons was in danger of becoming formless and deficient, and ultimately of collapsing into ruin. All the Aeons flew to the Father and implored him to calm down the Sophia, who was distressed about her offspring.

It is easy to see that this myth claims to explain how the finite comes forth from the absolute, and that the finite can arise only from the absolute; and yet the finite does not fit well with the concept of the absolute. Even though the concept of syzygy and the concept of engendering already posit the finite as being within the absolute itself, and even though in the series of Aeons, with Aeons engendering Aeons, the difference posited there is always once again thought of as a difference offset by their oneness, in the end it must all come down to a breaking away from the absolute without any further mediation, if the finite is otherwise said to come about as finite. Thus a breach took place within the absolute itself, a rift, a cleavage placing in question the absoluteness of the absolute. The task can then only be, on the one hand, to keep the concept of the absolute intact in its purity despite this breach, and on the other hand, to detach the finite from the absolute, to cut it free from the absolute.

This is then where the specifically Christian idea of restitution or restoration comes into play in this system. Because the Father had compassion for the tears of the Sophia, and heeded the pleas of the Aeons, he commanded a new projection to fill out the number of Aeons to thirty. From Nous and Aletheia there now issued Christ and the Holy Spirit, in order to give form to the aborted product and to separate it [from the world of Aeons], and to comfort and calm the Sophia. Christ separated the formless aborted product off from the collective Aeons so that the sight of its formlessness would not be disturbing for the perfect Aeons. So that this product would no longer be visible to them, the Father issued forth Stauros, yet another Aeon who, in portraying within himself the Father's greatness and perfection, and in holding the collective thirty Aeons together within himself, was supposed to be the pleroma's boundary post. This one is called Horos because he is the boundary between the pleroma and the defective thing (ὑστέρημα) found outside it; he is called the Sharer (μετοχεύς) because he also has a role in relation to the defective thing; and he is called Stauros (the Cross) because he stands immovably, such that nothing of the defective thing can even come anywhere near the Aeons found within the pleroma.

In addition to this Horos or Stauros there was the so-called Ogdoas, the Sophia found outside of the pleroma. As soon as Christ had formed her, he sprang, together with the Holy Spirit, back into the pleroma, to Nous and Aletheia, and all the Aeons were at peace and in unity. So harmony was restored within the pleroma, although this same process took a further course of its own outside of the pleroma, where the Sophia, separated from the one who formed her but then left her once more, was now terrified. In her longing and her suffering she implored him, and Christ and the other Aeons all pitied her. Jesus, or the Savior, who is called the common fruit of all the Aeons of the pleroma, appears in place of Christ. Christ and the other Aeons sent him outside the pleroma, as the σύζυγος (consort, or partner) of the external Sophia, in order to end the suffering she endured in her longing for Christ. This Jesus, or Savior, freed her from longing by divesting her of the various emotions constituting it, and by making these emotions into the psychical domain, the kingdom of the Demiurge.

The Gnostics thought of the psychical substance as being fiery, and they also called it "Place" and "Hebdomad" and "Ancient of Days."[38] The Demiurge has a fiery nature too, and Moses' statement (Deut 9:3) that "the Lord your God is . . . as a devouring fire" accurately describes the Demiurge. The Demiurge is essentially constituted by all that sets the psychical realm apart from the pneumatic realm. The Demiurge has no intelligent consciousness. Without him knowing what he is doing, the Sophia, hovering in the Ogdoad above him, does everything in and through him, whereas he supposes that he brings about the creation of the world on his own. Believing this about himself, he says, "I am God and there is no god besides me" (Deut 32:39). The Demiurge is the creator of the souls, to which he has given bodies consisting of physical and demonic substances. Thus the inner person, the psychical person, dwells in the physical or material body. [This dwelling is] sometimes for the soul on its own, sometimes for a soul together with demons, and sometimes for a soul together with λόγοι (rational principles).[39] These λόγοι, which come from above, from the common fruit of the pleroma and the Sophia, have been strewn into this world like seeds.

38. [*Ed.*] See *Philosophumena* (n. 11), 6.32.8 (ET 422–23).
39. [*Ed.*] See *Philosophumena* 6.34.6 (ET 428–29). There are three kinds of persons: physical,

This Jesus linked to the Sophia, who is outside the pleroma, is actually a second Christ along the lines of the first Christ. From this second Christ the Valentinians distinguish yet a third one, the Jesus born of Mary. The first Christ restored order to the pleroma, the second one restored order to the Ogdoad of the Sophia, and the third one is said to do the same for the world that now exists. But the Christ who comes not merely via the Demiurge, but also via the Sophia, can only bring about that restoration by revealing what was concealed even from the Demiurge. The Sophia had indeed already informed the Demiurge that he is not the one and only God; that there is one higher than him. So he had not been unaware of the great secret about the Father and the Aeons, although he had kept that to himself and imparted it to no one. Hence the revelation of the secret did not take place within the Demiurge's province. Instead Jesus was born of Mary when it was time to remove the veil obscuring the consciousness of human beings of the psychical realm and to bring all these mysteries to light.

Given this context, what else could Christianity be but making what the Demiurge already knew—but only in itself, in other words, just for or by himself—into a knowledge humankind was universally aware of? Therefore Christianity first enabled people to know that the Demiurge is not the most high God; that the world of Aeons or the pleroma, and the eternal Father, stand above the Demiurge. So Christianity first awakened people's consciousness of the absolute. But knowing this absolute is just the advance from the psychical level to the pneumatic or spiritual level. Indeed the Demiurge knows nothing of the higher world order standing above him, precisely because he is merely at the psychical level and what is psychical cannot take into itself what is pneumatic or spiritual. Thus when that knowledge is unveiled by Christ, but remains veiled to the Demiurge, this is, as such, the progression from the period of the psychical principle to the period of the pneumatic principle. Humankind enters upon a new and higher consciousness; it becomes aware of a higher world order, one lying beyond the earthly one, an order of what is existent in itself, of what is absolute and the absolute's relation to what is finite. However, it was indeed the pneumatic aspect itself that had first become the psychical aspect.

Accordingly, we have to distinguish two opposite aspects of the world's process of development. In one, the pneumatic descends into what is psychical, and in the other the psychical ascends into the pneumatic. So the psychical realm is just a transitional moment for what is spiritual. The pneumatic empties itself in becoming psychical, so as, in leaving the psychical, to regain itself within itself. Since the pneumatic principle is mind or spirit as distinct from matter, the series of moments in which the pneumatic becomes psychical, and the psychical then becomes pneumatic, is therefore spirit's process of engaging with itself. Spirit, or God as spirit in itself, goes out from itself, and the world has its origin in this self-revelation of God. The world in its distinction from God is also once again inherently one with God. But whether we look upon this immanent relation of God and world as God's self-revelation, or instead as the world's

---

psychical, pneumatic.

development, it is inherently a purely spiritual process, one grounded in the essence of spirit.

In the Aeons, which spirit issues forth from itself, spirit sets forth its own essence outside itself and over against itself. However, since the essence of spirit is, in itself, thinking and knowing, the process of spirit's self-revelation can therefore only consist of it being conscious of what it is in itself. The Aeons of the pleroma are the highest concepts of spiritual being and life; the universal thought forms in which what spirit is, in itself, it is for consciousness in a specific, concrete way. What is also posited together with spirit's self-knowing, with the self-consciousness of spirit distinguishing itself from itself, is not merely a principle of differentiation, but also—since God and world are inherently one—a principle of spirit taking on material or physical form. The more distant from the absolute principle are the concepts that impart the awareness of spirit, the more the spiritual consciousness becomes obscured. Spirit divests itself of itself; it is no longer clear and transparent to itself; the pneumatic sinks down to the psychical level; the psychical solidifies into material being; and at the extreme limits material being even gets involved with the concept of the demonic and the diabolical.[40] But since the psychical in itself is also a pneumatic nature, and the seeds

---

40. The most important point in the entire system is in fact the transition, depicted in the suffering of the Sophia, from the pneumatic to the psychical level. Spirit, wrestling with itself and despairing of itself, is in the greatest torment and distress when it is said to divest itself of itself and become something other than it is in itself. The passage in the *Philosophumena* (p. 191) [describing the fruit of the pleroma] says: "Thus he—being so great an aeon and an offspring of the entire Fullness—made her negative emotions depart from her and made them underlying substances. He made fear an animate substance, grief a material substance, and bewilderment the substance of demons. Finally, he made her yearning for return—her imploring, pleading, turning back, and her change of heart—a power of animate substance called 'the right hand'" [ET 420–23 from 6.32–36]. Cf. *Die christliche Gnosis* (n. 5), 134. [The passage continues, speaking of the Sophia and the Demiurge or "Artificer"]: "The Artificer is produced from fear. This, he says, is what the scripture means: 'The beginning of Wisdom is the LORD's fear.' It is this that is the beginning of Wisdom's wild emotions. For she was afraid, then grieved, then bewildered, and so rushed to implore and plead" [ET 422–23 from 6.32.7]. [*Ed.* The footnote to this passage in the ET cites Prov 1:7, "The fear of the LORD is the beginning of knowledge," but suggests it should be understood instead in the sense of *Philosophumena* 7.26.2, "The LORD's [fear is the beginning of wisdom.*"] There are therefore four states of this suffering. The psychical state arises from fear, the material or physical state arises from grief, and the demonic state from despair or bewilderment. A fourth element then follows, one seeming to be very different from the other three. Spirit can descend no lower than when it ultimately even transforms into the demonic. But for this very reason the fourth element or moment is the reversal and turning point. At the extreme point of its self-divestment, spirit goes back within itself and gathers itself together within itself, in order to find the way out of this agony or torment. Can the words ὁδός (way back), μετάνοια (change of heart), and δύναμις (power) have any other meaning than this?—In the Πίστις Σοφία, edited by Peterman (Berlin, 1851) from a Coptic manuscript, the suffering of the Sophia and her μετάνοια also provide the main contents of the first part. After his ascension, Jesus descends once more, simply to impart to his followers, openly and unveiled, the fullness of the truth from beginning to end. He tells them of the fall of the Sophia. When the Πίστις Σοφία was in the thirteenth [position] of the Aeons, in company with all her sisters, the ἀόρατοι (unseen) who themselves are the twenty-four προβολαί (defenders) of the great ἀόρατος (unseen realm), at the behest of the primary mystery, she looked into the heights and saw the light of the καταπέτασμα (veil) of the θησαυρός (treasure house) of the light. She longed to go to that place but was unable to do so. Instead of performing the mysteries of the thirteenth Aeon, she

of the spiritual life survive everywhere, the pneumatic aspect therefore must once more break through the material obscuring the spiritual consciousness at the level of psychical life and cast off the covering that, in the world of the Demiurge, lies over the spiritual consciousness.

The entire development of the world is the continuation of this same spiritual process. Hence there must also be a turning point at which spirit returns to itself, coming back from its self-divestment and returning to the clear awareness of what it is in itself. This is the Gnostic conception of Christian revelation. "Those who know" in the Gnostic sense of this expression, the pneumatic ones who as such also have within them the truly Christian consciousness, are a new element of the general religious life, the highest stage of God's self-revelation and of the world's development. This period of the world's course begins when Christ appears and ultimately ends when, via Christ and the Sophia, all that is spiritual is taken up again into the pleroma. Christ is active at every stage of the world's development, and thus also of course in the highest regions of the world of Aeons from which everything has its point of departure. From the very outset onward Christ has arranged this outcome for the whole, since he is the principle restoring and maintaining everything in oneness with the absolute. In the Gnostic worldview, Christ most certainly has the significance of an absolute world principle.[41]

The Valentinian system lets us see, more clearly than any other, the distinctive character of Gnosis, the internal coherence of its worldview, and the deeper spiritual content of the whole. No other Gnostic school had so many adherents. It had many branches, and the most prominent followers and successors of Valentinus were

---

directed her hymns to the place on high. Because of this, all the archons of the twelve Aeons hated her, because she was lax in her own mysteries and sought to be above them. The one who hated her most of all was the great and willful τριδύναμος αὐθάδης, who was the thirteenth τριδύναμος in the thirteenth Aeon. He sent forth from himself a great power with the face of a lion, and sent forth from his ὕλη (matter) a great many προβολαὶ ὑλικαί (physical defenders) that he dispatched to the lower regions, into the chaos, in order to waylay the Πίστις Σοφία and strip her of her power. When the Sophia saw in the depths the light-power that had proceeded from the willful one, she believed she was seeing the light she had seen from on high, and in desiring this light she descended into the chaos, where she was tormented by the physical defenders from the willful one. In her distress she called out for help from the light she had seen at first. She had had faith in this light from the beginning, and with her unfailing confidence in the power of the light, a confidence accounting for her name Πίστις Σοφία (Faithful Sophia), she addressed her μετάνοια (change of heart) to it. In twelve μετάνοιαι (expressions of penitence) she bewailed her distress and torment, and begged forgiveness for her sins. The twelve expressions of penitence correspond to her errors with respect to the twelve Aeons, and after that a thirteenth one because she had descended from the thirteenth Aeon, which is the τόπος δικαιοσύνης (place of justice or righteousness). With this thirteenth penance her time is fulfilled, the series of her afflictions is ended. Through the Jesus sent to her aid by the primal mystery, she is led back from chaos and to on high. See K. R. Köstlin, "Das gnostische System des Buches Pistis Sophia," *Theologische Jahrbücher* 13 (1854) 1–104, 137–96.

41. In this account [of the Valentinians] I have stuck mainly to the new source of the *Philosophumena*. See 6.29, pp. 184ff. The main points of this system are very clear in the *Philosophumena*, and the account above can readily be augmented by the fuller presentation in *Die christliche Gnosis*, 124ff., which relies on the essential consensus of other sources [in the church fathers].

Secundus, Ptolemäus, Heracleon, and Marcus.[42] They elaborated this system further in their respective schools, by presenting it in various forms.

Basilides

Various Gnostics were contemporaneous with Valentinus and his followers and those belonging together with them. These other Gnostics included the two Syrians, Bardesanes and Saturninus, as well as the most significant and independent ones, the two Egyptians, Basilides[43] and his son Isidore. Since the *Philosophumena*, a recently-added source, has enhanced and modified what we previously knew about Basilides' system, we are now in a better position to present its main features concisely.[44]

On the whole the Gnostics could not find a way to express the idea of the absolute sufficiently, so they ultimately just defined the absolute negatively, as what is above and beyond any expression or concept. Thus Basilides made the apex of his system that which is utterly nothing (*Nichts*), in order to speak of God too as "not-being" (*Nichtseiende*) rather than as being (*Seiende*). The apex was utterly nothing—not matter, nor substance, nor substanceless, nor simple, nor composite, nor human, nor angel, nor God—thus nothing from all that a human being can perceive or envisage. Yet the not-being God created a not-being world from the not-being, although of course only in such a way that also nothing positive is said about this creating, or about the divine act of will.[45] Basilides' general supposition was that the terms we use in speaking of things are not adequate to the things they name; and that can apply even more so when speaking of the absolute, where all positive and negative statements are just indications of what one wants to say.

---

42. The name Colarbasus, which up to now has customarily been paired with that of Marcus [cf. Irenaeus, *Against Heresies* 1.12–13] is to be removed henceforth from the series of Gnostics. G. Volkmar's essay in the *Zeitschrift für historische Theologie* (1855) 603ff., has incontestably and quite correctly shown this. His conclusion is that: "The Gnosis of Colarbasus reduces to the Valentinian Gnosis of the Kol-Arbas, the highest tetrad of the thirty Aeons, in the way it would be elaborated by the Marcosians in their appealing to the direct revelation of this tetrad itself, or of the Sige or silence, the mother of secrets in this tetrad." The only remaining question is whether we should think of Kol as the voice or sound in contrast to silence, instead of as all four members of the tetrad collectively.

43. [*Ed.*] Basilides taught in Alexandria from 117 to 138. Only fragments of his writings survive, and he is known mostly through his opponents.

44. *Philosophumena* 7.19.9–7.27.13 (pp. 230ff.) [ET 502–37]. See: J. L. Jacobi, *Basilidis philosophi gnostici sententias* . . . (Berlin, 1852); C. K. J. Bunsen, *Hippolytus und seine Zeit* (Leipzig, 1852), 1:65ff.; G. Uhlhorn, *Das Basilidianische System mit besonderer Rücksicht auf die Angaben des Hippolytus* (Göttingen, 1855); A. Hilgenfeld, "Das System des Gnostikers Basilides," *Theologische Jahrbücher* 15 (1856) 86–121; and *Die jüdische Apokalyptik* (Jena, 1857), 287ff. See also my article, "Das System des Gnostikers Basilides und die neuesten Auffassungen desselben," *Theologische Jahrbücher* 15 (1856) 121–62.

45. *Philosophumena*, 231. This God "wanted to make the world without conception, without perception, without will, without volition, without emotion, and without desire. I use the phrase 'God wanted,' he [Basilides] says, 'to signify an act that was without will, without thought and without perception'" [ET 508–9 from 7.21.1–2].

We see clearly that nothing would be more difficult for Basilides to express than the beginning of everything. God is, and is not. Likewise, the world too is, and is not, and one does not know how the world came to be: it just is. In order to dismiss any notion of an emanation or projection of the world from God,[46] he thought of the world as it is in the book of Genesis, as posited solely by the spoken word. Yet he also had no hesitation about speaking elsewhere of the world as a divine προβολή (projection). Basilides' standpoint differs from Valentinus, inasmuch as the fundamental focus of his system is not so much on everything going forth from God as it is on everything going back into God.

One major concept in Basilides' system involves the separating or differentiating of the various powers and elements. What can become separated must first be combined and connected. Basilides therefore assumed an original combination, or intermingling and co-existence, of what subsequently had to separate in the course of development and, in stages, had to become distinct elements. In this context we always have to take into account the σύγχυσις ἀρχική (mingling of the ruling elements) that Clement of Alexandria[47] says is characteristic of Basilides' system, without rightly knowing how we are to understand this point. According to our new source for knowledge of his system, we can only regard this mingling of the elements as a necessary postulate if the development he envisages is to have a beginning. When Basilides speaks systematically about development, he says that everything seeks to rise up from below, to rise from what is bad to what is better, whereas nothing is so foolish as to descend from what is better. He could not explain how a σύγχυσις ἀρχική came about, and yet he had to presuppose there was one if he wanted to view the world's development from the perspective of a process of separation.

To do so, Basilides spoke of a σπέρμα τοῦ κόσμου (cosmic seed) that contains within it, as in the tiniest seed, everything constituting the entire sum and substance of the world.[48] After this embryonic world is once posited outside God, as the world-

---

46. *Philosophumena*, 232: "Basilides entirely avoids and fears the idea of beings born through emanation" [ET 510–11 from 7.22.2]. He compares the process of emanation with a spider spinning its threads out of itself. In opposition to the concept of emanation, which assumes the full reality of existent being, Basilides makes the abstract concept of not-being into his starting point.

47. See *Die christliche Gnosis* (n. 5), 211ff.

48. *Philosophumena*, 231. "The world seed contained everything in itself just as the mustard seed comprises everything in the tiniest space, the roots . . . . In this way, then, the nonexistent God made the nonexistent world from entities that did not exist. He sowed and planted a single seed, which had in itself the entire mixture of the world's seeds" [ET 508–11 from 7.21.3–4]. Everything was in this seed, but as yet undeveloped and without form [cf. Gen 1:2]. Thus he called this πανσπερμία (seed mixture) an ἀμορφία τοῦ σωροῦ (formless heap) (p. 239 [ET 522–23 from 7.24.5]). The σπέρμα is something οὐκ ὄν (nonexistent), just as God is a "nonexistent God, having all the seeds treasured up and lying within himself, as if they did not exist. The nonexistent God planned beforehand to bring them into existence" (p. 233 [ET 512–13 from 7.22.5]). [*Ed.* The translation from the ET has been slightly modified to reflect the wording of the Greek Baur provides. The ET itself has, more consistently and with different Greek, "the seed (singular) contained all things . . . as if they (the things) did not exist."] The highest concept of the system is the oneness, or immanent relationship, of

principle, the world's development now first takes its specific course. Basilides calls the divine seeds contained in the primal world "the Sonship" (υἱότης),⁴⁹ and he distinguishes three different constituents of this Sonship. No sooner had the initial projection of the σπέρμα (seed) taken place, than the most subtle part of the Sonship turned directly back to the nonexistent one, with a speed Basilides describes using the poetic expression ὡσεὶ πτερὸν ἠὲ νόημα ("like a winged bird or thought").⁵⁰ Every nature is drawn to the nonexistent because of its superabundant beauty, each striving toward it in one way or another. The coarser part strives to follow the subtler part, but it remains back in the σπέρμα. Nevertheless it furnishes itself with wings, like the soul in Plato.⁵¹ The element supplying wings is the Holy Spirit, which functions in relation to this second part of the Sonship such that the two are interdependent, like the wing and the bird, for neither can rise to the heights without the other. So the Spirit indeed rises up and draws near to that most subtle part of the Sonship. However, the Spirit's nature could not tolerate the most subtle region, exalted above every name, of the nonexistent God and the Sonship, so it stayed back. However, just as a vessel filled with fragrant perfume still retains the fragrance even when it is emptied, so too the Holy Spirit likewise has a fragrance of the Sonship, and this fragrance coming down from the Holy Spirit penetrates right down to the formless world below.

After these first and second upward movements on the part of the Sonship, the Holy Spirit remains in between the superworldly realm and the world.⁵² After these two parts of what is existent have been separated by a firmament, the great Archon, the ruler of the world, tears himself loose from the σπέρμα κοσμικόν (cosmic seed), and from the πανσπερμία τοῦ σωροῦ (seed mixture of the formless heap). Not knowing that there is something above him that is wiser, mightier, and better, he regards

---

existence (being) and nonexistence (not-being); the concept that there is no existence not inclusive of a nonexistence within itself, and no nonexistence not presupposing an existence. This oneness, thought of so negatively, and as abstractly as possible, in the οὐκ ὂν θεός (nonexistent God), has, in the phrase σπέρμα οὐκ ὄν (nonexistent seed), already become a concrete way of looking at things. The God-world relation is grasped as an immanent transition from the abstract to the concrete; from the ideality of something thought to the reality of what is actual. The moving principle is the tendency to take the antitheses that are still passively related within the oneness and to set them forth outside of the oneness, by allowing them to emerge in their opposition, as a clear antithesis. This occurs precisely because the abstract antithesis of existence and nonexistence becomes the concrete antithesis of what is spiritual and what is material.

49. According to Clement of Alexandria, it is the ἐκλογὴ κόσμου (choosing the world). See *Die christliche Gnosis*, 223ff. The expression υἱότης (Sonship), used for what is spiritual, could have seemed to refer to the fact that the Son stands at the higher stage in this development proceeding from below to above. Thus the Archon's Son is more intelligent than the Archon himself. Nevertheless, we should take it in the sense of the υἱοὶ θεοῦ (children of God) in Rom 8:12–17. See *Philosophumena*, 238 [ET 522–23 from 7.25.1].

50. Homer, *Odyssey*, 7.36.

51. [*Ed.*] The *Philosophumena*'s Greek text mistakenly refers to Plato's *Phaedo*. Instead Basilides is apparently alluding to his *Phaedrus*; see 246a–e, 248b–c, 249a–d, and 356d.

52. Hence it is the πνεῦμα μεθόριον (boundary spirit). In speaking of this same mediating activity (its εὐεργετεῖν, doing good), Clement of Alexandria calls it the πνεῦμα διακονούμενον (serving spirit).

himself as the lord, master, and wise architect of the world, and begins to create all the individual things of the world. In keeping with the plan the nonexistent God had already made beforehand, when he laid the foundation of the world in the seed mixture, the first thing the great Archon did, because he did not want to be alone, was to create for himself a son from the material of his world at hand. This son was far better and wiser than the Archon was himself. Surprised by his son's beauty, the Archon set him at his right hand. With the son's help, he created the ethereal or heavenly world, which Basilides called "the Ogdoad"—the realm of the great Archon. After he completed this ethereal world, which extended down as far as the moon, another Archon rose up from the seed mixture, one even greater than all that is under him, though not greater than the Sonship still remaining behind. His place is the Hebdomad, and he too has a son who is more intelligent and wiser than he is himself.

Distinct from these worlds there is then the region Basilides calls the σωροῦ (heap) and the πανσπερμία (seed mixture); it is the basis for the world's entire development. This region has no supervisor, caretaker, or Demiurge of its own. The thought or design the nonexistent one infused in it upon creating is sufficient for that purpose. The third Sonship stays behind in it, must be revealed too, and be brought up to where, above the spirit, the first two parts and the nonexistent are. This is [the world of] the groaning creature, waiting for the revelation of the children of God.[53] Basilides says that we are these children; that we are spiritual ones left behind here.

When we, the children of God for whose sake the creation groans, were supposed to be revealed, the gospel came into the world. It did not come by the blessed Sonship of the inconceivable, blessed nonexistent God descending into the world. Instead, just as naphtha ignites a fire from afar, the son of the great Archon or Ruler thus received the intended plan of the Sonship, via mediation by the Spirit. The Archon recognized that he is not the God of the whole, for he has the unnamable, the nonexistent, above him. He went back within himself, became alarmed about his previous ignorance, and then was instructed by the son seated alongside him who now gets called Christ, about the one who is the nonexistent, about what the Sonship is, about what the Holy Spirit is, and about how the whole is arranged and whence it has come. Also, for the fear seizing the Archon, Basilides referred to the phrase ἀρχὴ σοφίας φόβος κυρίου ("The fear of the LORD is the beginning of knowledge," Prov 1:7), and for his repentance acknowledging the sin of self-exaltation, Basilides referred to Ps 31:5.[54] The same instruction was imparted to the entire Ogdoad, and the gospel then also came from it to the Hebdomad.

---

53. [*Ed.*] See Rom 8:21–22: "that the creation itself will be set free from its bondage to decay, and will obtain the freedom of the glory of the children of God. We know that the whole creation has been groaning in labor pains until now." Also, v. 19: "For the creation waits with eager longing for the revealing of the children of God."

54. [*Ed.*] Ps 31:5: "Into your hand I commit my spirit; you have redeemed me, O LORD, faithful God."

The son of the great Archon sent the light he had received from on high, from the Sonship, down to the son of the Archon of the Hebdomad. Enlightened by it, the son proclaimed the gospel to the Archon of the Hebdomad, and it produced the same impression on him as it did on the Archon of the Ogdoad. After all these regions—with their endlessly many ἀρχαί (rulers), δυνάμεις (powers), and ἐξουσίαι (authorities), as well as the 365 heavens ruled by the great Archon Abrasax—had been enlightened by the gospel, the light also had to go down to the ἀμορφία (formlessness, or chaos) in the lowest world where we are. For the previously unknown secret had to be revealed to the Sonship who had been left behind in the ἀμορφία, which was like an ἔκτρωμα (abortion). Thus the light from the Sonship came down, via the spirit, into the Ogdoad, from there to the Hebdomad, and then to Mary, and it enlightened her son Jesus. The power of the Most High, which overshadowed Mary, is the power of the κρίσις, of separation or differentiation. The world must persist until the entire Sonship follows Jesus, who is the support or rescue for the souls remaining behind in the chaos, and return purified. The world will become so subtle that, like the first Sonship, it soars up on its own.

We now have to give particular attention to this κρίσις and the ἀποκατάστασις (restoration) it is supposed to bring about.[55] The whole gospel story is so arranged, from beginning to end, such that Jesus accomplishes the separation of everything, apart from the Ogdoad and the Hebdomad, that is still formlessly mixed together. This separation, involving everything still left behind, occurs in the same way as it does with regard to Jesus himself. The sole purpose of his passion was the separation of what is mixed together. His bodily aspect, coming to him from the formlessness or chaos, was what in him underwent the suffering. This bodily aspect returned to the formlessness, and his psychical aspect, from the Hebdomad, returned to the Hebdomad. What came from the higher region of the great Archon returned to this Archon, and what was of the spirit remained with the spirit. But the third Sonship, still left behind, rose up through all of these regions to the blessed Sonship. Thus everything comes back again to its place; and when it is in that place it is supposed to remain there. For everything that remains in its place is everlasting, but what oversteps its natural bounds is transitory.

Hence in the same epoch when Christianity revealed what had previously been secret, the whole world was supposedly caught up in great ignorance, so that no one would desire anything contrary to its nature. The Archon of the Hebdomad does not know what is above him, so that he will not ask for what is impossible, nor experience sadness and sorrow. The same ignorance takes hold in the great Archon of the Ogdoad. The universal ἀποκατάστασις (restoration) therefore consists in everything

---

55. *Philosophumena*, 244: "This is their whole theory about blending and the 'heap,' as it were, of the seed mixture, the differentiation and the restoration of the blended parts to their appropriate places. Jesus was the first fruits of the differentiation" [ET 534–35 from 7.27.11–12].

arriving, at its proper time, at the place where it belongs, according to its natural properties—in other words, everything being recognized as what it is in itself.[56]

The same basic idea is all-pervasive in the systems of Basilides and Valentinus. The spiritual principle empties itself into the psychical and material realms, and therefore must return into itself once more from this externalization. This is the process of the world's development, a process culminating with Christianity. But this process can only be completed by the spiritual natures becoming conscious of what they are in themselves, that is, conscious of the absolute, supramundane spiritual principle that is existent in itself, and with which they too are inherently one in their own being as this oneness is concealed and obscured by the psychical and material realms. The very essence of Christianity consists of this consciousness of what is existent in itself and supramundane. Thus Basilides even defines Christianity in this way.[57] Although what reaches its fulfillment in Christianity is already prepared for in the earlier stages that the process of the world's development goes through, it first attains its full reality where spirit's going down within itself reaches its deepest point.

Just as Valentinus has a threefold Christ, Basilides' Jesus presupposes the son of the Archon of the Ogdoad and the son of the Archon of the Hebdomad. These three are inherently one; the same principle mediates between these individual spiritual beings and the primal principle, establishing and maintaining their connection with it and leading them back to oneness. And as with Valentinus, Basilides' Christ also stands alongside the Holy Spirit, who is in the same capacity as subordinate to Christ. The Sophia of Valentinus coincides with Christ and the Holy Spirit for Basilides. He has no Sophia, because his system as such lacks the more concrete concept of syzygy.

The gospel has simply expressed in general terms what was the case beforehand, but only as a mystery. The farther back one goes, the more fully [the meaning of] this mystery was concealed.[58] What at first was veiled in the utmost darkness was then indeed expressed, although it initially was just like a dim light. The mystery had first to make itself known in the creation waiting for the revelation of the children of God. Then there came, in Christianity, the bright daylight of the spiritual consciousness

---

56. *Philosophumena*, 242: "In this way, then, the restoration of all things will occur, when all things are naturally established in the seed of the universe that existed in the beginning and are restored to their proper times" [ET 532–33 from 7.27.4].

57. *Philosophumena*, 243: "According to them, the gospel is knowledge of supercosmic realities" [ET 532–33 from 7.27.7]. Only when one knows what transcends the world can one also know what the world itself is.

58. This is the sense in which Basilides said that the Ogdoad is ἄρρητος (indescribable), but the Hebdomad is ῥητός (describable) (p. 238 [ET 524–25 from 7.25.4]). The Archon of the Hebdomad said to Moses, "I am the God of Abraham, the God of Isaac, and the God of Jacob" (Exod 3:6), "but by my name 'the Lord' I did not make myself known to them" (Exod 6:30)—namely the ἄρρητος θεός (indescribable God), the name of the Archon of the Ogdoad. In the period from Adam to Moses, which is actually the period of the Archon of the Ogdoad, πάντα ἦν φυλασσόμενα ἀποκρύφῳ σιωπῇ (everything was guarded by the concealment of silence) [ET 524–25 from 7.25.3]. The two Archons designate the two world periods.

that is internally clear and transparent. This is also the very time period when God let a great ignorance come over the entire world, and it was to hinder everything from overstepping the bounds of its nature. This ignorance is also a very characteristic element in the standpoint of the system. It designates none other than the advance in the course of world history, in virtue of which each world period counts as the highest one, as absolute, so long as the self-developing spirit has not yet gone on to a higher level; a world period such that the preceding one appears to be so inferior and debased in contrast to it, that all that past glory is as though overcast with the darkness of ignorance. It is the two Archons who are most especially afflicted with this ignorance. But in the end this kind of ignorance, this darkening of consciousness, is always the general lot of what had been so great and significant in its day and, self-consciously like these Archons, regards itself as the power ruling the world—when the advancing world spirit has moved on beyond that point.

Hence according to Basilides, everything has its specific limits and its specific time. Knowing always in turn becomes not-knowing. When the world-historical process makes further progress, it takes back into itself once again the shapes of the spirit that has gone deeply within itself, shapes spirit has set forth from out of itself and ones of apparently independent importance. These shapes disintegrate internally and what ultimately remains is just the abstract concept, the natural law immanent in the existing world order, as the actual content of consciousness.[59] This is the point where the realism and idealism of the Gnostic perspective are so intertwined that the process unfolding in this worldview is not so much the real process of the world as it is the phenomenological process of spirit. The highest or absolute point from which everything proceeds, and on which everything depends, does not consist of the real principles behind the world's origin in itself. Instead, they are the focus only to the extent that the consciousness of knowing and thinking spirit becomes clear, for its own part, about them as its necessary presupposition for conceptualizing all the antitheses of the existing world order in their full extent.

This very way of thinking is also the genuinely Gnostic concept of the ἀποκατάστασις (restoration). The main thing is not that something not yet existing is realized in the realm of things that exist objectively. Instead, what is said to be established is only that what is already in itself is recognized, in the consciousness of the subject that knows it, as what it is in itself, that is, recognized in such a way that what is existent in itself also is an object for consciousness.[60] The more fully the objec-

---

59. Basilides says, about the world order at that time, that it has no leader like the Archons were: "For them, the plan of the Nonexistent suffices, a plan that he charted when he made [the world seed]" [ET 522–23 from 7.24.5].

60. The ἀποκατάστασις (restoration) is the third of the related elements, following upon the σύγχυσις (blending) and the φυλοκρίνησις (differentiation); *Philosophumena*, 244 [ET 534–35 from 7.27.11]. When Gnosis is defined in this way, its highest task is to know "the identity of the Nonexistent, the Sonship, the Holy Spirit, the construction of the universe, and where these things will be restored" (p. 239 [ET 526–27 from 7.26.2]). How else is this achieved except by "the construction of

tive being of things is also something known subjectively, and the more nearly being and consciousness thus come together as one, the more completely the goal of the world's development is then reached. This shows us clearly that the supreme topic dealt with in all the Gnostic systems is in the final analysis always that of knowledge, and recognition or realization (*Erkennen*). This is Gnosis in its distinctive and absolute significance. That is why the system of Basilides, in the form now known to us, occupies such a distinguished place in the history of Gnosis. For it lets us see, in more depth than any other of these systems, the inner essence of Gnosis, the spiritual process taking place in it.[61]

Marcion

If one regards a dualistic worldview as the basic characteristic of Gnosis, then this way of defining it does not fit very well with the two systems we have been speaking about in detail here as the main representatives of Gnosis. Although they cannot conceal their dualistic foundation, it nevertheless stays in the background. Thus dualism can hardly be viewed as their main feature. From this perspective, Gnosis would have fully formed its distinctive character for the first time in the system we must set apart from those already presented, because of its stricter dualistic form. We must consider this stricter dualism to be a new stage in the development of Gnosis. However, this is only a relative way of distinguishing these systems, since they all never abandon the spirit-matter antithesis no matter how differently they may modify it.

---

the universe" being known and recognized, in the consciousness of the knowing subject, for what it is in itself? In this sense it is "a restoration of the blended parts to their appropriate places" [ET 534–35 from 7.27.11]. Everything existent comes to its due and proper place, when what is diverse in itself is recognized in its difference in principle and is kept distinct. This is what knowledge and recognition are all about. Ignorance (ἄγνοια) in the sense discussed above is an essential moment of the restoration that is accomplished in this way.

61. Hilgenfeld contends that the portrayal of the system of Basilides in the *Philosophumena* is very discrepant with that in the sources previously known to us, and so has to be regarded as a secondary product; cf. A. Hilgenfeld, "Das System des Gnostikers Basilides" (n. 44). But see the contrary view in my "Das System des Gnostikers Basilides" (n. 44). What Hilgenfeld additionally maintains in the appendix to his *Die jüdische Apokalyptik* (n. 44), 287, adds nothing essentially new on this point. It is clearly evident that, in the respective systems of Basilides and Valentinus, we cannot determine exactly what is from the founder himself and what is from further elaboration by his followers. But what we can justifiably maintain, in a general history of Gnosis, is that the presentation in the *Philosophumena* incontestably portrays the form in which the specific character of the system of Basilides leaves its most definitive imprint. The teaching of Basilides seems to have taken different forms, for the name of Basilides is even linked with Manicheanism (see my *Das manichäische Religionssystem* [Tübingen, 1831], 84) and with Priscillianism (see Gieseler, *Lehrbuch der Kirchengeschichte* [n. 3], 1.2:98). There was indeed one form in which the blending of the Archons was specifically put at the head of the system, as a duality of principles. Yet this is no obstacle to our viewing the presentation in the *Philosophumena* as deriving from authentically Basilidean elements. [*Ed.*] Priscillianism was a Gnostic-Manichean system developed in the fourth century on the Iberian Peninsula by Priscillian, an ascetic who attracted many followers.

But how do things stand with this antithesis itself? As rigid as it seems to be, we have already seen, from our previous examination of these systems and as their very typical feature, that the two principles are not purely antithetical; that one principle always already involves something of the other. When spirit cannot resist the longing to assume material form, it therefore already has the principle of matter within it; and when matter is likewise moved by the impulse to come into contact with spirit, then it also already has a spiritual element within it. Therefore on the whole they just interrelate like two mutually attracting and repelling powers of one and the same substance. Thus we can just as well call the general character of the Gnostic systems "pantheistic" as "dualistic." Accordingly the difference always just hinges on how, within the unity of the antitheses, the center of gravity lies toward one side or the other, or else how the two are in equilibrium, to the extent that is possible. Depending on the particular system, the dualism is more or less in the background.

The system of Valentinus—in which spirit and matter are basically related as substance and accident, where the spiritual element is what is existent and the material element is what is non-existent, i.e., non-being—is the least dualistic one. The converse is the case with Basilides, since his system designates the spiritual element as the non-existent and the material element as the existent one. Spirit cannot be more completely subordinated to matter than when Basilides says they are so immediately one that, in this oneness, the antithesis is sublated in an indifference, on account of which the development here proceeds not from above to below, as it does with Valentinus, but instead from below to above. As opposed to these two systems, we see dualism in its truest form presented by Marcion,[62] who installs the clear antithesis of the two principles at the apex of the system, although even this form of dualism is simply a modification of the same fundamental relation.

Although the main issue for Marcion was the strictly dualistic separation of law from gospel, he still quite rightly belongs in the series of Gnostics. That is because his view of law and gospel rests on the general antithesis of the two principles determinative of his worldview. He not only assumed that there is a matter co-eternal with the supreme God, for he also related the creator of the world—to be distinguished from the supreme God—in such a way to God and to matter, that this creator could only be conceptualized as together with matter, and coming under one and the same basic perspective or heading as matter.[63] This stricter dualism thus gave Marcion's overall system an essentially different character from that of the other Gnostics.

Marcion's system has nothing in common with the other Gnostic systems except these four principles: the supreme God, matter, the Demiurge, and Christ. Marcion's

---

62. [*Ed.*] Marcion of Sinope (c. 85—c. 160) advocated a dualism between the God of the Old Testament (the Demiurge) and the God of the New Testament, for which he was declared a heretic. He published the earliest extant collection of New Testament books. After his excommunication, he returned to Asia Minor where he led a group of Marcionite churches. His writings are known only through his opponents.

63. See *Die christliche Gnosis* (n. 5), 276ff.

system has no pleroma, no Aeons, no syzygy, no suffering Sophia. The roles of all these other features, in introducing and mediating the world's general process of development, are just to advance things to the point at which what is inherently already present in Christianity is said to become real and complete. Therefore in Marcion's system everything takes place directly and without preparation, in an abrupt and sudden way. Quite intentionally, he arranges everything so as to completely sever the connection between Christianity and what preceded it. Without this connection, paganism has no relation at all to Christianity. Even Judaism is so inferior to Christianity that Marcion can only regard the two of them as being most harshly antithetical.

For Marcion, the Demiurge is not merely a limited, imperfect being; he is instead a being hostile and opposed to the supreme God, and to Christ.[64] Whereas for Valentinus and Basilides the Demiurge bows down before Christ and enters into him, for Marcion he is the one who brought about Christ's death. The main predicate of the Demiurge or Creator is of course "just" or "righteous," although in Marcion's view goodness and righteousness are such different things that righteousness only amounts to being strict and harsh. Also, the concept of righteousness is simply said to mark how different Judaism is from Christianity; how antithetical it is to Christianity. Hence Marcion stresses nothing more emphatically than he does how Christianity is utterly new, direct, unprecedented, and inexplicable. The God revealed by Christ is a completely unknown God. People had no presentiment at all of such a God in either the pagan world or in Judaism.

From this it follows that, as compared to the form of Gnosis mainly represented by Valentinus, the Marcionite Gnosis has a tendency directly opposed to Valentinianism. All the systems belonging to the former kind of Gnosis have a common orientation. They introduce as many members of the system as possible, intermediate between the absolute beginning and the point at which Christianity appears as a new element or moment. Their direct intention is to make the representation of the whole process of development as vivid and concrete as possible—the process in which Christianity is apprehended in such a way that its entire existence and essence can only be conceptualized based on all those prior factors that serve as its presupposition. Everything is entirely different with Marcion. Having an exactly opposite orientation, he seeks instead to remove all the ideal beings those other systems use to fill up the sphere [between the beginning and Christ], all that could have had a mediatorial role in the appearing of Christianity. Instead one should simply hold fast to the pure antithesis.

Yet however mutually contrary the two orientations seem to be—when one of them is very receptive to, and inclusive of, factors other than Christianity, while the other is entirely unconnected to, and cut off from, these factors—the difference between these views can only be a relative one. Inasmuch as Marcion's system, as well as those of Valentinus and Basilides, belong under the heading of Gnosis, they are all

---

64. *Philosophumena* (n. 11), p. 254 (7.31.5): "the Artificer is evil, Marcion claims, along with his products" [ET 560–61].

just different forms and modifications of one and the same overall outlook. When we examine the situation more closely, we see that it cannot be otherwise. However suddenly and unexpectedly the God revealed by Christ might appear and enter into world history and the history of religion, this is just the outwardly appearing, and revelation to human consciousness, of the previously unknown God, a revelation that presupposes God's absolute being. Therefore, although Marcion's Demiurge differs from the creator as our other two Gnostics see him, even on Marcion's view the God revealed by Christ cannot appear before the kingdom of the Demiurge, who rules the pre-Christian period of the world that has preceded that revelation. When the whole of world history and the history of religion get divided into these two periods in this way, with one period necessarily presupposing the other one, and when this very relationship can only be conceptualized based on a principle in which the antithesis itself is in turn unified, then the feature these Gnostic systems share is that everything belonging to the essence of Christianity, and constituting the essential contents of Christian consciousness, must be conveyed in light of a factor that is antithetical to Christianity.

Accordingly, neither dualism on its own, nor the Demiurge by itself, is basic to the essence of Gnosis. Instead what is basic is simply the relation in which the Demiurge stands to Christ; that Christ himself cannot be without the assumption of the Demiurge. On this point Marcion is as good a Gnostic as any of the others. If we further take into account that the Gnostic Demiurge itself is none other than a mythical personification in the same sense as the ancient worldview customarily symbolized and personified its concepts, then we see right away that Marcion's own Christian consciousness, wanting nothing to do with the pre-Christian world, is all the more entrenched in that world's ways of envisaging things. He too cannot contemplate the pre-Christian world as distinct from the Christian world without visualizing it in a being such as the Demiurge. He too occupies a standpoint where his own Christian consciousness is essentially determined by the universal antithesis of his general worldview.

There is of course something typically setting Marcion apart from the other Gnostics but also following from his strictly antithetical stance toward all that is pre-Christian. It is indeed his conceptual transition from the transcendent sphere of an objective consciousness of the world—wherein the world's development takes place in the antithesis between spirit and matter, or between the pneumatic and the psychical—to the sphere of subjective consciousness in which the course of the world's development is preeminently bound up with the ethical concept of law and gospel, of righteousness and goodness, of fear and love.[65] Marcion relegates to the background the general Gnostic antithesis of spirit and matter, so that the basis for his examination of the world, or for his own religious consciousness, is mainly just the antithesis between the visible and the invisible, as a way of keeping law and gospel apart to the fullest extent.

65. *Die christliche Gnosis*, 251ff.

The Pseudo-Clementine Homilies

The Aeons drop out in Marcion's Gnosis, but he retains the Demiurge and in doing so intensifies the dualism. So the question is whether there is a third form of Gnosis that downplays both the Demiurge (to which Marcion for the most part gives a pagan character, in setting him apart from the supreme God) and the dualism, while still continuing to be characteristic of the essence of Gnosis—one that at least considers Christianity from the perspective of the world's general process of development. The answer is that we do find such a form in the system contained in the *Pseudo-Clementine Homilies*.[66] It is of course so different from the systems usually reckoned to be Gnosis that we can, justifiably, ask whether it is to be classified with the other systems of Gnosis. On the other hand, however, it does bring together within it all the Gnostic concepts, in such a way that we can only take it to be a novel form of Gnosis.

Were we to follow the usual practice, by looking upon the separation of the world's creator from the supreme God as the main criterion for counting a system as Gnosis, then one like the Pseudo-Clementine's system, which so explicitly speaks out against this separation, would not be regarded as Gnostic. However, one can fully acknowledge that criterion and yet maintain that the system inherent in the *Homilies* has a thoroughly Gnostic character. It not only does sound anti-Gnostic, but is also intentionally and wholly anti-Gnostic, when the *Homilies* states, as though enunciating the basic truth of all religion, that the supreme God is also the creator of the world; furthermore that these two concepts are so inseparable and unavoidably linked that, as the *Homilies* puts it, even if the world's creator were the most awful being of all, we human beings would still owe him our complete adoration, for he alone is the source of our existence. Thus for religious consciousness the two concepts, God and the world's creator, are utterly identical.[67] However, it is also apparent how the *Homilies* draws a line between these two concepts, notwithstanding their identity.

First of all, according to the *Homilies*, God is not the creator of matter. Also, it knows of no creation from nothing, for it too assumes a primordial matter present with God as his co-eternal body, a matter from which the four elements and primal substances emerge because the spirit pervades this co-eternal body and changes it into various forms.[68] Also, to the extent that God is the world's creator, he is at least not

---

66. [*Ed.*] The *Pseudo-Clementine Homilies* contains a fictitious narrative report purportedly written by Clement of Rome, the second (or third) successor to Peter as bishop of Rome, about discourses of the Apostle Peter and circumstances surrounding Clement's accompaniment of Peter on his travels. Baur believes that it reflects the views of Christian Ebionites who regarded the Apostle Paul as an apostate and attached themselves to Peter as the true representative of Christianity. It plays a large role in Baur's reconstruction of early Christianity, a role that has been debated since his time. See also Part 2, n. 54.

67. *Homilies* 18.22. [*Ed.*] Baur uses the edition by Albert Dressel, *Clementis Romani, quae feruntur, homiliae viginti nunc primum integrae* (Göttingen, 1853). ET in *ANF* 8.

68. There is more detailed information about how matter is related to God in the conclusion, *Homilies* 20.5, first added in Dressel's edition. Cf. Uhlhorn, *Das Basilidianische System* (n. 44), 179ff.

directly the creator, for he only creates via the Sophia as intermediary. The Sophia, as soul always bound to God, is the world-creating principle through which God goes forth from himself and the monad becomes the dyad. Hence the Sophia is expressly called "the world-creating (*demiurgische*) hand of God."⁶⁹ So the difference from the Sophia of the Gnostic systems would only be that the Sophia of the *Homilies* is not separated from God; instead she is placed in the same kind of immanent relation to God as matter's relation to God. The system of the *Homilies* is further analogous to the other Gnostic systems in that God is not actually the ruler of the world. Instead the ruler is a being who fully occupies the position of the Gnostic Demiurge, except that "world creator" cannot be predicated of him.

When the four basic kinds of material (*Grundstoffe*) had come forth from God's body and had become mixed together, there arose from them a being that was eager to bring ruin to the bad ones. This being is from nowhere else than God, for all beings are from God. Yet it did not get its evil disposition from God, because that wickedness first arose apart from God; it arose from a will of its own on the part of the mixture of basic materials. Yet this did not occur contrary to God's will and certainly not independently of it, since no being, and least of all one exercising authority over a large number of other beings, can come to be in that position just by chance, apart from God's will. God has delegated rulership over the currently existing world to this very being, one we have described, so far at least, as evil. This rulership extends to enforcing [God's] laws and punishing evildoers. Accordingly, the whole world order is divided into two kingdoms, which are the presently existing world and the future world—in other words, the left hand of God, and the right hand or power of God. Over against the evil ruler of the present world there stands Christ, the good ruler of the future world.⁷⁰ So this evil one is also a being who enforces God's law by punishing evil, and who, in doing so, presents the concept of righteousness, as does Marcion's Demiurge; except that, with all that separates him, as an evil being, from God and makes him the demonic principle, he is not the kind of antithesis to God that Marcion's Demiurge is. For the *Homilies* makes Marcion's Demiurge the main target of the polemic it directs against all the older Gnostic systems—a Demiurge who is a world-creator [wholly] distinct from the supreme God, and who stands alongside the absolute one as a second god.

The general tendency of this system is not the utter rejection of Gnostic concepts and points of view, or even Gnostic dualism. Instead it just aims to limit and modify dualism in such a way that no harm is done to the fundamental doctrine of God's

---

69. *Homilies* 16.12: χεὶρ δημιουργοῦσα τὸ πᾶν.

70. *Homilies* 19.7, 7.3, and 3.19. The conclusion of the *Homilies* is where it first enlarges upon and fully elucidates the doctrine of the Devil as the ruler of this world. Just as the Devil is not actually an evil being but is instead a just being that serves God, so too the Devil, and evil, are finally transformed into what is good. While the Devil has an evil προαίρεσις (purpose), deriving from the κρᾶσις (mixing), he thus gains a προαίρεσις ἀγαθοῦ (good purpose) from the μετασύγκρασις (remixing, or transformation). *Homilies* 20.9.

absolute monarchy. This system simply makes the antithesis of two mutually opposed principles into a duality immanent in the being of God. In doing this, it even has a character quite analogous to the Gnostic systems, in likewise having its own process of the world's development, albeit in the form of syzygies of its own. The *Homilies* adopts the concept of syzygy in a different sense than Gnosis does elsewhere, since the concepts forming a syzygy are related chiefly by their antithetical character.[71]

The law of the universe is the law of the antithesis, in other words, of the syzygies. God himself, who is one from the beginning, has split everything into antitheses: right and left, heaven and earth, day and night, light and fire, life and death. However, the order of the syzygies was reversed when human beings appeared. Prior to that, the better one of the pair came first and the lesser one followed; but now the worst of the pair was first and the better one was second. Adam, the human being created by God, was followed first by the unrighteous Cain, and only then by the righteous Abel. Adam himself had been created according to that initial divine arrangement. In the syzygy he forms together with Eve, he comes first as the better one of the pair, and Eve follows as the worse one. In this system the turnabout within the syzygies is the same as what happens in the Valentinian system when, by the Sophia's fall out of the pleroma, a fissure occurs in the entire order of the world—something that must occur at some time but which admits of no further explanation. The way the syzygies exist, as the duality of a male and a female principle, as the split within the antitheses, is indeed a deficiency inherent in the finite nature of the world. This deficiency, this weak aspect of the entire world, becomes all the more prevalent and predominant by the female going before the male, by what is worse always being first and having to be overcome by what is better.

Here the process of world history therefore unfolds under this arrangement. The moving principle here is not the real antithesis between the pneumatic and the psychical, but the ideal antithesis between true and false prophecy. There are two kinds of prophecy, a male kind and a female kind, and they are related, respectively, as truth is to error, or as the future is to the presently existing world. How the present world stands in relation to the future is the type for [i.e., is foreshadowed by] the sequence in which the members of the syzygies are arranged. The minor or lesser member comes first and the major member comes second, like world and eternity. The present world is temporal, while the world to come is eternal. First there is ignorance, then knowledge. The prophets also fit into this same pattern. The present world is female and, as mother of children, gives birth to souls; whereas the future world is masculine and, as father, receives the children. So too the prophets in this world are the successors who, with their true knowledge, appear as sons of the future world.[72]

---

71. *Homilies* 2.15, is the main passage expressing the concept of syzygy: that God διεῖλεν (divided) everything at its apex διχῶς καὶ ἐναντίως (into twos and opposites).

72. *Homilies* 2.25.

I. Gnosis and Montanism

This law of the syzygies bears upon the world's history, and the history of religion, only insofar as Adam is said to reappear at various times under different names, before the flood in Enoch and after it in Noah, Abraham, Isaac, Jacob, Moses, and finally in Christ. In Christ the syzygy emerges definitively, and is seen clearly, in his antithesis to his forerunner John the Baptist, or to Elijah. The two [members of the syzygy] are related as moon and sun. The same relationship is repeated then in that between Simon Magus—who was indeed first among the followers of the Baptist and succeeded him as leader after his death—and the Apostle Peter. Therefore this same antithesis, portrayed in terms of the relationship between the present world and the future world, extends throughout the present world in various forms, for what is worse always precedes as the female aspect, and what is better follows as the male aspect.

However, if the same antithesis is just perpetually repeated, and at the end Christ is only the same as what, already at the beginning, was the Adam identical with him, then what is the overall goal of the development? It can only be that the present world rises up to the world to come and passes over into it. This does not happen via a process of development, as Gnostic systems elsewhere depict it. The general way of visualizing things that underlies the system of the *Homilies* is not so much one involving time and movement in time as it is one involving space and extension in space. The one true God—who, in the most perfect way, presides over the whole and, as the heart of the whole and everywhere that he is, is at the center of what is infinite—sends forth into the infinite, from himself as center, the six dimensions: height and depth, right and left, forward and backward. When it is then stated that, by looking upon these six dimensions as upon a number equal in all respects and accomplishing or completing the world in six temporal periods, the basic visualization is nevertheless a spatial one, of being resting in space. As the resting point of all existence, God has his image in the future endless age, as the beginning and end of all. The six infinite directions go back to the one true God, and everything has its extension into the infinite from him. That is the secret or mystery of the number seven. For the one true God is the point at which everything comes to rest. Whoever imitates his greatness on the small scale lets that one come to rest within himself.[73]

At least we can say this is no conception of the process of the world's development as a movement forward in time. And yet the system of the *Homilies* remains true to the fundamental character of Gnosticism, in that it too must be mediated by antitheses. In Marcion's system the antithesis of the principles of the real world, of spirit and matter, is simply the foundation and presupposition for the law-gospel antithesis, in order to understand these two supreme ethical principles as mutually

---

73. *Homilies* 17.9. Inasmuch as dualism gets superseded by the monotheism of the system, the duality of principles becomes a characteristic immanent in the essential nature of God. For matter is the body animated by the spirit of God, and the Sophia in her oneness with God, as the soul of God, is both monad and dyad. Thus Gnostic pantheism, as the basic outlook of this system, emerges all the more strikingly in that the world is immanently related to God. God and world are related as center and periphery, as οὐσία (being) and μετουσία (participation in being).

exclusive and to know, absolutely, the nature of each. In similar fashion, in the system of the *Homilies* the same authentically Gnostic concern to know expresses itself in the fact that the system's cosmogonic and metaphysical features also exist only in order to elevate ethical religious consciousness to the standpoint of absolute knowledge. What law and gospel are for Marcion, false and true prophecy or religion are in the *Homilies*.

There is both true prophecy and false prophecy, and the two kinds together constitute the contents and the course of world history and the history of religion. Now because the distinction between the two kinds of prophecy is great beyond measure, and nothing is so humanly important as our recognizing this distinction, there must also be a test for distinguishing between them, so that human beings can know, absolutely, what is the falsehood in false prophecy and what is the truth in true prophecy. That is why God has based the order of the world wholly on the law of the syzygies. As the teacher of truth who makes it possible for human beings to have knowledge of what is existent,[74] God has set the canon of the syzygies clearly before our eyes in the nature he created, so that in it, as the supreme and universal criterion, the truth can be known and error can be set apart from truth. Using this canon, one recognizes Simon Magus to be a false prophet from the fact that Peter came just after him, and followed upon him as light follows after darkness, knowledge follows ignorance, and recovery follows illness. What must happen initially is for the false gospel to come via a deceiver. Only then can the true gospel be spread abroad to refute incipient heresies. After the gospel is preached, the Antichrist must come forth and only then does the true Christ, Jesus, appear, whereupon the eternal light dawns and all darkness will disappear.[75] This is how one antithesis follows another, so that the antitheses mediate or bring about recognition of truth in an increasingly intensive and universal way.

Since from the beginning the truth is one and the same, there is no essential difference even between Mosaic religion and Christianity as to the identity of their contents. Thus the entire development can only aim at bringing about the recognition of truth, and introducing truth into humanity's general consciousness. Christianity marks an epoch of its own only by spreading the gospel among the Gentiles so that it becomes fully universal. However, this factor also shows once again this system's engagement with Gnosticism. Here too the significance of Christ is his being a universal world principle. The entire world-historical process, with the law of syzygies as its motive principle, has its unity in the fact that there is always just the same one true prophet. The one true prophet is the human being created by God, and endowed with the Holy Spirit of Christ, who, from the beginning of the world's course, appeared as

---

74. *Homilies* 2.15 [quoted by Baur in Greek]: "It is truly said that God, teaching human beings about the truth of being, divided all things at the apex into twos and opposites. As the only God, and sufficient in his own being, he created heaven and earth, day and night, life and fire, sun and moon, life and death" [*ANF* 8:231]. Cf. *Homilies* 3.16.

75. *Homilies* 2.17.

various figures and under different names, until, at his appointed time and because of the task he had undertaken, mercifully anointed by God, he attains everlasting rest.[76]

In the final analysis, the system of the *Homilies* differs from that of the older Gnostic systems in that, by strictly adhering to the principle of unity or oneness, the *Homilies* significantly remains within the scope of monotheism. Furthermore, the general worldview of the *Homilies* leaves behind the transcendent metaphysics of the Gnostic cosmogony, by entering into the sphere of world history and the history of religion, in order to mark the course, taken within this sphere, by the antitheses that enable the recognition and knowledge of what is true in itself and existent in itself. In the older Gnostic systems, crossing over to gain this knowledge is of course grounded in the concept of the pneumatic or spiritual element. Knowledge is the element of pneumatic natures; for they are spirit knowing what is true in itself—spirit freed from material and psychical elements obscuring its consciousness; self-conscious, knowing spirit. Gnosis in all its forms is knowledge of the absolute, is absolute knowledge. The only difference is how the object of this knowledge is defined. In the older systems the object is the absolute as such, together with the antithetical principles. For Marcion, the antithesis is between the pre-Christian and the Christian elements, in other words, between law and gospel. In the *Homilies*, the antithesis is between false prophecy and true prophecy.

The Three Basic Forms of Gnosis

We can also distinguish the three forms of Gnosis, presented in its historical development so far, as three forms of religion in which various different elements shape the content of Gnosis.

In the earlier systems, the symbolic, mythical outlook of pagan antiquity is still for the most part dominant, although the pre-Christian content is already the prelude to the Christian content, and there is basically just a fluid distinction between the two of them. Marcion's system is largely dealing with the pure concept of Christianity, disengaged from any elements foreign to it. In the system of the *Homilies*, Christianity is just a purified and expanded Judaism.

Whereas the older systems located Judaism at a very subordinate stage, Marcion even denied that Judaism has any religious value at all. To the contrary, the system of the *Homilies* saw Judaism as the absolute religion. However, the *Homilies* could grant this significance to Judaism only by dint of the arbitrary way it interpreted all the Old Testament passages the older Gnostics used to support their downgrading of Judaism. The *Homilies* declared that these passages—which served as the main evidence for those Gnostics' contention that the Demiurge, as God of the Jews, is only a weak and limited being—are counterfeit additions to the Old Testament scriptures. In this way

---

76. *Homilies* 3.20.

one form of Gnosis is the denial of the other form, and therefore they are mutually antithetical in historical terms too. When Marcion rejected allegory, he came out in opposition to the older Gnostics who based so much of their thinking on allegory. Then the system of the *Homilies* in turn rose up in opposition to his teaching. There can be no doubt that the erroneous teaching about Simon Magus that the *Homilies* contests, as a new form of pagan polytheism, is Marcionite Gnosticism.

Since these forms of Gnosis do not merely form a historical sequence but also are mutually and internally interconnected, and are complementary in their mutual opposition, altogether they exhaust the concept of Gnosis and complete its progression.[77] If Gnosis is essentially none other than the endeavor to understand the moments in the history of religion as what they are in themselves, that is, comprehend them philosophically, then Gnosis could regard the absolute standpoint it took up as itself a form of Christianity approaching as closely as possible to paganism, or else as a pure Christianity, or even as a form of Christianity identical with Judaism.[78]

---

77. [*Ed.*] In *Die christliche Gnosis* (n. 5), Baur describes the internal connection of the Gnostic systems in terms of how they relate Christianity to paganism and Judaism. In the first main form Christianity is linked to both Judaism and paganism (Valentinus, Basilides, the Ophites); in the second main form, Christianity rejects both Judaism and paganism (Marcion); in the third main form, Christianity is linked to Judaism but rejects paganism (the *Pseudo-Clementine Homilies*). A fourth major form, in which Christianity is linked to paganism and rejects Judaism, is logically possible, but it dissolves into philosophy and is visible only in Manicheanism. See Volker Henning Drecoll, "Ferdinand Christian Baur's View of Christian Gnosis," in *Baur and the History of Early Christianity* (n. 4), 125–26.

78. The aforementioned Πίστις Σοφία (n. 40) is yet another distinctive form of Gnosis that doubtless already belongs to a later era and has roots in Manicheanism. In his article, "Das gnostische System des Buches Pistis Sophia," *Theologische Jahrbücher* 13 (1854) 1–104, 137–96, K. R. Köstlin has undertaken, in very commendable fashion, the difficult task of showing clearly the connection of the main ideas in this text and providing an overview of its entire system. As Köstlin characterizes it, this system is set apart from other Gnostic systems in part by its monistic character and in part by its practical religious orientation. Here too the basic outlook is driven by the antithesis of spirit and matter, although matter, albeit impure, is no initially evil principle. The whole universe has come into being via emanation. The highest region, infinitely exalted above all worlds and heavens, is the region of the divine realm of light, in which the Ineffable One with his free will sends forth from himself the beings of light resting in his bosom, to stream forth each to its own existent reality. This is such an exceedingly pure spiritual realm of complete regularity and harmony that the Sophia is unseated from her place in the Valentinian pleroma and sent down into a more distant sphere. Throughout, this system is dealing with the idea of a falling-away from the infinite and the return to the infinite. It does so indeed by making the destiny of the Sophia, both her fall, and her repentance and redemption, the type prefiguring what is to take place for humankind in wholly the same way. The world has been created by, that is emerges from, the Ineffable via the initial mystery, simply in order to realize, in the full scope of a universe unavoidably giving rise to them, this mystery and the other *mysteria purgatores et remissores* (mysteries of purgation and remission)—which are the aforesaid hidden powers of the deity in the removal of the world's sin via conversion and repentance, also specifically including the activity of overcoming the falling-away and the resistance to the good. This whole cycle is able to present the divine's eternal transcendence over all finitude, and the infinitely reconciling and life-giving power and abundant life of the good principle. —The doctrine of the mysteries is an especially distinctive feature of this system. The concept of the mysteries brings together everything on which the existence and salvation of the world and of humankind depend. The mysteries give rise to, rule over,

I. Gnosis and Montanism

Docetism

We have not yet examined more specifically the aspect of Gnosis usually falling under the heading of docetism. Here too we are dealing with an issue going right to the heart or essence of Gnosis, one of particular interest for our understanding of Gnosis.

When Gnosis increasingly viewed Christianity in a more general, sweeping and extravagant way, the pressing issue had to be how Gnostic Christianity stood in relation to historical Christianity. Does Gnosis place in doubt the reality of the historical facts of Christianity and Christianity's historical character as such? Does it do so in a way that is incompatible with Christian consciousness? The name "docetism"[79] shows that this really happened, insofar as the Gnostics' view of Christianity was labeled as more or less docetic.

Docetism is understood to include the contention that Christ did not come in the flesh; that is, he did not truly have an actual body like other normal people.[80]

---

reconcile and rescue the beings subject to them. Hence the whole of Christianity is none other than the imparting of the mysteries via Christ, his bringing them down into the world. His imparting them is said to make the world acquainted, reconciled, and eternally united with the mysteries. —Righteousness and grace are the two equally essential and basic ideas of the system. Evil must disappear either through conversion and change for the better, or by being completely nullified. The final goal of the entire world-process must be reached: the universe purified of all that is unworthy and perverse. So this brings very much to the fore the issue of religious practice. The whole is calculated to make people aware, in all its magnitude and severity, of their finitude, of their dependence on the powerful beings of the lower worlds, and of their own inability to rise above these things without a higher force delivering them. But it also likewise assures them that a power of deliverance is actually present in the cosmos and has appeared in Christ. Therefore in this instance this practical concern is essentially conditioned by the Gnostic metaphysical foundation of the system. The glimpse into the infinite grandeur and glory of the supra-celestial region of light, and its principles, must have first opened one's eyes if one wants to comprehend the manner in which the finite returns to the infinite; or, in other terms, to comprehend how the finite is once again united with itself, and taken up into itself, by that very infinite from which it came forth. —Thus the system of the Πίστις Σοφία is closely related to the first systems belonging to this main form, especially to that of the Ophites. However, it rises above them in virtue of its moral spirit and its being freer from Gnostic dualism and particularism. According to Köstlin (pp. 188ff.) this system is living proof that even the later epoch of Gnosis was not merely a time of decline and disintegration, for it also included bringing Gnostic teaching once more into harmony with the spirit of Christianity and the challenges of ethical consciousness. It did so by bold speculation about the world above, by concern to maintain this speculation intact, and by seeking to combine all elements needed for this purpose, from already existing systems, with elements of its own. All this is presented most clearly in the part of the book from which the title derives, in the teaching about the Sophia. Although the foundation is thoroughly Ophitic, nevertheless, as for Valentinus, the Sophia is understood at the same time in a more spiritual way, as representing the finite spirit's longing for knowledge of the infinite. That is where the ethical element comes in, for she was at the same time the model of faith, of repentance and hope.

79. [*Ed.*] From the Greek for "seem" or "appear."

80. See the *Epistle of Ignatius to the Smyrnaeans*, ch. 5: ". . . but blasphemes my Lord, not confessing that he was [truly] possessed of a body?" [*ANF* 1:88]. [*Ed.*] In the text at this point Baur interpolates the remark: "as it is already stated in 1 John 4:3." First John 4:2–3 reads: "and every spirit that confesses that Jesus Christ has come in the flesh is from God, and every spirit that does not confess Jesus is not from God."

Now since the body is the material basis of human existence, this directly involves the further element that, if Christ truly had no actual body, then that entails calling into question the reality of the historical facts associated with his person, as well as the historical character of Christianity. Thus everything said to have happened to his body did not actually happen, for instance, his suffering. The supposition then is just that this occurrence is merely for show, just δοκήσει (fanciful) or κατὰ δόκησιν (apparent), something merely docetic.[81]

The ways in which the Gnostic systems regard the nature of Christ's body, with their various modifications, thus also involve views deviating to different degrees from the historical view of it held by Christianity. Basilides seems to have remained closest to the conventional idea of Christ's body and his birth from the Virgin Mary.[82] However, according to Valentinus and other Gnostics, Jesus was not said to be born from Mary, but only through (διά) Mary, having passed through her as though through a canal; so his birth was merely an apparent birth.[83] The Valentinians in any event just

---

81. See, among other sources, ch. 2 of Ignatius' epistle (n. 80): ". . . not, as certain unbelievers maintain, that he only seemed to suffer, as they themselves only seem to be [Christians]" [ANF 1:87]. Although docetism is a feature of Gnosis as such, the docetists are sometimes spoken of as a particular Gnostic sect. In *Stromata* 3.13, Clement of Alexandria calls Cassian—who came from the school of Valentinus and, together with Tatian, shared the principles of the Encratites—the ἐξάρχον τῆς δοκήσεως (chief of the docetists). —Without naming a founder of the sect, the author of the *Philosophumena*, in the eighth book, introduces the docetists as a sect of their own, along with his mentioning the sects of Monoïmes, Tatian, Homogenes, the Quartodecimans, the Montanists, and Encratites, and he specifically calls them "docetists" [*Philosophumena* (n. 11), 8.1–7; ET 580–81]. He says they conceived of God as the first principle, using the image of a seed that comprises what is infinitely great within what is infinitely small. The world grew from God as the fig tree does from the seed; and just as the fig tree consists of trunk, leaves, and fruit, so three Aeons arose from the first principle and, because ten is a perfect or complete number, they multiplied themselves tenfold to become thirty Aeons. The redeemer is someone produced in common by the collective Aeons, and expresses their unity or oneness. In other words, the redeemer is the oneness of the principle's having become, in all things, identical with itself. Just as there are thirty Aeons, so too the redeemer takes thirty forms (ἰδέας). That is why each heresy has a different conception of the redeemer, and each takes the way it conceives of him to be the only true way. "But these places are different. This is why there are so many Christian sects who hotly contest the nature of Jesus. He belongs to them all but appears different to each group because he is viewed from a different place. Each soul is drawn to Jesus and hastens toward him, he says. Each soul supposes this to be the only Jesus, its own kinsman and fellow citizen" (*Philosophumena* 8.10.10, p. 268 [ET 592–95]).—Accordingly this docetic doctrine also just expresses the general character of Gnosis, with the basic outlook understood as follows. In contrast to the objectivity of the one absolute principle, the diverse perspectives from which the reflective consciousness envisages all that has come into being are just subjective representations. Since Gnosis itself speaks of ἰδέαι (ideas), Gnostic docetism, put succinctly, is the aspect of Gnosis that we can quite properly call "idealism." In its effort to conceive of the absolute, that is, to impart to consciousness what is existent in itself, Gnosis itself was compelled to realize that it operated with a purely phenomenological procedure, and that its own metaphysics did not extricate it from the subjectivity of consciousness. Right where its structural elements were supposed to wed Gnosis to the concrete reality of existence, as in the case of the redeemer's person, for Gnosis this existing being dissolved into a mere δοκεῖν, or seeming.

82. Even the *Philosophumena* says that, in Basilides' teaching, Jesus is straightforwardly called ὁ υἱὸς τῆς Μαρίας (the son of Mary) (7.26.8, p. 241 [ET 528–29]).

83. See Tertullian, *Against Valentinus*, ch. 27 [ANF 3.516]; Theodoret, *Heretical Tales* 5.11.

ascribed a psychical body to Christ, although this was a very contentious issue for them, for they split into two schools over it, the "Eastern" and the "Italic" schools. The Italic school, to which Heracleon and Ptolemaeus belonged, maintained that Jesus had a psychical body, and that is why the spirit descended upon him at his baptism. However, the Eastern school (specifically, Axionicus and Adresianes) held the savior's body to be pneumatic, or spiritual, because the Holy Spirit, that is, the Sophia and the demiurgic, formative power of the Most High, came down upon Mary.[84] Marcion's teaching is the most decidedly docetic one. According to him, Christ's entire manifestation is mere appearance, a sheer phantasm. To not have him in the slightest contact with the realm of the Demiurge and the material life belonging to it, Christ was not even said to be seemingly born; instead he came down directly from heaven to earth.[85]

Our juxtaposing these different opinions indeed shows the close connection between the docetism of the Gnostic systems and their dualism. If, in the Gnostics' teaching, redemption consists in freeing the pneumatic element from the material and psychical elements, then that entails the concept of the redeemer as himself having as little contact as possible with the psychical element.[86] The material element is also a substantial component of a human body. Yet the more mutually repellent the two antithetical principles of spirit and matter are, the more the dominance of the pneumatic element must exclude everything material. Hence the redeemer's body quite naturally lacks the concrete reality of human existence; and if the redeemer nevertheless appeared to have a human body, such a body was a representation of a human body without any corresponding reality.

However, what holds good for Christ's body also holds good for his personality or personal features. Just as Christ's body lacks a material substrate, so too his personal features lack the concrete content of a human existence. The Gnostic Christ is too non-material a being to plant his feet firmly on the earth and to become integrally and organically connected with human life. His self-consciousness has its center of gravity in the transcendent region of the world of Aeons. He floated down suddenly from on high in order to exist for a brief time in the form of a human being. Such a one is no human being.

Add to this the fact that, according to the Gnostic doctrine as such, we cannot think of anything that would be regarded as the result of the redeemer's personal actions. The redeemer's work is redemption. But the Gnostics' view of redemption is of course evident in their well-known affirmation of a φύσει σώζεσθαι (being saved by one's nature). If those who become blessed do so because of their nature, that is, in virtue of the fact that ultimately, as pneumatic or spiritual in nature, they can simply come back again into the pleroma, then we cannot see what a redeemer has to do with

---

84. *Philosophumena* 6.35.5, p. 195 [ET 432–33].

85. Cf. *Die christliche Gnosis* (n. 5), 255ff.

86. *Philosophumena* 7.31.5, p. 254, states: "For this reason, Jesus came down unborn; he [Marcion] says, to be free from all evil" [ET 560–61].

their blessedness. In the Gnostic view, blessedness is not conditional upon some deed or ethical accomplishment. Instead, it is just a matter of knowing. Knowledge as such, recognition of the absolute, is itself redemption and blessedness.[87]

Therefore, when the original spiritual principle in those with a pneumatic nature, by gradually developing, breaks through the material and psychic elements obscuring it, this principle that can never be wholly extinguished so enlightens human consciousness that a person rises up beyond the world of the Demiurge and becomes aware of being one with the pleroma. This is how the highest level of the spiritual life, the level that as such is a blessed life, is attained and redemption is completed. Then when the Gnostic systems consider this to be also the redeemer's doing, they are just visualizing externally, in his appearing and activity, what is inherently a process interior to the spiritual life. What constantly recurs in this same way in the endless multiplicity of spiritual persons—as the same act of the spirit going back from its self-divestment and into itself, and elevating itself to its original state of being—is a process summed up in its unity in Christ, as the universal principle and bearer of the spiritual life. What is concrete, individual, and personal forever dissolves once more into the universality of the concept. The Gnostic Christ just represents a principle, the spiritual principle underlying all the forms and stages of the development.

The system of the *Homilies* generally sets itself apart from the other Gnostic systems by its more rigorous, unitary character. It presents, in a more definite and unified way, the principle that lacks coherence in the other systems with the various ways they depict Christ. This principle is that one and the same prophet of truth is present throughout all ages of the world, appearing under different names and in different figures. If so, then what significance can Christ's outward manifestation and human birth have in the *Homilies*? In this system Gnostic supernaturalism apparently sought to become completely unmasked, by expressly declaring that the external revelation is none other than spirit's immanent self-revelation. What makes a prophet to be a prophet, the *Homilies* states, is his ἔμφυτον καὶ ἀέvναον πνεῦμα (implanted and eternal spirit).[88] This spirit is attributed not merely to the prophet, but in general to all pious people. For, as people everywhere say, in the pious person the truth wells up from the indwelling, pure spirit. Thus the *Homilies* has the Apostle Peter[89] speaking about this same thing:

> Thus the Father also revealed the Son to me; so I know from my own experience what the revelation means. As soon as the Lord questioned me (Matt 16:14), [the answer] rose up in my heart and I know not how this happened to me, for I said, "You are the Son of the living God" [Matt 16:16]. He who therefore counted me blessed first said to me that it was the Father who revealed this. Afterward I realized what revelation is: something occurring within,

---

87. See *Die christliche Gnosis* (n. 5), 139ff., 489ff.
88. *Homilies* (n. 67) 3.15.
89. *Homilies* 17.18.

apart from one's being taught outwardly or having visions or dreams. This is also the case because the seed of all truth is contained in the truth God has planted within us. God's hand either conceals or discloses this truth, since God works according to his knowledge of the worthiness of each individual.

Therefore inner revelation replaces outward revelation. Revelation from without can only make us aware of what is already inherently deposited in human beings' spirit as the seed and principle of truth.

This account gives us insight into the inner, underlying principle that connects all the Gnostic systems at their foundations, despite their different outward forms. If the same divine spirit that was in Adam also appeared in Christ, then, since the divine spirit imparted to Adam also had to pass down to his human descendants, the divine principle in Christ is not essentially different from the divine element in all other human beings, and thus is not something utterly supernatural. It is the same divine spirit in humankind, the Holy Spirit of Christ, which, in the seven pillars of the world, pervades all the periods of world history, but which also is the indwelling, innermost principle in all human beings. The difference is just that, whereas this spirit comes forward as that [original divine spirit] in its substantial strength and purity, as the pure, archetypal human being, it is more or less obscured in all other people. Yet it is also not obscured and dimmed so much in them that it cannot break through what conceals it—whether it does so owing to the inner strength of its principle or because of outward prompting—and regain the full illumination of its self-consciousness.

This Adam-Christ is, so to speak, the male principle, a principle that in individuals has simply become so obscured and weakened by its being tied to a female principle that became dominant. The male principle is the spiritual and rational principle; the female principle is the sensuous and weak one, the aspect of human nature subject to error and sin. That is why, in the *Homilies*, the phenomena proving to be false prophecy, or demonic paganism, are in the final analysis always traced back to their source in a principle indwelling human beings. Hence what Judaism and paganism are for world history on the large scale, the two principles of reason and sensuality are that, respectively, in the setting of individual human beings and human nature in and for itself. In each of these contexts there is the same duality of a male principle and a female principle.

So it is simply a matter of stripping away the symbolic and mythical covering Gnostic supernaturalism has wrapped around itself, and taking these shapes, in which it has personified its concepts, for what they are in themselves. Then the Gnostic worldview, as their actual kernel, emerges as a very lucid rationalism basing itself on spirit's immanent self-consciousness. Even though the Gnostics may not have been very directly aware of this rationalism, the principle of rationalism is inherent in the concept of Gnosis. Hence we can simply regard docetism as the point at which the rational tendency, as an inherent feature of Gnosis, became its most visible external manifestation.

It is quite natural and unavoidable that, to the extent all the emphasis gets placed on general ideas of a speculative nature or on general religious content, the historical reality of the facts of Christianity moves to the background. In contrast to the idea, factual matters have only secondary significance, or even just become pictorial reflections of the idea. This is what Gnostic docetism is all about; what it states, first of all, with reference to Christ's body, inherently holds good for Gnosis in general. Just as Christ's body lacks the concrete reality of a human body, so too the general character of Gnosis is the evaporation or complete generalization of the positive contents of historical Christianity. Gnosis locates Christianity within its own overall worldview and understands it as being one moment of the general process of the world's development. The Gnostic Christ is a general principle, one in the older Gnostic systems determining the real-world process of the world's development, or at least, as in the system of the *Homilies*, a principle determining the knowledge of truth.

Christianity involves both of the following issues.[90] First: How is a human being saved, or how does one become blessed? Second, the general issue of the beginning, course, and goal of the world's development: How is it possible to know, in an absolute way, what is true, what is existent in itself? From a standpoint taking the salvation issue by itself, Christianity is at risk of being subsumed into the particularism of Judaism. From the standpoint of Gnosis, Christianity is in danger of dissolving into the concept, into the generality of a transcendent worldview. In the process of becoming the church, the catholicizing tendency of Christianity had to oppose exclusive emphasis on either of these positions. Yet before we turn to this aspect of the history of the Christian Church's development, Montanism calls for our attention.

2. MONTANISM

Gnosis and Montanism

Gnosis and Montanism are alike in that both are dealing with an issue that in principle relates to the general course of the world. They differ in that, whereas Gnosis looks to the beginning point from which all things emerge, the absolute principles that condition God's process of self-revelation and the course of the world's development, in Montanism the main factor motivating this whole outlook is the end of things, the denouement (*Katastrophe*) toward which the world's course is headed. Another equally important difference is that, whereas Gnosis takes for its horizons the most general worldview, one expanded and enriched by the most speculative ideas of the current philosophies, Montanism confines itself to the sphere of the Jewish messianic idea.[91]

---

90. [*Ed.*] Baur here summarizes the course of his argument so far. "First" refers to Part Two of this book. "Second" refers to Part Three.

91. [*Ed.*] Montanism takes its name from Montanus, a second century prophet in Asia Minor, who with two female colleagues, Prisca (Priscilla) and Maximilla, had ecstatic visions inspired by the Holy Spirit and advocated a morally rigorous life in preparation for the second coming of Christ. Tertullian

Notwithstanding these differences, we also have to highlight what the two have in common. These two phenomena we are discussing together here also both originated from the way that early Christianity looked at the world.[92] The Apostle Paul already came close to a Gnostic way of regarding the world, when he placed the two world-periods, the Christian and the pre-Christian periods, under the heading of general principles determining humankind's development, and distinguished different moments of a world-course that returns into the absolute oneness of God. And Montanism is wholly rooted in the early Christian belief in Christ's parousia, a belief shared by the Apostle Paul. Therefore here is the place, as we transition to discussing Montanism, for us to consider first of all this belief so characteristic of early Christian consciousness. Belief in Christ's parousia, and the reaction against a way of viewing the world that had already dispensed with this belief, are the two main elements in explaining the origin of Montanism and its character.

Belief in the Parousia

What ties Christianity most directly and closely with Judaism is the Jewish idea of the messiah. Nevertheless this bond at the same time involves the sharpest antithesis, one in which Judaism and Christianity definitely are at odds.

While people believed they saw in Jesus the promised messiah, come to fulfill their messianic hopes, his death certainly seemed to shatter forever all these hopes before they had been fulfilled. However, in the consciousness of his followers who believed in the messiah, the gap between Jewish messianic belief and the fact of Jesus' death all too soon closed. Although he had not fulfilled what people hoped he would as the living messiah, yet as the resurrected one who ascended to heaven he could certainly have come again from heaven in order to then accomplish all that remained to be done. For his first followers, Christ's parousia was a necessary postulate of faith; and as they were hardly able to renounce the content of their former belief, even in its new form, it seemed even more pressing for that belief to be fulfilled in the near future.

Thus many passages in the New Testament scriptures attest to how much this belief dominated Christian consciousness in the earliest days. There was no essential difference between the Apostle to the Gentiles, and the writer of the Book of Revelation, on this point. The Apostle Paul was among the first preachers of the gospel who saw Christianity's destiny, in becoming the universal religion of the whole world, as first being fulfilled in the distant future. Yet Paul's belief in the parousia is rooted in the

---

was deeply influenced by Montanism and conveyed many of its moral teachings (see, e.g., n. 103). On Baur's treatment of the origin of Montanism, see below, pp. 196–97.

92. [*Ed.*] Baur holds the old view, now disproved by subsequent discovery of additional texts, that Gnosticism originated on the soil of Christianity rather than pre-existing it.

conception that the end of all things already draws near, and he thought that he would live to see the great denouement himself.

Yet such a belief was far too vulnerable to refutation for it to persist as a strong and vital conviction. The longer this belief went unfulfilled, the more it had to lose its grip on the general consciousness of the times. Indeed we can trace the various modifications it gradually underwent within the New Testament writings. What a great distance there is between the Book of Revelation—easily the most extraordinary scripture in this regard, where this belief burns most brightly and has its most concrete form in chiliasm—and the Second Epistle of Peter! The writer of this epistle speaks of scoffers (3:3–4) who come "in the last days" and, "indulging their own lusts," say: "Where is the promise of his coming? For ever since our ancestors died, all things continue as they were from the beginning of creation!" Instead of renouncing the object of their contempt, he just seeks to refute them by treating belief in the parousia as a byproduct of acknowledging the general truths that underlie it. So this passage shows us clearly how things already stood then regarding this belief. However, although it was no longer a universal Christian belief, at least not in its original form, there nevertheless were some who, at odds with the growing worldliness of Christian consciousness manifest in this decline of belief in the parousia, just became more strongly attuned to it and held fast to it with renewed enthusiasm.

Chiliasm and Prophecy

The Montanists belong in the aforementioned category, because chiliasm[93] is one of their most prominent traits.

However widespread chiliasm may still have been at this time, the Montanists were in any event its most fervent exponents. The main factors fueling this fervor were their ecstatic enthusiasm and the inspired deliverances of their prophets in proclaiming the impending Judgment Day when Christ returns, his thousand-year reign, and the end of the world—with all this depicted in the most vivid images. The pronouncement of their prophetess, Maximilla, shows how vitally occupied they were with the end of the world. She said: "After me, there is only the end of the world."[94] As chiliasts, the Montanists could not see the end of the world occurring quickly enough. Their daily prayer was the expression of their chiliast outlook in the phrase "thy kingdom come" in the Lord's Prayer. They counted the kingdom of God and the end of the world as identical concepts.[95] Therefore, even though the entire generation to whom

---

93. [*Ed.*] Chiliasm comes from the Greek word χιλιάς (thousand) and refers to the belief in a thousand-year reign of Christ after his second coming (see Rev 20:2–3). It is often referred to as "millennialism" or "millenarianism." Postmillennialism believes the second coming will follow the thousand-year reign.

94. Epiphanius, *Against Heresies* 48.2. [*Ed.*] Baur's footnote gives the Greek for this sentence, in which συντέλεια refers to the completion or consummation (of everything).

95. See Tertullian, *On Prayer*, ch. 5, where he says about "thy kingdom come": "And so, if the

Christ's parousia supposedly was promised had hoped for it in vain, people did not abandon the belief itself—that the kingdom of God would begin in the near future. The Montanists knew the place where the heavenly Jerusalem would descend, and they even already had an exemplary vision of its descent from heaven.[96] While the chiliastic belief had become weaker and more half-hearted in other circles, that only made it stronger and more vital among the Montanists. They couple their chiliasm closely with their ecstatic prophecy, an equally characteristic feature of their belief system. When one's life is consumed with thoughts of the parousia and the future, and one sees before one's own eyes, and close at hand, the events said to introduce and accompany the coming world denouement, how can this vision of the future not of its own accord become prophecy in the present? It is very significant for Montanism that prophecy expressed itself in the form of ecstasy, even though ecstasy was hardly unusual in other circles. Since ecstasy was for them intensified prophecy, it was quite natural that, when chiliasm gained new energy among the Montanists, prophecy, as the expression of chiliastic inspiration, received such a powerful impetus in tandem with that chiliasm. Ecstasy makes the finite subject utterly passive in relation to the divine principle. This is apparent in the statement of Montanus comparing the human being to the lyre and the Paraclete to the pick, calling the human being the one who is sleeping and the Paraclete the one who awakens.[97] It is also evident in the fact that the instruments of the Holy Spirit are said to be chiefly female persons, prophetesses such as Maximilla and Priscilla. Each belief [in chiliasm and in ecstatic prophecy] of its own accord intensified the other one.

Believers in the parousia did not let the length of time that had already gone by deter them, for they simply believed that had to make the great denouement even more imminent. Everything was now at the final stage, was in the καιρὸς συνεσταλμένος (appointed time) (1 Cor 7:29). Because of that, the spirit, the πνεῦμα ἅγιον (Holy Spirit), as the principle of Christian consciousness, also had to become more strongly focused and thus express itself more directly and unambiguously. This increased focus and more direct expression were implicit in the awareness that they were living in the *dies novissimi* (last days). Tertullian's whole theory of the different periods of development

---

manifestation of the Lord's kingdom is subject to the will of God and we anxiously await it, how do some pray for the current age to continue ([Baur's interpolated version:]) how can many demand that the kingdom of God involves itself still longer in the temporal course of the word—that chiliasm was thus no longer so universal a belief) when the kingdom of God, which we pray may arrive, will mean the consummation of this age? Our wish is, that our reign be hastened, not our servitude protracted. Even if it had not been prescribed in the prayer that we should ask that 'thy kingdom come,' we should, unbidden, have called for it, so our hope would be soon realized." [ANF 3:683]

96. Tertullian, *Against Marcion* 3.24. [*Ed.*] ANF vol. 3 skips from ch. 23 to ch. 25 of Book 3, or more likely, ch. 24 is mislabeled as ch. 25. A portion of ch. 25 of Book 3 in *ANF* 3 (p. 342) reads: "And the word of the new prophecy which is part of our belief, attests how it foretold that we would see an image of this very city, as a sign prior to its manifestation. This prophecy, indeed, has been very lately fulfilled in an expedition to the East."

97. Epiphanius, *Against Heresies* 48.4.

is simply his analysis of the concept of the *novissima*. He says that first the plant grows from the single seed, and finally the fruit arises from the flower; and in similar fashion *justitia* (justice), originally in the natural state, advanced to childhood through the law and the prophets, whereupon it opened out to youth and now is brought to maturity by the Paraclete.[98]

People want to be quite clear about what in the "last things" are truly the last, by ruling out what are not yet final events so that they can attend only to what is final. But as the Montanists see it, in these last days everything is nearing the end and coming to a head, and would become more concentrated, more magnified, more intensive. Tertullian says that "in all cases it is the later things which have a conclusive force, and the subsequent which prevail over the antecedent."[99] This is a universal law for human affairs and thus also for the divine order of things, most especially with regard to the last days. Tertullian very often mentions the prophecy of Joel [2:28, "I will pour out my spirit on all flesh"] as what was to be fulfilled in the last days. The more all things draw to a head and intensify in this period where *tempus in collecto est* (time comes together), the more powerfully the spirit pervades a Christian's entire consciousness and fills it with its divine content, illuminating all darkness.

In the Book of Revelation we see essentially the same relation between the last things and the spirit's activity expressed in this setting. The book's contents are all the ensuing individual moments of the great denouement, and the book's writer is solely the instrument of the divine inspiration that has come over him. He too is ἐν πνεύματι (in the spirit), that is, in the state of ecstasy (1:10). Here we have a purely prophetic and visionary state, just as the ecstatic states of the Montanists take the forms of both prophecy and vision. The spirit animating Christians from the very beginning, and awakening them to prophetic inspiration and ecstasy, is also the principle of Montanism. The reason why this spirit was preeminently called the Paraclete then is that, in the trials and tribulations of the end time, the Paraclete was said to be not only the guide to all truth but also the advocate, support, and comfort for all those in whom it was the ecstatic, governing power. In any event the Holy Spirit, now referred to in particular as the Paraclete, had his very special significance firmly established for this final world-period, the time when a Montanist saw everything pressing toward its conclusion.

---

98. Tertullian, *On the Veiling of Virgins*, 1.

99. Tertullian, *On Baptism*, 13 [*ANF* 3:676]. Compare also Tertullian, *Martyrdom of Perpetua and Felicitas*, and Epiphanius, *Against Heresies* 4.8, with Schwegler, *Montanismus*, 39. [*Ed.*] In the text this note is placed after the next sentence, but it applies to the quotation here. The full title of Albert Schwegler's book is *Der Montanismus und die christliche Kirche des zweiten Jahrhunderts* (Tübingen, 1841).

The Reactionary Tendency of Montanism

The Paraclete's activities in the real [as opposed to the spiritual] world fall under the heading of morality. Thus he not only expresses himself most energetically in prophetic ecstasy, so as to fathom future mysteries and to shed light on all that is obscure for consciousness; he also most forcefully presents the moral requirements of Christianity in practice.

Therefore as the *spiritus sanctus, ipsius disciplinae determinator, institutor novae disciplinae* (the Holy Spirit, who determines disciplines and establishes new disciplines), the Montanist Paraclete is the exacting spirit of serious moral rigor, the declared enemy of all laxity and indifference in matters of morality. It is his inherent nature to actualize discipline in the moral realm. When Tertullian sums up all the features comprising the concept of the Paraclete, he puts this practical role first and foremost. He brings the scriptures to light, clarifies the intellect, lifts up to a higher level of perfection. But what is primary, his practical goal, is giving proper direction to discipline.[100]

The Montanists increased the severity of Christian discipline by several of their distinctive precepts. Examples include χειροφαγία (eating with hands), prolonging the *dies stationum* (stations of the day) into the evening, and their requirements regarding marriage and martyrdom. But the fundamental idea, the source of all these regulations, was that the Christian lived in the last days and stood at the end of the whole course of the world. How this theoretical idea fully occupied the Montanist's consciousness also had to determine where one stood in practical matters. Someone whose life was still seized by this single idea of the world's ending, and who saw in all the surrounding world just signs of the already impending world denouement everywhere, must have been inwardly and completely disconnected from the world. Therefore such a person could also simply consider carrying out this break with the world in all of life's circumstances, and completely undoing the ties still binding one's existence in the flesh to this world.

It has been correctly noted[101] that the moral requirements of Montanism are nothing new; that they are only novel inasmuch as they are a reaction; that the issue between the Montanists and their opponents within the church only concerns stricter enforcement of older precepts that, even conceptually, had fallen into disuse; that the Montanists' legislation regarding fasting and marriage simply aimed at observing in practice what had been recognized as God's eternal commands, as the legislation set forth in the Old and New Testaments. This reactionary tendency was based solely on the Montanists' belief that theirs was the better understanding of the time in which

---

100. Tertullian, *On the Veiling of Virgins*, ch. 1. [*Ed.*] The ET of this passage (*ANF* 4:27) reads: "What, then, is the Paraclete's administrative office but this: the direction of discipline, the revelation of the Scriptures, the re-formation of the intellect, the advancement toward the 'better things'?"

101. Albrecht Ritschl, *Die Entstehung der altkatholischen Kirche*, 1st ed. (Bonn, 1850), 513; 2nd ed. (Bonn, 1857), 497ff.

a Christian now lived; that they recognized it for what it was, as the end time. They asked: How much did this original consciousness, rooted in belief in Christ's parousia, have to have already diminished, when people are so dismissive of the duty of martyrdom that entire congregations have paid money for wholesale exemption from persecution, and when bishops and clergy themselves were the ones who encouraged this cowardice and took the lead by exemplifying it.[102]

The conclusion from this is how far things have also come from the strictness of the older morality. The church has already made its peace with the world. The direction Montanism took is therefore correctly understood as a reactionary stance. Montanism fought with all its energy against the ever-increasing worldliness of Christianity. The principle of this Montanist tendency could only be that it reverted to the original standpoint of the Christian consciousness that had rid itself of all worldly interests by affirming the same two beliefs: the parousia of Christ and the imminent end of the world. Hence again and again we see this as the underlying theme of all of Tertullian's precepts and exhortations.[103]

This is now the place to consider the particular question: How is the Paraclete related to the spirit acting in the apostles? The Paraclete does not wish to introduce anything new into dogmatics or morality. As Tertullian puts it, the Paraclete is *restitutor potius, quam institutor* (more a restorer than an introducer), and yet he goes beyond Christ and the apostles in that, what they declared to be morally permissible, the Paraclete can no longer overlook as weakness of the flesh. The basis for this too is that the nearer the world's end, the less indulgence there will be for weakness of the flesh. Every impediment to the sanctity of the flesh must be completely eradicated.[104] In post-apostolic times the spirit follows with stricter requirements, which is not to say the apostles had aimed at anything less; they were just less outspoken and direct about it. As Tertullian sees it, strictness is always nevertheless accompanied by a certain leniency that is only explainable as accommodation. Like the apostles did, the Paraclete also made accommodations. An exact understanding of Christ's meaning should have meant the Paraclete would not even consent to first marriages. Only out of forbearance, from accommodation to human weakness, did the Paraclete not wholly forbid marriage, as he inherently should have done.

Seen from this perspective, the whole of world history continually involves accommodations. As a result, what is initially allowed and freely granted must later be increasingly curtailed and withdrawn. What Moses enjoined Christ suspended because it was not so from the outset. Now the Paraclete can likewise disallow what Paul still condoned, if only the result of doing so is worthy of God and Christ. Just as it was formerly worthy of God and Christ to tone down hardness of heart when its time was

---

102. Tertullian, *On Flight in Persecution*, chs. 11 and 13.

103. See, for example, his *To His Wife*, 1.5.

104. Tertullian, *On Monogamy*, ch. 3: "But the flesh is taught sanctity; and in Christ the flesh was holy" [*ANF* 4:61].

past, it is now likewise worthy of them to eradicate the weakness of the flesh, since the end time draws near. Hardness of heart was the rule until Christ, and weakness of the flesh had its day up until the Paraclete set to work, whereupon the Lord set aside what at that time still could not be endured.

The Paraclete of course only carried out what Christ and the apostles already had intended implicitly. But because his own activity comes after theirs, he can now accomplish for the first time what could not have been done earlier on. So the general rule is that everything has its appointed time. In itself the flesh, the sensuous aspect of human nature, has no moral justification. Making allowances for the flesh is merely a concession. It is natural that, with the approaching end of the world, this concession is less and less appropriate as the flesh itself must become increasingly anxious, uncouth, and repellent in its relation to the spirit. With the present order of the world breaking down, so too the principles of spirit and flesh become mutually antithetical to the fullest extent. The material principle must give way to the spiritual principle and become unconditionally subordinate to it, since from the outset the material principle was only supposed to secure room in the world so that the spiritual element can operate in this space with its own absolute power. The flesh is like a woodlot people allow to grow up, only so as finally to cut it down to the roots.[105] The standpoint from which to consider everything is always the last point, the end of things, in which the finite as such stands out clearly in its finitude.

Hence the Paraclete itself is none other than the spirit—aware of the world's finitude, and withdrawing from the world and going within itself—now becoming aware, in its own self-consciousness, of its power over the flesh and the world. In this consciousness on spirit's part, a consciousness heightened by the Paraclete, every deceitful illusion with which the flesh surrounds the spirit vanishes of its own accord; and, with this illusory world removed, spirit has a clearer vision of the temporal order of things as something in itself empty, as already now collapsing internally. Thus the moral teaching of the Montanists is concentrated in the simple demand to cut one's ties with the world, for, in the Montanists' prophetic vision, the world is collapsing internally. Their doctrine is to dissolve the bonds spirit has to the flesh, just as one is to conceive of the world as being in its own process of dissolution.

Montanism Compared with Gnosis[106]

As soon as we have correctly understood the basic outlook of Montanism, we can grasp more clearly Montanism's essential nature, and it appears even more justifiable to set it alongside Gnosticism.

---

105. Tertullian, *On Exhortation to Chastity*, ch. 6.

106. [*Ed.*] Baur's text has a paragraph break at this point but no corresponding heading in the table of contents.

Both movements adopt a transcendent perspective. Both the Montanists and the Gnostics see the actual essence of Christianity as far removed from present-day reality, with the Gnostic looking back to a past time when everything has its absolute origin, and the Montanist looking toward a future when it all comes to an end and what is "down here" vanishes in face of what is "up there." For both, Christ is the absolute world-principle, with the Gnostic constructing his own entire system of the world's development based on this principle, whereas for the Montanist the Christ-principle is significant just for the world's destruction. As the Messiah made manifest, the [Montanist] Christ is only present to bring everything to an end, and to produce the great world-denouement by which the current world order passes over into the world to come. In the Gnostic systems too Christ, as the principle determining the process of the world's development, is the turning point at which everything goes back in order to join the end to the beginning. Whereas in Gnosticism everything takes an endless course, Montanism cannot have the final denouement come soon enough. For Montanism, as soon as Christ [re]appears—and he certainly shall appear in the immediate future—the world comes to its end. In Christ, right at the outset, the current world order is in principle superseded by the future one. In both systems the final goal is an ἀποκατάστασις (restoration, or reinstatement), in which the principles separate themselves and stand over against each other in their pure forms. In Gnosis these principles are spirit and matter. In Montanism, they are spirit and flesh.

Although the Gnostics and the Montanists associated different concepts with the pneumatic or spiritual element, each of these movements wanted to be the pure instrument of the spiritual principle. The Gnostics saw themselves, first and foremost, as the ones with spiritual natures, and they assigned the other Christians just to the level of psychical life. In similar fashion, the Montanists made the distinction between πνευματικοί (spirituals) and ψυχικοί (psychicals) normative, in order to look down disparagingly on those who did not believe in their doctrine of the Paraclete, i.e., the Catholic Christians. The two movements shared the same antithesis, although the Montanists did so within far more limited horizons.

The Origins of Montanism

Once we know what Montanism is, it becomes less important to investigate the external circumstances in which it came about. That is because what makes it distinctive are elements already present from the beginning of Christianity.

Montanism's alleged ancestry in a person named "Montanus" is scarcely any information at all. Therefore it is hardly worth the effort to join Neander in getting worked up over those who even wanted to question whether this apocryphal person ever existed. The earliest Greek writers call them not "Montanists" but "Cataphrygians" (οἱ κατὰ Φρύγας), from where they were located, and "those who expected the descent of the Heavenly Jerusalem." What we can say about Montanus is only that he appeared as a prophet alongside, and earlier than, the two well-known prophetesses, Priscilla and Maximilla.[107] The only basis for supposing that he claimed to be God the Father, or the Paraclete, is that, given the nature of ecstasy, the subject doing the speaking was not the ecstatic prophet but God himself, or the Holy Spirit.

Montanism as a historical phenomenon appeared about the middle of the second century. From that time onward it attracted increasing public attention as the issues it raised affected more deeply both life practices in general and most especially the circumstances of the ecclesiastical community that was taking shape. Working from this foundation, we can trace Montanism's further history from the side of those who opposed the phenomena we have discussed so far.[108]

---

107. Even the *Philosophumena* (n. 11) does not say he was the actual founder of the sect. It only says (8.19.1; p. 275): "They also equally glorify the earlier figure Montanus as a prophet" [ET 612–13].

108. The foregoing account of Montanism is the essential content of my treatise, "Das Wesen des Montanismus nach den neuesten Forschungen," in the *Theologische Jahrbücher* 10 (1851) 538–94. The treatise also contains a critique of recently-published views on Montanism, those subsequent to the work of Neander and Gieseler. Research in greater depth on this topic began with A. Schwegler's book, *Der Montanismus und die christliche Kirche des zweiten Jahrhunderts* (Tübingen, 1841). Even Neander had understood Montanism in a very one-sided way, and he went astray mainly in being misled by vague indications as to the person of Montanus. He explains the character of Montanism based on the nature-elements of the old Phrygian religion and the Phrygian mindset, as they were exhibited in the ecstasies of the priests of Cybele and Bacchus. He repeats this so often that it subsequently distracts us from the correct perspective.

II. The Catholic Church as the Antithesis to Gnosis and Montanism

1. THE DOGMATIC ANTITHESES

The Idea of the Catholic Church

Christian life of the first post-apostolic period was most fully productive and most vigorously energetic in Gnosis and in Montanism.

Gnosis gives the clearest proof of the great world-historical significance Christianity already had at that time. It is mainly in Gnosis where we see the powerful attraction the new factor of Christianity held for the intellectual life of the pagan and Jewish worlds in those days. Gnosis contained such diverse elements, and had blended together so much that was Hellenic and Jewish. In Christianity all this material acquired a new and shared focal point as the basis, in a large number of Gnostic systems, for ever-new combinations of elements in the most diverse ways. These systems continually tackled the same task, one indeed occupying the most thoughtful minds at that time and also subsequently remaining the most important issue for Christian religious philosophy—how to conceptualize Christianity from the perspective of a general worldview. Montanism likewise provided a new and energetic impetus, and it raised new and important issues, not merely for practical life but also for understanding Christianity as such.

So, if we take Gnosis and Montanism together, these phenomena as a whole present us with the spiritual and intellectual movement at that time. But they also show us very vividly the unsettled, fermenting conditions in which so much was topsy-turvy, and where the most diverse orientations intersected.

All these widely-divergent movements necessitated a reaction if Christianity was not to lose its own original character. Christianity not only had to hold firmly to the practical religious concerns of which it was directly aware, over against the transcendent speculation of the Gnostics. It also had to first secure the ground on which Christianity could set its feet firmly within the world, over against the chiliastic enthusiasm of the Montanists that precluded any possibility for its historical development. Above all, therefore, this called for a unifying point that could serve as a counterweight to positions related to Christianity and held in conjunction with it, as well as to all those other heterogeneous and eccentric orientations. This counterweight is the idea of the Catholic Church, which already—as a higher power standing above all their antitheses—had united Jewish Christians and Gentile Christians in a common enterprise. Thus, in opposition to the Gnostics and Montanists, a more definitive [Christian] consciousness developed, one taking a more cohesive shape and with an ever-widening scope.

The great struggle with Gnosis, a struggle ongoing throughout the second century and one so important for the history of Christianity's development and for the development of the Christian Church, was of a twofold kind, both dogmatic and ecclesiastical. On the whole Gnosis has a character so alien to Christianity that, in each of its forms, Gnosis had to conflict anew with Christianity. It could not have been otherwise, given the elements from which Gnosis emerged. The two had to be antithetical because many elements of Gnosis formed a very decided antithesis to the fundamental outlook of Christian consciousness. These antithetical features of Gnosis are: the dualism on which Gnosis relies and Gnosticism's antipathy to all that is material; the series of Aeons said to mediate God's relation to the world; replacing the Jewish and Christian concept that the world is freely created with the doctrine that the world emanated from God; the separation of the world's creator from the One High God; grouping Christ together with other divine beings where this can only be seen as detracting from Christ's absolute worth; the entire process of the world's development, into which Christianity is interlaced in such a way that the events of the redemption accomplished by Christ not only must lose their moral and religious meaning, but also even lose their historical character. Christian dogma was still so undeveloped at this time that it only came to be spelled out more precisely, and be given set form, mainly in opposition to Gnosis. So this is why at first there was a Christian rebuttal (*Antithesis*) to each Gnostic doctrine.

On the other hand, however, Gnosis also was very akin to Christianity and involved so much that harmonized with it. As soon as Christianity had spread further among the higher social classes, every person who was educated, and conversant with the leading ideas of the time, felt called upon to answer for himself the same questions the Gnostics were endeavoring to puzzle out. So the time came when Christianity's relation to Gnosis could by no means be just one of hostility and rejection. Hence the church fathers as a whole took various positions regarding Gnosis.

The Stance of the Church Fathers toward Gnosis

Clement of Alexandria, Origen, and Their Relation to Gnosis

Those who operated within the same intellectual setting from which the most important leaders of Gnosis itself had come were the least able to simply come forward as opponents to Gnosis. Alexandria, the native land of Gnosis, is also the birthplace of Christian theology, which in its own initial form sought to be none other than a Christian Gnosis.

Clement and Origen stand closest to the Gnostics. Since they position γνῶσις above πίστις, and place the two of them in such an immanent, mutual relationship that the one cannot be without the other—that there is no knowledge apart from the actual contents of faith, and no faith without elevating faith's contents into the form of knowledge—these theologians occupy the same standpoint as the Gnostics. They do so in order to conceptualize Christianity in its historical context, and to be conscious of its contents in intellectual terms, by utilizing all that the contemporary philosophy has to offer.

Clement[109] is in fact so convinced that the idea of the absolute is the essential content of Christianity that, like the Gnostics, he recognizes the highest task of his own Gnosis as being one's self-elevation from the finite to the absolute. The only difference is that, whereas the Gnostics, in the context of the entire development of the world, have everything pneumatic or spiritual returning into the absolute, the pleroma, Clement transfers this process from the real world into the knowing subject.

Clement says that the world and natural life move in cyclical fashion according to the number seven. So too the Gnostic reaches his absolute goal only through the hebdomad [set of seven]. Whatever else the hebdomad may refer to, whether it be a time that reaches its completion via a course of seven specific periods, or it be seven heavens numbered in ascending order—or whether the unchanging sphere that is close to the intelligible world be called the ogdoad [the number eight]—in any event the Gnostics must work their way through the world of birth and sin. That is why for seven days sacrificial animals are offered for sinners; and why there are seven "days" instead of seven "purifications," because in this number of days what is coming to be reaches its completion. However, the consummate way to appropriate [the goal] is belief in the gospel, acquired by grace via the law and the prophets, and that purity obtained via complete obedience and linked to renunciation of all worldly things, a renunciation in which the soul gratefully returns the tabernacle after it has made use of it. The true Gnostic belongs among those who, as David says (Ps 15:1), will find their

---

109. [*Ed.*] Clement of Alexandria (c. 150—c. 215) taught in the catechetical school of Alexandria. He was a convert to Christianity and well-educated in Greek philosophy and literature, by which he was influenced to a greater extent than any other Christian thinker of his time. Origen was one of his pupils.

rest "on the holy mountain of God," in the highest church where God's philosophers will assemble—the true Israelites, who are pure in heart and free of falsehood.[110]

Gnostics, in Clement's sense, who are at this highest level, realize in a twofold way the supreme task of their Gnosis, or of Christianity as the absolute religion. They do so both theoretically and practically. They do so theoretically by bringing together in their unity the components of the body of truth, which, so to speak, is fragmented into endlessly many scattered points; for whoever brings together again, and unites, what is separated will, without risk [of error], behold the perfect Logos, the truth.[111] They do so practically by directing their entire sensibility and life toward the absolute in a completely unemotional way, in order to become, in their dispassionate state, like their teacher the Logos; for the Logos of God is purely spiritual, which is why the spirit's image is seen in human beings alone, and why a good human being is, in soul, like unto God and godlike in form, and why, in return, God is human-like, since spirit is the characteristic form of each.[112]

For Clement's Gnostic, the idea of the Logos contains all that Christianity essentially is. In contrast to the absolute God who, like the Gnostics' primal being, is utterly unknowable in his abstract being-in-self, the Logos is simply the mediating principle through which the idea of the absolute realizes itself, theoretically and practically, in the Gnostic. However, for the Gnostics and for Clement too, the idea of the Logos is so constitutive of Christianity's substantial content that the historical character of Christianity fades away into docetism. The Gnostic Christ is so very much a being belonging to the world of Aeons that he cannot have any direct contact with the material, sensible world. Clement's Logos is likewise much too exalted and transcendent to be able to enter into the full reality of a genuinely human existence. Clement himself nevertheless spoke rather openly about his docetism when he could say, about Christ's human manifestation, that the Logos assumed the mask or guise of a human being and, taking form in the flesh, enacted humankind's salvific drama.[113]

Clement neither shared the dualism of the Gnostics, nor could he agree with them in separating the creator of the world from the supreme God. He had most affinity for the monotheistic form of Gnosis as we find it in the *Clementine Homilies*. He even identified Christianity with Judaism, not only in the same manner as the *Homilies* did, by accepting spurious additions to the Old Testament scriptures, but also, in truly Alexandrian fashion, he employed the method of allegorical interpretation that he and Origen utilized most extensively. For Clement the main thing is the

---

110. *Stromata* 6.16; 7.10; 4.25; 6.14. [*Ed.*] Baur paraphrases various passages from Clement's *Stromata* (The Miscellanies). Reference to the tabernacle appears to be an allusion to Ezekiel ch. 44, which speaks of the temple as a sanctuary. The tabernacle was a tent sanctuary the Israelites used after the Exodus, and it was later replaced by the temple as a permanent structure.

111. *Stromata* 1.13.

112. *Stromata* 6.9.

113. *Exhortation to the Heathen*, ch. 10.

scriptural interpretation received from the Lord; in other words, the church's norm of the harmony and agreement of the law and the prophets with the testaments provided owing to the Lord's appearing.[114] Allegorical interpretation therefore has the task of demonstrating the complete identity of the Old Testament with the New Testament. It accomplishes this purpose so completely that Christianity is shown to be essentially just Judaism unveiled. Since allegory never wants to be merely arbitrary and subjective, Clement also regards it as a traditional practice. Just as the Gnostics customarily traced their movement back to a specific authority from which they professed to have received their doctrines as secret teachings, so too Clement appealed to his own sources, from which his own Gnosis, consisting essentially of exploring the allegorical meaning of scripture, supposedly came to him via a secret tradition.[115]

Given so many points of contact between the Alexandrians' teaching and Gnosis, it is especially important to emphasize that, in contrast to the Gnostics' fatalistic and naturalistic doctrines, Clement and Origen held all the more firmly to the principle of the freedom of the will that is active in moral striving. However, when we proceed from Clement to Origen[116] with this issue in mind, this idea of freedom just gives us a new proof of how, at a deep level, the Alexandrian and the Gnostic outlooks are related. We see how, at that time, one could still just always erect a system analogous to Gnosis, as soon as one sought to set forth one's vision not merely in the scattershot manner of the *Stromata*, but instead as a self-consistent whole.

In Origen's system, everything depends on the idea of freedom. Freedom is the principle of morality. Hence Origen constructs his system not from the metaphysical standpoint of the Gnostics, but instead from the ethical standpoint. However, his system itself takes a course like that of the Gnostic systems. So as not to compromise in any way the idea of moral goodness, Origen affirms that the spirits created by God were originally and equally in possession of the same freedom of the will to do either good or evil. Every difference existing in the world has its basis in freedom, in the different uses made of freedom. The material world itself originated as the result of what the spiritual subjects in the higher world had actually done with their freedom.

If the principle of freedom is a given, not only is evil a possibility; also, no further explanation is needed for the fact that there can be actual evil. Thus in the development of Origen's system, as in the Gnostic systems, the main factor is the Platonic idea that spiritual beings fall from the higher world into the material world. The entire origin and organization of the world is simply conditioned by the idea of a morality that rests on the principle of freedom. In Origen's moral worldview, the material world

114. *Stromata* 6.15.

115. *Stromata* 1.1.

116. [*Ed.*] Origen (c. 184—c. 253) was a Greek scholar, ascetic, and prolific Christian theologian, who was born and spent the first half of his career in Alexandria. Many of his views were controversial, and later he was anathematized by the church and never declared a saint. He was the first Christian systematic theologian. Baur provides no citations, but his summary of Origen's system is based mainly on *De principiis* (On First Principles).

is regarded as a place of punishment for the fallen spirits, each of which, residing in a material shell, has been placed in the circumstances in the world that spirit deserved because of its moral [or immoral] conduct in the higher, intelligible world.

Yet a falling way (*Abfall*) also involves a return (*Rückkehr*). Beginning from the same principle of freedom always in turn involves this same possible consequence arising from it. Therefore, in the constant cycle of falling away and return, there is also an endless succession of finite worlds. Looked at in this way, God himself is simply the idea of the world's moral order, an idea immanent in the world, inasmuch as the moral standing of good and evil actions results in specific consequences based on the idea of divine justice. With the endless number of individual spirits, freely going off in such different directions, this divine justice alone restores an inner unity, an orderly, cohesive arrangement that gives unity to this freedom.

For Origen, the relation of spirit to matter is of course different than it is for the Gnostics. But when Origen says only God is pure, absolute spirit in the absolute sense, and that in the fallen spirits the spiritual fire cools into being soul, and the spiritual power reduced commensurate with the fall is unable to resist its material shell and the decisive influence of matter, then in the end Origen too falls back on the antithesis of spirit and matter. In any event we find ourselves facing the very doctrine that subsequent and more settled dogmatic consciousness found most objectionable, the doctrine of the pre-existence and fall of souls. The shift is to a set of ideas wholly related to Gnosis. Here the positive contents of historical Christianity are in peril. We also clearly see the same thing especially in Origen's christology, which tends toward docetism and presents the same danger of dissolving into general, speculative ideas. This therefore makes it clear that an opposition battling successfully against Gnosis could never emerge from this quarter.[117]

The Opposition of Irenaeus and Tertullian to Gnosis and to Philosophy

Irenaeus and Tertullian,[118] church fathers from the western part of the empire, took a quite different stance toward Gnosis. With them we encounter for the first time the Christian polemic that delves more deeply into the essential nature of Gnosis, although they too were able to achieve their goal not so much in terms of dogma as they did simply by an ecclesial strategy.

While the arguments with which these two church fathers sought to refute individual Gnostic doctrines, as well as refuting the whole way of looking at things that underlies the Gnostic systems, are largely astute and pertinent, this kind of

---

117. See Baur, *Die christliche Gnosis* (n. 5), 502ff., and "Der Begriff der christlichen Philosophie und die Hauptmomente ihrer Entwicklung," *Theologische Jahrbücher* 5 (1846) 81ff.

118. [*Ed.*] Irenaeus (c. 130—c. 202) was bishop of Lugdunum in Gaul (modern-day Lyon). His major work was *Adversus haereses* (Against Heresies), a detailed polemic against Gnosticism. Tertullian (c. 155—c. 240), from Carthage in Africa, authored an extensive corpus of Latin Christian literature. He created theological concepts that shaped western doctrinal discussion for many centuries.

polemic just led to a philosophical and dialectical battle that could never be definitively resolved. With Christianity, as the Gnostics understood it, losing its distinctive character, the issue for Christianity became one of positioning itself in opposition to the Gnostics from a standpoint that could, most decisively, give full value to specific Christian concerns. First and foremost, the Gnostic tendency of antagonism to the essence of Christianity as such had to be exposed.

Tertullian raised this point when, in his polemic against Marcion, he also made especially clear the consequences of Gnostic docetism. Tertullian says that if the flesh of Christ is a deception, a lie, then it also follows that everything done by Christ's flesh becomes deceitful; that Christ just seems to have associated with human beings, to have lived together with them. Even Christ's suffering deserves no credence, for whoever has not truly suffered has not suffered at all. So this subverts the whole of God's work; it denies the entire significance and outcome of Christianity, Christ's death, which the Apostle Paul makes the foundation of the gospel.[119] Therefore if Christianity is merely what it supposedly is as Gnosis sees it, then Christianity has no objective historical reality. Gnosis changes Christianity's factual component into something merely illusory, imaginary, and purely subjective. Gnosis could have this tendency so antagonistic to the historical character of Christianity only because Gnosis itself was something quite different from Christianity.

A major element of the polemic against Gnosis by these two church fathers is thus their response citing the pagan origin of Gnosis. They not only contended as much, for they also sought to demonstrate, on individual points, that the Gnostics borrowed everything in their systems partly from the theogonies of the ancient Greek poets and partly from the systems of the philosophers. The Gnostics just changed the names, although by looking at the subject matter itself one sees that, in all they pass off as their own secret wisdom, there is nothing not also to be found already in the teachings of Thales and Anaxagoras, of Heraclitus and Empedocles, of Democritus and Epicurus, of Pythagoras and Plato. Hence the dilemma with which Irenaeus summarizes the results of his marshalling of the evidence: The pagan poets and philosophers the Gnostics so closely align themselves with either knew the truth or they did not know it. If they knew the truth, then the redeemer's coming into the world is superfluous. But if they did not know the truth, then we cannot see how the Gnostics can sing the praises of such lofty knowledge, since by doing so they themselves are just agreeing with those who do not know God.[120]

This challenge to Gnosis made people more specifically aware of how not merely Gnosis, but Greek philosophy too, stood in relation to Christianity. Thus it became natural for them to also oppose philosophy itself as the source of Gnosis. In comparing

---

119. Tertullian, *Apostolic Constitutions* 3.8.

120. [*Ed.*] Baur footnotes *Die christliche Gnosis* (n. 5), 485ff. and 469ff. On p. 471 Baur provides a similar statement of this dilemma, part of which is directly reproduced here in our text, as it appears in Irenaeus, *Against Heresies* 2.14.7.

these church fathers with the Alexandrians, we see how entirely different is their assessment of the value of philosophy. Tertullian, for instance, had no reticence about expressing his views in the most extreme fashion. These writers looked upon philosophy as contradictory to Christianity, as irreconcilably antithetical to Christianity. They stated openly, and as a fundamental principle, that philosophy and Christianity can have nothing in common. The Alexandrians considered faith to be simply the foundation and first step, from which the advance to knowledge, which itself is faith's completion, had to take place; whereas these writers, to the contrary, wanted to stick with nothing but faith, by showing that any concern with a knowledge going above and beyond faith detracts from faith's purity.[121]

Since philosophy itself used the term "heresies" for the different views and opinions of the schools and sects into which it divided up, people naturally adopted this term as the customary way of designating all those modifications of doctrine that could be seen as simply in conflict with Christian consciousness. So they believed themselves completely justified in calling philosophy "the mother of all that is heretical." The more decidedly Christian consciousness understood and anchored itself internally in this way, as antithetical to Gnosis and philosophy, by holding firmly to its own specific contents and repelling everything alien to it, the more energetically it opposed Gnosis and philosophy. Nevertheless, no solid results could be achieved in this way. By seeking to engage their opponent to such an extent, these theologians still shared with the opponent a domain in which a new stage of the developing struggle simply emerged.

One would have thought that the dispute with the Gnostics, about what did or did not count as truly Christian teaching, could have been easily and simply resolved based on the apostolic scriptures that both sides recognized. However, although the respective opponents did not discount the authority of these scriptures, they did limit it in various ways since, by drawing upon different general principles, they did not hold everything in the scriptures to be equally divine and authentic. Furthermore, even where there was agreement about what books counted as scripture, there were very different views about what they mean. Thus on this terrain, since each side just interpreted the scriptures in its own way, it was just one opinion versus another. With each side entitled to claim the support of scripture, this dispute concerning scripture could only be settled by a different principle, one taking precedence over scripture itself. What principle was this to be?

---

121. Tertullian, *The Prescription against Heretics*, ch. 7: "What indeed has Athens to do with Jerusalem? What concord is there between the Academy and the Church? What agreement between heretics and Christians? Our instruction comes from 'the portico of Solomon,' who himself had taught that 'the Lord should be sought in the simplicity of heart.' Away with all attempts to produce a mottled Christianity of Stoic, Platonic, and dialectic composition! After Jesus Christ, we want no curious disputations; after the gospel, no investigations! With our faith, we desire to believe nothing beyond it. For this we believe first of all, and there is nothing we ought to believe beyond it." [*ANF* 3:246]

Scripture and Tradition; Catholicism and Heresy

Here we are at the point where the emerging Catholic Church took a new and significant step; where the church was first becoming conscious of the idea of the church as "catholic." In the controversy with the Gnostics, tradition for the first time gained the position it has occupied ever since in relation to scripture, in the doctrinal system of the Catholic Church.

In a time when the canon of what counted as apostolic scripture was not yet definitely set, what Christianity was in reality was something resting entirely on tradition. However, coping with opponents first made Christians aware of what the concept of tradition involved in principle. One could not dispute with opponents without doing so from a standpoint going back behind scripture and standing above it. Tertullian is the most important champion of the Catholic Church in this instance. No doubt he had learned often enough from experience that an argument basing itself merely on scripture is by no means conclusive. He therefore takes us right to the central point here when he declares: *ergo non ad scripturas provocandum est* ("our appeal, therefore, must not be made to the scriptures").[122] [Tertullian continues:] One ought not resort to a battlefield where, even at best, victory is always in doubt. Even when both sides are evenly matched in such a contest, the subject matter inherently still requires first of all posing the questions: Who holds the correct belief? To whom do the scriptures belong? From whom, and through whom, and when, was that teaching handed down by which one becomes a Christian? Wherever it is manifest that the truth of the teaching and of the Christian faith is present, there too will be the truth of scripture and scriptural interpretation, and all the Christian traditions.

But to locate the point on which the whole of Christianity's truth depends, we need only retrace the path by which Christianity has come down to us. Christ is the first preacher of Christian truth. After him there are the apostles, the term for which, *apostolici* or *missi* (ones sent), expresses the principle one has to adhere to.[123] If Christ has sent the apostles out to preach, then we are to acknowledge no other preachers than those he appointed. That is because no one knows the Father but the Son, and those to whom the Son has revealed him. The Son has not revealed him to others except the apostles he sent out to teach what he revealed to them. What they preached, that is, what Christ revealed to them, cannot be known otherwise than through the churches the apostles founded, both by the living word of their preaching and by the epistles they sent to them afterwards. If this be the case, then it is also firmly established that the doctrine agreeing with the faith of the apostolic core- and mother-churches is

---

122. *The Prescription against Heretics*, ch. 19. [*Ed.*] The following is a paraphrase of the remainder of this brief chapter.

123. [*Ed.*] Beginning with this sentence and continuing to the end of the paragraph, Baur paraphrases Tertullian. Note that the proof of the authority of tradition rests on a scriptural proof-text, namely, that no one knows the Father but the Son, and those to whom the Son has revealed the Father (Matt 11:27 and parallels).

II. The Catholic Church as the Antithesis to Gnosis and Montanism

to be taken as the truth, because it without a doubt comprises what these churches received from the apostles, what the apostles received from Christ, and what Christ received from God. All other teaching is presumed to be false, insofar as it is contrary to the truth of these churches, of the apostles, of Christ, and of God. The apostolic tradition, in other words agreement with the teaching of the apostolic churches, is therefore the witness to the truth, the criterion of truth.[124]

Tertullian's statement already includes all the elements belonging to the concept of tradition. Tradition is conceived of as mediation, the movement back and forth between two more or less distant points, the mediation for consciousness between past and present. If the tradition is to bear witness to the truth of Christian doctrine, it must provide assurance that what a later time deems to be Christian is one and the same with the original teaching of Christ. It of course goes without saying that truly Christian doctrine can be none other than the teaching proclaimed by Christ and handed down by the apostles. But which doctrines are those handed down by the apostles and proclaimed by Christ? As Tertullian says, their origin is important but not alone the key, inasmuch as *omne genus ad originem suam censeatur necesse est* ("it is necessary to evaluate the origin of every kind [of doctrine]"); and it is not merely a matter of what has transpired in the interim. For the third pertinent factor is starting out from the point that alone can get one back to the original teaching. This is Tertullian's argument when he points to the apostolic churches as those containing the authentic teaching of Christ. However, since there are multiple apostolic churches, not just one, the authentic teaching can be seen only in those points on which the collective apostolic churches are in agreement.[125] Thus there are three factors equally essential in spelling out the concept of tradition: origin from Christ, transmission via the apostles, and agreement among the churches. Each of these presupposes the other two. Without the agreement of the churches, one does not know the point from which to begin. Without the origin from Christ, the whole of doctrine is not unified in principle. Without transmission via the apostles, there cannot be continuity between the past and the present.

Insofar as Christian doctrine rests on tradition, these three factors, taken together, give the doctrine the character of objective truth. Inherent in the concept of tradition is the fact that it is, purely and simply, a given, and that it was originally imparted by divine revelation. Whatever does not concur with the tradition, and deviates from

---

124. *The Prescription against Heretics*, ch. 21. *Communicamus cum ecclesiis apostolicis, quod nulla doctrina diversa, hoc est testimonium veritatus* ("We are in communion with the apostolic churches because our doctrine is no different. This is the witness to the truth").

125. This agreement is the criterion of their common apostolic origin. "So all are primitive and all apostolic, while all are one. And this unity is proved by the peace they share, by their title of brotherhood, by their contract of hospitality; for these privileges have but one ground, the one tradition of the same revelation (*sacramentum*)." *The Prescription against Heretics*, 20 [ET from Henry Bettenson, ed., *Documents of the Christian Church* (Oxford, 1967), 70]. See also ch. 28: "that which is deposited among many . . . is not the result of error, but of tradition" [*ANF* 3:256].

it to one degree or another, is therefore just a subjective opinion, an arbitrary human notion, in other words, a heresy. Heretics are those who, as individuals, stand opposed to a majority counted as catholic and who have higher regard for truths they have concocted or chosen on their own than they do for the objective truth of the Catholic doctrine.[126] As opposed to what is heretical, what is Catholic consists of an agreement on doctrine that excludes all capricious differences of opinion. To make people aware of this harmony, the teachings were condensed into concise propositions, ones supposedly viewed as the essential expression of their shared convictions, and which articulated in positive terms the rebuttal to the antithetical statements of the opponents. These propositions are the *regulae fidei* (rules of the faith) to which Irenaeus and Tertullian appeal in their refutations of the Gnostics. They are the first attempts at a symbolic firming-up of the belief system, attempts that, like the later symbols of the faith, have been occasioned by the attacks of adversaries.[127]

Since the second of Tertullian's three factors is the intermediary connecting and binding the other two together, it is the most important one and the element in which the tradition carries on. The truth that originated from Christ could become the agreed-upon teaching of the collective Christian churches only via the intermediary role of the apostles. Yet the apostles themselves are to be regarded simply as transmitters of Christ's teaching. Thus they themselves are just the first members in a series of transmitters growing ever longer as time goes on. Hence although the apostolic foundation of the church is very important, it is nevertheless just as important to know who were the successors to the apostles; to know whether Christ's teaching was also handed on continuously, by subsequent members of the series, in as authentic and unadulterated a form as it had been received from the hands of the apostles.

The Gnostics cast doubt on the traditional authority of the apostles, by contending that the apostles themselves did not know all of the teaching; or that if the apostles did also know it, they did not impart all of it to everyone. In doing so, the Gnostics appealed to the dispute between two apostles, Peter and Paul, mentioned in the Epistle to the Galatians, with Paul's own stern words scolding Peter for what he taught.[128] They said that therefore the proof from tradition had to become increasingly suspect as the series of members transmitting the teaching became longer. But the church fathers just gave even greater weight to something they maintained emphatically, that only in their midst could one point to an ongoing and unbroken succession of the kind that had preserved, with the same fidelity, the teaching handed down by the apostles.[129]

---

126. Tertullian, *The Prescription against Heretics*, ch. 37: "heretics . . . cannot be true Christians, because it is not from Christ that they get what they pursue of their own mere choice, and from the pursuit incur and gain the name of heretics" [*ANF* 3:261].

127. Irenaeus, *Against Heresies* 1.10 and 3.4. Tertullian, *The Prescription against Heretics*, ch. 13; *Against Praxeas*, ch. 2; *On the Veiling of Virgins*, ch. 1.

128. Tertullian, *The Prescription against Heretics*, ch. 22. [*Ed.*] See Gal 2:11–14.

129. *The Prescription against Heretics*, ch. 32. "Let them produce the origins of their churches; let them unroll the list of their bishops, an unbroken succession from the beginning so that the first

The bishops are the successors of the apostles, and as such they are the bearers of the apostolic tradition. In the historical development of the Catholic Church, the episcopacy therefore is synonymous with tradition. If tradition is the substantial element of the Catholic Church, and is the principle that, however much the scope of the church expands, makes it the one apostolic church, then the episcopacy is where the tradition itself gains its concrete reality. Hence the further history of the Catholic Church unfolds in terms of the conception of the episcopacy. However, if we are to follow this historical course, we must, first and foremost, understand what the episcopacy as such is, and how it came about. Doing so will make it evident that the episcopacy and the tradition stand on the same footing, for they each have the same concern for unity that the idea of the Catholic Church summoned up in opposing Gnosis. It realized this idea in the form of tradition and also carried it on in the episcopacy, by which the Catholic Church first became an established organization.

2. THE HIERARCHY AS ANTITHESIS

The Local Authority and Autonomy of the Churches

Had the bishops been successors of the apostles in the sense the church's tradition held them to be, then there would be a very simple answer to the question about the origin of the episcopacy.[130] However, in no case was a bishop the direct successor of the apostles. Before there was an ἐπίσκοπος (bishop) in the actual sense, there were πρεσβύτεροι (presbyters, or elders) and διάκονοι (deacons).

The Book of Acts apparently assumes that, as a matter of course and analogous to the Jewish synagogues, the first Christian churches had presbyters as their leaders in addition to apostles. In speaking about the Jerusalem church, Acts just refers to the installation of διάκονοι (deacons), chosen, as proposed by the apostles, for the task of poor relief (Acts 6:1–7). So the churches already had presbyters. In the case of churches elsewhere, in contrast, the installation of presbyters is mentioned (Acts 14:23) as the first provision the apostles made for their initial leadership. It is entirely natural to assume that, when the apostles established a Christian church, they also arranged for its initial organization. Distant as we are from that time, we cannot be too cautious about supposing that the whole structure of the church had to be that of an apostolic institution. We ought not assume any more than the nature of the case warrants. Have

---

bishop had as his precursor and the source of his authority one of the apostles or one of the apostolic men who, although not an apostle, continued with the apostles. This is how the apostolic churches report their origins; thus the church of Smyrnaeans relates that Polycarp was appointed by John, the church of Rome that Clement was ordained by Peter. In the same way too the other churches present their predecessors as having been appointed to their episcopal seats by apostles, and as being those who transmit the seed planted by the apostles" [ET from Bettenson (n. 125), 71; cf. *ANF* 3:258]. See also ch. 36. Also Irenaeus, *Against Heresies* 3.2.2; 3.3.1–2; 4.26.2.

130. [*Ed.*] Baur published a major study, "Ueber der Ursprung des Episcopats in der christlichen Kirche," in the *Tübinger Zeitschrift für Theologie* (1838) no. 3, pp. 1–185. See below, n. 150.

we considered how frail the early Christian churches were in their initial stages, how small was their membership, and how limited in their structural choices the founders of churches were, even if they already had a complete plan for their organization?

If only a few families made up the initial foundation of a Christian congregation in process of formation, or indeed only a single family, then it is readily apparent that the family serving as the core group that others had then joined held the prominent position from which it assumed leadership of the whole congregation. They are the ἀπαρχαί (first fruits, or first converts) mentioned not only in chapter 42 of the First Epistle of Clement of Rome to the Corinthians, but also already in the Apostle Paul's First Epistle to this same church (1 Cor 16:15–16). Clement says here that, when the apostles proclaimed the gospel in the countryside and in the towns, they appointed the first fruits, that is, those who were the first ones to accept the Christian faith, εἰς ἐπισκόπους καὶ διακόνους τῶν μελλόντων πιστεύειν (as bishops and deacons for those who would later become believers). Here the bishops stand alongside the deacons, as also in the Epistle to the Philippians (1:1), where those heading the church are called bishops and deacons. Here in Philippians, where we first find mention of bishops, they can only have the same significance as the presbyters, since they are spoken of in the plural, as are the deacons and presbyters.[131] The two titles, bishops and presbyters, denote the same persons, according to whether they are considered as leaders and deputies of the congregation, or as those with oversight of it as a whole.

The bishops then go together with the presbyters, and it also therefore appears that the deacons were originally the local authorities in Christianity. As Clement puts it, the apostles appointed those first fruits, or initial converts, as bishops and deacons, not so much over those who already believe, but rather for those who should become converted to the faith. While the term "deacon" seems to indicate the kind of role the Apostle Paul commends in the household of Stephanas, as the ἀπαρχή or first fruits from Achaia, where the members have taken up the διακονία (deaconate) for the Christians,[132] we see, on the other hand, that in Clement's Epistle to the Romans the deacons are mentioned alongside the bishops. Thus if the diaconate of which the apostle speaks is, as a whole, a leadership group in the congregation, then it can simply assume the task of meeting all the immediate needs of this kind that arise in a church first taking shape. The Apostle's summons to obey the leaders makes it likely that διακονία is to be understood in this sense. The term itself can signify every kind of service to the congregation.[133] Since in the initial stage of a congregation just forming, the first converts had to undertake so many tasks that simply gave their activity the

---

131. See Acts 20:17, 28; Titus 1:5–7; 1 Tim 3:1–8; 1 Pet 5:1–3.

132. [Ed.] 1 Cor 16:15: "Now, brothers and sisters, you know that members of the household of Stephanas were the first converts in Achaia, and they have devoted themselves to the service of the saints."

133. In the Book of Acts the term is used for the apostolic office. See 1:17 and 25; 20:24; 21:19 [where it is translated as "ministry" in the NRSV]. According to Eusebius, *Ecclesiastical History* 5.1, the term in Rom 11:13 is διακονία τῆς ἐπισκοπῆς (diaconate of the episcopacy).

II. The Catholic Church as the Antithesis to Gnosis and Montanism

appearance of a service rendered to others, the term could most likely have designated general leadership of the church.

However, if we juxtapose the deacons to the bishops, then in these two we already have different, albeit essentially complementary, roles in the original structure of church offices. One involves the supervisory authority overseeing the whole congregation and keeping it unified, while the other embraces another sphere of official activity, comprising lesser service activities of a different kind, in particular those serving economic functions and support for the poor. Hence the deacons in these latter roles, from which the name derives, could have simply been subordinate to the bishops.[134] With Clement of Rome we have before us the original view of these two essential aspects forming the offices of the Christian churches, the bishops and the deacons. However, it is just the opinion, and way of looking at it, from a later time period, that it was the apostles themselves who established the episcopate and the diaconate as these standing offices of the churches, so as to give them their specific organization right from the outset.

The Apostle Paul is the first one we think of when it comes to founding Christian churches. Acts 14:21–23 reports that he appointed standing offices for the first churches he founded.[135] But had Paul thought doing this was so necessary, then there had to have been some indication of the existence of these church offices, appeals to bishops and deacons, in his epistles acknowledged to be authentic, in which he had such ample opportunity to do so, together with the precepts he issued, the disorderliness he reprimanded, and the contributions he called for. In the series of the gifts of the Spirit, where he takes into account the personal factor as the special capacity for various purposes and functions in the organic life of the Christian church, he does indeed include the deaconate, or ministry (Rom 12:7), as well as ἀντιλήμψεις or forms of assistance and κυβερνήσεις or forms of leadership (1 Cor 12:28), which we recognize as being more general expressions for the concrete terms "deacon" and "bishop." But there is no indication of a form of standing office, and even in speaking of the deaconate of the first converts of Achaia, he only treats it as a freely undertaken service of leadership.

In the later canonical scriptures, and in the epistle by Clement of Rome that belongs in the same category, we first encounter the bishops and deacons as church officials, and their mention is manifestly in the interest of validating the church structure at that time by the authority of the apostles. Clement states (ch. 44 and elsewhere) that the apostles recognized that there will be controversy about the term ἐπισκοπή (episcopate). He says there that, with their perfect foresight, they established bishops and

---

134. Thus Cyprian, in *Epistles*, 3.3, reminds the deacons that the apostles indeed constituted the deacons for (*sibi*) the episcopate and for the ministry of the church.

135. [*Ed.*] This passage says he traveled with Barnabas to Derbe, Lystra, Iconium, and Antioch, and "they appointed elders for them in each church."

deacons, and afterwards issued the additional regulation¹³⁶ that, after one of these men died, another worthy man shall be his successor in this service to the church. Those who had been appointed by the apostles, or those later appointed by other estimable men, with the approval of the entire congregation, and have blamelessly performed their service in the army of the Lord, cannot justifiably be removed from their church offices (their λειτουργία or divine service or, as Clement directly afterward calls it, the episcopate, in referring to the office of elder).

According to this account these church officials were chosen by both the ἐλλόγιμοι ἄνδρες (eminent men) and the πᾶσα ἐκκλησία (whole congregation). The more distinguished members of the congregation conducted the election and made the nomination, but the nominee's acceptance depended on the assent of the congregation. Since those members of the congregation who are just designated as persons of note are not themselves clergy, the right to vote was, as a rule, still vested in the congregation. These first steps toward the whole resulting hierarchy trace back indisputably to an original conception of autonomous congregations. This is the same autonomy not only recognized in the Book of Acts, where the selection of the first deacons took place, of course at the instigation of the apostles yet only with all the followers participating; but also presupposed by the Apostle Paul when, in 1 Cor 5:3–5, the prospective excommunication can be carried out only with the consent of the congregation, and likewise by Paul making the issue of reconciliation and reacceptance wholly dependent, in his judgment, on the congregation (2 Cor 2: 5–10).

We see how this autonomy was very much a feature of the original character of Christian congregations, from the fact that it still continued unchallenged later on in a congregation's being entitled to vote, right up to when Cyprian, the bishop of Carthage, spoke out for a clergy fully conscious of its own rights.¹³⁷ Even those functions that the clergy consequently performed, in virtue of their official, specified roles, had originally just been the province of the congregation, and not exclusively, distinct from the congregation, the province of persons standing at the head of the congregation. Later exceptions to this practice attest to what had been the general right of the congregation in earlier times.

Paul assumes there is widespread authority to teach, since he only excludes women from speaking in church (1 Cor 14:34). He also states (1 Cor 12:28) that "God has appointed in the church first apostles, second prophets, third teachers." So he speaks

---

136. "Regulation" is doubtless the meaning of ἐπινομή here. See R. A. Lipsius, *De Clementis Romani Epistola ad Corinthios priore disquisitio* (Leipzig, 1858), 20ff. It would not be understood that these offices should continue on in the future unless one had in mind a special regulation from the apostles. [*Ed.*] The Greek word derives from ἐπινέμω, which concerns the continuation of the right to graze cattle (on another's land).

137. In *Epistle* 33, to the presbyters, deacons, and the people generally, he wrote: "In ordaining clergy, we usually seek your advice beforehand, and in deciding for the common good we consider the conduct and merits of the individuals." In *Epistle* 67 he said, with respect to the people, that "the clergy themselves have the power to both appoint worthy priests and to root out bad ones."

of teachers as in a class of their own. The writer of the Epistle of James does not want too many to be teachers (James 3:1). In Hebrews 3:7, the reader is exhorted to "remember your leaders, those who spoke the word of God to you." Ephesians 4:11 refers to apostles, prophets, evangelists, pastors, and teachers. The *Shepherd* of Hermas[138] mentions *episcopi* (bishops), *doctores* (teachers), and *ministri* (deacons). No doubt we should not understand *doctores* to mean presbyters as distinct from bishops, for the *episcopi* (who are not distinct from presbyters) are named first simply because, in their case (as we also see from the word προεστώς, "set in front," in Justin Martyr's *First Apology*, ch. 67), they combine both offices, teaching and oversight, and that does not preclude there being other *doctores* in addition to them.

All this taken together shows clearly that, even though the teaching activity was linked to an official church position, it was not bound exclusively to it because, even later on the right to teach could not absolutely be denied to the laity. The only requirement was that instructional sessions be held in the bishop's presence and with his approval.[139] Nor do we find early on the later specific distinction drawn between clergy and laity in the administering of baptism or the Lord's Supper. As Tertullian says,[140] the right to baptize is conferred on the senior priest, who is the bishop, and after him on the presbyters and deacons, although not without the bishop's approval. He says that, in addition, the laity should also have this right, for what is received *ex aequo* (equally) can also be equally given. His proviso is that the laity should do this only when necessary [i.e., when these church officials are not present to do so]. The same applies to the Lord's Supper. The Christian custom was that the leader alone administered it, as also indeed according to Justin the προεστώς is the one who blesses the bread and wine. But Tertullian asks: "Are not the laity priests too?" Then he even says: "Where only three, albeit laity, are gathered together, there is the church."[141] Therefore Tertullian claimed for the laity, as a universal Christian priestly right, all that the clergy subsequently sought to have preeminently theirs alone, by their considering it to be the clergy's distinctive attribute.[142]

---

138. Vision 3, ch. 5. In the Greek text, known only via Simonides, it just says "bishops and teachers," but not "ministers." Yet directly thereafter we find ἐπισκοπήσαντες καὶ διδάξαντες καὶ διακονήσαντες (those serving as bishops and those serving as teachers and those serving as deacons), in a single series. See A. Dressel, *Patrum apostolicorum Opera* (Leipzig, 1857), 579.

139. See what Eusebius says about Origen, in his *Ecclesiastical History* 6.19.

140. *On Baptism*, ch. 17.

141. *On the Exhortation to Chastity*, ch. 7.

142. See Ritschl, *Die Entstehung der altkatholischen Kirche* (n. 101), 1st ed., 367ff.; 2nd ed., 347ff. Ritschl demonstrates very precisely and fully that, in the original understanding of church officials' relation to the congregation, as leaders of worship, or as priests, they had no specific role that set them apart from the congregation. This is also the case regarding the authority to forgive sins, the laying on of hands at baptism, and absolving lapsed church members.

The Clergy, the Presbyters, and the Bishops

Although at this time congregations still had a lively awareness of their former autonomy, and although this former right was still asserted even where it was no longer the practice, there was already a special class of ecclesiastical persons whose official activity encompassed all those functions pertinent to the congregation as a whole. Thus the church had already divided into two mutually distinct groups.

Clergy and laity, in other words the *ordo* (leading body) and the *plebs* (people), had these respective designations, although it is very noteworthy that this distinction itself originally carried with it no hierarchical overtones.[143] Even though these terms articulated a definite distinction [of these persons], the concept of the clergyman does not yet involve anything doing away with the original and essential equality of the two

---

143. Things would have been different if, as Jerome, in his *Epistle* 52, referring to Deut 10:9 and 18:2, says, the clergy would have been designated in that way because *de sorte sunt domini* (they are leaders "without allotment and inheritance"); in other words because *dominus ipse sors* ("the Lord is his allotment"), that is, *pars clericorum est* (the clergy's share). Neander, *Kirchengeschichte* (n. 4), 1st ed., 299ff., raised doubts about this interpretation because it is not justifiable when one goes by the history of these terms. But Neander's interpretation sticks too closely to the concept of allotment. In my essay, "Ueber den Ursprung des Episcopats" (n. 130), 93ff., I have pointed out that κλῆρος seems to mean "class," "rank," or "status," in particular a higher class, in the documents of the churches in Lyon and Vienne, according to Eusebius, *Ecclesiastical History* 5.1, where there is mention of κλῆρος μαρτύρων (rank of the martyrs), and in a few passages of the *Epistles* of Ignatius. Ritschl (*Entstehung* [n. 101], 1st ed., 398 ff; 2nd ed., 390), goes into this in greater detail. Κλῆρος means "rank" or "station." An example of this is when Eusebius (*Ecclesiastical History* 4.5), says that the sixth bishop of Alexandria "succeeded to the government of the diocese." So κλῆρος is equivalent to τάξις (military rank). Since there are distinct classes within Christian officialdom, the classes are a sequence of offices or degrees. Thus Irenaeus states (*Against Heresies* 3.3.3), about Bishop Eleutherius of Rome, that "in the twelfth place from the apostles," he held "the inheritance of the episcopate." Here inheritance or class means "rank," as in Acts 1:17 and 25, where the apostolic office is designated as "his share in the ministry." In the same sense there is mention of "a class of martyrs." An entire congregation is even called a κλῆρος, as when Ignatius (*Epistle to the Ephesians*, ch. 11) expresses the wish that he will be found "in the same class as the Ephesian Christians, who have always been of the same mind as the apostles." Thus the Christians of Ephesus took precedence over the others. So here the word κλῆρος is already linked to the concept of a higher rank. The special meaning of this word, its being conferred exclusively on a particular class, those who were church officials, is doubtless analogous to how we use the terms "rank" and "class." Although everyone belongs to a certain rank or class, we still speak of rank and class chiefly regarding those occupying a higher position in social life. Since the permanent officials were superiors over those who were fortuitously meritorious, such as through their martyrdom, the customary practice is to call these clergy "persons of rank and standing" in the original sense of this expression. In 1 Pet 5:3, where the elders are admonished to "not lord it over those in your charge," the κλῆροι (those in your charge) are synonymous with the ποιμνίον (flock), and are simply the various classes or groups that form the congregation, the multitude. So here κλῆρος still has its broader meaning. We first encounter the narrower meaning in Clement of Alexandria, *Who Is the Rich Man that Shall Be Saved*, ch. 42, where he says that the Apostle John went from Ephesus to the surrounding areas "here to appoint bishops, there to set in order whole churches, there to ordain such as were marked out by the Spirit" [ANF 2:603]. That is, where a collegium already existed, he installed one member to be the permanent clergy. Synonymous with κλῆρος is Tertullian's term *ordo* (class), which he sometimes characterizes as meaning utterly set apart from the *plebs* (people), and sometimes as *ecclesiasticus* (church official) or *sacerdotalis* (priest).

classes, as Tertullian also clearly states.[144] The clergy were just more highly esteemed than the other members of the congregation. By this time they do have priestly standing, for their *ordo* is not merely the *ordo ecclesiasticus* (ecclesiastical class) but is also the *ordo sacerdotalis* (priestly class). In direct contrast to the priesthood, the terms λαός and λαϊκοί acquire their distinctive meaning. As Clement of Rome defines this concept (in ch. 40 and elsewhere), a λαϊκὸς ἄνθρωπος (lay person) is anyone who is neither ἀρχιερεύς (high priest) nor ἱερεύς (priest), nor Levite. Therefore, although the λαός is the congregation of the people of Israel, the laity are those who simply belong to it without holding any special position in this congregation. However, the existence of a priestly role does not set up an antithesis between clergy and laity. The laity are indeed also priests, and the sacrificial offering [the performance of which] makes the priest into a priest, is simply prayer, namely the prayer of thanksgiving at the Lord's Supper, in conjunction with the offerings brought for it by the congregation.[145] Notwithstanding these descriptive labels, the difference between the two classes was always supposed to be still merely a fluid one, and the congregation's autonomy was not said to be set aside.

The distinction between *presbyteri* (presbyters, or elders) and *episcopi* (bishops) worked in the same way. Even after bishops had become a wholly different group from the presbyters, the term "bishop," and the conception associated with it, always still overlapped with that of "presbyter," and this term "presbyter" still encapsulated for the longest time the original consciousness of congregational autonomy. For Clement of Alexandria and for Irenaeus there is merely a relative distinction between presbyter and bishop. Clement does of course speak of deacon, presbyter, and bishop as a three-stage sequence of church officials, although he only differentiates between two official functions, those of presbyter and deacon, since he describes the presbyter's activity, related to teaching and discipline, as an edifying function, and the deacon's activity as a serving function.[146] Irenaeus often uses the two terms *presbyteri* and *episcopi* as completely synonymous, and he speaks about the succession of presbyters in the same sense as that of bishops. He even calls the bishops of Rome πρεσβύτεροι, and directly calls the office of presbyter the *episcopatus*.[147]

So there is agreement that, in the exercise of official authority, there was still no strict line of demarcation between bishop and presbyter. On the one hand, nothing was supposed to be done in the congregation without the bishop's consent—no baptism, no ordination, without his complete approval. On the other hand, however, the presbyters were also capable of performing such acts, which could not have been

---

144. *On the Exhortation to Chastity*, ch. 7: "The difference between the leading body and the people is constituted by one's ecclesiastical authority and the honor of being consecrated by the governing assembly."

145. See Ritschl, *Entstehung* (n. 101), 1st ed., 404–5; 2nd ed., 396.

146. *Paidagogos* [the Instructor] 3.12; *Stromata* 6.13 and 7.1.

147. *Against Heresies* 3.2.2–3, and 4.26.2.

the case if people had thought there is an essential difference between the offices of presbyter and bishop. This is how the relation of the two appears in a canon of the Synod of Ancyra, in 314. The fourth Council of Carthage in 398 said the same thing, stipulating that, at the ordination of a presbyter, the assembled presbyters should join the bishop in simultaneously laying hands on the head of the candidate. This can only have been an ancient custom from a time when presbyter and bishop stood as equals, with the bishop only *primus inter pares* (first among equals) alongside the presbyters. This original equality of presbyters with bishops was kept intact for the longest time in the Alexandrian church where, up until Bishop Demetrius (190–232), there was only the one bishop of Alexandria for all of Egypt; and where the twelve presbyters, reportedly appointed originally by Mark the Evangelist, had the right to choose one of their number as the bishop or patriarch. Soon after the beginning of the fourth century, Bishop Alexander was, for the first time, completely successful, in Alexandria too, in bringing the presbyters into the subordinate relation to the bishop that was the practice elsewhere.[148]

The Episcopate

We must consider all these relationships, so constitutive of the original, autonomous character of Christian congregations, as things stood then if we are to understand correctly the significance of the episcopate for the Christian Church's course of historical development. The autonomy of Christian congregations did not entirely disappear as long as the distinction between presbyters and bishops was just a relative and fluid one. The change the episcopate introduced made this relative distinction absolute and spelled it out.

The Concept of the Episcopate

There are multiple presbyters, whereas the conception is that [a church has] just one bishop, and that makes the one bishop essentially different from the presbyter, who is just one member of the body of presbyters. The central issue involved here can be

---

148. See Ritschl, *Entstehung* (n. 101), 1st ed., 431ff.; 2nd ed., 419. He refers to Jerusalem in answering the question as to the origin of the episcopate, an issue also appearing in the foregoing citations regarding Alexandria, as to the original form of congregational governance. See p. 434. The appointing of a bishop and twelve presbyters, said to have been done in Caesarea and Tripoli by the Ebionite Peter ([Pseudo-Clementine] *Recognitions* 3.66 and 6.15; *Homilies* 11:36), is paralleled by the relation of the Lord with the twelve apostles. However, this relation was retroactively attributed to the governance of the Jerusalem congregation in the declaration by Hegesippus (according to Eusebius, *Ecclesiastical History* 2.23.3–4) that "the charge of the church was passed to James the brother of the Lord, together with the Apostles." This distinctively Jewish Christian episcopate is to be distinguished from the Gentile Christian kind, which developed from the office of presbyter.

posed as the difference between an officer of the congregation, and being an official of the [larger] church.[149]

If the bishop too is but an officer of the congregation, then he is just what the presbyter is, albeit at a higher level. Hence if there is supposedly a more specific distinction, it can only be that what the bishop is, in relation to an individual congregation that he leads, does not exhaust the concept of the bishop. For, as congregational leader, the bishop at the same time represents the church as such. He is the general embodiment of church unity and authority. Since the church stands to the congregation as what is universal or all-encompassing stands to what is particular, the issue involved here is actually whether the universal is to be determined by the particular, or the particular by the universal.

Starting out with congregational autonomy means that the congregation unites around the presbyters and bishops, conceived of in their unity as its deputies. Thus the presbyters and bishops are, so to speak, simply a distillation of the indeterminate multiplicity of individuals who collectively make up the congregation. As the deputies and instruments of the congregation, these officials just stand in turn for what the congregation itself essentially is. They are nothing apart from it, and all that they are is just because of it. However, if instead of going from the many to the one, from the particular to the universal, the sequence reverses, then the relationship changes, for the unitary aspect is no longer merely a distillation of the congregational multiplicity, because instead the unity determines the multiplicity, the universal element overrides the particular element. This is how the bishop in the proper sense is related to the congregation, when he is absolutely and specifically set apart from the presbyters, and not just relatively so. The congregation depends on the bishop as its head, for only through him is it in essence what it is.

So it is only in this latter sense that we can say the issue of distinguishing congregational officials from officers of the church comes into play. If we see in the bishops not the individual congregation but the church as such, then the church is related to the congregation as what, from a universal standpoint and in principle, determines the congregation. The question to take up is therefore: What brought about the reversal by which the bishops, instead of belonging together with the presbyters as before, set themselves above the presbyters and the congregation in such a way that congregations lost their autonomy and now stand in utter dependence on the bishop?[150]

149. See R. Rothe, *Die Anfänge der christliche Kirche und ihre Verfassung* (Wittenberg, 1837), 153 ff.

150. This is where the different viewpoints diverge. According to Rothe, in the aforementioned work (n. 149), the episcopate was directly instituted by the apostles still living after the year 70, in order that the power of the keys, its exclusive, absolute power and sovereign governing authority, the divine right with which they presided over the church, should not cease to exist upon their death. This action established the organization of the Christian Church that, according to the Ignatian epistle, had finally come about (Rothe, 354 ff.). Rothe supports his contention with historical data in a way that obviously lacks any cogency, so it merits no further consideration. See my own essay, "Ueber der Ursprung des Episcopats" (n. 130), which is directed at Rothe's position. See also Ritschl, *Entstehung* (n. 101), 1st ed., 423 ff; 2nd ed., 410ff. In Rothe's case the main factor is actually his view of the authenticity

The Origin of the Episcopate, from Concern for Unity and in the Opposition to Heresy

This striving toward unity was already inherent in the concept of the church. As representatives of the congregation, the presbyters must have seen the need for one of their number to assume a position of seniority and become the leader of the whole. But as everything increasingly was drawn to the leader and became concentrated in a single focal point, the unity where everything converged increasingly had to gain, in the end, absolutely preponderant influence, and to make all else subordinate to it and dependent on it.

To this we must add the consideration that each congregation—as is generally true about the church to which the individual congregations belong as members of the one body—inherently has its principle of unity in Christ. The more vividly people became conscious of Christ's relationship to the church as a whole, as well as to each individual congregation, the more this prompted them to have an external way of portraying this relationship to the One Lord of the church, via a representative standing at the head of the Christian community, one in whom they beheld, as it were, Christ himself in his relation to the community.

Quite understandably, people had already seen an expression of the idea of the episcopate in the angels to whom the writings destined for the seven churches in the Book of Revelation are dictated [chs. 2–3]. The number seven here stands in general for the church as consisting of different individual congregations. In Rev 1:20, the seven golden lampstands are seven churches, and the seven stars in the right hand of Christ are seven angels. So the concept of a single church or congregation here involves its having an angel; and since the seven stars, corresponding to the seven angels, are all held together in the hand of Christ [1:16], they therefore have their unity in him. So the angel each congregation or church has expresses none other than the relation binding it to Christ as the One Head of all the congregations and of the entire church. Christ's relation to a community cannot be envisaged as vital and inward if it cannot be grasped as a personal relationship, a concrete, personal unity seen in someone representing the community in himself. So the person of the bishop, standing

---

of the Ignatian epistle. Ritschl also takes this epistle to be authentic, although only in the Syrian text of it. Thus it only serves him in a quite limited sense for backdating the origin of the episcopate to the beginning of the second century. In his *Epistle to the Romans*, ch. 2, Ignatius calls himself a bishop. In his *Epistle to the Ephesians*, ch. 1, he likewise calls Onesimus their bishop. In ch. 6 of his *Epistle to Polycarp*, "the bishop of the church of the Smyrnaeans," he distinguishes him specifically from the presbyters and deacons. Polycarp's *Epistle to the Philippians* is our warrant for attributing this same form of church governance to the congregation in Smyrna, about the middle of the second century. However, Ignatius knows the episcopate as just a congregational office, not as a church office. Therefore the monarchical form of the episcopate rightly existed at the beginning of the second century in the congregations in Antioch, Ephesus, and Smyrna, with features that make it appear as solely a congregational office, and as related to the congregation in a way entirely comparable to how Clement of Rome presents it. (See Ritschl, *Entstehung*, 2nd ed., 402ff.). See A. Hilgenfeld, *Die apostolischen Väter* (n. 22), 271ff., for doubts about the authenticity of Polycarp's *Epistle to the Philippians*.

at the head of the community, came to represent in actuality this same relationship arising from the concern for unity that we find in those angels of the Apocalypse, as ideal representatives of the congregations who, in their role as intermediaries between Christ and their congregations, graphically demonstrated this relationship.

We see clearly, from the position James held in the Jerusalem congregation, as recounted in the Book of Acts and in the Epistle to the Galatians, how very much people needed to see Christ's relation to his community also mediated in a personal way. As the Lord's brother, James was the leader in Jerusalem, in other words the bishop of the Jerusalem congregation (at least the Pseudo-Clementine writings called him the bishop), with Simeon as his successor in the same position because he was a blood-relation to Jesus.[151] From this we see very clearly expressed the endeavor to give as much concrete reality as possible to the bond linking the community to Christ. So this explains how the Christians' view as to the organic nature of their religious community always seemed to be lacking something if they did not have, directly before their eyes, a personal mediator of this bond, in the figure of the bishop as representative of both the community and Christ himself.

However, these factors would not have been enough to so decisively put an end to the original identity or equivalence of the *episcopi* with the presbyters, and to elevate the *episcopi* to what we could call their sovereign status over the presbyters and the community, had circumstances not arisen that initially gave that striving for unity its full energy and very practical significance. It is doubtless the case that the episcopate, in the specific form of its elaboration in the course of the second century, was a counterweight to the heresies threatening the Christian community, heresies increasingly taking hold of, and eating away at, the unity of the whole. The widespread movement originating with Gnosticism not only brought the idea of the Catholic Church to the forefront of people's consciousness; it also had the no less important consequence of provoking a reaction that could only achieve its specific goal in the episcopate. The episcopate not only counteracted the eccentric, rambling, disintegrative, and destructive tendencies of the heresies, from a secure, cohesive, central point that assumed complete control of all factors connected with the faith. It also took the Christian outlook that was focused on the transcendent regions of the supersensible world, and joined it together with the soil of historical reality and the needs of the present. The episcopate sought to arrive at an understanding as to the form a Christian church could take. It was the episcopate that toned down and calmed the excesses of millenarian beliefs, so that they increasingly gave way to a temperate presence of mind fixing its eyes on practical matters. The episcopate took Christian consciousness that was disconnected from the world and reconciled it with the world, to such an extent that, on the broad basis of a Catholic Church, Christianity was able to enter on the road of its historical development.

---

151. See Eusebius, *Ecclesiastical History* 3.11 [where it says Simeon was reported to be Jesus' cousin].

The Pastoral Epistles

In the Pastoral Epistles of the New Testament canon we already see how closely the heretical phenomena of the post-apostolic era are connected with the direction the church was headed as it constituted itself by settling upon, and finalizing, the episcopate. These epistles originated at a time when the main features of the heretics they depict can only mean that these heretics were Gnostics of the second century. The Gnostics had already attracted a great deal of public attention. The principal aim of all three epistles is combating these heretics. Nothing serves better for opposing them than sticking faithfully to the traditional teachings, and having a well-ordered system of governance for the congregations, one under qualified leaders. So these epistles contain a series of admonitions and precepts mainly with reference to church governance.

Second Timothy, the earliest of the three, is already aware of the full magnitude of the calamity threatening the church owing to the heretics. However, it is limited to directly calling upon Timothy himself to exert his best efforts in dealing with this calamity.[152] The epistle does not go into the structure of more general arrangements in Christian congregations. Only in the admonition of 2:2 do we see any concern about this, a concern with an eye to the future.

In contrast, the Epistle to Titus begins right away in 1:5 with general instructions regarding the presbyters and the *episcopos*. Verses 10–16 deal with heretics, for they are the reason behind the directions given here. Titus paints with a very broad brush in its directions and reminders, ones applicable not merely to the congregational leaders but generally to all the members of the Christian community.

First Timothy does the same thing even more fully. Right in the introduction, the heretics with their distinctive features are front and center. Beginning with chapter 3 it makes the transition from general human circumstances to those of the church. It draws attention to the requisites for the offices of bishop (vv. 2–7), deacon (vv. 8–13), and presbyter (5:17–20).

The tendency toward the episcopate in the narrower sense is already quite apparent in these epistles, although they do not speak of it in that way. But they do give us increasing insight into the shape it is gradually taking, although here we in the main just have the general issue of how the governance system of Christian congregations should be grounded. Even though we are not yet to think of the bishop in the later sense of the office, it is nevertheless noteworthy how in this case the ἐπίσκοπος (in the uniform descriptions of Titus 1:7–9 and 1 Tim 3:2–7) is already set apart from the multiplicity of deacons and presbyters.[153]

---

152. See the synopses of the Epistle's main contents in 2:14–19, 3:1–9, and 4:1–5.

153. See my book *Die sogenannten Pastoralbriefe des Apostels Paulus aufs neue kritisch untersucht* (Tübingen, 1835), 8ff. and 54ff.

II. The Catholic Church as the Antithesis to Gnosis and Montanism

Pseudo-Ignatius and Pseudo-Clement

The principal documents recounting the history of how the idea of the episcopate evolved are writings, in both cases pseudonymous, that have come down to us bearing the names of Ignatius, Bishop of Antioch,[154] and Clement of Rome.

It is all the more remarkable that they concur on the idea of the episcopate, since each represents a quite different orientation. Ignatius is a decided Paulinist, whereas Clement stands up for the strictest Judaism, in the name of Peter, the apostle he follows. Just as emphatically as the two of them warn about heresies and schisms, and vividly present the dangers they pose, these writers also forcefully present the episcopate as the sovereign power of the church that, within itself, represents God and Christ. Each of these writers is animated in the same way by the basic idea that, for the individual as well as for the whole church, there is no salvation apart from the unity that is headed by the bishop and ascends from him to Christ and God; that as soon as one forsakes this unity one is exposed to all the dangers of erroneous teaching and sin, of the most deplorable divisiveness and disunity.

---

154. The much-discussed issue as to the authenticity of the epistles of Ignatius has taken a turn owing to the recent discovery of a Syrian recension, a critically revised version, containing just three epistles, those to the Ephesians, to the Romans, and to Polycarp. Scholars unwilling to dismiss them as not being documents from an apostolic era church father, and yet are put off by such a decidedly outspoken hierarchical tendency already at such an early time, as well as by other features of these epistles, are nevertheless completely content with the brevity of the Syrian text. In contrast, the number of those who still defend the authenticity of the seven epistles in Greek continually decreases. One of the latter group is G. Uhlhorn, in his essay "Das Verhältniss der kürzeren griechischen Recension der Ignatianischen Briefe zur syrischen Uebersetzung," in Niedner's *Zeitschrift für historische Theologie* (1851) no. 1. Those in the former group include: C. K. J. Bunsen, in *Ignatius von Antiochen und seine Zeit* (Hamburg, 1847), and *Die drei ächten und die vier unächten Briefe des Ignatius von Antiochen* (Hamburg, 1847); Ritschl, *Entstehung* (n. 101), 1st ed., 577 ff, and 2nd ed., 402, 453ff.; R. A. Lipsius, "Über die Aechtheit der syrischen Recension der ignatianischen Briefe," in Illgen's *Zeitschrift für historische Theologie* (1856) no. 1. Lipsius contends (p. 62) that, because of its christological views, the heresies it combats, and finally because of its doctrine of the episcopate, the Greek text of the seven epistles presupposes a date that cannot be earlier than 140, whereas the Syrian text of the three epistles points to an earlier time in all these respects and has every claim to recognition as authentic. The Syrian text was discovered in the desert of Nitria, and was edited by Cureton; see *The Ancient Syriac Version of the Epistles of St. Ignatius* (London, 1845), and *Corpus Ignatianum* (London, 1849). The result has been that, the greater the inclination to regard the epistles in this Syriac form as authentic, the less doubt there is as to the inauthenticity of the Greek epistles, an inauthenticity already previously demonstrated for sound reasons. In historical terms, the most significant result of all this is that the inauthentic epistles provide us with a very meaningful documentation of the governance of the Christian Church at the middle of the second century. On this basis, the question as to the authenticity or inauthenticity of the Syrian text is intrinsically of no great import, although the answer can only be that it too is spurious. On this issue, see my book disputing Bunsen's view, *Die ignatianischen Briefe und ihr neuester Kritiker* (Tübingen, 1848); and Hilgenfeld, *Die apostolischen Väter* (n. 22), 187ff. and 274ff. Lipsius had supplemented his earlier essay by "Über das Verhältniss des Textes der drei syrischen Briefe des Ignatius zu den übrigen Recensionen der Ignatianischen Literatur," in *Abhandlungen für die Kunde des Morgenlandes* (Leipzig, 1859), 1ff. [*Ed.*] The dates of the historical Ignatius are c. 35—c. 107, and those of Clement of Rome are c. 35–99.

The most urgent and oft-repeated admonition of Pseudo-Ignatius is to align oneself with the bishop. We must hold to the bishop alone and do nothing without his assent, just as the Lord Christ, in his oneness with the Father, did nothing apart from him. If we are subject to the bishop, and so to Christ, then we live not in the human way but rather in the way of Christ, who died for us so that we might escape death by faith in his death.[155] The Spirit commands us to do nothing apart from the bishop, to love being united with him, to avoid dissension, and to be like Christ as Christ is like the Father.

Most especially, nothing involving the church can take place apart from the bishop. The eucharist is valid only if it is performed by the bishop or as approved by him. The congregation is said to be where the bishop is, just as the Catholic Church is present where Christ is present. It is not allowed to baptize or to hold a love feast (*Agape*) apart from the bishop, for such things please God only if they are authorized by the bishop; this authorization alone confers certainty and validity on all that one does. Whoever honors the bishop is honored by God. Whoever does anything [connected with the church] without the bishop's knowledge serves the Devil. Whoever belongs to God and Christ also belongs with the bishop. We cannot praise too highly the blessed ones who are united with the bishop as the church is with Christ and Christ with the Father, with everything concurring in unity. Whoever is outside this altar does not partake of God's sustenance. When the prayer of one or two is so effective, how much more so is the prayer of the bishop and the whole congregation! That is why one may not oppose the bishop. To be subject to God, one must look to the bishop as though to the Lord himself, and honor him as one honors Christ, the Son of the Father.[156]

Therefore the bishop is forthrightly called God's representative, the προκαθήμενος εἰς τόπον θεοῦ (leader in God's stead). Whoever obeys him, obeys not him but obeys the Father of Jesus Christ, as the ἐπίσκοπος πάντον (bishop of all). Whoever deceives the bishop is not deceiving the visible bishop but is instead betraying the invisible [i.e., God]. The visible bishop in the flesh (ἐν σαρκὶ ἐπίσκοπος), bodily and sensibly, is what God or Christ is in an invisible, spiritual way.[157] The basic idea underlying all the passages of these epistles that refer to the episcopate is therefore correctly spelled out as follows:

> The bishops are essentially the representatives and instruments of the church's unity, inasmuch as, in conformity with the specific character of the episcopate, they are the direct representatives, plenipotentiaries, and instruments of God and of Christ. In them Christ has, so to speak, replicated himself, for in them he has given himself a sensibly perceptible ubiquity within the realm

---

155. Ignatius, *Epistle to the Magnesians*, ch. 7, and *Epistle to the Trallians*, ch. 2.

156. Ignatius, *Epistles: To the Philadelphians.*, chs. 3, 7; *To the Smyrnaeans*, chs. 8 and 9; *To the Ephesians*, chs. 5 and 6; *To the Trallians*, ch. 3.

157. *To the Magnesians*, chs. 6 and 3; *To the Ephesians*, ch. 1.

of Christianity. He is what is essential in every congregation, acting through his instrument the bishop and guiding the activity of its life. This one and the same Christ therefore in essence stands at the head of every single congregation, although doing so by means of different individual representatives and instruments. And accordingly all the individual congregations are then of course bound together in the most thoroughgoing unity, although utterly conditional upon each one being organically attached to its bishop.[158]

The Pseudo-Clementine writings contain this same view of a system of church governance based on the idea of the episcopate. Just as they identify Mosaic religion with Christianity, and derive both from a primordial revelation and primordial religion, so too these writings see the episcopate as the bearer of a tradition that links the unity of the church with the unity of the human race. Christ is not only the omniscient, true prophet; he is also the primal human being who, to reveal the truth, appeared repeatedly in the patriarchs and in Moses. When he appeared for the last time, he then also appointed the twelve apostles as proclaimers of his word, and his brother James as bishop of Jerusalem. Because of his blood-relationship to the Lord, James has the prerogative that all teachers must be accredited as such by him. The teaching of the true prophet, a teaching propagated by James and the apostles, is so very much the immanent principle of the world's development that Peter, as its defender against Simon Magus, is reckoned in tandem with Simon as one of the syzygies that were predetermined in the world from its beginning. That is why the bishop, whose ordination makes him the possessor of the true doctrine of the faith, is, for his congregation, the representative of God and Christ, so that any honor or disrespect shown to the bishop redounds to Christ. Thus, within this sphere the bishop is the instrument of the one truth. Peter assigned these attributes to the episcopate when he ordained Zacchaeus as bishop of Caesarea.[159]

In the *Homilies* the principles of this system are further elaborated as follows.[160] The church is likened to a ship that, in the most violent storm, carries people from the most diverse regions. God is the captain, Christ is the pilot, the bishop is the chief oarsman, and the passengers are the great body of Christians. At journey's end the ship arrives at the longed-for harbor of eternal happiness. Hence the foremost need is for the church to have a well-ordered system of governance. This can only be the case if one person rules. The cause of many wars is that there are many kings, whereas if there were only one ruler then there would be everlasting peace on earth. This is why God has appointed one to rule over those who become worthy of eternal life, and that one is Christ. Therefore Christ is indeed Lord of the church, although there also has to be a visible representative of Christ's role, and this representative is the bishop.

158. R. Rothe, *Die Anfänge der christliche Kirche und ihre Verfassung* (n. 149), 477.

159. *Recognitions* 3.61; *Homilies* 3.60.

160. *Epistle of Clement to James*, ch. 14; *Homilies* 3.62ff. [*Ed.*] The apocryphal *Epistle of Clement to James* is prefixed to the *Homilies*.

The bishop occupies the place of Christ (Χριστοῦ τόπον πεπίστευται, is entrusted with the place of Christ), and whoever transgresses against the bishop sins against Christ. Honoring the bishop is honoring Christ, for the bishop has the power to bind and loose. Salvation depends on this tie with the bishop, because through him the individual is led to Christ, and from Christ to God. Hence whoever proves obedient to the bishop will attain salvation, and God will punish whoever is not.

On the other hand, it is not the duty of the bishop to dictate in tyrannical fashion, like the pagan sovereigns; rather it is to protect the afflicted like a father, to visit the sick like a physician, to watch over his flock like a shepherd; in short, to care for the salvation of everyone. He may not engage in worldly occupations, for these belong to the laity. His entire concern must focus on heavenly things. He has to oversee the salvation of everyone, most especially as this involves his charge of maintaining pure doctrine. The presbyters are tied to the bishop and the deacons to the presbyters. The central point of the entire Christian community is the bishop of Jerusalem, as the ruling bishop, ἐπίσκοπος ἐπισκόπων (bishop of bishops), who therefore is pre-eminently charged with maintaining doctrinal purity in the entire church, and to whom even Peter himself has to continually give an account of his effectiveness.

In comparing the idea of the episcopate as developed here, with the form still taken by the governance of Christian congregations in Clement of Rome's *Epistle to the Corinthians*, we see a considerable distance between them. Clement's epistle still has no place in its setting for a bishop in the sense of Pseudo-Clement and Pseudo-Ignatius. For Clement the idea of the episcopate is still so remote that even Christ is not called ἐπίσκοπος, but instead is just called προστάτης (leader, or protector) in ch. 58. However, we see how much the interest in this idea has grown, from how it has now become emphasized, and imposed on the entire system of church governance hinging upon it. In this context it is especially noteworthy that these writings, coming from otherwise such different principal orientations, concur on this matter. Also noteworthy is the unusual phenomenon that the writings working toward this common goal are pseudonymous writings. We also see clearly the resoluteness and concern with which this route, prescribed by contemporary circumstances, was taken.

This pseudonymous literature of Clement of Rome plays a role of its own here— [supposedly] the very same Clement to whom the idea of the episcopate is still so foreign in his own *Epistle to the Corinthians*. The Apostle Peter is the ἀπαρχή (first fruits) of the Lord, the first of the apostles; and so too Clement is the ἀπαρχὴ τῶν σωζομένων ἐθνῶν (first fruits of the saved Gentiles), the first Gentile converted by Peter, the apostle to the Gentiles.[161] As such and as the apostle's constant companion on his missionary journeys, as his most trusted follower who heard all his speeches and learned about church administration from him, Clement was ordained as bishop of Rome by Peter, and appointed as his successor in ruling over the Christian Church, which was spreading across the Gentile world through the apostle's missionary activ-

---

161. *Epistle of Clement to James*, chs. 1 and 3.

ity. All [powers] sufficient for governing the church are vested in him; he is personally responsible for establishing church law; his name is attached to a whole class of writings addressing this issue.[162]

Thus the governance of Christian congregations by relying on the idea of the episcopate has a Jewish Christian origin. What other conclusion than this is possible? As the increasing spread of the Christian Church, by the conversion of Gentiles, took place very much along Jewish Christian lines, the mindset in doing so was to sustain the Christian Church by a system of governance originally having an authentically Jewish Christian character, a system built on the idea of theocracy and the principle of strict and all-pervasive unity. At least this tendency is clearly expressed in the Pseudo-Clementine writings. Gentile Christianity as the work of Paul had no legitimacy so long as it still lacked the backing of Jewish Christianity. Gentile Christianity first received this backing in virtue of Peter replacing Paul as apostle to the Gentiles. Thus the entire governance of the church also was supposed to be thought of as an institution resting on the authority of the Apostle Peter and the original Jerusalem congregation. According to the fundamentally monarchical viewpoint of the Pseudo-Clementine writings, the character of the Christian Church can be maintained in its purity, and be preserved from all impure pagan influences imperiling its unity, only in circumstances where this original principle of unity is made secure.

Although these writings, in particular the *Homilies*, bear only the trace of a particular faction, at least we can still affirm that their contents as to church governance are those of a particular perspective. The idea of the episcopate they so emphatically validate is certainly the same idea actualized historically in the Catholic Church. Accordingly what follows from the particular concern that the factions represented in these writings have for the idea of the episcopate, is simply the Judaic origin of the church governance dependent on this idea. If in this context the striving for unity is so characteristic of these writings, does it indeed belong as such to the original character of Judaism? Or, is it not the same tendency—never losing sight of the connection with the original congregation, and monitoring the entire Christianity community in the interest of unity and correct belief—that we also meet with in Hegesippus and even in the pseudo-apostles, and that the Apostle Paul had so many run-ins with? This striving for unity has, at the same time, an overall anti-Pauline tendency that comes to a head in the *Homilies*, although in the Pastoral Epistles, and even more so in the epistles of Ignatius, we also see Paulinism suffused with the same concern for unity. This is the very thing that makes Pseudo-Ignatius so especially noteworthy in contrast

---

162. For the Jewish-Christian origin of the *Apostolic Constitutions* and for Clement's role as the intermediary through whom, traditionally, the apostolic constitutions came about specifically for Gentile Christians, see my treatise, "Ueber der Ursprung des Episcopats" (n. 130), 126ff.; A. Schwegler, *Das nachapostolische Zeitalter* (Tübingen, 1846), 1:406ff.; Hilgenfeld, *Die apostolischen Väter* (n. 22), 302ff.

to Pseudo-Clement. As a Paulinist, he comes forward on behalf of the same concerns for which the Petrine Pseudo-Clement is the main representative.[163]

Thus actualizing the idea of the episcopate, as a necessity grounded in the circumstances at that time, was so urgent that even the Paulinists could not refrain from recognizing this need. They simply wanted to adopt that idea for themselves without its Petrine associations. Just as for the Jewish Christians everything was linked to Jerusalem (and for Roman Christians who connected Clement of Rome with Jerusalem, that was the case too), the Paulinists, in contrast, directed their gaze back to Antioch, the initial site of Pauline Christianity. Antioch is where the followers were said to have been first called "Christians" (Χριστιανοί), as distinct from Jews—a point the Book of Acts (11:26) especially emphasizes. The Paulinists did so in order to counterpoise Bishop Ignatius to the Petrine Clement, the supporter of the Jewish-Christian tradition, for Ignatius likewise belonged to the apostolic age. They sought to reawaken the mental image of the Apostle Paul to serve their present goals—the image of Paul in captivity, traveling from east to west, escorted by Roman soldiers, to his death in Rome as a martyr.[164] In each case, Pseudo-Ignatius and Pseudo-Clement, there is the same underlying fiction. From this we also see how engrained in the mindset at that time was the introduction, into general consciousness then, of ideas, principles, and institutions arising from practical concerns, and doing so in the name of such figures and in such a fashion.

The Most Exalted Idea of the Episcopate and the Principle of Its Unity

The most exalted idea of the episcopate, and one about which Pseudo-Clement and Pseudo-Ignatius are in agreement, is the idea of the bishop as the representative of God and of Christ. But what is the basis of this idea, the reason for it?

In fact the *Homilies* simply present it as an assertion when they say (3.66), about the bishop, that "Christ's place is entrusted to the one occupying this seat." Or, in Ignatius' *Epistle to the Magnesians*, ch. 6, when it says that "the bishop presides in God's place." The statement in his *Epistle to the Ephesians*, ch. 3, amounts to the same thing: "Jesus Christ, our inseparable life, is the Father's will, just as the bishops appointed in various places are God's will." That is why one must adhere to what the bishop wills. This text even portrays the bishop's relation to Christ as involving the same substantial

---

163. The author of these epistles is caught up in the same idea of unity that engrosses the monarchical mind of the writer of the *Homilies*. In the *Epistle to the Philadelphians*, ch. 8, the Pseudo-Ignatius calls himself "a man well-equipped for unity," right on the heels (in ch. 7) of proclaiming loudly: "Adhere to the bishop and to the presbyters and to the deacons—never separate from the bishops—love unity," and so on.

164. See my "Ursprung des Episcopats" (n. 130), 179ff. The writer of the Pseudo-Ignatian *Epistle to the Ephesians* shows clearly that he is a Paulinist. In ch. 12 he calls himself a successor of the apostle highly praised on account of his martyrdom. The *Apostolic Constitutions* has Peter saying (7:46) that, in Antioch, he had appointed Evodius as a bishop and Paul had appointed Ignatius as a bishop.

unity as that existing between Christ and God. Therefore, just as Christ is the substantially hypostasized will of God, so too the bishops are said to be the substantially existent will of Christ. This view just relies on the assumption that oneness with Christ makes it necessarily so. However, it is inherently a leap to look upon the bishop as the direct representative of God and Christ, since bishops are initially just successors of the apostles. Furthermore, if the bishop's chief role is keeping the unity of the church intact in the purity of its doctrine, as well as warding off heresies and schisms, where else does he get the doctrine he is said to preserve, but from the hands of the apostles?

It is therefore noteworthy that this idea, set forth so starkly in these pseudonymous writings, was not one held by the church fathers of the next generation. Instead those theologians highlighted far more directly what stood intermediate between Christ and the bishops. For Irenaeus and Tertullian, the bishops are not representatives of God and Christ. Instead they are just successors to the apostles and custodians of the teachings handed down by the apostles. So here we of course have a further element in the development of the idea of the episcopate, and we thus have to distinguish the two different views of it.

The idea of the episcopate did not originate from a view of the church as a whole; instead it emerged from the domain of individual congregations. As long as a number of presbyters headed up a congregation, the whole still seemed to lack a unifying and cohesive bond. Since the role Christ has for the entire church he also has for each individual congregation, the ideal unity that each congregation has in Christ had to also become a unity in reality. This came about by one person coming to be head of a congregation as Christ's representative. They had to have the bishop, above all, be that person, in order to envisage in that person what all [the bishops] were together, collectively—the entire church as one.

But in order to present this united front, the bishops had to embody a real principle of unity. This could only be the teaching or doctrine they had in their custody. With all of them united by agreeing on doctrine, they joined together in the real, concrete unity of a closely-knit, whole body. However, they did not receive the doctrine, of which they had custody, directly from Christ; instead the apostles were intermediaries. Hence as soon as bishops were no longer merely the points of unity in individual congregations, but instead were representatives of the unity of the church as a whole, they could no longer be thought of as representatives of Christ. Now they were simply conceived of as successors to the apostles.

This transition from one role to the other is evident in the *Homilies*. Here the bishop is indeed also Christ's representative, but at the same time he is as well the guardian of the truth handed down by the apostles.[165] Since the truth transmitted by the apostles must be preserved, the *Homilies* have the office of bishop instituted by the apostles, although it is merely the Apostle Peter who also installs bishops everywhere

---

165. He is the "protector of the truth," the "ambassador of the truth." *Epistle of Clement to James*, chs. 2, 6, and 17.

that he establishes congregations. For the church fathers beginning with Irenaeus, apostolic succession is the main conception underlying the office of bishop. According to Irenaeus and Tertullian, bishops are essentially custodians and transmitters of the apostolic tradition. For them, the unity of the church is presented in the fact that all the bishops agree on one and the same doctrine. Thus we may simply trace the lines of succession of the bishops in order to arrive at the unity in principle of the doctrine.[166]

Cyprian, the chief representative of ecclesiastical and episcopal consciousness in his day, is even more strongly infused with the unifying idea of the episcopate. For him, church and episcopate are the same unity. The principle of the episcopate is not so much the apostolic succession as it is the Holy Spirit imparted to the bishops. The episcopate has the principle of its unity in this Spirit, and therefore there can be no differences of opinion among those in whom one and the same Spirit is present.[167] This one Spirit infuses each individual in the multiplicity of bishops, so that each bishop has in turn the same [understanding] as every other one. In the unity of the episcopate, all are as one. They are a unanimous, united whole in which no one stands on his own, for each individual at the same time presents in himself the unity and totality of the whole.[168]

If the bishops have their episcopal standing not as individuals on their own but instead only within the unity and totality of the whole body of bishops, then no one of them is any more or any less than the others. No one may command another or be commanded by another. Each one may consider himself a representative of the whole body of bishops, but may not set himself up as an *episcopus episcoporum* (bishop of bishops).

The Throne of Peter

Notwithstanding that, Cyprian confers a new meaning on the concern for the unity of the episcopate, namely that the unity presented by the collective bishops was said to have proceeded from a specific point of unity. Although the rest of the apostles were

---

166. The main passage on this point is Irenaeus, *Against Heresies* 4.33.8 [*ANF* 1:508]: "True knowledge is [that which consists in] the doctrine of the apostles and the ancient constitution of the church throughout all the world, and the distinctive manifestation of the body of Christ according to the successions of the bishops, by which they have handed down that church which exists in every place." On this passage, see Rothe, *Die Anfänge der christliche Kirche* (n. 149), 486. See also Ritschl, *Entstehung* (n. 101), 2nd ed., 442: "Because the office of bishop hands on the correct doctrine, for Irenaeus it counts as the continuation of the office of the apostles that they themselves put in place. For this reason the church consists in the totality of the bishops of the individual congregations in their concurrence with the apostolic teaching." See above, p. 208.

167. Cyprian, *Epistles* 73 and 68.

168. Cyprian, *Epistle* 52: "There is one church, divided by Christ throughout the whole world into many members and also one episcopate diffused through a harmonious multitude of many bishops" [in *ANF* 5:333 this quotation is from *Epistle* 51]. Also, *On the Unity of the Church*, ch. 3: "The episcopate is one, in which each individual is part of the whole."

Peter's peers, his colleagues equal in honor and power, the church of Christ begins from unity and so appears as one. The Lord gave the *potestas* (power) first of all to Peter, *unde unitatis originem instituit et ostendit* (whence he instituted and revealed the origin of the unity).[169]

Irenaeus and Tertullian had assigned preeminence to the Roman church alone, because it was founded by the two most glorious apostles. Cyprian now transfers this preeminence to the bishop of Rome himself. As the "throne of Peter," the Roman church is the "original church from which the sacerdotal unity has arisen." People also had to see this same unitary and central point in the person who sat on this same throne (*cathedra*), as successor to the Apostle Peter in the Roman church. Very soon the Roman bishops expressed this same conviction.[170] Here we already have the premises that led consistently to the papacy. If Peter was the first bishop in Rome, then the bishops of Rome had to be his successors, and thus had to have the same primacy as he had.

However, people dubbed Peter the bishop of Rome because he was said to have once been in Rome, and because one could only suppose, especially after the proceedings against the Apostle Paul, that Peter had been in Rome as the first apostle to be there in the capital of the world. The political importance of the city of Rome is the initial motive behind the traditional legend regarding Peter. Since the papacy itself rests on this legend, we are to seek the origin of the papacy simply in the importance Rome had as the world's capital city at that time, an importance carrying over to the bishop of the congregation in Rome.[171] To be sure this statement involves the apostles having a leader of the group. Yet this element by itself would not have amounted to much, since exclusive leadership or primacy is not ascribed to Peter, and one need not suppose that Christ's declaration must be understood in this sense. Only in Rome could there be bishops who, in claiming to be successors to the primacy of the Apostle Peter, also claimed actual primacy in the church.

169. Cyprian, *On the Unity of the Church*, ch. 4; *Epistle* 73 [72 in *ANF*].

170. In a letter to Cyprian (in Cyprian's *Epistles*, 75 [74 in *ANF*]), Firmilian, bishop [of Caesarea] in Cappadocia, emphasizes that Bishop Stephanus of Rome "glorifies the bishopric where he is and claims to hold it as successor to Peter."

171. A well-known passage in Irenaeus (*Against Heresies* 3.3) mentions both the political and the apostolic character of the city of Rome, and the *potentior principalitas* (preeminent authority) attributed to it. It is the *ecclesia maxima* (great church) as the congregation of the capital city. "For it is a matter of necessity that every church should agree with this church, on account of its preeminent authority, that is, the faithful everywhere, inasmuch as the apostolic tradition has been preserved continuously by those [faithful men] who exist everywhere" [*ANF* 1:415]. It seems to me that this passage, which has been interpreted in such different ways, is most correctly understood in the following way: that the first part expresses what cannot be otherwise, given how things stand, and the second part expresses what is actually the case. So I would render it as follows: "Because of the prominence of Rome as capital city and as an apostolic church, every church must be guided by this church. For of course the faithful from all quarters come to Rome, and so all those faithful ones who have links to Rome are also those who continually have upheld the apostolic tradition, both in the Roman church and in the church as a whole."

Cyprian, the bishop of Carthage (until 258) and his contemporaries, Cornelius and Stephanus who were bishops of Rome, provide the best yardstick for determining how the Roman church, already recognized as being the throne or seat of Peter, was already related to the Christian Church at that time, toward the end of the third century and the beginning of the fourth century. The greater Stephanus's pretensions became in the controversy over baptism by heretics, the more forcefully Cyprian and Firmilian stressed the independence of the churches of Africa and Asia Minor over against him. As for the disputed issue itself, it can seem contradictory that the bishop of Rome appears to sacrifice concern for unity to defending the validity of baptism by heretics. However, his opponents were not entirely justified in saying this.[172] For the characteristic feature of the Roman church is not merely a concern for unity; instead, it also involves the concurrent, and authentically Catholic, effort to open the arms of the one salvific church as widely as possible to all who are receptive to it. Only from this perspective could Stephanus conceive of the objectivity of the sacrament in such an external fashion, by declaring that mere laying-on of hands is sufficient for receiving all those who had been in some fashion baptized in the name of Jesus Christ,[173] and by considering defenders of one baptism in the one and only true church, as rebaptizers.[174]

Montanism and the Episcopate

Let us look back to the circumstances providing the first occasion and impetus for the development and realization of the idea of the episcopate. It is indisputable that the episcopate first gave the Christian Church the consciousness of its unity, grounded in faith in Christ, and enabled it to gain firm stability for its historical existence. This consciousness gave the Catholic Church the power to overcome all heresies and schisms, to overarch all partisan issues, to excise all extreme positions, and to unify all elements related to it.

172. Firmilian responded that, the more Stephanus boasted of his bishop's seat, the more foolish it is that, as successor to Peter "on whom the foundations of the church were laid, he should introduce many other rocks." [Ed.] See Cyprian, *Epistle* 74.17 (ANF 5:394).

173. See Cyprian, *Epistle* 74 [73.5–7 in *ANF*]: "If they attribute the effect of baptism to the majesty of the name, so that they who are baptized anywhere and anyhow, in the name of Jesus Christ, are judged to be renewed and sanctified . . . . Why does not the same majesty of the same name prevail in the imposition of hands?" How are those "able to be sons of God who are not born in the church," heretics such as Marcionites and Valentinians?

174. See Eusebius, *Ecclesiastical History* 7.5. The "second baptism" that, according to *Philosophumena* (n. 11), 9.12 [ET 656–57], was first ventured under the Roman bishop Callistus, is not, as J. Döllinger supposes (*Hippolytus und Callistus* [Regensburg, 1853], 189ff.), to be understood as referring to heretical baptism. Instead he says it refers to the baptism by Alcibiades the Elchasaite in Rome (*Philosophumena* 9.13.4 [ET 662–63]). Doubtless for good reasons, Stephanus appealed to the tradition of his church for the laying-on of hands. He had not yet made a dogmatic ruling about it. Cyprian did not contradict him on the point, but only said that the human tradition now no longer outweighed the "divine dispensation," that "custom" no longer outweighed the "truth."

II. The Catholic Church as the Antithesis to Gnosis and Montanism

However, what was the use of a church existing in this specific form, and organized for continuing into the future, if the church had no future and no possibility of historical development in the offing? What future if, with its belief in the parousia, it anticipated the end of the world at any moment? This issue takes us back to Montanism. Montanism kept the church most energetically focused on the thought that the denouement was at hand in the immediate future, and fixed its eyes on its end, right at the very threshold of its existence. Thus what first made possible the existence and historical development of the Christian Church was the episcopate, as the opponent of Montanism.

The controversy between the Montanists and their opponents points to a deep-seated bifurcation or ambivalence within Christian consciousness at that time. The opponents of Montanism saw its moral requirements as impractically strict. Thus they did not share the Montanist views that the end of the world was already so imminent and that there was nothing as urgent as cutting oneself off from the world in order to stand in readiness for the great denouement. Since belief in the parousia had not yet been fulfilled, they drew from this the natural conclusion that it still would not come about in the near future, and so the end of the world was not yet so imminent.

As the unnatural tension due to anticipation of the parousia increasingly lost its hold on people, this change had to have influenced all of a Christian's conduct when it came to practical affairs. People could no longer go on living in such total disregard for, and rejection of, the world. Instead they had increasingly to accommodate themselves to the world. But since Montanism could see this as simply a growing worldliness on Christianity's part, Montanism can only be understood, from this perspective, as a reaction to this worldliness. The Montanist faction thought the prevalent ethic of accommodation was too lax; so the Montanists became stricter about the practical matters of the Christian life, by affirming their own moral requirements, some of which they introduced for the first time, and some of which they said had always held good. Once these different views and factions had become so opposed, an open and intensified conflict was unavoidable. As it unfolded, each side far too publicly denied the Christian character of the other side. What ought the resolution to be in circumstances such as these?

In fact the actual issue here was not whether those who fell short in Christian character were still to be recognized as Christians. Instead the issue was whether, by the power of the keys imparting forgiveness of their sins, those people could be accepted back into the fellowship of the church. Here the general difference separating the Montanists from the Catholic Church directly became an issue of practice. The Montanists utterly refused to forgive those who had committed what they called a deadly sin, because such a sin was committed against God himself and could only be forgiven by God. Or else, since God is the Spirit, they said such a sin could be forgiven by the church insofar as the church is the Spirit, although those speaking in the new prophets, that is, through the Paraclete, declared their opposition to doing so.

Whereas the opponents of the Montanists not only affirmed the principle that even deadly sins could be forgiven; they also ascribed to themselves the authority to do so.[175]

This dispute, which started out as a dogmatic controversy, became important for the history of the Christian Church's governance that was taking shape in the episcopate. That is because the main opponents facing off against the Montanists, and in fact against their prophets, as instruments of the Paraclete, were the bishops. It is very probable that, right from the outset, bishops in Asia Minor were the leaders of the anti-Montanist movement. Tertullian[176] provides us with the main evidence for the bishops' stance on the Montanist issue. He tells of an important event when the bishop of Rome declared publicly that all those offenses the Montanists designated as the deadly sins of adultery and fornication shall no longer absolutely exclude someone from the fellowship of the church; that instead the guilty ones shall receive forgiveness after they have done penance.[177] Indeed Tertullian just speaks ironically about this imperious edict putting an end to the controversy, an edict the Roman bishop issued as "the *Pontifex Maximus*, that is, the bishop of bishops."[178] In any event this edict must have played a decisive role in the ultimate outcome of the controversy.

Prior to this the bishops of Rome had not spoken out decisively against the Montanists. When Praxeas came to Rome, probably when Eleutherius was pope [c. 175–189], they had even entertained the idea of uniting the ecclesial community with the Montanists. Thus it was very significant when the bishop of Rome (who was Victor I, from c. 190 to 200, or Zephyrinus, from c. 200 to 215), put an end to any doubt about the position of the Roman church on the Montanists, via the edict Tertullian mentions. So Rome hardly approved of the Montanists' moral principles. Tertullian himself gives us to understand that the bishop of Rome did not stand alone on this matter; that other bishops shared the same concern guiding him. We see that Tertullian was aware of this,[179] from his antithetical, Montanist contention that the church (*ecclesia*) should be the Spirit via a spiritual person (*spiritus per spiritalem hominem*),

---

175. Tertullian, *On Modesty*, ch. 21.

176. *On Modesty*, ch. 1.

177. Tertullian reports (ibid.) the bishop's edict as saying, among other things: "I remit, to such as have discharged [the requirements of] repentance, the sins both of adultery and of fornication" [*ANF* 4:74].

178. [*Ed.* Ibid. (*ANF* 474).] Gieseler (*Kirchengeschichte* [n. 3], 1.1:288) will have it that these phrases apply to the bishop of Carthage, although he has no basis for this and it contradicts the entire historical context of Montanism. These appellations certainly fit the bishop of Rome, who arrogated to himself a status he did not in fact possess. And if (according to Jerome, *Catalistus*, 53) Tertullian already had strained relations with the Roman clergy prior to his becoming a Montanist, then that further explains his irony here. Zephyrinus is probably the bishop of Rome Tertullian is referring to. The *Philosophumena* (n. 11) 9.12, pp. 290ff., provides new information about practices in Rome regarding the forgiveness of sin. [*Ed.*] *Philosophumena* 9.12.14–25 (ET 650–59) tells of Callistus I, or Calixtus, a favorite of Zephyrinus and his successor as pope (218–22), appointing clergy who were adulterers, and allowing other kinds of moral laxity.

179. [*Ed.*] See *On Modesty*, ch. 21.

not the church as a number of bishops (*non ecclesia numerous episcoporum*). Therefore, despite so many bishops espousing the anti-Montanist principle that the church can forgive even such [deadly] sins, in this instance the judgment of the Spirit, as it speaks in a spiritual person, alone can render the verdict.

The Montanists' concerns show us what the antithetical interests of the bishops were. The Montanists utterly rejected any forgiveness of mortal sins. In view of the impending end of the world, the Montanists drew the reins of church discipline as tightly as possible, making them tighter as a large segment of the Christian Church at that time had become more lax. Given their worldview, the bishops, in contrast, could only suppose that the time may have come to set the stage for a longer duration of the church in this temporal world. Right then is when, for the first time, the episcopate provided the church with an organization geared to its duration, and gave it the idea that the bishops latched onto so significantly—the idea of a continuous succession (*continua successio*). The bishops' eyes had to be directed forward, in considering the future lying before the church, as well as back to the apostles whose successors they claimed to be. If the bishops regarded themselves to be the custodians of the church ongoing in the world rather than a church already vanishing from the world into the time to come, then they had to have felt naturally impelled to remove from the Christian fellowship all vestiges of the excessively heightened early Christian consciousness that stood in such harsh opposition to the world. That consciousness could only too easily serve to derail the church from the track on which it was supposed to take its orderly course within the world.

The church could not carry on within the world unless it learned how to be on better terms with the world. This was not possible as long as people looked for the world to end at any moment. One can only imagine how those who thought constantly about Christ's parousia, and the denouement to accompany it, must have experienced a singular and conscious tension, as though suspended between existing and not existing. How could a fellowship where such a belief persisted plant its feet firmly within the world, when it saw the very ground of its existence as increasingly unstable, and it anticipated that, in the near future, the orderly world around it would collapse from within? When, as befitted this belief, moral requirements were to have been intensified in a way that exceeded the reach of ordinary human powers, then on this score too the conditions for existing harmoniously with the world as it is were no longer present.

What excessive moral requirements the Montanists imposed when they demanded, from members of the Christian fellowship, that they should remain utterly free of those transgressions the Montanists conceived of as being mortal sins! This was so unworkably severe that a community professing this principle had to see the moral force needed for its continued existence very soon eaten up from within. A concession made with regard to forgiveness for mortal sins was the first step taken in the transition from the transcendence of the Montanists' never-to-be realized idea to the soil of the given, empirical reality where this community could really become actual as an ongoing church. If it was impossible for there to be no sins, then it must at least be possible for sins to be forgiven. The church as purely ideal did indeed vanish, but the idea of the church had become an idea put into practice.

Therefore the church did not just consist of saints who remain totally untainted by any so-called deadly sin. It consisted of those the church, in virtue of the power of the keys, could recognize as true members of the Christian fellowship. And if, as the Montanists too acknowledged, the church had the right to forgive sins, why should it not have also exercised that right? In taking the lead as the opponents of Montanism, on the issue of allowing forgiveness for mortal sins, the bishops by doing so gave proof, in a way very typical for their position, that their Christian spirit had recovered from all the excessive tension, internal as well as external, of early Christian consciousness. In this way they first made possible the historical existence of the Christian Church, developed along the lines of the continuous succession of bishops. When in fact the bishop of Rome was the one in this succession whose authority had the most decisive influence, then it is even more noteworthy how, already at that time, the bishops of Rome were entering upon a path where they understood only too well, in both theory and practice, how to have the church and the world go hand in hand from then on.

Here we see the initial stages of Christianity's becoming a worldly religion, something that was always just a possibility but is now a reality in the Roman church. These initial steps are innocently undertaken, and justified given the circumstances. In short, there now exists a procedure for indulgences for the sins that the Montanists could only call "the highest crimes" of adultery and fornication, a procedure that begins the entire, and so notorious, history of granting indulgences in the Roman church. As though correctly foreseeing the entire historical significance of the edict of the bishop of bishops, Tertullian[180] already speaks of an earthly temple of God in which the bride of Christ, as the true, modest, saintly virgin, must suffer such liberality as was previously said to be posted on the gates of the sensual appetites, even just as something defiling her ears—a den of adulterers and fornicators.[181]

---

180. [Ed.] Baur quotes several Latin phrases from Tertullian's *On Modesty*, ch. 1, here given only in translation (*ANF* 4:74–75).

181. The *Shepherd* of Hermas is an important source for tracing the relation of the Roman church to Montanism, going back before Tertullian's day. (Ritschl first demonstrated this in detail in his *Entstehung* [n. 101], 1st ed., 546 ff; 2nd ed., 529ff.) The main theme of the *Shepherd* is the issue of forgiveness of sins subsequent to one's baptism. A second repentance is allowed after one's baptism, but only within a limited time frame, only "after a certain day, which has been fixed. For the repentance of the righteous has limits. For all the saints, the days of repentance are filled up. For the pagans, repentance will be possible even to the last day" (Vision 2, ch. 2 [*ANF* 2:11]). Here "pagans" means those not yet baptized. Vision 3, ch. 5, defines these limits more precisely, using the image of building a tower as representing the church. One can repent as long as "the tower is under construction. For if the building be finished, there will not be more room for any one, but he will be rejected." But this tower "will soon be finished" (Vision 3, ch. 8). Therefore the interval allowed for the second repentance is just the time during which the tower is still being built, up until the imminent second coming of Christ (Similitude 9, chs. 7 and 10). As Ritschl quite aptly shows, the completion of the tower signifies the

Once the possibility of forgiveness of sins within the church was stated in principle (as we see it in the edict of the bishop of Rome), this was therefore viewed as a major step forward. After that the church could proceed on a track for which even the sinful nature of its members posed no obstacle to its realization as an institution. One can now show, step by step, how people abandoned everything that had with new energy been enforced in Montanism as the original form of Christian consciousness, or else they just adopted it in an essentially modified form. Everything here is closely connected with the crisis in consciousness at that time, and how the episcopate resolved it.

The Bishops as Instruments of the Spirit

Cyprian no longer speaks of the "drastic measures of the time," the "distresses of the end time drawing near," which lay so heavy on the heart of Tertullian and made him so gloomy. However, Cyprian is indeed of the same mind. He too is convinced that the world will not last much longer. However, in this circumstance he simply sees the general truth—unrelated to belief in Christ's parousia, or to the church as such—that the world has already become old and lost its vigor.[182]

To the extent that, in this context, people increasingly adopted the generally-held view of the world, they also relaxed the strict practical requirements of that overwrought Montanist view. For Tertullian, "cut away the desires of the flesh" had been an absolute command of the Paraclete, and disregarding it could only be regarded as a deadly sin. Cyprian now reduces this rule to just doing what a Christian's moral consciousness recommends and advises that one should do so. Following this

---

very same epoch of the church said to be introduced by Montanism, except that Montanism thought this point in time was already so near that it discounted the possibility of a second repentance. That is why, for Hermas, the church appears in the first vision in the form of an aged woman, and scolds him for having secret desires and for devotion to worldly matters. In the second vision she appears with a youthful air, but with grey hair. In the third vision she is young and cheerful. Since in these latter visions she discloses that the time for a second penance is over, this shows clearly that the rejuvenation of the church and the renewal of the spirit are said to have been brought about by none other than the abolition of the second repentance, so as to counteract the increasing worldliness of the church as that is depicted in the first vision. In addition, Ritschl shows how the *Shepherd* of Hermas also takes its stance in opposition to the clergy who, with their authority, defended the church's conformity to the world and the second repentance policy. Thus the antithetical relation of the *Shepherd* to the clergy is the same as that between the Montanists and the Psychici. So the same issue that came to a head most contentiously in Montanism had already also emerged independently of Montanism, in the Roman church about the middle of the second century, when the *Shepherd* of Hermas was written. Ritschl writes (p. 538) that: "Hermas marks a local prologue to the phenomena that, beginning from Phrygia, were upsetting and disruptive in almost all parts of the church. He commenced the series of separatist movements that occupied the next century and that almost continuously commanded the attention of the Roman church. The secession of Hippolytus at the onset of the third century fell in between the Montanist movement in Rome and the Novatian schism."

182. In the treatise *Ad Demetrianum*, ch. 3, ed. Krabinger (Tübingen, 1859), 156. [*Ed.*] This is Treatise V in *ANF* 5:457–65; citation is from 458.

recommendation is meritorious, and entitles one to a greater reward. Not following it at least does not detract from what moral perfection one otherwise has.

However, the extent to which people strongly recoiled from the fanatical tendency that the Montanist vision had so greatly excited, is especially evident with regard to chiliasm. Antipathy to millenarianism became increasingly widespread. Now there was even an energetic concern to combat it and to repudiate the principle behind it. This happened not only in the Alexandrian church, which had always opposed chiliasm, but also mainly in the Roman church, indeed about the same time when it completely broke with Montanism. These changes are characteristic of this turning point in the historical development of the church. Even though Gaius, a Roman presbyter and one of the main representatives of this tendency, did not go so far as declaring the Johannine Book of Revelation to be a work of the heretic Cerinthus, he did nevertheless, in referring to Cerinthus, even more strongly contest the sensuous chiliasm of Judaism.[183]

Chiliasm now stood for the sum and substance of all that had been left behind in the effort to get completely away from everything that still tied Christianity to Judaism. In this setting people could just relinquish what had now lost its grip on their minds, what was now foreign to them, even though holding on to that view in a different form. They did not abandon the moral and ascetic demands of the Montanists; they just accommodated them to a catholic [i.e., all-inclusive] church. Even less so could they regard the Holy Spirit, Montanism's principle of revelation, as exclusively a Montanist principle. Each side presupposed that the Spirit and the church essentially belong together; that the church has the truth of its essential being in the Spirit, and the Spirit has the actuality of its existence in the church. However, the greatest objection from the catholic side was to the vagueness, arbitrariness, and randomness of Montanist prophecy; to its seeking to introduce novelty and, in the individuals it made its instruments, to establish a new principle of faith. In this sense they said the folly of the Montanists was in seeking to make one's own way of thinking count as the catholic way. People drew from the Montanist doctrine the conclusion that, in believing they were the first to receive the Paraclete promised by Christ, the Montanists were denying that the Paraclete came to the apostles—and they called this denial heresy.[184]

The Catholic Church therefore took a position wholly analogous to Montanism, except that now the working of the Holy Spirit—which, in the Montanist Paraclete, was operative in the free and full scope of the subjectivity of individuals who had the gift of prophecy—became settled and regulated by the Catholic Church. The keys of the power to bind and loose, which the Montanist prophets claimed for themselves, came to be exclusively in the hands of the bishops. Thus the bishops were now also the

---

183. Eusebius, *Ecclesiastical History* 3.28. Cf. [Eduard Zeller in] *Theologische Jahrbücher* 12 (1853) 157ff. [*Ed.*] The Judaizing Gnostic Cerinthus, according to Gaius, depicted an earthly kingdom of Christ filled with lust and pleasure, a marriage feast lasting a thousand years.

184. Schwegler, *Montanismus* (n. 99), 225 and 238.

only recognized instruments or intermediaries for the Holy Spirit. To the principle of individuality, on which Montanist prophecy relied, the bishops counterpoised the principle that the Holy Spirit, as the governing principle of the church, speaks only in the whole body of its representatives; and that these representatives themselves may more confidently believe they are inspired by the Spirit, the more indubitably they are fully aware of their representing the church. Thus what was such an indefinite and unstable affair in the revelations of the Montanist Paraclete got channeled into the organized and orderly procedure of the councils representative of the church. Continuity with the Spirit working in the apostles was firmly established in dogma, in contrast to the apparently so weak and so easily dissoluble bond the Montanist Paraclete had with it. Consequently the decrees of the councils are just the content of the apostolic tradition immanent in the church, and made known to everyone.

This form of revelation of the Spirit obviously ruled out the individualized ecstasy of Montanist prophecy. Through the working of the Spirit in ecstasy, the mind of an individual can simply get so outside itself that one loses all self-control. However, if the Spirit speaks in the collective consciousness of a number of individual subjects, then it is unthinkable that the group product, said to count as the expression of the Spirit, can come about in any other way than by reflection guiding their shared deliberation. According to Tertullian, the individual cannot help being outside himself when seized by the Spirit. So Tertullian has no hesitation in locating the essence of prophecy precisely in loss of control over one's own mind, or *amentia*.[185] Prophecy simply has its basis in how the individual, as he is, stands in relation to the Spirit, inasmuch as the individual is just passively related to the Spirit and must let it work in him so as to displace him from his own center of consciousness and cause him to be outside himself. It is thus clear that the Spirit's relation to the consciousness of a number of individuals, as presented in the bishops assembled in council, inherently cannot have the same external and fortuitous character as in Montanism. Setting no limit to the number of persons inspired by the Spirit eliminates the inadequacy of Montanism, and also makes it possible to think of the Spirit simply as the substantial principle immanent in the collective bishops. So it was entirely fitting that there was no longer any place for the ecstatic prophecy of the Montanists, as soon as the instruments of the Spirit were no longer individuals, as they are fortuitously, but instead were the bishops considered in their prescribed role as representatives of the church. Also in this case, the bishops' opposition to Montanism signaled the transition from the unsettled conditions experienced by the earliest Christians, to the secure and orderly stability of the Catholic Church.

What lay behind all this, as the ultimate cause for the ecstatic prophecy of the Montanists, we can recognize simply as the transcendent view of the world that was the form of consciousness typical of the earliest Christians, so long as, with their belief

---

185. *On the Soul*, ch. 11. [*Ed.*] What Tertullian says here is that the Spirit that comes upon a person in ecstasy is an operation of the soul but not a part of the soul's nature.

in Christ's imminent parousia, they still stood with one foot in their contemporary world and the other foot already in the world to come. In such a state one's consciousness is not, in itself, an undivided whole (*Beisichsein*) but is instead outside itself (*Ausersichsein*). Here ecstasy is its characteristic form. Hence there can be no clearer signpost of the general crisis that then ensued, than the specific declaration that ecstasy as such befits neither the prophetic spirit nor Christian consciousness.[186]

After this time it became the orthodox conception that the Old Testament prophets certainly did not prophesy in an insensible state of ecstasy; instead they prophesied consciously and with an understanding of what they said. Ecstasy is held to be a degrading condition typical of demonic paganism; whereas from the standpoint of Christian consciousness, the inspired person's self-composure is regarded as an essential feature of a theory of inspiration. Christian consciousness—after having secured a firm foothold in the existing world, and upon seeing, in the Christianity taking shape in the Catholic Church, the foundation for a newly developing order of things—now feels strong enough to maintain its composure in the face of the working of the divine Spirit, and to hold firmly to its own self-awareness.[187]

The Church Councils (*die Synoden*)

From the account so far it is clear how important the episcopate is for the church's structure and development. The episcopate gave a specific form to the church. What Christ himself had imparted to the apostles, what it was their greatest privilege to receive, could now be thought of as handed down to the bishops. The person of the bishop is where the church as a whole was concentrated and set forth, in essence and according to its own proper principle.

The Holy Spirit is the principle of Christian consciousness for Christians as such. It is the Spirit that properly animates them and makes them to be ἅγιοι (holy ones) just as Christ himself, being infused with, or anointed by, the Holy Spirit, the principle of messiahship, is the ἅγιος absolutely. The Holy Spirit is the principle operative in the Christian community, working with its divine power wherever the needs of Christianity require it. And the Holy Spirit does all of this in the bishops, in the most exalted and most concentrated sense. They are pre-eminently the bearers and possessors of

---

186. Eusebius, *Ecclesiastical History* 5.17, refers to a writing by Miltiades, from Asia Minor, in opposition to the Montanists and entitled περὶ τοῦ μὴ δεῖν προφήτην ἐν ἐκστάσει λαλεῖν (Why Prophecy Ought not Speak Ecstatically). See Schwegler, *Montanismus* (n. 99), 277.

187. It is noteworthy that the *Pseudo-Clementine Homilies*, in exalting prophecy as it does, also speaks openly in opposition to tolerance of ecstasy in divine matters. In sharing the same concerns as the Catholic Church, it too considers ecstasy to be something incompatible both with the orderly governance of the church as it exists in the system of the episcopate, and with a more highly developed stage of Christian consciousness. It explicitly opposes demonically deceptive ecstasy, and instead affirms the immanent consciousness of the "indwelling and eternal spirit," which is not only in the prophets but is in all pious people everywhere. See above, pp. 186–87.

the divine Spirit immanent in the church. Just as Christ, by imparting his spirit to the apostles, also bestowed on them the authority to forgive sins, so too in the bishops' case this privilege, as the highest power bestowed on the church, is linked to their possession of the spirit. This same power passes down from the apostles to the bishops and from one bishop to another through apostolic succession and vicarious ordination. Just as Christ, in giving the apostles the authority to forgive sins, granted them the greatest privilege he could leave to them, the supreme attribute of the office of bishop is therefore the power of the keys.[188]

The initial self-awareness of the church as such emerged with the institution of the bishop. The whole power of the church is concentrated in the bishops, its leadership and its vital unity. Since they are the church as self-aware, this awareness must also find its expression in them in a specific form. This form is a function of the fact that each bishop has the same standing as all the others have, and yet he has this standing not when regarded by himself alone, but only in concert with all the other bishops. Hence the consciousness of the church, represented by the bishops, cannot express itself in a single bishop, by himself alone; it can only express itself in a larger or smaller number of assembled bishops. So it was inevitable that, when governance by the bishops began, there were also councils (*Synoden*). When issues of common concern arose that called for concerted action, it was the occasion for consultation and decisions about them. This first took place regarding the Montanists, and regarding the Easter controversy. But very soon it also became customary to hold assemblies of this kind at regular intervals. As these assemblies themselves resulted from the

---

188. See Cyprian, *Epistle* 75 [74 in *ANF*], where Bishop Firmilian says, after making reference to John 20:21–23: "Therefore the power of remitting sins was given to the apostles, and to the churches which they, sent by Christ, established, and to the bishops who succeeded them by vicarious ordination" [*ANF* 5:394]. Here the original congregational power is not yet entirely forgotten, for bishops have apostolic authority only via the link with churches founded by the apostles. As for this passage in John ["Jesus said to them again, 'Peace be with you. As the Father has sent me, so I send you.' When he had said this, he breathed on them and said to them, 'Receive the Holy Spirit. If you forgive the sins of any, they are forgiven them; if you retain the sins of any, they are retained.'"], those who can only take the Gospel of John to be post-apostolic will readily believe that the question regarding its stance on this matter is analogous to the Easter controversy. In the designation of the Holy Spirit as the Paraclete, the Gospel concurs with the Montanists. Apostolic authority to loose and to bind is vested in the power to forgive sins, in the same sense in which the Montanists and their opponents disputed about this; and it is grounded in the same principle on which everything rested for the Montanists, the Holy Spirit, whereas in affirming this power Matt 16:19 and 18:18 do not mention the Holy Spirit. John takes the side of those who hold to the Catholic position on this issue, as he also does on the Passover issue [in the Easter controversy (see above, pp. 123–33)]. When John 20:21 has Jesus saying, "As the Father has sent me, so I send you," when he imparts the Holy Spirit to the disciples, this statement also expresses the concept of apostolic succession and the principle that it must also be successors of the apostles who have this same power to forgive sins. It is striking that John 20:21–23 is indeed cited by Cyprian and Firmilian, in *Epistles* 73 [72] and 75 [74], but not by Tertullian. Cyprian also said: "Whence we perceive that only they who are set over the church and established in the gospel law, and in the ordinance of the Lord, are allowed to baptize and to give remission of sins" [*ANF* 5:381]. Therefore it also seemed to him that what this passage says about the apostles likewise holds good for the bishops and only for them. But Tertullian could not concede this point.

bishops' ecclesial consciousness, they also had to serve for the most part to strengthen the bishops' consciousness of their status, and to give the councils the character of representing the church as a whole.[189]

An essential feature of such a system of representation is that it gains in significance as the number of participants grows. Thus even before governance by the episcopate had surpassed the stage of titular metropolitans, conciliar governance had already reached its proximate goal with the first general council. As an ecumenical council, it was inclusive of all bishops of the Roman Empire. As each bishop could regard himself preeminently as an instrument of the Holy Spirit, and as what was true of one must be even more true of a number of bishops, then the ecumenical council also came to fully manifest the underlying principle of the system of church governance. In the Book of Acts (15:28), the council held by the apostles in Jerusalem issued its decisions in the name of the Holy Spirit. Subsequent provincial councils made use of the same formula.[190] Therefore the collective bishops assembled at an ecumenical council had to carry even more weight, as the ones through whom God's will is revealed, under the influence of the Holy Spirit.[191]

3. THE SYSTEM OF THE HIERARCHY

The system whose development we have set forth already embodied the elements of the most comprehensive and thoroughgoing hierarchy. We see its beginnings as emerging quite naturally from circumstances at that time. Its greatest feature is the simplicity of the models on which it relies. The basic model is the bishop's relation to the congregation of which he is the head. This always remains the model, however the system may develop, expand, and undergo modifications. The bishop of the smallest congregation has essentially the same position as the pope at the highest level of the papacy.

The same basic model recurs at all levels of this hierarchical system. The greatest feature of this basic model is its ability to be extended indefinitely. Since the bishops are of course always qualitatively the same, yet their areas of responsibility can be quite different quantitatively, their episcopal equality also allows for subordination

---

189. In *On Fasting* 13, Tertullian writes: "Throughout Greece, councils of the whole church are held in certain places, assembled to deal with the greater issues. That these councils represent the whole, in the name of Christianity, is celebrated and greatly venerated" [*ANF* 4:111]. In Cyprian, *Epistle* 75 [74], Firmilian says: "It happens of necessity among us, that year by year we, the elders and prelates, assemble together to arrange those matters which are committed to our care, so that if any things are more serious they may be directed by the common counsel" [*ANF* 5:391].

190. For instance, the assembly in 252 in Carthage, under the leadership of Cyprian, says: "We have determined, by the suggestion of the Holy Spirit . . . ." See *Epistle* 54 [53].

191. See Socrates, *Ecclesiastical History* 1.9, where Constantine, in writing to the church in Alexandria about the Council of Nicaea, says: "It pleased three hundred bishops, knowing God's decree, so many men of such a kind and so great, men devoted to reason and in whom the Holy Spirit is present, to make known the divine will."

via a series of ascending stages and their occupants. This arrangement is a model not merely having the widest possible application, but also making possible a fully articulated, organic structure. The very concept of hierarchy involves this distinctive feature of a system taking form, via subordination, as ascending and different levels. There is no hierarchy in which all the members are equal. The bishop must outrank the presbyter and the deacon, and the presbyter outrank the deacon. The distinctions among these three levels form the prototype determining the entire system, however many stages it may rise to include.

In one respect, with the bishops all being colleagues of the same rank, the system tends to have the broadest base. On the other hand, with distinctions also drawn between the bishops, the system likewise strives very much to concentrate at its apex and to wind up in a supreme unity. Subordination is characteristic of this ecclesiastical system; but no less characteristic is the principle of this subordination, which is that the system is not merely hierarchical, but is also theocratic. The theocratic character likewise essentially belongs to the simple, basic form on which the system rests. The subordination the system calls for is an absolute demand having the same character of inner necessity as the subordination in which the human must be subordinate to the divine. The fundamental conception of the bishop is certainly that he is the representative of God and of Christ; that he is the instrument through which the Holy Spirit, as the immanent principle of the Christian community, preeminently speaks. Everything rests on divine authority. In the bishop's relation to his congregation we see the same relation of Christ to the church. On the one hand, this relationship posits an unconditional subordination, inasmuch as everything utterly proceeds from unity: as there is one God and one Christ, so there can also be just one church and one episcopate, and everything must be utterly subordinate to this oneness. On the other hand, however, there is also the factor of piety, and it is linked to all the pious feelings comprised in a human being's religious relation to God and Christ. The bishop should be the spiritual father of his congregation, and its members should cling to him with childlike trust.[192] Hence if we understand the original elements of this system, then we see that it is essentially the product of a stage of religious development where people felt the need to have a visible representative of how Christ, the Lord of the church, is related to the church. Just as the apostles took the place of Christ who sent them, so

---

192. The *Apostolic Constitutions* 2.34 [*ANF* 7:412], states that "You ought to love the bishop as your father, and fear him as your king, and honor him as your lord." What applies to the bishop also applies to the clerical office in general. Based on the Old Testament idea of the priesthood, which Cyprian, the chief defender of the idea of the episcopate, backs to the fullest extent, priests are set apart from the world as having the same absolute superiority as the bishop has over the congregation. Therefore, when priests concern themselves with worldly matters and affairs, it simply degrades their office. [*Ed.* Baur quotes several fragmentary statements from Cyprian, *Epistle* 66 (65 in *ANF*), which reiterate reasons for priests not getting involved in worldly affairs. He continues:] Here we have expressed, in Cyprian's words, the great practical importance of this principle, and the view of the clergy's priestly character on which it rests. See also Clement, *Epistle to James*, ch. 5, and *Homilies* 3.71.

too people could look upon the bishops, who were successors of the apostles, as being simply the representatives of Christ.

Part 4

Christianity as the Highest Principle
of Revelation, and as Dogma

The Transition to Dogma

In reviewing the presentation thus far, we see that in this sphere there are two outlooks or ways of thinking in which the idea immanent in Christianity realized itself in Christian consciousness. Above all, the limitation that the particularism of Judaism wanted to impose on the Christian principle of salvation had to be overcome, and Christian universalism had to be established. This could only happen by doing away with the wall of separation between Judaism and paganism or the Gentile world, and by regarding the entirety of humankind—the wide domain in which the idea of Christianity should actualize itself—as both needing Christian salvation and being receptive to it. In this regard, however, just as Christianity had from the outset the tendency to expand into a universal movement, it on the other hand had, from this universal standpoint, an equal concern to hold firmly to its specific content and character. In wanting to be just as specific—that is, personal, individual, and historically concrete—as it was universal, Christianity had to relate these two aspects adequately to each other.

Christianity's universalism situated it in the broad domain of a worldview pervaded by pagan elements. It brought Christianity into the closest contact with a way of looking at things in which Judaism had already been so compromised by ideas from Greek philosophy that this affected Christianity too. Christianity, being drawn into the same circle of ideas, could only take on a character more or less related to pagan polytheism. This would have changed the Christian process of salvation into a general process of the world's development, one in which Christ himself became just one of the various world principles that condition the course of the world's development. In brief, becoming worldly was the danger that threatened Christianity from the side of its universality.

In simply basing itself chiefly on its moral and religious perspective, Montanism believed it had to counter this very danger of Christianity becoming worldly. It claimed to have made a complete break with the world and to have made the Jewish-messianic end of the world the principle of its own worldview. Therefore Christian consciousness also had the opposite task, from this perspective, of leading Christianity on a path where it could pursue the historical development commensurate with its original idea.

The Catholic Church unified in itself all these elements coming under consideration from various angles. Its Catholic consciousness united all the elements that very much kept the universality of Christianity intact, with those on the other side that sought to keep their distance from everything that tarnished the specific character of Christianity by Jewish or pagan influence and that seemed to go too far to one side or the other.

At first the idea of the Catholic Church existed only in those who, being conscious of it, formed the dominant majority and labored most successfully to realize it and give it a solid basis. But by taking shape in this negatively antithetical way, by opposing everything inadequate in Christian terms, the Catholic Church was still just a merely formal idea that had first to be filled out with its own specific content. But although the Christian consciousness expressed by the majority in the church largely agreed about what views are to be avoided and rejected, what very much mattered was affirmation as opposed to negation. The church had to spell out in a positive way what should count as the absolute content of Christian consciousness. The church had constituted itself in a specific way ever since it came to have bishops who could be regarded as the bearers and representatives of the apostolic tradition, and of the church's consciousness. However, this consciousness itself was still just something very undefined, a mere form without content, so long as dogma—the content of the apostolic tradition, or Christian revelation—had not, in its development and gradual elaboration, come to be definitively conceptualized and expressed.

The Council of Nicaea, which concluded the first period of the Christian Church's historical development, gives us a very clear picture of the connection between these two features: the form of governance the church acquired in the bishops who represented its unity; and the dogma, as the content said to be expressed by those interpreters of the tradition and vehicles for the church's consciousness, and said to be settled as universally enforceable doctrine. As an ecumenical council, Nicaea most fully represented the episcopacy and the church. Therefore, in its dogma of the *homoousian* [of the Son], it expressed the supreme thing that Christian consciousness can have for its dogmatic content.

So we are now at the point where dogma as such has its specific place. If the church had not had its definite content in its Catholic dogma, within bounds firmly spelled out by the church itself but also converging from all sides in the idea of a Catholic Church, then the church would otherwise have been a mere form. In its first period the church did of course concentrate the entire development of dogma in the doctrine of the person, or divine status, of Christ. All the dogma belonging to the content of the Christian faith that emerged then was just dogma as it more or less pertained to this main [christological] dogma.

Yet however high the standing of this dogma [of Christ's person], it is not in fact the most immediate and direct focus of Christian consciousness. Since Christ simply comes in order to bring messianic salvation, he himself just stands as the means to this end. So it must be the case that, in the development of the dogma, the one factor must be conditioned by the other. Throughout the entire history of dogma we can perceive how the doctrine of Christ's person, in the various forms in which it got elaborated, is simply the reflection and concrete expression of the view one has of the work of Christ, of the significance and nature of the messianic salvation he has brought about. Each age and each faction confers upon Christ's person all the characteristics that seem to be necessarily presupposed if he is capable of being the redeemer in the specific sense he was said to be.

The Christology of the Synoptic Gospels, and Paul's Christology

Since our standpoint involves a critical examination of the gospel story, there is one thing we should never forget. It is that what we know about Jesus' teaching as such, as well as all he himself teaches us about his personal significance and status, we know only through what the New Testament writers tell us. So in this instance too we have to keep the historical perspective strictly separate from the dogmatic perspective. Hence we can just confine ourselves here to the issue of how the person of Jesus is presented in the various theological frameworks within the canonical scriptures, since all else belongs in a domain involving, in one way or another, assumptions and contentions that are grounded dogmatically.[1]

With this understanding we first of all take up the christology of the Synoptic Gospels. It is incontestable that there is not the slightest justification for supposing that in the Synoptics we have anything more than the representation of a purely human Messiah. There can be no clearer proof that the idea of pre-existence still lies outside the Synoptics' horizons than the narrative of Jesus' supernatural birth. All that elevates him above the human level, but does not do away with the purely human element of his person, is simply traceable back to the causality operating in his conception. Or, in a different account, it is traceable back to the πνεῦμα ἅγιον (Holy Spirit) first imparted to him at his baptism, which, as the principle of the messianic epoch, is also constitutive of Jesus' own messianic person.

The substantial foundation of the Synoptics' christology is the concept of the Messiah, designated and conceived of as the υἱὸς θεοῦ (son of God). All the features of this concept rely on the same assumption of an inherently human nature. "But God raised him up, having freed him from death, because it was impossible for him to be

---

1. [*Ed.*] In referring below to the *Pseudo-Clementine Homilies*, Baur contrasts its "Jewish form of christology" with that "on the way to the Catholic dogma." But this "Jewish form of christology" is in the first instance that of Paul and the Synoptic Gospels. See my editorial introduction to Baur's *Lectures on New Testament Theology*, ed. P. C. Hodgson, trans. R. F. Brown (Oxford, 2016), pp. 32–38, 48–50. I argue that, according to Baur, Paul, despite his critique of Jewish particularism and the conflict over circumcision, interprets Christ and the redemption accomplished by his death in very Jewish categories; and that, likewise according to Baur, the Synoptic Gospels are heavily dependent on Old Testament texts and types for their portrayal of Jesus as the Messiah of Israel.

held in its power" (Acts 2:24). It is impossible that the Messiah be subject to death, for one subject to death would no longer be the Messiah. Therefore, even if the Messiah dies, in him death in itself is raised up into life, albeit not in the supernatural feature of his person, yet in his messianic stature. It is in this same sense that the concept of the Messiah involves his being the Prince [or Author] of life (Acts 3:15). The highest thing predicated of Christ by the Synoptics' christology is [Jesus' saying that] "all authority in heaven and on earth has been given to me" (Matt 28:18). In other words, he "sat down at the right hand of God" [Mark 16:19], which indicates that he shares directly in the divine power and governance of the world. As a human being, he is exalted to that place by his death and resurrection. The ascension is the point where this connection between heaven and earth is mediated. It is where he is even seen to float upward, in visible form, from earth to heaven.

Here we see clearly that the general perspective governing this christology is the elevation of the human to the divine; that, based on the concept of the Messiah, the human element is always also already given with the divine one. Over against this standpoint is that of the Johannine idea of the Logos, which makes the inherently divine element of Jesus' essential being the substantial concept of his person. There the entire thought process proceeds from above to below, not from below to above. According to it, the human element is only something secondary and just added on.

Pauline christology occupies a position of its own, one in between these other two mutually opposed standpoints. So in Paulinism we can get a handle on the transition from the Synoptics to John. On the one hand Paul's Christ is essentially a human being, while on the other hand he is more than that. In Christ the human aspect is already so augmented and idealized that he is in any event a human being in a different sense than in the Synoptics' way of envisioning Christ, which has him firmly based in the historical, human appearance of Jesus. Christ is a human being not merely according to one aspect of his essential nature, but absolutely so, because he is indeed a human being, like Adam. What distinguishes him from Adam is only that the distinctive element of his being is the pneumatic or spiritual element, not the psychical one. Notwithstanding his pneumatic nature, he is human, and what follows from this is just that both the pneumatic and the psychical aspects constitute an integral element of his human nature.

As opposed to the "one man" through whom sin and death "came into the world," there is "the one man, Jesus Christ" in whom "the grace of God . . . abounded for the many" (Rom 5:12, 15). "For since death came through a human being, the resurrection of the dead has also come through a human being" (1 Cor 15:21). "The first man was" like Adam, ["from the earth, a man of dust"]; "the second man is from heaven" (v. 47).[2] Thus Christ is essentially a man like Adam, only "man" in a higher sense. The

---

2. Important for a correct understanding of Pauline christology is the fact that the most recent critical authorities say κύριος (the Lord) does not belong in the text of 1 Cor 15:47. That obviously removes any obstacle to connecting "from heaven" directly with "man." Accordingly the Apostle says

question can only be: On the substantial foundation of human nature, what higher concept do we have to connect with the person of Christ?

The Apostle identifies the higher principle in Christ's person as the spiritual or "heavenly" element in him, but not as though a divine principle different from the human nature would have been first added to it. Instead the higher principle is just the purer form of the human nature itself. As the pneumatic human being who has come here from heaven or is of a heavenly origin, he is the archetypal human being, presenting within himself the fullness or perfection of human nature. Adam, as the earthly, psychical human, is the human being come under the power of sin and death; Christ, as the spiritual, heavenly man, as the one in whom the lower aspect of human nature is lifted up into the higher aspect, is the man without sin. An essential feature of the concept of Christ is that he "knew no sin" (2 Cor 5:21). Just as Adam, with the sin that initially began to express its power in him, also had within him the principle of death, so Christ, on the contrary, with freedom from sin was also free from death. Not only was Christ not subject to the principle of death; he also had within him instead the opposing principle of life, the life-giving spirit.

Hence although Christ had a bodily nature as all other human beings do, his σάρξ or flesh still had nothing of the principle of sin and death in it. Owing to his sinlessness, his flesh was only a ὁμοίωμα σαρκὸς ἁμαρτίας (likeness of sinful flesh) (Rom 8:3). As free from sin, Christ also ought not to have died. For he submitted to the necessity of death not on his own account, but only because he took upon himself the sins of human beings. This presupposes that the flesh is inherently mortal, even apart from sin. If the flesh of Christ is only a "likeness of sinful flesh"—since sin is not to be separated from the σάρξ inasmuch as it as such is the seat of sin, and it as such has in it a predisposition to sin and sin's seed, σάρξ as such[3]—then the σάρξ is a mere accident of Christ's being, the actual substance of which can only be the πνεῦμα or spirit.

As the Apostle states without qualification in 2 Cor 3:17, "Now the Lord [Christ] is the Spirit"—is spirit in himself, according to his substantial being. The Apostle conceived of the essence of spirit as spiritual light-substance, as a radiance or glory in the same sense as he speaks of the glory streaming from the face of Moses (2 Cor 3:7–18). God's own eternal being of light is mirrored in this glory of Christ (2 Cor 4:4). Christ's entire relation to God rests on the fact that Christ is essentially spirit, because it is inherent in God's spiritual nature of light to reflect himself in a radiance

---

both things about Christ in the same way: as a "man," he is "from heaven." [*Ed.*] If κύριος is included in the text, it would read: "the second man is the Lord from heaven."

3. The fact that, where the σάρξ is without sin, the Apostle just speaks of a "likeness of flesh," or where he mentions σάρξ and sin together he speaks of a "likeness of sinful flesh," proves in the clearest way that he thinks of ἁμαρτία or sin as the essence of the σάρξ itself. Where the σάρξ is not a sinful flesh, that is a σάρξ not having sin belonging to its essential being, that is not anything that can properly be called σάρξ. It is no "sinful flesh" and so not actually flesh; it is a mere "likeness," only something ὅμοιος, similar to flesh. Pauline christology distinguishes σάρξ (flesh) from σῶμα (body). There is a "spiritual body" (1 Cor 15:44), but there is no "spiritual flesh," because "flesh and blood cannot inherit the kingdom of God" (v. 50).

or glory. Hence just as Christ is spirit, so he is also "the Lord of glory" (1 Cor 2:8). He is essentially spirit and light, not just in consequence of his exaltation but inherently so, since by his exaltation he was simply able to attain the full realization of what he already was before it.

This of course also involves the idea of pre-existence. Although the pre-existing personal being (*Persönlichkeit*) of Christ is said to have been already essentially human, and to have been conceived of simply as the spiritual light-figure of the heavenly or archetypal human being, analogously to how the *Pseudo-Clementine Homilies* depicts the primal human being who first came forth from God, this personal being is also called "the Spirit of Christ" in virtue of the wisdom dwelling with God's eternity, or the Holy Spirit, which, by indwelling Christ in the highest sense, accordingly constitutes his very own essential being. Hence the Apostle Paul must have assumed a twofold primal human being: an earthly being who from the outset was from [i.e., made of] earth and a psychical nature; and a heavenly, archetypal nature pre-existing in heaven until, as "the second man . . . from heaven" (1 Cor 15:47), he appeared in the flesh at the appointed time as the "second Adam," in other words as the ἔσχατος, the "last one," as he is called with regard to his earthly appearance in inaugurating the second or final period of the world. However, this is all we can say about how the Apostle conceived of Christ's birth in the flesh and his entry into humanity. Although when Galatians 4:4 and Romans 8:3 speak about "the sending of the Son," they presuppose that he already existed, we still just have here the same pre-existence as in the phrase "from heaven" in 1 Cor 15:47. These passages too provide no further information about the way in which Christ came to appear in the flesh.

On the whole, Pauline christology is marked by the fact that, while it presupposes Christ's pre-existence, the Apostle is forward-looking rather than focused on what Christ was beforehand. Romans 1:3–6, which is important for Paul's christology, is to be understood especially from this perspective. Here the Apostle assembles all the elements belonging to the messianic standing and role of Christ. As descended from David, he is the Messiah. But a more important measure of his messianic status is his resurrection from the dead. What Christ is bodily as son of David, he is spiritually because of his resurrection. His resurrection is the spiritual attestation to his messianic status, because the resurrection was able to provide the factual demonstration that the Spirit, which made him alone to be the Messiah, was also truly in him. This is the concept of the πνεῦμα ἁγιωσύνης (spirit of holiness). It is the Holy Spirit inasmuch as it produces the holiness through which Christ is the holy one and Christians are the saints; that is, it is active as the messianic principle and it realizes the idea of messiahship.

If we combine this with the other elements of the Pauline christology, then the concept of Christ's personal being is spelled out as follows. 1) In himself, Christ is spirit with regard to his substantial, essential being; and Christ's spiritual nature of its own accord comprises within it the concept of pre-existence, in the ideal figure of the primal human being. 2) As the essential element of Christ's personal being, the spirit becomes, in Christ's earthly-human appearing, the messianic spirit; it becomes the spirit of holiness. 3) Just as Christ first makes himself known as God's Son in the highest sense by the resurrection, so the spirit of holiness first shows itself in its full import through its being active as the πνεῦμα ζωοποιοῦν (life-giving spirit) (1 Cor 15:45). What the messianic spirit is for the person of Christ himself, the life-giving spirit is for humankind in general, as the life-principle working within it, abolishing sin and death within it, and transfiguring the mortal σάρξ into the image of the heavenly human being. The idea presenting itself in Christ as the primal human being is then fully realized when all humanity is "conformed to the image of his Son" as God ordained it (Rom 8:29).[4]

The teaching about Christ's higher status was first solidified in dogmatic terms by the Apostle Paul. Even though the more exalted concept of his person was, of its own accord, a feature in the belief in Jesus' resurrection and exaltation, and in his messianic status that this belief in effect confirmed, the important thing was then to understand the particular elements of this belief. The resurrection was the initial point from which the entire development proceeded. People could not think of the risen one, who through his resurrection had become the victor over death and had entered into a higher life, without envisaging him in a state of glorification and supremely close to God. Thus he became the subject of all those characteristics comprised in the idea of the Lord, as he was called without qualification, in keeping with his exaltation.

However, everything people ascribed to Christ as the risen one, and as elevated to the right hand of the Father, still lacked a sufficient basis if he had no equally illustrious pre-earthly condition comparable to his post-earthly state of glorification. Thus

---

4. One question remains. Although Christ was "from heaven," does his designation as the "second man" and the "last Adam" just date only from his earthly-human appearing? But what is Christ supposed to have been as spirit if his spiritual, personal being is not conceptualized in the form of human existence? The effort was made to apply to the Pauline christology as well the contention that the pre-existing subject appearing in Jesus is to be thought of as an angel, in conformity with an especially popular notion widespread in the earliest church based on combining angelology with the messianic idea already present in Judaism (J. Hellwag, "Die Vorstellung von der Präexistenz Christi in den ältesten Kirche," *Theologische Jahrbücher* 7 [1848] 239ff.). However, there is no trace in Paul of Christ being an angel or an angel-like being, and we have no right to devalue one of two representations in favor of the other: his being spirit, and his being essentially human. The Apostle Paul unquestionably makes it very plain in 1 Cor 8:6 that he attributes to Christ not merely pre-existence but also the creation of the world. On the other hand it also cannot be denied that, just as the context of the phrase "from whom are all things" points to "God," the context of "through whom are all things" is the concept of "the Lord." Here the concept of the Lord refers only to what Christ became by his resurrection and exaltation, not to what he was in his state prior to the world. If (as stated above) "the Lord" does not belong in the text of 1 Cor 15:47, then that passage too is no exception with regard to the meaning associated with the term κύριος (Lord). Anyhow, the passages in 1 Cor 10:4 [Christ, "the spiritual rock"] and 2 Cor 8:9 ["our Lord Jesus Christ"] are no proof to the contrary. In their regard we simply see how arbitrarily people have expanded and diluted the concept of Christ's divinity in Pauline christology. On this issue, see my book, *Paulus, der Apostel Jesu Christi. Sein Leben und Wirken, seine Briefe und seine Lehre* (Stuttgart, 1845), 623.

people could arrive at a more lofty picture of Christ's personal being only if he was essentially the same already before his appearing humanly on earth. Then people could no longer look upon Christ's having been elevated to a higher status after his death as merely an extraordinary role just bestowed on him by an act of God. This status was inherently due him; it was inherently grounded in the essence of his personal being; hence his human existence was for him only a moment he passed through in order to be, also in this concrete form determined by his human existence, what he actually was in himself.

The idea of pre-existence is now the main point around which the further development of christology then takes place. The tendency of this development is entirely to do away, as much as possible, with the distinction between God and Christ, by linking the condition of pre-existence ever more with the predicates that accomplish this. Indeed the Apostle Paul advances from the idea of pre-existence to the idea of the world's creation. Although in his case this predicate of world-creator still has an indeterminate and ambiguous character, soon after him it took on a more definite meaning. The Apostle Paul was the one who gave this higher impetus to christology, and that is without question linked to the more exalted way in which he depicts Christ's calling and what Christ does.

Paul was the first to understand Christianity from a higher and more universal perspective, and to recognize its significance as that of a general principle shaping the entire course of the world and the path of humanity's development. This standpoint gave Paul the vision, as his necessary presupposition, that Christ must be more than human, a supraworldly being. This vision was then the beginning of the process by which the concept of Christ's person got increasingly enhanced, right up to his absolute oneness with God, and every analogous feature that contemporary philosophy had to offer got assigned to him.

The Christology of the Book of Revelation

The christology of the Book of Revelation comes next in time after the christology of Paul. It too follows the same trustworthy rule of thumb, according to which the greater the anticipated denouement accompanying Christ's parousia, the more exalted must be the representation of the person who brings it about by his parousia. In the same way as we saw in the Apostle Paul's case, the Christ of the Apocalypse also attains supreme divine power and glory through his death and resurrection.

The author of Revelation brings together the greatest and the least matters, the antithesis of life and death, of heaven and earth, in one and the same vivid picture of the "Lamb that was slaughtered" (5:6 and 12; 13:8) standing before the throne of God. Christ, in the direct presence of God, not only shares with God the same power and dominion, the same adoration; he also receives predicates that seem to allow for no essential difference between him and God. In the same sense in which God is called the ruler of all things, he "who is and who was and who is to come," Christ too is called "the Alpha and the Omega," the beginning and the end (1:8).

The "new name" given to the Messiah (3:12), the name "that no one knows but himself" (19:12), is the name "Jehovah," which is not to be uttered. Indeed, Christ not only has as his attribute "the seven spirits of God" (3:1), the individualized form of the power of the divine governance of the world, overseeing and ruling over all things; he is also the "origin of God's creation" (3:14) and "the Word of God" (19:13). Yet all these predicates are just externally related to the person of the Messiah. The Messiah is of course called Jehovah, or God in the highest sense. But that is only a way of speaking about him and does not allow us to infer from this name that a truly divine nature is ascribed to him as well.

The same applies to designating the Messiah as "The Word of God." The writer considers Jesus' entire appearing under the heading of the word of God, inasmuch as he both discloses and fulfills it. Christianity itself is the "word of God" (1:9), and all the constituents of the apocalyptic visions' contents are "true words of God" (19:9). Jesus is he who reveals God's decree and also carries it out. What has once been expressed as God's decree must also be realized. In this context too Jesus is the word of God. Here Jesus' efficacy is compared to a sharp sword coming from his mouth (19:15). The fact that this sword emerges from his mouth clearly points to the sword in fact being likened to the word proceeding from his mouth, the word of God that he reveals. It is a sharp sword inasmuch as Jesus carries out God's entire decree with irresistible power, as strict punishment. That is why he is first called by this name, "The Word of God," in this passage (19:13) of the Book of Revelation, where he descends from heaven to the earth as a judge who punishes. The basic concept is the word of God, in other words the divine will and decree carrying itself out in the strictness of the divine punishment.

Since this expression involves no metaphysical concept and articulates nothing about a relationship belonging intrinsically to the nature of the subject or individual in question, it also makes evident the sense in which to take the additional, and even more especially remarkable, predicate that Revelation gives to Jesus when it describes him as the "origin of God's creation" (3:14). Although, as the beginning of creation, Jesus is just the first one created, this phrase still clearly enough seems to involve the concept of pre-existence. But if, on the other hand, we ponder that, just previously, the heavenly name of the Messiah is called a "new name" (3:12), and that nowhere else in this entire scripture is the pre-existence of the Messiah clearly enunciated, then it is very likely that this is no dogmatic designation. Instead it is merely an honorific, an intensified way of expressing the notion that, upon creation, the Messiah is the highest creature to which consideration would have been given from the outset.

The Book of Revelation's christology thus has the distinctive feature that, as a rule, while it does indeed confer the highest predicates on Jesus as the Messiah, all these predicates are just terms transferred to him in external fashion, ones lacking an internal connection with the essence of his person. Still missing is an internal interplay between the divine predicates and the historical individual said to bear or possess them.[5] Hence it is remarkable how, even at this time, Christian consciousness contained the impulse to give such high standing to the person of Jesus. But we can hardly overlook how the whole sum and substance of these predicates is nevertheless a transcendent form, one having no concrete contents grounded in Jesus' own personal being. These predicates are still no immanent features arising from the substantial being of Jesus' person itself. It is simply for the sake of the major eschatological expectations that the Messiah, as their main subject, must also have sufficient standing. Any metaphysical content remains beyond the horizons of the Book of Revelation. It still looks at things from here below and soon after the Messiah's death, in assigning to him everything that gives him a higher, divine status. See Rev 5:12.[6]

---

5. See Eduard Zeller, "Beiträge zur Einleitung in die Apokalypse," *Theologische Jahrbücher* 1 (1842) 709ff.

6. [*Ed.*] Rev 5:12 has myriads of angels sing: "Worthy is the Lamb that was slaughtered to receive power and wealth and wisdom and might and honor and glory and blessing!"

Christology in the Epistle to the Hebrews, and in the Deutero-Pauline Epistles

The Epistle to the Hebrews and the Deutero-Pauline Epistles mark a further stage in christology's development, one in which Christ is now already understood as an inherently divine being.

The concept of the Son is the fundamental christological concept in Hebrews. It is as the Son of God in the strict sense that Christ is the subject of all the predicates assigned to him here. As the Son, Christ is the radiance, the direct reflection, of God's glory. He is the one who intrinsically bears "the exact imprint of God's very being" (1:3) in the concrete reality of his personal existence. In virtue of this, Hebrews places Christ, as the Son of God, utterly above the world. He is an essentially divine being, different from the world. He does share with the world the fact that, like everything else, he has proceeded from God, which we see in his being called, in 1:6, the πρωτότοκος or firstborn one. And yet he is the one who "sustains all things by his powerful word" (1:3), the one through whom God "created the worlds" (1:2), the present world and the world to come, or the visible world and the invisible world. The christology of Hebrews takes itself so far above the human dimension that it sets out first of all to pinpoint precisely the concept of the Son as being distinct from the angels, with the Son transcending them by far. It does so by reserving the term "Son" for him alone, and by the other predicates it assigns to him (1:4–14).

In general terms, therefore, the christology of Hebrews is intermediate between the christologies of Paul and John. Whereas, for the Apostle Paul, however highly Christ is placed he is still always essentially a human being, the "second man, from heaven," the author of Hebrews completely sets aside the "primal human being" aspect. For him Christ, as a purely divine being, is assigned to the supersensible realm. On the other hand, however, the Son is still not the Logos in the Johannine sense. He is not the Logos, but instead just "sustains all things by his powerful word" (1:3). So it is rather odd that the writer of Hebrews stops at this point and does not go on to identify the Son with the Logos, since he does to some extent personify the Logos of God (4:12–13), and that naturally leads to treating the two concepts as identical.

Notwithstanding this construal of the Logos of God as a real existent (*dieser Hypostasirung*), the two concepts, Son and Logos, are nevertheless hardly interrelated. The concept of the Pneuma or Spirit, not the concept of the Logos, is what defines the divine nature of the Son. The reconciling power of Christ's death rests on his being "the eternal Spirit" (9:14). He reconciles the world with God because he offers himself to God in the element of the Spirit; because the eternal Spirit, not the blood of rams and bulls, is the means of atonement, the factor determining and mediating the actual nature and efficacy of this death. What makes Christ the eternal high priest, what gives him the power of indissoluble life such that the absolute life-principle is an immanent characteristic of his being, is the Spirit, the fact that he is a purely spiritual being, just as God himself is Spirit and "the Father of spirits" (12:9).

At the same time the writer thinks of the Son's relation to the Father as one of strict subordination. The Son is so dependent on the Father that the Father is the active subject even in matters directly involving the Son. The Father has "for a little while" made the Son "lower than angels" (2:7).[7] "So also Christ did not glorify himself in becoming a high priest, but was appointed by the one who said to him, 'You are my Son, today I have begotten you'" (5:5). This statement is from Psalms 2:7, which Hebrews cites as in principle involving the concept of sonship. This account of sonship can only be understood as a relationship established by God's will, whereas the terms "radiance" and "imprint" (1:3) signify it as a natural relationship. Thus in Hebrews the elements of these two representations of the relationship of the Father and the Son always form the main antithesis. Since in either of these ways the Son is, in himself, a divine being, human existence is something he must first enter into.

In any event the writer of Hebrews does not yet see his path to a well-defined concept of the incarnation. He only says about it that Christ became like human beings in all ways: in their moral weakness, by his being susceptible to temptation or testing (2:18); in their powerlessness and finitude, by his being made "lower than the angels" (2:6–9); and above all by his own ability to suffer. As this incarnation took place for the purpose of redemption, with Christ, as the eternally appointed high priest cleansing human beings of their sin, what we have on the whole here is the idea of a process of moral development as the perspective from which to understand the whole of Christ's personal being. Because of Christ's submission, God heard his prayer for rescue from destruction and death. Christ was brought back from the realm of the dead (13:20), was taken up again into heaven, and once more exalted above the angels he had been made lower than (4:14, 7:26, 1:4). He was "crowned with glory and honor" and with joy (2:9; cf. 1:9, 12:2), and received a seat at the right hand of God forever (1:3, 8 and 13; 8:1; 10:12).

All of this together makes up the concept of the consummation in which, as Hebrews sees it, the end gets integrated with the beginning. The process taking its course in the person of Jesus simply presents the universal process in which the imperfect

---

7. [*Ed.*] Heb. 2:6–7 says this about human beings, but 2:9 says it about Jesus.

raises itself up to what is perfect, the present gives way to the world to come, and Judaism is succeeded by Christianity. In sum, the idea works its way through its still untrue shape in order to attain its true, concrete reality. The idea of the high priest is already prefigured in the Old Testament in the person of Melchizedek. It is realized when the true high priest, offering up himself and by his death putting an end to the imperfect Levitical priesthood, and striding through the heavens with his blood, appears before the face of God and takes his seat at the right hand of glory, on the throne of grace (9:11, 10:12).

The christology of the Deutero-Pauline Epistles has this same character, except that what emerges in them, indeed in a more specific form, is the speculative, metaphysical perspective related to the Gnostic ways of thinking as they pertain to the person of Christ.

Here too, in a manner similar to Hebrews, Christ in his inherently divine nature is called "the image" of God (Col 1:15). He is the reflection of God in which the intrinsically invisible essence of God is beheld in visible form. This passage goes on to state, more specifically, that "in him all things in heaven and on earth were created, things visible and invisible, whether thrones or dominions or rulers or powers" (v. 16). Thus everything from the highest regions of the spirit world down to what is below has its being and continued existence in him. This no longer has to do merely with using the concept of the Son to give him his specific place as opposed to the angels. Here he already has the significance of a principle mediating between God and the world, as someone standing absolutely at the apex of all spiritual beings. As "the firstborn of all creation" (Col 1:15), he is indeed placed in the same sequence with creatures. Although he is prior in time and in rank to all the other creatures, he is nevertheless created by God as they are. But inasmuch as he supports and sustains all else that is created, it all has the substantial ground of its unity in him; he stands absolutely over all else. Thus Christ is absolutely different from the world, but at the same time his relation to the world can only be described as an immanent relation to it.

This is indeed how we are to understand Col 1:16 when it says all things were created "in him," rather than saying "through him." This way of speaking most especially involves carrying over to Christ the unusual concept of the πλήρωμα (pleroma, or fullness), where Christ's immanent relation to the church is understood simply as the more concrete form of the general relationship in which he stands to the world as such. Ephesians and Colossians both have the specific concept that Christ is the pleroma, because it is in Christ that the intrinsically self-existent God first comes forth from his abstract being and opens himself up to the fullness of concrete life (Col 1:19; 2:9; Eph 1:22–23; 3:19; and 4:13). Christ is the pleroma in the highest or absolute sense. He is the one "who fills all in all" (Eph 1:23). He is the pleroma or fullness of God, as the one in whom what God is, in an abstractly ideal way, fills itself with its specifically concrete and real content. The pleroma of Christ is the church, as the concretely real being with which Christ fills himself as his own content. The term "pleroma" designates a concretely real being, as the content of another being with which this pleroma combines in a unity of form and contents.

The concept of the σῶμα (body) functions in a way similar to that of the pleroma. The church is "the body of Christ" (Eph 1:23, 4:12). However, Christ himself is also called the body, for he is the body of the deity inasmuch as "in him the whole fullness of deity"—what fills the idea of deity with its specific, concrete content—"dwells bodily" (Col 2:9). But if he is himself the body of the deity, then the church can only be his body in a more concrete sense since, as the body of the deity, he is the head of the church and the principle on which the whole, internally articulated organism of the church depends (Eph 4:16; Col 2:19).

These ways of designating Christ's relation to the church first acquire their full meaning from the general idea underlying the christology of these epistles. Christ's being the head of all things, their principle and central point, is the expression in his person of a general idea taking the form of a definite worldview. It belongs to the essence of the idea (as such) that it also is in reality what it is in itself. Therefore the idea embodied in the person of Christ must also realize itself in a series of specific moments. This takes place through the "gathering up" (ἀνακεφαλαιώσασθαι) of all things in Christ (Eph 1:10), through his "reconciling" (ἀποκαταλλάξαι) all things to himself (Col 1:20). This is the basic idea of the two epistles. Everything proceeds from him and so everything is said to be brought back once more to its unity in him. The work of Christ is, in this sense, considered to be the overall reconciliation and unification of the entire universe. This includes not merely the earth but also the underworld, the entire universe insofar as it is inhabited by rational beings. Christ's redeeming activity extends to all of it, filling all things with its influence and linking together what is highest and what is lowest (Eph 4:8–10). Everything must surely be recapitulated or summed up in Christ and be reconnected to that original unity, in which it has the substantial ground of its being and continued existence in him.

The Epistle to the Philippians operates within the same outlook, insofar as it not merely distinguishes the "form of God" from "the form of a slave" or servant (Phil 2:6–7), but also sets "being equal to God" in contrast to "being in the form of God." Thus here too Christ must make his way through the specific moments of an ongoing process. Only after he has actualized his inherently divine nature on the path of moral striving, by his obedience being tested, is Christ what he is in himself—also truly and in actuality possessing the full reality of divine being.[8]

---

8. On the christology of the Epistle to the Hebrews and that of the Deutero-Pauline Epistles, see: K. R. Köstlin, *Der Lehrbuch des Evangeliums and der Briefe Johannis* (Berlin, 1842), 352ff., 387ff.; Albert Schwegler, *Das nachapostolische Zeitalter* (Tübingen, 1846), 2:286 ff; my book *Paulus, der Apostel Jesu Christi* (Stuttgart, 1845), 417ff., and articles ("Zur neutestamentlichen Kritik" and "Ueber Philipper 2, 6 f.") in the *Theologische Jahrbücher* 8 (1849) 501ff., and 11 (1852) 133ff. See the latter articles also for the christology of Philippians, and on the denial that Gnostic ideas can simply explain a "robbery" (ἁρπαγμός) by which the one existing "in the form of God," but still not identical with God to the point of "being equal to God," would have anticipated attaining, directly and powerfully, without such

The Johannine Concept of the Logos

If we set the christology developed thus far alongside the Johannine form, we see that there is not far to go to reach Johannine christology. The only thing basically remaining is to conceptualize and express in a more specific way the elements already at hand. This is what the Johannine concept of the Logos did.

The supreme expression of all that constitutes the distinctive contents of Christian consciousness with regard to the person of Jesus is found in the concept of the Logos. This concept indeed designates as God the very same subject that, in his appearing outwardly in time, is the human being Jesus, in describing him as an independent divine nature standing in the most direct connection with God. In John 1:1, the statement θεὸς ἦν ὁ λόγος, "the Word was God," the Logos, although not declared to be the absolute God, is declared to be God, in other words a divine being.

Indeed the concept of the Logos and the entire description given of him entails that he can only be thought of as a divine being subsistent on his own. This is also indicated in particular by the fact that he is said to have been πρὸς τὸν θεόν or "with God" (1:2), and is the one ὢν εἰς τὸν κόλπον τοῦ πατρός, "who is close to the Father's heart" (1:18). The particular way in which εἶναι is linked with εἰς ("to be close to"), and πρός is linked with the accusative case ["with God"] is supposed to signify that the Logos being "with God" is not merely a passive state but instead an active state; that the Logos is in constant activity and motion, and that the object of his activity and motion is the essential being of God. It expresses his immanent relation to God in virtue of the fact that, as the one "who is close to the Father's heart," he is, so to speak, active himself in the heart of God; and that, in his oneness with God, he seeks to cancel out everything that separates and distinguishes him from God. However, this very feature also presupposes that he is at the same time aware of the distinction of his person from God. The absoluteness of his own being thus resides in the interpenetration (*Ineinandersein*) of these two elements, in that his relation to God is just as much distinction in unity as it is unity in distinction.

---

arrangements, what he should have attained but only could do so by the route of a moral mediation. In the background here is the Gnostic version of their Aeon's well-known outrageous deed that brings about the unnatural but sudden rift between the finite and absolute domains and is to that extent metaphysically necessary. [*Ed.*] On "robbery" (rather than "exploitation") as a translation of ἁρπαγμός in Phil 2:6, see Baur's *Lectures on New Testament Theology* (n. 1), 264 n. 46.

However, that the gospel writer signified this higher divine standing, the status he wanted to ascribe to Jesus, by making such unequivocal and unqualified use of the concept of the Logos, can only be explained by the fact that this Logos-idea was not at all foreign to the ideas in circulation in the time and place at which this Gospel appeared. We all know how significant the Logos-idea indeed was in the Alexandrian religious philosophy. It would contravene every analogous historical situation if we wanted to assume that the gospel writer arrived at his teaching about the Logos wholly apart from contemporary conceptions, entirely unrelated to the Logos-idea so widespread at that time. Of course he could not have taken the content of the Logos-idea itself from the contemporary philosophy, for, if this content would not already have been an essential feature of Christian consciousness—that is, owing to Christ's higher status, placing him in the relationship of identity with God, a relation the Logos concept expresses—then the writer could not have thought to carry over to Christ this conception widespread at that time. Therefore we can simply think of the matter as follows. If the higher standing Christian consciousness assigned to Christ was to be conceptualized and expressed in a specific way, then it seems this could be done in no more adequate way than via the Logos concept. What can have facilitated doing so, as a mediating factor, is that the Christian teaching, whose source is Jesus, was called "the Logos of God" or even just "the Logos," or Word. The Book of Revelation too calls Jesus the Word of God.

With the concept of the Logos we must always hold fast to the meaning "word," that is, "instrument of revelation," for the term Logos also means "reason," but only inasmuch as thinking is also a speaking. However, the Gospel of John also stands very closely related to the Gnostic set of ideas, in fact closely related to the Gnostic teaching about the Aeons, where the same concepts—λόγος (word), ζωή (life), φῶς (light), πλήρωμα (fullness), χάρις (grace), ἀλήθεια (truth)—are found in a wholly analogous combination. The evident difference is the distinctiveness and practical character of the original Christian way of looking at things. By setting aside all those multifarious representations that the Gnostic imagination and speculation uses to fill out the supersensible world, the Gospel of John just holds firmly to the single concept of the Logos, and in it captures all those points that, for Christian consciousness, were said to count as the highest expression of how it viewed Christ's person.

But however precise the distinction one may draw between form and content in the Johannine Logos concept, even with reference to the elements already at hand, the adoption of this idea in Johannine christology can only be explained from the fact that the Gospel writer shares, with the Alexandrine religious philosophy and Christian Gnosis, the same standpoint of the absolute idea of God. The Logos-idea in the higher sense can only find its place where God's essential nature, in its purely abstract being-in-itself (*Ansichsein*), is removed to such transcendent heights that God's relationship to the world can be mediated only by an instrument of revelation such as the Logos. Yet the more transcendent this way of looking at things is, the more too we have here, as Philo of Alexandria already had, the same incompatible representations. On the one hand, the entire significance of the Logos rests on the fact that, because the most high God himself cannot come into any direct contact with what is finite, the Logos is a being different from God; on the other hand, however, if the divine is to be communicated to the world, the Logos must be identical with God.[9]

The gospel writer himself has expressed in clear terms his absolute standpoint in apprehending the idea of God. "No one has ever seen God" (1:18), because God's essential being as such absolutely transcends everything finite and is, by its nature, invisible. God and spirit are utterly identical concepts (4:24). This transcendence makes it necessary to have a being mediating God's relation to the world. This is the concept of the Logos as the divine instrument of revelation. However, the Logos can only be such a one in his direct oneness with God. Only as the only begotten Son, who is in the bosom or heart of the Father, can he reveal and express what, apart from him, is, for human beings, closed off in God's absolute, essential nature. In this identity with God, the Logos is the only begotten Son (1:14, 18). Since the Logos is explicitly called "God," then the predication "Son" simply refers to his essential being in common (*Wesensgemeinschaft*) with God. Of its own accord the concept of the Son involves the concept of begetting. He is not created, in the way the world and all that exists have been created through him. Instead he is begotten, and therefore in the Gospel of John the term "Son of God" has an entirely different significance than it has in the Synoptic Gospels. What the "children of God, who were born . . . of God" are in a relative way, he, as the only begotten, is in an absolute way (1:13–14). Therefore, God is his Father in a wholly distinctive way (5:18; 10:36).

The basic concept of this relation is the concept of oneness with God and equivalence to God. As Son, the Logos is so very much one with the Father that the Son is in fact simply the concrete appearing of the Father. "Whoever has seen me has seen the Father" (14:9). "The Father and I are one" (10:30; cf. 10:38 and 17:21). The Father and the Logos, or Son, are indeed two distinct persons, with each of the two having his own personal self-consciousness. However, the distinction of persons is superseded by the fact that each of the two recognizes his own personal self in that of the other. The oneness binding the two of them together therefore can, in the relation of oneness, be defined simply as a moral relationship, although doing so posits as just a free act what belongs intrinsically to its essential nature. Each one of the two relinquishes

---

9. See Eduard Zeller, *Die Philosophie der Griechen*, 3 vols. (Tübingen, 1844–52), 3.2:627. In *Die philonische Philosophie in ihrem Hauptmomenten*, 2nd ed. (Gothenburg, 1858), Maurice Wolff states on p. 20: "The absolute, existent in itself, makes itself objective in the Logos, becomes concrete, a spirit living within itself; whereas when it is understood merely from the perspective of being, the absolute is the wholly contentless, abstract God. Being is only one element of the divine, and the deity becomes fulfilled only in unity with the other element, the Logos, in which God appears as spirit, as living, creative spirit. The divine becomes an other to itself, although this other is not something foreign to it, something separate from it. Instead the other is within it." God is essentially both at the same time, but also only in unmediated fashion.

his own self to that of the other, so that he knows himself to be one with the other and merges his own self-consciousness in that of the other.

In virtue of this oneness in their essential nature and will, the Son also has truly divine attributes in his human appearance. "For just as the Father has life in himself" in an absolute and original way, "so also does the Son through the impartation of the Father" (5:26). The absolute power of the Father also belongs to the Son; the Son works with it (5:19–23), and there is likewise no limit to his knowledge (1:49–51; 2:25; 4:19; 6:64; 11:4 and 14).

In this oneness with God, the Logos is the supreme instrument of revelation. But since he proves to be active in the world, as such an instrument and as the principle of light and life for human beings, he has his antithesis in the darkness. The more deeply he enters into the world of antitheses, the more the other side of his nature comes to the fore in him, the finite and human character that belongs to him as distinct from God. The Logos is not only "the light shining in the darkness" (1:5); he is also "[the Word] become flesh" (1:14), with all that results from appearing in the flesh.

The incarnation of the Logos is the transition from the eternal Logos, existent in himself, to the historical Messiah appearing in the person Jesus. Here as nowhere else it is so evident both how disconnected are the two aspects the idea of the Logos comprises, and how different Johannine christology is from the christology of the Synoptic Gospels. While the Synoptics have the Messiah, who is the subject of the gospel account, first beginning to exist concretely through the working of the Holy Spirit, and they display Jesus' birth most vividly as the starting point of the gospel story,[10] the Gospel of John is content with the simple statement, "the Word became flesh" (1:14). So John's account hardly seems to allow for further analysis. Yet at the same time the incongruity between the human and divine elements in the Johannine Christ is unmistakable.

Indeed the true sense of the term σάρξ or "flesh" not only calls to mind simply a body assumed by the Logos; also, in the context of the prologue to John, the phrase σὰρξ ἐγένετο ("became flesh," 1:14) can be understood as his flesh being merely a secondary characteristic. From the beginning the Logos is so decidedly the same self-identical subject that, in the entire course of his operations, nothing can arise that would have made him for the first time into this specific subject, or into a different subject than he was before. His existing in the world already has its full reality in that he is the light shining in the darkness.

Just as the Logos is the same subject from the beginning, so too those who in faith become one with him are, in the same circumstance, already "children of God" (1:12). For those who receive him into themselves, the incarnation of the Logos is just the highest manifestation of his glory. Hence "becoming flesh" by no means has the significance it apparently has to have as the act of in fact "becoming human." "Became

---

10. [*Ed.*] With the exception, of course, of the Gospel of Mark, which begins with the baptism of Jesus.

flesh" was only an accidental feature of the personhood of the Logos, which remains forever self-identical.

But if this statement "became flesh" has once established, as utter fact, the identity of the Logos with the historical person of Jesus, then the entire gospel account is essentially the self-presentation of the Logos. The Logos identical with the person of Jesus presents himself in Jesus' works, his teaching and his death. In all these settings what matters is that, in faith in his person, he be recognized as the one he inherently is. This very self-presentation of Jesus as the Logos is also his ongoing glorification, and his death is its most important element. In the Gospel of John the resurrection has a spiritualized meaning, in the coming of the Lord in the Spirit, which is identical with it. Thus in him the end comes together with the beginning in the most inward way. Jesus returns to the Father from whom he has come, returning "to where he was before" (6:62). For, prior to this, before he came into the world and became flesh, he was the purely divine Logos not yet become flesh. Thus he cannot subsequently be anything other than the Logos. So what necessarily follows from this is that, because he is indeed simply "the spirit that gives life," whereas "the flesh is useless" (6:63), he also in turn set aside the earthly shell of the flesh he initially assumed, in order to be purely the one he is in himself, in immediate oneness with the Father, with whom he can only be one in spirit, as the Father himself is utterly spirit in the highest, absolute sense (4:24).[11]

---

11. See my *Kritische Untersuchungen über die kanonischen Evangelien* (Tübingen, 1847), 77ff.

The Apostolic Fathers and the Early Church Fathers

The overwhelming tendency in John is to grasp Jesus' whole appearing and his person from the standpoint of his supersensible being, and to subordinate the human dimension to the divine one in such a way that the entire reality of his personal being falls on the side of the divine nature; or else just to say that the two aspects, the divine and the human, stand side-by-side, are unconnected. The way the Logos-idea had become, in the Gospel of John, the firm foothold for Christian consciousness, reached the point from which Christian dogma could go on to develop its own specific theological contents.

Even by the middle of the second century, however, the Logos-idea, with the essential features the Johannine theological framework attached to it, was by no means so firmly established that it could pass muster as the objective expression of the collective dogmatic consciousness, as one would rightly have expected had there been widespread familiarity with the Gospel of John since the end of the first century. At that time dogmatic consciousness instead still wavers for a long time between two different conceptions until, in the second half of the second century, the Logos-idea in its Johannine form gradually becomes the overarching view. The following three elements should be considered in this context.

The first element is the principal concept used to designate the divine aspect of Christ's person. It is not the concept of the Logos but the concept of the spirit, and there are two versions of it. The first version understands the spirit to be the spiritual principle belonging on the whole to the essence of God. The second one regards the spirit as an angel, as one of the natures in which the spiritual principle individualizes itself in a concrete form of its existence. We find the first version in the *Epistles* of Clement of Rome, and to an extent in the *Epistle* of Barnabas. This view distinguishes the divine in Christ as spirit, from the human element, his body.[12] The second version seems to be the view of the *Shepherd* of Hermas, in which the Son of God, who is more ancient than all the creatures and stood as advisor at the Father's side during the

---

12. See the second *Epistle* of Clement of Rome to the Corinthians, ch. 9, and the *Epistle* of Barnabas, ch. 7. [*Ed.*] The second epistle is no longer ascribed to Clement.

act of creating, and who supports and upholds the entire creation, is indeed termed the *spiritus sanctus* (holy spirit), but only in the sense in which the angels as such are "holy spirits."[13] This was a very widespread and popular conception in the earliest church, and also typical of the Ebionites, in thinking of the pre-existent subject appearing in Jesus as an angel. In Justin Martyr too his angelology seems very closely connected with his christology.[14] So this enabled people to think of the incarnation too as just the assumption of a body, and of the body as only the vessel in which the spirit resides.[15]

The second element also appears where the Logos-idea is already applied to Christ. But here it is such a nonspecific and fluid concept that it cannot be straightforwardly identified with the Johannine concept of the Logos. It still has no more specific dogmatic significance when the first *Epistle* of Clement of Rome (ch. 27) states about God that "by the word of his might he established all things, and by his word he can overthrow them." But we can simply understand Christ as being "the word of his might," and likewise "the scepter of his majesty" (ch. 16) and "the brightness of his majesty" (ch. 36). In the Pseudo-Ignatian *Epistles* even where God is made the subject directly identical with Christ in the patripassian sense, only the lack of a more specific spelling out of the Logos-idea deters an interpretation along the lines of Clement.[16] However, when in these very epistles Christ is not merely called the one who has come forth from the one Father and gone back to this one, but also, as the Son of God through whom the one God has revealed himself, Christ is called God's "everlasting Logos, not coming forth from silence," then this gets quite close to the Johannine concept of the Logos.[17]

These factors must make it seem odd that for Justin Martyr, in contrast, the representation of the Logos, so frequent in him too, nevertheless hardly concurs with the Johannine concept. For Justin, Christ, or the Son of God, is a being numerically or personally distinct from God. He is begotten by the Father or, from an emanationist perspective, he proceeded from the Father as fire kindles more fire without a lessening of its substance. The Son is the first-born of the entire creation who was already together with the Father prior to the creation, and the Father created everything through him. The Son himself is also God, although, notwithstanding all these predicates, he is so subordinated to the Father that, seeing as he is indeed also expressly called the servant of the world's creator, he belongs only in the category of beings through whose

---

13. Hermas, *Shepherd*, Similitude 9, ch. 12; and Similitude 5, chs. 2ff. [esp. ch. 5].

14. See Justin, *First Apology*, ch. 6; Hermas, Similitude 5, ch. 6; Epiphanius, *Against Heresies* 30.3, 16.

15. On this form of the most ancient christology and the data pertaining to it, see in particular the treatise by J. Hellwag, "Die Vorstellung von der Präexistenz Christi in der ältesten Kirche," *Theologische Jahrbücher* 7 (1848) 144ff.; and A. Hilgenfeld, *Die apostolische Väter* (Halle, 1853), 169ff.

16. See Ignatius, *Epistle to the Ephesians*, ch. 1, and *Epistle to the Romans*, ch. 6. Cf. my book in response to Bunsen, *Die ignatianische Briefe und ihr neuester Kritiker* (Tübingen, 1848), 108ff.

17. See Ignatius, *Ephesians*, chs. 7 and 19; and *Magnesians*, chs. 7–8.

agency God works. The term "Logos" is nevertheless hardly the Son's own specific designation, for it is only one of the quite varied titles given throughout to this divine being of the second rank.[18]

In Justin's day, accordingly, the Logos-idea appears to be a conception also prevalent in the Christian Church. However, Justin's writings clearly show that the Gospel of John is not in fact the original source of this conception. How do we square with the great significance of the Logos-idea for Justin, the fact that he should have completely ignored the supreme authority the Gospel of John had to have had for him in this respect? The cause of his silence can only be that he was unfamiliar with this Gospel even though it was not unavailable. This omission is unexplainable if this Gospel had already been long regarded as apostolic.

The third element shows that the Logos-idea was not merely the more precise way of firming up, in dogmatic terms, the higher divine status linked to Christ. For the Logos-idea also contained an element setting Christian God-consciousness more definitively apart from that of Judaism. As long as people thought of the divine aspect in Christ only in terms of the concept of spirit, or else in the form of angelology, there could be no conflict with the strictly monarchian idea of God in Judaism. However, despite the origin of the Logos-idea having been the soil of the Alexandrian religious philosophy, such a conflict was unavoidable. The Johannine Logos-idea already involved the essential stipulation that the Logos is God; and even Justin, however modest his representation of the Logos, nevertheless explicitly states that the Logos is God.[19] This is then the stipulation that brought the christology on the way to the Catholic dogma, into an antithetical relation with the Jewish form of christology.

The christology of the *Pseudo-Clementine Homilies* presents the Jewish view of Christ's person in its most developed form. Thus in characteristic fashion the *Homilies* most acutely grasps the point at which the christology resting on the Logos-idea seems to infringe on God's monarchical status, so that the *Homilies* wants nothing at all to do with a Son of God who is himself God. "Our Lord neither asserted that there were gods except the creator of all, nor did he proclaim himself to be God, but he with reason pronounced blessed him who called him the Son of that God who has arranged the universe."[20] With this statement we can imagine ourselves plunked down in the time of the Arian controversies, when in this very passage of the *Homilies* we see the difference between the Father and the Son spelled out by the antithesis between the two concepts, "unbegotten" and "begotten," with the result that Father and Son are separated by an unbridgeable chasm. Thus since the Son is someone completely other

---

18. On this point see Hellwag (n. 15), 258ff.; and especially A. Hilgenfeld, *Kritische Untersuchungen über die Evangelien Justin's* (Halle, 1850), 297ff., and *Das Evangelium und die Briefe Johannis* (Halle, 1849), 130ff.

19. *First Apology*, ch. 63: "The Son, being the first-begotten Word of God, is God from the beginning" [*ANF* 1:184].

20. *Homilies* (Part 3, n. 66), 16.15 [*ANF* 8:316].

than the Father, he may not be given the same name of "God." That is because the "begotten" cannot have the same name as the "unbegotten," not even when the begotten one is of the same essence as the begetter. The name "God" ought only be used for what is proper to God alone, and is utterly incommunicable to an other.

So the Johannine thesis that the Logos is God, to which this Pseudo-Clementine polemic can alone refer, has no authoritative status at all for the standpoint holding firmly to the strictly Jewish concept of God. This makes it clear that the Logos-idea belongs to a religious domain where the constraints of a Jewish God-consciousness had already been set aside to a great extent. And yet in the Johannine theological framework the Logos, or Son, who is declared to be God, is so subordinated to the endlessly greater Father that the difference between the two was still great enough. But as soon as the Father and the Son were once put on a par by just using the same term "God" for both of them, this foreshadowed the end point toward which the further development of dogma would be headed. Once begun, this movement could not rest until the identity of Father and Son had been finalized as much as possible and in every respect.

We have now indicated in general terms the further course taken by the dogma of Christ's divinity as it advanced with reference to the Logos-idea. The basic form in general use for thinking about the divine aspect of Christ then became the Logos-idea. With it people sought to establish, for dogmatic consciousness, the specific elements in the concept of Christ's divinity. While one cannot demonstrate that Justin had knowledge of the Gospel of John, the influence of the Johannine Logos-idea becomes ever more clearly and definitely recognizable in his immediate successors: Tatian, Athenagoras, and Theophilus.

However, there are two aspects to the Logos-idea. In addition to the Logos being identical with the Father there is the equally important element of the personhood of the Logos himself. The meaning of the second factor, the personhood, is above all the main thing to be spelled out. In order to conceptualize the full reality of the Son being the Logos, one had to formulate a more specific way of representing his origin. As the Son, the Logos could only arise from, or be begotten from, God's essential being. Thus there had to have been a definite point of time when he originated, and this could have been none other than that very time when everything at all first came into being. The creative word calling everything into being is indeed in itself the same word to which the concept of the Logos as the Son refers. However, if, at a specific point of time and through a specific act of God, the Logos first came to be the Son, then that does not rule out his having already also existed as Logos beforehand, only in a different way than afterward, after he as Logos had also become the Son. Thus the twofold meaning of the term "Logos" led of its own accord to the distinction Theophilus first introduced into the currently accepted terminology: the distinction between the λόγος ἐνδιάθετος (immanent Logos) and the λόγος προφορικός (expressed Logos).

Thus the general relation of the immanent thought to the expressed word, or the self-existent idea to its actualization in reality, became the fundamental way of looking at the relation of the Father and the Son. However, since one could only think of the external word going forth from the inner thought, in other words the self-realizing idea, as analogous to a natural process in which life propagates itself from life—and since God, as the primal substance and primal power of all being and life, has within him the natural impulse to bring forth from himself something other to himself, in other words, to have it emanate from himself—what took shape in this way was a theory of emanation or subordination. In this theory, in the emanations and projections of the divine essence in the successive stages of the Father and the Son, and in which of his own accord the Holy Spirit followed as the third member, the important thing was to delimit the sequence as a trinity so that it would not form an unbroken series in any way continuous with the remaining created beings. The main representative of this form of the trinitarian idea in its most physical and most concrete form is Tertullian.[21]

However, this idea bore the stamp of a quasi-physical approach to the issue and so could not fail to elicit a reaction. The point where an overly-physical approach to the idea of God had to be countered was above all the divine act of begetting the Son. The quasi-physical way of thinking would have introduced into God's essential being the very categories of temporal becoming, and the same sensible emotional states, that these Christian writers criticized in Gnostic thinking. Hence we can take it as a reaction against fashioning the Logos-idea in too physical a way, when such early church fathers as Athenagoras and Irenaeus as a rule did not spell out the Son's proceeding from the Father as one particular element. Yet since the Son's subsistence as a person even depends on this element, we see that these church fathers downplayed the aspect of the Son's difference from the Father too much, in favor of their oneness. This view insufficiently disengaged the Son from his identity with the Father.

Those who in general were more decidedly averse to all anthropomorphism and notions of emanation, most especially the Alexandrians, had to find it even more difficult to stick so firmly to the Son's distinction from the Father in the way called for by the concept of the two as personally distinct natures. This trait is more striking in Clement of Alexandria than in any other church father. In his theology the Son is given extravagantly exalted predicates reflective of the Father's absolute essence, and the character of the Logos as mediating the God-world relationship almost wholly disappears in the oneness of the Logos with God.

The abstract Alexandrian concept of God, in the final analysis purely negative [with respect to mediating the relationship], and the physical realism of a Tertullian who could only think of God's being as a corporeal substance, presented the antithesis

---

21. In connection with the preceding and the following accounts, one can turn to the more detailed explanation, supported with textual citations, in my *Die christliche Lehre von der Dreieinigkeit und Menschwerdung Gottes*, 3 vols. (Tübingen, 1841–43), 1:163ff.

of the dominant views to the greatest extent. Commensurate with this antithesis, the two features supposedly securely united in the concept of the Son, that is, his being a subsisting person and his identity with the Father, still remained forever separate and unmediated. Either we just have a Son who is not personally distinct from the Father; or we have the kind of Son who, although begotten by, or emanated from, the essence of the Father, has a temporal beginning to his existence and is by far subordinate to the Father, and so just belongs in the category of created beings.

That the Son must be at the same time both one with the Father, and also in turn a person distinct from the Father, was already the increasingly prevalent teaching with a certain claim to authority in the church at the time of Irenaeus, Tertullian, and Clement of Alexandria, although these church fathers themselves were not entirely of one mind about this. However, we have to qualify the statement about the general acceptance of this teaching. For another group opposed these church fathers, one that could by no means accept the idea of a lesser God who went forth from God to have an ongoing personal subsistence. These are called "Monarchians." Their standpoint is indicative of an abstract Jewish monotheism, and they sought to keep their distance from any notion of emanation presupposing an internal distinction and life-process in God. They opposed everything the church fathers were accustomed to represent using the term "economy"[22] in the sense that those theological constructs involved multiple divine beings or essences. Still other elements came into play alongside these monotheistic concerns, and that gave this kind of teaching an important place, so that, throughout the whole of the third century, it remained an open question as to which side would ultimately gain a decided advantage.

---

22. [Ed.] Greek οἰκονομία means the management of a household or a world. The later trinitarian discussion distinguished between the immanent or preworldly Trinity (God's inner self-relations) and the economic or worldly Trinity (God's relations to the world through the Son and the Spirit).

The Monarchians

FIRST GROUP

Praxeas and Callistus

Praxeas is among the first in this series of Monarchians. We only know about him from Tertullian's *Against Praxeas*, written in opposition to him. It is striking that he is not mentioned by Theodoret, or by the author of the *Philosophumena*, who could not have failed to know of this heretic appearing in Rome, or by any other church father.

According to Tertullian, Praxeas distinguished the divine and the human aspects in Christ simply as "spirit" and "flesh." Praxeas said the same subject, Christ, as spirit is the Father, and as flesh is the Son. So here the unavoidable consequence is what we call "Patripassianism," a term applicable everywhere where the divine in Christ is located only in the πνεῦμα or spirit identical with the essence of God, and the σάρξ or flesh is considered to be the natural element correlative with the spirit. Praxeas himself did not even object to the patripassianist label, except that he did not want to speak without qualification of a *pati* or "suffering" by the Father; instead he only spoke of a *compati* or "suffering" by the Father "together with" the Son. That is plainly how his teaching is to be understood, for he said that the Father, as spirit, could only suffer via the intermediary of the flesh, only as spirit bound up with the flesh, in other words, only as the [spiritual] subject identical with the Son.

If we compare the teaching of Praxeas, as presented by Tertullian, with the teaching the author of the *Philosophumena* indicates as the teaching of Callistus (who, as a student of Cleomenes[23] and Noetus, appeared in Rome under Zephryrinus, the bishop of Rome[24]), then these two taught wholly the same thing. Like Praxeas, Callistus also maintained that the Father and the Son differ in name only. In themselves they are

---

23. This Cleomenes himself was the student of a certain Epigonus who, as "assistant and student" of Noetus of Smyrna, "sojourned to Rome and sowed this godless opinion" (*Philosophumena* [Part 3, n. 11], 9.7.1, p. 279 [ET 622–23]).

24. [*Ed.*] Callistus succeeded Zephryinus as pope, 217–222.

one, the indivisible Spirit. The Spirit become flesh in the Virgin Mary was not an other in addition to the Father, but instead one and the same Spirit. That is why, in John 14:11, Jesus says: "Believe me that I am in the Father and the Father is in me." What one sees as the human being is the Son. The Spirit, who has taken his own place in the Son is the Father, for the Father and the Son are not two Gods but are one; for the one whom the Father has become in the Son has taken on flesh, and, through their union, they are both God and bound up in unity. The one God is called "Father" and "Son." This one person cannot be two beings, and so the Father has suffered together with the Son.[25] The main factor is that not merely are the Father and the Son made identical, but "God" and "Spirit" are also taken to be utterly identical concepts. Father and Son coalesce therefore, just as spirit and flesh conjoin in a personal unity in Jesus, accordingly also without the Logos playing an intermediary role.

Noetus

Noetus of Smyrna is of course better known than Praxeas. He is historically important mainly as a forerunner of Sabellius. However one might classify these Monarchians, Noetus and Sabellius are in any event a pair of closely-connected thinkers whose teachings are guided not by monotheism but by a philosophical worldview we customarily place under the general heading of pantheism.

Some Christian writers, such as the author of the *Philosophumena*, do not just derive all that is heretical from Greek philosophy but also believe they must trace each heresy back to a specific philosophical system. These writers find the teaching of Noetus to be so closely related to that of Heraclitus that they say Noetus is plainly a follower of Heraclitus. Heraclitus looked upon nature as the harmony of opposites, as the unity of all things in which of course external appearances always have one thing in opposition to another, although inherently all the oppositions are overcome in the unity. He supposedly said about the world-all that it is both destructible and indestructible, both originated and not originated, both mortal and immortal.[26] Thus

---

25. *Philosophumena* 9.12, 18–19, p. 289: "In this sense, the Father suffered with the Son. [For he] does not want to say that the Father suffered [and says that there is one person—supposing in this way he escapes blasphemy against the Father]" [ET 652–53]. Tertullian says quite the same thing about Praxeas. See my *Dreieinigkeit und Menschwerdung Gottes* (n. 21), 1:251. In *Against Praxeas*, ch. 20, Tertullian also cites John 9:11.

26. *Philosophumena* (n. 23), 9.9.1: "Herakleitus affirms that the All is Divisible/Indivisible, Born/Unborn, Word/Eternity, Father/Son, God/Righteous One" [ET 624–25]. [*Ed.* The translator, Litwa, notes, p. 627, that scholars disagree as to whether all these are opposites, as the quotation reads.] In the series of extant fragments from Heraclitus, none reads literally as presented in this quotation. But those included by F. Schleiermacher in his treatise on Heraclitus (nos. 38 and 51, *Philosophische und Vermischte Schriften* [2 vols., Berlin, 1838–46 (*Sämmtliche Werke*, 3rd div.)], 2:80 and 122) have somewhat similar wording. But the word φησίν (he says, asserts, etc.), so often employed vaguely in philosophical texts (see E. Zeller in *Theologische Jahrbücher* 12 [1853] 149), is not to be understood as a literal quotation. *Philosophumena* 9.10.1 (p. 281) presents what it regards as the essential feature of Heraclitus' teaching: He "places apparent phenomena in the same rank as the unapparent and values

Noetus too is said to have not thought it contradictory that the same subject unites within himself opposite characteristics; that as Father he is invisible, unborn, immortal, but as Son he is the contrary; that God, as Father and Son, is both the one and the other, when and as he wills to be. Noetus apparently affirmed this as a view of the world that had what is God's intrinsically one and essential being both going forth into the changing, diverse realm of phenomena, and returning from it again by going back within himself. Nevertheless, Sabellius is the first one in whose teaching this general view—already present in Noetus, and perhaps present in Praxeas too—first emerges with clarity.

Sabellius

In order to understand correctly the teaching of Sabellius[27] (an essential point of which even Neander failed to grasp in his presentation[28]), the main thing is the significance he has given to the Logos-idea, unlike his predecessors. It is typical of Praxeas and Noetus that they have God becoming Father to the Son without any mediation on the part of the Logos. In contrast to them and in amplifying on the idea of the Trinity,

---

them equally, since, as we all agree, the apparent and unapparent are in some way one" [ET 632–33]. This is the main point of contact between Heraclitus' teaching and Noetus. Thus *Philosophumena* 9.9.11 (p. 284) presents Noetus' teaching as follows: "When the Father had not been born" (that is, so long as the One had not yet become the Father of the Son), "he was rightly called 'Father'" (that is, he was rightly called "Father of the World"). See also p. 283 (9.9.9–11): "What they say—There is one and the same God, the Artificer and Father of all.... But when the Father deigned to endure birth, he was born and became his own Son—not the son of another. In this way then he [i.e., Noetus] seems to establish a rule of one, claiming that Father and Son exist as one and the same. The Son is born not as one being from another but as himself from himself. He is nominally called 'Father' and 'Son' in the alternation of times" [ET 638–41]. The basic Sabellian notion of the πρόσωπα or persons [of the Trinity] is already found in this "alternation, or turning about, of times." In order to express the oneness of the Father and the Son, of the Invisible and the Visible, in the bluntest terms, the writer of the *Philosophumena* continues, in 9.10.12 (p. 284): "This is the one who in his Passion was fixed to a tree and committed his spirit to himself. He died and did not die, and raised himself on the third day. He was buried in a tomb, wounded by a spear, and fixed with nails. This one is the God and Father of the universe, as Kleomenes and his chorus chant. In doing so, they foist upon the masses the darkness of Herakleitus" [ET 642–43]. With Noetus' teaching seen in this light, its distinctive feature is therefore that it predicates of the person of Jesus, as a specific individual, what Heraclitus said held good for the πᾶν, the whole of everything, the world as such, and what Heraclitus quite sensibly took to be the unity of opposites. The same thing is thus often repeated in the history of christology, where people suppose that just replacing the individual character of the person of Jesus with something universal also enables one to conceptualize the personal aspect as such.

27. [*Ed.*] Sabellius (early 3rd c.) was the most famous of the "modalistic" Monarchians. The view that the Father, Son, and Holy Spirit are three modes or manifestations of one divine person is sometimes referred to as "Sabellianism." On the "dynamic" Monarchians, see n. 35. J. N. D. Kelly's description of the different types of Monarchianism is helpful (*Early Christian Doctrines* [London, 1958], 115–23).

28. [*Ed.*] Presumably in his *Allgemeine Geschichte der christlichen Religion und Kirche* (Part 3, n. 4).

Sabellius not only adopted the Logos-idea, which had already become an essential element in contemporary thinking; he also made it the principle of this doctrine.[29]

The characteristic feature of the doctrine of Sabellius involves both the distinction between a monad and a triad, and the way in which he has the monad becoming the triad. The Logos is the intermediary factor between these two aspects, the principle of the movement by which the monad passes over into being the triad. For Sabellius the Logos has a wholly different position or role than that given to him elsewhere. The usual conception is that the Logos proceeds from the Father in order to become the Son. However, for Sabellius the Logos is prior to the whole triad; and so the Father, who is the first member of the triad, already follows from the Logos as his presupposition. Since the first of everything that is to be comes into existence in the triad, the Logos of Sabellius is not even a self-subsistent being. The Logos is instead just the transition to being; it is being as first coming about; it is the principle of world-creating movement.[30]

The monad is what is first and primary; it is the principle serving as the necessary presupposition for all that has come into being. The monad is what is existent in itself and, as utter oneness, comprises everything within itself. In order to grasp the overall perspective from which Sabellius views the matter, we must hold firmly, above all else, to the distinction of the monad from the Father. What is still hidden away within the monad as oneness must go forth from it and be revealed. It is in this sense that Sabellius speaks of a silent and a speaking God, in other words of an inactive and an active God. The "speaking God" can only be the Logos in his relation to the monad, except that we would once again misconceive his meaning if we thought Sabellius was thinking of the Logos as the creative word expressed just once. In speaking of the God who is existent in himself, who is one and the same in substance but who takes different shapes as needed in each era, Sabellius said that God expresses himself (διαλέγεσθαι) now as Father, now as Son, now as Holy Spirit.[31]

---

29. The Sabellian doctrine involves the progression from the dyad to the triad. Originally the teaching of Sabellius was no different from that of Noetus. The υἱοπάτωρ or Son-Father, an expression denoting the teaching of Sabellius (see Gieseler, *Kirchengeschichte* [Part 3, n. 3], 1.1:299), is Noetus' merely nominal distinction between the Father and the Son. The *Philosophumena* first makes us somewhat better acquainted with Sabellius the person. [See *Philosophumena* (n. 23), ET 642–45, 650–53.] See Gustav Volkmar, *Hippolytus und die römischen Zeitgenossen* (Zürich, 1855), 122.

30. The Logos-concept is a most remarkable point of connection for the teaching of Noetus and Sabellius with the philosophy of Heraclitus. What the Logos is for Sabellius, as the principle of world-creating movement, is for Heraclitus the διὰ πάντων διήκων λόγος, or law of reason pervading everything, whose content and true significance is the law of oppositions, the identity of being and not-being, in its movement constantly shifting about in the antithesis of its elements and, in doing so, is identical with itself. This is how Lassalle characterizes the concept of the Heraclitean Logos, which forms the idea of becoming. See Ferdinand Lassalle, *Die Philosophie Herakleitos, des Dunkeln, von Ephesus*, 2 vols. (Berlin, 1858), 1:322ff. See also 281 and 259, as well as 2:263ff.

31. In *Epistle* 210, Basil stresses this feature that is especially characteristic of the teaching of Sabellius. [*Ed.*] In this footnote Baur presents the Greek of the statement he has substantially quoted in this sentence of our text. He then adds: "Basil introduces this statement as the actual words of

Thus it is clear that Sabellius did not conceive of the Logos as merely involved in the act of creating the world. Instead he considered the entire process of the world's development, running its course in the three forms of his trinitarian idea, as one and the same Logos, as an ongoing speaking, as a dialectical activity of God proceeding through different moments. Hence the Logos is the principle of the world's origin and of its development, and therefore the God who is immanent in the world first becomes actually existent in the world. The world's process of development is likewise the trinitarian process in which the God who in himself is one presents himself, in the concrete reality of his being, as Father, Son, and Spirit—in these three specific forms, which are likewise multiple moments in the course of the world.

Thus we have Sabellius' concept of the πρόσωπα or "persons." Here the immanent relation of God and the world, Sabellius' fundamental idea, already makes it apparent that the persons do not mutually co-exist but instead can only be thought of as successive stages. Just as the world becomes different from one period to the next, taking on a different character, so too God shows a different face, so to speak, in each of these periods. God changes his form, presenting himself in turn as Father, then Son, then Spirit, each time as a different specific person. Each "person" is a different "expression," and the three "persons" altogether are simply the concept of the Logos explicating itself in them. Thus it is very characteristic of Sabellius' general view that, as he himself expressly stated,[32] it attributes just lawgiving to the Father, not the world's creation. Since it is only through the Logos that the silent God becomes the speaking God, the world's creation as the changeover from being to becoming, as the beginning of the divine activity with relation to the world, can only be conceived as belonging to the Logos.

The series of "persons" forming the triad or Trinity can only develop or emerge in tandem with the concrete being of the world. The first period or phase of world history, the Old Testament period, is the time of the Father's πρόσωπον or person. In the second period of the world the same God appears in the person of the Son. Just as God makes himself known in the first period as Father and lawgiver, so the incarnation of the Logos is now what gives to the second period its distinctive character. This could easily foster the supposition that, in the person of the Son, the Logos has a different and more immediate relation [to this manifestation] than he does to the other two πρόσωπα or persons. But he is also already this same operative principle in the person of the Father, for the Father's lawgiving is the Logos' own work, as is the incarnation of the Son. The Logos enters into the one as he does into the other, in world history's course of development; except that he subsequently appears in a different form.

The same is the case in the third πρόσωπον or person. This divine-human oneness, presenting itself in the Logos become incarnate as a single individual with whom

---

Sabellius."

32. Theodoret says (*Heretical Tales* 2.9) that Sabellius only ascribes lawgiving to the Father in the Old Testament.

the Logos links himself in a personal unity, extends, in the form of the Holy Spirit, to the totality of faithful or spiritual subjects. Each of these subjects, by itself and in a relative way, is the same as what the Son is in an absolute way as the one God-man. In this series of persons, the different phases of his revelation, God draws ever closer together with the world and with humanity. Thus the third person—in which, in the form of the Holy Spirit, God unites himself with human beings, and in which each individual is severally conscious of his or her own oneness with God—is not merely the most universal of the divine persons but is also the most intensive interpenetration of the divine and the human spheres. The Logos as the speaking God is also the operative principle in the person of the Holy Spirit. Just as he is within the individual man in the person of the Son, so too he individualizes himself, in the person of the Holy Spirit, within the endless multiplicity of individual subjects.

However, the entire process of revelation and development, on the part of the divine nature immanent in the world, will ultimately conclude by the Logos also going back into God just as he has gone forth from God. Indeed the whole articulation of Sabellius' theory admits of no other outcome. But there is also explicit evidence that Sabellius spoke of a final return of the Logos into God, marking the end of all things. Since Sabellius' fundamental view of the divine nature involves it expanding and then withdrawing back within itself in this fashion, the ancient fathers of the church, for example Athanasius,[33] had to find the source of this teaching in Stoic philosophy. This contention is as justifiable as that tracing the teaching of Noetus and Sabellius back to the philosophy of Heraclitus. For the Stoic doctrine itself has the greatest affinity with the teaching of Heraclitus, where the main thing is the idea of a self-moving process, one engaging in the conflict of opposites and then taking everything back once again from this opposition—between being and becoming, oneness and duality, expansion and contraction—and into the unity of the principle. This was a very widespread worldview in antiquity, one we also come across in other Christian writings of that time.[34]

SECOND GROUP

Theodotus of Byzantium, and Artemon

If the teaching of the preceding group of Monarchians, when fully carried out, can only be designated as pantheistic, then this factor can serve as the hallmark for setting them apart from a different set of Monarchians, ones who likewise rejected a hypostatic Trinity as the church fathers saw it, but at the same time took a different kind

---

33. *Orations against the Arians*, 4.13 ["This perhaps he borrowed from the Stoics, who maintain that their God contracts and again expands with the creation, and then rests without end." *NPNF*[2] 4:437.] See also Gregory of Nazianzus, *Orationes*, 1 (ed. Paris, 1619, 1:16) [*NPNF*[2] 7:203ff.].

34. We find it in the *Pseudo-Clementine Homilies* and also in the apocryphal *Gospel of the Egyptians*. See Matthias Schneckenburger, *Über das Evangelium der Aegyptier* (Bern, 1834), 3 and 8.

of Monarchian direction.[35] From a pantheistic standpoint, the substantial element in Christ's person can only be located in the divine aspect, with the human aspect, in which the divine makes its appearance, held to be merely a nonessential feature of his person. The opposing standpoint would consider the human aspect as the substantial element of Christ's person, and relegate the divine aspect belonging to the concept of his person to just a secondary and subordinate status. This is the view of those the ancient church fathers characteristically described by saying that they teach a Christ κάτωθεν ("from below"); that is, a Christ who comes up from below inasmuch as he is in himself merely a human being, and all that makes him divine is just the extent to which the divine lets itself unite with him as an essentially human person.[36]

Theodotus of Byzantium and Artemon are leaders of this group of Monarchians. They held Jesus to be an ordinary man, but accepted that he is supernaturally begotten, and that at his baptism the Holy Spirit descended upon him in an entirely special way. Thus they agreed completely with the Synoptic Gospels' teaching about Christ, indeed in such a way that at the same time they also adhered strictly to points where the Synoptics differ from the Johannine teaching about the Logos. It is especially noteworthy that these figures made their appearance in the Roman church right when it underwent a notable turning point in its christological consciousness. According to the report Eusebius handed down from the writings of an opponent of Artemon's teaching,[37] the followers of Artemon contended that, until the time of Victor, the bishop of Rome, the same thing that they taught was also the teaching handed down by the apostles in the Roman church; and that only under Victor's successor, Bishop Zephyrinus, was this teaching "corrupted." Thus they described the teaching prevailing since that time, namely that Christ is inherently divine in nature, as a recent innovation.

If we simply take a more careful look back at the course taken by the dogma of Christ's person up to that point, and at what is now chiefly at issue, then doing so will readily convince us that the contention of the followers of Artemon is by no means such an empty pretext as is usually supposed. The inherently divine aspect of Christ's person was not yet established as long as the concept of the Logos had not yet been made a permanent predicate of Christ. If we keep this in mind, then how would the followers of Artemon have not been correct when they declared that the Logos doctrine was just recently introduced? The *Philosophumena*, which we have already frequently cited, provides a new proof of how unstable christology still was in the initial decades of the third century. From how he presents himself, its author shows us

---

35. [*Ed.*] Baur's second group of Monarchians are known as "dynamic" or "adoptionist" (Jesus adopted as divine at baptism) as opposed to "modalistic" (the first group).

36. See Eusebius, *Ecclesiastical History* 5.28.14, which says about the followers of Artemon: "him who comes from above they do not know"; and 7.30.11, about Paul of Samosata: "he says that Jesus Christ is from below" [LCL, *Eusebius*, 1:322–23, 2:220–21].

37. *Ecclesiastical History* 5.28.3.

that he was a very active participant in these controversies. Against the doctrine of a personal Logos, which he defended, others were still continually objecting that it set a second God alongside the one God.[38] And when Bishop Victor even sought to have Theodotus expelled from the ecclesial community because of his teaching, the Logos doctrine still hardly met with universal acceptance, with the result that not only did Callistus, the most notable of those Monarchians, subsequently become the bishop of Rome, but also Zephyrinus, his predecessor [and Victor's immediate successor] held the same view as Callistus. In any event the decisive period for this issue is during the papacy of Zephryrinus [c. 199–217]. The writer of the *Philosophumena*, and other opponents of the Monarchians, pushed back forcibly against the doctrinal outlook of the other side during the papacy of Zephyrinus, and their zeal is what made them increasingly able to gain the upper hand on this issue going forward.[39]

38. See *Philosophumena* (Part 3, n. 11), 9.11.15, pp. 284ff. The author says that their opponents call them Δίθεοι (ditheists) [ET 650–51]. Callistus replied to them (p. 289): "I will not speak of two gods—Father and Son—but one" [ET 652–53]. The author presents his own Logos doctrine in 10.33.1–8, pp. 334ff. [ET 748–53].

39. The preceding account requires still further discussion, since the credibility of the *Philosophumena*'s author has been seriously disputed in the interests of Catholicism. The author of this "Refutation of Heresies" may have been the Roman presbyter Caius, the case for which I made in opposition to Bunsen; or, as now commonly accepted, he was Bishop Hippolytus. In any event the author was a very prominent leader of a faction belonging to the Roman church. If we take the report of this writer to be accurate, then it gives us a very clear picture of the status of dogma in the Roman church at the beginning of the third century. In his *Hippolytus und Kallistus oder die römische Kirche in der ersten Hälfte des dritten Jahrhunderts* (Regensburg, 1853), J. J. I. von Döllinger contends (pp. 232ff.) that, in writing the *Philosophumena*, Hippolytus has introduced what are manifest contradictions and falsehoods into his portrayal of the form of Callistus' teaching. In my "Caius und Hippolytus," *Theologische Jahrbücher* 13 (1854) I sought to show (358ff.), in opposition to Döllinger, that such is not the case, for Döllinger himself was mistaken in how he interpreted the passages in question. —In opposition to me and by very earnestly accepting Döllinger's contention, J. E. Kuhn published "Die theologischen Streitigkeiten in der römischen Kirche und die Lehre derselben in der erste Hälfte des dritten Jahrhunderts," in the *Theologische Quartalschrift* (1853), 343ff., where he very emphatically accuses my interpretation of being the erroneous one. Since Callistus was a Roman bishop, Kuhn supposes that it would in any event be at least a point of interest to know that he was a Sabellian, as I have indeed identified him. Kuhn writes: "But why add that Callistus, the Roman pope, was a Theodotian? According to Hippolytus he was a Theodotian as well, and therefore even doubly a heretic! We say there is really just this alternative: that he is both a Sabellian and a Theodotian, or he is neither one. It is not very hard to decide. The issue is whether the passionate opponent of Callistus (namely, Hippolytus) recognized and stated the simple truth, or else his portrayal is one-sided, prejudicial, and tainted." — My reply is that the *Philosophumena* has recognized and stated the truth; that Callistus is not just doubly a heretic, but even triply so; that he is not just a Sabellian and a Theodotian, but also a Noetian; and that it is only possible to understand these controversies correctly if we take all of this into account. The writer of the *Philosophumena* declares in most particular terms (9.7 and 9.10, pp. 279, 284 [ET 622–23, 632–45, extending into 9.11.3]) that Callistus was an adherent of the dogma proceeding from Noetus of Smyrna, which, via Epigonus and Cleomenes, got introduced into Rome under Bishop Zephyrinus. That being the case, in the controversy about the issue of how to specify both the oneness of the Father and the Son, and their difference, Callistus could be characterized as a Theodotian just as well as a Sabellian. The difference between the teaching of Noetus and that of Theodotus is that, whereas Noetus posited the oneness of the Father and the Son absolutely and left it undefined, except for just saying that what one is visibly the other is invisibly, Theodotus used the concept of the Spirit

as the intermediary of their unity. According to the writer of the *Philosophumena*, Theodotus taught that only upon the baptism in the Jordan River did Christ descend from above upon the man Jesus in the form of a dove, for prior to this the divine was not operative in him; "the Spirit (which he calls 'Christ') descended and was shown to be in Jesus" (*Philosophumena* 7.35.2, p. 258 [ET 570–71]). — Callistus too took up the concept of the Spirit into his own view, in order to link it with the teaching of Noetus and thereby to spell out the relation of the Father and the Son. He said the two of them are one, as the "undivided Spirit.... Everything is full of the divine Spirit, both things above and things below. Moreover, the Spirit that was made flesh within the Virgin is not different from the Father but one and the same" (*Philosophumena* 9.12.17 [ET 650–53]). (According to Diogenes Laertius, *Lives of Eminent Philosophers*, 9.9, Heraclitus spoke of "the downward path" and "the upward path." The *Philosophumena*'s reference to "both things above and things below" is analogous to this. See Lassalle [n. 30], 1:275.) Callistus' view here is of course actually what we know to be the view of Praxeas, although inasmuch as it chiefly relies on the concept of the Spirit, an opponent could also have called it Theodotus' position. However, if Callistus is then said to have been not just a Noetian and a Theodosian, but also a Sabellian (according to *Philosophumena* 9.12.19, p. 290 [ET 652–53]), then that doubtless calls to mind the distinctive meaning Sabellius gave to the Logos-idea. One need only pay attention to the stance the *Philosophumena* attributes to Sabellius; for we first become better acquainted with Sabellius' general historical significance from this new source. On p. 285 (9.11.1 [ET 642–45]) it says that Callistus sometimes expressed himself in terms of the true doctrine, and sometimes along the lines of Sabellius—whom he "drove away"—as the one who could have led him on the right path. For whereas Sabellius was not unreceptive to the admonitions the writer of the *Philosophumena* said Callistus voiced to Sabellius, the latter, as soon as he was alone with Callistus, "was spurred by him to incline to the dogma of Cleomenes" (9.11.2 [ET 644–45]). The writer of the *Philosophumena* places the greatest emphasis on a personally subsisting Logos who is himself God (10.33.1–2, p. 336 [ET 748–51]). Sabellius agreed with him in also affirming the Logos-idea, although as a Monarchian he gave it a different meaning. So at least in this sense Sabellius held a position in between the two antithetical views, and Callistus concurred in this by taking the concepts of Spirit and Logos to be identical. On p. 330 (10.27.3–4) the writer designates Callistus' heresy as follows: "'God,' he says, is 'Spirit.' Thus God is not another being in relation to the Word, and the Word is not another being in relation to God. Thus there is one person distinguished by name, but not in essence" [ET 736–37]. See p. 289, where Callistus is reported as follows: "He claimed that the Word himself is nominally Son as well as Father. In reality, however, the Word is one, the undivided Spirit (9.12.16 [ET 650–51]). Just before this the writer expressly notes that Callistus concocted this heresy, in "publicly reviling" the writer's faction by stating: "'You are ditheists!' For these reasons—and still more because he was constantly accused by Sabellius as a transgressor of the pristine faith" (9.12.15 [ET 650–51]). Therefore Callistus concocted his heresy because he had been accused by Sabellius, who had advanced beyond his initial beliefs. The "pristine faith" can only be the teaching of Noetus, on which Callistus and Sabellius were in agreement, and the "transgressing" alleged by Sabellius constituted the progression of Callistus in elaborating his Logos doctrine, on account of which Callistus, as justification in face of Sabellius' rebuke, could only say that "the Word himself is nominally Son" and so on. Yet Callistus is also said to have cut his ties with Sabellius and even drove him out of Rome! —This is what Kuhn says mainly counts against my position. He says it is always easier to misconstrue and misrepresent words than it is actions. The fact that Callistus adopted a middle position between Hippolytus and Sabellius makes evident what is actually the key element in Hippolytus' entire diatribe against Callistus, and this fact, which is both indubitable and striking, ought not be overlooked. Indeed it appears to be the most reliable clue and the guiding thread for making our way out of the labyrinth of Hippolytus' presentation. Therefore, as with other points in my treatise, Dr. Kuhn also cannot grasp this one, the fact that I court Callistus as a Sabellian without even regarding the excommunication of Sabellius by Callistus as worth mentioning (Kuhn, 347). The expulsion of Sabellius is a fact, but the alleged intermediate position of Callistus is no fact, just an assumption. However, the fact of the expulsion is such a feature of the *Philosophumena*'s whole presentation that it calls for no further explanation. If, so long as Callistus was not yet the bishop and was concerned to win Sabellius over to his side, that gave him a reason to be

Beryllus of Bostra

There can no longer be any doubt that Bishop Beryllus of Bostra is to be reckoned as belonging not just to the first group of Monarchians [Praxeas et al.], but to our second group. We see this from the more thorough discussion of his teaching.

Since he declared his opposition to Christ's pre-existence as a personal being (κατ' ἰδίαν οὐσίας περιγραφήν, "in an individual existence of his own"), and to his having an inherently divine nature, the issue for Beryllus was most definitely establishing Christ's personal being as an essentially human person. He then also had to determine how, on this basis, one would have to think of the divine aspect that is ascribed to him. Although Beryllus did not accept that Christ had being prior to his human existence, he did allow as how Christ was predetermined in the mind of God and thus preexisted in at least an ideal way. The divine aspect added on to Christ's human person Beryllus designated by an expression that, while at least not pointing to any notion

---

accommodating to Sabellius' way of thinking, what would be more natural than for Callistus to cast off Sabellius after he achieved his goal [of the episcopacy], and by expelling him to seek to gain the favor of the opposing faction? *Philosophumena* 9.12.15 states that "Callistus... supposed that he had attained his quarry. He expelled Sabellius as unorthodox" (p.288 [ET 650–51]). —From all this we see with sufficient clarity the vacillating status of the trinitarian doctrine at that time in the church of Rome. Accordingly, the entire depiction of the circumstances in the Roman church that the writer of the *Philosophumena* provides for us confirms very forcefully the contention of those heretics, namely, that right up until the time of Bishop Zephyrinus, the Monarchian view was the conventional and prevalent teaching in Rome. I have already shown, in my *Dreieinigkeit und Menschwerdung Gottes* (n. 21), 1:279, that this contention of the Monarchians was, in its essentials, a completely true assertion. This has also been acknowledged by J. C. L. Gieseler, in his "Abhandlung über Hippolytus, die ersten Monarchianer und die römische Kirche in der ersten Hälfte des dritten Jahrhunderts," *Theologische Studien und Kritiken* (1853) 767ff. —Whatever form the Monarchian doctrine may also have taken, the main antithesis to it always remained the Logos doctrine, in the form in which it found its most decided defender, the author of the *Philosophumena*. (Kuhn, who assumes that Callistus taught none other than the purely orthodox, Nicene doctrine, has nothing to say about this latter point in his treatise.) The *Philosophumena*'s author has the same significance for the history of the doctrine of the Trinity in the Roman church, in this regard, as Tertullian has in the African church. In fact the contention of these heretics is in no way different from what we find in Tertullian's treatise against Praxeas, ch. 3 [*ANF* 3:598–99]: "The simple, indeed (I will not call them unwise and unlearned), who always constitute the majority of believers, are startled at the dispensation of the Three in One, on the ground that their very rule of faith withdraws them from the world's plurality of gods to the one only true God; not understanding that, although he is the one only God, he must yet be believed in with his own οἰκονομία. The numerical order and distribution of the Trinity they assume to be a division of the Unity; whereas the Unity which derives the Trinity out of its own self is so far from being destroyed, that it is actually supported by it. They are constantly throwing out against us that we are preachers of two gods and three gods, while they take to themselves preeminently the credit of being worshipers of the one God; just as if the Unity itself with irrational deductions did not produce heresy, and the Trinity rationally considered constitute the truth." This is wholly the same stance on the matter as that in the *Philosophumena*. The vast majority of the faithful just cling to the opposition to pagan polytheism and so do not want to hear of any Logos doctrine. This doctrine must therefore first carve a path for itself, although it takes itself to be the form of doctrine that captures the deeper and more concrete meaning of Christianity. Hence we see its connection with Montanism and Montanism's more earnest moral stance, something that also sets the author of the *Philosophumena* apart from Callistus.

of emanation, can only be understood as a free, spiritual action on God's part, one resting on God's moral oneness [with Christ].[40]

Deserving of our attention is how, in the teaching of Beryllus, the concept of the person [of Christ], his being "in an individual existence of his own," his personal being, is expressed as something circumscribed, delimited and set apart in his being-on-his-own (*Fürsichsein*). This of course indicates how important the concept of personal being is for determining the relation of the divine and the human aspects in the person of Christ. It provides the transition from Beryllus to Paul of Samosata, the two of whom are related in the same way as Noetus is related to Sabellius.

Paul of Samosata

Paul's christology is the perfect counterpart to the christology of Sabellius.[41] It is just as characteristic a representative of the one group of Monarchians as that of Sabellius is characteristic of the other one. If we can simply call the general character of Sabellius' view "pantheistic," then in contrast the view of Paul is "theistic," in a sense in which the pantheistic and theistic worldviews are, on the whole, essentially antithetical. From Sabellius' standpoint the human dimension, in its oneness with the divine, is just the manifestation of the divine; whereas in contrast the tendency of Paul's teaching is to hold the divine and the human as much apart as possible, and to set God and the man Jesus over against each other as two equally personal subjects, each subsisting by itself.

Like Theodotus and Artemon, Paul too set out from the point that Christ is in himself just human, even though he was supernaturally begotten. But a further element in his elaboration of this theory is that Paul for the first time spoke of a Christ who had become God (a τεθεοποιῆσθαι). If Christ is not by nature God, then he can only have come to be what he is as a divine nature. But how did he become a divine

---

40. Eusebius, *Ecclesiastical History* 6.33, uses the term ἐμπολιτεύεσθαι ("dwelling in") for Beryllus' view of the Father's being in the Son, a term taken from political and social life.

41. [*Ed.*] Paul of Samosata (200–275) is the most important of the dynamic Monarchians. He held that Jesus was a man who was inspired and filled by the divine Logos, Wisdom, or Spirit (not "God-become-man" but "man-become-God"), and he was one of the forerunners of adoptionist christologies. He was condemned at the Synod of Antioch in 268 or 269. Robert L. Calhoun devotes special attention to Paul of Samosata in his *Lectures on the History of Christian Doctrine* (private printing, 1948), 1:133–36. In Calhoun's interpretation of Paul (which agrees with that of Baur), Jesus "reaches a level at which he himself is assimilated with the divine. At his baptism, the Holy Spirit came upon him, and by this anointing he became Christ. The Logos is divine from all eternity; but it is not divine as a second God. Far from it. It is divine as the rational character of the one God, and it is that one Logos that guides and inspires and ultimately deifies the man Jesus, a Son of God by adoption. The unity of God and man in Jesus Christ is moral unity. One may even speak of moral identity, for in none of his acts did Jesus do anything other than what God wills." The emphasis on a moral union is similar to Jesus' teaching and self-understanding as Baur presents them in Part 1. The fact that Paul of Samosata was condemned shows how far Christian doctrine had drifted away from its historical founder already by the third century.

nature? The external way in which Theodotus had the divine imparting itself to Jesus, via the descent of the Holy Spirit in the form of a dove, no longer sufficed for Paul. So only the moral element could be that in which the divine and the human were bound together as a unity in Jesus. Christ as a human being, which is what he is in himself, became God and the Son of God only by the route of moral striving and moral perfection. On the other hand, however, if the human dimension was supposedly elevated to divine status by this moral element, then the moral element could not be thought of as a purely human factor apart from divine assistance.

This is therefore where the idea of the Logos comes into play for Paul as well, the Logos that now cannot be omitted from any theological framework. In order to rule out any thought of a personal Logos, Paul did not apply the concept of the Logos to Christ without simultaneously spelling out in general terms what the Logos is in God. In God, the Logos is the same thing he also is in human beings: the inward, spiritual principle of thinking and self-consciousness. In his Logos, God is the personal, self-conscious God, just as in human beings as well the Logos is the inner man or woman, the principle of one's personhood. Hence the Logos is what he is only as inseparably united with God. As he can hardly separate himself from this unity, so he can hardly exist in a personal way outside of God. Of course Paul also allows that the Logos is operative and indwelling in Jesus the man. However, this involves no substantial uniting of God with the human being, for it is instead just a divine activity in boosting Jesus' human power of understanding and his strength of will. So one cannot speak here about a unity of God with the human being. Instead there are simply two different personal subjects, and this entire way of looking at it is dualistic. The main concern here is to preserve an essential difference between what is divine and what is human.

An energetic movement arose against Paul and his teaching, and it did not rest until his teaching was condemned and he was forced out of his episcopal seat in Antioch. People made vindictive accusations against his character, for they linked his theory, which elevated the human side in Christ's person to preeminence, because they said it went hand in glove with a sensibility directed toward what is vile and worldly. There was great opposition to him on the part of the church. All of these reactions sufficiently show how people were already very comfortable in considering the dogma that Christ pre-existed as a person, prior to the incarnation, as the orthodox position.

The last one of the synods to deal with this issue, the synod that met at Antioch in 269, was in many respects already a prelude to the Council of Nicaea. Yet it is odd that the fathers meeting in Antioch felt they had to officially condemn the very same terminology that later came to crystallize Nicene orthodoxy. They declared explicitly that the Son of God is not ὁμοούσιος with ("the same being as") the Father. Athanasius could not regard the fathers meeting at the Synod of Antioch to be less orthodox than those meeting at Nicaea, and so did not allow an apparent contradiction to trouble his traditional ecclesial consciousness. Thus according to Athanasius this decision of

Antioch was only reached because it was the simplest way to counter the dialectical arguments of Paul of Samosata.[42] According to Athanasius in this passage, Paul had argued that, if it is not conceded that Christ is merely a man, then he must have been of the same being as the Father; but the Father and the Son stand as ὁμοούσιοι (the same or equivalent beings), so there must be one οὐσία (being) transcending and comprising both of them, as their common presupposition, as the unity to which they themselves are subordinated. So what would follow, Paul says, from the teaching of those Antiochene fathers that the Son is by nature God, is the inherently objectionable contention that the Father would not be the highest, absolute God.[43] Accordingly, they supposed that only by denying the *homoousian* could they circumvent this consequence that would lead directly to Sabellianism.

---

42. See Athanasius, *On the Councils*, ch. 45 [*NPNF*² 4:473–74.]

43. According to Athanasius there would then be μία προηγουμένη οὐσία (one antecedent being) alongside two οὐσίαι (beings) emanating from it. If we stress the concept of the *homousian* so much that the Father and the Son are fully coordinate natures, then one οὐσία must still stand above them, and they are both emanations of it in the same way. Athanasius provides the best solution in the passage of *On the Councils*, ch. 51, where he argues against this approach by stating: "It is not right to say that the Son is coessential [i.e., *homoousios*] with the Father, because he who speaks of 'coessential' speaks of three, one essence pre-existing, and that those who are generated from it are coessential: and they add, 'If then the Son be coessential with the Father, then an essence must be previously supposed, from which they have been generated; and that the one is not Father and the other Son, but they are brothers together'" [*NPNF*² 4:477]. The conception on which Paul bases his hypothetical argument is Sabellius' view of the issue, where the monad, as the one antecedent being or the one highest God, actually stands above the Son, the Spirit, and the Father, who are all on the same level. However, it is uncertain whether Sabellius had already made use of the term *homoousian* to indicate the coordinate status of his three πρόσωπα or persons.

The Further Development of the Doctrine of Christ's Divinity

We stand here at a point in the development of the doctrine of Christ's divinity where very different ways of envisaging it intersect in severely antithetical fashion. The notion making the divine aspect in Christ's person so insignificant, as compared to the human aspect, that he would have been regarded as only a human subject, faced the most decided opposition. However, the opposed view, starting out from the idea of God and in which Christ consequently was indeed a substantially divine nature, albeit just a transitory manifestation of the divine, presenting in itself one specific phase of the one divine essence, also could not prove satisfactory for Christian consciousness.

Christ's position seemed to require his already existing as a personal divine nature even prior to his human existence. But this view also posed many difficulties that could not be so easily avoided. Even if, despite the objections of the Monarchians, one dismissed how it conflicted with the doctrine of the oneness of God, in this view the position of Christ still seemed to be very much in question precisely because of what people believed they principally had to affirm. That is because they could think of the Son of God, or the Logos, as a subsisting person, only as a nature coming forth from God at one specific moment. Therefore that not only involved positing within God's nature a temporal change and an inclination toward the physical world, along the lines of the Gnostic emanation theories. It also had to arouse misgivings as to whether a nature that originated in such fashion and stood so far below the one, supreme God, could rightly be regarded as an inherently divine being.

ORIGEN

If we juxtapose all of these elements resulting from the course of development thus far, then we are at the point from which Origen understood the current task of theological speculation if it was to advance to a further stage in its development.[44]

---

44. [*Ed.*] Origen of Alexandria (c. 184—c. 253) is often regarded as the first Christian systematic theologian because of his book *On First Principles*, discussed by Baur below. He was an enormously

Origen's teaching, a new and very significant factor in the historical development of theology, had a decisive influence. We have to distinguish two elements in it that are essentially related to each other. On the one hand, Origen firmly held above all that the Son could only be a nature subsisting on its own, a person distinct from the Father. For if the Son is no mere power and attribute of God, then he exists outside of God, not within God. Therefore, as distinct from God, the Son can only have a dependent and subordinate relation to God. The idea of God as absolute is so very important for Origen that he could not have juxtaposed to the Father, as the absolute God, another nature, in the person of the Son, as perfectly equal to the Father. Accordingly, if we are to conceive of the Son, in his full reality, as being a hypostasis on his own, it is no less essential to specify that he is subordinate to the Father; and Origen has no reservations about describing the Son as in every respect a far lesser nature compared to the Father. For instance, he says the Father alone is good absolutely, but he does not want to say the same about the Son; and he limits the Son's agency to the rational or logical sphere in order to subordinate it to the Father's agency, which extends over all existent being generally.

On the other hand, however, while Origen widened the gulf between the Father and the Son by the foregoing specifications, he also sought to fill it in as much as possible. However far the Son stands beneath the Father, so that, in the nature of the case, he can hardly measure up to the Father's own absolute nature, the Son nevertheless shares in the Father's absoluteness in one point. Although he is begotten, he is begotten from eternity, not begotten in time at a specific moment of time before the creation of the world. With regard to time, the Son's existence is just as much without beginning, just as absolutely eternal, as that of the Father. Origen's entire teaching about the relation of the Father and the Son revolves around this main concept. His notion of a Son co-eternal with the Father was supposed to place the Son in an adequate relationship to God's absolute nature, and to remove any emanationist notions from the idea of God. It provided a counterweight to offset the Son's subordination, by linking the finite and the infinite in unity.

As with the eternal creation of the world, Origen also recognized in God's absolute nature the basis for an eternal begetting of the Son. Since one cannot conceive of a time at which God was not already what he is in his absolute nature, but instead had first to become it, God can therefore also simply have been, from eternity, not just the world's creator but also Father of a Son. If God is the ruler of all things, then there must also always have been that for the sake of which he is the ruler of all [i.e., the world]. Therefore he can also not have begun to be Father, since, unlike with human beings, there is no conceivable obstacle to God's becoming the Father. For, if God is always perfect and always has the power to be the Father, and it is good that he is the Father of such a Son, then what prevents him from also actually being the Father? If the Son's being eternal is grounded in this way in the absolute perfection of the divine

prolific writer, including his work against Celsus and his many biblical commentaries.

nature itself, then that also disposes of any view that, in the usual way of representing the begetting of the Son, is far too analogous with merely natural processes. Origen could think of the Son's begetting solely as an extra-temporal divine act that no kind of human thinking could categorize. That is because Origen's idea of God was totally incompatible with any view presupposing some feature in God's nature that changes in time or is bodily divisible.

While Origen sought to grasp the concept of begetting abstractly, as devoid of all positive features, he was nevertheless automatically confronted with an issue in which the resulting and differing representation of the Father-Son relationship divided to form a very specific antithesis. The issue is whether the Son is begotten from the Father's own nature or being, or else is produced by an act of will on God's part. Although Origen never formulated the issue in this specific way, it nevertheless clearly underlies his vacillating explanations, which incline now to one view, now to the other. He ascribes to the Son an essential nature in common with the Father, and uses the term ὁμοούσιος in this context, even saying that the Son is begotten from the essential nature of the Father; and he compares the Son to an effluence, or a radiation of light. However, he also speaks in turn, and in the same sense, not of the Father's nature but of the Father's will. Although he does this just analogically, and only wants to have the Son be begotten from the Father in the way the will proceeds from the mind or spirit, without introducing division or being separate from it, Origen still at the same time specifically declares that the Father's willing is sufficient to produce whatever the Father wills; that even the hypostasis of the Son is begotten merely by the medium of the will.[45] If we combine this explicit declaration that the Father's will is the principle of the Son's subsistence, with all that Origen teaches about the Son's distinction from the Father, about his being another, about his subordination, his far lower standing and agency, then it cannot be wholly incorrect, for those who regard him as a major authority for the Arian theological framework, to even call him "the father of Arianism." And yet, all that Origen has to say unfavorably about the Son, especially about his subordination to the Father, is constantly outweighed by the lofty predicate of the Son's eternity, one no other church father before Origen had given to the Son with such a full awareness of its speculative significance.

When regarded in this way, Origen marks a very important turning point in the history of dogma. The two tendencies on this issue—ones that from the outset go side-by-side, with each being equally justified for its own sake, so as on the one hand to give the Son equal standing with the Father (to the extent that is possible) and to identify the Son with him in a oneness of their essential nature, while on the other hand distinguishing the Son from the Father and placing him in a specifically subordinate relation

---

45. See the passages demonstrating this in my work on *Dreieinigkeit und Menschwerdung Gottes* (n. 21), 1:196ff., and in E. R. Redepenning's *Origenes* (Bonn, 1841–46), 2:293ff. When Redepenning criticizes my speaking of Origen's vacillation as to the begetting of the Son, it seems to me that Redepenning has not sufficiently weighed the words of Origen that he himself cites.

to the Father—come together in Origen's thinking as having equal weight. However, in fact from this point on, because of how they differ, these tendencies diverge widely and co-exist as such. The further development of dogma then heads toward its next goal with very rapid strides in the period after Origen.

The students and the followers of Origen—including Dionysius, the bishop of Alexandria, who stood out as representative of a very prevalent way of presenting Origen's teaching—proceeded more or less along the lines of the Origenist theological framework that was predominantly interested in distinguishing and separating the Son from the Father. The fragments provided in the works of ancient writers do not tell us in detail about this teaching. In any event since these fragments repeat the customary comparisons drawing upon the concept of emanation, and refer to the Son as something created, and in other respects were found to be very objectionable by later orthodox church fathers, it is quite likely that these Origenists did not uphold Origen's teaching with regard to its main point: predicating eternity of the Son. Dionysius of Alexandria is expressly said to have spoken out in opposition to the Son's eternity, and to have come so close to the Arian theological framework that he even made use of the formulation, ἦν ποτε, ὅτε οὐκ ἦν ("there was a time when he was not"). Dionysius was also said to have set forth a theory of subordination, the most offensive expressions of which he subsequently found it advisable to tone down after several Libyan bishops with Sabellian tendencies had turned to the Dionysius who was the bishop of Rome with a complaint lodged against their own bishop of Alexandria. The Roman Dionysius then responded with the text of a Roman synod that was directed against both Sabellianism and tritheism.[46] The text affirmed a divine triad most closely connected with the monarchy of God—which indeed came near to the Nicene theological framework but also just juxtaposed these conceptions while leaving them unconnected. This vacillating condition, in which each conception constantly reacted against the other without also being able to support itself on a firm foothold of its own, only came to an end with the Arian controversy.

ARIANISM

What is characteristic of Arianism, what makes it momentous, is that it firmly and readily grasped what differentiated the perspectives coming from all quarters that were still always so varied and that intersected in so many ways. Arianism reduced

---

46. Dr. Kuhn (n. 39) has correctly shown (386ff.) that, in the fragment cited by Athanasius in his *On the Decrees of the Council of Nicaea*, ch. 26, Dionysius of Rome only apparently speaks of three different views, those of Sabellius, the tritheists, and Dionysius of Alexandria. Instead he just speaks out against two views, since the tritheist view is none other than that of Dionysius of Alexandria, who faces the twofold objection that he separates the oneness of God into three deities, and also says of the Son that he is a created being, something that first came into being. See Athanasius, *On the Sentences of Dionysius*, ch. 13, which also speaks of two views that Dionysius of Rome wrote against, the Sabellian view and the view sounding like Arianism.

them all to one clear antithesis that it expressed and established definitively. If one could not think of the Son, in his existence prior to the incarnation, as personally distinct from the Father—how one was supposed to conceive of him without putting him in a relation of dependence on, and subordination to, the Father, and without considering him a far lesser nature—then one also had to spell out more precisely what, in the final analysis, is the distinguishing element in the whole Father-Son relationship. Although the Son was originated, should he nevertheless be said to be begotten from the nature of the Father and to be essentially the same as what the Father is? If so, then how could one nevertheless place him so far beneath the Father? All the stipulations made about the relation of Father and Son always remained vague and vacillating as long as one did not seek, first of all, to answer the question: What in principle and absolutely constitutes their difference?

The ancient church fathers said that Arianism had a preeminently dialectical orientation, since of course from their own standpoint these fathers could only criticize the Arians for seeking to undergird their theory chiefly in dialectical terms and for devoting themselves so avidly to dialectic with this end in mind. What these fathers meant by this was the Arians' very methodical procedure of drawing sharp distinctions, keeping their eyes on specific conceptual elements and being consistent in their thinking. Had it lacked this character, Arianism could never have gained the historical significance that it did.

The founder of Arianism, the Alexandrian presbyter Arius, therefore set the task as simply looking first, and most penetratingly, at the relation between the Father and the Son: what it actually is, and what in principle constitutes the difference between them. But what issue concerning their relationship still waited to be settled if even eternity had already been predicated of the Son, so that the very concept of being generated was said to pose no obstacle to regarding him, in the unending duration of his existence, as just as absolute a being as the Father is? Yet when one nevertheless makes the Son comparable to the Father in such an emphatic way, and discounts any distinguishing features, there still always remains one thing that the Son can in no way share with the Father, one thing that separates him absolutely from the Father: the concept of being unbegotten. This is the point from which Arianism sets out, and based on which it develops its theses with strictly logical consistency.

If the Father alone is unbegotten, then the absolute, essential being of the Father himself involves being unbegotten. Since the Son is not unbegotten like the Father, for the Son is just begotten, the Son therefore cannot be equal in nature or essence to the Father. Instead the Son is just of an essentially different nature. Accordingly the Son is also not begotten from the Father's essential nature. As such, the Son is not begotten but is instead just made or created. Furthermore, if he is not begotten from the Father's essence, then there is nothing from which he could have been made. Thus one can only say about the Son that he was made or created from nothing. Had the Son been of the Father's essence, and thus essentially the same as what the Father is, then there would certainly be—what is self-contradictory—two equally unbegotten or equally absolute beings. However, if the Son was created from nothing, and therefore thus originated, then his being also had a beginning; and, if one also understands this passing out of non-being and into being as abstractly as possible, then one can only say about the Son that there was a time when he was not. Had he not originated but was instead eternal, then he would have been co-eternal with the Father. Yet the Father is nevertheless eternal only because he is unbegotten.

These two theses that are equally characteristic of Arianism—that the Son is ἐξ οὐκ ὄντων ("from non-being, or nothing") and that ἦν ποτε, ὅτε οὐκ ἦν ("there was a time when he was not")—affirm such a great gulf separating the Son from the Father that the Son can only belong to the category of created beings. What sets him above creatures is simply the fact that, although a creature himself, he is nevertheless the creator of the other creatures; and also the fact that, although he is originated, he does not have his origin in time, for instead it lies before time, and time itself first came about through him. In light of his preeminence, Arius calls him "God" in the full sense, although doing so does not in any way remove the absolute difference between the Son and the Father.

Thus the general heading under which Arius places the relation of the Son and the Father is the antithesis of the finite and the infinite. Just as the finite and the infinite are utterly opposed to each other, so too there can be no intermediary linking the Father and the Son, for which reason Arius also dismissed most definitely all physical analogies and notions of emanation. If the Father and the Son have nothing in common as to their respective essences, then the principle of the Son's existence can be posited only in the Father's will, not in the Father's essence. The Son is, or exists, sheerly in virtue of the Father's will, just as all else that is other than God has been created by an act of his will.

THE TEACHING OF ARIUS' OPPONENTS

The opponents of Arius' teaching could not object to all these specific points. Initially they could only maintain that, if there is supposedly the same difference and contrast between the Father and the Son as there is between the infinite and the finite, then the Son cannot still be even what Arius wanted to let him be in order to exalt him above the sphere of created being. They could rightly ask whether it is not contradictory for the Son, while himself being just a created being, to be at the same time supposedly the creator of the creatures. Furthermore, if he himself is originated and in his origin is subject to the category of temporality, they then asked whether, as the creator of time, he stands above all time.

There were even more consequences of the Arian theological framework. One had to carry through even more strictly with the antithesis of the finite and the infinite.

In the end one could only stop with a Son who, as an utterly finite being, no longer had any claim to divine predicates.

But what did such objections gain if one could not set a positively grounded position over against the Arian theological framework that denied the Son's divinity? For this to be done one had to point out, in the chain of the Arian argument, a place where one could, with good reason, counter the conclusions the Arians drew from their principle. In arguing from the concept of what it is to be "unbegotten," the Arians took being unbegotten and being eternal as equivalent concepts. Their opponents could not concede that the two concepts are identical if they did not wish, by doing so, to relinquish everything that gave the Son an inner point of contact within the essence of the Father. Hence for the Son to not be relegated to an utterly finite status, consistent with the Arian argument, above all one had to ascribe eternity to the being of the Son. As the Son, he could only be begotten, not unbegotten. Such could only be possible if there was a middle point between the finite on the one hand, and the infinite on the other hand, a middle point that was both at the same time, a nature both finite and infinite. This is the concept of the eternal generation of the Son as maintained by the opponents of Arius. As begotten, the Son has his existence from another, and therefore, like everything that does not have the cause of its own being within itself, the Son just belongs in the category of the finite. However, inasmuch as he is begotten from eternity, the dependence and conditioned character of his nature, its finitude, is said to be in turn superseded in his eternal being.

Hence whereas Arianism employed the abstract antithesis of the finite and the infinite, as mutually exclusive, to define the relation between the Son and the Father, according to the contrary teaching of their opponents the characteristic concept of the Son's person conjoins the finite and the infinite as one in him. However, the question is simply whether this oneness, which as the unity of the finite and the infinite is a purely abstract concept, is also a conceivable condition corresponding to concrete reality. Although the relation of the Father and Son, spelled out in the concept of the Son's eternal generation, is said to be so unusual that it does not fit with the customary categories of human thinking, it must nevertheless be able to be made concrete and comprehensible so that we can represent it to ourselves in some way or other.

Yet here we have the weakest point in this anti-Arian theory. All that the church fathers taking the anti-Arian side knew how to say in justifying it was simply the well-known, and already so often repeated, analogy to the natural relationship between light and the ray emitted by the light. As the ray is inseparable from the light that emits it, so too the Father was said to be hardly thinkable without the Son begotten from him. Yet if the Son is related to the Father simply as the ray proceeding from the light, then how do things stand regarding the Son's subsisting as a person? That is no less an essential feature of the concept of the Son. Is the Son also just an accident of the Father's substance, merely a nonessential reflection of it? To say that the very point distinguishing the analogy of the Father's relation to the Son from these natural relationships is the fact that, in his oneness with the Father, the Son at the same time has his own existence as a person, is to lose the foundation of the natural way of looking at it from which one set out. Then this entire way of representing the relationship no longer has any foothold. Either one could therefore just think of God's eternal process of generating [the Son] as analogous to a natural process, a view apparently pulling God's supersensible nature down into the sensible domain and a view that always calls forth once again the same objections to this way of representing it; or else one would have a completely transcendent and contentless concept.

THE NICENE DOGMA

If we understand the two theological frameworks, at odds here, from the perspective of their antithetical, essential specifications, then we will obviously see how these same conceptions that, in their antithesis, have, with various modifications, pervaded the whole previous history of the development of dogma, now simply confronted each other in a new and more focused way. However, the sharper the antithesis had become, the more certainly it also had to arrive at a final resolution.

Favoring the anti-Arian approach was the fact that, in the development of doctrine thus far, people were always mainly inclined toward the presentation seeking to hold firmly to two factors deemed essential—the Son's oneness with the Father, and his being a person distinct from the Father—and to give the two equal importance. However, one could hardly show any inner connection between these two separate affirmations. But when Arianism emerged with such energy and, with its analytical dialectic, insisted even more forcefully on clear and specific concepts, it had to be even more difficult to maintain a presentation of doctrine with such little internal basis as the one advanced by Arianism's opponents.

However, the circumstances now giving the Christian Church a wholly different position in the world exerted the greatest influence on the resolution of this controversy. When the persecution of Christians had ended, and Christianity was already coming to be conceived as the Roman state religion, the political condition of Christians now contributed to the way in which the Arian controversy gained far greater scope and significance than had been the case for any dispute before this time. Thus under an emperor who was a Roman and had become a Christian, and united the two in himself, the resolution of the Arian controversy became most intimately connected with the state interests of Rome. As the sole ruler, Constantine made it his task everywhere to smooth over existing tensions, to reconcile opposing parties, and to establish a new order of things in which Christianity too should take the place befitting it. He also took hold of the Arianism issue with the same methodical approach, in order to establish calm and order and a generally peaceful world on this issue as well. The Council of Nicaea, summoned by Constantine as the first ecumenical council representing the Christians of the entire Roman world, was epoch-making chiefly because it manifested, on such a grand scale, how Christianity was one with the Roman state, and displayed the twofold interest this unity involved, both for the Christian Church and for the Roman state. How very important, therefore, must have been the decisions reached at such a council! The outcome of the Council of Nicaea was the rejection of Arian teaching and the affirmation of belief in the Son as expressed in the formula that he is "begotten from the essence of the Father, is God from God, light from light, true God from true God, begotten not made, the same in being (ὁμοούσιος) as the Father."

Thereafter the concept of the *homoousian* was permanently established by the church as the means of expressing the Son's relation to the Father. The development of the dogma of Christ's divinity reached its apex with this term, for the initial tendency from this direction, identifying the Son as much as possible with the Father, could go no further if there was still said to be any difference between the Father and the Son. The concept of the *homoousian* of the Son was said to express the most decided antithesis to how the Arians separated the Son from the Father. We might turn to such an authentic source as Athanasius for the more specific sense of this expression, because he was indeed one of the main spokespersons for the anti-Arian faction. Yet from his explanation we just see that one hardly knew how to attach a clear and specific concept to this term. Athanasius says that in no way ought one to think of any corporeal relation; that one must leave aside all sensuous considerations and apprehend, with pure thinking alone, the unique relation of the Son to the Father, of the Logos to God, and the perfect likeness of the reflected splendor to the light.

Since here we are speaking exclusively of what is incorporeal, the light's oneness of nature, its identity, is something that is indivisible. It is altogether necessary to stick to the image of light and the light's reflected splendor. Just as the sun's rays or reflected splendor are nothing alien to, or unlike, the sun in that example; just as light and its rays are one and the same, so that in the one we always at the same time see the other; therefore, also with regard to the relation of the Father and the Son, this oneness and natural distinctiveness can only be designated by the term ὁμοούσιος. Accordingly the fathers of the Nicene Council wished to express this meaning with their formula.[47] Therefore, right where it seems we must think, first of all, about the natural relationship in which two substances stand to each other, in virtue of derivation or emanation, that is not how this formula was said to be understood. Yet on the other hand this very analogy to the physical realm ought to have been the requisite way of looking at it, the one through which alone we could form a notion of this unique relationship.

In any event the very emphatic protest of Arius and his followers, against anything in the idea of God that is suggestive of emanation, was so influential that, mainly from this angle, they believed they had to be leery of the formula. That is why, even at the council itself, where the proposed formula aroused a lively controversy, it could

---

47. The foregoing summarizes the account in Athanasius, *On the Decrees of the Council of Nicaea*, chs. 20–25. [*Ed.*] Athanasius (c. 296–373) was archbishop of Alexandria and a major defender of Nicene doctrine.

only be adopted with the express proviso that using it about the Son is not said to affirm any physical affect or state on his part, or any separation or isolation from the Father. That is certainly the case because nonmaterial, spiritual, incorporeal nature excludes all bodily affects. Putting it this way simply expresses the point that the Son has no likeness to creatures, for he is simply in every way like unto the Father who has begotten him. But how was he said to have been begotten from the Father if one did not know how to say anything about the manner of the begetting? However positive the formula sounded, it just provided an ill-defined, contentless, negative concept, and very great effort was expended in getting the formula adopted, an effort that would have proved unsuccessful without the intervention of imperial authority.[48]

To be sure, church fathers such as Athanasius were unwilling to say that adoption of the formula depended on this intervention. However, Eusebius' account leaves no doubt about the emperor's decisive personal involvement in the final outcome of the council. At first the emperor declared himself in favor of a different meaning,[49] a factor supporting the supposition that Alexandrian influence is what later decided him to favor the ὁμοούσιος formula. At a time when they had already become so powerful, hierarchical interests are where to look for the ultimately controlling factor in this matter as well. Just think back to the very beginning of the controversy. It lay in the fact that, in Alexandria, where the presbyters were for a long time at odds with the episcopacy and had maintained a freer role for themselves, one presbyter parted ways with his bishop over the doctrine of Christ's divinity. How could the disagreement have been decided other than the bishop ultimately emerging victorious over the presbyter who contradicted him? The further history of dogma shows clearly enough how closely the theological framework now counting as Catholic was bound up with the hierarchical interests of the bishops.

---

48. [Ed.] From Baur's point of view, the Nicene formula contained irresolvable contradictions that the church struggled to explain for centuries. Greek metaphysics and Roman politics were part of the problem. Modern speculative philosophy, he believes, provides a more adequate basis for understanding the union of God and humanity in Christ.

49. See Constantine's letter to Alexander and Arius, in Eusebius, *Life of Constantine* 2.69.

The Big Picture:
The Doctrines of God, Moral Freedom, and the Church

A dogma that is such a prominent feature of the theological activity overall, as the doctrine of Christ's divinity was in the pre-Nicene period, is justly regarded as the characteristic expression of the general dogmatic consciousness at that time. How could precisely this doctrine have gained such overwhelming importance, and been able to be ultimately decided upon in such a form as the concept of the *homoousian*, if the entire consciousness at that time had not been focused on the supersensible, metaphysical, transcendent realm? Even when it came to Christ's person, the human element had to take such a back seat to the divine element that everything belonging to the human side was, in principle, still not a topic for dogmatic reflection.

Yet with all the thinking at that time very much immersed in the idea of God and directed toward purely "theo-logical" matters, and very much just still absorbed in abstract, contentless determinations—and with all the efforts to provide a definite, dogmatic concept for the idea of God by means of the trinitarian relationships—the teaching about God nevertheless did not have the kind of content that enabled it to have a very specific influence on the other teachings of the Christian faith. It is typical of the first period generally that the various elements making up the contents of Christian religious consciousness are still just very externally related to one another. When, in his περὶ ἀρχῶν (*On First Principles*), Origen first attempted a systematic presentation of the Christian faith, he organized its essential contents under three main headings (God, the world, and freedom), and set each of these three principles independently alongside the others. The result was that each of the three divisions of the whole was at the same time the whole itself, as just seen from a different perspective.

We should not regard this as just idiosyncrasy on Origen's part. Instead it is completely consistent with the overall standpoint of dogma at that time. God, the world as what is finite, and human beings as rational subjects, are still three independent topics treated in parallel fashion. Origen's system certainly does of course take up the entire relationship of human beings with God, in other words the treatment of God and the world, as though these topics are in principle running on two entirely separate tracks, with the idea of God on one track and the idea of freedom on the other. Furthermore, all that constitutes specifically Christian contents in the later ecclesial system, regarding the doctrine of the God-man, and all those means by which salvation is imparted to human beings, have hardly any place at all here. The actual concept of grace and the effects of grace, in the later ecclesial sense, is still absent from the church leaders' teachings in this period. Instead they only speak of God's love, goodness, and benevolence, or of a divine providence and general governance of the world. Thus when it comes to human beings, the major emphasis is on freedom of the will.

None of the important teachers of the church fails to explicitly acknowledge that if one is not free—so that, as a free, self-determining subject, one would be the uniquely responsible initiator of one's own actions—then the difference between good and evil, between virtue and vice, would be eliminated, as well as all else that marks out Christianity as a moral religion different from paganism. Everything giving a person moral and religious value in God's sight is therefore vested in human free will. In the nature of the case, accordingly, attaining a salvific Christian faith can only be a matter of practical conduct, of actively obeying the divine commandments. This is a concept of freedom that of its own accord rules out anything in the antithesis of sin and grace that could restrict this freedom in one way or another. In particular, it also rules out identifying the concept of sin with the concept of nature—although Tertullian was of course inclined to affirm this identification in the full sense. Not only did this concept of freedom become securely established in opposition to the pagan view of a blind fate and chance, and the Gnostic doctrines about an astrologically determined destiny; with it people also sought to eliminate the difficulties God's foreknowledge, or belief in prophecies, or apparently deterministic scripture passages, seemed to present for the idea of human freedom.

Since one could scarcely think of a human being's relation to God otherwise than as shaped by the fact of moral freedom, Origen, the first of the church's teachers to set forth a theory of his own about the relation of the divine and the human aspects in Christ's person, certainly believed he could posit freedom as alone the bond of Christ's divine-human unity. In the well-known Platonic trichotomy to which Origen subscribed, the soul [*psyche*] is the mind-body mediator [or mediation], and is the principle behind the will's complete freedom to decide in favor of either the mind or the body.

What is the case in an absolute way regarding the soul of Jesus is only relatively so, to a greater or lesser degree, in all the other souls. For, as rational essences created by God, they fell away from God and, in their descent from the higher world, they first became souls, as cooled-down spirits. Jesus' soul alone is so inseparably bound to the divine Logos from the beginning, because its willing is unwavering and the warmth of its love is inextinguishable, that his soul merges wholly with the essence of the Logos and the two are no longer two but are essentially one. What was at first simply the will's free self-determination has become its nature, which is why Origen visualized this all-pervasiveness of the human by the divine in Christ's person by employing the image, so often used subsequently, of iron made red-hot by fire.

The same principle of moral free will belonging to the concept of rational beings, and having such great importance for anthropology and christology, also extends to angelology and demonology. The fact that there are not just angels but also demons, in the higher region between God and human beings, has its basis simply in free will and the possibility of using it for evil as well as for good. The antagonism between these two realms also places the domain of Christian revelation under the heading of a dualistic worldview, with Christ's death as a struggle against the Devil, and with the struggles of Christian martyrs who, following in Christ's footsteps, incessantly strike back victoriously against the attacks of the demons.

Angelology and demonology on the one hand, and eschatology on the other, offered very wide latitude not merely for fantasizing freely about the supersensible world, but also for the influence of pagan and Jewish notions. Consequently such elements also reminded Christianity that its origins had common ground with paganism and Judaism. Thus what then took shape, in light of this, was not merely the very specific expression of distinctively Christian dogma, as in the doctrine of the Trinity, but also the character of Christianity in the process of forming itself into the church—namely, the doctrine of the church itself.

The dogma of the only salvific church already had its basis at that time, and Cyprian stated it in the thesis that those who do not have the church for their mother also do not have God for their father.[50] Once the idea of the Catholic Church had become so extensively realized, Cyprian's precept followed from two premises: whoever did not adhere to the church's tradition also could not belong to its fellowship; and, Catholic dogma is given its specific contents in the doctrine of Christ's divinity.

Already in the controversies with the Montanists and the Novatians, where the doctrine of the church itself first came into play, one nevertheless had to become aware of how the predicates assigned to the church came into mutual conflict, as antinomies, when the one apostolic church was said to be not merely the Catholic Church, but also the holy church. The Montanist and the Novatian view of the church's essential being so highly valued the attribute of holiness that, as the church of the spirit, the church was said to consist only of *spiritales* or spiritual persons, not of *psychici* or psychic persons. That is why these sects wanted to exclude from the fellowship or communion of the church said to be holy, all those whose acknowledged transgressions made their

---

50. Cyprian, *On the Unity of the Church*, ch. 6: "He cannot have God for his father who has not the church for his mother. Since no one not on Noah's ark escaped the flood, no one outside the church is rescued" [Henry S. Bettenson, *The Early Christian Fathers* (London, 1956), 73]. The *Shepherd* also contains the same teaching where the church is portrayed using the image of building a tower, for which only those stones described in the text can be used (Vision 3.4) [*ANF* 2:13–14]. The *Shepherd* has the exalted idea of the church that "she was created first of all" and "for her sake the world was made" (Vision 2.4) [*ANF* 2:12].

joining it impossible.⁵¹ Hence they had to make the concept of catholicity subordinate to that of holiness in this way, just as the Catholic Christians, being *psychici*, had to set limits to the norm of holiness so as not to take away anything from the church's catholicity.

According to those sects, what makes a person unworthy of fellowship or communion with the church, as a holy church, are the specific kinds of sins that the Montanists considered to be mortal sins. Yet what is lost because of sin can be regained by the forgiveness of sin. Hence the issue of the possibility of forgiving sins, and the authority to do so, is directly involved with the doctrine of the church. The Montanists allowed that forgiveness of sin is possible, and did not absolutely deny that the church has the right to receive back into its fellowship someone guilty of a mortal sin, provided that the sin is assuredly forgiven. But since the Montanists maintained⁵² that absolution could be given only by prophets who, as instruments of the spirit, have standing equal to that of the apostles, and that in no case could it be granted by the clergy, by the bishops of the Catholic Church, they regarded forgiveness of sin as a direct act of God, not an act of the church. Hence they refused to give ecclesiastical absolution to repentant sinners but left open to them the prospect of receiving God's grace. They called upon sinners to be contrite and repent, and offered intercessory prayers for them, but left the outcome up to the mercy of God.

It has been correctly noted⁵³ that this Montanist position draws a distinction in principle between the individual's relation to the church and the individual's relation to God. It assumes that salvation could also be gained apart from the communion of the church. It relinquishes the exclusive role of the church and even the concept of the visible church, although without being aware of the consequences of doing so. Thus only God can forgive sins. The prophets are of course fully authorized to forgive sins, but the reason they make no use of this power is lest still more sins be committed after those sins have been forgiven.⁵⁴ The worrisome prospect the Montanists foresaw, one subsequently borne out clearly enough by practice in the Catholic Church, was that forgiveness of sins could itself become a device that encourages or fosters sins. To prevent this from happening, they wanted to not grant forgiveness of sins at all, because what is done once can just as well also be done repeatedly.

In any event, since forgiveness of sins calls for contrition and repentance, when it comes to repentance we are dealing with the same larger issue involving the doctrine

---

51. In this sense the Novatians called themselves "the pure ones," the Καθαρούς, making this the first time the term "Cathari" acquired its special significance. Eusebius, in speaking of the Roman presbyter Novatus, otherwise known by his Roman name Novatian, recounts that, as founder of the Novatians, he "became the leader of a separate sect of those who, in their pride of mind, styled themselves Puritans [Καθαρούς]" (*Ecclesiastical History* 6.43.1).

52. See above, pp. 231–32.

53. See Schwegler, *Montanismus* (Part 3, n. 99), 232.

54. In *On Modesty*, ch. 21, Tertullian reports a Montanist prophet as saying: "The church has the power to forgive sins; but I will not do so lest they commit other sins."

of the church. The possibility of repenting a second time, after first having done so in the forgiveness of sins accompanying baptism itself, was also a major factor in the conflict between the Catholic Church on the one side, and the Montanists and Novatians on the other. The *Shepherd* of Hermas,[55] and even Tertullian too in his earlier period,[56] allow for repenting at least one more time subsequent to the initial repentance at one's baptism, as the outer limits of divine indulgence. However, as a Montanist, Tertullian declared that post-baptism repentance is utterly in vain, is fruitless. This is the pivotal issue in the conflict between the Catholic Church and the Montanists, a topic we covered earlier. Cyprian criticized the contradiction on the part of such opponents, who urge repentance and yet deny that penance is a means of salvation.[57] On this point the Novatians fully agreed with the Montanists. As late as the Council of Nicaea, the Novatian bishop Acesius defended the Montanist tenets regarding repentance and absolution.[58]

---

55. In Book 2, Fourth Commandment, ch. 1 [*ANF* 2:21]. See also Part 3, n. 181.
56. *On Penitence*, ch. 7.
57. *Epistle* 55.
58. Socrates, *Ecclesiastical History* 1.10.

Part 5

Christianity as a Power Dominant in the World, in Its Relation to the Pagan World and to the Roman State

The Transition to a Position of Power[1]

When we consider the various aspects of Christianity as a historical phenomenon, we see that it developed and realized, in ever wider scope, the absolute idea, which is Christianity's essential content. It could not have asserted itself as the principle of salvation had it not abolished the particularistic limitations with which Judaism sought to counter it. Christianity did so by affirming universal salvation as its principle. In addition, Christianity could not have set its foot firmly in the world as a truly historical phenomenon unless, with the idea of a catholic church, it cut all ties with two forces that, in comparable ways, would have to have made Christianity's historical development impossible.

Under one of them, a Christianity with a Gnostic Christ would have dissipated its specific content in the idea of a general world process, and dissolved itself into the generality of a speculative worldview. Under the other, with a Montanist Christ, Christianity would have come into the world only in order to remove, as soon as possible, the soil of its own historical existence, with a denouement ultimately demolishing all of history. Thus Christianity could not even become conscious of the content of its own dogma, as the absolute truth immanent in the Catholic Church, without presenting itself as God's supreme and absolute revelation, in its concept of the *homoousian*, in the idea of a Christ identical in essence with God.

Yet even with this affirmation Christianity had not yet done all it had to in realizing the absolute idea of its own essential nature. In all these circumstances we have discussed so far there is an inner antithesis prominent within the sphere of Christianity itself. But there is also an external antithesis as well; so we now look at the face of Christianity turned toward the non-Christian world. Inasmuch as the idea of the Catholic Church is supposed to realize its historical existence within the world, this already presupposes a power also extending over everything outwardly and overcoming every hostile opposition to it. If Christianity is the universal, absolute religion, then it must also be the world religion and become dominant everywhere.

Christianity and the Roman Empire could not coexist in the world without sooner or later becoming as one. People regarded it as the most unmistakable proof

---

1. [*Ed.*] The German simply reads *Übergang*; our heading parallels the *Übergang auf das Dogma* (transition to dogma) at the beginning of Part Four.

of Christianity's divine standing that this goal of their union had been reached in such a short time and by the most splendid victory. But it is even far more important to be aware of how this goal had been reached and of how internally coherent this very great, world-historical change proved to be, by following up this change from its earliest beginning and through all its twists and turns. Christianity could not have become the dominant religion of the Roman Empire without its dominant position in the world having been simply the outward manifestation of the power it had gained within the consciousness of the time.

Hence, in our historical presentation of the topic now before us, we by and large have to distinguish two issues. The question, first and foremost, is: How did that whole turnabout happen in the contemporary consciousness of the paganism standing opposed to Christianity? Then we ask: How did the outward stance of Christianity toward the Roman state increasingly correlate with the inner course of this spiritual process?

I. The Internal Aspects of Christianity's Relation to the Pagan World and to the Roman State

In looking back to the earliest beginnings of this world-historical process of development, what we see juxtaposed are Christianity as the most insignificant factor, and the Roman Empire as the greatest one. Yet this most insignificant factor was not merely the bearer of the seed of world dominance, for from the outset, and at every point of its development, what this seed expressed was the consciousness of its own power to overcome the world.

THE WORLD-CONSCIOUSNESS OF CHRISTIANS

This world-consciousness is already expressed as the general character of Christianity in Jesus' words to the disciples: "You are the salt of the earth" (Matt 5:13). This is the guiding idea that already inspired Christians right from the beginning, at a time when their external circumstances could not but contrast greatly with this world-consciousness of Christianity, even though in various ways it repeatedly manifested itself in them in very characteristic fashion. They are more or less clearly aware that they are the heart and soul of the world, the center substantially holding it all together, the axis around which world history revolves, those who alone have a future for themselves.

Melito, the bishop of Sardis during the reign of Marcus Aurelius, sent an *Apology*, written about 170, to the emperor. In it he reminds the Romans that Christianity appeared in the world at the same time as the epochal reign of Caesar Augustus, when the Roman Empire was at the height of its success. Melito says that since then they have both co-existed in the world in a mutually advantageous way.[2] Thus Melito

---

2. See Eusebius, *Ecclesiastical History* 4.26.7–8, where, in the main passage cited there from Melito's book *To Antonius*, it says: "Our philosophy [*Baur*: Christianity is called a 'philosophy' as it also is elsewhere by the Apologists; see Tatian's *Address to the Greeks*, ch. 35] first grew up among the barbarians, but its full flower came among your nation in the great reign of your ancestor Augustus, and became an omen of good to your empire, for from that time the power of the Romans became great and splendid. You are now his happy successor, and shall be so along with your son, if you protect the philosophy which grew up with the empire, and began with Augustus. Your ancestors nourished it together with the other cults, and the greatest proof that our doctrine flourished for good along with the empire in its noble beginning is the fact that it met no evil in the reign of Augustus, but

was able, from his standpoint, to simply attribute to Christianity the good fortune the Roman Empire had experienced since Augustus, as a new source of well-being inaugurated for it in the world.

At that time it seemed to Christians that indeed everything essentially conducive to the welfare of the Roman Empire just had its basis in Christianity. Therefore, from the conjunction of these two factors one could simply conclude that the world's well-being had a more secure foundation to the degree that the bond uniting them was strengthened. Before he became a Montanist, Tertullian's view of the world bore the imprint of the same world-consciousness indwelling other Christians. We see it in his notion that those alone are Christians who by their prayers halted the world's destruction, and in doing so kept the Roman Empire intact; that only because of them did God hesitate to do away with everything.[3]

The anonymous author of the *Epistle to Diognetus* is the most vocal of the early church teachers with this consciousness. No one is more suffused with it than he is, or expresses it in a finer or more energetic way. After depicting, in a pointedly antithetical fashion, the distinctive and puzzling conduct of the Christians as it contrasts in so many ways with their surroundings, he sums up his characterization with the following statement.

> To sum up all in one word—what the soul is in the body, that are Christians in the world. The soul is dispersed through all the members of the body, and Christians are scattered through all the cities of the world. The soul dwells in the body, yet is not of the body; and Christians dwell in the world, yet are not of the world. The invisible soul is guarded by the visible body, and Christians are known indeed to be in the world, but their godliness remains invisible.

---

on the contrary everything splendid and glorious according to the wishes of all men" [LCL, *Eusebius*, 1:390–93]. How fitting and suggestive it is here to call Christianity the philosophy that grew up with the Empire, in its relation to the Roman state since Augustus! Thus Christianity and Empire are, so to speak, linked like a pair of siblings.

3. Tertullian, *Apology*, ch. 32: "There is also another and a greater necessity for our offering prayer in behalf of the emperors, nay, for the complete stability of the empire, and for Roman interests in general. For we know that a mighty shock impending over the whole earth—in fact the very end of all things threatening dreadful woes—is only retarded by the continued existence of the Roman Empire. We have no desire, then, to be overtaken by these dire events; and in praying that their coming be delayed, we are lending our aid to Rome's duration" [ANF 3:42–43]. Also, in ch. 39: "We pray . . . for the welfare of the world, for the prevalence of peace, for the delay of the final consummation" [ANF 3:46]. (See above, pp. 190ff., for the Montanist antithesis to this prayer.) In ch. 7 of his *Second Apology*, Justin Martyr writes: "Wherefore God delays causing the confusion and destruction of the whole world, by which the wicked angels and demons and men shall cease to exist, because of the seed of the Christians, who know that they are the cause of preservation in nature. Since, if it were not so, it would not have been possible for you [the Roman Senate] to do these things, and to be impelled by evil spirits; but the fire of judgment would descend and utterly dissolve all things" [ANF 1:190]. The Christians are aware of their being the world-preserving principle. Therefore everything in the world depends on them, so that even what "you pagans" do against the Christians is limited, for the Christians' sake, by God's not yet being willing to let the world come to ruin. For if there were no Christians, it would not even be possible for you pagans to do this, and for the evil demons to incite you to do it.

I. The Internal Aspects of Christianity's Relation to the Pagan World and to the Roman State

The flesh hates the soul, and wars against it, though itself suffering no injury, because it is prevented from enjoying pleasures; the world also hates the Christians, though in nowise injured, because they abjure pleasures. The soul loves the flesh that hates it, and [loves also] the members; Christians likewise love those that hate them. The soul is imprisoned in the body, yet preserves that very body; and Christians are confined in the world as in a prison, and yet they are the preservers of the world. The immortal soul dwells in a mortal tabernacle; and Christians dwell as sojourners in corruptible [bodies], looking for an incorruptible dwelling in the heavens. . . . God has assigned the Christians this illustrious position, which it were unlawful for them to forsake.[4]

Those who in this way know themselves to be the soul of the world must have the reins of worldly dominion fall naturally into their hands since, without question, the time for that will come.

THE HOSTILITY OF THE PAGANS, AND THE POWER OF CHRISTIANITY QUIETLY AT WORK

However, a great deal of ground was to be covered before Christians came to hold the reins. There was still much aversion to Christianity and its followers, much abhorrence and antagonistic hostility to be overcome in the minds of the pagan world.

From the Christian perspective, the whole of paganism was regarded as the kingdom of those demons who used the arts of deception to mislead human beings by trickery and guile, so that people would revere them as gods. Despite all their defeats, these demons are relentless as the bitterest enemies of the Christians, because they hate nothing more than all that opens the eyes of human beings to the light of truth, and that destroys the snares with which they deceive people.

From the other side, the pagans saw in Christians a race hostile to humankind and scarcely deserving to be called human beings.[5] In Christianity itself, what they see too is anything but what could make just the remotest claim to be called a religion. As we learn from the writings of the Apologists,[6] all that is irreligious and immoral could always just be laid at the door of Christianity, with all of it comprised in the three, generally current, accusations of atheism, eating human flesh, and promiscuous intercourse.[7] The fact that to the pagans the Christians appeared to be "atheists"

---

4. [Ed.] Baur gives a German translation of this passage from the *Epistle to Diognetus*, ch. 6, but does not have a footnote locating where it occurs. We have presented, with several minor modifications, the English translation found in *ANF* 1:27, which was made from the original Greek.

5. Tertullian, *Apology*, ch. 37: "Yet you choose to call us enemies of the human race" [*ANF* 3:45].

6. The list of pertinent passages includes: Justin Martyr, *First Apology*, ch. 26, and *Dialogue with Trypho*, ch. 10; Tatian, *Address to the Greeks*, ch. 25; Athenagoras, *Plea for the Christians*, ch. 31; Tertullian, *Apology*, ch. 7; Minucius Felix, *Octavius*, ch. 9; Origen, *Against Celsus* 6.27 and 6.40.

7. [Ed.] Here Baur gives the Greek customarily used to state these accusations. "Atheism" is ἀθεότης. The other two accusations are stated in terms referring to figures in Greek mythology; see also the

(ἄθεοι, as they were so often called) is quite natural, since the Christians not only did not recognize the pagan deities, for Christianity was hardly perceived as bearing the marks of a religious cultus in its own right. They were also said to commit acts of such a horrible kind among themselves, the kind of acts only recounted in ancient myths from a time far removed from all civilized and humane life, and this attests to an abnormal level of hatred on the part of the pagans. Whatever may have been the source of such accusations,[8] as soon as they had once become current as folk legends, they not only got elaborated into incredible narratives; there was also the general predisposition to believe them all the more willingly the more they seemed to be confirmed by so many features setting Christians apart from Jews and pagans. With Christianity becoming so widespread, features that became increasingly obvious included the Christians' custom of holding their gatherings at night, with the customary meals at that time, as well as their intimate fraternization, which aroused the suspicion of their

---

following footnote, by Baur. "Eating human flesh" is Θυέστεια δεῖπνα, using an allusion to Thyestes, who was tricked into eating the flesh of his own sons at a banquet. "Promiscuous intercourse" is Οἰδιπόδειοι μίξεις, alluding to Oedipus who (unwittingly) married his mother.

8. The fact that such accusations utilize allusions to ancient Greek myths was no obstacle to regarding Jews as their main originators. In *To the Nations* 1.14, Tertullian writes about this: "For what other set of men is the seed-plot of all the calumny against us?" [ANF 3:123]. The lies and calumnies in the Talmud are analogous. See below, n. 19. What primarily gave rise to these charges is doubtless the early Christians' custom of commemorating the night on which the Lord was betrayed and prior to that had celebrated the Eucharist with the disciples (1 Cor 11:23–26). They did so by gathering in the evening, and by referring to their principal act as eating the flesh and blood of the Lord. The main accusation was therefore that of ἀνθρωποφαγία (cannibalism), and Tatian confines himself to just protesting against this charge (*Address to the Greeks*, ch. 25). However, Justin was of course aware (*First Apology*, ch. 26 [ANF 1:172]) that, in the Christians' case, the charge involved not merely ἀνθρωπείων σάρκων βοραί (using the human body as food), but also (*Dialogue*, ch. 10 [ANF 1:199]) λυχνίας ἀνατροπή (extinguishing the lights) and ἀνέδην μίξεις (promiscuous intercourse), acts said to follow in due course. With Tertullian we see all this portrayed in a scene combining everything that is horrible and could inflame people's imagination as they opposed such a sect. "Monsters of wickedness, we are accused of observing a holy rite in which we kill a little child and then eat it; in which, after the feast, we practice incest, the dogs—our pimps, forsooth, overturning the lights and getting us the shamelessness of darkness for our impious lusts" (*Apology*, ch. 7 [ANF 3:23]). See also *To the Nations* 1.7: ". . . an infant . . . to be sacrificed, as well as some bread to be broken and dipped in his blood; you also want candles, and dogs tied together to upset them, and bits of meat to rouse the dogs" [ANF 3:115]. In his *Octavius*, ch. 9, Minucius Felix has the pagan Caecilius recount the "accursed fable" in which the actions are most especially contrived for "the initiation of young novices" [ANF 4:177]. Subsequently we encounter the same fable with the Manicheans of the Middle Ages, indeed in the form in which the child is the offspring of copulation depicted as it is above; and that the ashes of his body, which was burned after eight days, have the demonic power of keeping firmly in the sect whoever has eaten even a little of them. In this version the Devil also plays his role along with the demons. This legend had crossed over to these Manicheans from the Euchites, who came to Thrace from Western Asia. Michael Psellus, writing about the middle of the eleventh century, recounts this same story of putting out the lights at night and incestuous sexual promiscuity, of murdering and burning the resulting children, and the magical effect of their ashes mixed together with their blood, in his *De operatione daemonum*, ed. Boissonade (Nuremberg, 1838), p. 8. Tertullian's mention of sacramental infanticide stands intermediate between this form of the fable, which resulted from ancient Eastern ideas of demons with their works of darkness (on which see my *Das manichäische Religionssystem* [Tübingen, 1831], 134ff.), and that old, simple form. But what is the origin of that version itself?

being a secret society. There was also their reclusive conduct in withdrawing from public life, and other features of this kind.

As Tacitus so strikingly wrote about Christianity, this was then that "deadly superstition" (*exitiabilis superstitio*), notorious because of their "shameful crime" (*flagitia*). Thus we must take his verdict about the matter as expressing the authentically Roman view in his day. To understand him correctly, and to comprehend in a general way how even the most educated Romans, and not merely the masses, could reach such a verdict, we must not overlook another factor unmistakable in Tacitus. It is that people looked upon the Christianity coming out of Judea (the *origo hujus mali*, origin of this evil) as simply a product of Judaism, as simply what, to a heightened extent, embodied everything in Judaism that had already fully aroused the antipathy of the Romans.[9] Tacitus could only explain the character of the Jews—so very antagonistic to the ideas, customs, and practices of all other people, with everything that made them in their own way such a unique people—on the basis of the rancorous hatred toward all others that filled them from the very outset and was in fact the principle of their national identity. Thus when it came to Christians, they too were completely characterized by "hatred of humankind" (*odium generis humani*), and it seemed that they had to be utterly excluded from the environs of the whole civilized and cultured world.

If we in fact consider educated men who thought like Tacitus as being authentic representatives of the Roman world at that time, then there can be nothing more antithetical than the relationship between Christianity and the Roman Empire in his day—no greater incompatibility, no greater mutual harshness and repugnance. One can scarcely imagine how the faith of a sect that, at all levels of society, from the lowest to the highest, had public opinion so very much against it, was ever able to overcome such a great social disadvantage. But its still so narrow scope did not keep Christianity from growing beyond its initial size. However, in the second half of the second century its opponents criticized Christianity because its followers were to be found neither in the great mass of the populace nor in the educated class of ordinary citizens, but instead among the craftsmen and people who would most prefer to keep to themselves and avoid the public arena.[10] This gives us the best picture of how Christianity gradually and steadily gained influence, by quietly attracting hearts and minds to itself.

The converts to Christianity were those whose loss of faith in the ancient deities had left a desolate emptiness in their religious consciousness. They felt the need for a new spiritual content, the kind for which people should have been already prepared, in the quiet, internally-focused religiousness of the Christians. Its features are:

---

9. Tacitus' depictions of the Jews (*Histories*, 5.2–3) and of the Christians (*Annals*, 15.44) are mutually complementary, for he is always also thinking about the Jews when he writes about the Christians. He very emphatically expressed his overall impression of Judaism in the statement that "the ways of the Jews are foolish and vile" (*Judaeorum mos absurdus sordidusque*).

10. For this criticism of Christianity, by Celsus, see Origen, *Against Celsus* 3.55.

self-denial, or acceptance of privation, in an avaricious world; Christianity's internal cohesiveness during an almost universal dissolution of the most important social ties; the equally important consolation of the gospel's promises; the lively expectation of the great denouement aroused by faith in the parousia, for which one must await in readiness. Because of the inner power that Christianity exercised over the hearts and minds of people, it won over a far greater proportion of the pagan populace in this way than would have been outwardly apparent. When Christianity's ever more visible advances also provoked more violent countermeasures, the result was simply what Tertullian pointed out in reply, toward the end (ch. 50) of his *Apology* addressed to the pagans, in these words: "Nor does your cruelty, however exquisite, avail you; it is rather a temptation to us. The oftener we are mown down by you, the more in number we grow; *the blood of Christians is seed*" [ANF 3:55].

THE APOLOGISTS

This persecution occurred right when more and more philosophically educated persons were becoming Christians. The admiration they had to have for the steadfastness of the Christian martyrs also compelled them to acknowledge that a teaching making its adherents so contemptuous of death also had to rest on a deeper foundation of truth, and could certainly not be an instigation to sensuous appetites.[11] Indeed, as philosophers they made the practical application of philosophical principles to their own lives the main purpose of philosophy. So it seemed to them that Christianity, with its own strictly moral and practical orientation, is also itself philosophy. Then, as Christians, they continued the same kind of life dedicated to philosophy that they had already pursued as philosophers, just doing so under a different label.[12]

What Justin, philosopher and martyr, has to say along these lines, about his own motive in going over to Christianity, is certainly also the story of the conversion of so many others with the same orientation.[13] For us he is the main representative of those who, in being called "the Apologists," form a group in its own right. That is indeed because now these figures well-acquainted with Greek culture and philosophy, who had gone over to the enemy camp, introduce a new epoch in the relation of Christianity to the pagan world.

The overall project of the Apologists was to justify Christianity to the world hostile to it, and in particular to make this case to those who had the most decided

---

11. Justin Martyr, *Second Apology*, ch. 12: "for what sensual or intemperate man . . . could welcome death that he might be deprived of his enjoyments" [ANF 1:192].

12. Even as Christians they wore the pallium or cloak of the philosophers. See Justin Martyr, *Dialogue with Trypho*, ch. 1. Tertullian, *On the Pallium*, ch. 6, concludes by declaring: "Joy, Mantle, and exult! A better philosophy has now deigned to honor thee, ever since thou hast begun to be a Christian's vesture!" [ANF 4:12]. Also see August Neander, *Antignostikus, Geist der Tertullianus und Einleitung in dessen Schriften* (2nd ed., Berlin, 1849), 307.

13. *Dialogue with Trypho*, ch. 8.

influence on how Christianity related to the Roman state and to public life, and on the circumstances of the Christians themselves. The Apologists sought to achieve this by portraying, as absurd and empty, the crass accusations currently made against Christians, and to put an end to the prejudices confronting Christianity in public opinion. By a more detailed explanation of the teachings and principles, the ethics and customs, the entire social and moral conduct, of the Christians, the Apologists sought to substantiate a more accurate representation of Christianity's essential nature, and by doing so also to undergird the conviction that the Christians pose no danger to the state. The main point in all this was acquainting people with the true nature of Christianity. Once they just knew what it is, then it seemed they also could not refuse to tolerate it in civil society.

Nevertheless the Apologists did not simply stop at this point. Whereas the pagans' accusations against Christianity, and their thoughts about its relation to the entire pagan world, could not have been expressed with greater coarseness and repugnance, the picture the Apologists painted from the other side about this relationship was no less an exaggeration. They claimed that Christianity was hardly something new and unheard of, something just coming all at once into the world to conflict with everything heretofore passing muster as ethics, humaneness, and culture, and in doing so being universally detested by humankind. The Apologists supposed instead that, if people just opened their eyes they would behold everywhere, right in the midst of the pagan world itself, the clearest proofs of Christianity's presence in the world already prior to its actual appearance. In order to convince the Jews of Christianity's truth and divinity, Christians directed the attention of the Jews to the Old Testament, which, if just understood correctly, in its more profoundly spiritual meaning, is seen to already contain all that in fact belongs to the essential nature of Christianity, all the elements of the gospel story, discoverable in prophetic and typological terms right down to the smallest points. In entirely the same fashion, the apologetic aimed at the pagans was said to reach its apex in explaining to them that, without their knowing it, there are Christians in the midst of the pagan world who have internalized Christianity as the immanent truth of their own consciousness.

To be sure, nothing sounds stranger than Justin's rhetorical address to the pagans,[14] when he points out that the form of the cross is visible everywhere, in order to make the truth of Christianity very vivid for them and to set it before them. For, how

---

14. *First Apology*. [*Ed.* What follows in our text is a paraphrase from ch. 55.] Compare Tertullian, *Apology*, ch. 16: "If any of you think we render superstitious adoration to the cross, then you share that adoration with us.... Every stake fixed in an upright position is a portion of the cross; we render our adoration, if you will have it so, to a god entire and complete. We have shown before [ch. 12] that your deities are derived from shapes modeled from the cross. But you also worship victories, for in your trophies the cross is the heart of the trophy. The camp religion of the Romans is all through a worship of the standards, and sets the standards above all gods. Well, as those images decking out the standards are ornaments of crosses, then all those hangings of your standards and banners are robes of crosses" [*ANF* 3:31].

can they persist in their unbelief even now, when they see the universal significance of the cross before them in all the instruments or tools they use in their occupations, in navigation and agriculture? This is also the case with respect to the erect stature that distinguishes a human being from the animals; indeed, even so with the banners and victory emblems they display publicly as symbols of their power and dominance, and in the images of their deceased emperors. What deep insight these examples give us, into the distinctive way of looking at things belonging to those for whom Christianity hardly appears to be something that contrasts with the world around them. For them what seems instead to now arise, for the first time, is their clear consciousness regarding what they had already been [i.e., Christians] and had before their eyes [i.e., Christianity]! Although such an outlook was initially just a vague play of the imagination, they certainly knew how to find an even deeper and more solid foundation for their Christian universalism.

We should not regard it as accidental that the Logos-idea became the prevalent concept at the very time when there was such great concern to accommodate Christianity to the consciousness of the pagan world, and to have the differences separating them seem as slight as possible. For example, the form this idea took in Justin's case was most especially adapted to serving as a bridge between what is Christian and what is non-Christian. The very same Logos that became a human being, as foretold by the Jewish prophets, also brought about everything found to be true and rational in the pagan world. So Justin even contended, without any reservations, that what is rational as such is also Christian. All those who have lived rational lives (μετὰ λόγου) are Christians, even though they were said to be godless people. The excellent accomplishments of philosophers and lawgivers did not happen without their sharing in the Logos. They were simply unaware of the Logos in its entirety, which is also why they so often contradicted one another.[15]

To spell out this relationship, Justin turned to the Stoic doctrine of the Logos Spermatikos, in order to distinguish what the Logos is in his unity and totality, as the universal reason, from what he is in the individual person, only in a particular way. This same insight is foundational for the worldview held by Clement of Alexandria. The difference between what is Christian and what is non-Christian in this respect, is simply that, after the whole Logos has appeared in Christianity, this makes Christianity, in an absolute way, what that which is indeed also found outside of Christianity is in just a relative and particular way, just imperfectly and fragmentarily. What follows from this is that everything the Logos Spermatikos has brought about was not so imprinted in human consciousness that it could also become what the uneducated people believed; that those people gained no inspiration and capacity for sacrifice in the cause of truth, of the kind Christians demonstrated by their showing contempt for

---

15. Justin Martyr, *First Apology*, ch. 46; *Second Apology*, chs. 10 and 13. [*Ed.*] In ch. 13, Justin says that "they who contradict themselves on the more important points appear not to have possessed the heavenly wisdom" (*ANF* 1:193).

death. Despite the analogies between Socrates and Christ, this feature shows how they differ. At the same time, since the Christian element in the Logos concept is essentially the rational element, what is Christian and what is non-Christian have such a close inner relationship that, in the pagan world too, Christianity encounters kindred elements and points of contact everywhere, ones to which it can attach itself.

Similar to how Justin declared that what is rational is also Christian, Tertullian saw "a testimony of the soul that is by nature Christian" (*testimonium animae naturaliter christianae*),[16] in the simplest expressions of the religious consciousness where the pagan willingly casts aside the polytheistic character of his idea of God. Thus one may simply revert to something that dialectical consideration also calls for—the original and immediate element that polytheistic belief has as its necessary presupposition. Then pagans and Christians stand on the same ground of universal reason and natural God-consciousness; and in Christianity, through the Logos having become a human being, what is expressed clearly and vividly for popular consciousness too is simply what each person must acknowledge as being inherently true and rational.

We do not know if these apologetic writings made a direct impression, or even if they just remained in the hands of those who were initially their intended recipients. Generally speaking, it is undeniable that their essential contribution was to draw the attention of a larger sector of the public to Christianity, and to have it be seen in a quite different light than before.

THE PHILOSOPHICALLY EDUCATED OPPONENTS OF CHRISTIANITY

Literary manifestos now took the place of the sinister folk legends that heretofore had so often been the murky sources from which people drew their information about Christianity. One could not disregard these writings, which gave any interested persons the opportunity to form their own independent judgments; writings calling for doing so in a tenor that had to be even more provocative.

The more that people became knowledgeable about Christianity in detail, the less they could fail to appreciate the significance Christianity had increasingly gained as a new phenomenon of those times. They had to see the necessity of accounting, seriously and fundamentally, for how things stood with Christianity as such, for what it involved, for what claims to truth it had to make. It was now impossible to ignore Christianity or to just dismiss it scornfully and contemptuously. If one could not deign to believe in it, one did have to make the attempt to refute it. The more such an investigation made one aware of the vast difference between the Christian worldview and the pagan worldview, the more one also had to go back to the ultimate foundations on which each of these worldviews rested.

---

16. *The Soul's Testimony*, chs. 1–6. See also *Apology*, ch. 17. [*Ed.*] The Latin is from the latter document, translated in *ANF* 3:32 as "O noble testimony of the soul by nature Christian."

Celsus

In the second half of the second century there was no shortage of opponents of Christianity who were fully aware of how important this issue is. Evidence of that is the remarkable writing against Christianity composed by the Greek philosopher Celsus. We have no specific knowledge of him apart from it.[17]

---

17. It is no longer possible to ascertain the identity of this Celsus whom Origen opposed in composing his famous apologetic work, for Origen himself knew nothing more about him. What we do know, and can take into account is as follows. In *Against Celsus* 1.8, Origen informs us that there were two individuals named Celsus, both of them Epicureans; that one lived in Nero's day, and "this one" in the time of Hadrian and after. That the latter Celsus, presumably the author in question, was an Epicurean, is evident from others of his writings. In 4.36, Origen speaks of "this Epicurean Celsus . . . (if it be the same Celsus who composed two other books against the Christians)" [*ANF* 4:513]. In 1.68 Origen speaks of a Celsus who wrote several books in opposition to magic. Although Origen considers his Celsus to be someone presenting himself as an Epicurean, or else as the Celsus known to be an Epicurean, he says here that he is unsure if his opponent is the Celsus who wrote those books opposing magic. [*Ed.* The "magic" in question here is Jesus' performance of miracles, considered to be tricks.] From the *Pseudomantia* of Lucian we learn of an Epicurean Celsus who wrote in opposition to magicians. At the request of his friend Celsus, Lucian wrote this account of Alexander of Abonuteichos, about the middle of the second century, and dedicated it to Celsus while speaking very highly of Epicurus. This Alexander was a notorious sorcerer who passed himself off as a prophet. No doubt Lucian's Celsus is the Epicurean Celsus known to Origen from other writings, although it is quite dubious whether this one is also the Celsus who opposes Christianity and is rebutted by Origen. It is hardly possible to assume that he is, since this latter Celsus is such a pronounced Platonist in his philosophical views and principles that one can hardly think of him as actually being an Epicurean or even just an eclectic philosopher. So the oft-discussed question as to the identity of Origen's Celsus has not been definitively answered. (See in particular C. W. J. Bindemann, "Ueber Celsus und seine Schrift gegen die Christen," in Illgen's *Zeitschrift für historische Theologie* 12 [1842] no. 2, 58ff.) Nevertheless we might be done with this issue of Origen's Celsus and the Epicurean Celsus, if we interpreted, more correctly than it usually is, the passage 4.36, where Origen does designate his Celsus as an Epicurean, but adds: "if it be the same Celsus who composed two other books against the Christians" [*ANF* 4:513]. August Neander (in his *Allgemeine Geschichte der christlichen Religion und Kirche*, 1st ed. [Hamburg, 1825–31], 1:274), rightly notes that this reference to "other books" can mean none other than the one Origen is rebutting, and Origen's concern is only whether the Epicurean Celsus wrote it. The issue as to whether this Epicurean wrote "two other books against the Christians" is a separate matter. The only thing Neander does not explain is how Origen could speak of "two books" when he is focused on just this one book of Celsus. But that is fully accounted for by Origen's remark to his friend Ambrosius at the very end (8.76): "You must know, however, that Celsus had promised another treatise as a sequel to this one, in which he engaged to supply practical rules for living to those who felt disposed to embrace his opinions. If, then, he has not fulfilled his promise of writing a second book, we may well be contented with these eight books [i.e., a treatise in eight parts] which we have written in answer to his discourse. But if he has begun and finished that second book," Ambrosius might be on the lookout for it and send it "so that we may answer it" [*ANF* 4:669]. Without a doubt by "two books" Origen meant the work of Celsus he wrote in opposition to, and the other one mentioned in 8.76, since in 4.36 he presupposes that Celsus has actually carried out his intention. So in any case there was only one Celsus who wrote in opposition to the Christians, not two of them. [*Ed.*] Celsus' book was banned in 448, along with the works of Porphyry, and all extant copies disappeared.

I. The Internal Aspects of Christianity's Relation to the Pagan World and to the Roman State

The Significance and the Structure of Celsus' Book

The title of Celsus' book, ἀληθὴς λόγος (*True Reason*), was doubtless supposed to indicate the concern for truth that made him determined to challenge Christianity in this way.

The abundant extracts from this now lost treatise, preserved for us by Origen in the eight books of his work of rebuttal, sufficiently show the seriousness with which Celsus pursued his intention, as well as the effort and care he bestowed on his work. He not only knew the Christians' religious texts, a fact clearly demonstrable with reference to multiple passages from the New Testament canon we use today; he also knew about the Christians' principles, practices, and organization, and the factions into which they split up—everything that characterized Christians at that time and had to be especially noticeable to a pagan opponent of them. His mental acuity, dialectical skill, and multifaceted philosophical and general education, are second to none among the opponents of Christianity. So we are seldom surprised to see him already, and very aptly, raising the same general and decisive considerations to which all the subsequent opponents of Christianity always once again return, albeit in other forms and from their very different standpoints.

Hence we should be very interested not only in becoming better acquainted with the principal points in his challenge to Christianity, but also mainly in answering the question as to the verdict he finally reached and stated about the nature and character of Christianity as such by drawing together all of his reflections over so many pages. Also, what does his verdict tell us about the general viewpoint at that time regarding Christianity's relation to the world standing opposed to it?

The work by Celsus seems to have been organized very methodically, and to some extent rather artfully. Yet a more definite judgment on this point cannot be made. That is because, while Origen takes up his opponent's text as a connected whole, he nevertheless also passes over much of it and so leaves us unsure to what extent the many repetitions and digressions in Origen's reporting were actually due to the original author. The fact that different figures are the vehicles for presenting the material enables us to see better how Celsus' work was structured.

The Initial Attack from the Jewish Standpoint

Before Celsus comes forward in his own right, he uses the figure of a Jew to articulate his objections from a Jewish perspective. This approach does not just serve to give the presentation dramatic vitality. His principal intention, in setting apart these issues a Jew could have raised from a Jewish standpoint, was instead to give a more cutting edge and significance to the main objections that were the nobler province of the pagan opponent, ones that could ultimately be settled only in the realm of philosophy.

In his separate role the Jew is preeminently assigned all the issues bearing on the credibility of the gospel story, on the inherent likelihood of its contents. He attacks the narrative of Jesus' birth from the Virgin and contends that, to the contrary, Jesus was born from a poor woman supported by her own labor, and whose husband had charged her with adultery. Cast off and homeless, she gave birth to Jesus while hiding in disgrace. Jesus, whose poverty forced him to become a servant in Egypt, learned secret arts there. After returning from Egypt and using them successfully, he declared himself to be a god.[18] Celsus correctly has his Jew making this accusation, for he seems to have gotten it from what Jews were doubtless saying at that time.[19] Most of the Jew's other objections are put in more negative terms, in that he seeks to point out what are disreputable and improbable contents of the gospel accounts. In taking this tack with reference to the birth of Jesus, he asks whether God was enamored of Jesus' mother because she was beautiful, and also how the fact that God allowed her to be cast off squares with the kingdom of God.[20] He also asks why the child Jesus was taken to Egypt. Was God also fearful that the child would be killed? There was an angel sent from heaven with the command to flee. But could not the great God who had already sent two angels for Jesus' sake, not have kept his own son safe at home? And from the accounts of Jesus' death one can see that he did not have the kind of blood that Homer says flows in the blessed gods.[21]

The ancient myths about the sons of the gods—about Perseus, Amphion, Aeacus, Minos—deserve no credence, although the great and admirable deeds of these figures nevertheless lend plausibility to such status. But what great thing have Jesus' words and deeds accomplished? Even though the Jews in the temple called upon him to demonstrate by a clear sign that he is the Son of God (Matt 12:38; also 16:1–4), he provided none.[22] How then could they regard as a god someone who not only did none of all the things he promised, but who also hid when the Jews found him guilty, condemned him and deemed him worthy of death, and who was seized while shamefully fleeing and was betrayed by those he called his disciples? A god would not have fled, and ought not to have been bound and led away. However, least of all ought the one whom people regarded as the redeemer, as the son of the greatest God, as an angel, have been forsaken and handed over by those who were together with him,

---

18. Origen, *Against Celsus* 1.28.

19. In 1.32 Origen quotes Celsus' statement that Jesus' father was "a certain solider named Panthera." According to Nitzsch, in the Talmud Jesus is called "the son of the paramour"; see K. I. Nitzsch, *Theologische Studien und Kritiken* 1 (1840) 115. The term πάνθηρ or *panthera* passed from Greek to Chaldean. Like the Latin term *lupa* ("she-wolf," also "prostitute"), it depicted the covetous sensual pleasure, the avaricious wantonness, of the kind of person who preys on everyone, eagerly pursuing them all. So it is just another way of expressing the concept of πορνεία or fornication.

20. Origen, *Against Celsus* 1.39.

21. 1.66. [*Ed.*] The reference is to the ethereal fluid (ἰχώρ) that, according to Greek mythology, is the blood of the gods and other immortals.

22. 1.67.

who shared everything with him in an intimate fellowship, and who had him as their teacher.[23]

Celsus' Jew places special emphasis on the fact that Jesus was betrayed by his own disciples. This would never have happened to any competent general, even to the leader of many thousands of men. Any head of a band of robbers would better understand how to bind his people to himself by gaining their favor.[24] The Jew also has various objections to Jesus' foretelling of his own fate. If any god or demon or rational person knew ahead of time that such things would befall him, would he not avoid them instead of plunging headlong into them? If he foretold to one of his disciples that he would betray him, and to another that he would deny him, why would they not be in such great awe of him, as a god, that the former would not betray him and the latter would not deny him? However, if he made these predictions as a god, then it was necessarily the case that what he predicted must happen. If so, then this god "led on his own disciples and prophets, with whom he was in the habit of eating and drinking, to such a degree of wickedness, that they became impious and unholy men."[25]

It is just as inconceivable to the opponent how anyone could have proven himself to be God and the Son of God in the way Jesus supposedly did. As the sun manifests itself by illuminating everything, the Son of God was said to have done likewise. What did he do in this regard that was worthy of God? Was it that he showed contempt for people and derided what befell him? If not beforehand, why did he not in the end manifest himself as God? Why did he not dispense with this ignominy, and revenge himself and his Father on those who attacked him? Celsus' Jew therefore asks how one could blame the Jews for not taking him to be a god. Since not once in his life did he convince his own disciples to view his impending death as something he would have to undergo for the benefit of humankind, how could one blame the Jews for not adopting such a view themselves? The opponent asks the Christians: Is it not contradictory that they die with him, whereas those who were his companions in his lifetime, who heard him speak and benefited from his instruction, neither died with him nor for him when they saw him suffer and die, and could not be moved to have contempt for death?[26]

From the series of objections belonging to the same category, we might just include here those involving Jesus' resurrection. The Jew asks how one could be convinced that it took place. Even granting that his resurrection had been foretold, there are of course so many other instances of those who found it in their interest to persuade gullible people by such allegations. The examples include: Zalmoxis, the slave of Pythagoras, among the Scythians; Pythagoras himself in Italy; Rhampsinitus in Egypt; Orpheus among the Odrysae; Protesilaus in Thessaly; Hercules in Taenarus;

23. 2.9.
24. 2.12.
25. 2.20 [*ANF* 4.439].
26. 2.30–45 [correcting a misprint].

Theseus.[27] But something to ponder is whether anyone who was actually dead was ever resurrected with the same body. How can Christians suppose that what others say are just myths, but that their own dramatic events included not just Jesus' outcry on the cross when he died, the earthquake and darkness, but also the most glorious and convincing denouement when he, who while living could not help himself, rose up again when dead, showing the marks of his passion, the deadly wounds and pierced hands? Who were witnesses to it? An overwrought woman, as they themselves state, or whatever others belonged to the same band of conjurers and were inclined to believe it, or else to fantasize about it as they wished, as of course many others have done. Alternatively, and even more plausibly, they were those who wished, by such a miracle, to astonish other people and to manipulate them by other deceptions. If Jesus had truly wanted to manifest his divine power, he should have appeared to his enemies, to his judges, in general to everyone. If he could have proven his divinity by instantaneously vanishing from the cross, he ought to have done so. From these and other similar arguments the Jew draws the final conclusion that Jesus was the kind of human being that the truth shows him to have been, the kind that is susceptible to rational analysis.[28]

Celsus' Disdainful Verdict

Celsus himself describes the role he has his figure of the Jew play as merely a prelude to his own dialectical battle with Christianity. In his eyes the contest between the Jews and the Christians is so foolish that he compares it with the proverbial dispute about "the shadow of an ass."[29] What Jews and Christians are disputing about is not important, since both groups believe that the divine Spirit has prophesied that a redeemer of humankind is to come, and they are only in disagreement as to whether the one prophesied about has already come. So the task now is to contest the assumptions from which the Jews and the Christians set out, and in doing so to challenge the supernaturalist worldview as the soil on which they both stand.

---

27. [Ed.] Zalmoxis, freed from slavery, dwelt among the Getae, where he lived underground for three years, after which he re-emerged, seeming to return from the dead (Herodotus, *The Histories* 4.94–96). Pythagoras is said to have descended to Hades and then returned (Diogenes Laertius, *Lives* 8.21 and 4.1). Rhampsinitus and his hidden treasure chamber is an Egyptian legend (Herodotus, 2.121–22). Orpheus descended to the underworld to bring back Eurydice (Ovid, *Metamorphoses* 10.1–85 and 11.1–66). Protesilaus was killed upon landing at Troy, but was allowed by the gods to return for three hours to his grieving wife (Homer, *Iliad*, 2.695ff.). Hercules dragged Cerberus up from Hades, through the entry place in the cave at Taenarus. Theseus, aided by Ariadne, slew the Minotaur and found his way up from the Labyrinth.

28. Origen, *Against Celsus* 2.55, 63, 68, and 79.

29. [Ed.] In 3.4, it is apparently Celsus himself who says that searching through prophecies, to score points favorable or unfavorable to Christian claims about Jesus, is comparable to searching for "the shadow of an ass."

I. The Internal Aspects of Christianity's Relation to the Pagan World and to the Roman State

Before Celsus proceeds with the weightier arguments on this issue, he expresses in various ways his general view of Christianity, namely, that overall he finds nothing in it that could claim one's respect and approval. On the whole Christianity has no sound, rational foundation. The Jews separated from the Egyptians as the result of religious dissension, and likewise in the Christians' case what drives them is arbitrariness and mania for change, rebelliousness and a sectarian spirit. They base their faith simply on such factors, and on the fear they instill in others, especially by terrifying pictures of future punishments.[30]

Far more rational than the Christians are the Greeks, with their beliefs in figures who, as men, were held to be gods because of their meritorious deeds: Hercules, Asclepius, Dionysus. Also, their legends tell of men who were similar to Jesus but were not regarded as gods: Aristeas of Proconnesus, Abaris the Hyperborean, Hermotimus of Clazomene, and a Cleomedes of Astypalaea. The Christians' cultus offered to their Jesus was in no respect better than Hadrian's cultus of Antinous.[31] The Christians have no reason to laugh at the worshipers of Zeus because people point to his tomb in Crete, since they do not know what the Cretans intend by doing this, and since they themselves certainly worship someone who was entombed.[32]

Furthermore, one can see what Christianity is like from the fact that no educated, wise, or rational people turn to the Christians; that ignorant and foolish ones may do so trustingly. Christians regard such people as deserving of their God, and publicly declare that they can and will have no others in their number. Since the Christians at that time for the most part belonged to the lower classes, Celsus therefore gave special attention to these traits in his characterization of Christianity. To him the Christians seemed to belong in the class of those who ply their simple trades in the public square and have no place in respectable society. In homes one sees them as woolworkers, cobblers, and tanners, as uneducated and uncultured people who dare not utter a word in the presence of the senior and more intelligent masters of the house. However, if they are able to interact with the household's children and women by themselves, then they tell them the most wondrous things and give them the notion "that they ought not give heed to their father and their teachers" but instead should only follow these Christians themselves; that their fathers and teachers are caught up in vain pursuits and cannot do anything really worthwhile; that they, the Christians, "alone know how one ought to live" and that "if the children obey them, they will be happy themselves and will make their home happy also."[33] Celsus does not believe he is judging Christians too harshly in this account.

---

30. 3.5ff. and 14.

31. [*Ed.*] The handsome Antinous was Emperor Hadrian's favorite, and was deified by the emperor after he drowned in the Nile.

32. Origen, *Against Celsus* 3.22, 26, 36 and 43.

33. 3.50, 52, and 55 [cf. *ANF* 4:486]. See J. A. Möhler, "Bruchstücke aus der Geschichte der Aufhebung der Sklaverei," in *Gesammelte Schriften* (Regensburg,1839–40), 2:85, where he understands

Celsus has an even stronger reproach to make. He says that, whereas in other mystery cults those called to be cleansed of transgressions are the pure ones who have no consciousness of guilt and have lived good lives, in Christianity it is the opposite. There every sinner, fool, and hapless person is promised acceptance into the kingdom of God. Celsus is most especially offended by Christianity's predilection for sinners and for the forgiveness of sins. His general view is that the forgiveness of sins is not possible, since everyone surely knows that those who, by their habits, have reinforced the natural tendency to sin, are not changed by being punished, and even less so by compassionate treatment. The most difficult thing is to completely change one's nature. Also, forgiveness of sins is hardly compatible with the idea of God. The Christians represent God as like people who are less severe out of compassion. By pitying those who cry out, God goes easy on bad people, but he spurns those who do nothing of the kind. To be sure, the Christians think that God can do all things. But it is clear that their doctrine cannot win over any reasonable person.[34]

Celsus' Opposition to Revelation

Indeed in all these respects Christianity therefore cannot be attractive to rationality. Yet its conflict with reason emerges even more starkly when we investigate the foundation on which Christianity ultimately rests. Christianity presupposes a special manifestation and revelation of God. So in the end we come to the concept of revelation. Celsus not only challenges this concept with arguments that have also been advanced against the possibility of revelation as such ever since his time. He also traces the main issue at stake back to the difference between a theistic and a pantheistic view of the world, in order to show how far apart these two standpoints are.

It is disgraceful how the Jews and the Christians fight about whether God, or God's Son, has already come down or is still to come. The real issue is what rational notion of such a descent of God ought one to entertain at all.[35] Celsus asks: Why did God come down? Was it to see how things stand with human beings? Did God not know everything? Did God know it? Had he not made things better, and could he not have done so, using his divine power? Could God not have set things right without sending someone for this purpose? If human beings still did not know him and he thought that made him somehow lacking, perhaps God wanted to become known and see who believed in him and who did not! Celsus' own answer to all these questions is that God would gain nothing for himself by becoming known, but instead just

---

the terms ἐριουργοί (woolworkers), σκυτοτόμοι (shoemakers), and κναφεῖς (fullers) to indicate slaves. He introduces this passage as evidence that Christians were very actively and successfully converting slaves. But this is not what this passage (3.55) indicates, and it is incorrect to assume that handworkers such as those mentioned were just slaves in ancient times. Why name separate occupations if the writer just wished to designate them as being slaves?

34. Origen, *Against Celsus* 3.63, 65, 70–71.

35. 4.2–3.

imparts this knowledge to us for our own benefit. But then he asks why it occurred to God to set our human lives right only after such a long time had passed. Did God not think of doing that before?[36]

To probe more deeply into the matter, Celsus returns to the concept of God. He says he does not wish to introduce anything new, but only to state what has long been acknowledged. "God is good, and beautiful, and blessed," the sum and substance of what is most beautiful and best. "But if he comes down among us, he must undergo a change . . . from good to evil," from beautiful to homely, from blessed to wretched. Who then would wish to undergo such a change? "It is the nature of a mortal, indeed, to undergo change and reshaping, but of an immortal to remain the same and unaltered." The kind of change Christianity presupposes is thus inherently impossible for God.[37]

Of course the Christians suppose that God can actually change himself into a mortal body. But since this is impossible, we are just left to think that, without actually changing, God just appears to observers as having made such a change. However, if he were to do this he would be a liar and a deceiver. Lying and deception are always bad, and are only to be resorted to among friends simply in order to heal them when they are ill and out of their minds, or else to escape danger from enemies. But neither case applies to God.[38]

Notwithstanding the fact that a revelation is inherently impossible, if we nevertheless assume that one has actually occurred we must also be able to think of it as serving a definite purpose. The believer in revelation can only look at the world teleologically. Yet a teleological view of the world leads to particularism [i.e., partisanship, or a narrow viewpoint], and that is most closely linked to an anthropomorphic and anthropopathic notion of God. So in this part of his work, where the most important issues of philosophical principle get expressed, Celsus carries further the train of thought in his polemic. He states the two partisan views as follows. The Jews contend that, since life is filled with all sorts of evils, someone sent by God must come to punish the wicked and purify everything, just as occurred with the Great Flood in Genesis. The Christians modify this point by saying that God has already sent down his Son, because of the sins of the Jews, and that the Jews have incurred God's wrath (χόλος) because they punished him with death and gave him gall (χολή) to drink.

Celsus does not hesitate to mock this situation, by comparing Jews and Christians alike "to a flight of bats or to a swarm of ants issuing out of their nest, or to frogs holding council in a marsh, or to worms crawling together in the corner of a dunghill, and quarreling with one another as to which of them were the greater sinners." They say that "God shows and announces to us all things beforehand," adding that for our sake he has abandoned the whole world, heaven and earth; that in order to associate

36. 4.8.
37. 4.14 [cf. ANF 4:502].
38. 4.18.

with us he has sent his messengers and cannot cease from forever sending new messengers, because for him it all involves our being with him always. The worms say that there is a God and they come next after God, and are like him in every way; that God has made everything else subject to them—earth, water, air, stars; that all else exists for their sake and is assigned to serve them. However, the worms add that "since certain among us commit sin, God will come or will send his Son to consume the wicked with fire, that the rest of us may have eternal life with him."[39]

This comparison already indicates the very ingenious turn Celsus' argument takes in order to direct his attack now at the Old Testament in particular, by making quite vivid, in its history of revelation, the anthropopathic character of the Christian concept of God. Christians and Jews can simply be compared to the aforementioned kinds of animals, since the Jews are runaway Egyptian slaves and have never done anything noteworthy. They show that their race is derived from the most ancient charlatans and deceivers, by appealing to obscure, ambiguous, mysterious utterances, which they interpret for ignorant and stupid people. Sitting in their corner in Palestine, totally uneducated and knowing nothing about Hesiod and other divinely-inspired men, they have concocted the most unbelievable and crudest creation story. So here Celsus turns to Old Testament history in order to deride it because of how tasteless he finds it. Many Jews and Christians do of course interpret it allegorically. Yet their doing so just proves that they are ashamed of these things.[40]

Celsus' purpose in this entire discussion is simply to show most emphatically how this sensuous way of thinking involves God's being drawn so deeply into the human and earthly realm, in contrast to the Platonic view in which God made nothing at all that is mortal, but only made what is immortal—that the soul alone is the work of God, whereas the body's nature is different [i.e., non-divine]. For Plato, the nature of the world as a whole is forever one and the same; so there is always the same amount of evil in the world.[41] Evil is not from God; it is a feature of matter and of mortal natures, and remains ever constant in the recurring fluctuations of past, present, and future. Hence the overall purpose of the world lies not in human beings but only in the maintenance of the whole. For all individuals pass away, and what seems evil to one or another of them would not in itself be something evil if it serves the purpose of the whole.

In order to refute, in its full compass, the teleological proposition that God has created everything for the sake of human beings, a thesis that is the foundation of the Christian view of revelation, Celsus engages in an extensive comparison of human beings with the animals. In it he seeks to take each prerogative conceded to human beings and offsets it very much to the advantage of the animals, such that humans

---

39. 4. 23 [*ANF* 4:506].
40. 4.31ff. and 48ff.
41. 4.54 and 62.

stand beneath the animals rather than above them. In concluding, he expresses his overall view in these words:

> All things, accordingly, were not made for man, any more than they were made for lions, or eagles, or dolphins, but that this world, as being God's work, might be perfect and entire in all respects. For this reason all things have been adjusted, not with reference to each other, but with regard to their bearing upon the whole. And God takes care of the whole, and his providence will never forsake it; and it does not become worse; nor does God after a time bring it back to himself; nor is he angry on account of men any more than on account of apes or flies; . . . each one of which has received its appointed lot in its proper place.[42]

In its essentials, this is the same view that major opponents of a supernaturalistic belief in revelation have adhered to from Celsus' time right down to today.

This opposing view has become even more dangerous to belief in revelation, in proportion to how it has been elaborated beyond its still rough form in Celsus' case, and has become a philosophically grounded theory. If the world is a whole that is complete on its own, then God and world belong together and the two can only be thought of as immanently related. Then everything that is particular, or that has a teleological or supernaturalistic character, vanishes of its own accord in the universal oneness of the whole. This cuts away the roots of the justification for a concept of revelation. The fact that there is no God distinct from the world, standing above the world and acting upon it by his personal will, means that there also cannot be any revelation in a Jewish or Christian sense. God and world are simply co-extensive (*in einander*). Everything takes place within the same order or system that is established once and for all, in an eternal cycle constantly returning unto itself.

Various Arguments of Celsus in Line with Polytheism, or else with Platonism

Here at the height of his polemic against Christianity, Celsus stands as the advocate for a view that is antithetical to it in principle. Yet he cannot maintain this lofty standpoint. Since his way of representing the pantheistic worldview was also most closely associated with the old polytheistic religion, he had to face the question as to whether his verdict about Christianity from a polytheistic standpoint had to be the same as the verdict from his pantheistic viewpoint.

Although in Christianity the one supreme God of course did not come down into the world himself, the founder of Christianity can certainly seem to be one of the higher, superhuman beings that the Christians, Jews, and pagans all assume exist. They just use different names for them, since some call them angels and others call them demons. Accordingly, all the arguments previously advanced against the divine

---

42. 4.99 [*ANF* 4:541].

character of Christianity have still not proven that Christianity is not of a higher, divine origin. In *Against Celsus* 5.2 [*ANF* 4:543], we find him saying, according to Origen: "O Jews and Christians, no God or son of a God either came or will come down [to earth]. But if you mean that certain angels did so, then what do you call them? Are they gods, or some other race of beings [such as] demons?"

This would then be a further issue that needs to be addressed. Yet it is odd that Celsus does not set out to answer this particular question directly. Instead, he proceeds as if he had to grant the possibility that Christianity is, in the foregoing sense, divinely revealed. He now attacks the Jews and the Christians mainly regarding various features of the contents of their religion, in particular by also comparing it to Greek philosophy and so seeking to gain the higher ground over against them. He has hardly mentioned the angels when he expresses amazement that the Jews "should worship the heaven and the angels who dwell therein," and yet do not esteem "its most venerable and powerful beings, the sun, the moon, and the other heavenly bodies."[43]

Right after this Celsus takes up the doctrine of the resurrection. He says that in this case too it is foolish to suppose that after God, like a cook, has ignited a fire and everything is roasted in it, those believers alone will remain unharmed, and even the ones who were long dead shall rise up from the earth with their own flesh. Worms might hope to do so, but what human soul wishes to have a decayed body? Even a few of the Christians declare that this is both ghastly and an impossibility. How could a wholly ruined body be restored to its original condition? Since they have no answer, they take refuge in the most nonsensical thesis that, for God, all things are possible. Celsus replies that God cannot possibly do anything improper, nor does he will what is perverse. God is the rationality of all existing beings and cannot act contrary to reason or contrary to himself.[44]

In continuing, Celsus concedes to the Jews that they are as equally entitled as others are to have laws for their own nation. However, the Christians have parted ways with the Jews, and the Jews ought not think that their laws make them wiser and better than other people.[45] As though he were only now arriving at his actual theme, Celsus wants to concede to the Christians that their teacher is in fact an angel, but would insist that he is not the first and only one to come. Celsus says that other angels came before him, as is also maintained by those who accept a different and higher God and

---

43. 5.6 [*ANF* 4:545].

44. 5.14. It is noteworthy that we already find here the well-known distinction between "against nature" (*contra naturam*) and "above nature" (*supra naturam*). Celsus says God wills nothing παρὰ φύσιν (against nature). But in 5.23 Origen replies to this, saying that a distinction must be made. "If things happen according to the word and will of God, they are not necessarily contrary to nature.... So we must say that, as compared with what is generally understood as 'nature,' there are certain things which are beyond its power, which God could do at any time" [*ANF* 4:553].

45. 5.25, 33, and 41.

Father than the creator of the world.⁴⁶ Origen's account is not entirely clear as to what Celsus is supposedly saying, or what his polemical point is here.

On the other hand, Celsus is very clear in the remainder of his work, where he proceeds to compare Christianity to Greek philosophy, specifically to Platonic philosophy. There he seeks to show that, if Christianity has some elements that a rational person could find attractive, it is nevertheless not where these elements are exclusively to be found. They are just widely-known insights that were already expressed in a far better way by the Greeks, and without involving those religious threats and promises from God or a Son of God.⁴⁷ Celsus refers to Platonic statements, and extols Plato in particular for not passing off his teaching as supernatural revelation, and for not preventing those who wished to from seeking the truth for themselves. He did not demand that they first of all believe it. He did not say "there is a certain sort of God who has a Son like him, and the Son himself has come down and has spoken with me." Even when, as things stand, no further explanation is available for what is being investigated, Plato always offers rational arguments. He would not pretend to have found some novel element or proclaim it as having come from heaven. He would state where he got it. Some Christians appeal to this authority and some to that one, but all alike insist: "Believe it if you want to be saved, or else go away." When they say this, what should someone do who truly wants to be blessed? Should one let a roll of the dice decide what course to take and whom one is to follow?⁴⁸ Here the advantage is decidedly on Plato's side.

Thus Celsus seeks to demonstrate, in individual instances as well, that the Christians have borrowed a great deal from Plato, while at the same time simply misunderstanding and misrepresenting it. The most godless errors of the Christians derive overall from their inability to understand the divine mysteries. Celsus puts the Christian doctrine of Satan as God's adversary especially in this category. The ancients—Pherecydes, Heraclitus, and others—have of course spoken in enigmatic terms about a war of the gods. The Christians distorted it and turned it into their doctrine of Satan. The Son of God is overcome by the Devil, and he forewarns the Christians about Satan yet to come, who will do great and wondrous things and will lay claim to the glory of God. The Son says the Christians ought not lose their faith in him when this occurs. From all this we just see instead that this Satan or Antichrist is a cheat and a liar like Jesus, who quite naturally fears him as his rival.⁴⁹

---

46. 5.52. [*Ed.*] As Baur says in the next sentence, Celsus' point here is not entirely clear. In ch. 52, what he says about angels coming before him perhaps refers to the "sons of God" in Gen 6:2–4, who fathered the Nephilim. The latter part of this sentence would correspond somewhat to the Demiurge in Plato's *Timaeus*, vis-à-vis the Good itself.

47. 6.1ff.

48. 6.8 and 10. See also 1.9, where Celsus similarly reproves Christians for their ἀλόγως πιστεύειν (believing irrationality).

49. 6.42ff.

Celsus continues by saying that Christians speak of a Son of God because the ancients call the world a child or offspring of God because it arose from God.[50] This leads Celsus to speak of the doctrine of the world and the world's creation, and of the Mosaic creation story. In criticizing the Mosaic account, he sets his Platonic doctrine of God over against its crude anthropopathisms, which he denounces. In the Platonic doctrine, God, as the cause of all existence, is wholly without color, shape, or motion, and transcends all our words and concepts. At this point Celsus mentions something Christians could say in reply to him in light of this Platonic concept of God, the related issue of the possibility of having knowledge of God. They could say that, precisely because God is so great and so difficult to know, God has infused his own Spirit into a body like ours and sent it here to us, so that we can heed God and learn about him.

However, this just gives Celsus the welcome opportunity to ridicule anew such a sensuous mode of representation. Had God wished to send forth his own Spirit, why was it necessary to instill it into the body of a woman? Since God already understood how to form human beings, he could also construct a body for his Spirit without casting it into such a loathsome medium. If his Spirit were to appear suddenly, coming down from on high, disbelief would have been impossible. But if the divine Spirit was to have once appeared in a body, then he also should have surpassed all others in magnificence, in beauty, and in the striking impression made by his entire being. But certainly he would hardly have been so undistinguished as to have been so very insignificant and homely. Perhaps God was like the Zeus depicted by the comic poets, who awakened from a long slumber and wanted to rescue the human race from all its ills. If so, then why did he then send what Christians call his Spirit into one little corner of the world? Surely God should have enlivened many such bodies and sent them throughout the whole world. In order to get laughs in the theater, the comic poets had Zeus, awakened from his slumber, send Hermes to the Athenians and the Spartans, although it would be far more ridiculous had God sent his Son to the Jews.[51]

Celsus then turns his particular attention to Old Testament prophecies. In addition to attacking their other faults, he argues most forcefully by utilizing the antithesis the Gnostics posited between the Old and New Testaments. He says that, if God's prophets among the Jews foretold the coming of Jesus as God's Son, how then could God have enjoined them, through Moses their lawgiver, to prosper, to rule, to populate the earth, to slay their enemies, to destroy them all, as God himself has indeed done before the very eyes of the Jews;[52] whereas God's Son, the Nazarene, commands exactly the opposite by denying that the rich, the power hungry, those striving for wisdom and honor, have access to the Father. This Son calls upon people to worry less about food and its supply than do "the birds of the air," or less about clothing

---

50. 6.47ff.

51. 6.69ff. [see esp. 6.78].

52. [*Ed.*] See Gen 9:1–7: "God blessed Noah and his sons, and said to them, 'Be fruitful and multiply, and fill the earth . . .'" Moses is traditionally the author of Genesis, in which this passage appears.

than do "the lilies of the field" (Matt 6:25–33). He demands that "if anyone strike you on the right cheek, turn the other also" (Matt 5:39). Who therefore is the liar, Moses or Jesus? When the Father sent Jesus, had he perhaps forgotten his commandments given through Moses? Or perhaps he regretted his own legislation and sent a messenger with antithetical commandments![53]

The question Celsus now puts to the Christians is: Where are you headed and what do you hope for? He interprets the doctrine of the resurrection as though Christians wanted it to be the path to God and to knowledge of God. This leads him once again to the question as to whether, and how, God is knowable. Celsus says Christians continually ask: "How can we know God and see God if there is no sensory knowledge of God? How can one know anything without sensory perception?" Celsus replies that this is a question not posed by the person or the soul, but one put only by the flesh. If the faint-hearted race that clings to the body[54] is willing to listen, one can simply say to these people that they will only "see God" when they close off their senses and look upward with their spirit; when they turn away from the eyes of the flesh and open the eyes of the soul; and when, in seeking a guide on this path, they should flee deceivers and sorcerers and those who recommend idols. Otherwise they make themselves completely ridiculous, since on the one hand they are maligning as idols those shown to be gods, and on the other hand they are worshiping that other God of theirs, who is in fact even more deplorable than the idols, is not even an idol but is instead a dead man, and they seek after a Father like him.

Celsus holds up to them the Platonic declaration about the Creator and Father of all, saying that it is difficult to discover him and that, when one has done so, it is impossible to speak of him in a way understandable to everyone. That is the true path on which godly persons seek the truth, the path that, to be sure, those with their sensibility bound wholly to the flesh, and seeing nothing clearly, cannot follow. If they believe that a Spirit of God has come down to proclaim the truth, this can only be the Spirit who proclaims that with which men of antiquity such as Plato were imbued. If they cannot understand anything of this then they ought to keep silent and conceal their ignorance. They ought not call those who do see "blind," nor call those who walk "lame," for they are quite lame and crippled in soul themselves, and only live on as lifeless bodies.[55] If they are looking for something new and must have anyone at all to hold on to, in any event they ought to have chosen someone who died a noble death

---

53. 7.18. See also 6.29, where Celsus accuses the Christians of a contradiction. Under Jewish pressure they acknowledge having the same God as them; but when their teacher Jesus makes their law something entirely different from that of Moses the Jew, they maintain that they have a different law. [*Ed.*] This accusation makes sense only if one pits the Marcionite position against the anti-Marcionite position.

54. The Greek of 7.36 is δεῖλον καὶ φιλοσώματον γένος. These persons can therefore only represent God to themselves as if God were by nature a body (σῶμα), and, in 7.27, as "a body like a human being" (ἀνθρωποειδὲς σῶμα).

55. 7.28, 36, 42, and 45.

and is worthy of being the subject of a divine myth. If they did not find a Hercules or an Asclepius to their liking, then they might indeed have had Orpheus, who also died a violent death, or Anaxarchus or Epictetus, who were reportedly deserving of such status. To serve this purpose they make into a god someone who ended the most disgraceful life with the most ignominious death. Jonah in the whale's belly, or Daniel in the lion's den, would have been a more suitable choice.[56]

Demonology as a Major Element of Affinity and of Difference

After all these attacks by an adversary as keen and skillful in the arguments and sophisms of his dialectic as he is sarcastic in his derision, there was still one more point on which Celsus had to engage with Christians. It is the doctrine of demons,[57] inasmuch as that seemed to be a point of contact between the Christians and the pagans.

We have already noted the context in which the polemical discourse of Celsus took up this topic, only to turn soon to other matters. Hence it was still not comprehensible how an adversary with this mortal hatred for Christianity should have found it so easy to concede that Christianity had a divine origin, albeit not as Christians understood it but rather along the lines of the pagan doctrine of demons. So this point must be made clearer. Doing so will show it was no accident that Celsus came to speak of the doctrine of demons particularly at the conclusion of his book.

The fact that Celsus found the Christians' aversion to temples, altars, and images inexcusable provided the transition to the issue of demons. Celsus says the Christians utterly repudiate images of the gods. If they do so because an image made of stone, wood, bronze, or gold cannot be a god, then that would be a ridiculous kind of wisdom because only a fool takes such things to be anything other than merely votive offerings and images. However, if their view is that there should be no images of the gods because the gods have a different form, then the Christians ought to say so; for they certainly do believe God created human beings in his own image, and thus a human being resembles God. What they do say can only mean that they think those to whom the images are dedicated are not gods but instead demons, and they suppose that a worshiper of God ought not render any service to demons. It is clear that they worship neither a god nor a demon, but just a dead man.

But why should one not worship demons? "Does not everything proceed from divine providence? Does not the law governing everything that is done—whether by a god, by angels or other demons, or by heroes—come from the supreme God? Is not each of these placed over the domain for which God has empowered him? According

---

56. 7.53.

57. [*Ed.*] The word "demon" does not necessarily denote an evil spirit for ancient people as it does for the modern world. To the Greeks and Romans a demon (δαιμόνιον) was just one of a race of lesser divine beings. So a "demon" could preside over some constructive feature of life, and be a suitable object of worship.

to the Christians it is not right for those who worship God to therefore worship these ones who have received their power from God. That is because, as the Christians say, 'No one can serve two masters' (Matt 6:24)."[58] So this is the proposition we are dealing with regarding the cultus of demons. In light of it, the task is to show whether or not the Christians and the pagans can reach a mutual understanding on the issue of demons.

From the fact that the Christians associate a quite different concept with demons than the pagans do, one should have thought that the issue is already settled; for the Christians are totally unwilling to think of demons as divine beings. Yet from the Christians' standpoint this view of demons is a derivative notion, a secondary matter. The reason demons are not really gods is simply because, in the Christian outlook as such, nothing but the one God can be acknowledged as truly divine. So this is the main thesis governing the matter. By expressing it in terms of the Gospel of Matthew's declaration that "no one can serve two masters," Celsus is using it as the basis for contesting the Christian view of demons. He states that this contention [about serving two masters] can only be made by those who take turmoil and dissension as their guideline, "who separate themselves and stand aloof" from the rest of humankind. Whoever speaks in that way is transferring his own emotional states to God. It could well be the case that human beings regard it as an imposition if one's servant also serves another. But that surely does not apply to God. The person who worships multiple gods also honors the supreme God by doing so, in honoring those who are associated with the supreme God.[59] Celsus maintains that it is impious to speak of God as the one Lord, for that is as though there were an adversary [to God], and that would just bring division and disunion into the kingdom of God.

Perhaps the Christians would have been able to stick to their thesis if they had just worshiped no one other than the one God. But they pay excessive reverence to someone who has just recently appeared, and believe that their honoring God's servant is no offense against God. Also, the fact that the Christians worship God's Son as well as worshiping God would make it self-evident that it is permissible to worship God's servant too, and not merely worship the one God. They are so eager to just worship the founder of their sect that, if it were proven to them that he is not the Son of God, they would not want to worship the true God, the Father of All, apart from him.[60]

It is entirely natural that, since the Christians did not believe the demons are gods, they also did not take part in the public cultus, in the sacrifices and feasts. So Celsus' criticism of them on this matter has no further significance. More telling seems to be the urgent choice facing the Christians, to either worship the demons or, by not doing so, to forfeit further claims to the sustenance they provide. If the

---

58. [*Ed.*] These sentences within quotation marks are Baur's paraphrase of Origen's quotation from Celsus in 7.68.

59. 8.2.

60. 8.11ff.

Christians shun those feasts, one can only wonder how they do not know that (when they dine) they are indeed tablemates with the demons, even though they were not present themselves at the sacrificial slaughter of the animal. The grain they eat, the wine they drink, the fruit they enjoy, even water and the air they breathe, are all things they also certainly receive from specific demons. Each demon has a special role in the care of everyone. Either one must entirely cease to live and walk the earth, or else, in partaking of this life, one must be grateful to the demons who are appointed the overseers of the earth. One must offer them the first-fruits and one's prayers throughout one's life, so that they are favorably disposed toward human beings.[61]

Celsus reiterates the simple choice facing the Christians.

> If they refuse to render due service to the gods, and to respect those who preside over this service, let them not come to manhood, or marry wives, or have children, or indeed take any share in the affairs of life; but let them depart hence with all speed, and leave no posterity behind them, that such a race may become extinct from the face of the earth. Or, on the other hand, if they will take wives, and bring up children, and taste of the fruits of the earth, and partake of all the blessings of life, and bear its appointed sorrows (for nature herself has allotted sorrows to all men, for sorrows must exist, and earth is the only place for them), then must they discharge the duties of life until they are released from its bonds, and render due honor to those beings who control the affairs of this life, if they would not prove to be ungrateful to them.[62]

The Christians too did not wish to be ungrateful for the good things of daily life. But they believed they owed them to the angels, not to the demons. Origen says "we Christians" also maintain that not only would the earth fail to bring forth its plants without the oversight of unseen cultivators and husbandmen; also, without them no water would flow in the springs and streams, and the air would not be kept pure and healthy. But we deny that these unseen, controlling powers are demons.[63] We know that angels "have been set over the fruits of the earth, and over the birth of animals, and we praise and bless them, as having been entrusted by God with the things needful for our race; but we do not show them the honor due to God."[64]

In the polemic on this point, the distance between Christianity and paganism has become quite small. Thus if the Christians could only have made up their minds to call their angels "demons" and to so regard them, that would of course set aside something the pagans found very offensive about Christianity; and the pagans would have been much more inclined to make concessions on other points they contested because of this particular disagreement. Yet how could Christianity have been able

---

61. 8.28.
62. 8.55 [ANF 4:660].
63. 8.31.
64. 8.57 [ANF 4:661].

I. The Internal Aspects of Christianity's Relation to the Pagan World and to the Roman State

to make just this one concession without being untrue to itself? Had the Christians honored as demons, in the pagan sense, the same beings that Christians called "angels," then they would surely also have stood up for pagan polytheism and wholly adopted a way of thinking typical of the pagan world as such. Christian opposition to the pagan doctrine of demons is therefore simply the point at which Christianity is profoundly and internally antithetical to paganism, and that becomes apparent in the most striking way. In repudiating the pagan doctrine of demons, the Christians were saying that they were disavowing the entire pagan worldview, were rejecting a way of looking at things that, time and again, annuls the absolute concept of the divine by failing to maintain with sufficient strictness the difference between the divine and the natural realm; that instead treats the boundary between the two as fluid. Whereas to the pagans the difference between their demons and the angels of the Christians seems minimal, the underlying antithesis between them runs very deep.

In the section of his work dealing with the doctrine of demons, Celsus conspicuously adopts the role of an apologist for paganism, and not so much an attacker of Christianity as such. At least at this point it is as though everything rests on convincing the Christians of the truth of the pagan religion. He tries very earnestly to bring home to them how, by disavowing the pagan doctrine of demons, they are denying their own innermost God-consciousness, are offending against the most sacred duties, and proving to be people who in no way deserve to live in the world. Why else could Celsus regard the Christian's opposition to the pagan doctrine of demons as being, in the final analysis, an open declaration of war against all of paganism, as the most decided rebellion against everything in the entire pagan world that counts as religious belief and as sacred custom, handed down from most ancient times? Hence it is very characteristic of Celsus to accuse the Christians of sedition (στάσις).[65] As rebels and insurgents, they have risen up against all the rest of human society and renounced it.[66]

However, in this regard the Christians have only done what their ancestors, the Jews, had already done, by in turn separating themselves from the Jews. For the Jews had their origin as the result of a rebellion (στάσις) in which they split off from the Egyptians, a group to which they initially belonged.[67] Rebellion, separation, and sectarianism are therefore features Judaism and Christianity have in common. Taci-

---

65. In 8.2 Origen says this about Celsus: "After having put this question for the purpose of leading us to the worship of demons, he represents us as answering that it is impossible to serve many masters. He goes on to say that 'this is the language of sedition, and is only used by those who separate themselves and stand aloof from all human society'" [*ANF* 4:640]. Hence in 8.14 [*ANF* 4:644] Celsus calls Christianity "sedition" (στάσις) and Christ "their leader in the sedition" (στάσις ἀρχηγέτης).

66. Indeed they have even conspired against it. That the Christians have no altars, images, or temples was supposedly "the typical sign of a secret and forbidden society"—that consequently they have become a secret association (8.17). See also 1.1: "The Christians entered into secret associations with each other contrary to the law" [*ANF* 4:397].

67. See 3.4ff., 4.31, and 2.1. In Celsus' view, Christianity's sectarian character is very much a part of its nature. In 3.9 he says that, if everybody wanted to become Christians, the Christians themselves would not want that to happen.

tus says that the Jews were detested by the pagans because they were opposed to all other religious practices (*contrarii ceteris mortalibus ritus*).[68] That also applied to the Christians to a far greater extent, since they had added to the older rebellion a new and far more exacerbating feature.

Celsus himself of course has mitigated the pagans' natural antipathy for the Jews to the extent that he even put them on a par with other peoples, and wished to have their religion, such as it may be, at least acknowledged to be a religion of a national group.[69] The obvious reason for this is that a people who have a national history such as the Jews do would also have had a historical justification for itself that nobody could deny. But how distant is the time when the Christians will have an equal claim to possessing such historical roots? Until Christianity has finally achieved such an existence, the Christians could only be regarded as rebels and renegades, as the sort who, like heretics, had fallen away from the all-embracing totality. Since one could not explain how Christianity, having such an origin, could have already gained such importance as had to be conceded to it at that time, Christianity must have established itself in the world by means of the most insidious artifices, deceit, and guile.

Christianity: Deceit and Delusion, Albeit a Force to Be Reckoned With

Therefore, although Christianity is no longer a notoriously "destructive superstition" owing to its "shameful acts,"[70] its essential nature is nevertheless simply deceit and delusion.

But who is in fact the one who initiated this deception? Where there is a deceiver there are also those who are deceived. No doubt Celsus viewed the great mass of Christians as simply victims of deceit. With his low opinion of the Christians as uneducated people belonging to the lower classes, and easily aroused by sensuous expectations, he saw them as ripe for deception on a grand scale. In looking for its source, the question is simply whether Jesus himself initiated the deception, or does the responsibility for it merely lie with his disciples? Celsus declared that Jesus' disciples were deceivers of the worst sort, just as he saw the entire company of Jesus' followers after his death as largely a band of charlatans, who in all likelihood directly intended to spread throughout the world the lie that Jesus had risen from the dead.[71] Celsus held the narratives of the gos-

---

68. Tacitus, *Histories* 5.4: "They profane all that we hold sacred, and on the other hand they allow what to us is defiling."

69. Origen, *Against Celsus* 5.25, and elsewhere.

70. It is remarkable that Celsus' text says nothing at all about all those calumnies against Christianity that even Tertullian is still refuting in such detail. Celsus had very accurate knowledge of Christianity, and took his task seriously, so he could not give credence to such accusations. We see this clearly from Origen, 6.27 and 40. See also Eusebius, *Ecclesiastical History* 4.7, where he explicitly states that "with the lapse of time the calumnies against the whole teaching were extinguished" [LCL, *Eusebius*, 1:318–19].

71. 2.55.

pel account to be largely concocted by the evangelists themselves, who quite evidently did not even know how to disguise their fiction. Like those who, in a drunken state, do violence to themselves, these writers altered the original text of the Gospels three and four times and even more, so as to disavow what in them had been shown to be false. Celsus denies any credibility especially to such narratives as those recounting the birth and the baptism of Jesus. For, he says, who has ever seen such phenomena as those accompanying Jesus' baptism, or has ever heard such a voice from heaven, except the very ones whose interest is served by alleging such things? The disciples also just concocted the belief that Jesus foresaw and foretold what was to befall him.[72]

But the disciples are not the only initiators of the deception by which Christianity got introduced into the world. The responsibility goes back to Jesus himself. Although it was only after Jesus' death that the disciples first abandoned the law of their fathers and founded a new sect, Jesus himself had already induced them to do so by deluding them in the most ridiculous way.[73] The initial deception came from Jesus himself. When Celsus depicts Jesus as previously having learned magical techniques in Egypt, ones he later used in his homeland to attract attention, Celsus can only have viewed Jesus' entire impact as a massive deception.[74] This is in fact the distinctive feature of Celsus' attack on Christianity. In order to avoid acknowledging that there is anything great about Christianity, anything calling for respect, he makes Jesus himself out to be a deceiver, and he seems totally unable to think of Christianity otherwise than as just gaining its place in the world through trickery and deception.[75]

Yet one can hardly mistake the fact that, when Celsus looks down upon Christianity with great contempt, and spews out so abundantly the bitter sarcasm he directs at it, this is basically just an outlook he pretends to have. A man like Celsus was unquestionably one of the most educated and enlightened, most knowledgeable and judicious, men of his time. Can there be any greater indication of the significance Christianity already had in the eyes of the thinking public at that time, than for the new phenomenon of Christianity to be important enough that someone like Celsus made it the object of his most meticulous and many-faceted examination? Celsus may even have thought that very much in Christianity seems objectionable and reprehensible, nonsensical and tasteless, too sensuous and sensual. He may not have conceded that it has any particular value overall, in either philosophical or religious terms. At the same time, in order to combat Christianity successfully, Celsus has to resort to the resources of Greek philosophy in opposing it, and can only do so from the lofty

72. 2.26ff., 1.40, and 2.13.

73. 2.1.

74. Celsus only concedes that Jesus worked wonders in order to class these wonders with those of the charlatans and others who learned from the Egyptians how to perform their great artistry in the marketplace for a few obols. They exorcised demons, banished illnesses, summoned the souls of heroes, simulated elaborate banquets, and caused inanimate objects to move as if they were alive (1.68).

75. Throughout his work Celsus describes Jesus as a deceiver. See also 2.49 and 6.42.

standpoint of a Platonic philosopher. If the issue for Celsus was mainly that the Christians did not worship the demons, and wanted no involvement in the popular religion of the myths, how could he be so earnest in accusing them of this? From his own philosophical position he was well aware that belief in the old gods could only be a tradition largely abandoned.

In all of this and from his own standpoint, Celsus certainly could have regarded Christianity as just an enterprise of deception. At least, then, it was supposedly not viewed as anything more serious than that. So we have proof that people were aware of how significant Christianity had then become, from the fact that such a phenomenon was thought to be explainable only by assuming a deception that had to be ever more enigmatic as it grew more influential. What else can one say except that Christianity had become a powerful movement at that time in some secret and sinister way for which there is no further explanation!

Lucian of Samosata

We do not know if the Celsus familiar to us from Origen's text is the same person as Celsus the friend of Lucian.[76] In any event Lucian should be discussed along with Origen's Celsus. That is because from Lucian's writings we can form a more specific understanding of how Christianity was reflected in the consciousness of its pagan contemporaries and increasingly became less incompatible with it, by gradually ceasing to make such a harsh and off-putting impression on them. Lucian was another who took a specific interest in Christianity. Although Lucian perhaps did not know the writings of the Christians, he was informed about the principal facts of the gospel story and about Christian ethics and practices. He had formed his own judgment about the overall character of Christianity.[77]

How Lucian Compares with Celsus

Lucian's standpoint was quite different from that of Celsus. Despite all the ridicule and derision in Celsus' treatment of Christianity, he nevertheless provided a very seriously intended refutation of it because, as a Platonist, he upheld the pagan worldview in opposition to the Christians' adversarial position. In contrast, an Epicurean[78] who

---

76. [Ed.] Lucian of Samosata (born c. 120) wrote a great many works in Greek, utilizing a variety of literary forms. While not a profound or consistent thinker, he is a skillful satirist with a wide range of contemporary targets.

77. See pp. 134ff. of my article, "Apollonius von Tyana und Christus," *Tübinger Zeitschrift für Theologie* (1832) no. 4, 3–235. See also A. Planck, "Lucian und das Christenthum," *Theologische Studien und Kritiken* 23 (1851) 826ff., esp. 886ff. on Lucian's familiarity with Christian writings.

78. [Ed.] The standard reference works do not say that Lucian was in fact an Epicurean. They say he had no consistent or genuinely philosophical position, and instead just reflected various approaches at different stages of his very extensive authorship. Perhaps the only basis for calling him an

had made pagan belief in the gods itself into merely a vehicle for his wit and frivolity, could not have had any further interest than just that.

In Christianity, Lucian simply saw a phenomenon offering him new material for the satirical picture of his time he sought to sketch in so many of his writings. In order to provide a vivid concept of the deception he regarded as the work of Christianity, Celsus had indeed grouped Christianity with other phenomena calculated to hoodwink and deceive. Lucian also understood how such phenomena in his day were akin, and that became his main perspective. For him, Christianity too was just one of the many aberrations, follies, and crazes he noticed in the colorful and confusing world of his day. That is why he principally drew upon just those features of Christianity and Christians that, with their eccentric tendencies, best served as topics of a satirical portrayal.

Lucian's Peregrinus Proteus

The work of Lucian entitled *Peregrinus Proteus*[79] is dedicated to this Cynic philosopher and recounts the story of his life and death. It belongs to the aforementioned class of Lucian's writings, and Christianity is a major component in the presentation. However, it is organized in such a way that Christianity is just presented in connection with similar phenomena Lucian wanted to classify with it. He especially emphasizes two features in his understanding of Christianity itself: the credulity of Christians, which quite simply explains the origin of Christianity, and the fanaticism of the Christian martyrs.

After committing many despicable crimes, and ultimately because he had strangled his own father, Peregrinus became a fugitive among the Christians in Palestine. After initially mastering their wondrous wisdom, Peregrinus soon surpassed his teachers, the priests and scribes, in this role to such an extent that they were like schoolboys as compared to him. Thereupon he became a prophet and leader of their cultus and their congregations, their all-in-one. In this capacity he was the interpreter of their books and the author of many himself, until finally they revered him as a god and regarded him as their lawgiver. This is obviously all intended as a parody of the story of Jesus, inasmuch as Lucian sought to show by it how easy it would be to become the leader of a sect composed of such people. Since Peregrinus had joined the already existing Christian community, he naturally could not gain as high a stature as that of Jesus himself. For the Christians of course continued to worship that great one who had been nailed to the post in Palestine, for he had brought these new mysteries to life.

Epicurean is that he does praise Epicurus in his dialogue *Alexander*.

79. [*Ed.*] Peregrinus, of Parium in Mysia, a Cynic philosopher nicknamed "Proteus" (after a Greek sea-god who can change shape at will), lived c. 100–165. Lucian's account that follows is almost the only source of information about this person. So it is hard to know how much here is accurate.

Lucian continues his narrative of Peregrinus' life with the Christians by telling how he was imprisoned for being a Christian. But because this enhanced his reputation, it just gave new fuel to his appetite for adventure and fame. The Christians regarded his imprisonment as a great misfortune and made every effort to get him released or at least to alleviate his hardship. Emissaries from the Christian congregations in the cities of Asia came to support and comfort him, with the result that Peregrinus became wealthy from being imprisoned. All these actions supposedly serve to illustrate further characteristics of the Christians. Lucian's aim here is to emphasize in particular how very industrious the Christians are in pursuing some goal once they become publicly involved with it. All that they have they give up forthwith, for these unfortunate folk are convinced that they are wholly immortal, body and soul, and will live forever. That is why they are also contemptuous of death and many yield willingly to it. So their first lawgiver persuaded them that they would all be brothers and sisters if, in becoming Christians, they renounce the Hellenic deities, and if they worship that sophist nailed to the post and live according to his laws.

From these characteristic features Lucian returns to the main thing about the Christians that stands out, namely, their credulity, which makes them far too easy prey for a deceiver. Because of their desire for brotherhood, they disdain everything equally and regard it all as common property, since they do not subject their beliefs to examination, but just accept all the tenets of this kind. If a deceiver and clever person, someone who knows how to have his way with their cause, should join them, he could quickly become very rich and then make fools of the simple-minded people.[80] In the final analysis Lucian accordingly regards Christianity as rooted in a deception, although he does not go on back to the source and nature of this deception. Instead, while pitying them to a certain extent, he is just content to regard the Christians as the deceived rather than the deceivers.

The second thing about the Christians that especially struck Lucian was their zeal for martyrdom. However, he regarded it as in part just fanatical excess, in part simply the vain, emotional impulse to make a name for oneself and to create a stir in the world. Lucian ends his *Peregrinus* with the major scene in which the protagonist casts himself into the flames of a bonfire before the people assembled at Olympia. Without a doubt this is pure fiction.[81] So in this scene Lucian can simply have in-

80. *The Death of Peregrinus*, chs. 11–13.

81. Nobody before Lucian's day or apart from him knows anything of such an event. See Planck (n. 77), 834ff. and 843. I do not understand how Ferdinand Gregorovius, in his *Geschichte des römischen Kaisers Hadrian und seiner Zeit* (Königsberg, 1851), 254ff., can accept Lucian's narrative as straight factual history. He does not even raise the question as to whether what we have here is, in whole or in part, a piece of Lucian's own composition. It is indeed also a portrait of a particular time, although no single individual existed who actually had all of these major features. Gregorovius places the figure of Peregrinus Proteus alongside the sorcerer Alexander of Abonuteichos [also portrayed by Lucian] and the Pythagorean holy man Apollonius of Tyana, as a third figure—all of whom are for him examples of the absolute derangement of reason and boundless fantasizing amidst the chaotic breakdown of moral and religious factors in Hadrian's day. In the case of Alexander of Abonuteichos, Lucian's exaggerating

tended to present a caricature of certain phenomena in his day. What else could have naturally come to mind in this connection but the scenes of Christians' martyrdom that just then were attracting public attention, during the persecutions under Marcus Aurelius? But what was the point of linking Peregrinus so closely with the Christians if Lucian had not wished to portray him as their follower in this, the main feature of the adventurous role he has him play? Indeed when Peregrinus, being among the Christians, was taken prisoner by the pagan authorities, this very circumstance largely reinforced his impulse to become famous via his adventures, something he strove to do successfully from that point on and for which he had been given new energy. The current governor of Syria, thinking Peregrinus did not even deserve a whipping, merely had him released because, as a philosophically-minded man, the governor did not want to give him any opportunity to satisfy his vainglorious quest for renown.

This is such an obvious allusion to the Christians' longing for martyrdom that the subsequent scene, where what previously could have taken place does now happen but even more ostentatiously, falls of its own accord under the same heading of martyrdom. The fact that, after Peregrinus parted ways with the Christians and Christianity, he is portrayed merely as a Cynic,[82] is no obstacle to our treating his death at Olympia in this context, since it is a feature of Lucian's presentation that he views the Christians' longing for martyrdom as not just a specifically Christian characteristic. Instead it is a widespread element in a depiction of those times. Lucian wants to display in graphic terms the vain striving, in the most extravagant way, to create a stir and play a role in the world; in other words, to exhibit a new form of the cynicism of that time, which so intentionally and brazenly drew public attention to itself.

Marcus Aurelius admonished those ready to die when their stance does not rest on their own convictions, but stems from mere defiance as in the case of the Christians. That is because the wise depart from the world calmly, rationally, and with dignity, and without any theatrics (ἀτραγῴδως).[83] Thus Lucian wanted to portray satirically in his *Peregrinus* these theatrical, self-satisfied extravaganzas on the part of the Christians. So he introduced Peregrinus as a figure of high tragedy, even more extraordinary than all the heroes of Sophocles and Aeschylus, in this singularly fantastic drama.

This extravagant contempt for death, this longing for martyrdom in which the Christians even outdid the tragic heroes, was now a phenomenon especially characteristic of the Christians. Celsus himself had little to say about it.[84] Now martyrdom

---

and idealizing depiction has obviously and greatly augmented the factual material. For he presents most vividly both the great skill of such a deceiver and how incredibly receptive the public was to such artifices. Although Lucian does not think much of the Christians in his *Peregrinus*, that is no obstacle to his juxtaposing them, as unbelievers and atheists, with the highly-regarded Epicureans in his *Alexander*. [*Ed.*] In his *Alexander*, Lucian portrays the protagonist as an imposter, and groups the Christians with the Epicureans as persons he excluded from the mysteries he conducted

82. [*Ed.*] According to Lucian, Peregrinus went to Egypt to study under Agathobulus the Cynic.

83. *Meditations* 2.3.

84. Only in Origen's *Against Celsus* 8.49, do we find him calling it a contradiction that the

had to have become increasingly manifest, for in Marcus Aurelius' day there were not only the usual persecutions; the punishment of death by fire was also common in its full splendor as the fate of heroic Christian martyrs, for instance when Bishop Polycarp of Smyrna died a martyr's death. It even became proverbial to speak of Christians, or Galileans, as those in a frenzy who, simply because it had become fashionable, did what is rationally possible only if one has insight into the laws governing the universe.[85]

The Fanaticism of Christianity

Even though, like Celsus, Lucian looks down upon Christianity with scorn and contempt, his own sentiments and views differ. We can regard him as representative of those who, with an Epicurean indifference to religion in general, not only consider a phenomenon such as Christianity more calmly, but also seek to account for it in terms of how they see the world themselves. They consider Christianity to be analogous to comparable phenomena and similar pathological conditions that afflict humankind.

Lucian does not express the bitter hatred of a Celsus, one that wants only to see Christians as a band of deceivers who have, as it were, plotted to destroy the rest of human society. For Lucian the Christians are just simpletons, credulous people, and fanatics who, fixated on one dominant idea, are therefore quite capable of playing the most fantastic role and providing the grandest demonstration of self-sacrifice. So people have become reconciled to Christianity at least to the extent of regarding it as no worse than what comes to light in so many other contemporary movements. Yet when one goes back to the ultimate source of Christianity, its origins are simply seen to lie in deceit and delusion. Although, unlike Celsus, Lucian did not call Jesus an outright deceiver, but only termed him a sophist,[86] it is hard for Lucian to express an inherently more favorable judgment about Jesus.

Christianity seemed less alien at least when regarded as one example of a broader social pathology. So too the pagans' views of Christianity could change if and when

---

Christians hope for a bodily resurrection "as though it were the best and most precious part of us; and yet . . . to expose it to such tortures as though it were worthless" [*ANF* 4:657].

85. See Arrian, *Discourses of Epictetus*, bk. 4, ch. 7, entitled "freedom from fear." [*Ed.*] The following passage, quoted by Baur in Greek, seems not entirely clear in isolation. Hence we add to the quote a subsequent sentence later in this chapter, which provides the larger context for this statement. The text, as translated by P. E. Matheson, in *The Stoic and Epicurean Philosophers*, ed. Whitney J. Oates (New York, 1940), 437–38, is as follows: "Yet if madness can produce this attitude of mind, even if habit can produce it in the Galileans, can reason and demonstration teach no one that God has made all things in the world . . . but its individual parts to subserve the whole?" To which we add p. 438: "If a man understands this, there is nothing to prevent him from living with an easy and obedient spirit, content with his past lot, and awaiting with a gentle spirit all that may yet befall him."

86. For what Lucian means by this term, which he also uses for Jesus in ch. 16 of his *Philopseudes*, see Planck (n. 77), 873 ff. For Lucian, the term "sophist" has both favorable and unfavorable senses, which suffices for Lucian because he does not wish to speak so disparagingly of Jesus as Celsus does.

they saw a way to find in it a religious dimension that could be assimilated into one of the worldviews current at that time. There was no prospect of gaining the favor of the Epicureans, who were indifferent to everything savoring of religion. Nor were the Stoics receptive, for they were so opposed to the Christians' fanaticism regarding martyrdom that they despised Christianity as something un-Roman. In contrast to these philosophies, Platonism, while scarcely seeming to be ready for such a move with a man like Celsus, was nevertheless sufficiently broad-minded and universal in outlook that it could make concessions to Christianity on the very issue of greatest importance, that it has a divine origin.

Philostratus

The religious eclecticism and syncretism that became widespread in the Roman Empire, directly after the time of the Antonine emperors,[87] and was based on the oriental cult of the sun, paved the way for this change in outlook, since the sun cult infused several of the rulers of the Empire with extreme religiosity.

Philostratus' Life of Apollonius of Tyana

We in fact have proof of the influence this syncretism had on the pagan world's view of Christianity, as seen in the *Life of Apollonius of Tyana*, written by Philostratus.[88] This work plays an important role in our account. It was written in the first decades of the third century, within the social circle of Empress Julia Domna, the wife of Emperor Septimus Severus.[89] We may doubtless assume that she shared in the kind of religious thinking that was so prominent later on in several members of the imperial dynasty and their families. The subject of Philostratus' work, the magician Apollonius of Tyana who lived in the second half of the first century, is also known to us from other sources. He was said to have attracted attention as a soothsayer and miracle worker mainly during the reign of Domitian [i.e., 81–96]. Not much else is said of him other than by Philostratus, who presents him in such an idealized light that one must assume he has a particular motive in doing so.

---

87. [*Ed.*] The Antonine emperors and the dates of their rule are: Antoninus Pius (137–61), Marcus Aurelius (161–80), Lucius Verus (Marcus' brother by adoption, and co-ruler, 161–69), and Commodus (joint ruler from 177, ruler 180–92).

88. [*Ed.*] Flavius Philostratus (c. 170–245) was a Greek Sophist who studied at Athens, and subsequently joined a philosophical circle in Rome that had the emperor Septimus Severus (ruled 193–211) as its patron. Baur's article, "Apollonius von Tyana und Christus, oder das Verhältnis des Pythagoreismus zum Christenthum," *Tübinger Zeitschrift für Theologie* (1832) no. 4, 3–235, examines the comparison of Apollonius and Christ encouraged by Philostratus' portrayal of the former as a wandering first-century philosopher, sage, and miracle-worker. Philostratus' work may have been commissioned by Empress Julia Domna, who had an interest in Apollonius.

89. *Life of Apollonius* 1.3. See *Lives of the Sophists* 2.30.1, also by Philostratus.

The features of Philostratus' depiction of Apollonius leave no doubt as to the aim of such a portrayal. Put succinctly, the rather disreputable magician and soothsayer has now become a moral and religious world-reformer who, had he actually been that in the past, would have surpassed all else the ancient pagan world has to show in the way of such efforts. As depicted here, he dedicated his whole life completely to activities with a religious focus. Wherever he appeared, he eagerly strove to disseminate correct information about the gods and divine things. He instructed people in the worship pleasing to the gods, by encouraging love for what is divine and a pious sensibility that honors the gods. To this end, he was primarily occupied everywhere with religious matters. During his constant travels he did not fail to stop at any sacred place whose past prompts pious feelings, or is even now still chosen, by gods and heroes, for visibly manifesting their accessibility and presence. He visited every temple, dearly loved to linger in them, and gave discourses there that influenced people to worship the gods more zealously. People came there in the hope of receiving more abundant gifts from the gods.

This depiction has Apollonius insisting just as zealously on virtue and morality. Wherever he went he had an extremely positive impact by bringing rigor to an age become lax, and guiding it back to the purer morality of the past. In doing so, he laid a firmer foundation so that nations could flourish. He most especially enjoined self-knowledge and careful attention to the moral judgment expressing itself in the voice of conscience. He located the norm governing moral judgment in the idea of justice or righteousness.[90] But he expressly stated that "doing no wrong" does not yet qualify as righteousness.

Apollonius sought to have the most widespread impact with his teachings and principles. He engaged in these same activities everywhere, and the purpose of his continuous travels through all the lands of the currently known world could only have been to make the wisdom he taught, and that he hoped to be able to utilize for the benefit of humankind, into a legacy for everyone. His impact was indeed a testimony to the universality of his way of thinking. There was nothing either partisan or secret about his teaching. His discourses were public and anyone who wished to could participate in them. He did of course have about him a smaller group of followers, although he seems not to have differed fundamentally in how he instructed this inner circle. The followers at his side were to guarantee that, in the future, the teachings he expected to be a new impetus for moral and religious life, would become universally acknowledged and firmly established.

As a moral and religious reformer, it naturally had to follow that he aroused a certain opposition from the world around him. The aim of his activity was to counter,

---

90. [*Ed.*] In the *Republic*, Plato refers to personal righteousness as "justice in the individual." People in Philostratus' day would have been very familiar with this equivalence of the terms "justice" and "righteousness" in discussing personal morality. It also fits well with the next sentence in our text, which contemporaries would recognize as resonating with Plato's refusal to accept merely "doing no wrong" as an adequate definition of personal justice or morality.

to the best of his ability, the ignorance and indifference with regard to divine matters, the moral deficiencies and defects, that were prevalent among his contemporaries, by correcting the various errors he noticed here and there on the part of individuals. By doing so he sought to remedy the disparity between what his contemporaries did, and the idea that in his view ought to be realized in human life. However, his activity also took a political direction that gave it an even more specific character. His public life fell in the period when the tyranny of Domitian[91] led to widespread terror in the Roman world. Apollonius opposed this tyranny with the courage of a sage undaunted by any danger and, by drawing upon all the teachings and principles the true philosophy has to offer, he became the defender of freedom.

Nevertheless it is not enough for a moral and religious reformer to devote his public activity to the idea that inspires him. Above all he must make this idea vitally and concrete perceptible in his own person. Thus Philostratus depicts the person of Apollonius in a way that presents us with such an ideal. The following traits of Apollonius thus call for special emphasis in this regard. Just as his higher knowledge made him far superior to ordinary people intellectually, and as all knowledge regarding matters divine and human came together in him as in a single focal point, so too in practical affairs he was in equal measure the consummate sage. Beginning with his youth, Apollonius had a secret and inexpressible love for the Pythagorean philosophy. He complied with the way of life it prescribed for its votaries as the only life that is holy, pleasing to God, and worthy of the sage, and he did so more strictly than anyone else. But since the consummate sage can appear in his true greatness only if he also overcomes the terrors of death, this element also has to be a feature of Apollonius' life. He did not shy away from the thought of sacrificing himself as a martyr for the cause of freedom. By his fearlessness and his contempt for death, he disarmed the inhuman cruelty of the tyrant Domitian.

All these traits combined made Apollonius the manifestation of a superhuman, divine figure: his extraordinary knowledge of matters divine and human; his spotless purity, which manifested the finest combination of all the virtues, the most authentic ideal of moral perfection; the noble vocation of his entire life in working for the good of humankind; his courage in facing death, by defending the cause of freedom in opposition to tyranny; and his decision to sacrifice his life in the consciousness of duty. His gifts of prophecy and miracle-working attested to the divinity of his nature, just as the marvelous events at his birth and at the end of his life invested his person with a glory all its own. Hence it was entirely natural for his contemporaries to see him as indeed a god.

On the one hand, this entire portrayal is unhistorical and idealized, and so can only be based on a specific intention; whereas on the other hand, all the main features

---

91. [*Ed.*] Domitian (ruled 51–96), became ruthless in the latter part of his reign (89–96) by, among other actions, terrorizing senators, confiscating property, and banishing the philosophers from Italy.

of this ideal result in a very striking parallelism of Apollonius with Christ. Thus many of the individual features show that Philostratus was well-acquainted with the gospel story. In considering these factors, we can only ask what the intention was in making Apollonius a counterpart to Christ in this way. Nothing here indicates a merely hostile intention. Even if Philostratus' portrayal just sought to say that the Christians have no cause to regard their Christ as such an extraordinary and singular figure—that the pagan world could even match him with a comparably ideal figure; that this can be indeed viewed as opposing Christianity—the thing to ponder, first of all, is what a great concession this makes to Christianity, in that the pagan ideal this sets up is just said to be a counterpart to the original one found in Christianity. When we look back to Lucian and Celsus, where before now do we find talk that came just short of acknowledging the priority of Christianity in this regard? As though any prejudice against Christianity were overcome, it is now conceded to be something very exalted and divine. Yet in order not to grant precedence to Christianity alone, the task that remained was to summon up all the pagan world can bring together in such a counterpart to Christ.

The philosophy ascribed to Apollonius himself claims to be Pythagorean. Doubtless the predilection for Pythagorean philosophy,[92] awakened since the beginning of the Christian era and gradually becoming more widespread, is what chiefly explains the reversal in contemporary pagan consciousness with regard to Christianity, the reversal we see as already an accomplished fact in the work of Philostratus. That is the case even though the work itself seems intentionally to ignore any connection to Christianity. Philosophy itself increasingly took a religious direction. As the consequence of its recent negativity, philosophy began to long for a higher revelation, and sought to satisfy its longing by drawing upon the traditions of earlier times and upon the religious teachings of the East.[93] Thus it had to be more inclined to give credence to a doctrine that also emerged making claims to be a divine revelation, and that after existing for more than two centuries could of course no longer be viewed as therefore a new one, as just a late-comer.

Religious Syncretism

This is how the religious syncretism principally deriving from Neopythagoreanism emerged. It believed the closest approach to absolute truth comes from combining the different forms of religion in a single, unitary conception, insofar as that is possible and to the extent that something higher and divine seems to be revealed in them. They

---

92. [Ed.] Neopythagorean philosophy at this time had become a kind of philosophical theology, which emphasized the distinction between soul and body, argued that the soul must be freed from its material prison by ascetic discipline, and regarded God as the principle of the good and the source of revelation. It together with Neoplatonism served as a counterweight to the secular strain in pagan thought.

93. See Eduard Zeller, *Die Philosophie der Griechen* (Tübingen, 1844–52), vol. 3.2, 490ff.

were all to stand side-by-side and to have equally relative claims to truth so that, all together, they are regarded as rays of light from one and the same principle of light.

Thus Christianity took its own rightful place alongside the other religions. Its founder was honored as were the founders of other religious institutions, and other sages from olden times were set beside him. In being content to juxtapose some other, and equally legitimate, element from the pagan world, to the exalted and divine features acknowledged in Jesus Christ—or, as might be supposed, even still more exalted and more perfect features from that world—was first of all to overlook the fact that this very move had to place Christianity in an entirely different relation to pagan religion and philosophy.

From its beginnings Platonism was closely related to Pythagoreanism. But when it had been elaborated in its new form as Neoplatonism, and had risen to become the dominant philosophy at that time, it had to see the necessity of engaging with Christianity in a specific way, in order to establish more precisely both what it approved of and acknowledged in Christianity, and what it had to reject in Christianity and regard as in principle antithetical to itself. We have become acquainted with a decided opponent of Christianity in the person of Celsus, and with an ambivalent, syncretistic, intermediate figure in Philostratus. Now we come to the Neoplatonist Porphyry, as the main representative of the third and only remaining form possible in the spiritual process under way here, a process in which we see the religious consciousness of the pagan world both drawn to Christianity on the one hand and repelled by it on the other.

Porphyry

Porphyry[94] falls under this twofold perspective. Nevertheless the church fathers consider him to be the most bitter and most intransigent opponent of Christianity.[95]

Porphyry's Polemical Work

Porphyry's work directed against the Christians, in fifteen books, was an even more famous polemical writing than that of Celsus. People were so aware of its importance that very detailed refutations of it were composed by the church's most respected teachers of that era, such as Methodius of Tyre, Eusebius of Caesarea, and Apollinaris

---

94. [*Ed.*] Porphyry (c. 232—c. 305) studied at Athens, acquired a reputation for his learning in many fields, and then went to Rome in 263 to become Plotinus' student and subsequently his biographer. In addition to his lost work *Against the Christians* (fragments translated by Robert M. Berchman, Leiden, 2005), he is noteworthy for popularizing Plotinus' thought, and for his important commentaries on Plato, Aristotle, and Plotinus.

95. For instance, Theodoret calls him "our implacable enemy, our most bitter enemy of all," in *Graecarum Affectionum Curatio* 10.12. [*Ed.*] Baur cites an edition by Schulz. A recent translation is *Theodoret of Cyrus: A Cure for Pagan Maladies* (New York, 2013; Ancient Christian Writers 67).

of Laodicea. Porphyry's attack on Christianity was not as comprehensive and multifaceted as that of Celsus, and it was not likewise aimed at the Christian worldview in general. For Porphyry was better equipped to address points where his arguments emphasized factual evidence that certainly seemed to be undeniable. The Christians' rebuttal documents also have not survived, so of course we know very little about the original and hated target of the Christians' scathing replies. Yet the few fragments that have been preserved from Porphyry's work do enable us to understand it as follows.

Porphyry mainly attacked the Christian scriptures and sought, with critical acumen, to point out the contradictions in them, contradictions that naturally must seem to detract from the character of godliness these scriptures supposedly have. One such point is where he looks in particular at Galatians, ch. 2, which mentions the conflict between the two apostles.[96] Porphyry reproaches one of them [Peter] for his erroneous idea and the other one [Paul] for his contentiousness, and from this whole account concludes that, if the very leaders of the congregations are so disunited, then their overall teaching could only be based on fabrication and lies.[97]

Porphyry accuses Jesus of duplicity and contradiction in his behavior, as stated in the gospel account itself (e.g., John 7:8 as compared to 7:14[98]).[99] Book twelve of Porphyry's work was especially famous. There he took up the prophecies of the prophet Daniel and sought to show that the Book of Daniel was in no way written by the prophet whose name it bears. Instead it was composed by a later author who lived in Judea at the time of Antiochus Epiphanes [i.e., early second century BC]. Daniel had not predicted future events. Instead this other person narrated the past events, and all of his account up to Antiochus contains true history; but since he did not know the future, all that comes after Antiochus is a later invention.[100]

In his critique of the story of Moses and of ancient Jewish history, in book four of his work, Porphyry mainly finds fault with the exegetes, most of all Origen, for their

---

96. [*Ed.*] Gal 2:11–14 presents, from Paul's viewpoint, his confrontation with Cephas (i.e., Peter) at Antioch. Paul confronts Peter by accusing him of hypocrisy regarding the policy of eating with Gentiles.

97. See Jerome, in the introduction to his *Commentary on Galatians*.

98. [*Ed.*] John 7:8: "Go to the festival yourselves. I am not going to this festival, for my time has not yet fully come." John 7:14: "About the middle of the festival Jesus went up into the temple and began to teach."

99. See Jerome, *Dialogue against the Pelagians* 2.17. Porphyry also seems to have located many untrue and intentionally false statements elsewhere in the gospel account. See Jerome, *Epistle 57, to Pammachius*, ch. 9, and *Quaestiones hebraicae in Genesim*. Jerome takes the words of Peter to Ananias and to Sapphira in Acts 5:1–11 as not a prophetic declaration of judgment by God, but only as an *imprecari mortem* (invocation of death). [*Ed.* In this chapter, Ananias and his wife Sapphira are each struck dead after hearing Peter's words about their misconduct regarding the proceeds of the sale of their land.] In his *Epistle to Demetriades* (in J. S. Semler's edition of the *Pelagii . . . epistolata ad Demetriadem* [Halle and Magdeburg, 1775], 156), Jerome cites this as "foolishness (*stultus*) on the part of Porphyry."

100. Jerome reports this about Porphyry in the introduction to his commentary on Daniel.

allegorical interpretations in which they pretentiously substitute mystery teachings in place of the clear sense of the five books of Moses.[101]

Three questions posed in dialectical fashion are especially characteristic of Porphyry's polemical method. If Christ says he is the way of salvation, is grace and truth, and leaves the souls of those believing in him hoping for him alone to return, what then were people doing throughout so many centuries before Christ? Why do the Christians refuse to make sacrificial offerings, when the God of the Old Testament has instituted them? How is sin related to eternal punishment when Christ nevertheless states that "the measure you give will be the measure you get" [Matt 7:2].[102]

The Critical Stance of Neoplatonism

These objections, and doubtless so many others too, show how trenchant Porphyry's polemic was. They also show how very much his whole way of framing arguments, to the extent we can discern it, manifests the spirit of a Celsus. Yet unlike Celsus, Porphyry in no way intended to deliver an utterly negative verdict about Christianity. All that he found fault with in Christianity, and objected to, was only supposed to weigh heavily against the Christianity that was then no longer the authentic and original version.

The challenge now was to combine two elements, showing the respect and recognition that Neoplatonism could not refuse to give Christianity, and maintaining the standpoint paganism had taken in its opposition to Christianity until now. The way to do this was to separate the teacher from his followers, and to replace a purely negative dialectic and polemic, one just seeking to set forth the falseness and vacuity of Christianity as a whole, with a critique adopting the task of distinguishing the original truth of Christianity from the false and spurious additions to it. Even now Christianity ought not to be exonerated from the charge of deception, since its significant place in the world could only be explained based on this assumption. However, the deception was now no longer said to go back to the founder himself; it only extended to the circle of those after him who distorted his true teaching and made the false additions to it that had to make it repugnant and abhorrent to the religious consciousness of the pagans.

The Neoplatonists were the first ones to adopt this stance toward Christianity. It can rightly be called a critical stance since it has the same tendency as every critical way of understanding Christianity thereafter. Such a stance had to look, first and foremost, at what in Christianity is intrinsically true and original, and what has been added to it

---

101. In his *Ecclesiastical History* 6.19.4, Eusebius speaks about the allegorical method of interpretation, and says that these Old Testament exegetes "boast that the things said plainly by Moses are riddles, treating them as divine oracles full of hidden mysteries, and bewitching the mental judgment of their own pretentious obscurity" [LCL, *Eusebius*, 2:56–57].

102. Augustine, *Epistle 102*, or *Six Questions to the Pagans*, qu. 2, 3, 4. See also Jerome, *Epistle 133, to Ctesiphon*, ch. 9.

by some other route. Augustine says those who added to it were "those vain eulogizers of Christ and those crooked slanderers of the Christian religion . . . [who] turn their blasphemies aside from Christ, and pour them forth against his disciples."[103] So what Celsus charged Jesus with doing is now laid at the door of the disciples, for they alone are the ones who denied the pagan gods and took such a hostile stance toward all the pagan popular beliefs. Jesus himself was far from doing so. He believed in the gods, honored them according to pagan customs, and with their help performed miracles as a wonder-worker, which gained him great fame.[104] In this Neoplatonist version, just as the disciples said things about their master that he himself never conceived of, so too their statement that he called himself God is said to be simply a false assertion. Conceding divine stature to Jesus would have been to make Christianity superior to paganism. Yet the Neoplatonists were willing to recognize and honor Christ as one of the wisest and most excellent of men.[105] However, Jesus was also just said to share in this excellence along with the wise and godly men of pagan antiquity, such that this parallel served not so much to exalt him as it did to eclipse him.

Philostratus had written his *Life of Apollonius*, and Porphyry and Iamblichus reflected like interests when each wrote a biography of Pythagoras. They endowed and glorified his life with all the elements that could make it a theophany of the same kind that the Christians beheld in their Christ. Quite intentionally they presented their divine Pythagoras not merely as the highest ideal of wisdom, but also as an incarnate god. Iamblichus says that even as a youth Pythagoras impressed people as being a god.[106] All those who saw and heard him looked upon him in wonderment, and many with good reasons expressed the conviction that he was the son of a god. Supported by the opinion people held about him, by the education he had received from childhood onward, and by his naturally godlike nature, he confidently proved to be all the more worthy of the excellent qualities that were his. He stood out because of his religiousness, his knowledge, the distinctive nature of his way of life, the healthy state

---

103. Augustine, *The Harmony of the Gospels*, 1.15 [*NPNF*¹ 6:86].

104. In 1.34–35 Augustine states that the Neoplatonists' "aim is to get Christ credited with the writing of some other composition, I know not of what sort, which may be suitable to their inclinations, and with having indulged in no sentiments of antagonism to their gods, but rather having paid respect to them in a kind of magical worship; and their wish is also to get it believed that his disciples not only gave a false account of him when they declared him to be the God by whom all things were made, while he was really nothing more than a man, although certainly a man of the most exalted wisdom, but also that they taught with regard to these gods of theirs something different from what they had themselves learned from him" [*NPNF*¹ 6:100]. See also ch. 9.

105. Augustine, *The Harmony of the Gospels*, 1.7: "they admit that all other men have been excelled by him in the matter of wisdom, although they decline to acknowledge him to be God" [*NPNF*¹ 6:82]. The pagan oracles too are said to have declared Jesus one of the most godly and wisest of men, and the Neoplatonists placed great weight on their pronouncements. See *The City of God*, 19.23, and Eusebius, *Proof of the Gospel*, 3.8.

106. *Life of Pythagoras*, ch. 2. [*Ed.*] "No one will deny that the soul of Pythagoras was sent to mankind from Apollo's domain" (*The Pythagorean Sourcebook and Library*, trans. Kenneth Guthrie [Grand Rapids, 1987], 58–59).

of his soul, his physical grace in all that he said and did, and an inwardly cheerful and inimitable equanimity that he did not let be disturbed by an onset of anger or laughter, of envy or contentiousness, or any other passion. Thus he dwelt in Samos, as a good demon or spirit appearing among human beings.[107] When he went to Italy and established the universally celebrated Magna Graecia,[108] he appeared here too as a god. The inhabitants received his laws and precepts as divine commands, from which the slightest departure was not allowed.

The entire society of his followers lived together in perfect unity. All the neighboring communities extolled it and praised it as blessed. The followers held all their possessions in common. They counted Pythagoras in the circle of the gods as a good demon, one friendly to human beings. A few said he was the Pythian Apollo, others the Hyperborean Apollo, others the Paeon, others one of the demons who dwell in the moon, and still others one of the Olympian gods who appear to the living in human form for the healing and restoration of the lives of mortals.[109] Hence Pythagoras is the salutary light of blessedness and of philosophy (the salvific philosophy) who is permitted to share in mortal nature.[110]

Iamblichus adds that no greater good has ever come than the one sent by the gods through this Pythagoras, and a greater good never will come. That is why the one nicknamed "the long-haired Samian" is spoken of with the greatest respect. Therefore, if there is also the kind of incarnation of God as the Christians maintain Christ is, in other words the kind of indwelling a human being on God's part (ἐπιδημία εἰς ἀνθρώπους θεοῦ), as the philosopher Eunapius[111] wanted to characterize Apollonius in the life of him by Philostratus, and as one can accordingly also call the life of Pythagoras depicted by Porphyry and Iamblichus, then Pythagoras [as the greatest good] stands alone and, next to him, Christ can only be regarded as a secondary figure. It is

---

107. "His influence, at Samos, was that of some beneficent divinity." [Ed.] Quoted by Baur in Greek. Iamblichus, *Life of Pythagoras*, 59 in the Guthrie edition.

108. [Ed.] The term is used for those Greek cities established in southern Italy (i.e., "Greater Greece"), beginning with Cumae about 750 BC. Iamblichus' *Life of Pythagoras* (who lived in the sixth century BC) credits him with being the founder of "Magna Graecia," although other Greek cities (such as Croton) were clearly there before his arrival (see ch. 5–6 of the Guthrie edition, 63).

109. [Ed.] The Pythian Apollo is the Apollo associated with the oracle at Delphi, presided over by the Pythia or prophetess there. The Hyperboreans were a legendary race living in the northern regions, and Apollo supposedly spent the winter months there. Apollo Paeon is a form of Apollo as a god of healing.

110. [Ed.] Baur's footnote, without specific citation, gives what appears to be the Greek he is paraphrasing up to this point in the text, beginning with "who appear to the living in human form." This statement is found in ch. 6 of Iamblichus' *Life* (p. 63 in Guthrie [n. 106]). Baur adds a reference to the New Testament, to Titus 2:11–13, which, along the same lines, reads: "For the grace of God has appeared, bringing salvation to all, training us to renounce impiety and worldly passions, and in the present age to live lives that are self-controlled, upright, and godly, while we wait for the blessed hope and the manifestation of the glory of our great God and Savior, Jesus Christ."

111. In the preface to the *Vitae Sophistarum*, ed. Boissonade (Amsterdam, 1822), 3. [Ed.] Eunapius (c. 345—c. 420) was an anti-Christian Sophist.

just an overstatement on the Christians' part if they make any more out of Christ than a god or divine man in the pagan sense.

Hierocles

Hierocles,[112] the governor of Bithynia, took a different view of Christ than the Neoplatonists did. He did not object to their view, yet he adopted the procedure of Celsus and his *True Reason* (Ἀληθὴς λόγος) by writing *Words of the Love of Truth* (Λόγοι φιλαλήθεις) in two books, against the Christians. The main point of his polemical writing seems to have been drawing a parallel between Christ and the Apollonius who was glorified by Philostratus. His only reproach against the Christians is that they do not know how to evaluate extraordinary phenomena of this kind in a more dispassionate and circumspect way.

Hierocles says the Christians make far too much out of Jesus' good deeds, by extolling him for enabling a few blind people to see again and for performing a few other miracles of this kind. What ought to be noted, however, is that the pagans hold a far more correct and reasonable view of such things and how they think about extraordinary persons. Hierocles then cites the examples of Aristeas of Proconnesus,[113] of Pythagoras and a few other ancient figures, but most especially Apollonius of Tyana, who first appeared during the reign of Nero. In introducing them he merely intended to contrast the pagans' well-founded judgment in each case with the irresponsible approach of the Christians. To be specific, the pagans regard such miracle-workers not as gods but only as people beloved by the gods; whereas the Christians declare their Jesus to be a god on account of a few insignificant, miraculous signs. It is also relevant to take account of the fact that Jesus' deeds have been embellished in every way by Peter and Paul and a few other similar people who were liars, fantasizers, and preoccupied with magic. On the other hand, the deeds of Apollonius have been described by those who were most highly educated and knew how to value truth, and who, out of love for humankind, did not want the deeds of a noble man, beloved of the gods, to be unknown.[114]

The most the pagans could concede to Christ was just a divine dignity in the same sense that, according to a polytheistic outlook, different forms of the divine could generally have in equal measure. Hence the worship of Jesus always presupposes that the worship of the pagan gods is equally justified. So the ultimate point of contention between Christians and pagans always involved the reality of the pagan

---

112. He wrote two books known only from their refutation in the *Against Hierocles* of Eusebius of Caesarea. [*Ed.*] Sossianus Hierocles was a Roman aristocrat and office-holder. In 303 he was transferred to Bithynia, where he became known for his anti-Christian activities.

113. [*Ed.*] In legends about Apollo, Aristeas serves the god in various ways by taking on a non-human shape, and by separating from his body so as to appear elsewhere.

114. See ch. 2 of Eusebius' *Against Hierocles*.

gods. The Christians could not acknowledge the pagan gods without contradicting the absolute character of their concept of God; whereas the pagans could not condone predicating something exclusively of one god that they were accustomed to thinking of as the attribute the many gods shared. Furthermore, since the Christians, as opposed to the pagans, were always just one sect that had arisen fairly recently, they were faulted for having forsaken the universal, popular belief, sanctified by ancient tradition. In the eyes of the Neoplatonists that was far more blameworthy than it was commonly thought to be.

In the Neoplatonic worldview, polytheism does not just befit a beautiful and many-faceted world. It is also mandated by the ruler of the universe, and thus results in a multitude of different peoples' religions, because each people has its own "superintending spirit."[115] Thus in the general order of the world determined by God, and in the position within it assigned to each individual, abandoning the religion of one's native land can also be regarded as simply a blasphemous transgression. In this sense Porphyry called honoring the deity in the manner of one's native land (τιμᾶν τὸ θεῖον κατὰ τὰ πάτρια),[116] the greatest fruit of piety. Porphyry set Ammonius Saccas and Origen side by side,[117] and pronounced the following judgment on the two of them. Porphyry said that, although born of Christian parents, as soon as Ammonius began to philosophize he turned to "the life of the law-abiding citizen" (ἡ κατὰ νόμους πολιτεία), but Origen, although raised as a Greek among Greeks, turned to "barbarian venturesomeness" and adulterated his Greek knowledge by living, in unlawful fashion, as a Christian.

The Authority of Tradition and the Principle of Religious Freedom

The syncretism of Neoplatonism interacting with the consciousness of the pagan world compensated for Christianity's initially being rejected as something hated and abhorrent, and in consequence being declared, at the least, as just deception and fanaticism. Things progressed to the point that the conflict between these two spiritual forces seemed to just involve the formal issue of whether it was permissible to change over from the received religion to a new religion. Each person could only answer this question based on the dictates of his or her own religious consciousness.

Even now, whoever has a religious consciousness unable to conceive of the heavenly realm as lacking the divine figures of the old belief system, had to answer in

---

115. The term used by Celsus, according to Origen, *Against Celsus* 5.25.

116. In ch. 18 of the letter to his wife Marcella, which was discovered by A. Mai, and published in 1816 [ET: *Porphyry's Letter to His Wife Marcella Concerning the Life of Philosophy and the Ascent to the Gods*, trans. Alice Zimmern (Grand Rapids, 1989)].

117. According to Eusebius, *Ecclesiastical History* 6.19. On Porphyry's contention, see the review of Heigl's 1835 paper that I published in the Berlin *Jahrbücher für wissenschaftliche Kritik* (1837) pt. 2, 652ff. Also see E. R. Redepenning, *Origenes* (Bonn, 1841), pt. 1, 422ff. [*Ed.*] Ammonius Saccas of Alexandria, a Platonist of the early third century, was the teacher of both Plotinus the pagan philosopher and Origen the Christian theologian. Originally a Christian, he converted to paganism.

the negative; whereas those no longer conscious of being impacted by the old gods, exercising such spiritual power, could give an affirmative answer. However, even those consciously and inwardly relieved and freed from all ties to the old belief system could feel outwardly bound to it, since, as individuals or as just a powerless minority, they confronted a very dominant majority. So the main issue now was already essentially the same one that subsequently became so very significant within the Christian Church itself: How is the subjective freedom and competency of the individual related to the force of custom and past practice, in other words, to the authority of a tradition counting as Catholic? Also, given all those concepts [of custom and tradition] that were tied to the old beliefs in the gods, and given the concepts of tradition that likewise gave the Christian Church its Catholic character, what rights do individuals therefore have if they cannot know that they have freedom of consciousness over against this [kind of external] power?

It is noteworthy how, when the earliest Christian apologists defended the Christian faith against the pagan belief system, they proceeded to affirm, against their pagan opponents, the Protestant principle of freedom of belief and conscience, as something intrinsically belonging to the concept of religion. Tertullian responds to those opponents by asking: Among the pagans, where does each one get the right to worship principally this god or that one? Where else does it come from but from religion itself, inasmuch as religion is inherently and essentially just a matter of free choice and free self-determination? Why should the Christians not also have the same right?[118]

The writer of the *Pseudo-Clementine Homilies* examined this same issue. He has the pagan grammarian Apion[119] maintaining that the greatest sin would be to abandon the customs of one's native land and turn to barbarian mores. But the writer answers the question whether one is to follow the forefathers in all things concerning God, by drawing a distinction between truth (ἀλήθεια) and custom (συνήθεια). To

---

118. Tertullian, *Apology*, ch. 24: "Let one man worship God, another Jupiter; let one lift suppliant hands to the heavens, another to the altar of Fides; let one—if you choose to take this view of it—pray to the clouds, and another to the ceiling panels; let one consecrate his own life to his God, and another to consecrate the life of a goat. For see that you do not give further ground for the charge of irreligion, by taking away religious liberty, and forbidding free choice of deity, so that I may no longer worship according to my inclination, but am compelled to worship against it. Even a human being would not care to have unwilling homage rendered him; and so the very Egyptians have been permitted the legal use of their ridiculous superstition. . . . Every province even, and every city, has its god. . . . In fact, we alone are prevented from having a religion of our own. We give offense to the Romans, we are excluded from the rights and privileges of Romans, because we do not worship the gods of Rome. It is well that there is a God of all, whose we all are, whether we will or no. But with you liberty is given to worship any god but the true God, as though he were not rather the God all should worship, and to whom all belong" [*ANF* 3:39]. Also, *To Scapula*, ch. 2: "It is a fundamental human right, a privilege of nature, that every man should worship according to his own convictions: one man's religion neither harms nor helps another man. It is assuredly no part of religion to compel religion—to which free will and not force should lead us—for even the sacrificial victims are required to be willing. You will render no real service to your gods by compelling us to sacrifice" [*ANF* 3:105].

119. [*Ed.*] Apion, an Alexandrian Greek of the first century BC, whose anti-Semitic position was the target of *Against Apion* by the Jewish historian Josephus.

disallow conversion from pagan religion to the Christian religion, on the grounds that it would be wrong to rebel against the customs and beliefs of one's forefathers, is to fail to appreciate the great difference between truth and custom. The ancestral practices are only to be continued if they are good ones. But pagan religion is indeed not good, because it is polytheistic.[120]

Origen says the same thing in replying to Celsus: that we know it is right to give up the age-old practices of individual lands when there are better and more godly laws, such as those given by Jesus, the supreme master; for it is wrong to not trust in the one who has proven to be purer and mightier than all rulers.[121]

Therefore, once one is convinced that there is a better way, then that in itself also means one is right to follow it and no power on earth can withstand it. The victory of Christianity was decided as soon as the Roman state saw itself obliged to grant external freedom to the religious conviction that the apologists had already shown Christianity entitled to have. What now follows is the demonstration of that process.

---

120. *Pseudo-Clementine Homilies* (Part 3, n. 66), 4.7ff.
121. Origen, *Against Celsus* 5.32.

II. The External Aspects of Christianity's Relation to the Pagan World and to the Roman State

The usual practice is just to assess Christianity's relation to the Roman state in terms of the series of persecutions Christians suffered from under one emperor or another. The Romans, being pagans, could of course simply persecute Christianity, and it seemed to be a matter of chance as to when they did or did not do so. But of course when we look more closely at the persecutions we see that they differed in kind and as to what motivated them. Thus the relation of the Roman state to Christianity varied as the pagan world's overall view of Christianity took one form or another.

The whole series of phenomena that are now our next topic are therefore simply the external reflection of what we already discussed as the internal process taking its course in the consciousness of the pagan world, and shaped by the state of affairs then. As surely as Christianity, with its overarching power of truth, increasingly and inevitably won a place in the consciousness of the pagan world, and ultimately had to become dominant in that world, so too there ultimately had to come a point where Christianity overcame the Roman state and took into its own hands all the state's power and sovereign authority.

TIBERIUS, CLAUDIUS, AND NERO

Christ, who was born during the reign of Augustus and was crucified under Tiberius, stands at the pinnacle of the most important epoch in Roman history.[122] Both of these equally significant world powers, Christianity and the absolute rule of the Roman emperor, made their appearance in world history at the same time. However, the first point at which they meet shows that they can hardly coexist as such. It is especially significant that the annals of Roman history also record the fact that the founder of Christianity was condemned to death by the decree of a Roman magistrate.

---

122. [*Ed.*] In 31 BC, Caesar Augustus became the sole ruler of the Roman world. Later declared emperor, he ruled until his death in AD 14. Tiberius, his stepson, succeeded him and ruled until AD 37.

II. The External Aspects of Christianity's Relation to the Pagan World and to the Roman State

The first Roman historian to mention Christianity and Christians writes: "During the reign of Tiberius, the instigator known as Christ received the death penalty from the procurator, Pontius Pilate."[123] It is as though the writer, quite intentionally and with diplomatic delicacy, sought to perpetuate in the annals of world history the point that this was done by a Roman and in the name of the Roman state. However, Christian legend has it that Tiberius himself acknowledged the divinity of Christ, and in the Roman Senate he proposed that Christ be worshiped. So this legend just wants to create a vivid impression of how the events reported from Palestine to the emperor, pertaining to the death of Jesus, must have affected the mind of a Tiberius, and by its doing so have the punishment Tiberius deserved fall more surely on Tiberius' head, as the one who had incurred this heavy load of guilt.

Yet there is no historical record of the Roman state having any contact with Christians during the reign of Emperor Claudius.[124] Suetonius tells us[125] that Claudius expelled from Rome the Jews "instigated by Christ" (*impulsore Chresto*) who were constantly raising an uproar. So it is very likely that the term *impulsor Chrestus*[126] is a faint echo of the fact that Christianity, having made inroads into Rome at that time, had split the Roman Jewish community into two factions, as it had also typically done elsewhere; furthermore, that this Christian faction had provided the impulse for the unrest that caused the emperor to take these measures. For in this case Christianity still appeared under the umbrella of the Jewish religion, as a permitted religion (*religio licita*),[127] and was protected only to the extent that it shared in the protection granted to the Jews.

During the reign of Nero [54–68] the Christians entered the annals of history for the first time in a manner that befitted them. Tacitus[128] tells us about the great

---

123. [*Ed.*] Tacitus, *Annals* 15.44 (translation from Henry S. Bettenson, *Documents of the Christian Church*, 2nd ed. [London, 1963], 2).

124. [*Ed.*] Claudius, who ruled 41–54, was the fourth Roman emperor, following the despotic reign of Caligula (37–41).

125. In 25.4 of the "Life of Claudius," in his *Lives of the Caesars*. Compare the statement that follows in the text with Acts 18:2 ["Claudius had ordered all Jews to leave Rome"]. Since Dio Cassius says the very opposite [in his *Roman History*], 60.6, that Claudius did not expel the Jews from Rome, the following is thought to be the best way to harmonize these two accounts. In AD 41 Claudius issued an edict prohibiting all Jews from residing in Rome. However, since there were so many of them that the decreed general expulsion could not be carried out without uprisings, only prominent individuals such as Aquila were in fact expelled. Instead of full compliance with the original edict, the order was merely to close the synagogues, and later in the same year a general edict of toleration was issued (Josephus, *Antiquities*, 19.5). Christians also enjoyed protection under this edict. See Hermann Lehmann, *Studien zur Geschichte des apostolischen Zeitalters* (Greifswald, 1856), 1ff.; also, *Claudius und Nero* (Gotha, 1858), 141ff.

126. The pagans customarily spoke of "Chresto" instead of "Christ"; see Tertullian, *Apology*, ch. 3. [*Ed.*] This statement is a "faint echo" because Suetonius (75–160) wrote long after the time of Claudius.

127. Tertullian, *Apology*, ch. 21.

128. [*Ed.*] Tacitus (c. 55–120), a Roman historian, whose *Annals* covered the time from Tiberius to Nero. See *Annals*, 15.44, for the following information.

conflagration in Nero's day when a major part of the city of Rome was destroyed and the persistent rumor was that Nero himself was the one who caused it. Tacitus says Nero sought to counteract this rumor by casting blame on others, and by inflicting the most cruel punishments on those the populace called "Christians,"[129] and who were hated for committing their foul deeds. In spite, "they were clad in the hides of beasts and torn to death by dogs; others were crucified, others set on fire to illuminate the night when daylight failed."[130] Tacitus says the Christians were convicted not so much because there was evidence supporting the charge that they started the conflagration, but rather because they were haters of the human race.[131] Therefore they were by no means convicted for starting the fire. Instead this particular charge that could not be brought against them was replaced by a general charge that made them deserving of punishment. It was that while there might be no proof of particular actions on their part, they could at least be regarded as capable of criminal acts not demonstrably provable against them.

The Christians' *odium generis humani* (hatred of the human race) was said to be a mindset so hostile to all other human beings that, in opposing the Christians, it was justifiable to disregard all the rules people are elsewhere obliged to follow in relation to others. Denying them any human consideration identified them as a class of people who, simply by their own doing, were said to completely lack any human character and culture. This is how the Roman public at that time viewed the Christians. Hence people were satisfied with such a *subdere reos* (way of subduing criminals), and found the whole situation quite in order. Tacitus himself shared this view, and had no misgivings about these cruel actions. Instead, the way he speaks about Christianity says clearly enough that he regards such measures against the Christians as sufficiently justified. Everything done to the Christians at that time was accordingly just the practical consequence of the pagan world's general view of Christianity.

A chance event led to Nero's persecution of Christians, so the purpose behind these actions apparently had little to do with the nature of Christianity itself.[132] For

---

129. *Quos . . . vulgus Christianos appellabat.* So already in Nero's day this was what people usually called them. According to Acts 11:26, "it was in Antioch that the disciples were first called 'Christians.'" (The word for "disciples"—χρηματίσαι, those who received a revelation—could just be a popular expression.) The adjectival *christianus* is not Greek but authentically Latin, which makes it unlikely that the term originated in a city with a Greek-speaking populace. No doubt it originated in Rome. The writer of Acts says it originated in Antioch because he thought of Antioch as the chief city of Gentile Christianity, where it was first established. Despite its Gentile origins, the Paulinists were happy to make this term their own. That is because, as Pseudo-Ignatius also emphasizes (see my essay, "Über der Ursprung des Episcopats," *Tübinger Zeitschrift für Theologie* [1838] no. 3 181ff.), the Paulinist writer of Acts expresses most directly, and in opposition to Judaism, the independent significance of the Christianity emancipated from Judaism.

130. [*Ed.*] Tacitus, *Annals*, 15.44 (Bettenson, *Documents* [n. 123], 2). Baur paraphrases in German.

131. [*Ed.*] Baur quotes the Latin text from *Annals*, 15.44.

132. According to Lehmann in his *Studien* (n. 125), the persecution resulted from Jewish hatred [of Christians] and is attributable to Nero's wife, Poppaea Sabina. According to Josephus (*Antiquities*, 20.8) this woman was a convert to Judaism, whereas according to Tacitus (*Histories*, 1.22) she kept

the pagans saw Christianity as something quite different from what it actually was. Still, the persecution was a deadly blow aimed directly at Christianity itself. While not an attempt at general suppression of Christianity, the declaration was in fact that it is to be destroyed just as all that is base and abominable cannot generally be tolerated. Thus as long as the Roman state's view of Christianity remained unchanged, this was just the beginning, and one had to anticipate that the persecution would occur again at every opportunity. That the two sides were inherently opposed had now become a major historical actuality, emerging in its full extent for the first time.

On the Christian side as well, this initial conflict with the Roman state could only result in the Christians becoming fully aware of how repellent they were to the state and the state was to them. This first actual persecution of Christians, with all its scenes of martyrdom, came at a time when they most eagerly anticipated the parousia of Christ and the tribulations to accompany it. It is inconceivable that the persecution would not have had a very unsettling effect, not merely on the Roman congregations but also on the Christians in all places that received news of it. Although this persecution may have been confined to the city of Rome, it could only be seen as the initial signal of the great denouement that was said to be on the verge of commencing.

In the Book of Revelation, written just a few years after this, we see the most striking and authentic testimony to the profound and lasting impression the persecution made on the entire Christian world. It is in fact none other than the Christian manifesto countering the Roman declaration of war actually made by that persecution. The bloody scenes of Nero's persecution of Christians clearly shine through all those images in which Revelation depicts the Roman Babylon, the woman drunk on the blood of the holy martyrs [Rev 17:3–6]. The tyrant Nero, who had himself first begun such a wicked outrage against the Christians and against Christianity itself, now counted everywhere as the Antichrist, as Revelation certainly declared him to be. Tacitus and Suetonius tell of a legend widely believed among the Roman populace, that Nero still lived and would come again, returning from the East as the sovereign. It is more likely that this legend originated with the Christians, and came about because Nero had to be set over against Christ, as the Antichrist.[133]

---

company with a large number of mathematicians, a group that included Jewish magicians, and her hand is recognizable in the persecution through her influence on Nero. This is pure conjecture. E. Böhmer, in the *Jahrbücher für deutsche Theologie* 4 (1859) 446, says this explanation even applies to the conflagration; that the plan was to destroy the old palace prior to founding the *regnum Hierosolymorum* (kingdom of Jerusalem) prophesied to Nero (according to Suetonius, *Lives of the Caesars*, ch. 40).

133. See my treatise on the Book of Revelation ("Kritik der neuesten Erklärung der Apokalypse") in the *Theologische Jahrbücher* 11 (1852) 325ff.; and E. Böhmer, "Zur Lehre vom Antichrist nach Schneckenburger," in the *Jahrbücher für deutsche Theologie* 4 (1859) 441ff. It seems to me that the Second Epistle to the Thessalonians is a not insignificant contribution to the history of this era, which was stirred up by belief that Nero would return as the Antichrist. I sought to show this in my essay, "Der beiden Briefe an die Thessalonicher," in the *Theologische Jahrbücher* 14 (1855) 141ff. The writer of the epistle, speaking in the name of the apostle, expressly warns them "not to be quickly shaken in

Therefore the Christians' view of the pagan world and of the Roman state was no different than the pagans' view of Christianity. The Christians also saw what they faced as simply a world deserving of destruction and rapidly headed for it. Therefore they would sooner break away completely from the presently existing world order, and see it demolished at a single stroke, in the most violent way, by the intervention of the Lord, appearing from heaven once more in his glory—all this, rather than entertaining the thought that the theater for realizing the idea of the kingdom of God should be within this world order, on the soil of the Roman Empire, which was still continuing to develop as a temporal domain. Later on, even when anticipation of the parousia was no longer in the forefront of people's minds in the same way as in the early days, the Christians could not rid themselves of this harsh way of understanding their relation to the Roman Empire. They saw the Roman Empire as, at the very least, the realm of demons with all the *pompa diaboli* (the Devil's retinue), and their Christian consciousness could only turn away in horror from any association with such a kingdom of darkness.

How many intermediate steps there had to be before these harsh antitheses could be reconciled in a unitary consciousness, before the Roman Empire and Christianity—as its dominant religion, as the state religion—were conceived of as one and the same! It is self-evident that this could not have happened without a long struggle, one taking various forms and passing through different phases.

Despite all that, for a long time there are no further historical reports about the lot of Christianity and Christians in the Roman Empire. The next to emerge as a new persecutor of Christians was Domitian, "a man of Nero's type in cruelty," as Tertullian calls him.[134] Yet we have no specific information about this from his time. It is without a doubt pure fiction that the Apostle John suffered martyrdom in boiling oil in Domitian's day. It is indeed remarkable how the name of a Clement also appears in the works of pagan historians during Domitian's rule. But it is anybody's guess whether

---

mind or alarmed. . . . Let no one deceive you in any way" (2:1–3). He warns them to not be led to believe that the day of the parousia is now dawning. It is very natural here to think of the well-known pseudo-Neronian incitements, and especially those Tacitus mentions in his *Histories*, 2.8. Concerning the time after the murder of Galba, when not only Otho and Vitellius but also Vespasian thought of resorting to arms, Tacitus writes: "About this time Achaia and Asia were terrified by a false rumor of Nero's arrival. The reports with regard to his death had been varied, and therefore many people imagined and believed that he was alive. . . . Then the alarm spread far and wide. Many came eagerly forward at the famous name . . ." (LCL, *Tacitus*, vol. 1, 172–73). Right in those provinces that were the main theater of this movement, in Achaia, by which Tacitus means Greece and Macedonia, including the city of Thessalonica, the Christians made up a considerable part of the population. See Heinrich Ewald, *Sendschreiben des Apostels Paulus* (Göttingen, 1857), 25. Ewald correctly notes that, although it does not follow from the passage in Tacitus that a pseudo-Nero had already appeared, it is all the more remarkable how the mere rumor of Nero's return and the belief in it, this laughing-stock of a false Nero, could have alarmed so many. This horrifying impression also calls to mind the Christians who were fearful of the Antichrist appearing. See my treatise on Revelation for how closely the Antichrist depicted in Second Thessalonians, ch. 2, is related to the Antichrist of the Book of Revelation.

134. *Apology*, ch. 5.

or not there is any connection between the Christian Clement, who occupies such an important place in the tradition of that time as bishop of the Roman community, and the Flavius Clemens whom Domitian ordered be put to death. Even where we find what is very likely a reference to Christianity, the text just speaks of atheism and of Jewish practices. That seems to justify the supposition that Christianity once again found itself under the umbrella of the Jewish religion, and at least attracted no special attention from the Roman state. It may be that in the provinces people could be aroused to hate the Christians, and so committed acts of persecution in one place or another. But these were isolated instances that had no great import for how Christians were generally regarded.

TRAJAN, HADRIAN, AND THE ANTONINE EMPERORS[135]

The edict of Trajan came in response to the famous letter of Pliny the Younger to the emperor.[136] Pliny, the governor of Bithynia in Asia Minor, reported that the number of Christians in that region seemed to have increased greatly in a short time.

Pliny's letter makes clear that the pagan religion had suffered a significant decline, its temples stood empty, its festivals were no longer celebrated in the customary way, and people were no longer purchasing the sacrificial animals. This prompted a reaction on the part of the pagans. Christians of all ages and social classes, and of both sexes, were being hauled into court, and now for the first time decisions were being made as to what right they had to be Christians. Pliny himself is quite explicit that these proceedings have very little to do with Roman law. He confesses that having Christians brought before his tribunal puts him in an awkward position. He has never before dealt with the interrogation of Christians, and so does not know what is punishable and what calls for further investigation. He is unsure whether to treat children and adults differently; "whether those who recant should be pardoned, or whether someone who has ever been a Christian should benefit from ceasing to be one; whether those innocent of crime should be punished for bearing the name 'Christian,' or just those committing *flagitia cohaerentia nomini* (crimes associated with the name)."

On the issue before him Pliny knew he could only rule that those professing to be Christians, and facing the consequences of doing so, were to be punished. For he

---

135. [*Ed.*] The Nerva-Antonine dynasty was a dynasty of seven emperors who ruled the Roman Empire from 96 to 192. They were Nerva, Trajan, Hadrian, Antoninus Pius, Lucius Verus, Marcus Aurelius, and Commodus. They were also known as the Adoptive Emperors because all but the last adopted the candidate of his choice to be his successor.

136. [*Ed.*] Trajan ruled 98–117. Pliny the Younger (61/62–113) was a Roman administrator, and a prolific writer of letters that reveal much about life in the empire, and that are noteworthy for their literary excellence. At the time when he wrote this letter to Trajan, Pliny was the Roman governor of Bithynia, in Asia Minor. Pliny published nine books of letters to his friends. Book Ten contains his official correspondence with Trajan. What follows in the next three paragraphs is from Pliny, *Letters*, 10.96, with (modified) translations by Bettenson (n. 123), 3–4.

says he is of the opinion that "whatever kind of crime it may be to which they have confessed, their pertinacity and inflexible obstinacy should certainly be punished." After all these very detailed and strictly conducted investigations regarding Christianity as such, Pliny's general verdict is that Christianity is a "depraved and unbridled superstition" (*prava et immodica superstitio*), a contagion that "has spread not only in the cities, but in the villages and rural districts as well; yet it seems capable of being checked" if the multitude of Christians were "given a chance of recantation."

This was a new issue for Pliny. So he took the matter to the emperor, in order to get more precise information and instructions as to the emperor's intentions. From the emperor's replies we learn more specifically how things then stood regarding Christians in the Roman state. Trajan approved of Pliny's views and procedures, and he himself admitted that this was the kind of situation not lending itself to a generic solution. He said the Christians "are not to be sought out; if they are informed against, and the charge is proved, they are to be punished, with this reservation—that if anyone says he is not a Christian and actually proves it, that is by worshiping our gods, he shall be pardoned as a result of his recantation, however suspect he may have been with respect to the past. Pamphlets published anonymously should carry no weight in any charge whatsoever. They constitute a very bad precedent, and are also out of keeping with this age." If we pay attention above all to this last point, then Trajan's decision seems as fair and moderate as was ever to be expected from a pagan emperor. The motive behind it may also have been the conviction that naked force would only make a bad situation worse, and that the kind of fanaticism he saw Christianity as being would most surely calm down of its own accord if forbearance were shown.

In this approach we see a change in consciousness at that time, for people were no longer regarding Christianity as "destructive" (*exitiabilis*), as Tacitus put it from the perspective of Nero's day. Instead they saw it as just a "depraved and unbridled superstition." Therefore it now no longer counted as something utterly incompatible with human moral and social life. Instead Christianity is just an overexcited movement that oversteps proper boundaries. As such, the Christians were no longer "seen by way of crimes" (*per flagitia invisi*). Instead one must first ask whether there are "crimes associated with the name." One only wanted to punish to the extent necessary; but as soon as Christianity came out into the open, of course such a conspicuous contradiction of the Roman state religion could not be tolerated. Thus Christianity supposedly was allowed to exist within the Roman state at least to the extent that it could be disregarded. But how long could it be disregarded when it was constantly gaining ground? And what did it then have to expect on the part of the state, when Pliny had already seen that it was no longer merely fanaticism, but was also an "inflexible obstinacy" that defiantly provoked use of the state's power over against it, and when the emperor himself, without any reservations, said about the Christians: "If they are arrested and convicted, they are to be punished"?

Put succinctly, Trajan's edict marks an epoch in which Christianity is formally and without reservation said to have no legal right to exist in the Roman state. Anyone calling himself a Christian, anyone who was at one time an acknowledged Christian and has not actually disavowed his Christianity, needs no further investigation as to his culpability and has, as such, become a criminal deserving the death penalty. Notwithstanding the fact that Trajan's edict hardly seems to say anything directly hostile to Christianity, it involves the severest possible stance against Christianity. From their own standpoint the Christian apologists could view it as simply an injustice at odds with all otherwise-valid concepts of justice, and as self-contradictory.[137] There was no change in how people had been regarding the Christians. The only difference was that, when the verdict absolutely condemning them was to be pronounced, it would be based not on general human considerations, but on the Roman standpoint.[138]

Under the governments of subsequent emperors Trajan's edict became the standard for legal proceedings against the Christians. Because of the name they bore, they

---

137. In ch. 2 of his *Apology*, Tertullian proclaims: "O miserable deliverance—necessarily a self-contradiction! This edict forbids them to be sought after as innocent, and it commands them to be punished as guilty, It is at once merciful and cruel; it overlooks and it punishes. Why do you play a game of evasion, O Judgment? If you condemn, why do you not also inquire? If you do not inquire, why do you also absolve? . . . Well, you think the Christian a man of every crime, an enemy of the gods, of the emperor, of the laws, of good morals, of all nature; yet you compel him to deny, that you may acquit him, which without his denial you could not do. You play fast and loose with the laws" [*ANF* 3:19]. In any event, only the Christians thought the edict was so unreasonable. They had no idea that the pagans were just treating them in a way that soon enough would become the Christian Church's own customary practice. When Pliny says he believes the Christians' "pertinacity and inflexible obstinacy" must be punished, he means their refusal, in disavowing the Christian faith, to acknowledge belief in the pagan deities. The Christians were therefore martyrs for their convictions, because the Roman state upheld the state religion, and the "godless ones" (ἀθέους), the self-declared deniers of the state religion, cannot go unpunished. This is also the main point of Tertullian's *Apology*: the fact that they are not punished "as Christians" is perfectly self-evident; that what principally opposes the authority of the state here is the innermost self-certainty of Christian consciousness. The following are further passages from Tertullian's *Apology*. "'You do not worship the gods,' you say. . . . So we are accused of sacrilege and treason. . . . We do not worship your gods, because we know that there are no such beings. . . . And punishment would be due to Christians if it were made plain that they were indeed divine. But you say, 'They are gods.' We appeal . . . to your knowledge . . . if it can deny that all these gods of yours were but men" (ch. 10) [*ANF* 3:26]. "We give offense to the Romans, we are excluded from the rights and privileges of Romans, because we do not worship the gods of Rome" (ch. 24) [*ANF* 3:39]. "Therefore, summoned to participate in the sacrifice, we are obliged to refuse for the sake of our own conscience, and the reason for this is our salvation, not obstinacy" (ch. 27) [our translation; cf. *ANF* 3:41]. What is noteworthy about Trajan's edict is that the norms he uses to spell out this relationship reflect the standpoint of the Roman state and the Roman state religion.

138. Sentencing "to the beasts," and transporting to Rome those so sentenced—which was said to have been the fate of Bishop Ignatius of Antioch—may not have been uncommon under Trajan as well. Although R. A. Lipsius defends the story of Ignatius' martyrdom, in the *Zeitschrift für historische Theologie* 26 (1856) 76ff., it seems, in light of the Ignatian epistles, even in the Syriac text, hardly likely to be true. What actually happened is that, in the year 115 in Antioch, when Trajan spent the winter there, Ignatius was martyred as a sacrifice to the people's rage because of the earthquake that year. See Henry F. Clinton, *Fasti Romani* (Oxford, 1845), vol. 1, 100. Because Trajan was there, the surviving account developed into the glorification of Ignatius' martyrdom.

were already considered to be guilty as criminals, as evil-doers who, without further proof, were assumed to be the worst sort of people. As their numbers grew, the hatred of the pagan populace also intensified. So Christians were increasingly accused, and were put to death merely for calling themselves Christians.[139] There was no possible recourse in face of such an unjust procedure, as long as no essential change occurred in the overall view of Christianity held by those in the Roman state. So it was to be expected that persons among the Christians with sufficient education and intellectual power to speak out forcefully on behalf of the Christian cause, would direct their main efforts in this setting toward influencing public opinion. Thus in the period directly following Trajan's edict the *Apologies*, composed by Christians as a defense of the Christian position and publicly addressed to the emperor, the governors of the provinces, and the wider public in general, were important works indicative of the times.

Whatever effect they may have had in gradually enlightening the Roman world regarding the nature of Christianity as such, they were unsuccessful with the powerful figures to whom they were directed. In no way can we view them as influencing the decrees of the emperors directly after Trajan, which supposedly shielded the Christians from the oppressive measures resulting from Trajan's edict. Those alleged decrees are quite clearly fictions. How can it be credible that a Roman emperor in those days would have issued an order like the one attributed to Antoninus Pius?[140]

The emperor is supposed to have written the following rescript, replying to the Κοινὸν τῆς Ἀσίας, the assembly of the delegates from the towns of Asia Minor. It reads as follows:

---

139. See Justin Martyr, *First Apology*, chs. 2–4, and especially the *Second Apology*, which tells of a very striking instance of this kind. Also see Eusebius, *Ecclesiastical History* 5.21. In ch. 2 of his *Apology*, Tertullian writes: "all that is cared about is having what public hatred demands—the confession of the name, not examination of the charge" [*ANF* 3:18]. In *To Scapula*, ch. 4, [after dismissing those who just pretend to be Christians,] Tertullian asks: "Who has complaint to make against us on other grounds?" [*ANF* 3:107]. According to Gustav Volkmar, "Die Zeit des Justin's des Märtyrers kritisch untersucht," *Theologische Jahrbücher* 14 (1855), 227ff. and 412ff., the two *Apologies* of Justin Martyr were written about 150, during the reign of Antoninus Pius. The same measures against Christians are evident in 1 Pet 4:14–19, where it so clearly and explicitly exhorts the recipients not to be in actuality an evildoer or criminal (κακοποιός), as people suppose the name "Christian" (Χριστιανός) indicates. From this it is evident that this epistle originated when Trajan's edict was in force. Albert Schwegler first demonstrated that in his *Nachapostolische Zeitalter* (Tübingen, 1846), 2:11ff.

140. According to Justin Martyr, *First Apology* 70 [not a numbered chapter, but a 70th part entitled "Epistle of Antoninus to the Common Assembly of Asia" (*ANF* 1:186)]. See also Eusebius, *Ecclesiastical History* 4.13. Eusebius presents it as an edict from Marcus Aurelius, although just prior to this (ch. 12) he says the emperor in question is the one to whom Justin addressed his *Apology*, thus Antoninus Pius. [*Ed*. However, "Antoninus" is also one of the names of Marcus Aurelius.] Also, [after giving the text of this decree,] at the end of ch. 13 Eusebius mentions (4.13.8) the "further testimony to these events" by Melito of Sardis, which cannot be confirmation that the edict was from Marcus Aurelius, else Melito, had he known that, would have mentioned it in his own *Apology* (cf. Eusebius, 4.26.2 and 4–11). So Eusebius' mention of Melito in 4.13 can only be with reference to his writings to Larissa et al. Without a doubt this fictitious edict was supposedly from Marcus Aurelius but got ascribed to his predecessor, Antoninus Pius, in order to magnify its impact as coming from the prior emperor.

II. The External Aspects of Christianity's Relation to the Pagan World and to the Roman State

> I know that the gods also take care that such people [the Christians] should not escape notice, for they would be far more likely to punish those who are unwilling to worship them than you are. But you drive them into tumult, for you confirm them in the opinion which they hold by accusing them as atheists, and they too when so accused apparently might well prefer death rather than life for the sake of their own God. Wherefore they are also conquerors because they sacrifice their lives rather than obey and do what you command. With regard to the earthquakes which have taken place and are still going on it is not out of place to remind you that when they happen you are depressed, and so set up a comparison between our position and theirs. They obtain increased confidence towards God, but you the whole of the time neglect the other gods and the worship of the immortal. But when the Christians worship him you harry and persecute them to death. And many of the provincial governors wrote formerly on behalf of such people to our divine father, and he replied that they were not to be interfered with unless they appeared to be plotting against the Roman government. And to me also many reported about such men, and to them I too replied consistently with my father's opinion. But if anyone persist in taking action against any one of such persons, on the ground that he is so [a Christian], let that one who is accused be released from the charge, even if it appear that he is such, but the accuser shall be liable to penalty.[141]

We perceive every word of this reply as something a Christian would say—someone who has the emperor severely reprimanding the pagans, and speaking about the Christians as they could always just desire to be judged and treated by powerful Roman officials. Indeed, the emperor even concludes by directly countermanding Trajan's edict.

Without a doubt the same emperor's written statements to Larissa, Thessalonica, Athens, and to the assembly of Greeks, supposedly favoring the Christians, belong in this same category.[142] Indeed Hadrian's rescript,[143] still accepted as authentic until recently, also looks equally suspect when examined more closely in this same context. The emperor is said to have written it to Minucius Fundanus, the governor of Asia Minor, so that the matter concerning the Christians, which Minucius' predecessor, Serennius Granianus, had brought to his attention, would not remain unresolved, lest there be unrest in the province and those shameless informers gain an opening for their evil deeds. Hence the emperor decreed that, in the future, a formal complaint shall be entered against the Christians only if the accuser appears before the court to speak and to answer questions, taking it upon himself to make the case that the

---

141. Eusebius, *Ecclesiastical History* 4.13.1–7 [LCL, *Eusebius*, 1:330–33].

142. In his *Apology* to Marcus Aurelius, Melito says "that no new measures should be taken concerning us" (this according to Eusebius, 4.26.10), without saying anything about their contents or explicitly mentioning the decree to the assembly of delegates.

143. See Justin, *First Apology*, 69; Eusebius, *Ecclesiastical History* 4.9.1–3.

Christians are acting illegally, and the judge then investigates the matter most carefully. Suitable punishment for the crime is to be imposed upon conviction. But the emperor declared that wrongful accusation against a Christian shall be severely punished according to how shameful the accusation is.

It has been correctly shown[144] that the rescript was not what it is usually thought to be, something directed against the unregulated and disorderly measures people were taking against the Christians. Instead, its background was the existing and not newly mandated practice, in particular the judicial format for bringing a charge, but in which of course the mere denunciation of someone as a Christian had sufficed to condemn that person. If Hadrian had indeed issued a contrary decree—that charges brought against Christians be carefully investigated, the strictest legal procedures be followed in their case, and the punishment imposed be just proportionate to the proven facts of the crime—it would have contradicted Trajan's edict, and it is not credible that he would do so.

Via a new rescript completely ignoring the previous one and rendering it invalid, the Christians would have instantaneously gained what they alone desired, that they could not be legally condemned for their identity as Christians (*nomen ipsum*), but only condemned for crimes associated with the name "Christian" (*flagitia cohaerentia nomini*). This is certainly the distinction drawn by the [fictitious] rescript of Hadrian, a distinction Trajan's edict did not want to make. Being unable to comprehend a procedure that already condemned them for their identity, and being aware that everything people associated with the label "Christian" is not merely unproven but also unprovable, the Christians thought they were entirely justified in calling their accusers "sycophants,"[145] or shameless informers. In the eyes of the Christians they were shameless informers. However, as long as Trajan's order, "when accused and convicted, they are to be punished," was still in force, and given the prevailing view that Christianity inherently had a criminal character, there were no accusations of this sycophantic kind. So this rescript is also a Christian fiction, for its contents are incompatible with the historical setting both before and after this time.[146]

144. In Karl Theodor Keim's essay, "Bedenken gegen die Aechtheit des hadrianischen Christen-Rescripts," *Theologische Jahrbücher* 15 (1856) 387ff.

145. The rescript uses this expression, and it is found in Melito's *Apology*, according to Eusebius, *Ecclesiastical History* 4.26, and Athenagoras, *Plea for the Christians*, ch. 2.

146. What Neander has to say in defending the authenticity of the rescript (*Allgemeine Geschichte* [n. 17], 1:173ff.) proves nothing. According to Eusebius, 4.26, Melito of course knew of it, but it is dubious whether Justin Martyr did, since the rescript is just something tacked on at the end of his *First Apology*. When oppression and persecution of Christians was increasing, they protested via rescripts allegedly the statements of earlier emperors. The words of Trajan, "they are not to be sought after" (*conquirendi non sunt*), could be interpreted to mean that Christians ought not be punished provided that they commit no crimes. Accordingly, the rescript of Hadrian would just have been a commentary on Trajan's edict, something one scarcely ought to have thought possible, just as that someone could also have dared to put forward such a thing as the statement of Antoninus Pius to the assembly of Asia. In any event the one, like the other, is new proof of what literary fictions that era was capable of if they simply seemed to be in the interest of Christianity; and proof of how readily the Christians

Under Antoninus Pius the Christians were of course more harshly oppressed than they were under Hadrian.[147] The persecution increased still more under Marcus Aurelius. In his *Apology*, written about 170 and addressed to the emperor Marcus Aurelius, Melito depicts the status of the Christians as follows:[148] "It has never before happened as it is now that the race of the religious should be persecuted . . . by new decrees throughout Asia. For shameless informers and lovers of other people's property have taken advantage of the decrees, and pillage us openly, harrying night and day those who have done nothing wrong." Melito doubts that a righteous emperor could ordain something so unjust. He says that if "this counsel and this new decree (and it would be improper even against barbarian enemies)" should originate from the emperor himself, "we beseech you all the more not to neglect us in this brigandage by a mob."

This is precisely the time of the first great persecutions of Christians carried out by the Roman state authorities. The first one, in 167, impacted the Smyrna community, and the second one, ten years later, beset the Gallic communities in Lyon and Vienna.[149] It can seem strange for an emperor so much renowned for love of justice and for moderation to have ordered such severe persecutions of Christians. However, aside from all that arose not directly from the emperor himself but instead is to be attributed to the local authorities, and even more to the fervor of vulgar mobs, these persecutions were simply carrying out Trajan's edict. Emperor Marcus Aurelius was the very man to find such proceedings fully compatible both with the interests of the Roman state and with his own Stoic principles. The way the Christians behaved in facing persecution, their heroic martyrdom, which filled so many with admiration and respect for Christianity, must have also turned against it those who, as Romans, were of course averse to nothing so much as they were to a religious fanaticism that got people emotionally aroused. Christianity increasingly counted as a "depraved and unbridled superstition," but one that, in its conflict with the Roman state, had become a punishable stubbornness, an unbending obstinacy that had to be broken by the power of the state.[150] Hence when Christians were brought before the court, "if any should recant they should be let go" without further punishment, as Marcus Aurelius had

---

accepted them, since of course Melito, like others, appeals to them at least in general terms and, in trusting them, cannot go far enough in promoting good will (*captatio benevolentiae*) toward Hadrian and the Antonines.

147. On Hadrian, see Keim (n. 144), 394.

148. See Eusebius, *Ecclesiastical History* 4.26.5–6 [LCL, *Eusebius*, 1:388–89].

149. [*Ed.*] Vienna was settled by Celts, who can be described as Gallic because the Gauls were Celts. Vindobona (a Celtic/Gallic name) became a Roman military camp in the first century BC, on the border of the Empire in the province of Pannonia.

150. The order of Marcus Aurelius was that whoever should introduce a new and unfamiliar religion—to be sure, the kind that makes the gentle human mind (*leves hominum animi*) become unstable and disturbed—shall, depending on that person's social class, either be deported or be punished with death. This order doubtless applied especially to Christianity. See the citation in J. C. L. Gieseler, *Lehrbuch der Kirchengeschichte* (4th ed., 6 vols., Bonn, 1844), 1.1:174.

directed.¹⁵¹ This remained the procedure for Christians throughout the entire time of the Antonine emperors.¹⁵²

SEPTIMUS SEVERUS, HELIOGABALUS, AND ALEXANDER SEVERUS

In 193, Septimus Severus became the sole ruler of the Roman Empire.¹⁵³ His reign marks a new epoch in the historical sequence of the Roman emperors, one which also saw a shift in perspective regarding the position of Christianity vis-à-vis the Roman state. A succession of rulers of foreign extraction meant that imperial power was now no longer in the hands of those from the old Roman nation.

Emperor Septimus Severus was a North African, and his wife Julia was from Syria. Emperors succeeding Septimus Severus—Caracalla, Heliogabalus, and Alexander Severus—came from the same lineage, so their physical appearance was more Oriental than it was Roman.¹⁵⁴ Through these emperors religious syncretism became the prevailing mode of religious thinking at this time. (From our examination of Philostratus' life of Apollonius of Tyana, we have already seen the facet of this syncretism that took Christianity into account). Emperors who were leaning in this direction could not have the same concern for the Roman state religion that the Antonine emperors had still clung to so doggedly. Of course Septimus Severus remains in the line of persecutors of Christians. During his reign the persecution in many places was said to have been so intense that, as Eusebius¹⁵⁵ tells us, people thought the "coming of the Antichrist was already near." But perhaps his strict prohibition of anyone converting to either Judaism or Christianity showed a syncretistic tendency if, in doing so, he only intended to counter how these two religions were harming the pagan religion by

---

151. Eusebius, *Ecclesiastical History* 5.1.47 [LCL, *Eusebius*, 1:428–29].

152. In Eusebius, 5.21, we find an example of this under Commodus. [*Ed.* It says that Apollonius, when accused by his servant, defended his Christianity and so had his legs broken and then was beheaded.] Dio Cassius, *Roman History* 72.4, writes about Marcia, the concubine of Commodus, who was favorably disposed toward Christians. *Philosophumena* (Part 3, n. 11), 9.12.10–11 [ET 648–49] also tells of "Commodus' concubine—a woman devoted to God." She inquired of Victor, the Roman bishop, about the Christian martyrs presently in the mines of Sardinia, and got Commodus to order their release. This is how Callistus, who fell into the same category, also got free.

153. [*Ed.*] He was the first of the Severan emperors and ruled 193–211. The others were Caracalla (198–217), Getra (209–11), Macrinus (217–18), Elagabalus (Heliogabalus) (218–22), and Alexander Severus (222–35).

154. [*Ed.*] Caracalla (Marcus Aurelius Antoninus), whose rule overlapped with his father's, was the eldest son of Septimus Severus. Heliogabalus, called Elagabalus because he had been the priest of a god by that name, was a Syrian. Alexander Severus was also a Syrian, the cousin and adopted son of Elagabalus.

155. *Ecclesiastical History* 6.7.

encroaching on it, and he meant to confine each religion to its own proper domain, in order to advance the time when the different religions could co-exist as such.[156]

In any case it seems permissible to assume that Empress Julia too was no stranger to the religious syncretism so indigenous in her own family. She was of Syrian descent herself, and through the grandchildren of her sister Maesa, that is, Heliogabalus (who himself had been a priest in the temple of the sun in the town of Emesa) and Alexander Severus, the oriental, Syrian cult of the sun became the foundation and basic form of all other forms of religion. Thus in the great pantheon Heliogabalus erected in Rome to his god—the god from whom he, as this god's priest, had taken his own name [Elagabalus]—the Jewish, Samaritan, and Christian religions were to be united with the Roman *sacra* (holy things). The pious emperor, Alexander Severus, dedicated his own *lararium*[157] to also honor Christ alongside the better ones of the Roman emperors, as well as such noble spirits as Apollonius of Tyana, Abraham, and Orpheus.

So now Christianity was no longer a disreputable, inordinate superstition. Although not the one true religion, it was as good a religion as any other. It too is one of the various forms in which the idea of religion manifests itself, as the sun does in the refracted rays of its light. So Christianity has the same right to exist within the Roman Empire, and to have its own cultus, as the other religions do. Emperor Alexander Severus reputedly intended to build a temple for Christ and to accept him as one of the Roman gods. Except for briefly during the reign of Maximus the Thracian [235–38], there was no persecution of Christians during this period, and there are individual signs of a favorable attitude toward Christianity. Indeed there was even an emperor, Philippus of Arabia [244–49], who was said to have been a Christian.[158]

DECIUS AND GALLIENUS

As is to be expected, the numbers of Christians grew very significantly during this lengthy period of toleration and calm. Yet when Trajanus Decius[159] assumed the imperial power, following the downfall of Philippus of Arabia, there began a new period of quite a different character.

Now the question was no longer what to make of Christianity: how it related to the general consciousness at this time and to the otherwise customary ways of thinking; that is, what place it had to be given alongside the other religions existing within the Roman Empire. We see clearly how, under the regimes of emperors not so disposed to things Roman in nature during the last period, Christianity had become

---

156. See Barthold Georg Niebuhr, *Vorträge über Römische Geschichte* (3 vols., Berlin, 1846–48), 3:250: "Characteristic was his propensity for foreign religions."

157. [*Ed.*] A *lararium* is a shrine dedicated to the Roman household spirits, the *Lares* et al.

158. [*Ed.*] According to the *Oxford Classical Dictionary*, this later tradition was certainly erroneous.

159. [*Ed.*] Decius ruled 249–51. He added "Trajan" to his other names to show he was sympathetic to the older Roman order.

in fact such an established power, that emperors now impelled by a forceful sense of the old Roman state could only see Christianity as an enemy they had to engage in a battle of life and death.

Therefore the persecutions of Christians that now began were typically initiated by the state leadership itself and not, as so often before, by the populace that, hate-filled and fanatical, drove the Roman authorities, frequently unwillingly, to do the persecuting. So these latter persecutions had a quite different character than the earlier ones did. As Origen says,[160] in the earlier persecutions "some, on special occasions, and these individuals who can be easily numbered, have endured death for the sake of Christianity." Now, however, as general mandates, the persecutions spread throughout the empire, were pursued as a matter of principle, were methodically organized, and had no other purpose than the total suppression of Christianity.

The emperor Decius was the first to formulate such a plan. Although it was carried out just sporadically, it remained in place throughout the reigns of the subsequent pagan emperors. In 250, soon after Decius had begun to rule, he issued an order to all the governors of the provinces, threatening to punish them if they did not take the most severe actions against the Christians, and bring them back to the Roman religion, by instituting all sorts of terror and martyrdom.[161] The governors began their execution of the emperor's order by announcing that, by a specific date, their Christian residents had to renounce their current religion and make sacrifices to the pagan deities. If they did not do so, then the next step would be judicial investigation and the use of force. There were now instances of heroic Christian martyrdom, but the recent lengthy period of tranquility had sapped the zeal and courage of the Christians, so that very many became openly unfaithful and others concealed their Christian beliefs. The plan behind such a persecution was for it to fall mainly on the bishops, as the leaders of the Christian communities. They were the particular targets of the death penalty, which was not at first imposed on the large majority of the Christians.

Persecution continued even after the death of Emperor Decius in 251. Public calamities for which the Christians were always blamed stirred up people even more against those who did not participate in the sacrificial offerings to appease the gods. After a brief period of quiet under Valerian [who ruled 253–60], the persecution resumed in 257, now beginning as planned with the leaders of the Christian communities. There followed an even more severe edict directed at all those leaders who professed the Christian faith, including bishops, presbyters, deacons, senators, persons of rank, Roman equites, matrons, and officials of the imperial court. There was no talk of punishing Christians as a whole. The calculation was that once Christianity would be expunged from the higher social classes it could not maintain itself in the mass of the population. Nevertheless what now ensued was a longer-lasting period of calm.

160. *Against Celsus* 3.8 [ANF 4:468].
161. Eusebius, *Ecclesiastical History* 6.41.

Gallienus[162] was the son of Emperor Valerian and co-ruler with him until Valerian died as a captive of the Persians. As sole ruler, Gallienus not only ended the ongoing persecution of Christians, but also issued edicts that can be viewed as the first laws of tolerance benefiting Christians and Christianity. He wrote to several bishops that he wanted their lives to be peaceful and secure, and he ordered the pagans to restore to the Christians their sacred meeting places and cemeteries.[163] However, we should not infer from this leniency that Christianity was gaining anything more than just temporary indulgence, the state's acknowledgment of its right to exist. Still, a number of the subsequent emperors took no action against Christianity. Diocletian himself was not at first hostile toward the Christians (even though his later great persecution of Christians made him a much-hated figure in the annals of Christianity). The Christian Church had never yet flourished to the extent it did at this time. Eusebius[164] makes the transition to his description of this last period by saying "It is beyond our powers to describe" how much the Christian Church has, in the meantime, grown in size and reputation. "The rulers have even entrusted the government of the provinces to our people." In the imperial palaces "the Christian religion may be practiced by the Christians who hold important offices at the court." How could this state of affairs change once again, and so suddenly?

DIOCLETIAN

It is generally acknowledged that Diocletian[165] was one of the Roman Empire's most competent rulers. Niebuhr[166] says that, as a man of uncommon intellect, Diocletian saw it as extremely dangerous to unite by force two differently oriented regions. So he devised the apparently unusual system of dealing with the many fissures between East and West by having separate governments for the two under separate rulers, but with the two rulers linked through a central point and together forming a single whole. Thus in other matters too Diocletian doubtless saw how little the heterogeneous

---

162. [*Ed.*] Gallienus was co-ruler (253–60), but only in Italy. He then ruled alone 260–68. Valerian died in captivity after being defeated by the Persians at Edessa in 260.

163. Eusebius, *Ecclesiastical History* 7.13.

164. *Ecclesiastical History* 8.1 [cf. LCL, *Eusebius*, 2:250–51].

165. [*Ed.*] Diocletian was declared emperor by his army in 284 (but just effectively so in Asia Minor). When his predecessor, Carinus, was assassinated in 285, Diocletian became sole emperor in the East, where he ruled until 305. The "Tetrarchy," proclaimed by Diocletian in 293, split the Empire into two halves, East and West, each to be ruled separately by a senior "Augustus" and a junior "Caesar." The rulers of the Tetrarchy (through 313) were Diocletian (ruled 284–305), Maximian (286–305), Galerius (305–11), Constantius Chlorus (305–6), Valerius Severus (306–7), Constantine the Great (306–37), Maxentius (306–12), Licinius (308–24), and Maximinus (311–13). Several rulers in this complex chronology are discussed by Baur.

166. *Römische Geschichte* (n. 156), 293. Albrecht Vogel also depicts him as a great emperor and as the inaugurator of a new era of the Empire, in *Der Kaiser Diokletian* (Gotha, 1857).

elements coexisting in the Roman Empire had any prospect of uniting at any point in common.

His thinking about religion we see best from the reasons he gives for the law he promulgated in 296, in opposing the Manichean sect, which had made incursions into the Roman Empire by that time.[167] Diocletian said: "In their providence the immortal deities have surely ordained and established what is true and good. Many good and wise men concur in holding unalterably and firmly to it. One may not take one's stance in opposition to this truth; an ancient religion may not be disparaged by a new one. For it is the greatest crime to undo what, from time immemorial, has had its own way of doing things, what has gained a firm foothold and permanence." This statement authentically expressed the Roman view of the state's relation to religion. It is very mistaken to suppose that, in this case, the issue as to whether the Roman state should recognize Christianity ought to have been decided according to our modern concepts of universal human rights, of tolerance and freedom of conscience. Such concepts and principles still lay wholly beyond the horizons of the ancient world. A person was simply to believe what counts as publicly acknowledged truth according to traditional authorities, not what he or she independently perceives as being true. Hence in religious affairs the issue was only whether something is old and established, or is new. It is from this perspective that Diocletian promulgated his law against the Manicheans. But how did it apply to Christianity?

Christianity too was a new religion as opposed to the Roman state religion, and from this perspective it had been treated so far as another new religion. But now, after Christianity had persisted for almost three centuries and had also become a significant force within the Roman state, one might justifiably have asked whether, even then, it was still to be regarded without qualification as a "new religion." In any event there was no ignoring the fact that, because it was firmly entrenched, Christianity could not be suppressed without the greatest efforts and without causing very dangerous public disturbances. We gain insight into these considerations from Lactantius' report[168] that Diocletian in his later years had resisted pressing demands to persecute Christians, when he "showed how pernicious it would be to raise disturbances throughout the world and to shed so much blood; although the Christians were eager to meet death, it would be enough for him to exclude persons of that religion from the court and the army." On the other hand, however, one could not cede to Christianity the power it held nor stand by as it spread further, without undermining the principle of the

---

167. See Gieseler, *Kirchengeschichte* (n. 150), 1.1:311. [*Ed.*] In a footnote Gieseler quotes from Diocletian's edict to Julian opposing the Manicheans. The following statement in the text is from Baur's German version.

168. *Of the Manner in Which the Persecutors Died*, ch. 11 [*ANF* 7:305]. [*Ed.*] Lactantius is writing about private discussions between Diocletian and Galerius, his eventual successor as emperor, in which Galerius called for harsh persecution of Christians. The title of the work reflects its topic, which is the ending of persecution and the overthrow of the persecutors, when Christianity finally triumphed in the empire.

Roman state. At a time when the empire had to muster all its forces against a multitude of enemies, everything depended on the armed forces and successful military undertakings. In keeping with pagan concepts, where else could one look for this success other than to the pagan deities? And how could the deities grant this success when, despite the sacrifices offered to gain this favor, they would be put off by the presence of so many Christians in the army and the hated sign of the cross?

Whatever one's view of Christianity might have been, its relation to the Roman state had now become a vital issue for the state. This was how the combative Galerius, Caesar of the East, relying on the Roman sacred rites, looked at the current condition of the empire. He and Hierocles, the governor of Bithynia, were the main drivers of this last decisive battle. As Eusebius explicitly states, it is significant that the persecution began with the army. Many Christians were high-ranking officers in the army, and had not previously been impugned because of their beliefs. Now, however, questions were increasingly raised about "profane persons" being present at the sacred rites. Soldiers who were unwilling to take part in the sacrificial rites were expelled from the army and sentenced to death. This was the start of the persecution, after Diocletian no longer stood in the way of Galerius' persistent badgering. Now the church felt its full force.[169]

---

169. The latest historian of this most noteworthy period in the annals of the Roman Empire is Jacob Burckhardt, who has closely examined the striking phenomenon of such a great turnabout in the previous circumstances, the shift from such exceptional toleration to the most fervent persecution. See *Die Zeit Constantin's des Grossen* (Basel, 1853), 325ff. It seems to him that, when we consider the immediate circumstances, the issue assumes a quite different shape. If the government had been entertaining the idea of future persecution it would not have allowed the number of Christians to multiply unopposed, so that Christianity became a force within the state. One could say that the Romans only belatedly and gradually became aware that, by being tolerated without qualification, the Christians would strive to gain the upper hand. But Diocletian was not so naïve as that. So the verdict must be that we are dealing with one of the greatest of the Roman emperors, someone who preserved the Empire and Roman civilization, and with the keenest judge of his times. Diocletian's political legacy would have been entirely different had he died in 302. So what has to be investigated is whether what tarnishes his legacy was simply an outburst of innate cruelty and brutality, or perhaps a superstitious reaction, or else just a pitiful concession to the co-rulers [the Caesars], who were subordinate to him. [*Ed.* Diocletian, as "Augustus," had appointed two "Caesars," of the East and the West respectively, who ruled under him.] Or perhaps in this instance the historian is obligated to seek some alternative explanation taking us beyond the written records. The alternative is based on the supposition that the Caesars believed they had detected a plot by Christians who, aware of their growing numbers, sought to take control of the Empire. Some of them, perhaps just a small number of Christian courtiers and a few Christian military commanders in the provinces, believed that, by a coup d'état, they could place the Empire in the hands of the Christians or their sympathizers, perhaps thinking that in the process they would spare the person of the emperor. This hypothesis relies on such an artificial and daring combination of facts that it can hardly be promising. Placing more stock in it than it warrants does not get us any further. If we start out by acknowledging Diocletian's statecraft and his greatness as a ruler, it still remains incomprehensible, in the face of such a puzzling catastrophe, how such an emperor could have taken these measures because of a plot supposedly confined to just a very small number of conspirators and not including Christians generally. No one would have foreseen better than Diocletian what far-reaching consequences such measures had to have for the state. So we have to look back at the general circumstances at that time. In doing so, Burckhardt has a very unfavorable

The three edicts issued in 303 in quick succession, were aimed at Christianity and the leaders of the Christian communities. The fourth edict in 304, directed at Christianity as such, gave free rein to the fanaticism of the people, and to the capricious actions and cruelty of the authorities. Especially after the initial storm had passed, however, the position of Christians differed quite a bit from one province of the Empire to another, depending on the mindset and political concerns of the local rulers who governed, or succeeded one another, over the next eight years.[170] Those writing from the church's perspective of course tend to exaggerate, for their depictions overemphasize how severe this persecution was, and paint its scene in colors that are overly vivid.[171] However, more important than rehearsing their accounts of martyrdom is keeping our eyes on the transitional elements where the main results ultimately turned out to be the opposite of the originally intended outcome. Galerius, the principal author of the plans that had been implemented, changed his mind when he saw they were not successful. In April 311, speaking from Nicomedia in concert with Constantine and Licinius, he issued the first of the remarkable edicts concerning

---

view of the work ascribed to Lactantius, *Of the Manner in Which the Persecutors Died*. Yet whether it was written by Lactantius or by someone else, and however slight its literary value is, it is indisputable that, with all its misrepresentation and exaggeration, it contains historical data that can be very useful for understanding this period. So Burckhardt reckons it utterly silly for the writer to say that, when Diocletian could "struggle no longer against" Caesar Galerius, "still he attempted to observe such moderation as to command the business to be carried through without bloodshed; whereas Galerius would have had all persons burnt alive who refused to sacrifice" [ANF 7:305]. Yet in the edicts there is no explicit statement about a "business accomplished [without] bloodshed"; so the way the author portrays things is quite credible. That is because the co-rulers with Diocletian only gradually drew him deeper and step-by-step into the procedures of persecution. Vogel too ([n. 165] p. 109) sees Lactantius justified in saying that Diocletian was not at liberty in this business but was subject to other factors, was under the influence of the [pagan] priests and of Galerius. Also, we cannot dismiss the possibility that this is all connected with the uprisings in 303. Except Vogel's opinion is that all of these factors would not have forced Diocletian to allow the fateful action if it would not have been a consequence of his own thinking, a consequence of his own principles, which until then his own feelings, his understanding, and the difficulties in consolidating his power, had prevented from being carried out. But how do we reconcile the two factors, his lack of freedom and his own inner inclinations? Also, if persecution of Christians is assumed to be compatible with his principles, how can he have done nothing of the kind for so long a time, and then embark upon it all at once? Therefore we are left with the fact that Diocletian just yielded to pressure from others, and after taking the first step also had to go the rest of the way. It can only have been for political reasons that he had not sought to do to Christianity what he had done in all severity to Manicheanism. But what is very apparent is that, in having himself worshiped as God in a way no other emperor did, in regarding himself as, so to speak, the high priest of a pagan state church, and portraying himself also outwardly as being bodily the Jupiter who rules the world (see Vogel, 29ff. and 39), his intention was to overcome Christianity with all the majestic splendor of an oriental Roman emperor, while sensing that the decline of this magnificence was imminent.

170. [*Ed.*] That is, from 303 to 311. In 312 Constantine the Great became emperor in the West and began to favor the Christians.

171. Even Niebuhr (n. 156) remarks (p. 295) that the persecution was not as terrible as we usually envision it being. He says Dodwell is correct that it was nothing like what the Duke of Alba has done in the Netherlands. [*Ed.*] The Duke of Alba, or Alva, a Spanish general, enforced Spanish control in the Netherlands (1567–73) by driving out thousands of Huguenots, and executing others, for rebellion.

religion.[172] The import of these edicts was that they openly expressed, as accomplished fact, the triumph of Christianity over paganism and over the Roman state.

THE RELIGIOUS EDICTS OF THE ROMAN EMPERORS

The First Edict, from Galerius, Constantine, and Licinius

This is what the three emperors stated in their edict[173]:

> Among our other regulations to promote the lasting good of the community we have hitherto endeavored to restore a universal conformity to the ancient institutions and public order of the Romans; and in particular it has been our aim to restore a proper attitude in the Christians who had abandoned the religion of their fathers. We do not know how such willfulness and folly had taken possession of them, so that instead of observing those ancient institutions, which possibly their own forefathers had established, they, through caprice, made laws to themselves, and drew together into different societies many men of widely different persuasions. After the publication of our edict ordering the Christians to conform to the ancient institutions, many of them were brought to order through fear, while many were exposed to danger. Nevertheless, since many still persist in their opinions, and since we have observed that they now neither show due reverence to the gods nor worship their own God, we therefore, with our wonted clemency in extending pardon to all, are pleased to grant indulgence to these men, allowing Christians the right to exist again and to set up their places of worship; provided always that they not offend against public order. . . . In return for this indulgence of ours it will be the duty of Christians to pray to [their] God for our recovery, for the public weal and for their own; that the state may be preserved from danger on every side, and that they themselves may dwell safely in their homes.[174]

This edict is conspicuously at variance with the past history of this issue. The persecution of Christians by Diocletian supposedly was not applicable to Christianity itself, but instead just to the sectarian spirit of Christians who were undermining Christianity. It was not undertaken with the intention of bringing Christians back to paganism, but only of making them true Christians once more. There is a great

---

172. See Lactantius, *Of the Manner in Which the Persecutors Died*, ch. 34. Also see Eusebius, *Ecclesiastical History* 8.18. [*Ed.*] At this time when Galerius was the emperor in the East, Licinius was "Augustus" in the West and so co-ruler with Galerius. He succeeded Galerius in the East, and Constantine I became the emperor in the West.

173. See K. T. Keim, "Die römische Toleranzedicte für das Christenthum (311–313) und ihr geschichtlicher Werth," *Theologische Jahrbücher* 11 (1852) 207–59. Burckhardt (n. 169), p. 395, just mentions these edicts briefly without discussing them in detail. Keim's essay is thus the one worthy of attention.

174. Lactantius, *On the Manner in Which the Persecutors Died*, ch. 34 [combining Bettenson, *Documents* (n. 123), 15, and *ANF* 7:315].

discrepancy because, although Christians did not obey the imperial order and persisted in their own ways, imperial favor and pardon is nevertheless now to be extended to those who worshiped neither the pagan gods nor the God of the Christians. We can only explain this discrepancy as based on the desire to change how Christianity is related to the state, without openly acknowledging any alteration in the previous view of Christianity. The edict presupposes as a longstanding relationship what it is said to be expressing now for the first time. It is as though the state had made its peace with Christianity long ago, and it merely wants to have things reflect what that status really is.

In order to make it seem that the act of recognition just then taking place was not something the state was forced to do, the edict presented what was supposedly the actual purpose of the latest persecution: restoring "a universal conformity to the ancient institutions [or laws] and public order of the Romans," that is, simply a return to "the ancient institutions," so that, without saying so outrightly, Christianity itself counts as one of the ancient institutions. It is as if the intention underlying the persecution was just to single out the mania for change coming from those who founded the Christian sects, and was not aimed at Christians as such. Because the persecution was unsuccessful, people came to look upon Christianity as one of the ancient institutions. What had withstood all the attempts to suppress it demonstrated, by doing so, that it was long-established.

Hence the state's resulting recognition of Christianity now took the following form: that Christianity shall have a lasting place in the state so long as it just is, and remains, what it was from the beginning, and does not degenerate into something arbitrary and innovative. This is in fact the concept of a legitimate religion (*religio licita*). For ancient peoples, nothing in matters of religion and politics was more offensive than making innovations (νεωτερίζειν). Their view was that the state could not, by a special act, make a religion into a "legal or legitimate religion." Instead, the religion makes itself into one by enduring historically and being deeply rooted. So all the state could do is just enunciate the religion's right to exist as a right based on its having originated in the past. This reversal in how Christianity was viewed also involved the fact that not only was it allowed to exist in the state, but also it even seemed to be in the state's own interest to extend to Christianity all the rights of a state-recognized religion. Whereas previously Christians were thought to be a subversive element in the state, now they were called upon to pray for the state's well-being, which was thought to rely on the Christian God as well as on the pagan deities. However, it is important to note that the state was only willing to place this confidence in one form of Christianity. The distinction the edict drew between original Christianity and sectarian forms of it served, first of all, as the legal factor behind the state's step in recognizing Christianity. But it also expressed the condition for that to take place, namely, that only the original, true, and unified form of it is valid Christianity, which means the Christianity of the Catholic Church, for it alone fits into the category of ancient institutions.

The Second and Third Edicts of Constantine and Licinius

In the spring or summer of 312, prior to the fall of Maxentius,[175] Constantine and Licinius followed this first edict by issuing a second one. We do not know exactly what it stated, since it has not survived. However, we can infer how it read from a third edict directly related to it and issued by the same two emperors at Milan early in 313.[176]

In the third edict, which is still extant, the two emperors declare:

> In our watchfulness, in days gone by, that freedom of worship should not be denied, but that each one according to his mind and purpose should have authority given to him to care for divine things in the way that pleased him best, we had given orders that both to the Christians [and to all others liberty should be allowed] to keep to the faith of their own sect and worship. But inasmuch as many and various conditions seemed clearly to have been added in that rescript, in which such rights were conceded to the same persons, it may be that perchance some of them were shortly afterwards repelled from such observance.[177]

The emperors continue[178]: "When we, Constantine and Licinius, met in Milan in conference concerning the welfare and security of the realm," in matters relating to religion, [we said] "it was right that Christians and all others" should have complete religious freedom, "so that the God who dwells in heaven might be propitious to us and to all under our rule." That is why the emperors regarded it as most salutary and appropriate, to in no way hinder the freedom to turn either to the cultus of the Christians or to the religion seeming to be most suitable for oneself, so that the highest deity one obeys with a free spirit should prove favorable and benevolent in all things. This is why the emperors resolved, by removing each and every condition as contained in

---

175. [*Ed.*] In 306, the Roman army in Britain proclaimed Marcus Aurelius Maxentius the emperor. Installed in Rome, he ruled there until he was slain by the forces of Constantine at the battle of the Mulvian Bridge in 312. The two edicts must therefore be taken together.

176. See Lactantius, *Of the Manner in Which the Persecutors Died*, ch. 48, and Eusebius, *Ecclesiastical History* 10.5. Eusebius begins his account with the introductory remarks in the edict, whereas Lactantius omits them and begins with the provisions.

177. [*Ed.*] Baur provides a mixture of quoted parts and abbreviated paraphrase. Our text is from Eusebius, *Ecclesiastical History* 10.5.1–3 (LCL, *Eusebius*, 2:444–47). Baur in his footnote gives the Greek for the sentence beginning with "But inasmuch as . . . ." He then remarks as follows: [*Baur*] This is the awkward passage that is mainly to blame for this edict being poorly understood until now. Eusebius uses the Greek word αἱρέσεις (which can mean "sects" as well as "choices") where Lactantius has *conditiones* (conditions). So people always supposed that this sentence had to be speaking about sects. Of course it is true that just before this Eusebius uses the term in this sense, but αἵρεσις is sometimes equivalent to *conditio*. Since Lactantius, in his original Latin text following this passage, speaks of *conditiones* where Eusebius has αἱρέσεις, one can hardly comprehend how this passage could have been so misunderstood. See Keim (n. 173), 225.

178. [*Ed.*] In the following, wording in quotes is from the text of Lactantius, in Bettenson, *Documents* (n. 123), 15–16. The rest is Baur's paraphrase.

the earlier edict with regard to the Christians,[179] to see to it that absolutely everyone who wanted to adhere to the Christian religion could do so without being "troubled or molested." Thus the emperors make it known that they have given the Christians absolute freedom and legal standing for their religious cultus; that others too shall have the same public and unrestricted religious freedom; and accordingly that everyone can worship as he or she wishes, because the emperors do not want to shortchange any cultus or any religion.

It is very evident how intentionally this edict repeatedly gives assurance of complete and unconditional religious freedom, indeed especially with regard to the Christians. From this fact we conclude that this was the respect in which the earlier edict had not been as satisfactory as one wished it was. For the new edict also expressly states that it now removes the circumstances people saw as still limiting religious freedom. Because of these restrictions the Christian religion had not been a possible choice for everyone, since pagans still were prohibited from converting to Christianity. So we must assume that, after the religious edict of 311 had once declared that Christianity was to be overtly permitted and recognized, very many people who were already Christians at heart, but still outwardly adhered to the pagan cultus, now went over openly to Christianity. This was doubtless the reason that the two emperors thought they had to intervene with preventive measures to restrain and limit these conversions, in order to at least impede such a massive changeover from paganism. The second edict, of 312, was supposed to accomplish this. However, since a third edict, one sounding so entirely at odds with the second one, followed so closely on its heels, we can infer from the contents and whole tenor of this third edict that the newly-enjoined religious compulsion of the second edict, which was still only pending, had caused commotion and unrest in the entire Christian population, especially in western lands. Discontent about this must have been expressed with such energy that the two emperors saw the situation calling for the most specific and unqualified declaration that, from then on, there shall be complete religious freedom; that there are no longer to be any anxious doubts about this, namely on the part of Christianity.[180]

179. [Ed.] Here Baur gives both the Latin, and Eusebius' Greek version, of the relevant sentence in Lactantius' version: ". . . without regard to any provisos in our former orders to you concerning the Christians, all who choose that religion are to be permitted, freely and absolutely, to remain in it and not to be disturbed in any ways, or molested" (ANF 7:320, much expanded from Baur's concise Latin).

180. Maximinus [Galerius Valerius Maximinus], the Augustus of the eastern lands, also issued similar proclamations along the lines of the three edicts and as ancillary to them. The Latin epistle from the prefect Sabinus, which Eusebius presents out of context, in [the Greek translation of] 9.1.2–6, corresponds to the edict of the three emperors. Sabinus could only have written it under the instruction of Maximinus. It allows for tolerance of Christians if they relinquish their subjective arbitrariness and come together in the tight-knit unity of their ἴδιον ἔθνος (own people), of their own religion, of their cultus. This edict was issued in early 311. Half a year later Maximinus was again persecuting the Christians (Eusebius, *Ecclesiastical History* 9.2). Soon after that, however, he issued the edict which, according to Eusebius, 9.9–10, correlated with the two edicts of the two emperors [i.e., Constantine and Licinius]. According to this edict, from 313, Maximinus had even sought, in the earlier edict of 312, to grant peace to the Christians, conditional upon their worshiping God in united assemblies as a

In retrospect, the Christians did not give much thought to the matter, since the majority of the pagan populace were no longer in favor of persecuting Christians.

CONSTANTINE

It would be a mistake to suppose that these three edicts [from Constantine and the other emperors]—especially the third, which completes the first two—are just all about establishing the principle of universal religious freedom. It is abundantly clear that Christianity is the focus of all the provisions contained in these edicts. It is also clear that they speak about the other religions, and about general religious freedom, only in connection with the position said to be given Christianity. The Christians are the central figures, and everyone should be allowed to join them. Christians are said to have complete freedom, and only because their freedom cannot be limited are the other groups said to have this freedom too.

The special provisions in the second part of the third edict, provisions benefiting the Christians, demonstrate this very point. Their meeting places and church properties were to be returned to the *corpus Christianorum*, the Christian Church. This should be done without delay or any demand for payment, and apart from the prospect of compensation by the state, whether those assets had been subsequently purchased by others or acquired as gifts. The governors should most forcefully initiate the prompt return of these possessions, and in the process should maintain public tranquility in this endeavor, thus in such great matters gaining divine favor in conjunction with the ruler's actions. Soon thereafter, Constantine added further decrees favoring the Christians. This favoritism included: the March 313 exemption of Christian clerics from rendering burdensome public service; the very deferential tone in which the documents from that time speak about the Christian Church; how obliging and generous Constantine then appeared to be toward the leaders of the Christian Church; how in 313 Bishop Hosius of Cordova stood alongside Constantine and consequently advised him in such weighty matters. In light of all this, and put succinctly, we see how the edict of 313 already took the step that would elevate Christianity to being the state religion.

Constantine's Concern for Unity

From the outset it was nevertheless very clearly understood that the state wanted, via its representatives, to enter into this new relationship solely with the Christianity of the Catholic Church. In the first edict the main objection against the Christians was their division into sects and factions. Thus the third edict repeatedly states that all

---

close-knit whole: "if any should wish to follow such a custom or the same religious observances, such a one should adhere to his purpose without hindrance" (Eusebius, *Ecclesiastical History* 9.9.8 [LCL, *Eusebius*, 2:376–77]). See Keim (n. 173), 216 and 229ff.

the favors shown to the Christians hold good only for the *corpus Christianorum*; that the Christians will share in them only insofar as they form a large body, that is, the Catholic Church.

This is indeed the core of the fondness Constantine felt for Christianity and the Christian Church, what drew him to it. Nothing is more characteristic of Constantine, or gives us deeper insight into the internal forces behind this remarkable time of transition, than the genuinely "catholic" concern for unity that led Constantine to the Christian Church, by starting from his own political standpoint. This was the very principle of the Roman Empire's rebirth, now taking place within Christianity. Diocletian had already striven to accomplish this with his system of reorganization, by so energetically shoring up, with a number of rulers, the unity of an empire that was falling apart. This is the point where Constantine had the greatest rapport with the Christian Church. This is where we see Constantine so consistently the same, from beginning to end.

Already in 313 and thereafter, Constantine is the emperor who has amicable relations with bishops, who very much wants to be a bishop, who wants his calling, as the supreme protector and guardian of peace [in the Empire], to be regarded as a divine office like that of the bishops, and would have counted himself happy if only the bishops also regarded him as their compatriot and colleague.[181] In the 313 edict, and in others of the emperor's writings found in Eusebius,[182] which are contemporary with it and related to it, what is in fact remarkable is the recurrence of this same characteristic feature: the concern for unity. Throughout, his first requirement is that there be brotherly harmony and oneness. Nothing troubles him more than a divided people, squabbling among the bishops. He views theological issues and controversies as just unpleasant affairs, contentiousness, private feuding, wretchedness, perversity, godlessness, insanity. He thinks those who precipitate controversies are people who lack character and restraint, are those who seduce the folk of the most holy Catholic Church, are those who not only forget their duty to brotherly unity but even forget the respect one owes to the most holy faith. These people make Christianity a laughing stock for the nonbelievers.

Hence Constantine ardently desired to nip controversies in the bud and bring everything back to dutiful service and faith. Already in the summer of 313 he spoke of his reverence for the Catholic Church, which impels him to insist that the bishops not tolerate schism and divisiveness anywhere, the kind that Miltiades, the bishop of Rome, was well aware of. Now Constantine already saw it as his right and his duty to restore this unity where it had been disrupted, because his heart was troubled that there would be dissension in the provinces divine providence had entrusted to him. The Donatist and Arian controversies, which were currently in full swing, provided abundant opportunities to act on these principles. The zeal with which Constantine

181. Eusebius, *Life of Constantine* 1.44, 2.68–69, 4.24.
182. *Ecclesiastical History* 10.5–7.

sought to reestablish the now-disrupted unity of the church arose from his fervent conviction that unity everywhere, but especially in religion, is the most essential condition for the strength and power of the Empire.

Constantine himself showed that this idea was very much the leading precept of his administration by expressing it, more clearly than anywhere else, in what he wrote to the leaders of the two factions in Alexandria, Bishop Alexander and Arius the presbyter, directly after receiving news of the outbreak of the Arian controversy.[183] Right at the beginning of his missive he states that the first thing he has undertaken is unifying the religion of all people so it has the same form and properties, and the second thing is restoring the very unhealthy body of civil society. He has given his attention to the first of these with the unseen eyes of the mind, and has sought to accomplish the second one by military power. He is convinced that, if he brought about the general unity he desires among all the servants of God, the fruit of doing so would also be a change in public affairs, corresponding to everybody's pious sensibility. Next Constantine says he is very exasperated by the insufferable mania that has taken hold in all of Africa because of the Donatist schism, and the mindless and irresponsible way that the communal religion has split into various heresies. And now it is most deplorable that he has to learn of a new and still more unpleasant conflict. The whole tendency of his missive is thus to insist most emphatically on everyone's duty to be united, and to emphasize this one thing as the supreme goal.

Constantine states that, in light of these concerns, the Arian controversy seems to be the kind of dispute just involving very minor and unimportant matters. As the supreme agent for peace, he wants to intercede between the contending parties, to entreat them to desist voluntarily from diabolical temptations. The great God and their mutual redeemer has enlightened them all, that they might approve of him [i.e., Constantine], God's servant and acting under God's providence, in bringing his endeavors to a good end by his responses and efforts and urgent admonitions, which are guiding God's congregations toward a common unity. If there is unity on the main issues, then division and schism involving such insignificant controversies will not be allowed to arise.

Constantine also addressed the Council of Nicaea [325] along these same lines. He declared it the greatest of all blessings to see before him a gathering where unanimity of insight and sentiment should prevail.[184] All of this, like all else we have been speaking about, is so closely connected with the program of his government, already set forth in the Edict of Milan [313], that it suffices as our concept of how the idea of unity and the striving for unity, the monarchical tendency, was the all-defining principle of his personality.

---

183. Eusebius, *Life of Constantine* 2:64ff.
184. Ibid., 3.12, 17, and 21.

Constantine's Politics and His Religious Sentiments

What further information do we need, then, in order to comprehend, in historical terms, the character of the epoch bearing the name of Constantine? Is the key to interpreting this epoch to be found in the legend of the wondrous vision Constantine wanted to have when he marched against Maxentius, according to an account so ambiguous and unauthenticated despite there being an authoritative informant?[185] Those who set more emphasis on minor personal matters than they do on the larger course of history, and give more weight to what is fantastically miraculous than they do to the simple truth of historical facts, may find this account satisfactory. In this historical domain there is certainly no deeper significance in the question people customarily regard as the height of pragmatic historiography: whether Constantine's conversion to Christianity, and subsequent elevation of Christianity to being the state religion, was more a political move or more a matter of his own inner religious conviction. This is not the correct approach, since it apparently wants to make the historical significance Christianity gained with Constantine depend on a feature of his personality, and the only uncertainty is whether this feature relates more to Constantine's politics or to his religious sentiments.

Viewed in a larger context, however, Christianity owed the significance it gained at that time to no one other than Constantine himself. In any event if we pose the question in the latter way, then the answer must favor Constantine's politics, inasmuch as politics is none other than correctly evaluating the circumstances that determine the crucial issues at a particular time. Christianity had become an objective force by then, and there was no way to avoid recognizing that fact. The greatness of Constantine, what makes him one of those world-historical figures who are individual expressions of the spirit of their times, is simply that Constantine understood the age in which he lived. Furthermore, he had the subjective capacity to internalize what the spirit (*Genius*) at that time within Christianity wanted to place in his hands, and knew how to make it one with his own person. After there had been such a significant cry of alarm between the second and third edicts, this was definitely the right time to become freely reconciled with Christianity. The recent and unsuccessful major efforts

---

185. This legend had to find a place in the treasury of anecdotes that is Neander's church history. Of course this incident cannot pass muster as a miracle, for it is based on the Christian view of history. However, a psychological analysis will serve, and by watering down history in this psychological fashion we get the following conclusion: "Now it can very well be that, either on his own or because of Christians in his company, Constantine believed that he perceived the sign of the cross in the shape of the clouds or in some other medium.... This gave him hope that he would be victorious through the power of the Christians' God"; and so forth [August Neander, *Allgemeine Geschichte der christlichen Religion und Kirche* (n. 17), 2:21]. Thus the great world-historical revolution at that time hinged on the kind of accidental cloud formation that amuses an imaginative child. On this view of Neander's, see the fitting criticism by Keim (n. 173), p. 251, and Burckhardt (n. 169), pp. 394ff. It is also inexplicable how Neander can separate the second and third edicts from the first one by assigning them to different time periods. [*Ed.*] The "authoritative informant" is apparently Eusebius. Neander cites *The Life of Constantine* 1.28; see also *Ecclesiastical History* 8.15–9.11.

against Christianity had just exposed the weakness and impotence of the pagan world, of an ancient faith in the process of disintegration. It was now evident that Christianity, as the *corpus Christianorum* with the solid and well-organized structure of the Catholic Church, was the only substantial force at that time. This was simply the form in which Constantine knew Christianity. What impressed him so much was just the magnificent unity the episcopal system of the church had already built up for itself by this time. So in the Christian Church Constantine saw the force by which the Roman Empire would gain the strength and capacity for the regeneration it needed. Thus the two sides converged, for it was in the interest of both to do so.

Christianity was the only real power at that time. Whereas all the cohesive structures of the ancient world were currently in disarray, Christianity alone had a solid, compact unity in which it could provide a new bodily form for a collapsing state. On the other hand, it was also quite in the interest of Christianity for it to have become the dominant force in the world, in the historically-rooted form of the Roman Empire. If there were also to be a continuation of the Roman Empire, then, simply put, that would be possible with a Christian emperor as its leader. Thus it was simply an inner necessity, one integral to this very set of circumstances, by which these two powers, Christianity and the Roman state, came to coincide in a new unity: Christianity, in the form of the church and the episcopate that also now would in turn build the bridge over which Christianity would advance to a new stage of its historical development; the state, insofar as it would continue to be, at least in name, what it no longer was in reality. The process at work here is very much just the objective course taken by these elements themselves. There is nothing in Constantine's own personal life that can be pinpointed as deciding his crossover to Christianity. He even postponed his own baptism to the end of his life, as though such a personal action was in no way requisite for him as the Christian emperor. Looked at in this way, the change we are dealing with here has a thoroughly and an inherently political character. It is in principle of no historical significance to ask how Constantine's own religious convictions relate to all of this.[186]

Yet to the extent that the religious element plays a part here, it does so in another way. We must also regard it as religious sensibility when someone recognizes what, by the route of historical development, has manifestly become objective reality, sees in it a divine sign, and in his own subjective consciousness bows before it as a higher power. We surely ought not deny that Constantine had this kind of religious consciousness, for he no doubt had this form of religion as the actual substance of his own religious consciousness. He manifested his religious frame of mind when he looked

---

186. I concur, but for entirely different reasons, with the essential point of Burckhardt's assessment of Constantine; see *Die Zeit Constantin's des Grossen* (n. 169), 346ff. and 389ff. Also, with regard to Eusebius, I can simply concur that, in everything to do with Constantine, Eusebius is a very problematic panegyrist who is guided by the interests of the Christian hierarchy.

upon the efforts of his opponents as nothing but a tyranny hostile to God,[187] for in opposing him, the friend of Christians and of Christianity, they could only find support in the residual power of paganism, and in doing so they were at odds with the spirit of their day. The opponents were the enemies and adversaries of God, because they did battle against what, in history itself, was obviously the declared will of God. They were tyrants precisely because there was therefore no justification for them having power and ruling. Hence when Licinius raised the banner of paganism one last time, it was thus an extremely futile and feeble undertaking, for the outcome on the battlefield had already been decided.

CHRISTIANITY VICTORIOUS

Relations between Christianity and the Roman state were initially turbulent, with each finding the other repellent, so they were most decidedly antithetical. But in the end they came together in peace and harmony, in a very close-knit unity. As their historical development proceeds from this point on, Christianity and the Roman state go hand-in-hand, and no earthly power seems able to separate these two forces that are so closely interconnected.

But what enabled Christianity to gain a victory that people ever since could only regard as one of the greatest wonders in world history? The reason for it was, first and foremost, the specificity and traditional importance of the forms or procedures by which Christianity bound its adherents together in the most intimate, mutual fellowship. No religion can become historically important without having a communal form resting on an authority of long standing. Faith in Jesus as the Messiah who has appeared and will soon come again, was such a distinctive communal bond for those who believed in him that this relationship, which bound them together ever more intimately, most definitely set them apart from the surrounding world. This left them with just two alternatives: overcome the world, or perish in the fight against it.

Once the Christian community had developed its christological consciousness to the point of being unable to think of Christ in his divine status, as Lord of the community, without the community also having at its head an overseer and leader acting on Christ's behalf, the episcopate became the form these ecclesial ties assumed. On the one hand this episcopal form was capable of endless extension [to any number of bishops], and on the other hand it served to unite all the church members most intimately, as well as both reaching back into the past and extending forward into the future. It is correct to say that the episcopate alone is what made Christianity's historical development possible and paved the way for its world-historical future. That is because the episcopate encompassed matters divine and human, spiritual and worldly, lofty and lowly, near and far. While it by no means ignored the transcendent element

---

187. According to Eusebius, *Life of Constantine* 3.12, the emperor spoke of this θεομαχία τυράννων (impious hostility of the tyrants).

in Christian consciousness, the episcopate also consistently recognized what are in fact the given conditions and needs of the present. As the history of Christianity unfolded, whenever there was a significant crisis, the episcopate always assumed a conciliatory role. Indeed it was the episcopate that averted the dangers and seductions of Gnosticism and Montanism, headed off the excesses of all the heresies, and constantly secured and created a broad basis for the Catholic Church. After the main impact of the latest persecutions had certainly, and for good reasons, especially targeted the bishops, they were the ones who worked constructively to steer the Christian Church and the Roman state toward the new forms of their mutual relationship.

But the question we must now ask is: Why did Christianity have such a great need for a formal structure enabling it to span every wider regions? What internal features accounted for its outward expansion? The simple answer to this question seems to lie in how Christianity has to impress and affect all souls who are receptive to it. Yet history tells us little about that. The annals of history do not record how many had converted to faith in Christ because of the consolation of the gospel, and all the spiritual blessings it affords. This is just a matter of the human heart's private history, and there is hardly even a hint about it in the general history that is so quick to overlook individuals. Also, of course all that pertains to such matters naturally could not be the first and foremost effect Christianity had in its contact with the pagan world. In its own way every religion provides for forgiveness of sins, reconciliation, consolation, and a good conscience. All of this was also available in pagan religion if one just believed in the gods, who were said to bestow these highest blessings of the spiritual life.

But of course as soon as belief in the gods themselves had disappeared, there was also no longer any basis for hoping to receive these gifts from them. This is exactly why the main issue at stake in the struggle between Christianity and paganism, the essential element, was not so much the desire for salvation on the part of hearts seeking the consolation of the gospel; instead it was the intellect asking, above all, about the truth of its conceptions. The only real issue at this time was whether there was still any truth and significance in the religious consciousness in paganism, the belief in the deities of the pagan religion. When people considered Christianity as opposed to the pagan world, and the huge consequences of Christianity's first three centuries, from this perspective, how could it be surprising that Christianity had won such a widespread and decisive a victory over the pagan world by this time? How many people might there still be whose imagination was still captivated by the old mythological teaching about the gods, with its appeal to fantasy?

From the large number of proselytes gained in the early days of the Empire by Judaism, a religion so firmly opposed to pagan concepts, we see how easily pagan religious consciousness turned away from the old gods. If we consider how clearly and energetically Christianity set itself at odds with the whole of pagan polytheism, and how in all the conflicts between Christianity and paganism the issue always in principle involved either acknowledging the pagan gods or denying their existence,[188] then it can by no means be surprising that victory was no longer in doubt. For who were the ones most active in defending the old beliefs? One group was the vulgar, fanatical rabble, for whom these beliefs had become out-and-out superstition and who were driven simply by blind hatred of Christians. The other group was just those who either had to keep this belief system intact because it was in the interest of the state to do so, or else, more or less unconsciously, had imputed a different meaning to it, in light of their Platonic idealism.

Yet there was also a very important class that fell in between these other two groups. Its numerous members belonged neither to the ruling aristocracy or the philosophically erudite, nor to the lower social strata. They made up the group of ordinary citizens who were to some degree skilled or educated. This social class was comprised of those Celsus and Lucian spoke about so contemptuously, as "Christians"—artisans, weavers, shoemakers and tanners, people who stayed in the background but proved to be so active, covertly and unto themselves, in matters of their faith. From the beginning Christianity found the most receptive soil for its impact in the unassuming, modest minds of these very people. They were the ones least held back by all the presumptions and concerns of the other social classes. Being of a sober and practical mindset, they were therefore receptive to completely cutting the weak ties that still bound them to belief in the old deities. People of this kind could hardly play any sort of role in the arena of public affairs, especially under the current political conditions. So that made it easier for Christianity to quietly make ever-greater inroads among them, and to an ever-increasing extent undermine belief in the existence of the old gods, until at last a new generation had arisen right within the pagan population. The existence of this new generation suddenly caused the rulers to see that the pagan state stood on the brink of an abyss.

Whatever one may make of the rhetorical flourish with which Tertullian depicts the strength of the Christian population in his day, it nevertheless suffices for us to realize how important Christianity had already become by then in the provinces of the Roman Empire. This inspired apologist for Christianity cries out to the pagans:

> We are but of yesterday, we have filled every place among you—cities, islands, fortresses, towns, market places, the [military] camp itself, tribes, companies, palace, senate, forum—and we have left nothing to you but the temples of your gods. For what wars should we not be fit, not eager, even with unequal forces, we who so willingly submit to the sword, if our religion did not count it better to be slain than to slay? Using no weapons, and raising no banner of insurrection, but simply hostile to you, we could carry on the contest with you by just breaking away in discontent. For if such multitudes of men were to break away from you and go to some remote corner of the world, why, the very loss of so many citizens, whatever sort they were, would cover the empire with shame.

188. For instance, see Tertullian's refutation of the pagan belief in gods, in his *Apology*, chs. 10ff.

Our forsaking you would be our revenge. Why, you would be horror-struck at the solitude in which you would find yourselves: an all-prevailing silence and the stupor as of a dead world. You would have to seek subjects to govern. You would have more enemies than citizens remaining. For now it is the immense number of Christians that makes your enemies so few, since almost all the inhabitants of your various cities are followers of Christ. Yet you choose to call us enemies of the human race, rather than enemies of human error.[189]

Now just think how much more all this must have been the case after another century had passed, after such a long period of quiet and such unsuccessful persecutions. Emperor Maximinus,[190] the last fervent persecutor of the Christians, certainly spoke the truth when, in his 312 edict issued to put a stop to the hostilities, he stated that Emperors Diocletian and Maximian[191] had seen that almost everybody had abandoned the cultus of the old deities and had merged into the Christian population.[192] When Constantine was carried along by the course of events, and raised high the sign of the cross in the place relinquished by the old deities, the soil of the ancient religion had, for all intents and purposes, already been long abandoned.

---

189. Tertullian, *Apology*, ch. 37 [*ANF* 3:45]. [*Ed.*] Written about 200.
190. [*Ed.*] See n. 180.
191. [*Ed.*] Senior co-emperor with Diocletian, 286–305.
192. See Eusebius, *Ecclesiastical History* 9.9.1. He speaks here of an ἔθνος Χριστιανῶν (nation of Christians), just as the 311 edict spoke of a *corpus Christianorum*.

Part 6

Christianity as a Moral and Religious
Principle, in Its Universality
and Its Limitations at This Time

Introduction

The founder of Christianity began his preaching of the gospel by stating that those who profess faith in his teaching are not merely "the poor in spirit" to whom belongs "the kingdom of heaven" (Matt 5:3), but also "the meek" who "will inherit the earth" (vs. 5). His words would also be fulfilled in this latter sense in the outward history of Christianity, in the world-historical course of its first three centuries.

We cannot properly understand the point at which Christianity stands in the major epoch known as the age of Constantine, without looking back to its beginnings, and to the principle giving rise to all those phenomena comprising the first three centuries of Christianity's history. What now stands before us in the full force of an overarching principle, one overcoming the world, is that sense of poverty in which, when confronting the world, the first followers of Jesus regarded themselves as the poor, but as "the poor in spirit" whose poverty in material things was for them just the symbol and pledge of this material poverty's direct opposite, given their conception of the kingdom of heaven. All that it has become outwardly over the course of time Christianity simply owes to its own principle, as the force at work within it. The greater the impact of this principle, the more certainly this impact attests to the divinity of Christianity's origin.

There are multiple ways in which we can specify what this divine element is in Christianity's origin and principle. We can designate it as the Son of God having become incarnate in humanity; or as the Spirit poured out upon the initial fellowship of those who believed in Jesus; or as the Spirit in the sense in which the Apostle Paul identified the divine Spirit, working directly in the faithful, with a Christian's own immediate self-consciousness, such that this Spirit can only be thought of as the principle of Christian consciousness.

The Universality and the Energy of Christianity's Moral and Religious Principle[1]

In any event, if we link the principle with its effects, it can only be regarded as the kind of principle that genuinely has an inherently moral character. Indeed the only way any religious movement can make its divine origin and principle operative is by the moral effects it produces, by its moral effectiveness and the energy it unleashes in its adherents.

Without a doubt there has never been a greater and more all-pervasive change in the world than the one Christianity brought about; none so completely epochal in its external scope and its inner significance. However, what would all these alterations in humanity's religious faith and conceptions have amounted to—namely, the turn from polytheism to monotheism; and, instead of setting one's hopes on a messiah to come, believing he has already appeared and worshiping him as the Son of God in the highest sense—if there had been no change in the world's moral sensibility and its ethical conduct? What if the immorality of the ancient world, those phenomena so typical of it, had not been replaced by authentic moral virtue and religious piety? The way Christianity wants to shape human beings, the essence of the transformation it is said to accomplish, Christianity itself calls a rebirth and complete renovation of the person. Therefore this efficacy in transforming persons would also be evident in history, by moral rebirth occurring in the public life of humankind. For this is certainly the most important feature of Christianity's first three centuries, when we consider this period from the most universal perspective, namely, the moral dimension of religion.

Here we must focus our attention not on what Christianity is in the individual person, in the hidden depths of one's inner life, but instead on its large-scale effects, what emerges in the shared public life of various peoples as Christianity's noblest fruit. From this perspective we can rightly state that the world has in fact become a morally purer and better place owing to Christianity, albeit just in the limited sphere to which its influence first of all spread.

---

1. [Ed.] Baur often uses the adjectival expression *sittlich religiöses*, which we translate as "moral and religious." What he means is a religious principle with a moral focus or emphasis. Baur holds to this Kantian conviction throughout his career, even after he comes under the influence of Hegel. It is found in both his early sermons and his later writings.

The Good Features of the Christian's Approach to Morality

The moral improvement (and it naturally could not have been otherwise) is evident at all those points where Christianity came into the closest and most direct contact with the moral corruption prevalent in the pagan world. This is an indisputable historical fact. The pagan opponents of Christianity were never willing to credit it with being a moral religion. They even accused it of the uttermost moral perversion and depravity. The Christians responded by pointing to all those features of their lives that manifestly attested to the truly moral character of Christianity.

Just read the writings of the second century Christian apologists and judge for yourself whether they would have been able to speak in such terms in defending and characterizing Christianity had things in fact been quite different than they said they were; had the following attributes not actually been those that set the Christian community apart from the pagan world in the most unambiguous way. The list includes the Christians' sincere, unfeigned piety and fear of God; their dread of everything immoral and forbidden, because of constantly thinking about the presence of a God who sees even into what is hidden and judges in accord with strict justice; their integrity, honesty, and rectitude in all the circumstances of social life; their moral purity and chastity in renouncing all sensual pleasures; their heartfelt, self-sacrificing human kindness not even excluding enemies and those who abuse them; their humble and persistent forbearance that holds good in suffering as the distinctively Christian vocation, the supreme act of the moral self; in sum, all those virtues that at all times have counted as the fairest fruits and surest signs of a truly Christian sensibility.[2]

---

2. See in particular: Justin Martyr, *First Apology*, chs. 12–13; Athenagoras, *A Plea for the Christians*, chs. 31ff.; Tertullian, *Apology*, ch. 39. Also, the Christians questioned by Pliny gave proof of the blamelessness of the Christian life from the fact that they "bind themselves by an oath, not for the commission of any crime but to abstain from theft, robbery, adultery and breach of faith, and to not deny a deposit when it was claimed" (cf. 1 Pet 4:15) [Pliny the Younger, *Epistle* 10, in Bettenson, *Documents of the Christian Church* (Part 5, n. 123), 4]. Justin emphasizes (ch. 17) how honest and conscientious the Christians are in paying taxes to the state. In his *Apology*, ch. 42, Tertullian has this to say about it: "But your other taxes will acknowledge a debt of gratitude to Christians; for the faithfulness which keeps us from defrauding a brother makes us conscientious in paying all that is due. Thus by ascertaining how much is lost by fraud and falsehood in the census declarations—the calculation may

AVERSION TO SHOWS OR SPECTACLES

This difference had to have been especially noticeable, for the Christians did not participate in so many practices that were typically part of life in the ancient world, because they could not reconcile these practices with their Christian concepts.

The Christians not only avoided everything bringing them into contact with the pagan cultus of demons; they also kept their distance from places where they could seem to be seeking idle pleasure by sharing in the barbarous delight in shows or spectacles, in the brazenly shameless pagan customs. Consider, in this regard, Tertullian's verdict about participating in the pagan spectacles (a view he held wholly apart from his morally rigorous Montanism). He states that

> God has enjoined us to commune calmly, gently, quietly, and peacefully with the Holy Spirit, because these things are alone in keeping with the goodness of his nature, with his tenderness and sensitiveness. We are not to vex him with rage, ill nature, anger, or grief. Well, how shall this compare with the shows? For the shows always lead to spiritual agitation. . . . Are we not, in like manner, enjoined to put away from us all immodesty? On this ground, again, we abstain from the theater, which is immodesty's very own abode, where nothing is reputable other than what elsewhere is disreputable.[3]

Tertullian most decidedly rejected the phony arguments by which even Christians sought to justify such pleasures as permissible, because nowhere in the scriptures are they explicitly forbidden.

He continues:

> Never and nowhere is what God condemns free from blame. Never and nowhere is it right to do what you may not do at all times and in all places. The freedom of the truth from all change of opinion and varying judgments is what constitutes its perfection, and gives it its claims to be the complete master, to be ever revered, to be faithfully obeyed. That which is really good or really evil cannot be otherwise. For in all things the truth of God is immutable. . . . The pagans, who lack a full revelation of the truth because they are not taught of God, regard something as evil or good as it suits their self-will and passion, making what is good in one place evil in another, and what is evil in one place good in another.[4]

---

easily be made—you could see that the ground of complaint in one department of revenue is offset by the advantage others gain" [*ANF* 3:49]. (That is, what the state loses from the fact that the Christians do not participate in the pagan sacrificial cultus is sufficiently made up for by their honesty in other matters.) One of the finest attestations to the truly moral spirit with which Christianity confronts the pagan world is contained in Tertullian's treatise, *Of Patience*. See in particular the conclusion, in ch. 15, where Tertullian summarizes the features of patience depicted as the soul of Christianity in practice—the truly Christian, heavenly traits as opposed to those of the deceptive, disgraceful gods of the earth.

3. *The Shows* (*De Spectaculis*), chs. 15, 17 [*ANF* 3:86].

4. Ibid., chs. 20, 21 [*ANF* 3:88].

All that is not from God, or that displeases God, is from the Devil. All this belongs to the Devil's ostentatious display and, as the mark of our faith, we renounce it.

> We should have no connection with the things we abjure, whether in deed or word, whether by looking on them or looking forward to them. But do we not abjure and rescind that baptismal pledge, when we cease to act faithfully to it? Must we ask the pagans themselves? Let them tell us, then, whether it is right for Christians to attend the shows. Our rejection of these amusements is the chief sign to them that a person has adopted the Christian faith. . . . May God keep his people free from any passionate eagerness to enjoy such a cruel entertainment![5]

It is self-evident that such principles must also have been applied to so many other contexts in which Christians came into contact with public life in the ancient world. Because of this the Christians' view of life and their entire conduct must have had a serious and austere quality to it.[6]

WITHDRAWAL FROM POLITICAL AFFAIRS; THE CLOSENESS OF THEIR OWN COMMUNITY

There were many things in which the Christians could not take part without damaging or denying their moral sense. They kept themselves at arm's length from the pagan universe, and doing so had to alienate them from the public and political life of the ancient world. This circumstance naturally meant that the more they withdrew from public life, the more they formed an ever-closer community among themselves. Because the moral and religious bond they had lay wholly outside the horizons of the pagan world, they suffered the great injustice of people thinking they were just bound together as a political association, and assuming that was the purpose of their movement.

---

5. Ibid., chs. 24, 25 [ANF 3:89].

6. Here we should mention in particular the two of Tertullian's writings in which he exhorts Christian women to set themselves apart from pagan women by dressing conservatively and decorously (again, without being influenced by Montanist principles). These two texts comprise the two books of Tertullian's *On the Apparel of Women* (*De habitu muliebri* and *De cultu feminarum*). In bk. 2, ch. 11, Tertullian says to Christian women: "What reason do you have for appearing publicly in such grand attire, since you have no occasion to attend events calling for such exhibitions? For you neither make the rounds of the temples, nor want to attend public shows, nor have anything to do with the holy days of the pagans. People display all that pompous attire before the eyes of others when they attend these public gatherings, for all the 'seeing and being seen.' They do it to be voluptuous, as prostitutes, or else just for their own glory. You, however, have no reason to appear in public except for serious purposes. . . . You handmaids of God must be different from the handmaids of the Devil, so that you may be an example to them" [ANF 4:24]. Clement of Alexandria's *The Instructor* (*Paedagogus*) has an abundance of precepts for a Christian's moral conduct in books two and three. However, many of them deal only with special cases or stray into petty issues.

Tertullian says that, in fairness, this sect ought to have been included as one of the legally permissible associations, since it would not be guilty of any of the things one usually fears from banned associations. "We, who are indifferent to the pursuit of glory and honor, have no incentive to join your political associations. Nothing is more entirely foreign to us than the affairs of state. We acknowledge one all-embracing commonwealth—the world."[7] Yet given these conditions, this mandate to distance oneself from the public and political life of the pagan world was by no means to be understood as though the Christians wanted, with this move, to make themselves of no use in the practical purposes of life itself.[8] This is what Tertullian says in reply to the pagans who held that view of the lives of Christians:

> How in all the world can that be the case with people who are living among you, eating the same food, wearing the same attire, having the same habits, needing the same essentials of life? We are not Indian Brahmins or Gymnosophists who dwell in woods and exile themselves from ordinary human life. We do not forget the debt of gratitude we owe to God, our Lord and Creator. We reject nothing God has made, though certainly we exercise restraint ourselves, lest we make an immoderate use of any of his gifts. So we dwell together with you in the world, avoiding neither forum nor marketplace, nor bathhouse, workplace or any other places for life's ordinary transactions. We sail with you and do military service with you; we till the soil and engage in commerce. We take part in your occupations and provide our labor for your benefit.[9]

Thus a new community was said to be founded in the midst of the pagan world, a community resting on truly moral foundations. It increasingly contrasted with life in the pagan world inasmuch as the pagans became more deficient in the moral bonds that join people together with one another, namely, in love and mutual goodwill. Tertullian says this about the Christian community:

> It is mainly the deeds of a love so noble that lead many to distrust us. They say, "See how they love one another," whereas they themselves are animated by mutual hatred. They say, "See how they are ready to die for one another," whereas they themselves are ready to kill one another. Our calling each other brethren seems suspicious to them for no other reason than that for them all such relations are just pretence. We are also your brethren by dint of the nature we have in common, and which is the mother of us all—although human nature itself disavows you as unfitting brethren. At the same time, how much more fittingly those are called and counted as brethren who have been led to acknowledge the one God as their father, who have received the one Spirit of holiness, who from the same darkness of ignorance are awakened to the same

---

7. *Apology*, ch. 38 [*ANF* 3:45–46].

8. As Tertullian says in *Apology*, ch. 42, they did not want to be accused of being *infructuosi in negotiis* "useless in the affairs of life" [*ANF* 3:49].

9. *Apology*, ch. 42 [*ANF* 3:49].

light of truth! . . . And we, one in mind and soul, do not hesitate to share our earthly goods with one another. We hold all things in common, excepting only some things [namely, wives] that some others hold in common.[10]

MARRIAGE AND DOMESTIC LIFE

Tertullian makes this last statement particularly with reference to the married life of Christians, for marital life and domestic life belong most especially to the relationships in which the moral spirit animating the Christian community had to express its ennobling influence. The greater the value Christians assigned to chastity, and moral decency, the more they also had to regard marriage as a sacred bond.

Marriage itself counted as a religious matter, and from very early on the custom was that a couple not be married without religious consecration of the marriage and the approval of the church.[11] The following statement from Tertullian evidences a deep and tender sensibility as to the importance of the marital bond:

> Where are we to find words enough to describe the happiness of that marriage of which the church approves, the oblation confirms, its seal the angels announce, and the Father regards as ratified? Even on earth children do not rightly and lawfully wed without their fathers' consent. What a linking of two believers, with one hope, one mode of life, one and the same service! The two are brother and sister, fellow servants, united in spirit and flesh. They are truly "two in one flesh." Where there is one flesh there is also one spirit. They pray together, . . . fast together, mutually leading and exhorting each other. They are in God's church together . . . "for better and for worse." Neither hides anything from the other one or is troublesome to the other. Freely they visit the sick, support the needy. . . . They sing psalms and hymns and challenge each other as to who sings better to their Lord. Christ enjoys seeing and hearing this. . . . Where the two of them are, he is there also. The Evil One does not come where Christ is present.[12]

---

10. *Apology*, ch. 39 [*ANF* 3:46].

11. Tertullian, *On Monogamy*, ch. 11: "Grant now that you are married 'in the Lord,' in accordance with the law and the apostle . . . by a monogamist bishop, and presbyters and deacons bound by the same solemn oath. . . . They will join you together in a virgin church, the one betrothed of the one Christ" [*ANF* 4:67]. In this passage Tertullian speaks in opposition to second marriage. See also his *On Modesty*, ch. 4: "Among us secret ties—ones not first professed in the presence of the church—run the risk of being judged akin to adultery and fornication" [*ANF* 4:77].

12. Tertullian, *To His Wife*, ch. 2.8 [*ANF* 4:48; Baur cites 2.9 (lacking in *ANF*) and quotes this passage in German, which we translate here]. The two books of this text belong to Tertullian's pre-Montanist period. See August Neander, *Antignostikus: Geist des Tertullianus und Einleitung in dessen Schriften*, 2nd ed. (Berlin, 1849), 224ff. It is self-evident that such a marriage is only possible when both spouses are Christians. Thus Tertullian emphatically opposed mixed marriages. See *To His Wife* 2.3: "It is certain that believers contracting marriages with pagans are guilty of fornication, and are to be excluded from all communication with the brotherhood" [*ANF* 4:45]. See also *The Chaplet* (*De*

Glowing as this picture of the ideal marriage may be, it is nevertheless clear that the moral spirit of Christianity could alone have given birth to this idea of marriage.

However, such sincere mutuality in marriage is only possible where each partner has rights. Thus the concept of marriage in Christianity is essentially one in which the wife has a much freer and more independent relation to the husband than was otherwise customary in the ancient world. The Christian concept of marriage required that wives be emancipated from their former status. So Christianity itself brought about this emancipation of women because these women themselves, in the freedom of their Christian consciousness, had to know that they are freed from everything incompatible with this consciousness. The mixed marriages that were so commonplace at that time gave the Christian wives many opportunities to become aware of this freedom.

Even the Apostle Paul certainly acknowledged the right of the Christian wife in a mixed marriage to act freely and independently of the husband in religious matters.[13] Thus she had to have been aware of having the right to a freer standing in social life as such. The freer conduct the women in the Corinthian congregation took advantage of, especially in claiming equal standing with the men in their assemblies, demonstrates how early the Christian women's consciousness of their freer position was awakened. Although the Apostle Paul had every reason to limit their push for freedom, and to admonish them regarding their duty to be subject to their husbands,[14] there can be no doubt that the moral concept of Christian marriage was essentially shaped by the freer position Christianity was first able to confer upon women, in the consciousness of their religious freedom.

If marriage is the foundation of domestic life, then, just as Christianity newly consecrated marriage, by the same token it had to pervade domestic life as such with a new spirit. For it is inherently the case that Christianity's moral impact could not have a more fitting and truly kindred sphere of action than that of domestic life. The quite natural result of Christians being appalled by all those customs and immoral practices of pagan life, was that they turned their attention from without to within and sought, in the life within their own fellowship, the satisfaction that could not be found in the public life of their surroundings. Thus only a religion that especially saw the most important duty as turning away from that pagan world and searching within oneself—in earnest self-examination and self-knowledge, the constant occupation with the innermost concerns of a heart directed toward God—could cultivate a sense for the domestic life. There alone, in its tranquil, sacred environs, could one engage in and nurture so many of the elements belonging to the task of living a Christian life.

---

corona), ch. 13. Notwithstanding their harsh tone, Tertullian's arguments against entering into a second marriage express a truly moral spirit as to how he understood the essential nature of Christian marriage.

13. See 1 Cor 7:12–13. The wife has the same right to obtain a divorce (ἀφιέναι) as the husband does. "If any woman has a husband who is an unbeliever . . . she should not divorce him."

14. See my "Beiträge zur Erklärung der Korinthierbriefe," *Theologische Jahrbücher* 11 (1852) 563ff.

It is an especially typical feature of this specific Christian approach to life that, whereas life in the ancient world was predominantly focused on the outer world, the public and political domain, because of Christianity social life took quite the opposite direction, becoming more intensified internally. Christianity gave an inner significance to all the circumstances of private life, an importance they could never have had when civic and political life was both flourishing and glorified in the ancient world. In due course the decisive turnabout came at the time when Christianity and paganism were most at odds, most antithetical. It is surely reasonable to hold that this change was mainly caused by Christianity's influence, by the subtle power of its domestic and marital life. The aristocratic and despotic spirit of the ancient world, which considered the individual to be simply an instrument serving the general purposes of the whole, indeed had to give way to a more humane and less harsh way of thinking, one recognizing that all had equal rights and respecting the human dignity of even the humblest and lowliest ones.[15]

Christianity's truly moral spirit, which is the innermost principle of its historical development, makes itself evident in all of these settings and far more typically so than in those endeavors people usually esteem the most. For in the latter kind, appearances are often deceptive when we analyze more carefully the exaggerated way they are depicted by pretentious writers, or detect the impure motives sometimes behind them. Ultimately all that serves to glorify the heroism of the Christian martyrs is truly and entirely a function of the same moral seriousness that Christianity awakens in its adherents, and by which it has ever deeper and more lasting effects upon human life, as opposed to its heritage from all the transitory resplendence of its martyrs' crowns.

However, we ought not just stick to the good features we have seen in the phenomena emphasized thus far. There is also a less-favorable side to be mentioned here

---

15. Slavery in the ancient world also comes into the picture here. It was first mitigated and gradually done away with during the Christian era, although more humanely-minded pagans also favored doing so. (See my "Seneca und Paulus, das Verhältniss des Stoicismus zum Christenthum nach den Schriften Seneca's," *Zeitschrift für wissenschaftliche Theologie* 1 [1858] 212ff.). The Apostle Paul, convinced that someone of any social status could be a good Christian, did admonish slaves to accept their status even though they could become free (1 Cor 7:21–24). Yet based on his Christian view as expressed in Gal 3:28, the distinction between slave and free is abolished, such that what has no inherent reason for continuing must sooner or later also cease to be the practice. The Epistle to Philemon is kindly disposed toward slaves, for it speaks, in most sympathetic, Christian terms, about sending the slave convert to Christianity back as a fellow Christian to his Christian master. In his *Against Celsus* 3.54, Origen considers educating slaves to think freely as one of Christianity's humanitarian projects, in order "to heal every rational nature with the medicine of reason, and to bring them into fellowship with God, the creator of all things" [ANF 4:486]. One of the innovations for which Callistus, the bishop of Rome, was blamed by his adversary Hippolytus, was said to be a decree allowing marriages between slaves and free women, and recognizing them as legally valid. (See *Philosophumena* [Part Three, n. 11], 9.12.24 [ET 656–57].) See J. Döllinger, *Hippolytus und Callistus* (Regensburg, 1853), 158ff. According to J. A. Möhler, "Bruckstücke aus der Geschichte der Aufhebung der Sklaverei," *Gesammelte Schriften und Aufsätze*, ed. J. Döllinger, vol. 2 (Regensburg, 1840), 54ff., Chrysostom was the first one in the Christian Church to raise the issue of freeing the slaves.

if we are to present a true and accurate picture of the religious life of Christians during this period.

The One-Sided and Restrictive Character of Christian Morality

All that is moral has a pure and noble character in proportion to how free and clear is the religious consciousness it presupposes. Christian morality was essentially determined by the fact that, in his own religious consciousness, Christ had rid himself of everything in pagan polytheism that obscured moral awareness and impeded its purer and freer development. However, was the religious consciousness of the Christians themselves as free in this respect as their resolute opposition to pagan polytheism should have led one to suppose?

THE FEAR OF DEMONS

To be sure, the Christians did not believe in the existence of the pagan deities. However, they were now faced with demons everywhere in the pagan world instead of deities. The way they envisaged these demons impacted their Christian lives in many ways. The Christians' belief in these demons or spirits spawned a multitude of superstitious notions and practices that in turn gave a pagan cast to the Christians' own lives.

Christians saw themselves surrounded and secretly watched by demons everywhere, and most of all where they came into contact with the pagan world. They did everything they could to protect themselves from the demons' attacks and snares. Not only did this situation affect a person's whole demeanor, making people anxious, ill at ease and agitated; that had to play a major part in people's morale, and was hardly the mark of someone whose own moral and religious self-consciousness was healthy and happy. Also, in being in this constant struggle with the demons, these Christians believed they could ward off the demons by devices lacking any moral basis, even ones of just a magical sort. For how was it anything other than magic when the mere name of Jesus supposedly had the power to drive out demons?[16] Furthermore, although Christians were known to value the moral and religious power and importance of

---

16. In *Against Celsus*, even Origen says: "A similar philosophy of names also applies to our Jesus. His name has already been unmistakably seen to have expelled myriads of demons from people's souls and bodies, so great was its power" (1.25 [*ANF* 4:406]).

prayer, they all too often associated similar magical notions with it. And what was more natural than for human life and the human spirit to stand totally exposed to the influence of higher powers of this hostile kind, to the extent that the demonic world was making inroads everywhere?

MORAL RIGORISM CLASHES WITH THE PAGAN WORLD

The more a person's consciousness is not focused internally but instead externally, and not on the sensible world but instead on the supersensible world, the more the moral consciousness still lacks a firm, immanent principle. For belief in demons was equally disturbing and unsettling for Christian consciousness where it encountered this belief in its pagan form in the circumstances of daily life. When people found themselves existing within a network of connections to the pagan world, it was of course difficult to avoid everything that could burden a Christian's conscience with guilt for collaborating with paganism.

When Christians regarded every contact with paganism as a demonic contamination, that must have led to many clashes with paganism. Where the lives of Christians were so closely intertwined with the lives of pagans, it was hard for Christians to draw a line between what was allowable and what was not. Matters of conscience could so easily become matters of life and death. Tertullian declares that idolaters are not merely those who sprinkle frankincense for the gods, or sacrifice to them or perform some other act directly connected with the pagan cultus; for the term "idolatry" also encompasses all the arts, trades, and occupations that in any way contribute to the erection and adornment of idols. What should those people do whose livelihood depends on such occupations? Tertullian's harsh answer is that faith does not fear hunger, for faith knows that for God's sake it would have to be as contemptuous of starvation as it is of any other manner of death. He says that indeed for the Lord's sake the apostles also left their trades and occupations behind them; that none of those the Lord called to follow him said, "I do not know what my means of livelihood will be."[17]

However, if this moral rigorism itself was just based largely on the misconception of the pagan deities as being evil demons, hostile to God, then what a restrictive, one-sided character the moral actions it dictated must have had! Since each of these actions could not be looked upon as promoting pagan idolatry in equal fashion, it was always doubtful as to whether the moral consciousness was sufficiently motivated by the command to obey it, when doing so involved such a great sacrifice. Tertullian responded to these considerations by saying that the luxury and opulence of his day would provide a much larger field for workers in the arts and trades than they had in the realm of superstition.[18]

---

17. Tertullian, *On Idolatry*, chs. 11–12.
18. Ibid., ch. 8.

But what could prevent this same stringency from even further application, since everything could always involve some kind of indirect relation to pagan idolatry and the *pompa diaboli* (the Devil's retinue)? Tertullian even went so far as to declare the office of the *ludimagistri* (schoolmasters) and the other *professores literarum* (professors of literature) to be incompatible with Christianity. They too are implicated in idolatry in various ways, since they have to describe the pagan deities, to explain their names, their genealogies, the fables told of them, and everything about their honor and distinction. In this instance Tertullian himself cannot ignore the objection that, if such things ought not be taught, then one also ought not learn about them; but that this would deprive Christians of access to the general education they cannot do without, even in religious affairs. The only answer he has is that there is always a difference between teaching and learning, and the pupils have much less need to take part in pagan idolatry than the teachers do.[19] From this we simply see how such a restrictive way of looking at things constantly led to clashes [with the features of everyday life], and how in the end one could only get around them by petty subterfuges.

All those cases in which Christians came into conflict with the pagan state fall into this same category. How could a Christian hold any governmental post, when there were pagan practices and emblems associated with it? How could one serve in the military when those who do had to swear an oath to the pagan banners? How could a Christian obey the emperor, when the emperor was the head of a pagan state? It was just being consistent when Tertullian bluntly said "no" in answer to the first two of these three questions.[20] But what should one say in answer to the third question? The Christians honored the emperor, and rendered the obedience due him, for they acknowledged it as their duty to give "to the emperor the things that are the emperor's, and to God the things that are God's" (Matt 22:21). Indeed they even saw the emperors as the regents God installed to rule an empire enduring until the end of the world. The emperor was the human being standing closest to God.[21]

---

19. Ibid., ch. 10. This is the first time the oft-discussed issue of *secularia studia* (worldly education) is raised. Clement of Alexandria discusses the same issue, but in a different sense, in *Stromata* 1.5ff., with reference to "worldly education" or "the early study of Greek."

20. Ibid., ch. 18: "Demons are the magistrates (the dignitaries and powers) of this world. They bear the *fasces* and 'the purple' (i.e., high rank), the emblems of one body" [ANF 3:72]. Ch. 19: "There is no agreement between the divine and the human sacrament, between the standard of Christ and the standard of the Devil, between the camp of light and the camp of darkness. One cannot serve two masters—God and Caesar" [ANF 3:73].

21. See Tertullian's tract, *To Scapula*, ch. 2: "A Christian is enemy to none, least of all to the emperor of Rome, whom he knows to be appointed by his God. So he cannot but love and honor the emperor, and must desire his well-being, as also the well-being of the empire over which he reigns so long as the world shall stand—for Rome shall continue as long as that. Therefore we render to the emperor such reverential homage as is lawful for us and good for him. We regard him as the human being next to God, as one who received all his power from God and is just less than God. This accords with the emperor's will; for, as less than the true God, he is also greater than all others. Thus he is greater than the lesser gods, for they too are subject to him" [ANF 3:105–6].

However, when the entire structure of the state rests on the worship of the demons, and when the head of the state was himself the strongest supporter and the greatest patron of this cultus, then from the Christian perspective one could just as well look upon him as the viceroy of the Devil rather than as God's appointed ruler.[22] Of course the Christians could make their obedience to the authorities simply contingent on their not being obliged to do anything contrary to Christianity. But their obedience soon reached its limits if the emperor himself demanded something from them of a pagan or demonic nature. What other choice did they have but either to violate their Christian conscience, or to abandon a world in which the practice of Christian virtue was impossible without the moral subject's temporary capitulation.[23] A moral persuasion that adopts this view without reservation is most laudable, subjectively speaking. But what is the status of moral action confined within such narrow limits, action determined by conceptions belonging to such a restricted way of looking at things that is linked to Christianity by happenstance? For what is the basis in the essence of Christianity itself for the notion mainly operative here, that Christians stand in such a strained relationship with the Roman state?

THE DUALISTIC, ASCETIC VIEW OF LIFE

From the beginning, the task of a Christian's moral and religious life was defined as not merely a struggle with flesh and blood, but also a struggle with the powers of darkness.[24] From the features we previously singled out to characterize Christian morality, we have seen the stance Christians took in opposition to the demons or spirits, and to the paganism associated with them. However, Christians also saw an antithesis present in their own flesh, one having a distinctive effect on their moral view of life and their moral action. The dualism of spirit and flesh, and in particular the flesh component in this antithesis, occupied a very important place in the Christians' entire way of looking at things.

22. In the Book of Revelation this is Nero as the Antichrist. There is no greater contrast on this point than the Apocalypse vis-à-vis the Epistle to the Romans, 13:1–7. The Apostle Paul is speaking of the same Emperor Nero (who embodies the Antichrist in the Apocalypse) when he says the Christian has a duty to obey the authorities. Whereas the Apocalypse calls for the most determined resistance to the adversary (who is hostile to God and fighting the Lamb), Paul writes: "whoever resists authority resists what God has appointed" (vs. 2). For the early Christians the Pauline and the Johannine injunctions had to have clashed. The passage of time simply did away with the conflict, in that Nero was not the Antichrist the Apocalypse had spoken about. But in those early days this clash must have been a source of discomfort for one's conscience. [*Ed.*] Recall from Part Two that Baur regards the Apostle John as most likely the author of the Book of Revelation (but not of the Gospel of John).

23. Tertullian, *On Idolatry*, ch. 24: "Let no one say, 'Who will guard against this? We will have to abandon the world!' As though leaving it were not worth it, as compared to remaining in the world as an idolater" [*ANF* 3:75].

24. [*Ed.*] In the text Baur cites Ephesians 6:12. This passage says: "For our struggle is not against enemies of blood and flesh, but against the rulers, against the authorities, against the cosmic powers of this present darkness, against the spiritual forces of evil in the heavenly places."

In one respect the flesh was so valued and cherished by Christians that this was one of the main features marking the Christians' view of the world, and of life, as distinct from that of the pagans. Thus Celsus referred contemptuously to the Christians as "a race clinging to the body"; and in fact, although the Christians still had to fight so hard against their most dangerous enemy within the flesh, they could never abandon it. They had to continually make their peace with the flesh, since without the flesh there is surely no resurrection, and without a resurrection there is no enjoying all those blessings and delights said to be provided in the world to come, the Christians' true home. The earliest period of the Christian Church, when it opposed the pagans and the Gnostics, saw greater stress on the doctrine of the resurrection than at any subsequent time in its history. Several of the most prominent church fathers, men such as Athenagoras and Tertullian, made the resurrection the object of special attention, in order to highlight its importance and its truth. They sought to show that the body is also an essential element of our God-created nature and of our human personhood, and how it is unthinkable that the divine justice and mercy would not apply to the body as well. Also, the body was not so very important merely for the world to come. As though the body were a subject of its own, subsisting by itself, it was said to be cooperating essentially in one's present life, throughout all the stages in the Christian's path for attaining salvation, which could only be gained in and through the body. In the world to come the body will simply receive, as its reward, what it had earned in the present world.[25]

In any event this specifically Christian view of the flesh is only one aspect to consider. The other aspect that also influences the Christian view of life is the dualism of spirit and matter that is tied so closely to the outlook of the ancient world. Because of it, there seemed to be no higher demand placed on the Christian striving to live a moral life than to flee from the body, to mortify the flesh. Hence Christian morality took on an essentially ascetic character, one in which the spiritual orientation prevalent at that time got modified in a Christian fashion. In this dominant view even philosophy, in its practical aspect, had come to be regarded as an ἄσκησις, an ascetic discipline, and for that very reason it also seemed to be internally related to Christianity.

The overall task of asceticism involves not merely preventing superfluous sensual desires, but also, by adopting a specific way of life, limiting the satisfaction of one's intrinsically necessary sensory needs to the greatest possible extent. Thus from the

---

25. See Tertullian, *On the Resurrection of the Flesh*, ch. 8: "We see . . . how much this trifling and lowly substance is privileged in God's sight. . . . The flesh is the condition on which salvation hinges. The soul is chosen to serve God, but it is the flesh that makes it capable of such service. The flesh is washed that the soul may be cleansed; the flesh is anointed that the soul might be consecrated; the flesh is signed (with the cross) that the soul too may be fortified; the flesh is shadowed by the imposition of hands, that the soul may be illuminated by the spirit. The flesh feeds on the body and blood of Christ, that the soul may also be fed by God. Therefore those united in their works cannot be separated in their wages" [*ANF* 3:551].

very beginning Christian asceticism in particular included frequent fasting exercises in which their Christian element got expressed mainly by linking these exercises most especially with days and hours made holy by recalling the passion and death of the redeemer. There was nothing remarkable about these ascetic practices, whether they were carried out more or less strictly, in a freer or more structured format, although from time to time they were tied to particular types of abstinence. Far more important is the question as to the views the Christians of these early times held about marriage and celibacy. These are what will give us a more finely-tuned way to evaluate the ascetic character of this period.

MARRIAGE

No other time has seen the issue of marriage discussed so repeatedly, or the emergence of such a variety of very conflicting opinions about it.[26]

---

26. See my "Beiträge zur Erklärung der Korinthierbriefe" in the *Theologische Jahrbücher* 11 (1852) 1ff., concerning the Apostle Paul's view of marriage and what led to his discussion of marriage in 1 Corinthians 7. Now I can only summarize what I have stated more fully elsewhere. Paul's view of marriage here marks the point where the Christian's moral view of the world still had to break free from the ancient view, which was based on the antithesis of matter and spirit. The Apostle not only prefers celibacy for its own sake, and allows for marriage only to avoid the greater evil of sexual immorality (πορνεία). He also declares it best for those who are still unmarried to remain unmarried, manifestly because of "the impending crisis" (v. 26), for "the appointed time has grown short" (v. 29) and "the present form of this world is passing away" (v. 31). Hence at a time when everything was already unstable, changing, and transitory, Paul thought it hardly seemed worth the effort to alter one's external relationships when such change brings with it new cares and difficulties, and when one cannot count on anything to be lasting (vv. 26, 28). The influence this "impending crisis" has on moral judgments about such relationships of social life as marriage is clearly evident in this instance. If, from our place in history, we can recognize that earliest Christianity is simply determined to involve itself in all those relationships in which it has become a factor, and has set forth, for all to see, what it inherently is, then we see before us the moral task Christianity has set for itself. Our entire notion of Christianity's absolute worth is essentially formed by considering all that it has become for humankind in moral terms, during the course of its historical development. The deeper and more wide-ranging our insight into how it has permeated all the circumstances of moral and social life, the more certainly we see this as simply the realization of the idea of its essential nature. Hence if there is a standpoint that not only leaves the course of Christianity's historical development entirely out of consideration, but also precludes considering it because of looking upon this temporal development as already ceasing at the point where it is said to have just begun, then, as a matter of course, that standpoint relinquishes the moral task of Christianity in the aforementioned conditions, and the very life-circumstances we had to regard as most especially Christianity's moral domain, appear more or less a matter of indifference to this other perspective. The Apostle Paul's view of slavery is similar in this regard to his view of marriage. He admonishes the slaves to continue as slaves, because his general opinion is that each one ought to remain in the circumstances one is in when first called to be a Christian (vv. 17, 20, 24). Yet our own verdict can only be that the moral consciousness demands the abolition of slavery, in keeping with the spirit of Christianity. Therefore, even though the Apostle held these now-outdated views of marriage and slavery, the universality of the Christian principle is evident in the fact that, in the entire history of humankind, there is no advance in moral development that would not have been inherently based in Christianity and introduced by its quietly effective influence, apart from any revolutionary impulses.

The Gnostic View of Marriage

According to the dualistic worldview, which was still so very influential on this issue, the essential nature of sexual relations could not be explained without going back to the antithesis of the two principles, spirit and matter. With these principles serving as background, every view of marriage was very important. That background is the reason why this issue had to capture the attention of the Gnostics most of all. We must focus on their principles if we are to correctly understand the different conceptions of marriage we are dealing with.

Gnostics such as Valentinus and Basilides, who understood the spirit-matter antithesis in a less crude fashion, did not utterly reject marriage. Valentinus certainly thought of the Aeons of the spirit-world as conjugal pairs. Basilides had such high regard for the ethical aspect that he did not let it be too severely restricted by his Gnostic dualism. However, Clement of Alexandria separated the Gnostics with the most extreme views into two classes or categories.[27] He says that one class freely engages in promiscuous sexual relations, but the other one overdoes it in the opposite direction, by demanding an irreligious restraint or continence. However much these two differ in their views, both are nevertheless based on the same dualism. If the relation between spirit and matter is conceptualized in such a dualistic way that the two, as mutually antithetical, can never unite in an inner harmony, then instead of their uniting, spirit can simply endeavor persistently to come to terms as much as possible with matter. This can only happen in one of two ways: either by spirit entirely cutting any ties it has with matter; or by spirit co-existing with matter but remaining completely indifferent to everything taking place because of matter or facilitated by matter, thus all "works of the flesh"—which leaves the essence of spirit completely untouched by matter. The Nicolaitans, who took this latter stance, followed the principle "that the bodily nature of the Lord is to be disregarded"; that the flesh must be left to its own devices so that, on its own, it may wear down and exhaust itself; that the desires of the flesh must run their natural course and not be restricted in doing so.[28] As with some other Gnostic sects, the Nicolaitans were therefore said to have engaged in the most shameless licentiousness.[29]

Since the strictest dualists were also the most resolute opponents of Judaism, they included some whose antinomian outlook even made them hostile to, and contemptuous of, the moral law. Because of this orientation, the church fathers called

---

27. In the *Stromata*, bk. 3, ch. 5, where he treats the teaching about marriage very fully, Clement of Alexandria says that they divide "all the heresies into two groups. Either they teach a way of life which makes no distinction between right and wrong or their hymn is too tightly strung and they claim asceticism out of a spirit of irreligious quarrelsomeness" [Clement of Alexandria, *Stromateis, Books One to Three*, trans. John Ferguson, The Fathers of the Church (Washington, DC, 1991), 280].

28. Clement, *Stromata* 3.5. See also 2.20.

29. There was no particular sect called "Nicolaitans." Instead the term came from Rev 2:6 (see also v. 15), and it simply served as a general designation for pagan-Christian libertines.

such people "the resisters." They said that the creator of the universe is their natural Father, and everything he has created is good; but that one of those engendered from him has sown weeds and thereby produced the character of the evil in which he has ensnared us, since it pitted us against the Father.[30] They said: "That is why we too oppose him in order to avenge the Father, in our acting contrary to the will of this second one. If he said 'You shall not commit adultery,' we therefore say, 'We break the marriage vow in order to annul this commandment of his.'"[31]

From this antinomianism that rejects all positive law, it is a small step to the naturalism and communism that completely abolish the distinction between what is natural and what is moral. Carpocrates and his son Epiphanes taught the latter doctrine and sought to ground it in principle as a new theory of social life, based on the idea of justice. Epiphanes wrote a book on justice, in which he explicated his idea as follows. He said the justice of God is life in common, with equality. Heaven extends equally on all sides and surrounds the earth. Night displays all her stars equally, and God has caused Helios, the originator of daytime, the father of light, to shine from above for all to see. Everyone sees alike, for here there is no difference between the rich and the poor, between the people and the prince, between the rational and dim-witted people, between man and woman, freemen and servants. The same applies to beings devoid of reason. Since Helios shines down from above on all living beings, on the good and the bad, he establishes justice by the fact that no one could have more light, or could rob from his neighbor in order to have a double share of light for himself. The sun provides for the growth of foodstuffs for all creatures alike, and grants equal justice to all. All creatures are generated in the way that is common to their species, and there is no written law governing generation. Any such law would have been repealed long ago. All members of the same species share the same traits, just as the creator and Father of all, the same just lawgiver, has given everyone the same eyes for seeing without setting females apart from males, reasoning beings apart from those devoid of reason, or as a rule, one apart from another.

Epiphanes regarded the laws as a power hostile to this natural commonality. Since laws are unable to restrain them, people learned how to contravene the laws. The peculiar feature of laws is that they cut and eat away at the commonality under the divine law. This calls to mind the words of the Apostle Paul, "through the law comes the knowledge of sin" (Rom 3:20). The distinction of "mine" from "yours" came about through laws. People could no longer enjoy what they share in as something shared, neither the earth nor her blessings, and not even marriage. The creator made the grapevines to be shared by all, available alike to the sparrow and the thief. The same is true of grain and other crops. However, the [law's] transgressions against the commonality is what gave rise to someone being a thief of herds and crops.

---

30. [*Ed.*] In other words, this engendered being caused some things created by the Father to be called "evil." Hence it gave rise to the moral law these opponents reject.

31. *Stromata* 3.4.

Since God created everything for human beings to have in common, and brought the female and the male together in common, pairing all creatures in the same way, by doing this he manifested justice, which is commonality with equality. But those who originated in this way have denied the commonality that was their origin. Each one is now supposed to have one mate, whereas for the rest of the creatures all of them can take part freely. For maintaining the species, men were implanted with a stronger sexual desire, and it is God's decree that nothing can eradicate it, neither law nor custom nor anything else.[32]

Whereas the foregoing class or category of heretics replaced marriage with the loosest sort of sexual unions, thus exhibiting how aberrant and extreme this Gnostic tendency was in practice, those Gnostics taking an opposite course sought to have so little to do with marriage and sexuality that they even made it their fundamental principle to totally sever this link that binds human beings to the bodily world of matter. While the former Gnostics actually made marriage into πορνεία, or sexual immorality, as opposed to its own universal commonality, or freedom and equality, the latter group even viewed marriage as just πορνεία, simply so that they could reject it as hateful and abhorrent. As Clement says in 3.6, they were those who acted impiously against the creation, and against the holy God and creator of the world, the one ruler of all; and they did so in the guise of advocating continence. They rejected marriage and producing children on the basis that one ought not bring other unfortunate people into the world, and so provide death with any new fodder. Saturninus, who expressly declared that marrying and producing children are the works of the Devil,[33] belongs in this category. Other Gnostics, namely those from Syria, must also have been among these opponents of marriage, given their view of matter.

However, the Marcionites are the most notable representatives of this view of marriage. Clement says[34] that the Marcionites regard nature as evil because it originated from matter and was created by the world-creator proper [i.e., not by the supreme God]. So as not to populate the world made by this creator [a lesser being], they demand that people refrain from marriage. They resist their creator and hasten to the Good, to the one who has summoned them, but do not turn to the one who, as they say, is of a wholly different kind. They become continent not because they freely decide to, but instead from hostility to the world-creator. They do not want to utilize anything he has created because they do not wish to make any concessions to him. However, while they wage war against God with their impious attitude, and disdain thinking in natural ways, and are contemptuous of God's long-suffering and goodness, and while they are unwilling to marry, they nevertheless make use of created

---

32. *Stromata* 3.2.

33. Epiphanius, *Against Heresies* 23.2. Also, *Philosophumena* (Part 3, n. 11), 7.28.7 [ET 538–39].

34. *Stromata* 3.3. Also see, in my book *Die christliche Gnosis, oder die christliche Religions-Philosophie in ihrer geschichtlichen Entwicklung* (Tübingen, 1835), 268ff., what Tertullian says about Marcion as someone who detests marriage.

foodstuffs and breathe the air provided by the world-creator, for they are his creations and they remain in his world. They proclaim as gospel something they say is a wholly new knowledge. Yet they ought to be thankful to the lord of this world for it, since this gospel has been announced to them here, in this world. Thus Clement correctly remarks that this dualism gets itself entangled in huge contradictions.

But we also see what a powerful influence dualism still continued to have, and the deep inroads it made where the freer spirit of Christianity should long since have taken Christian consciousness beyond the abstract antithesis of spirit and matter. However, this deep intertwining of the pagan and Christian worldviews is precisely the essence of Gnosis, and these two so heterogeneous principles could not become disengaged without various confrontations and conflicts. Hence in certain individuals where the Christian principle had already become deeply rooted we see the Gnostic element repeatedly gaining the upper hand.

Tatian is a notable example of this happening. As one of the Apologists, he was very closely associated with Justin Martyr. Yet owing to his inclination toward Christian asceticism, Tatian is also properly numbered among the Gnostics. He wrote an essay on Christian perfection,[35] in which he seems to have given special attention to the issue of marriage. He contended that in 1 Cor 7:5, the marriage the Apostle Paul has in mind is only the spiritual union of the spouses in prayer, whereas he would declare marital cohabitation to be a corrupting intercourse that invalidates prayer. Tatian says the Apostle's words are not to be taken in a permissive sense, but instead as a deterrent, for Paul states that one ought not serve two masters. If the spouses are united and of one mind in prayer, then they serve God. If they are not, then they serve incontinence, fornication, the Devil. Hence Tatian is regarded as the founder of the Encratites, who, by following in the steps of Saturninus and Marcion, established the principle of celibacy and reproached the first human beings for having joined, as man and woman, in sexual intercourse and for begetting children. Tatian is charged with blasphemy in particular for denying salvation to the first created man ($\pi\rho\omega\tau\acute{o}\pi\lambda\alpha\sigma\tau o\varsigma$).[36] In genuinely dualistic fashion, he seems to have separated law and gospel, as though the god of the law would have been an entirely different being from the God of the gospel, not merely because the god of the law instituted polygamy, but also because he instituted marriage as such. As the title of his book shows, to support his view Tatian doubtless also appealed mainly to the life of the savior himself.

Clement couples Julius Cassian of the school of Valentinus, and the reputed founder of the Docetae, with Tatian. Julian authored a text of his own, dealing with continence, in other words with eunuchism. He maintained that we ought not infer, from the male and female sexual organs, that God intended them to be used for sexual

---

35. It has not survived, but it is described by Clement in *Stromata* 3.12. Its Greek title was Περὶ τοῦ κατὰ τὸν σωτῆρα καταρτισμοῦ (On Perfection According to the Savior).

36. Eusebius, *Ecclesiastical History* 4.29.2. [*Ed.*] In 4.29.3 Eusebius says of Tatian, "As his own contribution [to Marcion and Saturninus], he denied the salvation of Adam."

intercourse. If this natural human configuration were from the God we seek to approach, then God would not have glorified eunuchs and the prophet would not have said that they are no unfruitful tree.[37] But if we did make that inference, then we would also certainly have had to criticize the savior, in that he should transform us, and should deliver us from that error and from the use of the sexual organs for intercourse. On this point Cassian appeals to a saying of the Lord contained in the Gospel of the Egyptians. When it became clear what Salome was asking, the Lord answered: "When you have trodden upon the garment of honor, and the two become one, and in the unity of male and female there will be neither male nor female."[38]

Tertullian

The extreme heretical position is the utter rejection of marriage. Those within the Christian Church just wanted to avoid this extreme. However, no sooner had they done so than they wanted just as much to retain essentially the same view.

No one stuck closer to that view than Tertullian, who, as a Montanist, of course also just presents the Christian view and moral stance from the specific perspective of one particular group. However, since he was already quite close to the Montanist way of thinking even before the Montanist period of his life, that only serves to show what different modifications and shadings there were within one and the same basic outlook. With the Gnostics and the Encratites demanding total continence and celibacy, the Christian ascetics aimed at something akin to this but within the bounds of marriage, where they sought to approximate the same perfection.

Using his finely-honed, sophisticated dialectic and the full force of his fiery rhetoric, Tertullian fought all out for single marriage (*Monogamie*).[39] He says there can be only one marriage; that anything beyond this, namely a second marriage, invites the same abhorrence of πορνεία (fornication) seen in the Gnostic and Encratic rejection of marriage as such. For the accursed Lamech, the first person to have two wives, this was fittingly regarded as a second crime in relation to Lamech's initial crime of homicide.[40] Tertullian says this not only about double marriage, for to him it is in principle

---

37. Isa 56:3. [*Ed.*] Whereas Deut 23:1 banned eunuchs from "the assembly of the Lord," Isa 56:3–5 accepts "the eunuchs who keep my sabbaths." V. 3: "do not let the eunuch say, 'I am just a dry tree.'"

38. Clement, *Stromata* 3.13. [*Ed.*] Quoted from Baur's German text, which is very close to the Greek of the original. This is the Greek Gospel of the Egyptians (early 2nd c.), as opposed to the later Coptic Gospel of the Egyptians. Salome, a follower of Jesus, is mentioned briefly in the canonical Gospels but appears more frequently in apocryphal writings. Her familiar question is, "How long shall death prevail?"

39. See Albert Hauber, "Tertullians Kampf gegen die zweite Ehe. Ein Beitrag zur christlichen Sittengeschichte," *Theologische Studien und Kritiken* 18 (1845), 607ff.

40. Tertullian, *On Monogamy*, ch. 4. [*Ed.*] The account of Lamech's crime and double marriage is in Gen 4:19 and 23–25. Lamech was a descendent of Cain, who killed his brother Abel. Tertullian says (ch. 4.): "But where the first crime is found—homicide, begun in fratricide—no crime was so worthy of the second place as a double marriage" (*ANF* 4:61).

all the same whether one has two wives in succession or concurrently. In either case it is just adultery.[41] A wife who has lived with her husband in discord and has lost him to death must be all the more bound to him by the Lord's proceedings. But if she has lived in peace with him who died, she must also remain married to him she did not want to be separated from; and she must continue to pray for his soul and make an offering on the anniversaries of his passing away, and hope to be reunited with him at the resurrection. However, should she marry again she would have the first husband in spirit and the second one in the flesh, and this is adultery, when a wife divides her consciousness between two men.[42]

The remarkable thing here is that the same arguments Tertullian marshals against second marriages also apply to first marriages. What he sees in marriage is just the sensual act in which the flesh satisfies its burning desire. Of course he is speaking initially of second marriage when he calls it a kind of fornication or violation (*species stupri*). When Paul says that married people seek to please each other, Paul has in mind the desires of the flesh, the same desires that give rise to fornication. Whoever looks at a woman with a view to marriage does so with a view to fornication. This obviously holds good for marriage as such. But, as Tertullian himself says, it is only the laws that differentiate matrimony and fornication, because of what the laws prohibit and not owing to the nature of the thing itself.[43] Tertullian himself concedes that he is undermining marriage as such by this argument. But he does not think it wrong to do so, because marriage is essentially the same thing as *stuprum*, or fornication. Hence what is best is the holiness of the original chastity that has nothing at all in common with fornication.

If this reason for continence already holds good for marriage itself, then how much more telling is it against second marriage? God is lenient about our marrying one time, and we must be grateful for that. But we must not abuse his leniency by sinking ever deeper below the first level [of chastity] and below the second level, that of marriage.[44] In his essay on monogamy, Tertullian is especially zealous in opposing

---

41. [*Ed.*] Baur next presents Tertullian's position as it varies from that of the Apostle Paul, who in Rom 7:1–4 writes: "Do you not know . . . that the law is binding on a person only during that person's lifetime? Thus a married woman is bound by the law to her husband as long as he lives; but if her husband dies, she is discharged from the law concerning the husband. Accordingly, she will be called an adulteress if she lives with another man while her husband is alive. But if her husband dies, she is free from that law, and if she marries another man she is not an adulteress."

42. *On Monogamy*, ch. 10.

43. *On Exhortation to Chastity*, ch. 9, says that intermingling of the flesh leads to marriage and fornication alike. *On Monogamy*, ch. 15: "For what is adultery but unlawful marriage?" [*ANF* 4:71].

44. *On Chastity*, ch. 9. In ch. 1, Tertullian distinguishes the following kinds and levels of virginity. "The first kind is virginity from one's birth. The second kind is virginity from one's second birth, that is, from the baptismal font. In the marital state the second virginity is kept pure by the marriage compact; or else in widowhood it continues by one's choice. A third level is monogamy when the partners subsequently renounce sexual intercourse. The first is the virginity of happiness: total ignorance of what one later wishes to be free of. The second is the virginity of virtue: being contemptuous of the power you fully know. The remaining kind is in never remarrying after the spouse has died; its glory

second marriage. Yet although he writes from a Montanist perspective, this is the very point on which the Montanist view did not essentially differ from the general Christian view. The exaggerations by the Montanists and the opposition they provoked were what first swept aside the prevailing bias against second marriage, whereas until then it was generally disapproved of and held to be at best a less scandalous form of adultery.[45]

In this view of second marriage—which must necessarily have in turn impacted the view of first marriage, and could even have it appear to be just a lesser evil as compared to fornication—we recognize the moral and ascetic spirit so characteristic of that time. Most of all we see how undeveloped the idea of morality still was for Tertullian himself. Moral teaching that also in turn permits what it forbids, and whose principles and precepts only seem, because of that inconsistency, to be enunciated as strictly universal (and therefore can also in turn leave room for lax application), inherently has a very ambiguous character. Even more striking is how, right in the midst of exhortations to control and stifle one's sensuous impulses, people hear the language of sensuality and find the most carnal concerns intermingled with what is apparently the most earnest zeal for Christian asceticism.

What sensuous expressions and depictions Tertullian uses in speaking about marriage! In all he says about first and second marriage, what catches our attention is the most ardent desire for the very thing he combats as a physical impulse. In his Montanist outlook, how far from any more exalted and moral concept of marriage he is when, in his own words, he locates the entire nature of marriage, what gives it continuity, in the most sensuous act of sexual intercourse![46] In insisting so forcefully that a first marriage is to be the end of this [unfortunate business], Tertullian makes a first marriage seem to be just a capitulation to sensuality. So one ought not enter into a second marriage, because such a sensual person is incapable of controlling sensuous desire other than by keeping far away from its object. Hence what we ordinarily take to be Tertullian's moral rigorism, or in any event to be a most estimable moral seriousness, really amounts to an admission of a lack of moral power.

We also see this so clearly from Tertullian's zealous insistence on virgins wearing veils. He demands that virgins be veiled as soon as sexual awareness awakens in

---

is in both virtue and moderation" [ANF 4:50]. See also *To His Wife* 1.8, where widowhood is placed higher than virginity and is more meritorious, because virginity finds it "easy not to crave what you do not know, and to turn away from what you never desired. More glorious is the continence aware of its own law, and which knows what it has seen" [ANF 4:43].

45. See, for instance, Athenagoras, *A Plea for the Christians*, ch. 33: "A second marriage is a specious kind of adultery." Whoever withdraws from his first wife, even though she be deceased, is a covert adulterer. He takes matters out of God's hands and dissolves the bond of sexual mutuality that unites flesh with flesh. Even the *Pseudo-Clementine Homilies*, from its basically monarchical perspective and its abhorrence of fornication, could only have affirmed one marriage alone. See my *Christliche Gnosis* (n. 34), 374ff. and 400.

46. *On Chastity*, ch. 9: "Marriage itself consists of that which is the essence of fornication" [ANF 4:55].

tandem with their physical maturation. From that point on they are no longer young maidens, but are instead women who, as the Apostle Paul enjoins, must be veiled.[47] What concepts of chastity and holiness must we assume such a zealot for decorum and modesty must have held? For we find Tertullian stating so forthrightly, and as something so self-evident, that pious men and young women cannot look at one another without blushing shamefully—that they cannot meet in public without becoming sexually aroused![48] So there must be a barrier separating men and young women. But if this barrier is simply in place, then chastity is sufficiently protected behind this rampart and one need not deal with the inner desire itself.[49]

Here we have once again the same superficial morality where the moral requirements demand nothing more than drawing an external boundary to distinguish what is moral from what is immoral. This is not someone having a moral mindset. Instead it just defines external conduct in terms of do's and don'ts, with these being the highest moral norms a person has to satisfy. Hence there are actions and personal states that by themselves count as moral. Chastity is not the chaste sensibility of the married couple, for only the virgins and eunuchs are truly chaste—those who completely abstain from those things that cannot even be done in the legal form of marriage without degrading the doer to a lower moral standing. Thus the unmarried or celibate life is now regarded as the most worthy life. It is preferable to marriage because people regard it as the most certain and most direct way one can come to God.[50] Everywhere else where sensuous desire is not overcome within but its object just warded off externally, the same enemy one has supposedly conquered crops up again repeatedly, just appearing in a different form, in order to assert its ancient rights.[51] The same is true in the present instance.

47. *On the Veiling of Virgins*, ch. 12: "Recognize the woman, yes recognize the wedded woman, by the evidence of her body and her spirit, by changes in her consciousness and in her flesh. These are the early signs of readiness for betrothal and marriage. Place an external veil on one who is to be kept safe within. Let those be covered above who are not to be exposed below" [*ANF* 4:35].

48. Ibid., ch. 2: "Seeing and being seen are alike lustful. It is the mark of a pious man to blush when seeing a maiden as it is the mark of a maiden when looked at by a man" [*ANF* 4:28]. Notice how strong sensuous impulses are in the passionate African nature of a Tertullian as well as of an Augustine!

49. Ibid., ch. 15: "True and total and pure virginity is wary of nothing more than it is of itself.... It takes refuge behind a veil over the head, a kind of helmet or shield to protect its virtue from being struck by temptation or injured by scandals" [*ANF* 4:36].

50. See Athenagoras, *A Plea for the Christians*, ch. 33: "You would find many among us, both men and women, growing old unmarried, in the hope of living in closer communion with God.... Remaining in virginity and being a eunuch are what brings people closer to God" [*ANF* 2:146]. See Tertullian, *To His Wife*, 1.6: "How many are there who set the seal (of virginity) on their flesh from the moment they are baptized? How many by mutual consent set aside the marital obligation, and are eunuchs by choice because they long for the heavenly kingdom?" [*ANF* 4:42]. See also *On the Apparel of Women*, chs. 2 and 10.

51. [*Ed.*] Baur is alluding to the ancient custom of referring to the Devil as the Enemy, who in virtue of human sinfulness has rights over, or ownership of, human sinners. However, Baur is also simply making here the general observation that a temptation one has not overcome but just suppressed will

Those virgins who seemingly had forever renounced marriage also still wanted to marry and live in wedded intercourse. Although earthly marriage held no attraction for them, in its stead they even more dearly wanted to be brides of heaven, that is *nuptae Deo* (brides of God) or *nuptae Christo* (brides of Christ). This "being married" to God or to Christ was already now a very prevalent notion. The pious imagination of an age enthusiastically in favor of continence was very much absorbed in endowing heavenly marriage with everything that could serve as a substitute for the foregone joys of earthly marriage.[52] What is even more striking is how sensual concerns thrust their way into the ascetic practices themselves. In Cyprian's day it apparently was not uncommon for ascetics to live together in sexual intimacy, in order to dedicate themselves to the ascetic life and, as they supposed, to [learn to] suppress sensual impulses more forcefully by the very procedure of exciting them. This intimacy was nevertheless just said to have the character of a spiritual communion.[53] Apparently it was the clergy who exposed their own moral standing to such a dangerous test.

CLERICAL CELIBACY

The dualistic worldview so deeply ingrained in Christianity could only regard evil as the impure character of matter. So it could only locate the utmost moral requirement

---

reappear when the desired object is present.

52. Tertullian, *To His Wife* 1.4: "They prefer to be wedded to God. They dedicate their beauty and their youth to God. They live with him; they converse with him; they do everything in relation to him, day and night. They allot their prayers to the Lord as dowries. As often as they desire it, they receive his approbation as marital gifts. Thus they have gained for themselves an eternal gift from the Lord. While on earth and by abstaining from marriage, they are already counted as members of the angelic family. (Tertullian now speaks directly to his wife:) By training yourself to emulate the example set by these women, in spiritual affection you will rid yourself of the concupiscence of the flesh. The gaining of immortal blessings will compensate for the abolition of temporal and fleeting desires for beauty and youth" [*ANF* 4:41]. See also *Exhortation to Chastity*, ch. 13. In *On the Veiling*, ch. 16, he writes: "Be somewhat misleading as to your inner thoughts, in order to exhibit the truth to God alone. [*Baur interpolates*: By veiling her head the virgin presents herself outwardly as being what she is not in herself, inwardly in her own consciousness, where she is a *mulier*, a woman.] Yet you do not mislead about being a bride, for you are wedded to Christ and have given over your flesh to him, have pledged your maturity to him. Proceed in accord with the will of your betrothed. Christ, who bids the betrothed and the wives of others to be veiled, expects this even more from his own" [*ANF* 4:37].

53. According to Eusebius, *Ecclesiastical History* 7.30, these are the "συνείσακτοι or spiritual sisters, as the Antiochenes call them" [LCL, *Eusebius*, 2:220–21]. From Cyprian's *Epistle* 61 we see how this sort of asceticism was practiced in an unchaste and shameless fashion. He speaks of "virgins who have confessed that they have slept with men [in fact, with deacons] yet declare that they are chaste." Cyprian denounces such practices. "What shall Christ and our Lord and judge think when he sees his virgin, dedicated to him and destined for his holiness, lying with another? How indignant and angry is he? . . . Since it behooves everyone to by all means keep discipline, it is all the more correct for overseers and deacons to adhere to this themselves. . . . For how can they oversee the integrity and continence of others if the corruption and the teachings of sin initially proceed from themselves?" [*ANF* 5:357–58]. From the prohibitions of it we see that this unchaste practice continued.

in the tenet that everything defiling spirit, because of its contact with matter, must be cut off from the life of the spirit, must be expunged from it.

On this view of things marriage could only be seen as reprehensible, inasmuch as it is an element of physical and carnal life. On the other hand, however, spirit and matter, or spirit and the flesh, are so closely connected and the two spouses exist so essentially as one, that even the strictest dualistic outlook cannot put asunder what God has joined together. Thus however strictly one held fast to the antithesis as an abstract, universal principle, in the matter of practical life its impact always had to be mitigated. The only way to harmonize the two concerns was of course to concede the abstract principle while not turning one's back on the needs of practical life. There had to be a specific demarcation showing where each of these concerns had its own legitimacy and application.

This is the basis for the distinction so important for the history of Christian ethics, between a higher morality and a lower morality. It is also the basis for the principle that became of practical significance especially owing to the issue of marriage: that, even when one chooses not to accomplish the utmost moral task, there still remains a sphere of life in which one has the moral capacity to satisfy the requirements of Christian morality. As the Christian life gradually became more lax in practice, there naturally had to be wider scope for meeting lesser and subsidiary expectations, instead of striving for absolute perfection.

Whereas initially marriage seemed, as such, to be a concession to practical life, later on the prejudice against second and even more marriages faded away.[54] Also, people even thought it possible to establish an equilibrium between the more and less strict tendencies, in the form of two coexisting groups that had equal moral justification but different roles for their lives. Of course if a moral aristocracy or elite was to form within the moral domain, what was more natural than that it be most closely linked to the aristocracy emerging as the church hierarchy took shape? If celibacy counted as the greatest moral perfection, then it would be preeminently the attribute of those in the hierarchy. However, since the hierarchy itself was just taking shape, that process could not begin with what is best or highest, even in moral terms. So it was

---

54. The *Shepherd* of Hermas is already open to second marriage, but with a caveat: "There is no sin in marrying again.... If they remain unmarried, they gain greater honor and glory with the Lord; but if they marry, they do not sin" (Commandment 4.4 [*ANF* 2:22]). Yet Tertullian speaks angrily about that "spurious shepherd of adultery" and his "scriptures, which alone love adultery" and have been judged "false and adulterous by every council of churches, and a patroness of adultery's comrades" (*On Modesty* 10 and 20 [*ANF* 4:85 and 97]). Another striking statement of Tertullian's rigorism also aims at Hermas in this same passage (ch. 10): "Step forth you rope-walker of modesty and chastity and everything to do with the sanctity of sex, using a discipline of this kind, far from truth, walking suspended, balancing flesh with spirit, moderating the vital principle with faith, fearfully calming your eyes." The watchword here is: "God is good. He favors his own, not the pagans. A second repentance awaits you, for you will go from being an adulterer to being a Christian." The shepherd depicted "on your chalice" is a "prostituter of the Christian sacrament, deserving to be both the idol of drunkenness and the refuge of adultery, like a chalice from which you sip nothing of good cheer but the onset of the second repentance" (*On Modesty*, 10 [*ANF* 4:84–85]).

quite natural, at a time when a second marriage counted as a form of adultery, that the leaders and heads of the Christian congregations be required, above all, to refrain from marrying a second time. The Pastoral Epistles attribute to the Apostle Paul the rule that the ἐπίσκοπος (bishop) is to be married only once.[55] This is specified in the church discipline as it took shape in the course of the second century. Thus the purity and holiness of the church seemed to require this rule.[56] So second marriage was allowed for one group and prohibited for the other group.

But what was the general view of marriage underlying this difference? Tertullian could appeal, on solid grounds, to the fact that Christians in general have a priestly character, when he argued against those holding that allowing second marriages follows from the Apostle Paul, who did not forbid them for everyone but only for a specific class of Christians, the bishops. Tertullian said that all Christians are indeed priests in the same way; that accordingly the precept governing the leaders, and those among them who are the heads of the congregations, simply expresses what should hold good as the general norm for everyone.[57] But why, in its opposition to Montanism, did the Roman Church not then claim that the second marriage it contended was admissible, was equally consistent and generally applicable for it? It still could not decide to do that because its view of the holiness of the celibate group—a view not just originating with Montanism but one it had itself expressed in most specific terms—was so deeply rooted in the general consciousness at this time that one could not so easily part with it.[58]

Hence a truly Catholic accommodation served to hold the higher morality and the lower morality together. Neither one kind nor the other was said to be the norm for everyone. Each held good in one specific sphere of the church's life, where the absolute requirement for all, which had to be thought of as really expressing moral

55. [Ed.] Titus 1:6-7: ". . . someone who is blameless, married only once, whose children are believers, not accused of debauchery and not rebellious. For a bishop, as God's steward, must be blameless . . . ."

56. Tertullian, *To His Wife* 1.7: "The discipline of the church and the precept of the apostle declare how detrimental to faith and disruptive to holiness are second marriages . . . . God's altar is to be set forth as pure. The halo [luster of light] encircling the church is described as its holiness." The pagans also give this significance to celibacy. "For the Devil, this signifies envy. It is unlawful for the current ruler, the pontifex maximus, to marry a second time" [ANF 4:43].

57. *On Monogamy*, ch. 12: "It was therefore fitting that the entire form of the community's discipline be set out in advance, emphasized in a certain way as a future edict for everyone—one for their overseers that they must observe too. Also so those leaders will not be flattered in having honor or license because of occupying a privileged position" [ANF 4:69].

58. Of course there were also many leaders of congregations who had married for a second time. In *On Monogamy*, ch. 12, Tertullian asks: "How many with second marriages preside in your churches?" [ANF 4:69]. The *Philosophumena* (Part 3, n. 11) confirms this. In 9.12.22 (p. 290) its author says that under Callistus "there began to be bishops and presbyters and deacons appointed among the clergy who were married two or three times. And if someone was married while a member of the clergy, such a miscreant would remain in the clergy as if not having sinned" [ET 654-55]. According to Döllinger, *Hippolytus und Callistus* (n. 15), 140ff., the question at issue here was whether the second marriage occurred before or after one was baptized.

consciousness, was accordingly scaled down to apply only to some. Thus bishops were not permitted to marry a second time whereas the laity were allowed to do so. Yet since it was already a concession to merely keep bishops from marrying a second time, as opposed to the principle of marrying just once, there was pressure from the older view to oppose even single marriage for bishops. As the church increasingly became hierarchical in structure, a celibate life also increasingly came to be expected of the bishops and of clergy in general.

Already at the time of the Council of Nicaea, the bishops gathered there wanted to make it a general law of the church that priests—the bishops, presbyters, and deacons—have to abstain from all marital bonds. The Egyptian bishop Paphnutius, who led an ascetic life himself, therefore made a very strong impression when he came forward expressly as a defender of the honor and dignity of the married state. He correctly foresaw the disadvantages for the church were such a strict mandate of celibacy, one not all were capable of obeying, to become a formal law of the church. Thus the individual could freely choose whether or not to retain his marital status. The Council just ruled, according to the ancient tradition of the church, that someone gaining clerical rank is no longer allowed to marry, but those clerics who are already married are not required to divorce their wives.[59] However, given the higher status of the clergy in the church, and the never-surrendered view that the celibate life is a holy life, the only outcome could be that, once celibacy had become an issue, it sooner or later had to become something required in practice.

MORTAL SINS AND VENIAL SINS

The moral concepts in this time period have the same general character as the features we have emphasized in discussing marriage. In its abstract generality, the moral requirement is indeed something commanded absolutely. However, in its practical application it retains merely a relative force because the moral domain gets subdivided and limited in an arbitrary fashion. When it comes to moral action, one and the same deed may be either good or reprehensible, depending on the particular circle of the Christian life in which it occurs. For instance, the laity are allowed to marry a second time, but clergy are forbidden to do so.

A norm like this for moral judgments can only apply where moral action is generally something apart from one's own disposition or state of mind; where actual moral worth is located not so much in the inner state of one's disposition as it is in the outer aspects and particular properties of the specific, individual act. Thus there are set categories for the classification of specific acts according to their moral status, wholly apart from the disposition of the subject who performs them. So, Christian ethics now already knows both which acts are utterly sinful as such, and which acts

---

59. Socrates, *Ecclesiastical History* 1.11.

inherently have objective moral value, as good works. The Montanists introduced the division of sins into mortal sins and venial sins.⁶⁰ This division comes mainly from the same moral tendency we have been discussing: from the effort to set bounds to the absolute nature of the moral demand, by having it refer to only a certain part of the moral domain, or to only a certain class of moral acts. [However,] it is a feature of the religious character of Christian ethics that acts contrary to the moral law are regarded as sins to be forgiven only if the acting subject is morally disposed.

But when specific transgressions, such as the so-called deadly sins, are then said without qualification to be the kind of sins for which forgiveness is not impossible, yet must be doubtful, because forgiveness is left to God alone in this case, then that leaves the absolute concept of sin confined to a certain class of sins. Then all acts not falling in this category hardly count as sinning per se, and in principle are no longer to be looked upon as sin at all; so divine forgiveness can be assumed as a matter of course. However, if forgiveness of sins once becomes taken so lightly, even just for one specific kind of sin, then that can only result in this easy forgiveness getting extended to more and more sins. In church practice, even the forgiveness of the deadly sins increasingly became a less thorny affair than one would have supposed from the retention of the old nomenclature. As we of course see today, especially in the Roman Church, when it became easier to gain forgiveness of sins, even in troubling cases, then Christian ethics increasingly had to be taken less seriously.

As we have already seen, the sin of adultery and fornication, understood in the Montanist sense, was the first of the deadly sins for which the gates of forgiveness for sins were opened in the Roman Church. No doubt Tertullian is speaking of Zephyrinus, the bishop of Rome, as the one who issued such a repugnant and imperious edict as "a *pontifex maximus*, or bishop of bishops."⁶¹ Tertullian looked upon the leniency shown to adulterers as inconsistent and halfhearted if it did not also extend in the same way to idolaters and murderers, and thus completely undermine all moral discipline.⁶² The successor to Zephyrinus removed this inconsistency. As we learn from the

---

60. See Tertullian, *On Modesty*, ch. 2: "Some will be remissible, and some will not. So, no one will be in doubt that some deserve chastisement, and some deserve condemnation. Every sin can be paid for, either by forgiveness or by punishment: forgiveness after reproof, punishment by condemnation. . . . This way of distinguishing sins affects the possibility of penitence. Those that are venial are remissible, and those that are unpardonable are irremissible" [*ANF* 4:76–77]. In ch. 19 Tertullian says: "We are all liable for some sins that we commit every day. For no one is immune from being angry without cause or staying angry beyond sunset [cf. Eph 4:26]; from physical violence; from carelessly speaking evil, swearing rashly, breaking one's word, or lying because of shame or urgency. We face great temptations in business, in our official duties, in making profits, in our way of life, in what we see and hear. If none of these were pardonable no one would be saved. They will be pardoned by the entreaties of Christ our Lord. Their contraries, graver and more destructive, are unpardonable: murder, idolatry, fraud, apostasy, blasphemy, and of course adultery and fornication, and any others that may 'violate the Lord's temple.' Christ will not plead on behalf of these other sins" [*ANF* 4:97].

61. See above, p. 232, and *On Modesty*, ch. 1 [*ANF* 4:74].

62. *On Modesty*, ch. 5: "What do you do, most easygoing and most humane discipline? You are either morally bound to be lenient to all sins (for "blessed are the peacemakers," Matt 5:9) or, if not to

writings of an unidentified opponent of Callistus, even before he became the bishop of Rome, Callistus drew up a general regimen for the forgiveness of sins that completely set aside the previous way of thinking about so-called mortal sins. Now everyone who had committed such a sin was, after doing penance, completely free to resume his place in the fellowship of the church.[63] This was not a temporary arrangement. Instead

---

all, then morally bound to our side. Do you condemn the idolater and the murderer for all time, yet welcome the adulterer, who is mentioned after the idolater and before the murderer, but is the colleague of each?" [*ANF* 4:78]. [*Ed.*] The Roman Catholic and Lutheran Churches follow Deut 5:17–18 in placing the commandments in this order. The Jewish and other Christian traditions place the ban on murder before that on adultery, as in Exod 20:13–14.

63. See *Philosophumena* (Part 3, n. 11), 9.12.20–24 (p. 290 [ET 654–57]). The writer of this text says that Callistus "founded a school and in this way taught in opposition to the church. He first hatched a plan to permit human pleasures. He proclaimed to all those under his authority that their sins were forgiven." He said that when a Christian sins, "the sin is not counted against him if he runs to the school of Callistus." He declared this with particular reference to those who turned from a heresy or a sectarian congregation to the Catholic Church. He also taught that "if a bishop sins in any respect—even a mortal sin—he need not be deposed." He allowed the clergy to be married on the terms we mentioned just above. Finally, he even allowed a single, nubile young woman to freely marry a man, whether someone free-born and poorer, or a slave, and so contract a marriage not recognized under Roman law. See Döllinger, *Hippolytus und Kallistus* (n. 15), 125ff., which attempts to uncover the factual basis for these charges against Callistus and to justify the truth in them from circumstances at that time. According to *Philosophumena* 9.12.22–23, Callistus sought support for his new theory in passages such as Rom 14:4 and Matt 13:29–30, and with reference to Noah's ark, which grouped together "dogs, wolves, crows, everything clean and unclean," as "a symbol of the church." He pointed to and utilized everything he could in support of his dogmas, and that is mainly how he increased his followers. In this same context the *Philosophumena* speaks of an Alcibiades from Apamea in Syria (p. 294 [ET 658–65]). In Callistus' day this Alcibiades came to Rome with a book of revelation bearing the name of Elchasi, and he proclaimed a new forgiveness of sins based on this authoritative source. This forgiveness was supposedly received by being "baptized a second time into the name of the great and highest God and in the name of his Son, the great King," and by calling upon "the seven witnesses who are named in this book (heaven, water, the holy spirits, the angels of prayer, oil, salt, and earth)." A person's formal statement is: "I testify by these seven witnesses that I will no longer sin. I will not commit adultery, I will not steal, I will not harm, I will not be greedy, I will not hate, I will not deal treacherously, nor take pleasure in any evil" (9.15.6 [ET 668–69]). Alcibiades states: "Again I say, O adulterers, adulteresses, and false prophets—if you want to convert so that your sins will be forgiven and so that there will be peace for you and a portion with the righteous—the moment that you hear this book, be baptized a second time with your clothes" (9.15.3 [ET 666–67]). The information in the *Philosophumena* and in Epiphanius, *Against Heresies* 19.30 and 53, shows unmistakably that the Elchasites had an essentially Ebionite cast. Especially characteristic in this context is what Eusebius reports (*Ecclesiastical History* 6.38), from a homily of Origen on Psalm 82, as the teaching of an Elchasite: that "it entirely rejects the Apostle Paul." The writer of the *Philosophumena* tells us (p. 293; 9.13.5) that he strenuously opposed the new teachings of Alcibiades. So this Alcibiades is also a new figure in the controversy that for a long time pervaded both ethics and the trinitarian doctrine. It is remarkable how the Montanists, Tertullian, the writer of the *Philosophumena* (whether Hippolytus or someone else), and the Novatians all maintain in similar fashion that two elements belong to the truly orthodox concept of Christianity, namely, strict church discipline, in other words the concept of a church fellowship excluding, as far as possible, everything unholy, and also the concrete concept of the personal Logos; whereas those taking an opposed view in this case, specifically Callistus and the Elchasite or Ebionite figure Alcibiades, are lax about both of these points. The Ebionites certainly also reject the doctrine of the λόγος θεός (Divine Word). See A. Ritschl on the sect of the Elchasites, in the *Zeitschrift für historische Theologie* (1853) 573ff., and his *Enstehung der altkatholischen Kirche*, 2nd ed. (Bonn,

it became church practice from this time on, for soon after this it was reinforced in the deliberation about allowing those who had fallen from grace to resume their place in the church—those who had lapsed during the persecutions in the time after Callistus.

The document addressed to Cyprian, the bishop of Carthage, from the presbyters and deacons of Rome, provides the best information about the views and practices of the Roman Church regarding lapsed Christians. They wrote it while filling the episcopal seat of Rome after the martyrdom of Fabian [in 250]. According to this document the issue was no longer taking lapsed Christians back into the fellowship of the church, but only taking care that the church not heal these wounds too hastily, without requiring sufficient penance. This then passed muster as "the severity of old, the ancient faith, the old discipline." The writer of the epistle was the Novatian who did of course actually return later on to the strict penitential practices of old, but could only uphold them as a schismatic.[64]

GOOD WORKS

Good works stand in direct contrast to mortal sins. Good works are good in themselves, whereas mortal sins are sins without qualification. In good works, the acts one is duty-bound to perform are very much confined to a specific class of actions, for instance prayer, fasting, or almsgiving. Thus what does not belong to one or another of such categories seems to lack definite moral value.

Here we see very clearly and distinctly how the general moral norm, defining what moral actions is in this case, is not so much the qualitative measure of a person's disposition but rather the quantitative measure of what he or she does. Although each Christian is required to perform a greater or lesser quantity of good works, the greatest good works cannot be obligatory for everyone. However, someone can do more than he or she is actually obliged to do; and since every good act is a morally meritorious act, there are acts that are not merely meritorious but are even super-meritorious, or supererogatory in nature.

A very significant point about the moral teaching taking shape within the Catholic Church is the fact that this quite important and deeply rooted distinction regarding good works was drawn by the first writer from the Roman Church to spell out the domain of Christian morality. In the *Shepherd* of Hermas, in the fifth similitude of book three, the shepherd appears to Hermas in the form of an angel. Hermas is sitting on a mountain during a fast, and the angel instructs him about the true kind of fasting, using the example of a worker in a vineyard who does more than the master has directed him to do. This example shows that obeying God's commandments is the true fast.[65] The interpretation of the parable includes this statement: "Keep the com-

---

1857), 234. Also see A. Hilgenfeld in the *Zeitschrift für wissenschaftliche Theologie* 1 (1858) 417.

64. See Cyprian's *Epistles*, no. 31; cf. 52.

65. Book 3, Similitude 5, ch. 1: "God does not desire such an empty fasting. Fasting in this way

mandments of the Lord and you will be approved, and be counted among those who obey his commandments. If you do any good beyond what the Lord has commanded, you will gain greater glory for yourself, and God will honor you more that you would otherwise have been honored."[66]

We see that this is the typical moral mindset at this time, not just because a writer such as Hermas speaks of *adjicere aliquid boni* ("adding some other goodness"), but also because Origen himself treats Christian moral acts from the perspective of this twofold undertaking. Origen writes[67] that as long as someone merely does what he is supposed to do, that is, what he is commanded to do, then he is "an unprofitable servant" (Luke 17:10). But if he does something in addition to what he is commanded to do, then he is not merely an unprofitable servant, for he is called a "good and trustworthy servant" (Matt 25:21). In 1 Cor 7:25–40 the Apostle Paul gives us an example of surpassing what is commanded by doing more than one is obliged to do. Concerning the commandments, regarding marriage, someone who preserves his or her virginity is therefore no "unprofitable servant" but is instead a "good and faithful servant." The same is true when the Apostle Paul says (1 Cor 9:14–15) he has "made no use" of the right, ordained by God, that "those who proclaim the gospel should get their living by the gospel."

Despite the fact that it runs counter to the spirit of the gospel to suppose that there are such super-meritorious moral acts, several forces working together made this the natural conclusion. Its basis lay, first and foremost, in the way of looking at things we already mentioned, which formulated the issue as: *adjicere aliquid boni, addere aliquid praeceptis* ("adding some other precept is to add some other goodness"). This very strikingly expresses the quantitative perspective from which moral acts get considered. With the imposition of moral demands that are hardly able to be met with strict consistency in practice, such that they cannot be binding in the same way for everybody—as was naturally the case with respect to marriage—then this by itself gives rise not merely to the difference in standing between two classes of people, but also to a twofold virtue and thus a twofold merit. One virtue and merit suffices for ordinary people's lives, and the higher virtue and merit is for those who have within them the impulse and the calling to not rest content with meeting the norms for ordinary folk. Also, here moral action as such is wholly oriented to the church's rules for one's external life, to the effort to make specific precepts the norms governing moral affairs, to sort out acts into specific and distinct categories. This latter tendency had to underlie the supposition that a person could of course always do more than meet the external

---

contributes nothing to living a righteous life. Instead, offer to God this kind of fast: Doing no evil in your life and serving the Lord with a pure heart; obeying his commandments, walking in his precepts, and letting no evil arise in your heart; believing in God. If you do these things and fear him, and abstain from every evil thing, you will live unto God. If you do these things you will observe a great fast, one acceptable to God" [*ANF* 2:33].

66. [*Ed.*] In ch. 3 (*ANF* 2:34).

67. In his *Commentary on Romans* 3.3

requirements, but that meeting them within a specific setting would be meritorious enough to satisfy the requisites for Christian virtue and perfection.

THE IDEA OF THE CHURCH AS THE PRINCIPLE OF MORAL ACTION

While the essence of Christian morality is located primarily in external, everyday actions, this morality also receives its distinctive mark in particular from the fact that the actions it involves are not just ones prescribed by the church, but also ones forming a unified whole in the idea of the church.

In this regard it is noteworthy that, in the *Shepherd* of Hermas, all of a Christian's moral conduct is already spelled out using the idea of the church. The church is portrayed by the image of a tower with seven women standing around it and supporting it, as the Lord commands. The first woman is Faith, and God's chosen ones are blessed because of their faith. The daughter of Faith is Continence, and whoever follows her example by refraining from all evil works will be happy in life. The other five form a succession of daughters. Their names are Simplicity, Innocence, Modesty, Discipline, and Love. Continence springs from Faith, Simplicity from Continence, Innocence from Simplicity, Modesty from Innocence, Discipline and Love from Modesty. Whoever serves these seven, and is able to do as they do, will dwell in the tower with God's saints.[68] The ninth similitude elaborates on this same theme. Here twelve virgins serve to portray the church. The first four are the highest: Faith, Continence, Power, and Patience. Following them in order are: Simplicity, Innocence, Purity, Cheerfulness, Truth, Understanding, Harmony, and Love. Standing over against them are twelve women dressed in black: Faithlessness, Intemperance, Unbelief, Lasciviousness, Sadness, Wickedness, Desire, Anger, Falsehood, Folly, Arrogance, and Hatred. All the stones brought to build the tower that are not carried into it by these virgins and through the unshakable portal that is the Son of God, are rejected. The women dressed in black carry back to the place they came from, those stones declared to be unfit for this purpose.[69]

So, in realizing the idea of the church within itself, Christianity essentially consists in the practice of those virtues whose sum and substance is obeying the divine commandments. Faith, which stands at the apex of the virtues as a whole, is simply the root of virtue. Thus the gospel's concept of faith takes a back seat to the overriding focus on the practical and moral aspect. So in Hermas's sense, faith just amounts to the precept that precedes all the other mandated virtues, believing in one God who has created everything from nothing. This already expresses the fundamental idea of Catholicism, that the essence of Christianity is not so much faith as it is works, in other words, putting into practice the virtues, which, as the universal norms for moral

---

68. [*Ed.*] This account is Baur's abbreviated paraphrase of Bk. 1, Vision 3, ch. 8 (*ANF* 2:15–16).

69. Bk. 3, Similitude 9, ch. 15 [*ANF* 2:49].

conduct, simply gain their Christian character from the fact that the church (appearing to this end in the *Shepherd* of Hermas) is what assigns them this status and issues the relevant precepts in the form of divine commands.

The Purer Moral Principles of Clement of Alexandria

In all these phenomena, what typifies Christian morality in the period we are discussing is that its predominant tendency has the marks of subsequent Catholicism. On the other hand, however, there are also features in which we recognize the purer moral spirit of evangelical Christianity.

Among the church fathers whose views and principles call for the most consideration here, no one stands out more than Clement of Alexandria. Of course he is one of the main representatives of the extreme tendency in his day to divorce oneself from everything of a material nature, since in his own version of Gnosis he established the ideal of a perfection in which the supreme goal is the divinization of human beings by their becoming completely free from emotional states or passions.[70] Yet we see even more evident in Clement the inner power of the gospel's truth. For he was very keen on preserving a healthy sense of how Christianity in practice stays as far away as it can from the extreme position apparent in the pronounced one-sidedness of the ascetic mentality in his day.

None of the other church fathers has a view of marriage that is as sensible as Clement's. He declared that eunuchism is a special gift of God, and ascribed particular

---

70. [*Ed*. In *Stromata* 4.21, Clement presents his description of "the perfect man," or Gnostic.] *Baur*: See, for instance, *Stromata* 4.22: "Becoming like God, as far as we can, is guarding the mind in relation to material things. For the changeable state of mind arises from excessive desire for material things" [*ANF* 2:435]. But it is equally characteristic of Clement that he regards engaging in moral actions as superior to all that is achieved by withdrawing, in negative fashion, into oneself and away from material things, and being self-absorbed in one's own mind. What is truly Gnostic is taking up that moral standpoint energetically in practical terms. He regards this as the positive factor that must be added to the negative feature of withdrawal. See *Stromata* 6.7, where he states that the Gnostic soul is sanctified "by withdrawing from earthly fires, and the body in which it dwells being purified, gaining the purity of a holy temple. But the first purification, that of the soul in the body, is abstinence from evil things. Some consider this to be perfection, and it is in truth the perfection of the ordinary believer, the Jew and the Greek. But after this, which others regard as perfection, the righteousness of the Gnostic is his proceeding to actively doing good. For the one whose more forceful righteousness proceeds to doing good, his perfection consists in the set habits of doing good in likeness to God" [*ANF* 2:494]. In this same sense *Stromata* 4.6 enjoins that one does not become righteous solely by not doing evil, for, according to the Lord, one becomes perfect by doing good. The [Gnostic's] spirit goes back into itself, but only in order to act outwardly, and all the more energetically, in one's moral conduct.

honor to monogamy, but he did not object to second marriage. He took a stand against those who called marriage "fornication" and appealed to the example of Christ, who did not marry. Clement said that the Lord did not marry because the church was his bride; that, not being the ordinary sort of man, he had no need of any flesh-and-blood spouse. He likewise did not have to beget offspring since, as the Son of God, he abides eternally. However, Christ himself said that "what God has joined together, let no one separate" (Matt 19:6). Nor did the apostles reject marriage. Peter and Philip had children, Philip gave his daughter in marriage, and Paul too did not shrink from speaking of a σύζυγος, or "loyal companion," in Philippians 4:3.[71]

There is no virtue in being a eunuch if one does not enter into this state from love for God.[72] Clement does not give unqualified preference to marriage over the unmarried life. But he does recognize the moral import of marriage, because it shapes a sphere of social life all its own and a setting for one's moral activity. In modeling himself after the apostles, the true Gnostic or perfect man (*der Vollkommene*) truly shows his manly qualities by not choosing a solitary life. He surpasses other men by being married, begetting children and seeing to household affairs, while those cares do not draw him away from the love for God; for instead he withstands all the temptations arising from having children and a wife, domestic servants and possessions. Someone who has no household affairs remains free from many temptations, since he makes provision for himself alone and is of course able to attend to his own salvation. Yet in managing the household, the married man is superior since he is in fact a microcosm of the power that truly sustains the universe (*die wahren allgemeine Vorsehung*).[73]

Thus in treating marriage Clement returns to one's attitude in choosing either married life or single life. In the same way, in his own treatise entitled *Who Is the Rich Man That Shall Be Saved?*, Clement makes everything depend on one's personal attitude toward the physical goods one possesses, and the use one makes of them. The only truly rich person is someone who is rich in virtues and can live purely and faithfully in any station in life. The person not truly rich is someone rich in material terms, whose life relies on external possessions that come and go, that pass from one person to another and ultimately to nobody at all.[74] Thus Clement views life's various circumstances, and these issues especially important at that time, from a general perspective that is authentically moral and focused on the concerns of Christianity in practice. For instance, he states his view of martyrdom along the same lines. While greatly valuing martyrdom, he nevertheless disapproves of the fanatical craving for

---

71. [*Ed.*] Phil 4:2–3: "I urge Euodia and I urge Syntyche to be of the same mind in the Lord. Yes, and I ask you also, my loyal companion, help these women, for they have struggled beside me in the work of the gospel . . . ." Most commentators assume the reference is to a man, but Baur seems to imply that Paul's companion was a woman.

72. *Stromata* 3.1 and 6.

73. [*Ed.*] The foregoing is Baur's paraphrase of the key part of *Stromata* 7.12 (cf. *ANF* 2:543).

74. [*Ed.*] Baur's paraphrase from *Who Is the Rich Man*, ch. 19 (*ANF* 2:596).

it that recklessly puts one in jeopardy. Thus, unlike Tertullian, he does not so totally condemn someone who flees in a time of persecution.[75] For Clement the essential feature of martyrdom is that the martyr does, with notable success, cleanse himself of sins and willingly suffers all the consequences of professing belief in Christianity.[76] Because Clement was free from Montanist fanaticism and one-sidedness, as well as from belief that the parousia and the world's end were at hand, he was not in danger of having those positions and beliefs derail him from correctly understanding life's moral relationships and circumstances.[77]

---

75. See Tertullian's *On Fleeing from Persecution* [ANF 4:116–25].

76. Book 4 of the *Stromata* has an extensive discussion of martyrdom. See especially chs. 9 and 10.

77. What a contrast there is between Clement's views of marriage and having children, and those of Tertullian! In *To His Wife* 1.5 [ANF 4:41–42], Tertullian writes: "People's additional reason for marriage is their concern to have posterity and the most disagreeable pleasure of children. We are indifferent to this. Why should we be eager to have children when, after having them, and in view of the imminent catastrophe, we wish to send them ahead of us (to glory) and wish that we ourselves be taken out of this most wicked world?" Everything pertaining to married life is just "a burden of being married." So why should one marry, why have children, why get involved at all in those life circumstances that are the actual arena for moral action? Thus "flight from this age" becomes a flight from the world of moral action.

More Lenient Moral Practices

The moral spirit of an age is expressed in its prevailing views and principles. Yet whatever the nature of the views and principles prevalent in the general consciousness of an age might be, it is particularly important for us to have the correct measuring stick for appraising its moral character: how these views and principles are operative in practice, in everyday life. Is the predominant concern to uphold them in their original, rigorous form, or is it to become increasingly lenient?

As we have abundantly seen, the Montanist period was a critical time, for Montanism can simply be viewed as a reaction against the increasingly less strict practices in the lives of Christians. Tertullian's writings about matters of Christian practice at this time are, in this respect, an especially fertile source for the history of Christian ethics. From them we see the reasons behind the effort to defend and justify relaxing the former strictness, and the factors most obviously leading to the new, less restrictive approach.

As an example, the enthusiasm for martyrdom, where the moral force animating Christians reached its peak, had already cooled down quite a bit by Tertullian's day. We can conclude, from Tertullian's denunciation of those who fled in the face of persecution, that this was a common practice. People hardly had any reservations about using bribery or other means for avoiding persecution by the pagan authorities, and even entire congregations, led by their clergy, had recourse to such a way out of trouble.[78] That there were such varied kinds of departures from the former strictness shows us that courage and steadfastness declined, so that what often even ensued was a relapse into paganism. On the whole, as the persecutions subsided and the Christians' lives were outwardly calm and peaceful, the virtues customarily thought of as especially meritorious in earlier times became ever more uncommon, and exactly opposite personal attributes took their place. Eusebius even makes a special point of this when, in discussing the transition to Diocletian's persecution of the Christians, he

---

78. Tertullian, *On Fleeing from Persecution*, ch. 13: "Whole churches have imposed tribute *en masse* on themselves. I do not know whether to grieve or be ashamed when Christians join the exempted soldiers and spies, among the hucksters and con men and bathhouse thieves and gamblers and pimps, in paying tribute. Did the apostles, foreseeing this, make the bishops free to rule happily by concealing this kind of management?" [*ANF* 4:125].

says[79] this persecution was punishment for the "sloth . . . envy and fierce railing against one another, warring among ourselves, . . . the hypocrisy and pretence" that he saw having made inroads among the Christians. Several well-known examples show that even bishops now already had the aristocratic arrogance and desire for hierarchical power that has been the hallmark of their position ever since.

The moral spirit of the Christian religion strictly and energetically opposed the concepts and viewpoints of the pagan world. Yet this opposition diminished with the passage of time, as the prevailing views and principles gradually became less restrictive, more lenient, and as people increasingly turned their attention, first and foremost, to what was feasible in practice and suited to their circumstances. We now have to look at the way the Christian cultus initially developed from this same perspective.

---

79. *Ecclesiastical History* 8.1 [LCL, *Eusebius*, 2:252–53].

The Christian Cultus

THE ORIGINAL ELEMENTS

When the Apostle Paul addresses those Galatian converts from paganism to Christianity who are now inclined "to turn back again to the . . . elemental spirits" (Gal 4:9) common to pagan and Jewish beliefs, he represents the extreme antithesis to pagan and Jewish forms of worship. He asks (vv. 8–11) how they can reconcile this with their Christian consciousness of God, this turning back to "the weak and beggarly elements" they had formerly served, and to "observing special days, and months, and seasons, and years" (v. 10). To him all this seems so unworthy of a Christian—taking a free spirit, conscious of its communion with God, and dragging it down to the elements and phenomena of the external and natural life of the physical world, by binding spirit to it as though it could only reach God through these intermediaries.

This would be a Christianity independent of all external elements, conscious of its purely spiritual content but appearing outwardly naked, devoid of all formal means of worship. Even in Celsus' day, the pagans found the most striking thing about Christians the fact that they seemed to lack all the things making religion possible: temples, altars, images.[80] A religion's cultus should present the idea of the religion and make it clear in a concrete way, especially as that cultus assumes a dignified and appealing form. So Christianity must have lacked the fundamental requisite of a beautiful cultus, if Christians thought they must represent Christ himself as undistinguished in appearance, indeed even as supposed to have been homely.[81] This originally Pauline character of the Christian cultus was very influential during the early centuries of the church, as the cultus took on a one-sidedly ascetic, spiritualistic and puritanical tone.

---

80. See above, p. 236. Also see Minucius Felix, *Octavius*, ch. 10, where the pagan Caecilius raises this very point, in the form of a question.

81. Justin, Tertullian, Origen, and Clement of Alexandria state this explicitly. See Clement, *The Instructor* 3.1: "The Spirit tells us, via Isaiah, that the Lord himself was uncomely" [*ANF* 2:272]. [*Ed.* Isa 53:2: "He had no form or majesty that we should look at him, nothing in his appearance that we should desire him."] Here, as elsewhere (see 33–34 above), the gospel account is augmented by passages from the prophets.

We see this from the decree of a Spanish synod forbidding murals because it regarded such portrayals of sacred themes as a degradation of what is holy[82]—this at a time when the Christian cultus had found its home in stately edifices.

THE EUCHARIST AND THE LOVE-FEAST

As opposed to paganism and Judaism, Christianity hardly seemed fitted for a cultus analogous to either of theirs. Yet the fundamental outlook and tendency of its religious consciousness did contain the elements for a cultus of its own.

The entire basis for the Christian cultus was the reverence that bound the Lord's first followers to him, and of course because he had a very momentous and emotion-filled impact on them when they were together with him for the last time. So Christians wanted to be together with him again and again, in the way the disciples were with him back then. As often as they gathered together, they sought to be present to the Lord who was still there in the circle of those who belonged to him. They could not be together with him without doing what he had done when he was together with his disciples for the last time.[83] They ate the bread as his body and drank the wine as his blood.

The Apostle Paul, who was the first one to report the Lord's words on this occasion, as Paul himself had received them from the Christian tradition, was far removed from what the later dogmatic concept of the sacrament read into these words, and what thus precipitated huge controversies and schisms. For Paul regarded the repetition of Jesus' words and actions as simply an act of remembrance said to proclaim his death until he comes again. This act of remembrance was to serve in place of his bodily presence, which his death had prevented. The Lord himself had declared that the bread and wine are his body and blood. They make him present to the disciples as he was when about to face his death, about to shed his blood in instituting a new covenant and giving his body for his disciples. The Apostle Paul portrays the bread that is broken and shared as the community, seen as the body of the Lord, inasmuch as one and the same bread, in which all share, is paralleled by the many members forming this community as bound to one another, as all together in the unity of one and the same communion or fellowship.[84]

At his meal with his disciples, Jesus began this act of institution with a prayer of thanksgiving. Thus the Christian celebration of the Last Supper is commonly referred to as the Eucharist ("thanksgiving"). The thanks given were of course primarily for the nourishing gifts of nature provided for such a shared meal. However, in light of Jesus' words of institution, nature's gifts of bread and wine, as the eucharistic elements, were

---

82. The Synod of Elvira (303) stated (in canon 36): "It is agreed that there should not be paintings in a church, either for study and adoration, or as representations on walls."

83. See above, p. 127.

84. See 1 Cor 10:16–17, and 12:27.

consecrated in a distinctive way. In describing this ceremony, Justin Martyr says[85] that the deacons assisting the presiding priest not only distributed the elements blessed by the eucharistic words, that is, the bread, and the wine mixed with water, to all who were present, but also took them to those who were not present.[86]

This same ceremony was also called the agape, or love-feast. The meal in remembrance of the Lord's death was also said to be a meal of the bond of love linking the apostles to one another. However, many things that at first and quite naturally belonged together, and of their own accord found their place in the ordinary course of life, could not be maintained subsequently in the same way when the community became larger. Thus the term "agape" got transferred to meals that were separate from the Eucharist, ones where people mutually contributed to the shared meal and avoided any distinguishing between rich and poor participants. It was supposed to promote enduring brotherly love and a shared spirit in the earliest communities of Jesus' followers. Thus two features originally in combination became separate, and each underwent changes in its own way. The agape ceremonies became looser affairs but also, by their misuse, deteriorated into being associations for Christian social life; whereas, through its liturgical procedures, the Eucharist took on its specifically ecclesiastical character.[87]

---

85. *First Apology*, chs. 66–67.

86. This of course shows that they attached the concept of a physical medium of salvation to the eucharistic bread consecrated as the Lord's body, because they preserved it to be partaken of at other times. According to Tertullian (*On Prayer*, ch. 19), this is "the Lord's body . . . received and reserved" [*ANF* 3:687]. The same meaning applies when Tertullian (in *To His Wife* 2.5) asks the Christian wife of a pagan: "Will your husband not know what you taste in secret before eating any food? And if he knows it is bread, does he not know it is that very bread it is said to be?" [*ANF* 4:46–47]. (If you tell him it is bread, he will not believe it is what you say it is. He will not regard it as what, according to the letter from Pliny the Younger, the Christians gave assurance that it was—"ordinary and harmless food.")

87. We see from 1 Cor 11:20ff. that the meals bringing Christians together to celebrate the Eucharist were also love-feasts. The Apostle Paul says that the current divisions he admonishes the Corinthians about made it impossible, as things stood, to celebrate these meals as meals of the Lord, as "eating the Lord's Supper" (v. 20), that is, as the Eucharist. Divisions of this kind existed regarding the love-feasts, which Jude, v. 12, refers to using this term ["These are blemishes on your love-feasts"]. In his *Epistle to the Smyrnaeans*, ch. 8, Ignatius says: "Without the bishop it is not lawful either to baptize or to celebrate the love-feast" [*ANF* 1:90]. This statement includes the Eucharist as part of the love-feast. In *To His Wife* 2.4, Tertullian still speaks of a "feast of the Lord." But in ch. 39 of the *Apology* he speaks of a gathering, called a love-feast, which is just a meal not objectionable for being luxurious. At the end of his work *On Fasting*, where he speaks as a Montanist addressing the "Psychici" [his term for his Catholic Christian opponents], he has supported that very objection in the strongest terms. About their love-feasts he says (ch. 17): "With you, love is heated in sauce pans, faith is aroused in kitchens, hope lies in dishes of food. But 'the greatest of these is love' [an ironic allusion to 1 Cor 13:13], which is how your young men sleep with their sisters! As we all know, lasciviousness and voluptuousness are appendages of appetite" [*ANF* 4:113]. Did the love-feasts change so much in such a short time? Or does this just cast doubt on Tertullian's reliability as an apologist?

THE PASSOVER FEAST, SUNDAY, AND THE SABBATH

The original pious feelings giving rise to the Christian cultus took root in the purest and most direct way, and developed in its various aspects, in the Passover observance by the churches in Asia Minor. The document written by Bishop Polycrates of Ephesus[88] presents the particular reasons why these churches adhered so firmly and persistently, and with such heartfelt concern, to the fourteenth of Nisan, since that is when they traditionally observed Jesus' last meal with his disciples. Hence they restricted their observance to this one date (which can fall on different days of the week), apparently without its governing the days for the observance of Jesus' death and his resurrection.

To the contrary, the Roman Church felt that, above all else, it had to proceed according to firmly decided liturgical forms. Thus it made the permanently fixed day of the resurrection to be the Sunday following the week in which that original [Christian] Passover is observed, and that in turn controlled the days for observances both of the church year and of the religious week. Each Sunday reawakened thoughts of the resurrection, so the Wednesday and Friday of each week reminded the faithful Christian of what happened on the days in that first Passover week. On Wednesday the passion of the Lord had begun with the Sanhedrin deciding to have him arrested.[89] On Friday he died. These are the *dies stationem* (set days) on which the fasting Christian, as a *miles Christi* (solider of Christ), stands watch and then is relieved of his watch post at the appointed hour.[90] When these actual dates [of Easter week] came around again in the annual cycle, that called for even greater observances. Fasting became extended and the entire week took on the character of a holy week. The Gospel of John, in 12:1 and in harmony with the Roman Easter observance, treats this as a holy week. The vigils, at which people gathered the night before the festival, were supposed to enhance the observance of the Passover feast by the participants being awake to greet the dawning of the festal day.[91]

Not only did Jesus' final meal with the disciples naturally lead to the emergence and structure of a Christian cultus, for Sunday, the day made holy by Jesus' resurrection, also served as its starting point and anchor. Without a doubt Sunday is "the Lord's day" of Rev 1:10, when the seer of the Apocalypse experiences his ecstasy, and

---

88. See above, p. 124. [*Ed.*] See Baur's lengthy discussion of the Passover Controversy, pp. 123–33.

89. See the fragment of a writing about the passion by Bishop Peter of Alexandria, toward the end of the third century, as reported by Routh in *Religio sacrae* 3.343.

90. See Tertullian, *On Fasting*, ch. 10, which says that we follow the example of military stations, for we are God's army; and *The Chaplet*, ch. 14, which speaks about stations four and six.

91. Tertullian already speaks of the vigils as a part of the Passover observance when, in *To His Wife*, 2.4, he asks the Christian wife if her pagan husband would quietly allow her to spend the night away from him in solemn paschal observance [*ANF* 4:46]. On these vigils, see Eusebius, *Ecclesiastical History* 6.34, and Clement of Alexandria, *Stromata* 1.21. Likely the mention of "the Christians' nocturnal gatherings and meetings before daybreak" refers to these vigils. Likewise the mention, in Pliny's *Letter*, of the custom of convening to stand before daybreak.

"the first day of every week" in 1 Cor 16:2, when the Apostle Paul wanted collections to be gathered for his "gift to Jerusalem" (v. 3). According to Justin Martyr,[92] all those living in the cities or the countryside gathered on the day called "Sunday" for readings from the traditions handed down by the apostles and from the writings of the prophets, and for prayer and the celebration of Eucharist. That is because it was on this day that, after dispersing the darkness, God first created the world, and because it was the day on which Jesus Christ our Savior rose from the dead and appeared to his apostles.

The sacred day of the Jewish cultus is the Sabbath, the last day of the week, and the sacred day of the Christian cultus is Sunday, the first day of the week. Both are important, but for Christians Sunday was of the first importance because it is the day when they prayed not on their knees but standing, and when they never fasted.[93] To emphasize the contrast between Sabbath and Sunday even more strongly, in Tertullian's day it was customary for the Roman Church, with its anti-Jewish orientation, to extend the Friday fast to Saturday as well.[94] This in turn got closer to the long-established idea of the Sabbath, wherein on Sunday one refrains as much as possible from engaging in one's ordinary business affairs.[95]

FURTHER FORMS OF THE CULTUS

At the end of the second century and the beginning of the third century, Christianity had already adopted a number of diverse religious forms, some of its own and some borrowed from Judaism and paganism. Whereas Justin Martyr still described baptism and the Lord's Supper as simple religious acts, they were now tied to symbolic practices and mystical notions that also gave to these principal constituents of the Christian cultus meanings analogous to those of the pagan mysteries.[96]

92. *First Apology*, ch. 67 [*ANF* 1:186]. [*Ed.*] Baur abbreviates this passage in the text.
93. See Tertullian, *The Chaplet*, ch. 3 [*ANF* 3:94].
94. Tertullian, *On Fasting*, ch. 14: "You (the Psychici) sometimes continue to fast even over the Sabbath, a day never to be kept as a fast except at the Passover season" [*ANF* 4:112]. One was to fast only on the Saturday before Easter, but on no other Sabbath. As a Montanist, Tertullian believed that this consideration is owed to the Sabbath because Christ himself, "in expressing the Creator's wishes, honored the Sabbath by not fasting on that day" (*Against Marcion* 4.12 [*ANF* 3:363]). The Roman practice was so pervasive in the West that, in its canon 26, the Synod of Elvira declared: "It is agreed to correct the error, so that, for all Sabbaths, we observe the continuation of Friday fasting."
95. Tertullian, *On Prayer*, ch. 23: "We accept that, only on the day of the Lord's resurrection, we ought to guard against all matters of concern and duties, even setting aside our businesses lest we provide any opening for the Devil" [*ANF* 3:689].
96. See these passages from Tertullian on baptismal practices: *The Shows*, ch. 4; *Against Praxeas*, ch. 26; *On Baptism*, ch. 7; *The Chaplet*, ch. 3; *Apostolic Const*itutions 1.14. According to Cyprian, *Epistle* 70, through the chrism or anointing (which Cyril of Jerusalem calls "the antitype, or anointing with Christ," in *Catecheses*, 3.1), the person baptized is someone anointed by God, and can have within him the grace of Christ. That is, the significance of the name "Christ" in this rite is what makes one a Christian. In his *First Apology*, ch. 66, Justin sees an analogy between the Lord's Supper and the mysteries of Mithra, and in discussing this sacrament Origen speaks of "Christian mysteries."

We now of course see that, in the very circumstances wherein the Christian Church worked out a new hierarchy for itself, mainly under the influence of ideas of priesthood taken from the Old Testament, the affairs it had to manage inevitably became more weighty and shrouded in mystery. Quite understandably those Gnostics who wished to see what is Christian distinguished as sharply as possible from Jewish and pagan elements, were faulted by Tertullian for their ignorance of how the orderliness and dignity of the cultus called for distinctions among ranks and classes of the clergy.[97] Marcion in fact declared that the now-current practice of separating the catechumens from the faithful was un-Pauline.[98] The Christian Church now had its own altars,[99] its own priests and sacrifices. Cyprian indeed speaks not merely about the sacrificial prayers, but of the true and perfect sacrifice that the priest, standing in the place of Christ, offers in the church to God the Father by doing as Christ did at the Last Supper.[100]

Since Christ died during the Jewish festival of Passover, and in its cultus Christianity could not deny its overall connection with Judaism, Easter and Pentecost likewise remained major seasonal observances for the Christian cultus. The Apostle Paul already had written that "our paschal lamb, Christ, has been sacrificed" (1 Cor 5:7). So right where the Christian cultus made its connection with the Jewish festival, all of it was invested with higher significance, and that enriched and intensified the conflicting feelings and sentiments that are characteristic of every more highly developed cultus. In the time of fasting preceding Passover, the Christians, in sympathy with the Savior, felt all the pain of his suffering; whereas, joyful at the Savior's resurrection, in the fifty days [until Pentecost] that follow upon the forty fasting days [of Lent], we Christians should, as Tertullian puts it,[101] "spend our time in all exultation." By exalting and empowering their self-consciousness, this joy remains present in them throughout their daily lives as their basic frame of mind, overcoming all the dark and sad moments they might experience.

97. Tertullian, *Prescription Against Heretics*, ch. 41 [*ANF* 3:263]: "I must now speak of how frivolous is the conduct of the heretics—how worldly, how merely human, lacking seriousness, lacking authority, lacking discipline, as suits their creed. To begin with, it is dubious as to who is a catechumen and who is a believer. All have access alike, all hear alike, all pray alike—even pagans who chance to come among them. They cast what is holy to the dogs, and their pearls (albeit not real ones) they toss to the swine. They want simplicity by debasing discipline. [*Baur*: For they trample church order under foot and count that as simplicity.] Our concern for discipline they say is what a procurer does. . . . At one time they put novices in office. . . . Their ordinations are carelessly administered, capricious, changeable. . . . So it comes to pass that today one man is their bishop, tomorrow someone else. Today a deacon, tomorrow a reader. Today a presbyter, tomorrow a layman. They even give laymen priestly functions."

98. Marcion appealed to Gal 6:6 ["Those who are taught the word must share in all good things with their teacher"]. In his commentary on Galatians, Jerome tells us that this was how Marcion made his case.

99. Tertullian, *On Prayer*, ch. 14.

100. Cyprian, *Epistle* 63 [62 in *ANF*].

101. *On Fasting*, ch. 14 [*ANF* 4:112].

THE CULTUS OF THE SAINTS

Another branch of the Christian cultus also bears witness to that same joyfulness. It arose very early on, in part from the Christians' pious feelings and in part from a way of looking at the human realm and its relation to the divine realm, a perspective with its basis in pagan religion.

Christians of earliest times generally regarded remembering the deceased as a very sacred matter. They had a lively awareness of being in ongoing communion with them. They honored the deceased by prayers and religious offerings on the anniversaries of their deaths. So the dates on which the martyrs had ended their triumphant struggles were especially celebrated most joyfully as days of birth, not festivals of death. This is how the church in Smyrna marked the anniversary of the martyrdom of Polycarp, its bishop.[102] As embellished by a legend, in his miraculous death his body was not consumed by the flames but was pierced by a dagger, and a dove flew out of it.[103] The dove is a symbol of the power of the Holy Spirit infusing him, similar to how the eagle, which makes known the apotheosis of a Roman emperor at his funeral rites, is, so to speak, the emblem of the new cultus of the saints, raising up human beings to divine honor.

People honored the bones of martyrs as sacred relics and gathered in pious devotion at the places where they were buried. They wanted to be buried themselves at these same places. Theirs is like the great desire of the ancient Egyptian to share in the gravesite of Osiris as his companion.[104] The Christian likewise thought it most comforting to rest at the side of his martyrs.[105] As such the cultus of the martyrs is the

---

102. See Eusebius, *Ecclesiastical History* 4.15.10–48, which gives a very extensive account of Polycarp's martyrdom, drawing upon a document from the church in Smyrna. The cult of martyrs came from the same pious feelings that gave rise to the worship of Christ. In 4.15.42, the Smyrnaeans are reported as saying: "For him we worship as the Son of God, but the martyrs we love as disciples and imitators of the Lord; and rightly, because of their unsurpassable affection toward their own King and Teacher" [LCL, *Eusebius*, 1:356–57]. In *The Chaplet*, ch. 3, Tertullian speaks of "offerings for the dead, as birthday honors" [*ANF* 3:94]. In his *Epistle* 34, Cyprian speaks not merely of sacrificial offerings for them, but also of the legends "in commemoration of the martyrs' suffering and death, and their anniversaries."

103. See Thierry Ruinart, *Acta primorum martyrum*, 2nd ed. (Paris, 1713), 35 and 43. While the original account in Eusebius is full of legendary features, the story of the dove is an added element in the expanded version of his text. The prototype for the stabbing of Polycarp is in John 19:34: "One of the soldiers pierced his side with a spear, and at once blood and water came out." The blood is the sign of death, but the water is the symbol of the Holy Spirit (see John 7:38–39).

104. See Plutarch, *On Isis and Osiris*, ch. 20: "to be buried together with the body of Osiris." See my *Symbolik und Mythologie oder die Naturreligion des Alterthums*, 2.2 (Stuttgart, 1825), 412ff.

105. One of the most zealous in honoring the saints was Bishop Maximus of Turin (who lived at the beginning of the fifth century). His *Homily* 81 goes on at length about the Turin martyrs Octavius, Adventius, and Salutor. [*Ed.* Baur quotes the Latin text from J.-P. Migne, *Patrologia Latina*, 57:427.] See C. F. Bellermann, Über die ältesten christlichen Begrabnissstätten und besonders die Katakomben zu Neapel (Hamburg, 1839), 5. The cultus of the saints became more developed and profoundly important in the course of the fourth century. Here it essentially rested on the very early cultus of relics. The way of thinking that underlay the entire linkage of the cultus of relics with the cultus of saints

aspect of the Christian cultus where it is most directly related to pagan practices and conceptions, and where it is most inclined to welcome a very close and heartfelt bond with the paganism it had overcome. At the same time it is one of the main elements on the basis of which the edifice of the Christian Church later on became so imposing.

(as seen in Maximus) enables us to understand the religious significance their shared cemeteries had for the earliest Christians, as places of worship (see Eusebius, *Ecclesiastical History* 7.13) Before there was an actual ἐκκλησίας or "church" building as such—these structures first appeared in the period between Gallienus and Diocletian (see Eusebius, 8.1)—the cemeteries were the devotional sites and places for religious gatherings. The notions associated with these cemeteries, as places where the martyrs' bodies rested, also got transferred to the church buildings themselves.

Index of Persons

Abaris the Hyperborean, 317
Abel, 178, 405
Abraham, 50–51, 53, 59, 90, 105, 109, 111, 170, 178, 363
Acesius (Novatian Bishop), 298
Adam, 58, 91, 152, 156, 170, 178–79, 186, 249–51, 404
Adresanes, 185
Adventius (Martyr), 431
Aeschylus, 335
Agathabulus the Cynic, 335
Akembes (Kelbes) the Karystian, 156
Alba, Duke of, 368
Alcibiades from Apamea, 231, 414
Alexander (Bishop of Alexandria), 216, 293, 375
Alexander of Abonuteichos, 312, 334–35
Alexander the Great, 4–5, 17
Alexander Severus (Emperor), 362–63
Ammonius Saccas, 347
Ananias, 342
Anaxagoras, 204
Anaxarchus, 326
Anicetas (Bishop of Rome), 124, 129, 132
Antinous, 317
Antiochus Epiphanes (King of Syria), 342
Antoninus Pius (Emperor), 158, 337, 355, 358, 360
Apion, 348
Apollinaris (Bishop of Hierapolis), 124, 128–29, 133
Apollinaris of Laodicea, 341–42
Apollo (Deity), 344–46
Apollonius of Tyana, 334, 337–40, 345–46, 362–63
Aquila, 351
Aratos of Cilicia, 146–47
Ariadne, 316
Aristeas of Proconnesus, 317, 346
Aristotle, 13, 147–48, 341
Arius, 288–90, 292–93, 375
Arrian, 336

Artemon, 276–78, 281
Asclepius, 317, 326
Athanasius, 130, 276, 282–83, 287, 292–93
Athenagoras, 268–69, 305, 360, 387, 399, 407–8
Augustine, 343–44
Augustus, Caesar (Emperor), 5–6, 303–4, 350
Axionicus, 185

Bardesanes, 165
Barnabas, 46–47, 103–5, 211, 265
Basil of Caesarea, 274–75
Basilides, 148, 158, 165–74, 182, 184, 401
Baur, Ferdinand Christian, xxiii–xxiv, xxvii–xxxiii, 3, 8, 15, 19–22, 24, 28–29, 34, 42, 45–46, 52, 54–55, 62, 64, 66, 77, 82, 88, 97–98, 100–101, 104, 106, 111, 113–16, 125, 129–30, 133–34, 136, 144, 150, 155, 164–65, 167, 182–83, 189, 197, 217, 221, 248, 252, 259–60, 264, 269, 280, 286, 293, 332, 337, 347, 353–54, 386, 392–93, 400, 403, 430
Bauspiess, Martin, 23
Bellermann, C. F., 431
Benjamin, 59
Beryllus of Bostra, 280–81
Bindemann, C. W. J., 312
Böhmer, E., 353
Bunsen, C. K. J., 165, 221, 266, 278
Burckhardt, Jacob, 367–69, 376–77

Caecilius, 306, 424
Cain, 178, 405
Caius (Gaius), 113, 236, 278
Calhoun, Robert L., 281
Caligula (Emperor), 351
Callistus (Bishop of Rome), 230, 232, 271–72, 278–80, 362, 393, 414
Caracalla (Emperor), 362
Carinus (Emperor), 365
Carneades (Philosopher), 14
Carpocrates, 402

Index of Persons

Cassian, Julius, 184, 404–5
Celsus, 5, 307, 312–33, 336–37, 340–44, 346–47, 349, 380, 399, 424
Cephas (*see* Peter, the Apostle)
Cerdo, 158
Cerinthus, 153, 236
Chrysostom, John, 393
Cicero, Marcus Tullius, 13–14
Claudius (Emperor), 351
Clement (Bishop of Rome), 71, 86, 104, 106, 114–15, 146, 176, 209–12, 217, 221, 224–25, 241, 265, 354–55
Cleomedes of Astypalaea, 317
Cleomenes, 271, 273, 278–79
Clinton, Henry F., 357
Commodus (Emperor), 337, 355, 362
Constantine (Emperor), 240, 291, 293, 365, 368–69, 371–78, 381, 385
Constantinius Chlorus, 365
Cornelius (Bishop of Rome), 230
Cyprian (Bishop of Carthage), 49, 211–12, 228–30, 235–36, 239–41, 296, 409, 415, 428–30

Dähne, A. F., 20
Daniel, 326, 342
David, 200
Decius (Emperor), 363–65
Demetrius (Bishop of Alexandria), 216
Democritus, 204
Dio Cassius, 362
Diocletian (Emperor), 365–67, 369, 374, 381, 422, 431
Diogenes Laertius, 279, 316
Dionysius (Bishop of Alexandria), 287
Dionysius (Bishop of Rome), 287
Dionysius (Mythical Figure), 317
Dodwell, 368
Döllinger, J. J. I., 230, 278, 393, 411, 414
Domitian (Emperor), 337, 339, 354
Drecoll, Volker H., 142, 182
Dressel, Albert, 176, 213

Eichhorn, J. G., xxix
Eleutherius (Bishop of Rome), 214, 232
Elijah, 179
Empedocles, 148, 204
Epictetus, 14, 326
Epicurus, 11, 204, 312
Epigonus, 271, 278
Epiphanes, 402
Epiphanius, 71, 76, 133, 136–37, 156, 190–92, 266, 403, 414
Eunapius (Sophist), 345
Euphrates the Peratic, 156

Eurydice, 316
Eusebius of Caesarea, 4, 23, 65–66, 70–71, 76, 124–27, 130, 132, 158–59, 210, 213–14, 216, 219, 230, 236, 238, 277, 281, 293, 297, 303–4, 330, 341, 343, 346–47, 358–62, 364–65, 367, 369, 371–78, 381, 404, 409, 414, 422–23, 427, 430–31
Eve, 178
Evodius (Bishop of Antioch), 226
Ewald, Heinrich, xxix–xxxii, 354

Firmilian (Bishop of Caesarea), 229–30, 239–40
Flavius Clemens, 355

Galba (Emperor), 354
Galerius (Emperor), 366–69
Gallienus (Emperor), 365, 431
Georgii, Ludwig, 17–18
Gerdmar, Anders, 42
Getra (Emperor), 362
Gieseler, J. C. L., 127, 131, 142, 172, 197, 232, 274, 280, 361, 366
Gregorovius, Ferdinand, 334
Gregory of Nazianzus, 276

Hadrian (Emperor), 132, 158, 312, 317, 334, 355, 359–61
Hase, Karl, 116
Hauber, Albert, 405
Hegel, G. W. F., xxxii, 10, 14, 386
Hegesippus, 23, 70–71, 76, 158–59, 216
Heigl, 347
Helena, 153, 155
Heliogabalus (Elagabalus) (Emperor), 362–63
Hellwag, J. 252, 266–67
Heracleon (Valentinian), 165, 185
Heraclitus, 147–48, 204, 272–76, 279, 323
Hercules, 315–17, 326
Hermes (Mythical Figure), 324
Hermotimus of Clazomene, 317
Herodotus, 316
Hesiod, 320
Hierocles, Sassianus (Governor of Bythynia), 346–47, 367
Hilgenfeld, Adolf, 19–21, 34, 47, 62, 64, 71, 77, 82, 84, 86, 93, 100, 104–8, 116, 122, 129, 136, 154, 165, 172, 218, 221, 225, 266–67, 415
Hippolytus, xxiii, 127–29, 133, 146, 235, 278–79, 393, 414
Hitzig, Ferdinand, 107
Holsten, Karl C. J., 44, 47–48, 51
Homer, 167, 316
Hosius (Bishop of Cordova), 373

434

Index of Persons

Iamblichus, 344–45
Ignatius (Bishop of Antioch), 104, 184, 214, 217–18, 221–22, 225–26, 266, 357, 426
Irenaeus, 70–71, 74, 81, 112, 124–26, 129, 132, 136, 148, 153, 156, 159, 165, 203–4, 208, 214–15, 227–29, 269–70
Isaac, 170, 179
Isidore (Gnostic), 165

Jacob, 170, 179
Jacobi, J. L., 165
James (Brother of Jesus), 48, 72, 83, 102, 116, 216, 219, 223
Jeremiah, 146
Jerome, 67, 115, 214, 232, 342–43, 429
Jesus of Nazareth, 5–6, 22–23, 25–37, 43–46, 63–65, 70, 119–23, 126–32, 134–35, 146, 152–53, 156, 162, 169, 184–85, 248–49, 255, 261, 263–64, 314–16, 324–25, 331, 385, 425 (see also "Jesus Christ" in the Subject Index)
Jezebel, 68
John, the Apostle, 69, 73–75, 112, 116–17, 124–25, 131, 133–34, 209, 214, 354, 398
John the Baptist, 179
Jonah, 326
Joseph, 153
Josephus, Titus Flavius, 20, 348, 351–52
Julia Domna (Empress), 337, 362
Justin Martyr, 70, 74, 81, 84, 104, 108–12, 123, 132, 137, 266–67, 304–6, 308–11, 358–60, 387, 404, 424, 426, 428–29

Kant, Immanuel, 14, 19, 28, 386
Keim, Karl Theodor, 360–61, 369, 371, 373, 376
Kelly, J. N. D., 273
Köstlin, Karl Reinhard, 21, 23, 62–65, 78–79, 93, 104, 107, 116, 122, 164, 182–83, 259
Kuhn, J. E., 278–80, 287

Lactantius, 366, 368–69, 371–72
Lamech, 405
Landmesser, Christof, 42
Lassalle, Ferdinand, 274, 279
Lechler, Gotthard, V., 47, 82, 129
Lehmann, Hermann, 351–52
Licinius (Emperor), 365, 369, 371–73, 378
Linus, 115, 147
Lipsius, R. A., 107, 212, 221, 357
Lotze, Hermann, 19
Lucian of Samosata, 312, 332–36, 340, 380
Lucius Verus (Emperor), 337, 355
Lücke, Friedrich, 22

Macrinus (Emperor), 362
Maesa, 363
Mai, A. 347
Marcella (Wife of Porphyry), 347
Marcia (Concubine of Commodus), 362
Marcion, 64, 66–67, 77, 148, 158–59, 172–77, 179–82, 185, 403–4, 429
Marcus (Valentinian), 165
Marcus Aurelius (Emperor), 14, 303, 335–37, 355, 358–59, 361
Mark (Son of Peter), 114
Mary, the Virgin, 3, 152–53, 156, 162, 169, 184–85, 272
Matter, Jacques, 142
Maxentius (Emperor), 362, 371, 376
Maximian (Emperor), 381
Maximilla (Montanist), 188, 190–91, 197
Maximinus (Emperor), 365, 372–73, 381
Maximus (Bishop of Turin), 400–401
Maximus the Thracian (Emperor), 363
Melchizedek, 90–91, 93, 258
Melito (Bishop of Sardis), 4, 124, 303–4, 358–61
Methodius of Tyre, 341
Michael Psellus, 306
Miltiades (Bishop of Rome), 238, 375
Minucius Felix, 305–6, 424
Minucius Fundanus (Governor of Asia Minor), 359
Möhler, Johann Adam, 317–18, 393
Montanus, 188, 191, 196–97
Moses, 27, 41, 55, 72, 75, 84, 105, 119, 155, 157, 161, 170, 179, 194, 223, 324–25, 342
Musaios, 147

Neander, August, 8, 47, 142–43, 196–97, 214, 273, 308, 312, 360, 376, 391
Nero (Emperor), 61, 312, 351–54, 356, 398
Nerva (Emperor), 355
Niebuhr, Barthold Georg, 363, 365, 368
Nitzsch, Karl Immanuel, 314
Noah, 179, 296, 324, 414
Noetus of Smyrna, 271–75, 278–79, 281
Novatian, 297

Octavius (Martyr), 430
Oedipus, 306
Onesimus, 218
Origen, xxiii, 4–5, 67, 81, 112, 146, 200–203, 213, 284–87, 294–96, 305, 307, 312–32, 342–43, 347, 349, 364, 393, 395, 414, 416, 424, 429
Orpheus, 147, 315–16, 326, 363
Otho (Emperor), 354
Ovid, 316

Panthera, 314
Papias, 23, 70
Paret, Heinrich, 45
Paul, the Apostle, 26, 41–62, 64–68, 70–83, 85–91, 94, 97–99, 101–3, 106, 108, 111–17, 120–22, 134–36, 144, 189–90, 204, 208, 210–12, 225–29, 248–54, 256, 342, 392–93, 398, 400, 402–3, 406, 408, 411, 414, 416, 420, 424–26, 428–29
Paul of Samosata, 277, 281–83
Peregrinus "Proteus" of Parium (Cynic Philosopher), 333–36
Peter, the Apostle (Cephas), 34, 44, 47–49, 52–54, 62, 64, 71–75, 77, 81, 83, 85–86, 100–102, 106, 112–17, 136, 176, 179–80, 186, 208–9, 221, 223–25, 228–30, 342, 420
Peter (Bishop of Alexandria), 427
Pherecydes, 323
Philip, the Apostle, 124, 420
Philippus of Arabia (Emperor), 363
Philo of Alexandria, 18–20, 93, 145–47, 262
Philostratus, Flavius (Sophist), 337–41, 344–46, 362
Planck, Gottlieb J., xxx, 78–79, 332, 334
Plato, 12–13, 144–45, 147–48, 150, 167, 204, 320, 323, 338, 341
Pliny the Younger (Governor of Bythynia), 355–57, 387, 426–27
Plotinus, 15, 341, 347
Plutarch, 430
Polybius, 10
Polycarp (Bishop of Smyrna), 106–7, 124–25, 129–30, 132, 209, 218, 221, 336, 430
Polycrates (Bishop of Ephesus), 123–25, 129–31, 427
Pontius Pilate, 351
Poppaea Sabina (Wife of Nero), 352
Porphyry, 312, 341–45, 347
Praxeas, 232, 271–73, 279–80
Priscilla (Montanist), 188, 191, 197
Priscillian (Ascetic), 172
Proclus, 15
Protesilaus, 315–16
Ptolemaeus (Valentinian), 133, 165, 185
Pyrrho (Founder of Skepticism), 13
Pythagoras, 148, 204, 315–16, 344–46

Redepenning, E. R., 286, 347
Rhampsinitus, 315–16
Ritschl, Albrecht, 19, 26, 64, 66, 71, 78–82, 84, 85, 93, 100, 104–5, 107, 111, 123, 126, 136, 193, 213–18, 221, 234–35, 414–15
Rothe, Richard, 217–18, 223, 228
Ruinart, Thierry, 430

Sabellius, 272–76, 279–81, 283, 287
Sabinus (Prefect), 372
Salome, 405
Salutor (Martyr), 431
Sapphira, 342
Saturninus, 165, 404
Saul, 33
Schelling, F. W. J., xxxii, 14
Schleiermacher, Friedrich, 8, 14, 19, 22, 272
Schneckenburger, Matthias, 101, 276
Schwegler, Albert, 64, 78–81, 97, 104, 106–7, 192, 197, 225, 236, 238, 259, 297, 358
Secundus (Valentinian), 165
Seneca, 14–15
Septimus Severus (Emperor), 337, 362
Serennius Granianus (Governor of Asia Minor), 359
Silvanus, 100, 114
Simeon, 219
Simon Magus, 49, 72–77, 85–86, 148, 153–56, 179–80, 182, 223
Simonides, 213
Socrates (Church Historian), 130, 240, 298, 412
Socrates (Philosopher), 12–13, 311
Solomon, 33
Sophocles, 335
Steitz, G., 127, 129
Stephanas (Bishop of Rome), 210, 229–30
Stephen, 41–43
Suetonius, 351, 353

Tacitus, 307, 330, 351–54, 356
Tatian, 184, 268, 303, 305–6, 404
Tertullian, 66–67, 81, 112, 115, 147–48, 158–59, 184, 188–96, 203–9, 213–15, 227–29, 232, 234–35, 237, 239–40, 269–72, 280, 295, 297–98, 304–6, 308–9, 311, 330, 348, 351, 354, 357–58, 380–81, 387–92, 396–99, 405–11, 413–14, 421–22, 424, 426–30
Thales, 4
Theodoret, 156–57, 184, 271, 275, 341
Theodotus of Byzantium, 276–79, 281–82
Theophilus, 268
Theseus, 316
Thyestes, 306
Tiberius (Emperor), 350–51
Timothy, 89, 102–3, 220
Titus, 46, 103, 220
Trajan (Emperor), 100, 158, 355–60

Uhlhorn, Gerhard, xxviii, 71–72, 82, 84, 165, 176, 221

Index of Persons

Valentinus, 147–48, 158–66, 170, 172–74, 182–85, 401, 404
Valerian (Emperor), 364–65
Valerius Severus (Emperor), 365
Vespasian (Emperor), 354
Victor (Bishop of Rome), 123, 125, 129, 132, 232, 278, 362
Vitellus (Emperor), 354
Vogel, Albrecht, 365, 368
Volkmar, Gustav, 64, 77, 107, 115, 156, 158, 165, 274, 358

Weiss, Bernhard, 100

Weitzel, K. L., 126–29
Wolff, Maurice, 262

Xenophon, 12

Zacchaeus (Bishop of Caesarea), 223
Zalmoxis, 315–16
Zeller, Eduard, 12–13, 15, 19, 42, 47, 77, 84, 101, 149, 236, 255, 262, 272–73, 340
Zeno (Founder of Stoicism), 11, 147
Zephyrinus (Bishop of Rome), 232, 271, 277–78, 280, 413
Zeus (Deity), 317, 324

Index of Subjects

Acts of the Apostles
    local authority and autonomy of churches described in, 209–10
    its purpose to bring about a reconciliation between Paul and Peter, 101–3
    unreliable history of the early Christian community, 41, 101–2
    written from a Paulinist perspective, 101
Aeons (Gnostic archetypes of the finite world), 149, 159–61
Alexandrian church, 216, 236
Alexandrian idealism, 92–93
Alexandrian religious philosophy, 145–47, 261
Alexandrian theologians (Clement, Origen), 200–203, 269–70
allegory, 18, 67, 109, 144–47, 182
angelology, 252, 266–67, 296
antinomianism, 66, 402–3
antithesis, between Paulinism and Judaism in the early church, 41–77
apocalyptic, 69, 116–17, 254
Apologists, 4, 305, 308–11, 348, 387, 404
Apostolic Fathers, 104–8, 265–70
apostolic succession, 228, 239
Arianism, 287–90
asceticism, 398–400, 404, 407

baptism, 83–84, 95, 108, 213, 230–31, 248, 277, 298, 428
Barnabas, Epistle of, 104–5, 265
Basilidean system, 165–72
bishops
    in relation to presbyters and deacons, 209–16
    as instruments of the Spirit, 235–38
    see also episcopacy

Catholic Church
    achieves an equilibrium between opposing viewpoints, 78, 81, 87
    antecedents of in Deutero-Pauline Epistles, 96–97
    as the antithesis to Gnosis and Montanism, 198–242
    hierarchical structure of (the episcopacy), 209–42
    idea of, 198–99
    makes its peace with the world as opposed to moral rigor of Montanism, 193–94, 231, 233–34, 411
    no salvation outside of, 296
celibacy, 409–12
chiliasm, 190–92, 236
Christ
    as archetypal human being, 187–88, 249–52
    body of as the Christian Church, 96, 258–59
    compared with Apollonius of Tyana, 337–40
    and the Demiurge, 151–52
    divinity of, 284–93
    docetic views of, 183–88
    Gnostic concepts of, 160–62, 168–70, 180, 196
    as the incarnation of the divine Logos, 22, 118, 134, 260–64
    parousia of, 189–90
    pre-existence of, 251, 253
    as priest (high priest), 89–93
    and Socrates, 12–13
    stands at pinnacle of most important epoch in Roman history, 350–51
    as true Passover Lamb, 120–23
    universal reconciliation achieved through, 94–97
    as the Word of God, 254–55
Christian Church
    early churches as autonomous, 209–13
    takes shapes or emerges from Christianity, xxiv, 142
    see also Catholic Church
Christian cultus
    and the Eucharist or love-feast (*Agape*), 425–26
    original elements of, 424–25
    of the saints, 430–31

Christian cultus *(continued)*
    Sunday and Sabbath, 427–28
Christianity
    as absolute religion, 7, 9, 15
    its appeal to the middle class, 380
    attack on by Celsus, 312–31
    attack on by Lucian of Samosata, 332–36
    attack on by Philostratus, 337–40
    attack on by Porphyry, 341–43
    becomes state religion of the Roman Empire, 301–2, 373–81
    beginning of not a miracle but part of a historical nexus, 3–4, 20
    distinctiveness depends on the person of its founder, 21, 32–33
    its feeling of dependence, 14
    growing toleration of in Roman Empire, 369–72
    as ideal world-principle, 141–97
    as moral and religious principle, 385–431
    multiple ways of specifying the divine element in, 385
    name first used by Pseudo-Ignatius, 106
    persecution of in the Roman world, 308, 351–53, 361, 364, 367–68
    philosophically educated opponents of, 311–46
    as a power dominant in the world, 301–81
    and the pre-Christian religions (pagan and Jewish), 7–10
    principle of, 24–29, 32
    produced a moral rebirth in the public life of humankind, 386–90
    as a real, historically conditioned phenomenon (Catholic Church), 198–242
    its relation to Greek philosophy, 11–16
    its relation to the pagan world, 305–49
    as a religion of the spirit, 50
    its spiritual character makes it distinctive, 9
    as spiritualized Judaism, 17
    under the Roman Emperors, 350–77
    as the universal principle of salvation, 41–137, 245
    universalism of, 4–6, 59
    its victory over paganism, 378–81
    world-consciousness of, 303–5
christology (doctrine of the person of Christ)
    of the Alexandrine theologians, 268–69
    of the Apostle Paul, 249–53
    of the Apostolic Fathers, 265–68
    Arian, 287–90
    of the Book of Revelation, 254–55
    central dogma of the early church, 246–47
    concept of Christ's person increasingly elevated as doctrine develops, 253
    of the Deutero-Pauline Epistles, 258–59
    of the Epistle to the Hebrews, 256–57
    from above and from below, 277
    of the Gospel of John, 260–64
    Monarchian views of, 271–83
    Nicene, 291–93
    Origen's version of, 285–87
    of the Synoptic Gospels, 248–49
church fathers, their stance toward Gnosis, 200–208
circumcision, 26, 46–48, 50–51, 58, 83–84, 95, 105, 108, 136
Clement, Epistle of, 106–7, 265–66
Clementine writings, 71–73, 85–86, 223–26
Colossians, Epistle to the, 94–97, 258–59
Constantine
    his concern for unity, 374–75
    conversion of, 376–77
    religious edicts of, 373
    his religious sentiments driven by political interests, 376–78
Corinthians, Epistles to the, 52–55
cosmic seed, 166–68
councils, church, 238–40

deacons, 209–16
Demiurge, 149–51, 161–62, 174–75
demonology, demons, 296, 326–30, 395–98
Deutero-Pauline Epistles, 94–97, 258–59
docetism, 183–88, 201, 203–4
dogma (doctrine)
    first developed mainly in opposition to Gnosticism, 199–205
    transition to in early church, 245–47

Ebionites, 71, 136–37
Eclecticism, 14
Ephesians, Epistle to the, 94–97, 258–59
Epicureanism, 11, 13–14
episcopacy
    bishop as representative of God and of Christ, embodying unity, 226–28
    concept of the episcopate, 216–17, 378–79
    described in Pseudo-Ignatian and Pseudo-Clementine writings, 221–26
    as opponent of Montanism, 230–35
    as organizational structure of the Catholic Church, 209–42, 378–79
    origin of the episcopate (concern for unity in opposition to heresy), 218–19, 230
eschatology (doctrine of last things), 192, 296
Essenes, 19–20

faith
    of Abraham, 50, 90, 109, 111

of the church, 3
of the disciples, 41
in God, 58
in Jesus as the Christ, 32–33, 58, 134, 378, 379
justifying, 107, 111
and knowledge, 144, 200
and law, 50, 58, 80
and love, 51, 80, 107, 135
in the resurrection, 36–37
rule of, 107, 208
in the teaching of Jesus, 385
and works, 81, 88–89, 97–99, 417–18
flesh (*sarx*), 36, 44, 58, 94, 250, 263, 398–400
forgiveness of sins, 29, 97, 108, 235, 297–98, 318, 379, 413
freedom, 46, 50–51, 55, 79, 202–3, 294–96, 348, 366, 371–73

Galatians, Epistle to the, 49–51
Gentile Christianity, 42, 83, 101, 103, 225
  versus Jewish Christianity, 49–55, 62, 84–85
Gnosis
  concept and nature of, 141–44
  docetic, 183
  dualism of, 143, 148–49, 153–54
  early sects of, 153–58
  as a form of religious knowledge, 144, 151
  as knowledge (*gnosis*) in relation to faith (*pistis*), 144, 200
  major systems of, 158–81
  Montanist form of, 188–89, 195–96
  opposition of Irenaeus and Tertullian to, 203–5
  origin of, 145–48
  process of world-development in, 188
  relation of Clement of Alexandria and Origen to, 200–203
  spirit versus matter in, 148–49
  stripped of its mythical covering, a lucid rationalism, 187
  as theological or philosophical speculation, 142–43
  three basic forms of (relating Christianity to paganism and Judaism), 181–82
Gnosticism, *see* Gnosis
God
  all of creation take up into, 59
  of the Gentiles as well as Jews, 58
  Gnostic concepts of, 159–62, 176–79
  love of, 58, 134, 295
  as not-being rather than being, 165
  return of all things to, 59
  righteousness of, 57–58

  as spiritual process (going out from and returning to self), 162–63
  supreme God distinguished from the Demiurge, 149–51
  and world, 162–64
  see also kingdom of God
God-consciousness, 11, 15, 69, 150, 267–68, 311, 329
good works, 415–17
Greek philosophy, 11–16, 18, 145, 147–48, 150, 204, 245, 272, 322–23, 331

Hebrews, Epistle to the, 89–93, 256–58
heresy, 206, 208, 218, 236, 272, 279
Hermas, *The Shepherd* of, 107–8, 265
hierarchy, 67, 87, 209–42, 410, 429
historical actuality, involves life, movement, struggle, conflict, xxviii
historical examination/reflection (*geschichtliche Betrachtung*), 3
historical method, transposition into the objective reality of the subject matter itself, xxiv
history, periods of transition in, 10
Holy Spirit
  bishops as instruments of, 235–38, 240–41
  constitutive of Jesus' messianic person, 248, 251, 263, 277
  dove as symbol of, 430
  Gnostic view of, 160–61, 167–68, 170, 180, 187, 191
  Montanist view of, 191–92, 236
  as Paraclete, 191–96
  possession by (ecstasy), 237–38
  as the principle operative in the Christian community, 238
  Simon Magus claims to be empowered by, 75
  and the Trinity, 269, 274, 276
  working of settled and regulated by the Catholic Church, 236
homoousian, 246, 282–83, 292, 294, 301
human beings
  adopted by God through the Spirit, 58
  divine element in, 187, 419
  freedom of in relation to God, 294–96
  inherent rights of lay beyond the horizons of the ancient world, 366
  as material, psychic, and pneumatic (spiritual), 151, 162–64, 181, 186, 249–50
  must turn inward and grasp their own subjectivity, 12–14, 25–27, 31
  their reconciliation with God, 9, 94, 134
  renewal or rebirth of, 97, 99, 386
  rights of promoted by Christianity, 392–93

441

human beings *(continued)*
    their self-consciousness related to God-consciousness, 29
    unrighteousness of contrasted with righteousness of God, 57

James, Epistle of, 98–100
Jerusalem congregation, 41–42, 46–47, 49, 60–61, 219, 225
Jesus
    death and resurrection of, 36–37, 252 *(see also* resurrection)
    death of as interpreted by Paul, 43–44
    filled by (or is) the Holy Spirit, 248, 250, 252, 281–82
    as founder of Christianity, 21
    and the law, 25–27
    his messianic idea, 32–34
    represented as a purely human Messiah in the Synoptic Gospels, 248–49
    represented as the archetypal human being by Paul, 249–52
    his teaching as summarized in the Sermon on the Mount, 24–29, 385
    his teaching of the kingdom of God, 30–31
Jewish Christianity, 62, 71, 79–86, 87–88, 89, 94, 99, 101–3, 104, 107–8, 110, 133, 137, 225
John, the Apostle, 69, 116
John, Gospel of
    its Alexandrian orientation, 135
    its attitude toward Judaism, 119–20
    cannot be harmonized with the Synoptic Gospels, 21–22
    its Christ as the true Passover lamb, 120–23
    as a form of Christian consciousness surpassing Judaism and Paulinism, 133–35
    incarnation of the divine Logos in, 22, 118, 134, 260–64
    not written by the Apostle John, 22, 116–17
    its relation to the Book of Revelation, 116–17
Judaism
    Alexandrian, 18, 28, 109
    Hellenistic, 5, 17–18
    as interpreted in the Epistle to the Hebrews, 89–93
    particularism of, 17, 59
    Paul's engagement with in Romans, 56–60
    as precursor to Christianity, 17–20
    its pure and refined monotheistic concept of God, 17
    as a religion of the law, 50–51
Justin Martyr
    christology of, 266–67
    his stance that of Alexandrian Judaism, 109
    as a transitional figure between the Apostolic Fathers and the Catholic Church, 108–11

kingdom of God, 23, 29–31, 59, 64, 69, 108, 190–91, 314, 318, 327, 354

laity, 213–15
law, function of according to Paul, 58
Logos-idea, 260–68, 273–76
Logos Spermatikos, 310
love feast (*Agape*), 222, 425–26
love
    and faith, 80
    God's, 58, 134, 295
    the highest concept for Gospel of John, 134
    of neighbor, 28
Luke, Gospel of, 62–64

magician, miracle worker, 76–77, 337–40
Marcion
    his collection of New Testament writings, 66–67
    his Gnostic dualism, 67, 172–75
    his Paulinism, 66
marriage
    and domestic life, 391–93
    Gnostic view of, 400–404
    Paul's view of, 400
    and the priesthood, 409–12
    second, 405–9
    Tertullian's view of, 405–9
martyrdom, 42, 62, 194, 334–36, 353, 361, 364, 421–22
matter, *see* spirit, and matter
Matthew, Gospel of
    compared with the Gospel of Luke, 64–65
    Jewishness of, 63
    most reliable source for sayings of Jesus, 23
    Sermon on the Mount in, 24–28
mediation
    baptism replaces circumcision as a factor in, 83–84
    between antitheses in the early church, 78–115
    how it came about, 82
messianic idea, 32–34, 36, 44, 188
millennialism, 190–92
miracle
    as absolute beginning, 3, 20
    in the Book of Acts, 102
    in the Gospel of John, 22
    in the Synoptic Gospels, 33, 63
Monarchianism

dynamic, 276-83
modalistic, 271-76
Montanism, 188-97, 230-35, 296-97
morality
   higher and lower, 410-11
   and moral action, 417
   moral conscience as the heart of Christianity, 26-29, 30, 32
   and moral rigorism, 396-98
   and moral-religious principle, 385-431
   more lenient practices, 422-23
   purer moral spirit of evangelical Christianity (Clement of Alexandria), 419-21

Neoplatonism, 15, 343-45, 347
Nicaea, Council of, 246, 291-93
Novatians, 296-97

Ophites, 155-56

paganism, 7-8, 17, 51, 69, 76, 95, 142, 182, 305-49, 352, 380, 396
papacy, 228-30
parables, 30-31
Paraclete, 191-97, 236-37
parousia, 189-91, 194, 231, 233, 254, 353-54
Passover controversy (concerning date of Jesus' last meal and death), 121-33, 427-29
Pastoral Epistles, 97-98, 220
Patripassianism, 271
Paul, the Apostle
   authority of questioned because not an original apostle, 52-55
   his belief in the parousia of Christ, 189
   called to be the Apostle to the Gentiles, 43-48
   christology of, 249-53
   conversion of, 42-44
   and the earlier apostles, 44-48
   engages with Judaism most fully in Romans, 56-60
   his final journey to Jerusalem, 60-61
   as founder of Christian churches, 211-12
   his interpretation of the death of Christ, 43-44
   opposition to in Corinth, 52-55
   opposition to in Galatia, 49-51
   his relation to the Apostle Peter, 48, 101-3, 112-15
   relies on his experience of the living Christ, 45-46, 53-54
   as represented in the Clementine writings, 72-77
   and the teaching of Jesus, 45
   his view of circumcision, 46-48
   his view of marriage, 400
Pauline theology
   compendium of in the Epistle to the Romans, 55-60
   its emancipation of consciousness from external authorities, 55
Paulinism, 22, 41, 55, 62, 65, 66-67, 79-81, 85, 87-88, 101, 109, 133-34, 249
Peratai, 156-58
Peter, the Apostle
   legend of his primacy as bishop of Rome, 229
   Pauline universalism transferred to Peter, 85-86
   his relation to the Apostle Paul, 48, 101-3, 112-15
   as represented in the Clementine writings, 71-77, 85
Peter, Epistles of, 98-100, 113-14
Pharisees, 19, 25-27
Philippians, Epistle to the, 94-97, 259
Philosophumena, xxiii, 146, 148, 278-79
Pistis Sophia, xxii, 163-64, 182
Platonism, 11, 150, 323-25, 337, 341
Polycarp, Epistle of, 106
presbyters (elders), 209-20
prophecy, 178, 180-81, 190-92, 237-38
providence, 5, 8, 295, 326, 375
Pseudo-Clementine Homilies, 176-81, 223-26, 267
Pseudo-Ignatian Epistles, 104, 106-7, 221-22
Pythagoreanism, 340-41, 344-45

Quartodecimans, 125, 130, 132, 136

religion
   expression of innate human desire to know and commune with the divine, 8
   Protestant principle of freedom of belief intrinsic to, 348
   reconciliation as it essence, 9
   see also morality
religious syncretism, 337, 345, 362-63
resurrection
   of the body, 399
   day on which it is celebrated, 124-26, 130, 427
   of/from the dead, 249, 251-52
   as a fact in the consciousness of believers, 36-37
   lies outside the sphere of historical investigation, 36
   questions about raised by Celsus, 315
   spiritual meaning of, 264

return of all things to God (*apokatastasis*), 59, 169, 171
Revelation, Book of
 christology of, 254–55
 Jewish tenor of, 68–69
 probably written by the Apostle John, 69
righteousness
 as the adequate relation to God, 29
 in contrast to love, 134
 and justice, 338
 not given by law but by faith in Christ, 58, 97
Roman Empire, 3–6, 350–81
Romans, Epistle to the, 55–60

Sabellianism, 273–76
scripture
 allegorical interpretation of, 18, 133, 144–45, 202
 attack on (by Porphyry), 342
 canonical, 88, 104, 112–13, 248
 fulfillment of, 119
 post-apostolic, 89
 post-canonical, 104
 and tradition, 206–9
self-consciousness
 and God-consciousness, 12, 15, 28–29, 385
 autonomy and immediacy of, 54–55
 and other-consciousness, 263
 and world-consciousness, 25
Sermon on the Mount, 23–29, 31
serpent, 155, 157
Simon Magus
 as caricature of the Apostle Paul, 71–77, 86
 father of heretics, 77
 father of simony, 75
 leader of a Gnostic sect, 153–55
sins, mortal and venial, 412–15
Skepticism, 13–14

slavery, 393, 400
Socrates, and Christ, 12–13, 311
Sophia, 160–63
spirit
 and matter, 141, 148–49, 173, 175, 179, 182, 185, 196, 203, 399, 400–401, 404, 410
 as process of self-knowing and self-revealing, 162–63
Stoicism, 11, 13–15
Synoptic Gospels
 christology of, 248, 263
 difference from Gospel of John on date of Jesus' last meal and death, 121–22, 131–32
 messianic consciousness of Jesus affirmed in, 34, 277
 provide access to historical foundation of Christianity, 21–22
 relation to each other, 22–23
syzygy (conjunction or pairs), 153, 159–60, 170, 178–79

Therapeutae, 19
tradition, and scripture, 206–9
Trinity, 269–70, 273, 275–76, 280, 296
Tübingen School, xxvii–xxviii, 19

Valentinianism, 159–64

women
 apparel of, 389
 as companions of Paul, 420
 excluded from speaking in church by Paul, 212
 and moral virtues, 417
 rights of, 392
 young, 408
worship, *see* Christian cultus

www.ingramcontent.com/pod-product-compliance
Lightning Source LLC
Chambersburg PA
CBHW060416300426
44111CB00018B/2872